Solutions designed for the way you teach today's students . . .

W9-BZT-924

From the day you choose to adopt a Thomson South-Western text through the final exams, we are committed to providing the best materials available to support your teaching *and* your students' learning. That's why this text is supported by two FREE resources that provide great educational value while making your own course preparation easier than ever before.

Book Companion Website

Available 24 hours a day from any computer with Internet access, the *Book Companion Website* for this text provides invaluable resources that you and your students can access anytime, anywhere.

Students can access an unmatched array of interactive learning tools – for instance, self-testing, reinforcement activities, and links to the best and most relevant information on the Internet. For instructors, the site can feature course outlines and learning objectives, suggested activities and exercises, and much more.

* Specific resources can vary by title. For detailed information or a demonstration, contact your Thomson South-Western sales representative.

Resource Integration Guide

Your one-stop source for course organization and preparation!
Accessible from the *Book Companion Website*, the *Resource Integration Guide* is an indispensable tool that helps you get the most from your textbook and its supplementary package.

A detailed grid lists all of the resources you can use to enhance your course – such as lecture outlines, PowerPoint® presentations, animations and video clips, online resources, testing options, and much more. You'll soon wonder how you ever did without this valuable course preparation tool!

THOMSON
SOUTH-WESTERN

Preview the companion site for this text and download your *Resource Integration Guide* at:

http://mceachern.swlearning.com

ISBN 0-324-31783-2

Microeconomics

A Contemporary Introduction

7|e

William A. McEachern
Professor of Economics
University of Connecticut

THOMSON

SOUTH-WESTERN

Australia · Canada · Mexico · Singapore · Spain · United Kingdom · United States

THOMSON
SOUTH-WESTERN

Microeconomics: A Contemporary Introduction, 7e

William A. McEachern

VP/Editorial Director:
Jack W. Calhoun

VP/Editor-in-Chief:
Dave Shaut

Sr. Acquisitions Editor:
Michael W. Worls

Sr. Developmental Editor:
Susanna C. Smart

Sr. Marketing Manager:
John Carey

Sr. Production Editor:
Elizabeth A. Shipp

Sr. Technology Project Editor:
Peggy Buskey

Web Coordinator:
Karen L. Schaffer

Sr. Manufacturing Coordinator:
Sandee Milewski

Photography Manager:
John Hill

Photography Researchers:
Sam Marshall & Rose Alcorn

Art Director:
Michelle Kunkler

Internal Designer:
Chris Miller

Cover Designer:
Diane Gliebe/Design Matters
Cincinnati, Ohio

Cover Image:
© Digital Vision, Inc.

Production House:
Pre-Press Company, Inc.

Printer:
Quebecor World
Versailles, KY

For permission to use material from
this text or product, contact us by
Tel (800) 730-2214
Fax (800) 730-2215
http://www.thomsonrights.com

For more information
contact South-Western,
5191 Natorp Boulevard,
Mason, Ohio, 45040.
Or you can visit our Internet site at:
http://www.swlearning.com

William A. McEachern began teaching large sections of economic principles when he joined the University of Connecticut in 1973. In 1980, he began offering teaching workshops around the country, and, in 1990, he created *The Teaching Economist*, a newsletter that focuses on making teaching more effective and more fun.

His research in public finance, public policy, and industrial organization has appeared in a variety of journals, including *Economic Inquiry, National Tax Journal, Journal of Industrial Economics, Quarterly Review of Economics and Finance, Southern Economic Journal, Kyklos,* and *Public Choice.* His books and monographs include *Managerial Control and Performance, School Finance Reform,* and *Tax-Exempt Property and Tax Capitalization in Metropolitan Areas.* He has also contributed chapters to edited volumes such as *Rethinking Economic Principles, Federal Trade Commission Vertical Restraint Cases,* and *Issues in Financing Connecticut Governments.*

Professor McEachern has advised federal, state, and local governments on policy matters and directed a bipartisan commission examining Connecticut's finances. He has been quoted in or written for publications such as the *New York Times, London Times, Wall Street Journal, Christian Science Monitor, Boston Globe, USA Today, Challenge Magazine, Connection, CBS MarketWatch.com,* and *Reader's Digest.* He has also appeared on *Now with Bill Moyers,* Voice of America, and National Public Radio.

In 1984, Professor McEachern won the University of Connecticut Alumni Association's Faculty Award for Distinguished Public Service and in 2000 won the Association's Faculty Excellence in Teaching Award. He is the only person in the university's history to receive both awards.

He was born in Portsmouth, N.H., earned an undergraduate degree with honors from College of the Holy Cross, served three years as an Army officer, and earned an M.A. and Ph.D. from the University of Virginia.

To Pat

Brief Contents

Contents

Part 2

Introduction to the Market System

P a r t **3**

Market Structure and Pricing

Contents

Economics has a short history but a long past. As a distinct discipline, economics has been studied for only a few hundred years, yet civilizations have confronted the economic problem of scarce resources but unlimited wants for millennia. Economics, the discipline, may be centuries old, but it's renewed every day by fresh evidence that reshapes and extends economic theory. In *Economics: A Contemporary Introduction*, I draw on more than 25 years of teaching and research to convey the vitality, timeliness, and evolving nature of economics.

Leading by Example

Remember the last time you were in unfamiliar parts and had to ask for directions? Along with the directions came the standard comment, "You can't miss it!" So how come you missed it? Because the "landmark," so obvious to locals, was invisible to you, a stranger. Writing a principles textbook is much like giving directions. The author must be familiar with the material, but that very familiarity can cloud the author's ability to see the material through the fresh eyes of a new student. Some authors revert to a tell-all approach, which can overwhelm students who find absorbing so much information like trying to drink from a fire hose. Opting for the minimalist approach, some other authors write abstractly about good *x* and good *y*, units of labor and units of capital, or the proverbial widget. But this turns economics into a foreign language.

Good directions rely on landmarks familiar to us all—a stoplight, a fork in the road, a white picket fence. Likewise, a good textbook builds bridges from the familiar to the new. That's what I try to do—*lead by example*. By beginning with examples that draw on common experience, I create graphic images that need little explanation, thereby eliciting from the reader that light of recognition, that "Aha!" I believe that the shortest distance between an economic principle and student comprehension is a lively example. Examples should be self-explanatory to convey the point quickly and directly. Having to explain an example is like having to explain a joke—the point gets lost. Throughout the book, I provide just enough intuition and institutional detail to get the point across without overwhelming students with information. The emphasis is on economic ideas, not economic jargon.

Students show up the first day of class with at least 18 years of experience with economic choices, economic institutions, and economic events. Each grew up in a household—the most important economic institution in a market economy. As consumers, students are familiar with fast-food outlets, cineplexes, car dealerships, online retailers, and scores of stores at the mall. Most students have supplied labor to the job market—more than half held jobs in high school. Students also have ongoing contact with government—they know about taxes, driver's licenses, speed limits, and public education. And students have a growing familiarity with the rest of the world. Thus, students have abundant experience with the stuff of economics. Yet some principles books neglect this rich lode of personal experience and instead try to create for students a new world of economics—a new way of thinking. Such an approach fails to connect economics with what Alfred Marshall called "the ordinary business of life."

Because instructors can cover only a portion of the textbook in class, material should be self-explanatory, thereby providing instructors the flexibility to focus on topics of special interest. This book starts where students are, not where instructors would like them to be. For example, to explain the division of labor, rather than discuss Adam Smith's pin factory, I begin with McDonald's. And to explain resource substitution, rather than rely on abstract units of labor and capital, I begin with washing a car, where the mix can vary from a drive-through car wash (much capital and little labor) to a Saturday morning charity car wash (much labor and little capital). This edition is filled with similar down-to-earth examples that turn the abstract into the concrete to help students learn.

SEVENTH Edition Content and Changes

This edition builds on the success of previous editions to make the material even more student-friendly through additional examples, more questions along the way, and frequent summaries as a chapter unfolds. By making the material both more natural and more personal, I try to draw students into a collaborative discussion. Chapters have been streamlined for a clearer, more intuitive presentation, with fresh examples, new or revised case studies, and added exhibits that crystalize key points.

Introductory Chapters Topics common to both macro- and microeconomics are covered in the first four chapters. Limiting introductory material to four chapters saves precious class time, particularly at institutions where students can take macro and micro courses in either order (and so must cover introductory chapters twice). For this edition, the order of Chapters 3 and 4 have been reversed for a better flow of topics, moving from an introduction to economics in the first three chapters, to an examination of market theory in Chapter 4.

Microeconomics My approach to microeconomics underscores the role of time and information in production and consumption. The presentation also reflects the growing interest in the economic institutions that underpin impersonal market activity. More generally, I try to convey the idea that most microeconomic principles operate like gravity: Market forces work, whether or not individual economic actors understand them.

At every opportunity, I try to turn the abstract into the concrete. For example, rather than describing an abstract monopolist, the monopoly chapter focuses on the De Beers diamond monopoly. New microeconomic material in this edition includes added coverage of labor issues, more about government regulation in other countries, more emphasis on the role of technological change in undermining monopoly power, additional discussion of public choice around the world, a new section entitled "Pollution Rights and Public Choice," a state-by-state examination of poverty levels, and a broader comparison of U.S. and world poverty levels.

International This edition reflects the growing impact of the world economy on U.S. economic welfare. International issues are introduced early and discussed often. For example, the rest of the world is introduced in Chapter 1 and profiled in Chapter 3. Comparative advantage and the production possibilities frontier are discussed from a global perspective in Chapter 2.

International coverage is woven throughout the text. By comparing the U.S. experience with that of other countries around the world, students gain a better perspective about such topics as unionization trends, antitrust laws, pollution, conservation, environmental laws, tax rates, the distribution of income, economic growth, productivity, unemployment, inflation, central bank independence, and government deficits. Exhibits have been added to show comparisons across countries of various economic measures—everything from the percentage of paper that gets recycled to public outlays relative to GDP. International references are scattered throughout the book, including a number of relevant case studies. This edition reflects additional coverage of international trade and trade barriers—including the Doha Round of WTO negotiations and the Central American Free Trade Agreement

(CAFTA), and places more emphasis on the role of technological change in international trade, especially with regard to outsourcing.

Case Studies Some books use case studies as boxed asides to cover material that otherwise doesn't quite fit. I use case studies as real-world applications to reinforce ideas in the chapter and to demonstrate the relevance of economic theory. My case studies are different enough to offer variety in the presentation yet are integrated enough into the flow of the chapter to let students know they should be read. The four categories of case studies in this text are as follows: (1) *Bringing Theory to Life* draws on student experience to reinforce economic theory, (2) *Public Policy* highlights trade-offs in the public sector, (3) *The World of Business* offers students a feel for the range of choices confronting business decision makers today, and (4) *The Information Economy* underscores the critical role of information in the economy. All case studies have been either revised or replaced.

In addition, the book features an even tighter integration of text and technology. For example, all case studies include relevant Web addresses and end-of-chapter questions for further analysis. These links plus navigation tips and other information can also be accessed through the McEachern Interactive Study Center at http://mceachern.swlearning.com/.

Clarity by Design

In many principles textbooks, chapters are broken up by boxed material, qualifying footnotes, and other distractions that disrupt the flow of the material. Students aren't sure when or if they should read such segregated elements. But this book has a natural flow. Each chapter opens with a few stimulating questions and then follows with a logical narrative. As noted already, case studies appear in the natural sequence of the chapter, not in separate boxes. Students can thus read each chapter from the opening questions to the conclusion and summary. I also adhere to a "just-in-time" philosophy, introducing material just as it is needed to build an argument. Footnotes are used sparingly and then only to cite sources, not to qualify or extend material in the text.

This edition is more visual than its predecessors, with more exhibits to reinforce key findings. Exhibit titles are also more descriptive to convey the central points, and more exhibits now have summary captions. The idea is to make the exhibits more self-contained. Additional summary paragraphs have been added throughout the chapter, and economics jargon has been cut down. Although the number of terms defined in the margin has increased, definitions have been pared to make them clearer, more concise, and less like entries from a dictionary.

In short, economic principles are now more transparent (a textbook should not be like some giant Easter egg hunt, where it's up to the student to figure out what the author is trying to say). Overall, the seventh edition is a cleaner presentation, a straighter shot into the student's brain. It omits needless words without tightening things too much. Despite the addition of fresh examples, new topics, additional summaries, and new exhibits, this edition contains about 4 percent fewer words of text than the previous one had.

Form Follows Function In most textbooks, the page design—the layout of the page and the use of color—is an afterthought, chosen with little regard for how students learn. No element in the design of this book has been wasted, and all work together for the maximum pedagogical value. By design, all elements of each chapter have been carefully integrated. Every effort has been made to present students with an open, readable page design. The size of the font, the length of the text line, and the amount of white space were all chosen to make learning easier. Graphs are uncluttered and are accompanied by captions explaining the key points. These features are optimal for students encountering college textbooks for the first time.

Color Coordinated Color is used systematically within graphs, charts, and tables to ensure that students can quickly and easily see what's going on. Throughout the book, demand curves are blue and supply curves are red. In each comparative statics example, the curves determining the final equilibrium point are lighter than the initial curves. Color shading distinguishes key areas of many graphs, such as measures of economic profit or loss, tax incidence, consumer and producer surplus, output above or below the economy's potential, and the welfare effects of tariffs and quotas. Graphical areas identifying positive outcomes such as economic profit, consumer surplus, or output exceeding the economy's potential are shaded blue. Areas identifying negative outcomes, such as economic loss, deadweight loss, or output falling below the economy's potential are shaded pink. In short, color is more than mere eye entertainment—it is coordinated consistently and with forethought to help students learn. Students benefit from these visual cues (a dyslexic student has told me that she finds the book's color guide quite helpful).

Net Bookmarks Each chapter includes a Net Bookmark. These margin notes identify interesting Web sites that illustrate real-world examples, giving students a chance to develop their research skills. And these bookmarks are extended at our Web site with additional information on resources as well as step-by-step navigation hints. They can be accessed through the McEachern Interactive Study Center at http://mceachern.swlearning.com/.

Reading It Right Each chapter contains special pedagogical features to facilitate classroom use of *The Wall Street Journal*. "Reading It Right" margin notes ask students to explain the relevance of statements drawn from *The Wall Street Journal*. There are also end-of-chapter questions asking students to read and analyze information from *The Wall Street Journal*.

Experiential Exercises Some end-of-chapter questions encourage students to develop their research and critical-thinking skills. These experiential exercises ask students to apply what they have learned to real-world, hands-on economic analysis. Most of these exercises involve the Internet, *The Wall Street Journal*, or other media resources.

Homework Xpress! Exercises New end-of-chapter exercises tie in to the Homework Xpress! (http://homeworkxpress.swlearning.com) supplement available for packaging with the textbook. The exercises afford additional practice in applying chapter graphing concepts.

THE INTERNET

As mentioned already, we devoted careful attention to capitalizing on the vast array of economic resources and alternative learning technologies the Internet can deliver. I gave much thought to two basic questions: What can this technology do that a textbook cannot do? And how can Web-based enhancements be employed to bring the greatest value to teaching and learning?

It's clear that students learn more when they are involved and engaged. The Internet provides a way to heighten student involvement while keeping the introductory economics course as current as today's news. With these ideas in mind, we have designed the text's supporting Web site to tightly integrate the book and the Internet. We have done this in a way that exploits the comparative advantage of each medium and in a structure that optimizes both teaching and learning experiences. Each chapter opener presents a HomeworkXpress! icon to remind students to check the site for problems, information, videos, news, debates, and graphing that will enhance their understanding of the chapter. In addition, graphs throughout the textbook that are enhanced in HomeworkXpress! Graphing are identified with the HomeworkXpress! icon.

The McEachern Interactive Study Center (http://mceachern.swlearning.com/) The Web site designed to be used with this text provides a comprehensive chapter-by-chapter online study guide that includes interactive quizzing, a glossary, updated and extended applications from the text, and numerous other features. Some of the highlights include:

Quizzes Interactive quizzes help students test their understanding of the chapter's concepts. Multiple-choice questions include detailed feedback for each answer. Students can email the results of a quiz to themselves and/or their instructor.

Key Terms Glossary A convenient, online glossary enables students to use the point-and-click flashcard functionality of the glossary to test themselves on key terminology.

Extensions of In-Text Web Features To streamline navigation, the Study Center links directly to Web sites discussed in the Internet-enhanced in-text features for each chapter—Net Bookmarks, e-Activities, and end-of-chapter experiential exercises. These applications provide students with opportunities to interact with the material by performing real-world analyses. Their comments and answers to the questions posed in these features can be emailed to the instructor.

McEachern HomeworkXpress! Web Site (http:// homeworkxpress.swlearning.com This new Web-based product allows professors to assign end-of-chapter graphing problems for student completion as well as tests and quizzes. The program grades the assignments and tests and transfers the grades to a gradebook. The students not only get immediate feedback, but can access extensive Review and Tutorial materials. Problems that can be completed using Homework Xpress! Are identified with an icon.

McEachern Xtra! Web Site (http://mceachernxtra.swlearning.com/) Each student has an individual learning style, and different learning styles require different tools. By tapping into today's technology, this textbook can reach out to a variety of students with a variety of learning styles and can help instructors ensure that they address the needs of all students. The McEachern Xtra! available to be packaged with the textbook provides access to a robust set of additional online learning tools. McEachern Xtra! contains these key features:

Master the Learning Objectives This element is the central navigational tool for McEachern Xtra! Step-by-step instructions associated with each learning objective systematically guide students through all available textbook and Xtra! multimedia tools to deepen their understanding of that particular concept. Each tool is accompanied by icons that identify the learning styles (print, aural, tactile, haptic, interactive, visual) for which it is most appropriate. Students can thus choose the most appropriate tools to support their own learning styles.

Graphing Workshop The Graphing Workshop is a one-stop learning resource for help in mastering the logic of graphs, one of the more difficult aspects of an economics course for many students. It enables students to explore important economic concepts through a unique learning system made up of tutorials, interactive drawing tools, and exercises that teach how to interpret, reproduce, and explain graphs.

CNN Online Video segments from the Cable News Network (CNN) bring the real world right to your desktop. The accompanying exercises illustrate how economics is an important part of daily life and how the material applies to current events.

Ask the Instructor Video Clips Streaming video explains and illustrates difficult concepts from each chapter. These video clips are extremely helpful review and clarification tools if a student has trouble understanding an in-class lecture or is a visual learner.

Xtra! Quizzing In addition to the open-access chapter-by-chapter quizzes found at the McEachern Product Support Web site (http://mceachern.swlearning.com), McEachern Xtra! offers students the opportunity to practice by taking interactive quizzes.

e-con @pps Economic Applications EconNews Online, EconDebate Online, EconData Online, and EconLinks Online help to deepen students' understanding of theoretical concepts through hands-on exploration and analysis of the latest economic news stories, policy debates, and data.

None of these features requires detailed knowledge of the Internet. Nor are they required for a successful classroom experience if an instructor wants to assign only the materials contained within the textbook. The online enhancements simply offer optional paths for further study and exploration—new ways for students to use their individual learning styles and new ways for instructors to experiment with technology and a wider range of assignment materials.

The Support Package

The teaching and learning support package that accompanies *Economics: A Contemporary Introduction* provides instructors and students with focused, accurate, and innovative supplements to the textbook.

Study Guides Written by John Lunn of Hope College, study guides are available for the full textbook, as well as for the micro and macro "split" versions. Every chapter of each study guide corresponds to a chapter in the textbook and offers (1) an introduction; (2) a chapter outline, with definitions of all terms; (3) a discussion of the chapter's main points; (4) a *lagniappe*, or bonus, which supplements material in the chapter and includes a "Question to Think About"; (5) a list of key terms; (6) a variety of true-false, multiple-choice, and discussion questions; and (7) answers to all the questions. Visit the McEachern Interactive Study Center at http://mceachern.swlearning.com/ for more details.

Instructor's Manual The *Instructor's Manual*, revised by Christy Vineyard of Southwestern Tennessee Community College, is keyed to the text. For each textbook chapter, it includes (1) a detailed lecture outline and brief overview, (2) a summary of main points, (3) pedagogical tips that expand on points raised in the chapter and indicate use of PowerPoint slides, and (4) suggested answers to all end-of-chapter questions and problems. Tina Mosleh of Ohlone College revised each classroom economics experiment to include an abstract, an overview, a clear set of instructions for running the experiment, and forms for recording the results.

Teaching Assistance Manual I have revised the *Teaching Assistance Manual* to provide additional support beyond the *Instructor's Manual*. It is especially useful to new instructors, graduate assistants, and teachers interested in generating more class discussion. This manual offers (1) overviews and outlines of each chapter, (2) chapter objectives and quiz material, (3) material for class discussion, (4) topics warranting special attention, (5) supplementary examples, and (6) "What if?" discussion questions. Appendices provide guidance on (1) pre-senting material; (2) generating and sustaining class discussion; (3) preparing, administering, and grading quizzes; and (4) coping with the special problems confronting foreign graduate assistants.

Test Banks Thoroughly revised for currency and accuracy by Dennis Hanseman of the University of Cincinnati, the microeconomics and macroeconomics test banks contain over 6,600 questions in multiple-choice and true-false formats. All multiple-choice questions have five possible responses, and each is rated by degree of difficulty.

ExamView—Computerized Testing Software *ExamView* is an easy-to-use test-creation software package available in versions compatible with Microsoft Windows and Apple Macintosh. It contains all the questions in the printed test banks. Instructors can add or edit questions, instructions, and answers; select questions by previewing them on the screen; and then choose them by number or at random. Instructors can also create and administer quizzes online, either over the Internet, through a local area network (LAN), or through a wide area network (WAN).

Microsoft PowerPoint Lecture Slides Lecture slides, created by Dale Bails of Christian Brothers University, contain tables and graphs from the textbook, as well as additional instructional materials, and are intended to enhance lectures and help integrate technology into the classroom.

Microsoft PowerPoint Figure Slides These PowerPoint slides contain key figures from the text. Instructors who prefer to prepare their own lecture slides can use these figures as an alternative to the PowerPoint lecture slides.

Transparency Acetates Many of the key tables and graphs from this textbook are reproduced as full-color transparency acetates.

Economics in the Movies This edition now features a tie-in to Thomson's *Economics in the Movies.* The guide, created by G. Dirk Mateer of The Pennsylvania State University, borrows from feature films in a way that enhances core economics content. Concepts are visualized by utilizing short film scenes, including *Out of Sight, Seabuscuit, Erin Brockovich, Waterworld, Being John Malkovich,* and many others. Icons direct professors to where they can use this guide to tie economic concepts to scenes in popular films.

CNN Economics Video The CNN Economics Video provides a variety of brief video clips, taken from Cable News Network (CNN) programs, that illustrate various aspects of economics.

Market Sim Markets come alive in this new microeconomic simulation product. Students can participate in a barter or a monetary economy while competing with their classmates and learning how markets work with this Web-based program.

Online learning is growing at a rapid pace. Whether instructors are looking to offer courses at a distance or to offer a Web-enhanced classroom, South-Western/Thomson Learning offers them a solution with WebTutor. WebTutor provides instructors with text-specific content that interacts with the two leading systems of higher education course management—WebCT and Blackboard. WebTutor is a turnkey solution for instructors who want to begin using technology like Blackboard or WebCT but do not have Web-ready content available or do not want to be burdened with developing their own content. South-Western offers two levels of WebTutor:

WebTutor Toolbox WebTutor uses the Internet to turn everyone in your class into a front-row student. WebTutor offers interactive study guide features such as quizzes, concept reviews, flashcards, discussion forums, and more. Instructor tools are also provided to facilitate communication between students and faculty. Preloaded with content, ***WebTutor ToolBox***

pairs all the content of the book's support Web site with all the sophisticated course management functionality of either course management platform.

WebTutor Advantage More than just an interactive study guide, *WebTutor Advantage* delivers innovative learning aids that actively engage students. Benefits include automatic and immediate feedback from quizzes; interactive, multimedia-rich explanations of concepts, such as flash-animated graphing tutorials and graphing exercises that use an online graph-drawing tool; streaming video applications; online exercises; flashcards; and interaction and involvement through online discussion forums. Powerful instructor tools are also provided to facilitate communication and collaboration between students and faculty.

The Teaching Economist For more than a dozen years, I have edited *The Teaching Economist*, a newsletter aimed at making teaching more interesting and more fun. The newsletter discusses imaginative ways to present topics—for example, how to "sensationalize" economic concepts, useful resources on the Internet, economic applications from science fiction, recent research in teaching and learning, and more generally, ways to teach just for the fun of it. A regular feature of *The Teaching Economist*, "The Grapevine," offers teaching ideas suggested by colleagues from across the country.

The latest issue—and back issues—of *The Teaching Economist* are available online at http://economics.swlearning.com/.

Acknowledgments

Many people contributed to this book's development. I gratefully acknowledge the insightful comments of those who have reviewed the book for this and previous editions. Their suggestions expanded my thinking and improved the book.

Steve Abid
Grand Rapids Community College

Polly Reynolds Allen
University of Connecticut

Hassan Y. Aly
Ohio State University

Ted Amato
University of North Carolina, Charlotte

Donna Anderson
University of Wisconsin, La Crosse

Richard Anderson
Texas A&M University

Kyriacos Aristotelous
Otterbein College

James Aylesworth
Lakeland Community College

Mohsen Bahmani Mohsen Bahmani-Oskooee
University of Wisconsin, Milwaukee

Dale Bails
Christian Brothers College

Benjamin Balak
Rollins College

Andy Barnett
Auburn University

Bharati Basu
Central Michigan University

Klaus Becker
Texas Tech University

Charles Bennett
Gannon University

Trisha L. Bezmen
Old Dominion University

Jay Bhattacharya
Okaloosa Walton Community College

Gerald W. Bialka
University of North Florida

William Bogart
Case Western Reserve University

Kenneth Boyer
Michigan State University

David Brasfield
Murray State University

Jurgen Brauer
Augusta College

Taggert Brooks
University of Wisconsin, La Crosse

Gardner Brown, Jr.
University of Washington

Eric Brunner
Morehead State University

Francine Butler
Grand View College

Judy Butler
Baylor University

Charles Callahan III
SUNY College at Brockport

Giorgio Canarella
California State University, Los Angeles

Shirley Cassing
University of Pittsburgh

Shi-fan Chu
University of Nevada–Reno

Ronald Cipcic
Kalamazoo Valley Community College

Larry Clarke
Brookhaven College

Rebecca Cline
Middle Georgia College

Stephen Cobb
Xavier University

Doug Conway
Mesa Community College

Mary E. Cookingham
Michigan State University

James P. Cover
University of Alabama

James Cox
DeKalb College

Jerry Crawford
Arkansas State University

Thomas Creahan
Morehead State University

Joseph Daniels
Marquette University

Carl Davidson
Michigan State University

Elynor Davis
Georgia Southern University

Susan Davis
SUNY College at Buffalo

A. Edward Day
University of Central Florida

David Dean
University of Richmond

Janet Deans
Chestnut Hill College

Dennis Debrecht
Carroll College

David Denslow
University of Florida

Gary Dymski
University of California–Riverside

John Edgren
Eastern Michigan University

Ron D. Elkins
Central Washington University

Donald Elliott, Jr.
Southern Illinois University

G. Rod Erfani
Transylvania University

Gisela Meyer Escoe
University of Cincinnati

Mark Evans
California State University, Bakersfield

Gregory Falls
Central Michigan University

Eleanor Fapohunda
SUNY College at Farmingdale

Mohsen Fardmanesh
Temple University

Paul Farnham
Georgia State University

Rudy Fichtenbaum
Wright State University

T. Windsor Fields
James Madison University

Rodney Fort
Washington State University

Richard Fowles
University of Utah

Roger Frantz
San Diego State University

Julie Gallaway
Southwest Montana State University

Gary Galles
Pepperdine University

Edward Gamber
Lafayette College

Adam Gifford
California State University, Northridge

J. P. Gilbert
MiraCosta College

Robert Gillette
University of Kentucky

Art Goldsmith
Washington and Lee University

Rae Jean Goodman
U.S. Naval Academy

Robert Gordon
San Diego State University

Fred Graham
American University

Philip Graves
University of Colorado, Boulder

Harpal S. Grewal
Claflin College

Carolyn Grin
Grand Rapids Community College

Daniel Gropper
Auburn University

Simon Hakim
Temple University

Robert Halvorsen
University of Washington

Nathan Eric Hampton
St. Cloud State University

Mehdi Haririan
Bloomsburg University

William Hart
Miami University

Baban Hasnat
SUNY College at Brockport

Julia Heath
University of Memphis

James Heisler
Hope College

James Henderson
Baylor University

James R. Hill
Central Michigan University

Jane Smith Himarios
University of Texas, Arlington

Calvin Hoerneman
Delta College

Tracy Hofer
University of Wisconsin, Stevens Point

George E. Hoffer
Virginia Commonwealth University

Dennis Hoffman
Arizona State University

Bruce Horning
Fordham University

Calvin Hoy
County College of Morris

Jennifer Imazeki
San Diego State University

Beth Ingram
University of Iowa

Paul Isley
Grand Valley State University

Joyce Jacobsen
Wesleyan University

Nancy Jianakoplos
Colorado State University

Claude Michael Jonnard
Fairleigh Dickinson University

Nake Kamrany
University of Southern California

Bryce Kanago
Miami University

John Kane
SUNY College at Oswego

David Kennett
Vassar College

William Kern
Western Michigan University

Robert Kleinhenz
California State University, Fullerton

Faik Koray
Louisiana State University

Joseph Kotaska
Monroe Community College

Barry Kotlove
Edmonds Community College

Marie Kratochvil
Nassau Community College

Joseph Lammert
Raymond Walters College

Christopher Lee
Saint Ambrose University, Davenport

J. Franklin Lee
Pitt Community College

Jim Lee
Fort Hays State University

Dennis Leyden
University of North Carolina, Greensboro

Carl Liedholm
Michigan State University

Hyoung-Seok Lim
Ohio State University

C. Richard Long
Georgia State University

Ken Long
New River Community College

Michael Magura
University of Toledo

Thomas Maloy
Muskegon Community College

Gabriel Manrique
Winona State University

Barbara Marcus
Davenport College

Robert Margo
Vanderbilt University

Nelson Mark
Ohio State University

Richard Martin
Agnes Scott College

Peter Mavrokordatos
Tarrant County College

Wolfgang Mayer
University of Cincinnati

Bruce McCrea
Lansing Community College

Richard Salvucci
Trinity University

Rexford Santerre
University of Connecticut

George D. Santopietro
Radford University

Sue Lynn Sasser
University of Central Oklahoma

Ward Sayre
Kenyon College

Ted Scheinman
Mt. Hood Community College

Peter Schwartz
University of North Carolina, Charlotte

Carol A. Scotese
Virginia Commonwealth University

Shahrokh Shahrokhi
San Diego State University

Roger Sherman
University of Houston

Michael Shields
Central Michigan University

Alden Shiers
California Polytechnic State University

Frederica Shockley
California State University, Chico

William Shughart II
University of Mississippi

Paul Sicilian
Grand Valley State University

Charles Sicotte
Rock Valley College

Calvin Siebert
University of Iowa

Gerald P. W. Simons
Grand Valley State University

Phillip Smith
DeKalb College

V. Kerry Smith
Duke University

David Spencer
Brigham Young University

Jane Speyrer
University of New Orleans

Joanne Spitz
University of Massachusetts

Mark Stegeman
Virginia Polytechnic Institute

Houston Stokes
University of Illinois, Chicago

Robert Stonebreaker
Indiana University of Pennsylvania

Michael Stroup
Stephen Austin State University

William Swift
Pace University

James Swofford
University of South Alabama

Linghui Tang
Drexel University

Donna Thompson
Brookdale Community College

John Tribble
Russell Sage College

Lee J. Van Scyoc
University of Wisconsin, Oshkosh

Percy Vera
Sinclair Community College

Han X. Vo
Winthrop University

Jin Wang
University of Wisconsin, Stevens Point

Gregory Wassall
Northeastern University

William Weber
Eastern Illinois University

David Weinberg
Xavier University

Bernard Weinrich
St. Louis Community College

Donald Wells
University of Arizona

Robert Whaples
Wake Forest University

Mark Wheeler
Western Michigan University

Michael White
St. Cloud State University

Richard Winkelman
Arizona State University

Stephan Woodbury
Michigan State University

Kenneth Woodward
Saddleback College

Patricia Wyatt
Bossier Parish Community College

Peter Wyman
Spokane Falls Community College

Mesghena Yasin
Morehead State University

Edward Young
University of Wisconsin, Eau Claire

Michael J. Youngblood
Rock Valley College

William Zeis

To practice what I preach, I relied on the division of labor based on comparative advantage to help put together the most complete teaching package on the market today. John Lunn of Hope College authored the study guides, which have become quite popular. Christy Vineyard of Southwestern Tennessee Community College carefully revised the instructor's manual. Dennis Hanseman of the University of Cincinnati undertook a thorough revision of the test banks. And Dale Bails of Christian Brothers University revised the PowerPoint lecture slides. I thank them for their imagination and their discipline.

The talented staff at Thomson Business & Professional Publishing provided invaluable editorial, administrative, and sales support. I owe a special debt to Susan Smart, senior developmental editor, who nurtured the manuscript throughout the revision and production. I also appreciate very much the smooth project coordination by senior production editor Libby Shipp, the exciting design created by Chris Miller, the imaginative photography management of John Hill, the patient production assistance of Jan Turner of Pre-Press Company, and the thoughtful copyediting of Cheryl Hauser. Peggy Buskey, Pam Wallace, and Karen Schaffer have been particularly helpful in developing the McEachern Xtra! and Homework Xpress! Web sites.

In addition, I am most grateful to Jack Calhoun, vice president and editorial director; Dave Shaut, vice president and editor-in-chief; Michael Worls, senior acquisitions editor and problem solver; and John Carey, the senior marketing manager, whose knowledge of the book dates back to the first edition. As good as the book may be, all our efforts would be wasted unless students get to read it. To that end, I greatly appreciate Thomson's dedicated service and sales force, who have contributed in a substantial way to the book's success.

Finally, I owe an abiding debt to my wife, Pat, who provided abundant encouragement and support along the way.

William A. McEachern

The Art and Science of Economic Analysis

"How luscious lies the pea in the pod."
Emily Dickinson

© Julie Dennis/Index Stock Imagery

Why are comic-strip characters like Hagar the Horrible, Hi and Lois, Cathy, Monty, and FoxTrot missing a finger on each hand? And where is Dilbert's mouth? Why does Japan have twice as many vending machines per capita as the United States? In what way are people who pound on vending machines relying on a theory? What's the big idea with economics? Finally, how can it be said in economics that "what goes around comes around"? These and other questions are answered in this chapter, which introduces the art and science of economic analysis.

You have been reading and hearing about economic issues for years—unemployment, inflation, poverty, federal deficits, college tuition, airfares, stock prices, computer prices, gas prices. When explanations of these issues go into any depth, your eyes may glaze over and you may tune out, the same way you do when a weather forecaster tries to provide an in-depth analysis of high-pressure fronts colliding with moisture carried in from the coast.

What many people fail to realize is that economics is livelier than the dry accounts offered by the news media. Economics is about making choices, and you make economic choices every day—choices about whether to get a part-time job or focus on your studies, live in a dorm or off campus, take a course in accounting or one in history, pack a lunch or grab a sandwich. You already know much more about economics than you realize. You bring to the subject a rich personal experience, an experience that will be tapped throughout the book to reinforce your understanding of the basic ideas. Topics discussed include:

- The economic problem
- Marginal analysis
- Rational self-interest

- Scientific method
- Normative versus positive analysis
- Pitfalls of economic thinking

The Economic Problem: Scarce Resources, Unlimited Wants

Would you like a new car, a nicer home, better meals, more free time, a more interesting social life, more spending money, more sleep? Who wouldn't? But even if you can satisfy some of these desires, others will pop up. *The problem is that, although your wants, or desires, are virtually unlimited, the resources available to satisfy these wants are scarce.* A resource is *scarce* when it is not freely available—that is, when its price exceeds zero. Because resources are scarce, you must choose from among your many wants and, whenever you choose, you must forgo satisfying some other wants. The problem of scarce resources but unlimited wants exists to a greater or lesser extent for each of the more than 6 billion people around the world. Everybody—taxicab driver, farmer, brain surgeon, shepherd, student, politician—faces the problem.

Economics examines how people use their scarce resources to satisfy their unlimited wants. The taxicab driver uses the cab and other scarce resources, such as knowledge of the city, driving skills, gasoline, and time, to earn income. The income, in turn, buys housing, groceries, clothing, trips to Disney World, and thousands of other goods and services that help satisfy some of the driver's unlimited wants.

Let's pick apart the definition of economics, beginning with resources, then examining goods and services, and finally focusing on the heart of the matter—economic choice, which arises from scarcity.

Resources

Resources are the inputs, or factors of production, used to produce the goods and services that people want. *Goods and services are scarce because resources are scarce.* Resources sort into four broad categories: labor, capital, natural resources, and entrepreneurial ability. **Labor** is human effort, both physical and mental. It includes the effort of the cab driver and the brain surgeon. Labor itself comes from a more fundamental resource: *time*. Without time we can accomplish nothing. We allocate our time to alternative uses: we can *sell* our time as labor, or we can *spend* our time doing other things, like sleeping, eating, studying, playing sports, going online, watching TV, or just relaxing with friends.

Capital includes all human creations used to produce goods and services. Economists often distinguish between physical capital and human capital. *Physical capital* consists of facto-

---

ECONOMICS

The study of how people use their scarce resources to satisfy their unlimited wants

RESOURCES

The inputs, or factors of production, used to produce the goods and services that people want; resources consist of labor, capital, natural resources, and entrepreneurial ability

LABOR

The physical and mental effort used to produce goods and services

CAPITAL

The buildings, equipment, and human skill used to produce goods and services

ries, machines, tools, buildings, airports, highways, and other human creations employed to produce goods and services. Physical capital includes the taxi driver's cab, the surgeon's scalpel, the farmer's tractor, the interstate highway system, and the building where your economics class meets. *Human capital* consists of the knowledge and skill people acquire to enhance their productivity, such as the taxi driver's knowledge of city streets, the surgeon's knowledge of human biology, and your knowledge of economics.

Natural resources are all so-called *gifts of nature,* including bodies of water, trees, oil reserves, minerals, and even animals. Natural resources can be divided into renewable resources and exhaustible resources. A *renewable resource* can be drawn on indefinitely if used conservatively. Thus, timber is a renewable resource if felled trees are replaced to provide a steady supply. The air and rivers are renewable resources if they are allowed to clean themselves of pollutants. More generally, biological resources like fish, game, livestock, forests, rivers, groundwater, grasslands, and soil are renewable if managed properly. An *exhaustible resource*— such as oil, coal, or copper ore—does not renew itself and so is available in a limited amount. Once burned, each barrel of oil and each ton of coal are gone forever. The world's oil reserves and coal mines are exhaustible.

A special kind of human skill called **entrepreneurial ability** is the talent required to dream up a new product or find a better way to produce an existing one. The *entrepreneur* tries to discover and act on profitable opportunities by hiring resources and assuming the risk of business success or failure. Every large firm in the world today, such as Ford, Microsoft, and Dell, began as an idea in the mind of an entrepreneur.

Resource owners are paid **wages** for their labor, **interest** for the use of their capital, and **rent** for the use of their natural resources. The entrepreneur's effort is rewarded by **profit,** which equals the *revenue* from items sold minus the *cost* of the resources employed to make those items. The entrepreneur claims what's left over after paying other resource suppliers. Sometimes the entrepreneur suffers a loss. Resource earnings are usually based on the *time* these resources are employed. Resource payments therefore have a time dimension, as in a wage of $10 *per hour,* interest of 6 percent *per year,* rent of $600 *per month,* or profit of $10,000 *per year.*

Goods and Services

Resources are combined in a variety of ways to produce goods and services. A farmer, a tractor, 50 acres of land, seeds, and fertilizer combine to grow the good: corn. One hundred musicians, musical instruments, chairs, a conductor, a musical score, and a music hall combine to produce the service: Beethoven's Fifth Symphony. Corn is a **good** because it is something you can see, feel, and touch; it requires scarce resources to produce; and it satisfies human wants. The book you are now holding, the chair you are sitting in, the clothes you are wearing, and your next meal are all goods. The performance of the Fifth Symphony is a **service** because it is intangible, yet it uses scarce resources to satisfy human wants. Lectures, movies, concerts, phone calls, broadband connections, yoga lessons, dry cleaning, and haircuts are all services.

Because goods and services are produced using scarce resources, they are themselves scarce. *A good or service is scarce if the amount people desire exceeds the amount available at a zero price.* Because we cannot have all the goods and services we would like, we must continually choose among them. We must choose among more pleasant living quarters, better meals, nicer clothes, more reliable transportation, faster computers, and so on. Making choices in a world of **scarcity** means we must pass up some goods and services.

A few goods and services seem *free* because the amount available at a zero price exceeds

NATURAL RESOURCES
So-called gifts of nature used to produce goods and services; includes renewable and exhaustible resources

ENTREPRENEURIAL ABILITY
Managerial and organizational skills needed to start a firm, combined with the willingness to take risks

WAGES
Payment to resource owners for their labor

INTEREST
Payment to resource owners for the use of their capital

RENT
Payment to resource owners for the use of their natural resources

PROFIT
The reward for entrepreneurial ability; the revenue from sales minus the cost of resources used by the entrepreneur

GOOD
A tangible item used to satisfy human wants

SERVICE
An activity used to satisfy human wants

SCARCITY
Occurs when the amount people desire exceeds the amount available at a zero price

the amount people want. For example, air and seawater often seem free because we can breathe all the air we want and have all the seawater we can haul away. Yet, despite the old saying "The best things in life are free," most goods and services are scarce, not free, and even those that appear to be free come with strings attached. For example, *clean* air and *clean* seawater have become scarce. *Goods and services that are truly free are not the subject matter of economics. Without scarcity, there would be no economic problem and no need for prices.*

Sometimes we mistakenly think of certain goods as free because they involve no apparent cost to us. Subscription cards that fall out of magazines appear to be free. At least it seems we would have little difficulty rounding up about three thousand if necessary! Producing the cards, however, absorbs scarce resources, resources drawn away from competing uses, such as producing higher-quality magazines. You may have heard the expression "There is no such thing as a free lunch." There is no free lunch because all goods and services involve a cost to someone. The lunch may seem free to us, but it draws scarce resources away from the production of other goods and services, and whoever provides a free lunch often expects something in return. A Russian proverb makes a similar point but with a bit more bite: "The only place you find free cheese is in a mousetrap." And Albert Einstein said, "Sometimes one pays the most for things one gets for nothing."

Economic Decision Makers

There are four types of decision makers, or participants, in the economy: households, firms, governments, and the rest of the world. Their interaction determines how an economy's resources are allocated. *Households* play the leading role. As consumers, households demand the goods and services produced. As resource owners, households supply labor, capital, natural resources, and entrepreneurial ability to firms, governments, and the rest of the world. *Firms, governments,* and *the rest of the world* demand the resources that households supply and then use these resources to supply the goods and services that households demand. The rest of the world includes foreign households, firms, and governments that supply resources and products to U.S. markets and demand resources and products from U.S. markets.

Markets are the means by which buyers and sellers carry out exchange. Bringing together the two sides of exchange, demand and supply, markets determine price and quantity. Markets are often physical places, such as supermarkets, department stores, shopping malls, or flea markets. But markets also include other mechanisms by which buyers and sellers communicate, like classified ads, radio and television ads, telephones, bulletin boards, the Internet, and face-to-face bargaining. These market mechanisms provide information about the quantity, quality, and price of products offered for sale. Goods and services are bought and sold in **product markets.** Resources are bought and sold in **resource markets.** The most important resource market is the labor, or job, market. Think of your own experience looking for a job, and you get some idea of that market.

A Simple Circular-Flow Model

Now that you have learned a bit about economic decision makers, consider how they interact. Such a picture is conveyed by the **circular-flow model,** which describes the flow of resources, products, income, and revenue among economic decision makers. The simple circular-flow model focuses on the primary interaction in a market economy—that between households and firms. Exhibit 1 shows households on the left and firms on the right; please take a look.

Households supply labor, capital, natural resources, and entrepreneurial ability to firms through resource markets, shown in the lower portion of the exhibit. In return, households

---

MARKET

A set of arrangements through which buyers and sellers carry out exchange at mutually agreeable terms

PRODUCT MARKET

A market in which a good or service is bought and sold

RESOURCE MARKET

A market in which a resource is bought and sold

CIRCULAR-FLOW MODEL

A diagram that outlines the flow of resources, products, income, and revenue among economic decision makers

demand goods and services from firms through product markets, shown on the upper portion of the exhibit. Viewed from the business end, firms demand labor, capital, natural resources, and entrepreneurial ability from households through resource markets, and firms supply goods and services to households through product markets.

The flows of resources and products are supported by the flows of income and expenditure—that is, by the flow of money. So let's add money. The demand and supply of resources come together in resource markets to determine resource prices, which flow as *income* to households. The demand and supply of products come together in product markets to determine the prices of goods and services, which flow as *revenue* to firms. Resources and products flow in one direction—in this case, counterclockwise—and the corresponding payments flow in the other direction—clockwise. What goes around comes around. Take a little time now to trace the circular flows.

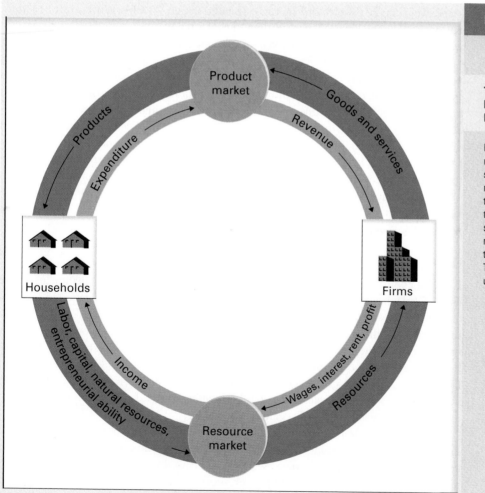

E X H I B I T **1**

The Simple Circular-Flow Model for Households and Firms

Households earn income by supplying resources to the resource market, as shown in the lower portion of the model. Firms demand these resources to produce goods and services, which they supply to the product market, as shown in the upper portion of the model. Households spend their income to demand these goods and services. This spending flows through the product market as revenue to firms.

The Art of Economic Analysis

An economy results from the choices that millions of individuals make in attempting to satisfy their unlimited wants. Because these choices lie at the very heart of the economic problem—coping with scarce resources but unlimited wants—they deserve a closer look. Learning about the forces that shape economic choice is the first step toward mastering the art of economic analysis.

Rational Self-Interest

A key economic assumption is that individuals, in making choices, rationally select alternatives they perceive to be in their best interests. By *rational*, economists mean simply that people try to make the best choices they can, given the available information. People may not know with certainty which alternative will turn out to be the best. They simply select the alternatives they *expect* will yield the most satisfaction and happiness. *In general, rational self-interest means that individuals try to maximize the expected benefit achieved with a given cost or to minimize the expected cost of achieving a given benefit.*

Rational self-interest should not be viewed as blind materialism, pure selfishness, or greed. We all know people who are tuned to radio station WIIFM (What's In It For Me?). For most of us, however, self-interest often includes the welfare of our family, our friends, and perhaps the poor of the world. Even so, our concern for others is influenced by the cost of that concern. We may readily volunteer to drive a friend to the airport on Saturday afternoon but are less likely to offer if the plane leaves at 6:00 A.M. When we donate clothes to an organization like Goodwill Industries, they are more likely to be old and worn than brand new. People tend to give more to charities when their contributions are tax deductible. TV stations are more likely to donate airtime for public-service announcements during the dead of night than during prime time (in fact, 80 percent of such announcements air between 11:00 P.M. and 7:00 A.M.[1]). In Asia some people burn money to soothe the passage of a departed loved one. But they burn fake money, not real money. The notion of self-interest does not rule out concern for others; it simply means that concern for others is influenced by the same economic forces that affect other economic choices. *The lower the personal cost of helping others, the more help we offer.*

Choice Requires Time and Information

Rational choice takes time and requires information, but time and information are scarce and valuable. If you have any doubts about the time and information required to make choices, talk to someone who recently purchased a home, a car, or a personal computer. Talk to a corporate official deciding whether to introduce a new product, sell over the Internet, build a new factory, or buy another firm. Or think back to your own experience of selecting a college. You probably talked to friends, relatives, teachers, and guidance counselors. You likely used school catalogs, college guides, and Web sites. You may have visited campuses to meet with the admissions staff and anyone else willing to talk. The decision took time and money, and it probably involved aggravation and anxiety.

Because information is costly to acquire, we are often willing to pay others to gather and digest it for us. College guidebooks, stock analysts, travel agents, real estate brokers, career counselors, restaurant critics, movie reviewers, specialized Web sites, and *Consumer Reports* magazine attest to our willingness to pay for information that will improve our choices. As

1. Sally Goll Beatty, "Media and Agencies Brawl Over Do-Good Advertising," *Wall Street Journal,* 29 September 1997.

we'll see next, *rational decision makers will continue to acquire information as long as the additional benefit expected from that information exceeds the additional cost of gathering it.*

Economic Analysis Is Marginal Analysis

Economic choice usually involves some adjustment to the existing situation, or status quo. Amazon.com must decide whether to add an additional line of products. The school superintendent must decide whether to hire another teacher. Your favorite jeans are on sale, and you must decide whether to buy another pair. You are wondering whether you should carry an extra course next term. You have just finished dinner at a restaurant and are deciding whether to have dessert.

Economic choice is based on a comparison of the *expected marginal benefit* and the *expected marginal cost* of the action under consideration. **Marginal** means incremental, additional, or extra. Marginal refers to a change in an economic variable, a change in the status quo. *You, as a rational decision maker, will change the status quo as long as your expected marginal benefit from the change exceeds your expected marginal cost.* For example, Amazon.com compares the marginal benefit expected from adding a new line of products (the added sales revenue) with the marginal cost (the added cost of the resources required). Likewise, you compare the marginal benefit you expect from eating dessert (the added pleasure and satisfaction) with its marginal cost (the added money, time, and calories).

Typically, the change under consideration is small, but a marginal choice can involve a major economic adjustment, as in the decision to quit school and get a job. For a firm, a marginal choice might mean building a plant in Mexico or even filing for bankruptcy. By focusing on the effect of a marginal adjustment to the status quo, the economist is able to cut the analysis of economic choice down to a manageable size. Rather than confront a bewildering economic reality head-on, the economist begins with a marginal choice to see how this choice affects a particular market and shapes the economic system as a whole. Incidentally, to the noneconomist, *marginal* usually means relatively inferior, as in "a movie of marginal quality." Forget that meaning for this course and instead think of *marginal* as meaning incremental, additional, or extra.

Microeconomics and Macroeconomics

Although you have made thousands of economic choices, you probably have seldom thought about your own economic behavior. For example, why are you reading this book right now rather than doing something else? **Microeconomics** is the study of your economic behavior and the economic behavior of others who make choices about such matters as how much to study and how much to play, how much to borrow and how much to save, what to buy and what to sell. Microeconomics examines the factors that influence individual economic choices and how markets coordinate the choices of various decision makers. Microeconomics explains how price and quantity are determined in individual markets—for breakfast cereal, sports equipment, or used cars, for instance.

You have probably given little thought to what influences your own economic choices. You have likely given even less thought to how your choices link up with those made by millions of others in the U.S. economy to determine economy-wide measures such as total production, employment, and economic growth. **Macroeconomics** studies the performance of the economy as a whole. Whereas microeconomics studies the individual pieces of the economic puzzle, as reflected in particular markets, macroeconomics puts all the pieces together to focus on the big picture.

MARGINAL

Incremental, additional, or extra; used to describe a change in an economic variable

[handwritten margin note:] Dessert: benefit – pleasure, satisfaction cost – money, time, calories

MICROECONOMICS

The study of the economic behavior in particular markets, such as that for computers or unskilled labor

MACROECONOMICS

The study of the economic behavior of entire economies

To review: The art of economic analysis focuses on how individuals use their scarce resources in an attempt to satisfy their unlimited wants. Rational self-interest guides individual choice. Choice requires time and information, and choice involves a comparison of the marginal cost and marginal benefit of alternative actions. Microeconomics looks at the individual pieces of the economic puzzle; macroeconomics fits the pieces together to shape the big picture.

The Science of Economic Analysis

ECONOMIC THEORY, OR ECONOMIC MODEL

A simplification of reality used to make predictions about cause and effect in the real world

Economists use scientific analysis to develop theories, or models, that help explain economic behavior. An **economic theory,** or **economic model,** is a simplification of economic reality that *is used to make predictions about the real world.* A theory, or model, such as the circular-flow model, captures the important elements of the problem under study; it need not spell out every detail and interrelation. In fact, adding more details may make a theory more unwieldy and less useful. The world is so complex that we must simplify if we want to make sense of things, just as comic strips simplify characters—leaving out fingers or a mouth, for instance. You might think of economic theory as a stripped-down, or streamlined, version of economic reality.

The Role of Theory

Many people don't understand the role of theory. Perhaps you have heard, "Oh, that's fine in theory, but in practice it's another matter." The implication is that the theory provides little aid in practical matters. People who say this fail to realize that they are merely substituting their own theory for a theory they either do not believe or do not understand. They are really saying, "I have my own theory that works better."

All of us employ theories, however poorly defined or understood. Someone who pounds on the Pepsi machine that just ate a quarter has a crude theory about how that machine works and what went wrong. One version of that theory might be "The quarter drops through a series of whatchamacallits, but sometimes it gets stuck. *If* I pound on the machine, *then* I can free up the quarter and send it on its way." Evidently, this theory is pervasive enough that many people continue to pound on machines that fail to perform (a real problem for the vending machine industry and one reason newer machines are fronted with glass). Yet, if you were to ask these mad pounders to explain their "theory" about how the machine operates, they would look at you as if you were crazy.

The Scientific Method

To study economic problems, economists employ a process of theoretical investigation called the *scientific method,* which consists of four steps, as outlined in Exhibit 2.

Step One: Identify the Question and Define Relevant Variables

VARIABLE

A measure, such as price or quantity, that can take on different values

The first step is to identify the economic question and define the variables that are relevant to the solution. For example, the question might be "What is the relationship between the price of Pepsi and the quantity of Pepsi purchased?" In this case, the relevant variables are price and quantity. A **variable** is a measure that can take on different values. The variables of concern become the elements of the theory, so they must be selected with care.

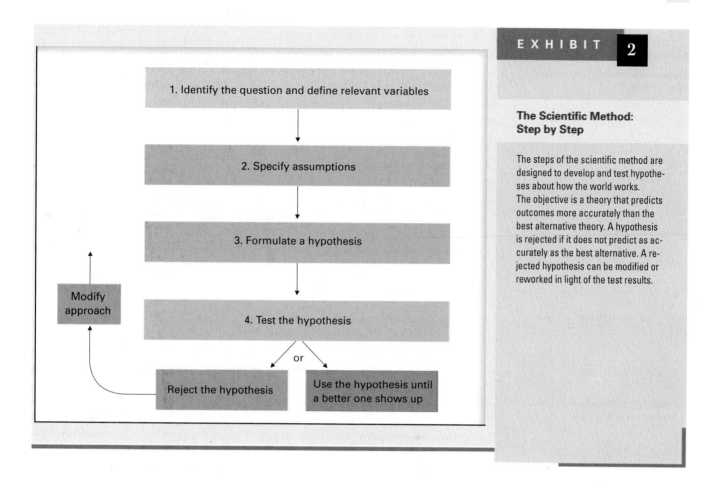

EXHIBIT   2

The Scientific Method: Step by Step

The steps of the scientific method are designed to develop and test hypotheses about how the world works. The objective is a theory that predicts outcomes more accurately than the best alternative theory. A hypothesis is rejected if it does not predict as accurately as the best alternative. A rejected hypothesis can be modified or reworked in light of the test results.

Step Two: Specify Assumptions

The second step is to specify the assumptions under which the theory is to apply. One major category of assumptions is the **other-things-constant assumption**—in Latin, the ceteris paribus assumption. The idea is to identify the variables of interest and then focus exclusively on the relationships among them, assuming that nothing else of importance will change—that other things will remain constant. Again, suppose we are interested in how the price of Pepsi influences the amount purchased. To isolate the relation between these two variables, we assume that there are no changes in other relevant variables such as consumer income, the average temperature, or the price of Coke.

We also make assumptions about how people will behave; these we call **behavioral assumptions.** The primary behavioral assumption is rational self-interest. Earlier we assumed that individual decision makers pursue self-interest rationally and make choices accordingly. Rationality implies that each consumer buys the products expected to maximize his or her level of satisfaction. Rationality also implies that a firm supplies the products expected to maximize profit. These kinds of assumptions are called behavioral assumptions because they specify how we expect economic decision makers to behave—what makes them tick, so to speak.

OTHER-THINGS-CONSTANT ASSUMPTION

The assumption, when focusing on the relation among key economic variables, that other variables remain unchanged

BEHAVIORAL ASSUMPTION

An assumption that describes the expected behavior of economic decision makers, what motivates them

HYPOTHESIS

A theory about relationships among key variables

Step Three: Formulate a Hypothesis

The third step is to formulate a **hypothesis,** which is a theory about how key variables relate to each other. For example, one hypothesis holds that if the price of Pepsi goes up, other things constant, then the quantity purchased will decline. The hypothesis becomes a prediction of what will happen to the quantity purchased if the price goes up. *The purpose of this hypothesis, like that of any theory, is to help make predictions about cause and effect in the real world.*

Step Four: Test the Hypothesis

In the fourth step, by comparing its predictions with evidence, we test the validity of a hypothesis. To test a hypothesis, we must focus on the variables in question, while carefully controlling for other effects assumed not to change. The test will lead us either to (1) reject the hypothesis, or theory, if it predicts worse than the best alternative theory or (2) use the hypothesis, or theory, until a better one comes along. If we reject it, we can go back and modify our approach in light of the results. Please spend a moment now reviewing the steps in Exhibit 2.

Normative Versus Positive

POSITIVE ECONOMIC STATEMENT

A statement that can be proved or disproved by reference to facts

NORMATIVE ECONOMIC STATEMENT

A statement that represents an opinion, which cannot be proved or disproved

Economists usually try to explain how the economy works. Sometimes they concern themselves not with how the economy *does* work but how it *should* work. Compare these two statements: "The U.S. unemployment rate is 5.7 percent" and "The U.S. unemployment rate should be lower." The first, called a **positive economic statement**, is an assertion about economic reality that can be supported or rejected by reference to the facts. The second, called a **normative economic statement,** reflects an opinion. And an opinion is merely that—it cannot be shown to be true or false by reference to the facts. Positive statements concern what *is;* normative statements concern what, in someone's opinion, *should be.* Positive statements need not necessarily be true, but they must be subject to verification or refutation by reference to the facts. Theories are expressed as positive statements such as "If the price of Pepsi increases, then the quantity demanded will decrease."

Most of the disagreement among economists involves normative debates—for example, the appropriate role of government—rather than statements of positive analysis. To be sure, many theoretical issues remain unresolved, but economists generally agree on most fundamental theoretical principles—that is, about positive economic analysis. For example, in a survey of 464 U.S. economists, only 6.5 percent disagreed with the statement "A ceiling on rents reduces the quantity and quality of housing available." This is a positive statement because it can be shown to be consistent or inconsistent with the evidence. In contrast, there was much less agreement on normative statements such as "The distribution of income in the United States should be more equal." Half the economists surveyed "generally agreed," a quarter "generally disagreed," and a quarter "agreed with provisos."[2]

Normative statements, or value judgments, have a place in a policy debate such as the proper role of government, provided that statements of opinion are distinguished from statements of fact. In such policy debates, you are entitled to your own opinion, but you are not entitled to your own facts.

Economists Tell Stories

Despite economists' reliance on the scientific method for developing and evaluating theories, economic analysis is as much art as science. Formulating a question, isolating the key

2. Richard M. Alston, et al., "Is There a Consensus Among Economists in the 1990s?" *American Economic Review* 82 (May 1992): pp. 203–209, Table 1.

variables, specifying the assumptions, proposing a theory to answer the question, and devising a way to test the predictions all involve more than simply an understanding of economics and the scientific method. Carrying out these steps requires good intuition and the imagination of a storyteller. Economists explain their theories by telling stories about how they think the economy works. To tell a compelling story, an economist relies on case studies, anecdotes, parables, the personal experience of the listener, and supporting data. Throughout this book, you will hear stories that bring you closer to the ideas under consideration. The stories, such as the one about the Pepsi machine, breathe life into economic theory and help you personalize abstract ideas. As another example, here is a case study about the popularity of vending machines in Japan.

A Yen for Vending Machines

© Paul Chesley/Stone/Getty Images

Japan faces a steady drop in the number of working-age people. Here are three reasons why: (1) Japan's birthrate has reached a record low, (2) Japan allows virtually no immigration—only 2 of every 1,000 workers in Japan are foreigners, and (3) Japan's population is aging. As a result, unemployment has usually been lower in Japan than in other countries. Because labor is relatively scarce there, it is relatively costly. To sell products, Japanese retailers rely on capital, particularly vending machines, which obviously eliminate the need for sales clerks.

Japan has more vending machines per capita than any other country on the planet—twice as many as the United States and nearly ten times as many as Europe. And vending machines in Japan sell a wider range of products than elsewhere, including beer, sake, whiskey, rice, eggs, vegetables, pizza, entire meals, fresh flowers, clothes, video games, DVDs, even X-rated comic books. Japan's vending machines are also more sophisticated. The newer models come with video monitors and touch-pad screens. Wireless chips alert vendors when supplies are running low. Machines selling cigarettes or alcohol require a driver's license, which is used to verify the buyer's age (and the machines can spot fake IDs).

Some cold-drink dispensers automatically raise prices in hot weather. Coca-Cola machines allow mobile phone users to pay for drinks by pressing a few buttons on their mobiles. Sanyo makes a giant machine that sells up to 200 different items at three different temperatures. Perhaps the ultimate vending machine is Robo Shop Super 24, a totally automated convenience store in Tokyo. After browsing long display cases, a customer can make selections by punching product numbers on a keyboard. A bucket whirs around the store, collecting the selections.

As noted earlier, it is common practice in the United States to shake down vending machines that malfunction. Such abuse increases the probability the machines will fail again, leading to a cycle of abuse. Vending machines in Japan are less abused, in part because they are more sophisticated and more reliable and in part because the Japanese generally have greater respect for property and, consequently, a lower crime rate (for example, Japan's theft rate is only about half the U.S. rate).

Japanese consumers use vending machines with great frequency. For example, 40 percent of all soft-drink sales in Japan are through vending machines, compared to only 12 percent of

U.S. sales. Japanese sales per machine are double the U.S. rate. Research shows that most Japanese consumers prefer an anonymous machine to a salesperson (Robo Shop 24's Web site notes, "Grumpy, nervous store clerks have been replaced by the cheery little Robo"). Despite the abundance of vending machines in Japan, more growth is forecast, spurred on by a shrinking labor pool, technological innovations, and wide acceptance of machines there.

Sources: Ginny Parker, "Vending the Rules," *Time*, 25 August 2003; and "In 2001 Japanese Spent $87.5 Billion on Vending Machines," *The Food Industry Report*, 3 March 2003; pictures and descriptions of Robo Shop 24 can be found at http://www.theimageworks.com/Robo/roboftur.htm.

This case study makes two points. First, producers combine resources in a way that conserves, or economizes on, the resource that is more costly—in this case, labor. Second, the customs and conventions of the marketplace can differ across countries, and this variance can result in different types of economic arrangements, such as the more extensive use of vending machines in Japan.

Predicting Average Behavior

The goal of an economic theory is to predict the impact of an economic event on economic choices and, in turn, the effect of these choices on particular markets or on the economy as a whole. Does this mean that economists try to predict the behavior of particular consumers or producers? Not necessarily, because a specific individual may behave in an unpredictable way. But the unpredictable actions of numerous individuals tend to cancel one another out, so the *average behavior* of groups can be predicted more accurately. For example, if the federal government cuts personal income taxes, certain households may decide to save the entire tax cut. On average, however, household spending will increase. Likewise, if Burger King cuts the price of Whoppers, the manager can better predict how much sales will increase than how a specific customer will respond. *The random actions of individuals tend to offset one another, so the average behavior of a large group can be predicted more accurately than the behavior of a particular individual.* Consequently, economists tend to focus on the average, or typical, behavior of people in groups—for example, as average taxpayers or average Whopper consumers—rather than on the behavior of a specific individual.

Some Pitfalls of Faulty Economic Analysis

Economic analysis, like other forms of scientific inquiry, is subject to common mistakes in reasoning that can lead to faulty conclusions. We will discuss three possible sources of confusion.

The Fallacy That Association Is Causation

In the last two decades, the number of physicians specializing in cancer treatment increased sharply. At the same time, the incidence of most cancers increased. Can we conclude that physicians cause cancer? No. To assume that event A caused event B simply because the two are associated in time is to commit the **association-is-causation fallacy,** a common error. The fact that one event precedes another or that the two events occur simultaneously does not necessarily mean that one causes the other. Remember: Association is not necessarily causation.

The Fallacy of Composition

Standing up at a football game to get a better view of the action does not work if others stand as well. Arriving early to buy concert tickets does not work if many others have the

ASSOCIATION-IS-CAUSATION FALLACY

The incorrect idea that if two variables are associated in time, one must necessarily cause the other

same idea. These are examples of the **fallacy of composition,** which is an erroneous belief that what is true for the individual, or the part, is also true for the group, or the whole.

The Mistake of Ignoring the Secondary Effects

In many cities, public officials have imposed rent controls on apartments. The primary effect of this policy, the effect on which policy makers focus, is to keep rents from rising. Over time, however, fewer new apartments get built because renting becomes less profitable. Moreover, existing rental units deteriorate because owners have no incentive to pay for maintenance since they have plenty of customers anyway. Thus, the quantity and quality of housing may decline as a result of what appears to be a reasonable measure to keep rents from rising. The mistake was to ignore the **secondary effects,** or the unintended consequences, of the policy. Economic actions have secondary effects that often turn out to be more important than the primary effects. Secondary effects may develop more slowly and may not be obvious, but good economic analysis takes them into account.

If Economists Are So Smart, Why Aren't They Rich?

Why aren't economists rich? Well, some are, earning over $25,000 per appearance on the lecture circuit. Others earn thousands a day as consultants. Economists have been appointed to cabinet positions, such as Secretaries of Commerce, Defense, Labor, State, and Treasury, and to head the Federal Reserve System. Economics is the only social science and the only business discipline for which the prestigious Nobel Prize is awarded, and pronouncements by economists are reported in the media daily. *The Economist,* a widely respected news weekly from London, argues that economic ideas have influenced policy "to a degree that would make other social scientists drool."[3]

The economics profession thrives because its models usually do a better job of making economic sense out of a confusing world than do alternative approaches. But not all economists are wealthy, nor is personal wealth the goal of the discipline. In a similar vein, not all doctors are healthy (some even smoke), not all carpenters live in perfectly built homes, not all marriage counselors are happily married, and not all child psychologists have well-adjusted children. Still, those who study economics do reap financial rewards, as discussed in this closing case study, which looks at the link between earnings and the choice of a college major.

FALLACY OF COMPOSITION

The incorrect belief that what is true for the individual, or part, must necessarily be true for the group, or whole

SECONDARY EFFECTS

Unintended consequences of economic actions that may develop slowly over time as people react to events

HOMEWORK Xpress! Ask the Instructor Video

College Major and Career Earnings

Earlier in the chapter, you learned that economic choice is based on a comparison of expected marginal benefit and expected marginal cost. Surveys show that students go to college because they believe a college diploma is the ticket to better jobs and higher pay. Put another way, for about two-thirds of U.S. high school graduates, the expected marginal benefit of college apparently exceeds the expected marginal cost. The cost of college will be discussed in the next chapter; the focus here is on the benefits of college, particularly expected earnings.

Case **Study**

The Information Economy

eActivity
The Federal Reserve Bank of Minneapolis asked some Nobel Prize winners how they became interested in economics. Their stories can be found at http://woodrow.mpls.frb.fed.us/pubs/region/98-12/quotes.cfm.

3. "The Puzzling Failure of Economics," *The Economist,* 23 August 1997, p. 11.

Among college graduates, all kinds of factors affect earnings, such as general ability, occupation, college attended, college major, and highest degree earned. To isolate the effects of college major on earnings, a National Science Foundation study surveyed people in specific age groups who worked full time and had earned a bachelor's as their highest degree. Exhibit 3 shows the median earnings by major for men and women ages 35 to 44. As a point of reference, the *median* annual earnings for men was $43,199 (half earned more and half earned less). The median earnings for women was $32,155, only 74 percent of the median for men. Among men, the top median pay was the $53,286 earned by engineering majors; that pay was 23 percent above the median for all men surveyed. Among women, the top median pay was the $49,170 earned by economics majors; that pay was 53 percent above the median for all women surveyed.

Incidentally, men who majored in economics earned a median of $49,377, ranking them seventh among 27 majors and 14 percent above the median for all men surveyed. Thus, even though the median pay for all women was only 74 percent of the median pay for all men, women who majored in economics earned about the same as men who majored in economics. We can say that economics majors earned more than most, and they experienced no pay difference based on gender.

Notice that among both men and women, the majors ranked toward the top of the list tend to be more quantitative and analytical. According to the study's author, "Employers may view certain majors as more difficult and may assume that graduates in these fields are more able and hard working, whereupon they offer them higher salaries."[4] The selection of a relatively more challenging major such as economics sends a favorable signal to future employers.

The study also examined the kinds of jobs different majors actually found. Those who majored in economics became mid- and top-level managers, executives, and administrators. They also worked in sales, computer fields, financial analysis, and economic analysis. Remember, the survey was limited to those whose highest degree was the baccalaureate, so it excluded the many economics majors who went on to pursue graduate studies in law, business administration, economics, public administration, journalism, and other fields (a separate study showed that lawyers with undergraduate degrees in economics earned more than other lawyers).

A number of world leaders majored in economics, including three of the last six U.S. presidents, Supreme Court Justice Sandra Day O'Connor, and Philippines President Gloria Macapagal-Arroyo, who earned a Ph.D. in the subject. Other well-known economics majors include eBay President Meg Whitman, Intel President Paul Otellini, Governor Arnold Schwarzenegger, aging rocker Mick Jagger, high-tech guru Esther Dyson, and Scott Adams, creator of Dilbert, the mouthless wonder.

Source: R. Kim Craft and Joe Baker, "Do Economists Make Better Lawyers? Undergraduate Degree Fields and Lawyer Earnings," *Journal of Economic Education*," Summer 2003; and Daniel E. Hecker, "Earnings of College Graduates, 1993," *Monthly Labor Review*, December 1995. For a survey of employment opportunities, go to the U.S. Labor Department's Occupational Outlook Handbook at http://www.bls.gov/oco/.

WALL STREET JOURNAL
Reading It Right

What's the relevance of the following statement from the Wall Street Journal: "With economics the most popular undergraduate major at many top colleges, demand for economics professors has led to a bidding war for the most highly-regarded candidates."

4. Daniel E. Hecker, "Earnings of College Graduates, 1993," *Monthly Labor Review* (December 1995): p. 15.

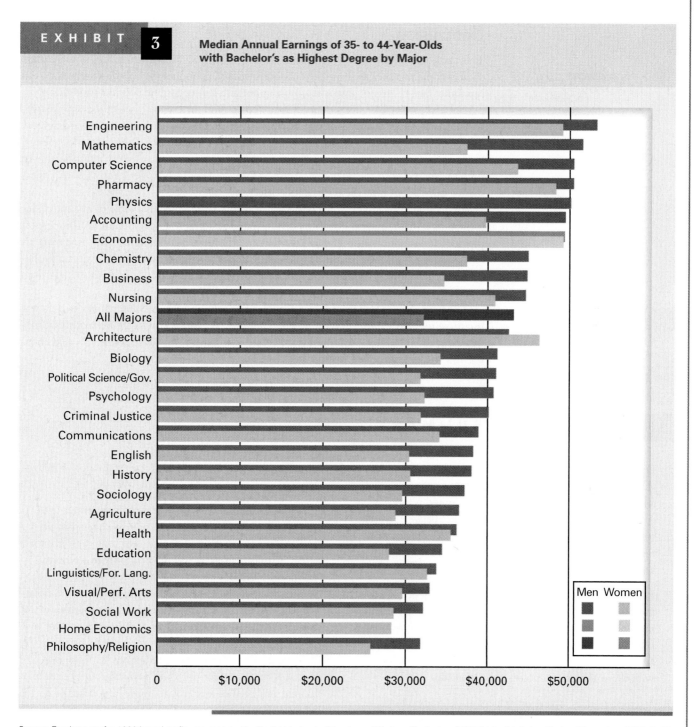

EXHIBIT 3

Median Annual Earnings of 35- to 44-Year-Olds with Bachelor's as Highest Degree by Major

Source: Earnings are for 1993 based on figures reported by Daniel Hecker in "Earnings of College Graduates, 1993," *Monthly Labor Review* (December 1995): 3–17.

Conclusion

This textbook describes how economic factors affect individual choices and how all these choices come together to shape the economic system. Economics is not the whole story, and economic factors are not always the most important. But economic considerations have important and predictable effects on individual choices, and these choices affect the way we live.

Sure, economics is a challenging discipline, but it is also an exciting and rewarding one. The good news is that you already know a lot about economics. To use this knowledge, however, you must cultivate the art and science of economic analysis. You must be able to simplify the world to formulate questions, isolate the relevant variables, and then tell a persuasive story about how these variables relate.

An economic relation can be expressed in words, represented as a table of quantities, described by a mathematical equation, or illustrated as a graph. The appendix to this chapter provides an introduction to graphs. You may find this information unnecessary. If you are already familiar with relations among variables, slopes, tangents, and the like, you can probably just browse. But if you have little recent experience with graphs, you might benefit from a more careful reading with pencil and paper in hand.

The next chapter will introduce key tools of economic analysis. Subsequent chapters will use these ideas to explore economic problems and to explain economic behavior that may otherwise seem puzzling. You must walk before you can run, however, and in the next chapter, you will take your first wobbly steps.

SUMMARY

1. Economics is the study of how people choose to use their scarce resources to produce, exchange, and consume goods and services in an attempt to satisfy unlimited wants. The economic problem arises from the conflict between scarce resources and unlimited wants. If wants were limited or if resources were not scarce, there would be no need to study economics.

2. Economic resources are combined in a variety of ways to produce goods and services. Major categories of resources include labor, capital, natural resources, and entrepreneurial ability. Because economic resources are scarce, only a limited number of goods and services can be produced with them; therefore, choices must be made.

3. Microeconomics focuses on choices made in households, firms, and governments and how these choices affect particular markets, such as the market for used cars. Choice is guided by rational self-interest. Choice typically requires time and information, both of which are scarce and valuable.

4. Whereas microeconomics examines the individual pieces of the puzzle, macroeconomics steps back to look at the big picture—the performance of the economy as a whole as reflected by such measures as total production, employment, the price level, and economic growth.

5. Economists use theories, or models, to help understand the effects of economic changes, such as changes in price and income, on individual choices and how these choices affect particular markets and the economy as a whole. Economists employ the scientific method to study an economic problem by (a) formulating the question and isolating relevant variables, (b) specifying the assumptions under which the theory operates, (c) developing a theory, or hypothesis, about how the variables relate, and (d) testing that theory by comparing its predictions with the evidence. A theory might not work perfectly, but it is useful as long as it predicts better than competing theories do.

6. Positive economics aims to discover how the economy works. Normative economics is concerned more with how, in someone's opinion, the economy should work. Those who are not careful can fall victim to the fallacy that association is causation, to the fallacy of composition, and to the mistake of ignoring secondary effects.

QUESTIONS FOR REVIEW

1. *(Definition of Economics)* What determines whether or not a resource is scarce? Why is the concept of scarcity important to the definition of economics?

2. *(Resources)* To which category of resources does each of the following belong?

    a. A taxicab
    b. Computer software
    c. One hour of legal counsel
    d. A parking lot
    e. A forest
    f. The Mississippi River
    g. An individual introducing a new way to market products on the Internet

3. *(Goods and Services)* Explain why each of the following would *not* be considered "free" for the economy as a whole:

    a. Food stamps
    b. U.S. aid to developing countries
    c. Corporate charitable contributions
    d. Noncable television programs
    e. Public high school education

4. *(Economic Decision Makers)* Which group of economic decision makers plays the leading role in the economic system? Which groups play supporting roles? In what sense are they supporting actors?

5. *(Micro Versus Macro)* Determine whether each of the following is primarily a microeconomic or a macroeconomic issue:

    a. Determining the price to charge for an automobile
    b. Measuring the impact of tax policies on total consumption spending in the economy
    c. A household's decisions about how to allocate its disposable income among various goods and services
    d. A worker's decision regarding how many hours to work each week
    e. Designing a government policy to affect the level of employment

6. *(Micro Versus Macro)* Some economists believe that to really understand macroeconomics, you must fully understand microeconomics. How does microeconomics relate to macroeconomics?

7. *(Normative Versus Positive Analysis)* Determine whether each of the following statements is normative or positive:

    a. The U.S. unemployment rate was below 6.0 percent in 2003.
    b. The inflation rate in the United States is too high.
    c. The U.S. government should increase the minimum wage.
    d. U.S. trade restrictions cost consumers $20 billion annually.

8. *(Role of Theory)* What good is economic theory if it cannot predict the behavior of a specific individual?

PROBLEMS AND EXERCISES

9. *(Rational Self-Interest)* Discuss the impact of rational self-interest on each of the following decisions:

    a. Whether to attend college full time or enter the workforce full time
    b. Whether to buy a new textbook or a used textbook
    c. Whether to attend a local college or an out-of-town college

10. *(Rational Self-Interest)* If behavior is governed by rational self-interest, why do people make charitable contributions?

11. *(Marginal Analysis)* The owner of a small pizzeria is deciding whether to increase the radius of its delivery area by one mile. What considerations must be taken into account if such a decision is to contribute to profitability?

12. *(Time and Information)* It is often costly to obtain the information necessary to make good decisions. Yet your own interests can be best served by rationally weighing all options available to you. This requires informed decision making. Does this mean that making uninformed decisions is irrational? How do you determine how much information is the right amount?

13. (*C a s e* **S t u d y**: A Yen for Vending Machines) Do vending machines conserve on any resources other than labor? Does your answer offer any additional insight into the widespread use of vending machines in Japan?

14. (*C a s e* **S t u d y**: A Yen for Vending Machines) Suppose you had the choice of purchasing identically priced lunches from a vending machine or at a cafeteria. Which would you choose? Why?

15. *(Pitfalls of Economic Analysis)* Review the discussion of pitfalls in economic thinking in this chapter. Then identify the fallacy or mistake in thinking in each of the following statements:

   a. Raising taxes will always increase government revenues.
   b. Whenever there is a recession, imports decrease. Therefore, to stop a recession, we should increase imports.
   c. Raising the tariff on imported steel will help the U.S. steel industry. Therefore, the entire economy will be helped.
   d. Gold sells for about $400 per ounce. Therefore, the U.S. government could sell all the gold in Fort Knox at $400 per ounce and eliminate the national debt.

16. *(Association Versus Causation)* Suppose I observe that communities with lots of doctors tend to have relatively high rates of illness. I conclude that doctors cause illness. What's wrong with this reasoning?

EXPERIENTIAL EXERCISES

17. *(Micro Versus Macro)* Go to the Bank of Sweden's page on the Nobel Prize in economic science at http://www.nobel.se/economics/. Review the descriptions of some recent awards, and try to determine whether those particular awards were primarily for work in macroeconomics or in microeconomics.

18. (*C a s e* **S t u d y**: College Major and Career Earnings) The Bureau of Labor Statistics maintains online copies of articles from its *Monthly Labor Review*. Go to the site http://stats.bls.gov/opub/mlr/mlrhome.htm, click on "Archives" and find the article by Daniel Hecker entitled "Earnings of College Graduates: Women Compared with Men" (March 1998). What can you learn about the payoff to college education for both women and men? (Note: You will need Adobe Acrobat Reader to get the full text of this article. You can download a copy of Reader at http://www.adobe.com/prodindex/acrobat/readstep.html.

19. *(Wall Street Journal)* Detecting economic fallacies is an important skill. Review the section titled "Some Pitfalls of Faulty Economic Analysis" in this chapter. Then use the *Wall Street Journal* to find at least one example of faulty reasoning. (Hint: Begin with the "Markets Diary" column in the "Money & Investing" section.)

HOMEWORK XPRESS! EXERCISES

*These exercises require access to McEachern Homework Xpress! If Homework Xpress! did not come with your book, visit **http://homeworkxpress.swlearning.com** to purchase.*

1. The price for a basic cheese pizza at Giorgio's is $5. Each additional topping is $1. Sketch a graph to illustrate the relationship between the price of a pizza and the number of toppings for up to 5 toppings.

2. Reproductions of the National Gallery of Art's *Girl with a Watering Can* by Renoir are offered for sale in the gift shop. The manager finds that if she sets the price at $20, no reproductions are sold. For every dollar she reduces the price, 10 additional copies are sold each week. Sketch a graph showing the relationship between the price of a reproduction and the number sold each week.

3. Economists studying consumption of pizza notice that households buy more pizzas per month as income increases, but only up to an income of $3,000 per month. At this income level, the average household consumes 10 pizzas per month. As income increases beyond this level, household consumption of pizzas declines. Sketch a graph showing a curvilinear relationship between household income and the number of pizzas consumed per month.

4. Nicer Pants Inc. found that at a price of $50 per pair, no one bought its product. For every dollar less it charged, it sold an additional 200 pairs of pants per month. Draw a graph to illustrate the relationship between the price of the pants and the quantity purchased per month. Label this as D for consumer demand.

   Due to an economics recession, the firm now finds that it has no sales at prices about $40 per pair. However, for each dollar it reduces the prices, it still sells an additional 200 pairs per month. Sketch a graph to illustrate this new relationship between the price of the pants and the quantity purchased each month. Label this as D1.

Understanding Graphs

Take out a pencil and a blank piece of paper. Go ahead. Put a point in the middle of the paper. This is your point of departure, called the **origin.** With your pencil at the origin, draw a straight line off to the right. This line is called the **horizontal axis.** The value of the variable *x* measured along the horizontal axis increases as you move to the right of the origin. Now mark off this line from 0 to 20, in increments of 5 units each. Returning to the origin, draw another line, this one straight up. This line is called the **vertical axis.** The value of the variable *y* measured along the vertical axis increases as you move upward. Mark off this line from 0 to 20, in increments of 5 units each.

Within the space framed by the two axes, you can plot possible combinations of the variables measured along each axis. Each point identifies a value measured along the horizontal, or *x,* axis *and a* value measured along the vertical, or *y,* axis. For example, place point *a* in your graph to reflect the combination where *x* equals 5 units and *y* equals 15 units. Likewise, place point *b* in your graph to reflect 10 units of *x* and 5 units of *y.* Now compare your results with points shown in Exhibit 4.

A **graph** is a picture showing how variables relate, and a picture can be worth a thousand words. Take a look at Exhibit 5, which shows the U.S. annual unemployment rate since 1900. The year is measured along the horizontal axis and the unemployment rate along the vertical axis. Exhibit 5 is a *time-series graph,* which shows the value of a variable, in this case the unemployment rate, over time. If you had to describe the information presented in Exhibit 5 in words, the explanation could take many words. The picture shows not only how one year compares to the next but also how one decade compares to another and how the rate trends over time. The sharply higher unemployment rate during the Great Depression of the 1930s is unmistakable. *Graphs convey information in a compact and efficient way.*

This appendix shows how graphs express a variety of possible relations among variables. Most graphs of interest in this book reflect the relationship between two economic variables, such as the unemployment rate and the year, the price of a product and the quantity demanded, or the price of production and the quantity supplied. Because we focus on just two variables at a time, we usually assume that other relevant variables remain constant.

One variable often depends on another. The time it takes you to drive home depends on your average speed. Your weight depends on how much you eat. The amount of Pepsi people buy depends on its price. A *functional relation* exists between two variables when the value of one variable *depends* on the value of another variable. The value of the **dependent variable** depends on the value of the **independent variable.** The task of the economist is to isolate economic relations and determine the direction of causality, if

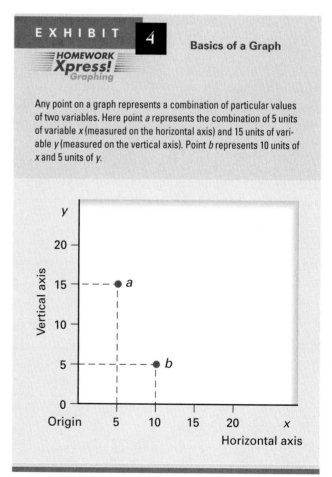

EXHIBIT 4

Basics of a Graph

HOMEWORK Xpress! Graphing

Any point on a graph represents a combination of particular values of two variables. Here point *a* represents the combination of 5 units of variable *x* (measured on the horizontal axis) and 15 units of variable *y* (measured on the vertical axis). Point *b* represents 10 units of *x* and 5 units of *y*.

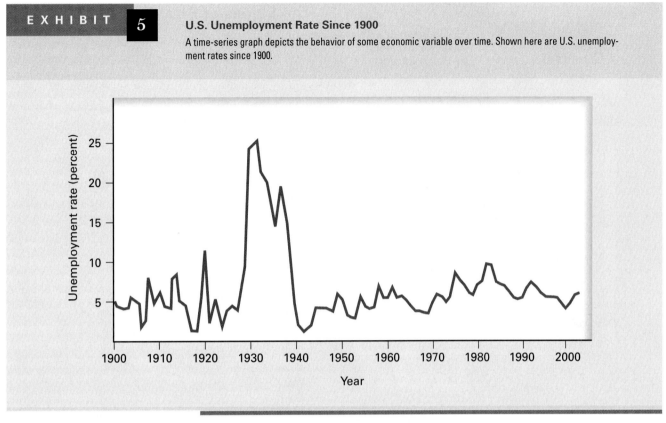

EXHIBIT 5

U.S. Unemployment Rate Since 1900

A time-series graph depicts the behavior of some economic variable over time. Shown here are U.S. unemployment rates since 1900.

Sources: *Historical Statistics of the United States,* 1970, and *Economic Report of the President,* February 2004.

any. Recall that one of the pitfalls of economic thinking is the erroneous belief that association is causation. We cannot conclude that, simply because two events relate in time, one causes the other. There may be no relation between the two events.

Drawing Graphs

Let's begin with a simple relation. Suppose you are planning to drive across country and want to determine how far you will travel each day. You plan to average 50 miles per hour. Possible combinations of driving time and distance traveled appear in Exhibit 6. One column lists the hours driven per day, and the next column lists the number of miles traveled per day, assuming an average speed of 50 miles per hour. The distance traveled, the *dependent* variable, depends on the number of hours driven, the *independent* variable. Combinations of hours driven and distance traveled are shown as *a, b, c, d,* and *e.* Each combination of hours driven and distance

EXHIBIT 6

Schedule Relating Distance Traveled to Hours Driven

	Hours Driven per Day	Distance Traveled per Day (miles)
a	1	50
b	2	100
c	3	150
d	4	200
e	5	250

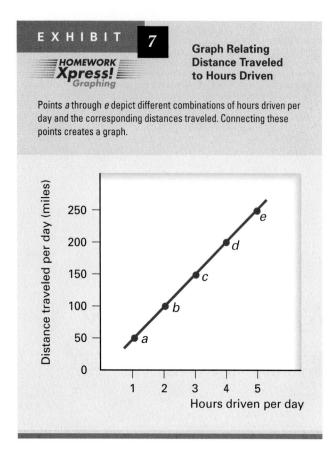

EXHIBIT 7

HOMEWORK
Xpress!
Graphing

Graph Relating Distance Traveled to Hours Driven

Points *a* through *e* depict different combinations of hours driven per day and the corresponding distances traveled. Connecting these points creates a graph.

The Slopes of Straight Lines

A more precise way to describe the shape of a curve is to measure its slope. The **slope of a line** indicates how much the vertical variable changes for a given increase in the horizontal variable. Specifically, the slope between any two points along any straight line is the vertical change between these two points divided by the horizontal increase, or

$$\text{Slope} = \frac{\text{Change in the vertical distance}}{\text{Increase in the horizontal distance}}$$

Each of the four panels in Exhibit 8 indicates a vertical change, given a 10-unit increase in the horizontal variable. In panel (a), the vertical distance increases by 5 units when the horizontal distance increases by 10 units. The slope of the line is therefore 5/10, or 0.5. Notice that the slope in this case is a positive number because the relation between the two variables is positive, or direct. This slope indicates that for every 1-unit increase in the horizontal variable, the vertical variable increases by 0.5 units. The slope, incidentally, does not imply causality; the increase in the horizontal variable does not necessarily *cause* the increase in the vertical variable. The slope simply measures the relation between an increase in the horizontal variable and the associated change in the vertical variable.

In panel (b) of Exhibit 8, the vertical distance declines by 7 units when the horizontal distance increases by 10 units, so the slope equals −7/10, or −0.7. The slope in this case is a negative number because the two variables have a negative, or inverse, relation. In panel (c), the vertical variable remains unchanged as the horizontal variable increases by 10, so the slope equals 0/10, or 0. These two variables are unrelated. Finally, in panel (d), the vertical variable can take on any value, although the horizontal variable remains unchanged. Again, the two variables are unrelated. In this case, any change in the vertical measure, for example a 10-unit change, is divided by 0, because the horizontal value does not change. Any change divided by 0 is infinitely large, so we say that the slope of a vertical line is infinite.

traveled is represented by a point in Exhibit 7. For example, point *a* shows that if you drive for 1 hour, you travel 50 miles. Point *b* indicates that if you drive for 2 hours, you travel 100 miles. By connecting the points, or combinations, we create a line running upward and to the right. This makes sense, because the longer you drive, the farther you travel. Assumed constant along this line is your average speed of 50 miles per hour.

Types of relations between variables include the following:

1. As one variable increases, the other increases—as in Exhibit 7; this is called a **positive,** or **direct, relation** between the variables.

2. As one variable increases, the other decreases; this is called a **negative,** or **inverse, relation.**

3. As one variable increases, the other remains unchanged; the two variables are said to be *independent,* or *unrelated.* One of the advantages of graphs is that they easily convey the relation between variables. We do not need to examine the particular combinations of numbers; we need only focus on the shape of the curve.

The Slope, Units of Measurement, and Marginal Analysis

The mathematical value of the slope depends on the units measured on the graph. For example, suppose copper tubing costs $1 a foot to make. Graphs depicting the relation between output and total cost are shown in Exhibit 9. In panel (a), the total cost of production increases by $1 for each

EXHIBIT 8 **Alternative Slopes for Straight Lines**

The slope of a line indicates how much the vertically measured variable changes for a given increase in the variable measured along the horizontal axis. Panel (a) shows a positive relation between two variables; the slope is 0.5, a positive number. Panel (b) depicts a negative, or inverse, relation. When the *x* variable increases, the *y* variable decreases; the slope is –0.7, a negative number. Panels (c) and (d) represent situations in which two variables are unrelated. In panel (c), the *y* variable always takes on the same value; the slope is 0. In panel (d), the *x* variable always takes on the same value; the slope is infinite.

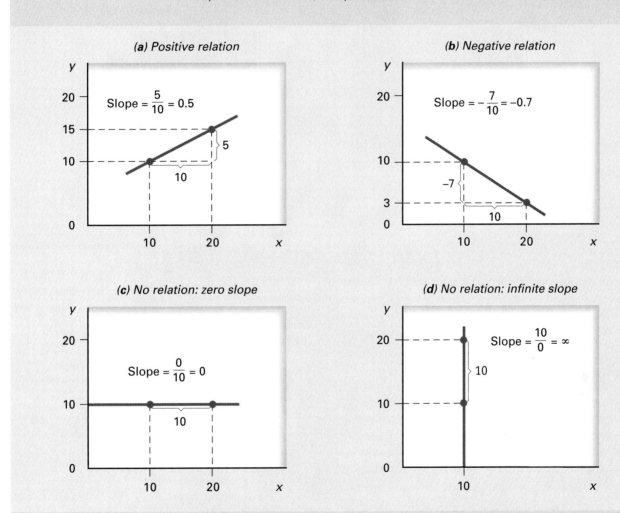

1-foot increase in the amount of tubing produced. Thus, the slope equals 1/1, or 1. If the cost per foot remains the same but the unit of measurement is not *feet* but *yards,* the relation between output and total cost is as depicted in panel (b). Now total cost increases by \$3 for each 1-*yard* increase in output, so the slope equals 3/1, or 3. Because different units are used to measure the copper tubing, the two panels reflect different slopes, even though the cost of tubing is \$1 per foot

in each panel. Keep in mind that *the slope will depend in part on the units of measurement.*

Economic analysis usually involves *marginal analysis,* such as the marginal cost of producing one more unit of output. The slope is a convenient device for measuring marginal effects because it reflects the change in total cost along the vertical axis for each 1-unit change in output along the horizontal axis. For example, in panel (a) of Exhibit 9, the

EXHIBIT **9**   **Slope Depends on the Unit of Measure**
The value of the slope depends on the units of measure. In panel (a), output is measured in feet of copper tubing; in panel (b), output is measured in yards. Although the cost of production is $1 per foot in each panel, the slope is different in the two panels because copper tubing is measured using different units.

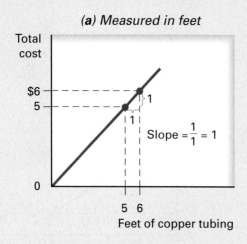

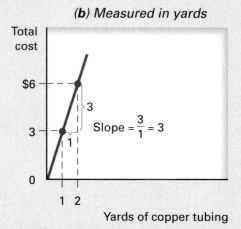

marginal cost of another *foot* of copper tubing is $1, which also equals the slope of the line. In panel (b), the marginal cost of another *yard* of tubing is $3, which again is the slope of that line. Because of its applicability to marginal analysis, the slope has special relevance in economics.

The Slopes of Curved Lines

The slope of a straight line is the same everywhere along the line, but the slope of a curved line differs along the curve, as shown in Exhibit 10. To find the slope of a curved line at a particular point, draw a straight line that just touches the curve at that point but does not cut or cross the curve. Such a line is called a **tangent** to the curve at that point. The slope of the tangent is the slope of the curve at that point. Look at the line *A,* which is tangent to the curve at point *a.* As the horizontal value increases from 0 to 10, the vertical value drops along *A* from 40 to 0. Thus, the vertical change divided by the horizontal change equals −40/10, or −4, which is the slope of the curve at point *a.* This slope is negative because the curve slopes downward at that point. Line *B,* a line tangent to the curve at point *b,* has the slope −10/30, or −0.33. As you can see, the curve depicted in Exhibit 10 gets flatter as the horizontal variable increases, so the value of its slope approaches zero.

Other curves, of course, will reflect different slopes as well as different changes in the slope along the curve.

Downward-sloping curves have a negative slope, and upward-sloping curves, a positive slope. Sometimes curves, such as those in Exhibit 11, are more complex, having both

EXHIBIT **10**   **Slope at Different Points on a Curved Line**

The slope of a curved line varies from point to point. At a given point, such as *a* or *b*, the slope of the curve is equal to the slope of the straight line that is tangent to the curve at that point.

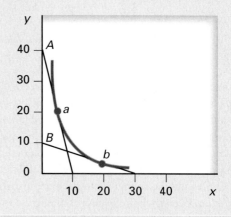

E X H I B I T **11**

Curves with Both Positive and Negative Slopes

Some curves have both positive and negative slopes. The hill-shaped curve has a positive slope to the left of point *a*, a slope of 0 at point *a*, and a negative slope to the right of that point. The U-shaped curve starts off with a negative slope, has a slope of 0 at point *b*, and has a positive slope to the right of that point.

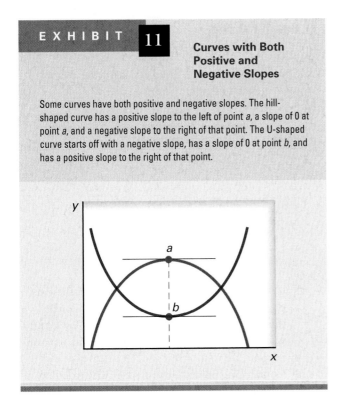

E X H I B I T **12**

Shift in Line Relating Distance Traveled to Hours Driven

Line *T* appeared originally in Exhibit 7 to show the relation between hours driven per day and distance traveled per day, assuming an average speed of 50 miles per hour. If the average speed is only 40 miles per hour, the entire relation shifts to the right to *T'*, indicating that each distance traveled requires more driving time. For example, 200 miles traveled takes 4 hours of driving at 50 miles per hour but 5 hours at 40 miles per hour. This figure shows how a change in assumptions, in this case, the average speed assumed, can shift the entire relationship between two variables.

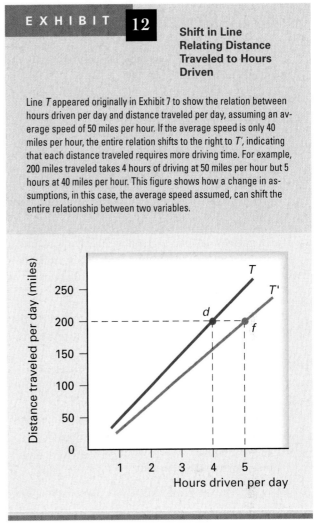

positive and negative ranges. In the hill-shaped curve, for small values of *x*, there is a positive relation between *x* and *y*, so the slope is positive. As the value of *x* increases, however, the slope declines and eventually becomes negative. We can divide the curve into two segments: (1) the segment between the origin and point *a*, where the slope is positive; and (2) the segment of the curve to the right of point *a*, where the slope is negative. The slope of the curve at point *a* is 0. The U-shaped curve in Exhibit 11 represents the opposite relation: *x* and *y* are negatively related until point *b* is reached; thereafter, they are positively related. The slope equals 0 at point *b*.

Line Shifts

Let's go back to the example of your cross-country trip, where we were trying to determine how many miles you traveled per day. Recall that we measured hours driven per day on the horizontal axis and miles traveled per day on the vertical axis, assuming an average speed of 50 miles per hour. That same relation is shown as line *T* in Exhibit 12. What if the average speed is 40 miles per hour? The entire relation

between hours driven and distance traveled would change, as shown by the shift to the right of line *T* to *T'*. With a slower average speed, any distance traveled per day now requires more driving time. For example, 200 miles traveled requires 4 hours of driving when the average speed is 50 miles per hour (as shown by point *d* on curve *T*), but 200 miles takes 5 hours when your speed averages 40 miles per hour (as shown by point *f* on curve *T'*). Thus, *a change in the assumption about average speed changes the relationship between the two variables observed.* This changed relationship is expressed by a shift of the line that shows how the two variables relate.

That ends our once-over of graphs. Return to this appendix when you need a review.

APPENDIX QUESTIONS

1. *(Understanding Graphs)* Look at Exhibit 5 and answer the following questions:

    a. In what year (approximately) was the unemployment rate the highest? In what year was it the lowest?
    b. In what decade, on average, was the unemployment rate highest? In what decade was it lowest?
    c. Between 1950 and 1980, did the unemployment rate generally increase, decrease, or remain about the same?

2. *(Drawing Graphs)* Sketch a graph to illustrate your idea of each of the following relationships. Be sure to label both axes appropriately. In each case, explain under what circumstances, if any, the curve could shift:

    a. The relationship between a person's age and height
    b. Average monthly temperature over the course of a year
    c. A person's income and the number of hamburgers consumed per month
    d. The amount of fertilizer added to an acre of land and the amount of corn grown on that land in one growing season
    e. An automobile's horsepower and its gasoline mileage (in miles per gallon)

3. *(Slope)* Suppose you are given the following data on wage rates and number of hours worked:

Point	Hourly Wage	Hours Worked per Week
a	$0	0
b	5	0
c	10	30
d	15	35
e	20	45
f	25	50

    a. Construct and label a set of axes and plot these six points. Label each point. Which variable do you think should be measured on the vertical axis, and which variable should be measured on the horizontal axis?
    b. Connect the points. Describe the curve you find. Does it make sense to you?
    c. Compute the slope of the curve between points *a* and *b*. Between points *b* and *c*. Between points *c* and *d*. Between points *d* and *e*. Between points *e* and *f*. What happens to the slope as you move from point *a* to point *f*?

Some Tools of Economic Analysis

© Digital Vision/Getty Images

W hy are you reading this book right now rather than doing something else? What is college costing you? Why will you eventually major in one subject rather than continue to take courses in different ones? Why is fast food so fast? Why is there no sense crying over spilt milk? These and other questions are addressed in this chapter, which introduces some tools of economics—some tools of the trade.

Chapter 1 introduced the idea that scarcity forces us to make choices, but the chapter said little about how to make economic choices. This chapter develops a framework for evaluating economic alternatives. First, we consider the cost involved in selecting one alternative over others. Next, we develop tools to explore the choices available to individuals and to the economy as a whole. Finally, we examine the questions that different economies must answer—questions about what goods and services to produce, how to produce them, and for whom to produce them. Topics discussed include:

- Opportunity cost
- Division of labor
- Comparative advantage
- Specialization

- Production possibilities frontier
- Three economic questions
- Economic systems

Choice and Opportunity Cost

Think about a decision you just made: the decision to read this chapter right now rather than use your time to study for another course, play sports, watch TV, go online, get some sleep, hang with friends, or do something else. Suppose your best alternative to reading right now is getting some sleep. The cost of reading is passing up the opportunity of sleep. Because of scarcity, whenever you make a choice, you must pass up another opportunity; you must incur an *opportunity cost*.

Opportunity Cost

Economics in the Movies

OPPORTUNITY COST

The value of the best alternative forgone when an item or activity is chosen

What do we mean when we talk about the cost of something? Isn't it what we must give up—must forgo—to get that thing? The **opportunity cost** of the chosen item or activity is *the value of the* best *alternative that is forgone*. You can think of opportunity cost as the *opportunity lost*. Sometimes opportunity cost can be measured in terms of money, although, as we shall see, money is usually only part of opportunity cost.

How many times have you heard people say they did something because they "had nothing better to do"? They actually mean they had no alternatives as attractive as the choice they selected. Yet, according to the idea of opportunity cost, people *always* do what they do because they have nothing better to do. The choice selected seems, at the time, preferable to any other possible choice. You are reading this chapter right now because you have nothing better to do. In fact, you are attending college for the same reason: College appears more attractive than your best alternative, as discussed in the following case study.

Case Study

Bringing Theory to Life

*e*Activity
Is college a sensible investment for you? Find out by reading "Sure You Should Go to College?" by Marty Nemko from the *Princeton Review* at http://www.princetonreview.com/college/research/articles/find/shouldyougo.asp.

The Opportunity Cost of College

What is your opportunity cost of attending college full time this year? What was the best alternative you gave up? If you held a full-time job, you have some idea of the income you gave up to attend college. Suppose you expected to earn $16,000 a year, after taxes, from a full-time job. As a full-time college student, you plan to work part time during the academic year and full time during the summer, earning a total of $7,000 after taxes. Thus, by attending college this year, you gave up after-tax earnings of $9,000 (= $16,000 − $7,000).

There is also the direct cost of college itself. Suppose you are paying $5,000 this year for in-state tuition, fees, and books at a public college (paying out-of-state rates would add another $5,000 to that, and attending a private college would add about $13,000). The opportunity cost of paying for tuition, fees, and books is what you and your family could otherwise have purchased with that money.

How about room and board? Expenses for room and board are not necessarily an opportunity cost because, even if you were not attending college, you would still need to live somewhere and eat something, though these could cost more in college. Likewise, whether or not you attended college, you would still buy items such as DVDs, CDs, clothes, toiletries, and laundry. These items are not an opportunity cost of attending college; they are personal upkeep costs that arise regardless of what you do. So for simplicity, assume that room, board, and personal expenses are the same whether or not you attend college. The forgone earnings of $9,000 plus the $5,000 for tuition, fees, and books yield an opportunity cost of $14,000 this year for a student paying in-state rates at a public college. Opportunity cost jumps to about $19,000 for students paying out-of-state rates and to about $27,000 for those at private colleges. Scholarships, but not loans, would reduce your opportunity cost (why not loans?).

This analysis assumes that other things remain constant. But if, in your view, attending college is more of a pain than you expected your next best alternative to be, then the opportunity cost of attending college is even higher. In other words, if you are one of those people who find college difficult, often boring, and in most ways more unpleasant than a full-time job, then the cost in money terms understates your opportunity cost. Not only are you incurring the expense of college, but you are also forgoing a more pleasant quality of life. If, on the other hand, you believe the wild and crazy life of a college student is more enjoyable than a full-time job would be, then the above figures overstate your opportunity cost, because the next best alternative involves a less satisfying quality of life.

Apparently, you view college as a wise investment in your future, even though it's costly and maybe even painful. College graduates on average earn about twice as much per year as high school graduates, a difference that exceeds $1 million over a lifetime. These pay gains from college encourage a growing fraction of college students to pile up debts to finance their education.

Still, college is not for everyone. Some find the opportunity cost too high. For example, Tiger Woods, once an economics major at Stanford, dropped out after two years to earn a fortune in professional golf. Some high school seniors who believe they are ready for professional basketball skip college altogether, as do most pro tennis players and many singers and actors. Some would-be actors even drop out of high school to pursue their careers, including Drew Barrymore, Tom Cruise, Cameron Diaz, Matt Dillon, Nicole Kidman, Demi Moore, Keanu Reeves, Kiefer Sutherland, and Catherine Zeta-Jones.

Sources: "College Tuition 101," *Wall Street Journal*, 15 September 2003; and Mary Beth Marklein, "College Braces for Bigger Classes and Less Bang for More Buck," *USA Today*, 27 August 2003; Greg Winter and Jennifer Medina, "More Students Line Up at Financial Aid Office," *New York Times*, 10 March 2003; and "2002–2003 College Costs," http://www.collegeboard.com/.

Opportunity Cost Is Subjective

Like beauty, opportunity cost is in the eye of the beholder. It is subjective. Only the individual making the choice can identify the most attractive alternative. But the chooser seldom knows the actual value of the best alternative forgone, because that alternative is "the road not taken." If you give up an evening of pizza and conversation with friends to work on a term paper, you will never know the exact value of what you gave up. You know only what you *expected*. Evidently, you expected the value of working on that paper to exceed the value of the best alternative. (Incidentally, focusing on the best alternative forgone makes all other alternatives irrelevant.)

Calculating Opportunity Cost Requires Time and Information

Economists assume that people rationally choose the most valued alternative. The idea of choosing rationally does not mean people exhaustively calculate the value of all possibilities. Because acquiring information about alternatives is costly and time consuming, people usually make choices based on limited or even incorrect information. Indeed, some choices may turn out to be poor ones (you went for a picnic but it rained; the DVD you rented stunk; your new shoes pinch; the exercise equipment you bought gets no exercise). Regret about lost opportunities is captured in the common expression "coulda, woulda, shoulda." At the time you made the choice, however, you thought you were making the best use of all your scarce resources, including the time required to gather and evaluate information about your alternatives.

Time Is the Ultimate Constraint

The sultan of Brunei is among the world's richest people, with wealth estimated at over $10 billion based on huge oil revenues that flow into his tiny country. He has two palaces, one for each wife (though he divorced one in 2003). The larger palace has 1,788 rooms, with walls of fine Italian marble and a throne room the size of a football field. The royal family owns hundreds of cars, including dozens of Rolls-Royces. Supported by such wealth, the sultan appears to have overcome the economic problem caused by scarcity. But though he can buy just about whatever he wants, he lacks the time to enjoy his stuff. If he pursues one activity, he cannot at the same time do something else, so each activity he undertakes has an opportunity cost. Consequently, the sultan must choose from among the competing uses of his scarcest resource, time. Although your alternatives are less exotic, you too face time constraints, especially toward the end of the college term.

Opportunity Cost May Vary with Circumstance

Opportunity cost depends on the value of your alternatives. This is why you are more likely to study on a Tuesday night than on a Saturday night. On a Tuesday night, the opportunity cost of studying is lower because your alternatives are less attractive than on a Saturday night, when more is happening. Suppose you go to a movie on Saturday night. Your opportunity cost is the value of your best alternative forgone, which might be attending a college game. For some of you, studying on Saturday night may be well down the list of alternatives—perhaps ahead of reorganizing your closet but behind doing your laundry.

Opportunity cost is subjective, but in some cases, money paid for goods and services is a reasonable approximation. For example, the opportunity cost of the new DVD player you bought is the value of spending that $100 on the best forgone alternative. The money measure may leave out some important elements, however, particularly the value of the time involved. For example, renting a movie costs you not just the $4 rental fee but the time and travel required to get it, watch it, and return it.

Sunk Cost and Choice

Suppose you have just finished shopping for groceries and are wheeling your grocery cart toward the checkout counters. How do you decide which line to join? You pick the shortest one. Suppose, after waiting 10 minutes in a line that barely moves, you notice that a cashier has opened another cash register and invites you to check out. Do you switch to the open line, or do you think, "Since I've already spent 10 minutes in this line, I'm staying put"? The 10 minutes you waited represents a **sunk cost,** which is a cost that has already been incurred and cannot be recovered, regardless of what you do now. You should ignore sunk cost in making economic choices. Hence, you should switch to the newly opened register. *Economic decision makers should consider only those costs that are affected by the choice. Sunk costs have already been incurred and are not affected by the choice, so they are irrelevant.* Likewise, you should walk out on a bad movie, even if it cost you $10 to get in. That $10 is gone and sitting through that stinker only makes you worse off. The irrelevance of sunk costs is underscored by the proverb "There's no sense crying over spilt milk." The milk has already spilled, so whatever you do now cannot change that.

Now that you have some idea about opportunity cost, you are ready to consider applying this idea to how best to use scarce resources to help satisfy unlimited wants.

Comparative Advantage, Specialization, and Exchange

Suppose you live in a dormitory. You and your roommate have such tight schedules that you each can spare only about an hour a week for mundane tasks like ironing shirts and typing papers (granted, in reality you may not iron shirts or type papers, but this example will help you understand some important points). Each of you must turn in a typed three-page paper every week, and you each prefer to have your shirts ironed when you have the time. Let's say it takes you a half hour to type your handwritten paper. Your roommate is from the hunt-and-peck school and takes about an hour to type a handwritten paper. But your roommate is a talented ironer and can iron a shirt in 5 minutes flat (or should that be, iron it flat in 5 minutes?). You take twice as long, or 10 minutes, to iron a shirt.

During the hour set aside each week for typing and ironing, typing takes priority. If you each do your own typing and ironing, you type your paper in a half hour and iron three shirts in the remaining half hour. Your roommate takes the entire hour typing the paper, leaving no time for ironing. Thus, if you each do your own, the combined output is two typed papers and three ironed shirts.

The Law of Comparative Advantage

Before long, you each realize that total output would increase if you did all the typing and your roommate did all the ironing. In the hour available for these tasks, you type both papers and your roommate irons 12 shirts. As a result of specialization, total output increases by 9 shirts! You strike a deal to exchange your typing for your roommate's ironing, so you each end up with a typed paper and 6 ironed shirts. Thus, *each of you is better off as a result of specialization and exchange.* By specializing in the task that you each do best, you are using the **law of comparative advantage,** which states that the individual with the lowest opportunity cost of producing a particular output should specialize in producing that output. You face a lower opportunity cost of typing than does your roommate, because in the time it takes to type a paper, you could iron 3 shirts whereas your roommate could iron 12 shirts. And if you face a lower opportunity cost of typing, your roommate must face a lower opportunity cost of ironing (try working that out).

Absolute Advantage Versus Comparative Advantage

The gains from specialization and exchange so far are obvious. A more interesting case is if you are faster at both tasks. Suppose the example changes in one way: your roommate takes

ABSOLUTE ADVANTAGE

The ability to produce something using fewer resources than other producers use

COMPARATIVE ADVANTAGE

The ability to produce something at a lower opportunity cost than other producers face

BARTER

The direct exchange of one good for another without using money

12 minutes to iron a shirt compared with your 10 minutes. You now have an *absolute advantage* in both tasks, meaning each task takes you less time than it does your roommate. More generally, having an **absolute advantage** means making something using fewer resources than other producers require.

Does your absolute advantage in both activities mean specialization is no longer a good idea? Recall that the law of comparative advantage states that the individual with *the lower opportunity cost* of producing a particular good should specialize in that good. You still take 30 minutes to type a paper and 10 minutes to iron a shirt, so your opportunity cost of typing the paper remains at three ironed shirts. Your roommate takes an hour to type a paper and 12 minutes to iron a shirt, so your roommate could iron five shirts in the time it takes to type a paper. Your opportunity cost of typing a paper is ironing three shirts; for your roommate it's ironing five shirts. *Because your opportunity cost of typing is lower than your roommate's, you still have a comparative advantage in typing.* Consequently, your roommate must have a comparative advantage in ironing (again, try working this out to your satisfaction). Therefore, you should do all the typing and your roommate, all the ironing. Although you have an absolute advantage in both tasks, your **comparative advantage** calls for specializing in the task for which you have the lower opportunity cost—in this case, typing.

If neither of you specialized, you could type one paper and iron three shirts. Your roommate could still type just the one paper. Your combined output would be two papers and three shirts. If you each specialized according to comparative advantage, in an hour you could type both papers and your roommate could iron five shirts. Thus, specialization increases total output by two ironed shirts. Even though you are better at both tasks than your roommate, you are comparatively better at typing. Put another way, your roommate, although worse at both tasks, is not quite as bad at ironing as at typing.

Don't think that this is simply common sense. Common sense would lead you to do your own ironing and typing, because you are better at both. *Absolute advantage focuses on who uses the fewest resources, but comparative advantage focuses on what else those resources could have produced—that is, on the opportunity cost of those resources.* Comparative advantage is the better guide to who should do what.

The law of comparative advantage applies not only to individuals but also to firms, regions of a country, and entire nations. Individuals, firms, regions, or countries with the lowest opportunity cost of producing a particular good should specialize in producing that good. Because of such factors as climate, workforce skills, natural resources, and capital stock, certain parts of the country and certain parts of the world have a comparative advantage in producing particular goods. From Washington State apples to Florida oranges, from software in India to hardware in Taiwan—*resources are allocated most efficiently across the country and around the world when production and trade conform to the law of comparative advantage.*

Specialization and Exchange

In the previous example, you and your roommate specialized and then exchanged output. No money was involved. In other words, you engaged in **barter,** where products are traded directly for other products. Barter works best in simple economies with little specialization and few traded goods. But for economies with greater specialization, *money* facilitates exchange. Money—coins, bills, and checks—is a *medium of exchange* because it is the one thing that everyone accepts in return for goods and services.

Because of specialization and comparative advantage, most people consume little of what they produce and produce little of what they consume. Each individual specializes then exchanges that product for money, which in turn is exchanged for goods and services. Did you make anything you are wearing? Probably not. Think about the degree of specialization that went into your cotton shirt. A farmer in a warm climate grew the cotton and sold it to someone who spun it into thread, who sold it to someone who wove it into fabric, who sold it to someone who sewed the shirt, who sold it to a wholesaler, who sold it to a retailer, who sold it to you. Your shirt was produced by many specialists.

Division of Labor and Gains from Specialization

Picture a visit to McDonald's: "Let's see, I'll have a Big Mac, an order of fries, and a chocolate shake." Less than a minute later your order is ready. It would take you much longer to make a homemade version of this meal. Why is the McDonald's meal faster, cheaper, and—for some people—tastier than one you could make yourself? Why is fast food so fast? McDonald's takes advantage of the gains resulting from the **division of labor.** Each worker, rather than preparing an entire meal, specializes in separate tasks. This division of labor allows the group to produce much more.

How is this increase in productivity possible? First, the manager can assign tasks according to *individual preferences and abilities*—that is, according to the law of comparative advantage. The worker with the toothy smile and pleasant personality can handle the customers up front; the one with the strong back but few social graces can handle the heavy lifting out back. Second, a worker who performs the same task again and again gets better at it (experience is a good teacher). The worker filling orders at the drive-through, for example, learns to deal with special problems that arise. Third, no time is lost in moving from one task to another. Finally, and perhaps most importantly, the **specialization of labor** allows for the introduction of more sophisticated production techniques—techniques that would not make sense on a smaller scale. For example, McDonald's large shake machine would be impractical in the home. Specialized machines make workers more productive.

To review: The specialization of labor takes advantage of individual preferences and natural abilities, allows workers to develop more experience at a particular task, reduces the time required to shift between different tasks, and permits the introduction of laborsaving machinery. Specialization and the division of labor occur not only among individuals but also among firms, regions, and indeed entire countries. The cotton shirt mentioned earlier might involve growing cotton in one country, turning it into cloth in another, making the shirt in a third, and selling it in a fourth.

We should also acknowledge the downside of specialization. Doing the same thing all day can become tedious. Consider, for example, the assembly-line worker whose sole task is to tighten a particular bolt. Such a job could drive that worker bonkers or lead to repetitive motion injury. Thus, the gains from dividing production into individual tasks must be weighed against the problems caused by assigning workers to repetitive and tedious jobs.

Specialization is discussed in the following case study.

Specialization Abounds

Evidence of specialization is all around us. Look at the extent of specialization in higher education. A large university may house a dozen or more schools and colleges—agriculture, architecture, business, drama, education, engineering, law, fine arts, liberal arts and sciences, medicine, music, nursing, pharmacy, social work, and more. Some of these include a dozen or more departments. And each department may offer courses in a dozen or more specialties. Economics, for example, offers courses in micro, macro, development, econometrics, economic history, health, industrial organization, international finance, international trade, labor, law and economics, money and banking, poverty, public finance, regulation, urban and

DIVISION OF LABOR

Organizing production of a good into its separate tasks

SPECIALIZATION OF LABOR

Focusing work effort on a particular product or a single task

C a s e **S t u d y**

Bringing Theory to Life

eActivity

Economics is a subject that has benefited from specialization and the division of labor. To get a feel for the many different subjects that economists investigate, take a look at the *Journal of Economic Literature*'s classification system at http://www.aeaweb.org/journal/jel_class_system.html.

regional, and more. Altogether, a university may offer courses in thousands of specialized fields.

How about a trip to the mall? Specialty shops range from luggage to lingerie. Restaurants can be quite specialized—from subs to sushi. Or let your fingers do the walking through the *Yellow Pages,* where you find thousands of specializations. Under "Physicians" alone, you uncover dozens of medical specialties. Without moving a muscle, you can witness the division of labor within a single industry as the credits roll at the end of a movie. There you will see scores of specialists—from gaffer (lighting electrician) to assistant location scout. TV is no different. An episode of *The Sopranos,* for example, requires contributions from about three hundred people.

Magazines also offer fine degrees of specialization, with tens of thousands to choose from. Fans of the Chevy Corvette, for example, can subscribe to *Corvette Enthusiast, Corvette Fever,* or *Vette.* The extent of specialization is perhaps most obvious on the Web, where the pool of potential customers is so vast that individual sites become sharply focused. For example, you can find sites for each of the following: miniature furniture, paper airplanes, musical bowls, prosthetic noses, tongue studs, toe rings, brass knuckles, mouth harps, ferret toys, cat bandannas, juggling equipment, and bug visors (for motorcycle helmets)—just to name a few of the hundreds of thousands of specialty sites. You won't find such specialists at the mall, but they can find their niche in the virtual world. Adam Smith said the degree of specialization is limited by the extent of the market. Sellers on the Web face the broadest customer base in the world.

Source: You can find online versions of the *Yellow Pages* at http://www.yellowpages.com/ and http://www.superpages.com/. Any search engine will turn up the specialty sites reported above.

The Economy's Production Possibilities

The focus to this point has been on how individuals choose to use their scarce resources to satisfy their unlimited wants or, more specifically, how they specialize based on comparative advantage. This emphasis on the individual has been appropriate because the economy is shaped by the choices of individual decision makers, whether they are consumers, producers, or public officials. Just as resources are scarce for the individual, they are also scarce for the economy as a whole (no fallacy of composition here). An economy has millions of different resources that can be combined in all kinds of ways to produce millions of different goods and services. This section steps back from the immense complexity of the real economy to develop our second model, which explores the economy's production options.

Efficiency and the Production Possibilities Frontier

Let's develop a model to get some idea of how much an economy can produce with the resources available. What are the economy's production capabilities? Here are the model's simplifying assumptions:

1. To simplify matters, output is limited to just two broad classes of products: consumer goods, such as pizzas and haircuts, and capital goods—physical capital, such as a pizza ovens, and human capital, such as higher education.

2. The focus is on production during a given period—in this case, a year.

3. The economy's resources are fixed in both quantity and quality during that period.

4. Society's knowledge about how these resources combine to produce output—that is, the available *technology*—does not change during the year.

The point of these assumptions is to freeze the economy's resources and technology in time so we can focus on the economy's production alternatives.

Given the resources and the technology available in the economy, the **production possibilities frontier,** or **PPF,** identifies possible combinations of the two types of goods that can be produced when all available resources are employed fully and efficiently. *Resources are employed fully and efficiently when there is no change that could increase the production of one good without decreasing the production of the other good.* **Efficiency** involves getting the maximum possible output from available resources.

The economy's PPF for consumer goods and capital goods is shown by the curve *AF* in Exhibit 1. Point *A* identifies the amount of consumer goods produced per year if all the economy's resources are used efficiently to produce consumer goods. Point *F* identifies the amount of capital goods produced per year if all the economy's resources are used efficiently to produce capital goods. Points along the curve between *A* and *F* identify possible combinations of the two goods that can be produced when *all* the economy's resources *are used efficiently*.

Inefficient and Unattainable Production

Points inside the PPF, such as *I* in Exhibit 1, represent combinations that do not employ resources fully, employ them inefficiently, or both. Note that point *C* yields more consumer goods and no fewer capital goods than *I*. And point *E* yields more capital goods and no fewer consumer goods than *I*. Indeed, any point along the PPF between *C* and *E*, such as point *D*, yields both more consumer goods and more capital goods than *I*. Hence, point *I* is *inefficient*. By using resources more efficiently or by using previously idle resources, the economy can produce more of at least one good without reducing the production of the other good. Points outside the PPF, such as *U* in Exhibit 1, represent *unattainable* combinations, given the resources and the technology available. Thus, *the PPF not only shows efficient combinations of production but also serves as the boundary between inefficient combinations inside the frontier and unattainable combinations outside the frontier.*

The Shape of the Production Possibilities Frontier

Focus again on point *A* in Exhibit 1. Any movement along the PPF involves giving up some of one good to get more of the other. Movement down along the curve indicates that the opportunity cost of more capital goods is fewer consumer goods. For example, moving from point *A* to point *B increases* the amount of capital goods produced from none to 10 million units but *reduces* production of consumer goods from 50 million to 48 million units. Increasing production of capital goods to 10 million units reduces consumer goods only a little. Capital production initially employs resources (such as heavy machinery used to build factories) that add little to production of consumer goods but are quite productive in making capital goods.

As shown by the dashed lines in Exhibit 1, each additional 10 million units of capital goods reduces consumer goods by successively larger amounts. As more capital goods are produced, the resources drawn away from consumer goods are those that are increasingly better suited to producing consumer goods. *Opportunity cost increases as the economy produces*

PRODUCTION POSSIBILITIES FRONTIER (PPF)

A curve showing alternative combinations of goods that can be produced when available resources are used fully and efficiently; a boundary between inefficient and unattainable combinations

EFFICIENCY

The condition that exists when there is no way resources can be reallocated to increase the production of one good without decreasing the production of another

EXHIBIT 1

The Economy's Production Possibilities Frontier

If the economy uses its available resources and technology fully and efficiently in producing consumer goods and capital goods, that economy is on its production possibilities frontier, *AF*. The PPF is bowed out to illustrate the law of increasing opportunity cost: additional units of capital goods require the economy to sacrifice more and more units of consumer goods. Note that more consumer goods must be given up in moving from *E* to *F* than in moving from *A* to *B*, although in each case the gain in capital goods is 10 million units. Points inside the PPF, such as *I*, represent inefficient use of resources. Points outside the PPF, such as *U*, represent unattainable combinations.

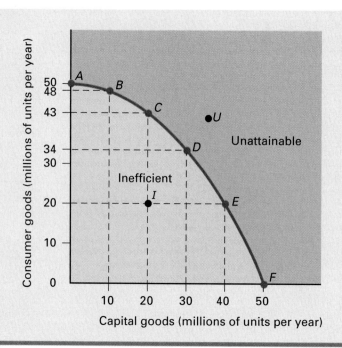

LAW OF INCREASING OPPORTUNITY COST

To produce each additional increment of a good, a successively larger increment of an alternative good must be sacrificed if the economy's resources are already being used efficiently

ECONOMIC GROWTH

An increase in the economy's ability to produce goods and services; an outward shift of the production possibilities frontier

more capital goods, because the resources in the economy are not all perfectly adaptable to the production of both types of goods. The shape of the production possibilities frontier reflects the **law of increasing opportunity cost.** If the economy uses all resources efficiently, the law of increasing opportunity cost states that each additional increment of one good requires the economy to sacrifice successively larger and larger increments of the other good.

The PPF derives its bowed-out shape from the law of increasing opportunity cost. For example, whereas the first 10 million units of capital goods have an opportunity cost of only 2 million units of consumer goods, the final 10 million—that is, the increase from point *E* to point *F*—have an opportunity cost of 20 million units of consumer goods. Notice that the slope of the PPF shows the opportunity cost of an increment of capital. As the economy moves down the curve, the curve becomes steeper, reflecting the higher opportunity cost of capital goods in terms of forgone consumer goods. The law of increasing opportunity cost also applies when moving from the production of capital goods to the production of consumer goods. If resources were perfectly adaptable to alternative uses, the PPF would be a straight line, reflecting a constant opportunity cost along the PPF.

What Can Shift the Production Possibilities Frontier?

Any production possibilities frontier assumes the economy's resources and technology are fixed. Over time, however, the PPF may shift if resources or technology change. **Economic growth** is an expansion in the economy's production possibilities and is reflected by an outward shift of the PPF.

Changes in Resource Availability

If people decide to work longer hours, the PPF shifts outward, as shown in panel (a) of Exhibit 2. An increase in the size or health of the labor force, an increase in the skills of the labor force, or an increase in the availability of other resources, such as new oil discoveries, also shifts the PPF outward. In contrast, a decrease in the availability or quality of resources shifts the PPF inward, as depicted in panel (b). For example, in 1990 Iraq invaded Kuwait, setting oil fields ablaze and destroying much of Kuwait's physical capital, thereby shifting Kuwait's PPF inward. In West Africa, the encroaching sands of the Sahara cover and destroy thousands of square miles of productive farmland each year, shifting the PPF of that economy inward.

The new PPFs in panels (a) and (b) appear to be parallel to the original ones, indicating that the resources that changed could produce both capital goods and consumer goods. For example, an increase in electrical power can enhance the production of both. If a resource such as farmland benefits just consumer goods, then increased availability or productivity of that resource shifts the PPF more along the consumer goods axis, as shown in panel (c). Panel (d) shows the effect of an increase in a resource such as construction equipment that is suited only to capital goods.

[handwritten margin note: similar if one only affects capital goods]

Increases in the Capital Stock

An economy's PPF depends in part on the stock of human and physical capital. The more capital an economy produces during one period, the more output can be produced in the next period. Thus, producing more capital goods this period (for example, more machines in the case of physical capital or better education in the case of human capital) shifts the economy's PPF outward the next period. The choice between consumer goods and capital goods is really the choice between present consumption and future production. Again, the more capital goods produced this period, the greater the economy's production possibilities next period.

Technological Change

A technological discovery that employs resources more efficiently could shift the economy's PPF outward. Some discoveries enhance the production of both capital goods and consumer goods, as shown in panel (a) of Exhibit 2. For example, the Internet has increased each firm's ability to identify available resources. A technological discovery that benefits consumer goods only, such as more disease resistant seeds, is reflected by a rotation outward of the PPF along the consumer goods axis, as shown in panel (c). Note that point F remains unchanged because the technological breakthrough does not affect the production of capital goods. Panel (d) shows a technological advance in the production of capital goods, such as improved software for designing heavy machinery.

What Can We Learn from the PPF?

The PPF demonstrates several ideas introduced so far. The first is *efficiency:* The PPF describes the efficient combinations of outputs, given the economy's resources and technology. The second idea is *scarcity:* Given the stock of resources and technology, the economy can produce only so much. The PPF slopes downward, indicating that, as the economy produces more of one good, it must produce less of the other good, thus demonstrating *opportunity cost.* The PPF's bowed-out shape reflects the *law of increasing opportunity cost,* which arises because some resources are not perfectly adaptable to the production of each good. And a shift outward in the PPF reflects *economic growth.*

Finally, because society must somehow select a specific combination of output—a single point—along the PPF, the PPF also underscores the need for *choice.* Selecting a particular combination determines not only current consumption but also the capital stock available next period. One thing the PPF does not tell us is which combination to choose. The PPF tells us only about the costs, not the benefits, of the two goods. To make a selection, we need

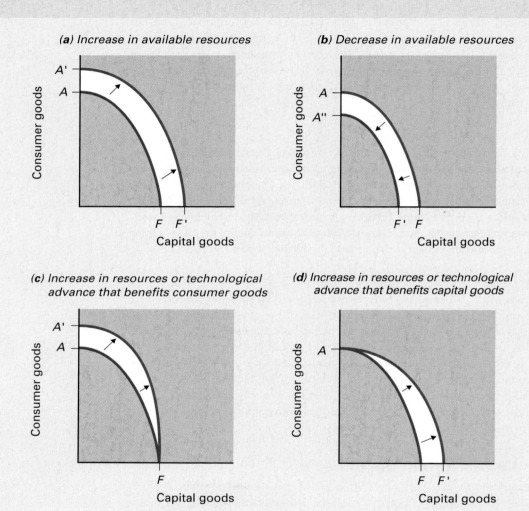

EXHIBIT 2

Shifts in the Economy's Production Possibilities Frontier
When the resources available to an economy change, the PPF shifts. If more resources become available or if technology improves, the PPF shifts outward, as in panel (a), indicating that more output can be produced. A decrease in available resources causes the PPF to shift inward, as in panel (b). Panel (c) shows a change affecting consumer goods production. More consumer goods can now be produced at any given level of capital goods. Panel (d) shows a change affecting capital goods production.

information on both costs *and* benefits. How society goes about choosing a particular combination depends on the nature of the economic system, as you will see shortly.

Three Questions Every Economic System Must Answer

Each point along the economy's production possibilities frontier is an efficient combination of outputs. Whether the economy produces efficiently and how the economy selects the most preferred combination depends on the decision-making rules employed. Regardless of how decisions are made, each economy must answer three fundamental questions: What goods and services are to be produced? How are they to be produced? And for whom are they to be produced? An **economic system** is the set of mechanisms and institutions that resolve the *what, how,* and *for whom* questions. Some criteria used to distinguish among economic systems are (1) who owns the resources, (2) what decision-making process is used to allocate resources and products, and (3) what types of incentives guide economic decision makers.

What Goods and Services Will Be Produced?

Most of us take for granted the incredible number of choices that go into deciding what gets produced—everything from which new kitchen appliances are introduced and to which roads get built and which movies get made (for example, movie studios pay for about 10,000 scripts a year but make only about 500 movies[1]). Although different economies resolve these and millions of other questions using different decision-making rules and mechanisms, all economies must somehow make such choices.

How Will Goods and Services Be Produced?

The economic system must determine how output gets produced. Which resources should be used, and how should they be combined to produce each product? How much labor should be used and at what skill levels? What kinds of machines should be used? What new technology should be incorporated into the latest video games? Should the factory be built in the city or closer to the interstate highway? Millions of individual decisions determine which resources are employed and how these resources are combined.

For Whom Will Goods and Services Be Produced?

Who will actually consume the goods and services produced? The economic system must determine how to allocate the fruits of production among the population. Should everyone receive equal shares? Should the weak and the sick get more? Should those willing to wait in line get more? Should goods be allocated according to height? Weight? Religion? Age? Gender? Race? Looks? Strength? Political connections? The value of resources supplied? The question "For whom will goods and services be produced?" is often referred to as the distribution question.

Economic Systems

Although the three economic questions were discussed separately, they are closely interwoven. The answer to one depends very much on the answers to the others. For example, an economy that distributes goods and services uniformly to all will, no doubt, answer the what-will-be-produced question differently than an economy that somehow allows personal choice. Laws about resource ownership and the role of government determine the "rules of the game"—the set of conditions that shape individual incentives and constraints. Along a spectrum ranging from the freest to the most regimented types of economic systems, *capitalism* would be at one end and the *command system* at the other.

Pure Capitalism

Under **pure capitalism,** the rules of the game include the private ownership of resources and the market allocation of products. Owners have *property rights* to the use of their resources and are therefore free to supply those resources to the highest bidder. **Private property rights** allow individuals to use resources or to charge others for their use. Any

1. As reported in Ian Parker, "The Real McKee," *New Yorker,* 20 October 2003.

ECONOMIC SYSTEM

The set of mechanisms and institutions that resolve the what, how, and for whom questions

WALL STREET JOURNAL

Reading It **Right**

What's the relevance of the following statement from the Wall Street Journal: *"Capitalism is supposed to be the one economic system that puts consumers at the center."*

PURE CAPITALISM

An economic system characterized by the private ownership of resources and the use of prices to coordinate economic activity in unregulated markets

PRIVATE PROPERTY RIGHTS

An owner's right to use, rent, or sell resources or property income derived from supplying labor, capital, natural resources, or entrepreneurial ability goes to the individual resources owners. Producers are free to make and sell whatever they think will be profitable. Consumers are free to buy whatever goods they can afford. All this voluntary buying and selling is coordinated by unrestricted markets, where buyers and sellers make their intentions known. Market prices guide resources to their most productive use and channel goods and services to the consumers who value them the most.

Under pure capitalism, markets answer the what, how, and for whom questions. That's why capitalism is also referred to as *market system*. Markets transmit information about relative scarcity, provide individual incentives, and distribute income among resource suppliers. No individual or small group coordinates these activities. Rather, it is the voluntary choices of many buyers and sellers responding only to their individual incentives and constraints that direct resources and products to those who value them the most. According to Adam Smith (1723–1790), market forces allocate resources as if by an "invisible hand"—an unseen force that harnesses the pursuit of self-interest to direct resources where they earn the greatest payoff. According to Smith, *although each individual pursues his or her self-interest, the "invisible hand" of markets promotes the general welfare.* Capitalism is sometimes called *laissez-faire;* translated from the French, this phrase means "to let do," or to let people do as they choose without government intervention. Thus, under capitalism, voluntary choices based on rational self-interest are made in unrestricted markets to answer the questions what, how, and for whom.

As we will see in later chapters, pure capitalism has its flaws. The most notable market failures are:

1. No central authority protects property rights, enforces contracts, and otherwise ensures that the rules of the game are followed.

2. People with no resources to sell could starve.

3. Some producers may try to monopolize markets by eliminating the competition.

4. The production or consumption of some goods involves harmful side effects, such as pollution, that affect people not involved in the market transaction.

5. Private firms have no incentive to produce so-called *public goods,* such as national defense, because private firms cannot prevent nonpayers from enjoying the benefits of public goods.

Because of these limitations, countries have modified pure capitalism to allow a role for government. Even Adam Smith believed government should play a role. The United States is one of the most market-oriented economies in the world today.

Pure Command System

PURE COMMAND SYSTEM

An economic system characterized by the public ownership of resources and centralized planning

In a **pure command system,** resources are directed and production is coordinated not by market forces but by the "command," or central plan, of government. In theory at least, instead of private property, there is public, or communal, ownership of property. That's why central planning is sometimes called *communism.* Government planners, as representatives of all the people, answer such questions through *central plans* spelling out how much steel, how many cars, and how many homes to produce. They also decide how to produce these goods and who gets them.

In theory, the pure command system incorporates individual choices into collective choices, which, in turn, are reflected in central plans. In practice, the pure command system also has flaws, most notably:

1. Running an economy is so complicated that some resources are used inefficiently.

2. Because nobody in particular owns resources, people have less incentive to employ them in their highest-valued use, so some resources are wasted.

3. Central plans may reflect more the preferences of central planners than those of society.

4. Because government is responsible for all production, the variety of products tends to be more limited than in a capitalist economy.

5. Each individual has less personal freedom in making economic choices.

Because of these limitations, countries have modified the pure command system to allow a role for markets. North Korea is perhaps the most centrally planned economy in the world today.

Mixed and Transitional Economies

No country on earth exemplifies either type of economic system in its pure form. Economic systems have grown more alike over time, with the role of government increasing in capitalist economies and the role of markets increasing in command economies. The United States represents a **mixed system,** with government directly accounting for about one-third of all economic activity. What's more, government regulates the private sector in a variety of ways. For example, local zoning boards determine lot sizes, home sizes, and the types of industries allowed. Federal bodies regulate workplace safety, environmental quality, competitive fairness, food and drug quality, and many other activities.

MIXED SYSTEM
An economic system characterized by the private ownership of some resources and the public ownership of other resources; some markets are unregulated and others are regulated

Although both ends of the spectrum have moved toward the center, capitalism has gained more converts in recent decades. Perhaps the benefits of markets are no better illustrated than where countries were divided by ideology into capitalist economies and command economies, such as Taiwan and China or South Korea and North Korea. In each case, the economies began with similar human and physical resources, but income per capita diverged sharply, with the capitalist economies outperforming the command economies. For example, Taiwan's production per capita in 2003 was 4 times that of China's, and South Korea's production per capita was 13 times that of North Korea's.

Recognizing the incentive power of markets, some of the most die-hard central planners now reluctantly accept some free-market activity. For example, about 20 percent of the world's population lives in China, which grows more market oriented each day, even going so far as to give private property constitutional protection. More than a decade ago, the former Soviet Union dissolved into 15 independent republics; most are trying to convert state-owned enterprises into private firms. From Hungary to Mongolia, the transition to mixed economies now under way in former command economies will shape economies of this new century.

Economies Based on Custom or Religion

Finally, some economic systems are molded largely by custom or religion. For example, caste systems in India and elsewhere restrict occupational choice. Family relations also play significant roles in organizing and coordinating economic activity. Even in the United States, some occupations are still dominated by women, others by men, largely because of tradition. Your own pattern of consumption and choice of occupation may be influenced by some of these factors.

Conclusion

Although economies can answer the three economic questions in a variety of ways, this book will focus primarily on the mixed market system, such as exists in the United States. This type of economy blends *private choice,* guided by the price system in competitive markets, with *public choice,* guided by democracy in political markets. The study of mixed market systems grows more relevant as former command economies try to develop markets. The next chapter focuses on the economic actors in a mixed economy and explains why government gets into the act.

SUMMARY

1. Resources are scarce, but human wants are unlimited. Because you cannot satisfy all your wants, you must choose, and choice involves an opportunity cost. The opportunity cost of the selected option is the value of the best alternative forgone.

2. The law of comparative advantage says that the individual, firm, region, or country with the lowest opportunity cost of producing a particular good should specialize in that good. Specialization according to the law of comparative advantage promotes the most efficient use of resources.

3. The specialization of labor increases efficiency by (a) taking advantage of individual preferences and natural abilities, (b) allowing each worker to develop expertise and experience at a particular task, (c) reducing the time required to move between different tasks, and (d) allowing for the introduction of more specialized capital and large-scale production techniques.

4. The production possibilities frontier, or PPF, shows the productive capabilities of an economy when all resources are used fully and efficiently. The frontier's bowed-out shape reflects the law of increasing opportunity cost, which arises because some resources are not perfectly adaptable to the production of different goods. Over time, the frontier can shift in or out as a result of changes in the availability of resources and in technology. The frontier demonstrates several economic concepts, including efficiency, scarcity, opportunity cost, the law of increasing opportunity cost, economic growth, and the need for choice.

5. All economic systems, regardless of their decision-making processes, must answer three fundamental questions: What will be produced? How will it be produced? And for whom will it be produced? Economies answer the questions differently, depending on who owns the resources and how economic activity is coordinated. Economies can be directed by market forces, by the central plans of government, or by a mix of the two.

QUESTIONS FOR REVIEW

1. *(Opportunity Cost)* Discuss the ways in which the following conditions might affect the opportunity cost of going to a movie tonight:

    a. You have a final exam tomorrow.
    b. School will be out for one month starting tomorrow.
    c. The same movie will be on TV next week.

2. *(Opportunity Cost)* Determine whether each of the following statements is true, false, or uncertain. Explain your answers:

    a. The opportunity cost of an activity is the total value of all the alternatives passed up.
    b. Opportunity cost is an objective measure of cost.

c. When making choices, people gather all available information about the costs and benefits of alternative choices.

d. A decision maker seldom knows the actual value of a forgone alternative and must base decisions on expected values.

3. *(Comparative Advantage)* "You should never buy precooked frozen foods because you are paying for the labor costs of preparing food." Is this conclusion always valid, or can it be invalidated by the law of comparative advantage?

4. *(Specialization and Exchange)* Explain how the specialization of labor can lead to increased productivity.

5. *(Production Possibilities)* Under what conditions is it possible to increase production of one good without decreasing production of another good?

6. *(Production Possibilities)* Under what conditions would an economy be operating inside its PPF? Outside its PPF?

7. *(Shifting Production Possibilities)* In response to an influx of illegal aliens, Congress made it a federal offense to hire

them. How do you think this measure affected the U.S. production possibilities frontier? Do you think all industries were affected equally?

8. *(Production Possibilities)* "If society decides to use its resources fully and efficiently (that is, to produce *on* its production possibilities frontier), then future generations will be worse off because they will not be able to use these resources." If this assertion is true, full employment of resources may not be a good thing. Comment on the validity of this assertion.

9. *(Economic Questions)* What basic economic questions must be answered in a barter economy? In a primitive economy? In a pure capitalist economy? In a command economy?

10. *(Economic Systems)* What are the major differences between a pure capitalist system and a pure command system? Is the United States more like a pure capitalist system or more like a pure command system?

PROBLEMS AND EXERCISES

11. (*C a s e* **S t u d y :** The Opportunity Cost of College) During the Vietnam War, colleges and universities were overflowing with students. Was this bumper crop of students caused by a greater expected return on a college education or by a change in the opportunity cost of attending college? Explain.

12. *(Sunk Cost and Choice)* You go to a restaurant and buy an expensive meal. Halfway through, despite feeling quite full, you decide to clean your plate. After all, you think, you paid for the meal, so you are going to eat all of it. What's wrong with this thinking?

13. *(Opportunity Cost)* You can either spend spring break working at home for $80 per day or go to Florida for the week. If you stay home, your expenses will total about $100. If you go to Florida, the airfare, hotel, food, and miscellaneous expenses will total about $700. What's your opportunity cost of going to Florida?

14. *(Absolute and Comparative Advantage)* You have the following information concerning the production of wheat and cloth in the United States and the United Kingdom:

Labor Hours Required to Produce One Unit

	United Kingdom	United States
Wheat	2	1
Cloth	6	5

a. What is the opportunity cost of producing a unit of wheat in the United Kingdom? In the United States?

b. Which country has an absolute advantage in producing wheat? In producing cloth?

c. Which country has a comparative advantage in producing wheat? In producing cloth?

d. Which country should specialize in producing wheat? In producing cloth?

15. (*C a s e* **S t u d y :** Specialization Abounds) Provide some examples of specialized markets or retail outlets. What makes the Web conducive to specialization?

16. *(Shape of the PPF)* Suppose a production possibilities frontier includes the following combinations:

Cars	Washing Machines
0	1,000
100	600
200	0

a. Graph the PPF, assuming that it has no curved segments.

b. What is the cost of producing an additional car when 50 cars are being produced?

c. What is the cost of producing an additional car when 150 cars are being produced?

d. What is the cost of producing an additional washing machine when 50 cars are being produced? When 150 cars are being produced?

e. What do your answers tell you about opportunity costs?

17. *(Production Possibilities)* Suppose an economy uses two resources (labor and capital) to produce two goods (wheat and cloth). Capital is relatively more useful in producing cloth, and labor is relatively more useful in producing wheat. If the supply of capital falls by 10 percent and the supply of labor increases by 10 percent, how will the PPF for wheat and cloth change?

18. *(Production Possibilities)* There's no reason why a production possibilities frontier could not be used to represent the situation facing an individual. Imagine your own PPF. Right now—today—you have certain resources—your time,

your skills, perhaps some capital. And you can produce various outputs. Suppose you can produce combinations of two outputs, call them studying and partying.

a. Draw your PPF for studying and partying. Be sure to label the axes of the diagram appropriately. Label the points where the PPF intersects the axes, as well as several other points along the frontier.

b. Explain what it would mean for you to move upward and to the left along your personal PPF. What kinds of adjustments would you have to make in your life to make such a movement along the frontier?

c. Under what circumstances would your personal PPF shift outward? Do you think the shift would be a "parallel" one? Why, or why not?

19. *(Shifting Production Possibilities)* Determine whether each of the following would cause the economy's PPF to shift inward, outward, or not at all:

a. An increase in average length of annual vacations
b. An increase in immigration
c. A decrease in the average retirement age
d. The migration of skilled workers to other countries

20. *(Economic Systems)* The United States is best described as having a mixed economic system. What are some elements of command in the U.S. economy? What are some elements of tradition?

EXPERIENTIAL EXERCISES

21. *(Production Possibilities Frontier)* Here are some data on the U.S. economy taken from the *Economic Report of the President* at http://www.access.gpo.gov/eop/.

Year	Unemployment Rate	Real Government Spending (billions)	Real Civilian Spending (billions)
1982	9.7%	$ 947.7	$3,672.6
1983	9.6	960.1	3,843.6
1996	5.4	1,257.9	5,670.5
1997	4.9	1,270.6	5,920.8

a. Sketch a production possibilities frontier for the years 1982 and 1983, showing the trade-off between public-sector (government) and private-sector (civilian) spending. Assume that resource availability and technology were the

same in both years, but notice that the unemployment rate was relatively high.

b. Sketch a PPF for the years 1996 and 1997. Assume that resource availability and technology were the same in both years but higher than in 1982 and 1983. Note that the unemployment rate in the late 1990s was much lower than in the early 1980s.

c. What lessons did you learn about the U.S. economy of the past 20 years?

22. *(Economic Systems)* The transitional economies of Eastern Europe are frequently in the news because they provide testing grounds for the transition from socialist central

planning to freer, more market-oriented economies. Take a look at the World Bank's Transition Newsletter at http://www.worldbank.org/html/prddr/trans/recent.htm. Click on "Recent Issues," open an issue, and choose a particular country. Try to determine how smoothly the transition is proceeding. What problems is that nation encountering?

23. *(Wall Street Journal)* The ability to measure the true (opportunity) cost of a choice is a skill that will pay you great dividends. Use any issue of the *Wall Street Journal,* and find an article that discusses a decision some firm has made. (Try the "Business Bulletin" column on the front page of Thursday's issue.) Then review this chapter's section titled "Choice and Opportunity Cost." Finally, make a list of the kinds of opportunity costs involved in the firm's decision.

HOMEWORK XPRESS! EXERCISES

These exercises require access to McEachern Homework Xpress! If Homework Xpress! did not come with your book, visit **http://homeworkxpress.swlearning.com** *to purchase.*

An economy producing only two goods—silver and potatoes—faces a bowed-out production possibility frontier. Draw one in the diagram and label it.

1. Suppose plant biologists develop a new type of potato that increases the quantity of potatoes produced without any additional resources. Show how the new production possibilities curve would differ from the original.

2. Suppose mining engineers find a new technique that results in extracting more silver from the mines than previously without using additional resources. Show how the new production possibilities curve differs from the original.

3. Suppose that immigrants arrive seeking work in both potato production and silver mining. Show how the new production possibilities curve will differ from the original.

Economic Decision Makers

I f we live in the age of specialization, then why haven't specialists taken over all production? For example, why do most of us still do our own laundry and perform dozens of other tasks for ourselves? In what sense has production moved from the household to the firm and then back to the household? If the "invisible hand" of competitive markets is so efficient, why does government get into the act? Answers to these and other questions are addressed in this chapter, which examines the four economic decision makers: households, firms, governments, and the rest of the world.

To develop a better feel for how the economy works, you must get more acquainted with these key players. You already know more about them than you may realize. You grew up in a household. You have dealt with firms all your life, from

Sony to Subway. You know a lot about governments, from taxes to public schools. And you have a growing awareness of the rest of the world, from international Web sites to foreign travel. This chapter will draw on your abundant personal experience with economic decision makers to consider their makeup and objectives. Topics discussed include:

- Evolution of the household
- Evolution of the firm
- Types of firms
- Market failures and government remedies
- Taxing and public spending
- International trade and finance

The Household

Households play the starring role in a market economy. Their demand for goods and services determines what gets produced. And their supplies of labor, capital, natural resources, and entrepreneurial ability produce that output. As demanders of goods and services and suppliers of resources, households make all kinds of choices, such as what to buy, how much to save, where to live, and where to work. Although a household usually consists of several individuals, we will view each household as acting like a single decision maker.

The Evolution of the Household

In earlier times, when the economy was primarily agricultural, a farm household was largely self-sufficient. Each family member specialized in a specific farm task—cooking, making clothes, tending livestock, planting crops, and so on. These early households produced what they consumed and consumed what they produced. With the introduction of new seed varieties, better fertilizers, and laborsaving machinery, farm productivity increased sharply. Fewer farmers were needed to grow enough food to feed a nation. Simultaneously, the growth of urban factories increased the demand for factory labor. As a result, many people moved from farms to cities, where they became more specialized but less self-sufficient.

Households evolved in other ways. For example, in 1950, only about 15 percent of married women with young children were in the labor force. Since then, higher levels of education among married women and a growing demand for labor increased women's earnings, thus raising their opportunity cost of working in the home. This higher opportunity cost contributed to their growing labor force participation. Today more than half of married women with young children are in the labor force.

The rise of two-earner households has affected the family as an economic unit. Households produce less for themselves and demand more from the market. For example, child-care services and fast-food restaurants have displaced some household production. Most people eat at least one meal a day away from home. The rise in two-earner families has reduced specialization within the household—a central feature of the farm family. Nonetheless, some production still occurs in the home, as we'll explore later.

Households Maximize Utility

There are more than 110 million U.S. households. All those who live under one roof are considered part of the same household. What exactly do households attempt to accomplish in making decisions? Economists assume that people attempt to maximize their level of satisfaction, sense of well-being, or overall welfare. In short, households attempt to maximize **utility.** Households, like other economic decision makers, are viewed as rational, meaning that they try to act in their best interests and do not deliberately make themselves worse off. Utility maximization depends on each household's subjective goals, not on some objective

UTILITY

The satisfaction or sense of well-being received from consumption

standard. For example, some households maintain neat homes with well-groomed lawns; others pay little attention to their homes and use their lawns as junkyards.

Households as Resource Suppliers

Households use their limited resources—labor, capital, natural resources, and entrepreneurial ability—in an attempt to satisfy their unlimited wants. They can use these resources to produce goods and services in their homes. For example, they can prepare meals, mow the lawn, and fix a leaky faucet. They can also sell these resources in the resource market and use the income to buy goods and services in the product market. The most valuable resource sold by most households is labor.

Panel (a) of Exhibit 1 shows the sources of personal income received by U.S. households in 2003, when personal income totaled $9.2 trillion. As you can see, 63 percent of personal income came from wages, salaries, and other labor income. A distant second was transfer payments (to be discussed shortly), at 13 percent of personal income, followed by personal interest at 10 percent, and proprietors' income at 8 percent each. *Proprietors* are people who work for themselves rather than for employers; farmers, plumbers, and doctors are often self-employed. Proprietors' income could also be considered a form of labor income. *Over two-thirds of personal income in the United States comes from labor earnings rather than from the ownership of other resources such as capital or natural resources.*

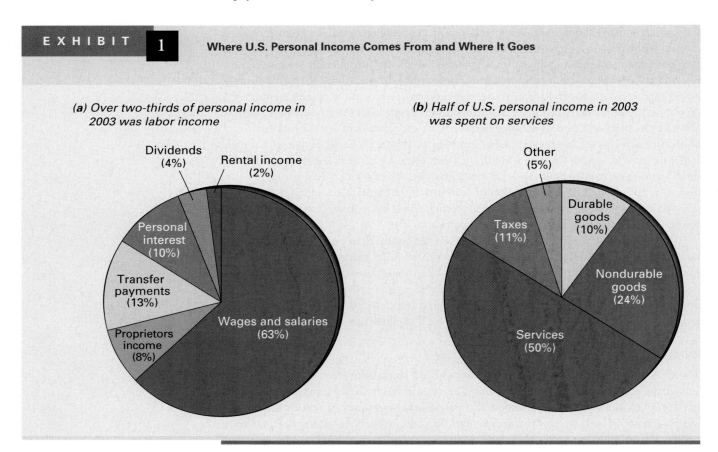

EXHIBIT 1   Where U.S. Personal Income Comes From and Where It Goes

(a) *Over two-thirds of personal income in 2003 was labor income*

- Dividends (4%)
- Rental income (2%)
- Personal interest (10%)
- Transfer payments (13%)
- Proprietors income (8%)
- Wages and salaries (63%)

(b) *Half of U.S. personal income in 2003 was spent on services*

- Other (5%)
- Durable goods (10%)
- Taxes (11%)
- Nondurable goods (24%)
- Services (50%)

Source: Based on figures from *Survey of Current Business*, Bureau of Economic Analysis, April 2004, Table B-1. For the latest figures, go to http://www.bea.doc.gov/bea/pubs.htm.

Because of a poor education, disability, discrimination, time demands of caring for small children, or bad luck, some households have few resources that are valued in the market. Society has made the political decision that individuals in such circumstances should receive short-term public assistance. Consequently, the government gives some households **transfer payments,** which are outright grants. *Cash transfers* are monetary payments, such as welfare benefits, Social Security, unemployment compensation, and disability benefits. *In-kind* transfers provide for specific goods and services, such food stamps, health care, and housing.

TRANSFER PAYMENTS

Cash or in-kind benefits given to individuals as outright grants from the government

Households as Demanders of Goods and Services

What happens to personal income once it comes into the household? Most goes to personal consumption, which sorts into three broad spending categories: (1) *durable goods*—that is, goods expected to last three or more years—such as an automobile or a refrigerator; (2) *nondurable goods,* such as food, clothing, and gasoline; and (3) *services,* such as haircuts, plane trips, and medical care. As you can see from panel (b) of Exhibit 1, durable goods in 2003 claimed 10 percent of U.S. personal income; nondurables, 24 percent; and services, 50 percent. Taxes claimed 11 percent, and all other categories, including savings, claimed just 5 percent. So half of all personal income went for services—the fastest growing sector, since many services, such as child care, are shifting from home production to market production.

The Firm

Households members once built their own homes, made their own clothes and furniture, grew their own food, and amused themselves with books, games, and hobbies. Over time, however, the efficiency arising from comparative advantage resulted in a greater specialization among resource suppliers. This section takes a look at firms, beginning with their evolution.

The Evolution of the Firm

Specialization and comparative advantage explain why households are no longer self-sufficient. But why is a firm the natural result? For example, rather than make a woolen sweater from scratch, couldn't a consumer take advantage of specialization by negotiating with someone who produced the wool, another who spun the wool into yarn, and a third who knit the yarn into a sweater? Here's the problem with that model: If the consumer had to visit each of these specialists and strike an agreement, the resulting *transaction costs* could easily erase the gains from specialization. Instead of visiting and bargaining with each specialist, the consumer can pay someone to do the bargaining—an entrepreneur, who hires all the resources necessary to make the sweater. *An entrepreneur, by contracting for many sweaters rather than just one, is able to reduce the transaction costs per sweater.*

For about two hundred years, profit-seeking entrepreneurs relied on "putting out" raw material, like wool and cotton, to rural households that turned it into finished products, like woolen goods made from yarn. The system developed in the British Isles, where workers' cottages served as tiny factories. This approach, which came to be known as the *cottage industry system,* still exists in some parts of the world. You might think of this system as halfway between household self-sufficiency and the modern firm.

As the British economy expanded in the 18th century, entrepreneurs began organizing the stages of production under one roof. Technological developments, such as waterpower and later steam power, increased the productivity of each worker and contributed to the shift of employment from rural areas to urban factories. *Work, therefore, became organized in large, centrally powered factories that (1) promoted a more efficient division of labor, (2) allowed for the*

INDUSTRIAL REVOLUTION

Development of large-scale factory production that began in Great Britain around 1750 and spread to the rest of Europe, North America, and Australia

direct supervision of production, (3) reduced transportation costs, and (4) facilitated the use of machines far bigger than anything used in the home. The development of large-scale factory production, known as the **Industrial Revolution,** began in Great Britain around 1750 and spread to the rest of Europe, North America, and Australia.

Production, then, evolved from self-sufficient rural households to the cottage industry system, where specialized production occurred in the household, to the current system of production in a firm. Today, entrepreneurs combine resources in firms such as factories, mills, offices, stores, and restaurants. **Firms** are economic units formed by profit-seeking entrepreneurs who combine labor, capital, and natural resources to produce goods and services. Just as we assume that households try to maximize utility, we assume that firms try to *maximize profit.* Profit, the entrepreneur's reward, equals sales revenue minus the cost of production.

FIRMS

Economic units formed by profit-seeking entrepreneurs who use resources to produce goods and services for sale

Types of Firms

There are about 25 million for-profit businesses in the United States. Two-thirds are small retail businesses, small service operations, part-time home-based businesses, and small farms. Each year more than a million new businesses start up and almost as many fail. Entrepreneurs organize a firm in one of three ways: as a sole proprietorship, as a partnership, or as a corporation.

Sole Proprietorships

SOLE PROPRIETORSHIP

A firm with a single owner who has the right to all profits and who bears unlimited liability for the firm's debts

The simplest form of business organization is the **sole proprietorship,** a single-owner firm. Examples are self-employed plumbers, farmers, and dentists. Most sole proprietorships consist of just the self-employed proprietor—there are no hired employees. To organize a sole proprietorship, the proprietor simply opens for business by, for example, taking out a classified ad announcing availability for plumbing, or whatever. The owner is in complete control. But he or she faces unlimited liability and could lose everything, including a home and other assets, as a result of debts or claims against the business. Also, since the sole proprietor has no partners or other financial backers, raising enough money to get the business going can be challenging. One final disadvantage is that a sole proprietorship usually goes out of business when the proprietor dies. Still, a sole proprietorship is the most common type of business, accounting most recently for 72 percent of all U.S. businesses. Nonetheless, because this type of firm is typically small, proprietorships generate just a tiny portion of all U.S. business sales—only 4 percent.

Partnerships

PARTNERSHIP

A firm with multiple owners who share the firm's profits and bear unlimited liability for the firm's debts

A more complicated form of business is the **partnership,** which involves two or more individuals who agree to contribute resources to the business in return for a share of the profit or loss. Law, accounting, and medical partnerships typify this business form. Partners have strength in numbers and often find it easier than sole proprietors to raise sufficient funds to get the business going. But partners may not always agree. Also, each partner usually faces unlimited liability for any debts or claims against the partnership, so one partner could lose everything because of another's mistake. Finally, the death or departure of one partner can disrupt the firm's continuity and prompt a complete reorganization. The partnership is the least common form of U.S. business, making up only 8 percent of all firms and 10 percent of all business sales.

Corporations

CORPORATION

A legal entity owned by stockholders whose liability is limited to the value of their stock

By far the most influential form of business is the corporation. A **corporation** is a legal entity established through articles of incorporation. Shares of stock confer corporate ownership, thereby entitling stockholders to a claim on any profit. A major advantage of the corporate form is that many investors—hundreds, thousands, even millions—can pool their funds, so incorporating represents the easiest way to amass large sums of money to finance the business. Also, stockholder liability for any loss is limited to the value of their stock, meaning stockholders enjoy limited liability. A final advantage of this form of organization is that the corporation has a life apart from its owners. The corporation survives even if ownership changes hands, and it can be taxed and sued as if it were a person.

The corporate form has some disadvantages as well. A stockholder's ability to influence corporate policy is limited to voting for a board of directors, which oversees the operation of the firm. Each share of stock usually carries with it one vote. The typical stockholder of a large corporation owns only a tiny fraction of the shares and thus has little say. Whereas the income from sole proprietorships and partnerships is taxed only once, corporate income gets whacked twice—first as corporate profits and second as stockholder income, either as corporate dividends or as realized capital gains. A *realized capital gain* is any increase in the market value of a share that occurs between the time the share is purchased and the time it is sold.

A hybrid type of corporation has evolved to take advantage of the limited liability feature of the corporate structure while reducing the impact of double taxation. The *S corporation* provides owners with limited liability, but profits are taxed only once—as income on each shareholder's personal income tax return. To qualify as an S corporation, a firm must have no more than 75 stockholders and must have no foreign or corporate stockholders.

Corporations make up only 20 percent of all U.S. businesses, but because they tend to be much larger than the other two business forms, they account for 86 percent of all business sales. Exhibit 2 shows, by business type, the percentage of U.S. firms and the percentage of U.S. sales. *The sole proprietorship is the most important form in the sheer number of firms, but the corporation is the most important in terms of total sales.*

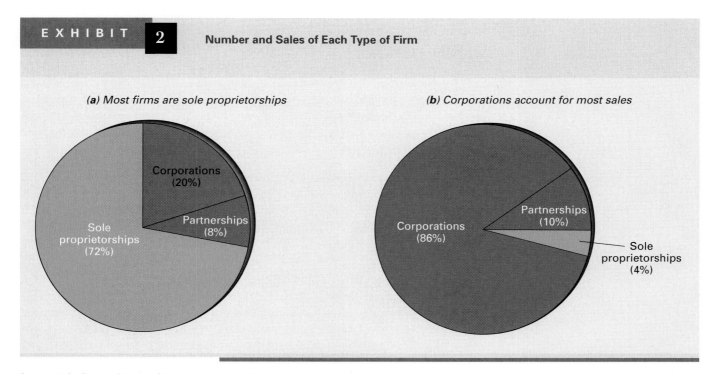

EXHIBIT 2   **Number and Sales of Each Type of Firm**

(a) Most firms are sole proprietorships

Corporations (20%)
Partnerships (8%)
Sole proprietorships (72%)

(b) Corporations account for most sales

Corporations (86%)
Partnerships (10%)
Sole proprietorships (4%)

Source: U.S. Census Bureau, *Statistical Abstract of the United States: 2003*, U.S. Bureau of the Census, Table No. 731. For the latest figures, go to http://www.census.gov/statab/www/.

Nonprofit Institutions

To this point we have considered firms that maximize profit. Some institutions, such as museums, ballet companies, nonprofit hospitals, the Red Cross, the Salvation Army, churches, synagogues, mosques, and perhaps the college you attend, are private organizations that do not have profit as an explicit goal. Yet even nonprofit institutions must somehow pay the bills. Revenue sources typically include some combination of voluntary contributions and service charges, such as college tuition and hospital bills. According to the U.S. Internal Revenue Service, there were 1.6 million tax-exempt organizations in the United States in 2001 and they controlled assets totaling $2.4 trillion. So the average tax-exempt organization controlled assets worth $1.5 million. Although the nonprofit sector is important, the *firms* discussed in this book will have profit as their goal.

Why Does Household Production Still Exist?

If firms are so great at reducing transaction and production costs, why don't they make everything? Why do households still perform some tasks, such as cooking and cleaning? *If a household's opportunity cost of performing a task is below the market price, then the household usually performs that task.* People with a lower opportunity cost of time will do more for themselves. For example, janitors are more likely to mow their lawns than are physicians. Let's look at some reasons for household production.

No Skills or Special Resources Are Required

Some activities require so few skills or special resources that householders find it cheaper to do the jobs themselves. Sweeping the floor requires only a broom and some time so it's usually performed by household members. Sanding a wooden floor, however, involves special machinery and expertise, so this service is left to professionals. Similarly, although you wouldn't hire someone to brush your teeth, dental work is not for amateurs. Households usually perform domestic chores that demand neither expertise nor special machinery.

Household Production Avoids Taxes

Suppose you are deciding whether to pay $3,000 to paint your house or to do it yourself. If the income tax rate averages one-third, you must earn $4,500 before taxes to have the $3,000 after taxes to pay for the job. And the painter who charges you $3,000 will net only $2,000 after paying $1,000 in taxes. Thus, you must earn $4,500 so that the painter can take home $2,000. If you paint the house yourself, no taxes are collected. The tax-free nature of do-it-yourself activity favors household production over market transactions.

Household Production Reduces Transaction Costs

Getting estimates, hiring a contractor, negotiating terms, and monitoring job performance all take time and require information. Doing the job yourself reduces these transaction costs. Household production also allows for more personal control over the final product than is usually available through the market. For example, some people prefer home-cooked meals, because they can season home-cooked meals to individual tastes.

Technological Advances Increase Household Productivity

Technological breakthroughs are not confined to market production. Vacuum cleaners, clothes washers and dryers, dishwashers, microwave ovens, and other modern appliances reduce the time and often the skill required to perform household tasks. Also, new technologies such as DVD players, high-definition TVs, and computer games enhance home entertainment. Indeed, microchip-based technologies have shifted some production from the firm back to the household, as discussed in the following case study.

The Electronic Cottage

The Industrial Revolution shifted production from rural cottages to large urban factories. But the **Information Revolution** spawned by the microchip and the Internet is decentralizing the acquisition, analysis, and transmission of information. These days, someone who claims to work at a home office is usually referring not to a corporate headquarters but to a spare bedroom. According to one recent survey, in the last decade the number of telecommuters more than doubled. Worsening traffic in major cities and wider access to broadband is pushing the trend. Nearly half the white-collar employees at AT&T work at home at least part of the time.

From home, people can write a document with coworkers scattered throughout the world, then discuss the project online in real time or have a videoconference (McDonald's saves millions in travel costs by videoconferencing). Software allows thousands of employees to share electronic files. When Accenture moved its headquarters from Boston to a suburb, the company replaced 120 tons of paper records with a huge online database accessible anytime from anywhere in the world.

To support those who work at home, an entire industry has sprung up, with magazines, newsletters, Web sites, and national conferences. In fact, an office need not even be in a specific place. Some people now work in *virtual offices,* which have no permanent locations. With mobile phones and other handhelds, people can conduct business on the road—literally, "deals on wheels." Accountants at Ernst & Young spend most of their time in the field. When returning to company headquarters, they call a few hours ahead to reserve an office. IBM is developing "Butler in a Dashboard" to help people work on the road. Speech recognition software allows the driver to dictate and send emails as well as send and receive voicemails. If traffic is too noisy, a tiny camera mounted on the visor reads the driver's lips. This Butler also provides directions and weather conditions, and warns of traffic tie-ups and flight delays. The model is expected to reach the market in 2005.

Chip technology is decentralizing production, shifting work from a central place either back to the household or to no place in particular. More generally, the Internet has reduced the transaction costs, whether it's a market report authored jointly by researchers from around the world or a new computer system assembled from parts ordered over the Internet. Easier communication has even increased contact among distant research scholars. For example, economists living in distant cities were four times more likely to collaborate on research during the 1990s than during the 1970s.

Sources: "IBM Envisions Butler in a Dashboard," *USA Today*, 25 June 2003; Jonathan Glater, "Telecommuting's Big Experiment," *New York Times*, 9 May 2001; and Daniel Hamermesh and Sharon Oster, "Tools or Toys? The Impact of High Technology on Scholarly Productivity," *Economic Inquiry*, October 2002. For a discussion of the virtual office, go to http://www.office.com/.

The Information Economy

eActivity

Economists have begun to study the economic implications of the virtual office and other virtual phenomena. Try visiting Google (http://www.google.com) and Excite (http://www.excite.com/). Search for the words *virtual* and *economics,* and see what you find.

WALL STREET JOURNAL
Reading It **Right**

What's the relevance of the following statement from the Wall Street Journal: "The rise of factories took work out of the home, and only now are we . . . rediscovering how to work and live in the same buildings."

INFORMATION REVOLUTION

Technological change spawned by the invention of the microchip and the Internet that enhanced the acquisition, analysis, and transmission of information

The Government

You might think that production by households and firms could satisfy all consumer wants. Why must yet another economic decision maker get into the act?

The Role of Government

Sometimes the unrestrained operation of markets yields undesirable results. Too many of some goods and too few of other goods get produced. This section discusses the sources of **market failure** and how society's overall welfare may be improved through government intervention.

Establishing and Enforcing the Rules of the Game

Market efficiency depends on people like you using your resources to maximize your utility. But what if you were repeatedly robbed of your paycheck on your way home from work? Or what if, after you worked two weeks in a new job, your boss called you a sucker and said you wouldn't get paid? Why bother working? The system of private markets would break down if you could not safeguard your private property or if you could not enforce contracts. Governments safeguard private property through police protection and enforce contracts through a judicial system. More generally, governments try to make sure that market participants abide by the "rules of the game." These rules are established through laws and through the customs and conventions of the marketplace.

Promoting Competition

Although the "invisible hand" of competition usually promotes an efficient allocation of resources, some firms try to avoid competition through collusion, which is an agreement among firms to divide the market and fix the price. Or an individual firm may try to eliminate the competition by using unfair business practices. For example, to drive out local competitors, a large firm may temporarily sell at a price below cost. Government antitrust laws try to promote competition by prohibiting collusion and other anticompetitive practices.

Regulating Natural Monopolies

Competition usually keeps the product price below what it would be without competition—that is below the price charged by a **monopoly**, a sole supplier to the market. In rare instances, however, a monopoly can produce and sell the product for less than could competing firms. For example, electricity is delivered more efficiently by a single firm that wires the community than by competing firms each stringing its own wires. When it is cheaper for one firm to serve the market than for two or more firms to do so, that one firm is called a **natural monopoly.** Since a natural monopoly faces no competition, it maximizes profit by charging a higher price than would be optimal from society's point of view. Therefore, the government usually regulates the natural monopoly, forcing it to lower its price.

Providing Public Goods

So far this book has been talking about private goods, which have two important features. First, private goods are *rival* in consumption, meaning that the amount consumed by one person is unavailable for others to consume. For example, when you and some friends share a pizza, each slice they eat is one less available for you. Second, the supplier of a private good can easily exclude those who fail to pay. Only paying customers get pizza. Thus, private goods are said to be *exclusive*. So **private goods** are both rival in consumption and exclusive, such as pizza. In contrast, **public goods,** such as reducing terrorism, providing national defense, and administering a system of justice, are *nonrival* in consumption. One person's benefit from the good does not diminish the amount available to others. Your family's benefit from a safer neighborhood does not reduce your neighbor's benefit. What's more, once produced, public goods are available to all. Suppliers cannot easily prevent consumption by those who fail to pay. For example, reducing terrorism is *nonexclusive*. It benefits all in the

MARKET FAILURE

A condition that arises when the unregulated operation of markets yields socially undesirable results

MONOPOLY

A sole producer of a product for which there are no close substitutes

NATURAL MONOPOLY

One firm that can serve the entire market at a lower per-unit cost than can two or more firms

PRIVATE GOOD

A good that is both rival in consumption and exclusive, such as pizza

PUBLIC GOOD

A good that, once produced, is available for all to consume, regardless of who pays and who doesn't; such a good is nonrival and nonexclusive, such as national defense community, regardless of who pays for it and who doesn't. Because public goods are *nonrival* and *nonexclusive*, private firms cannot sell them profitably. The government, however, has the authority to collect taxes for public goods.

Dealing with Externalities

Market prices reflect the private costs and private benefits of producers and consumers. But sometimes production or consumption imposes costs or benefits on third parties—on those who are neither suppliers nor demanders in a market transaction. For example, a paper mill fouls the air breathed by nearby residents, but the market price of paper fails to reflect such costs. Because these pollution costs are outside, or external to, the market, they are called externalities. An **externality** is a cost or a benefit that falls on a third party. A negative externality imposes an external cost, such as factory pollution or auto emissions. A positive externality confers an external benefit, such as driving carefully or beautifying your property. Because market prices do not reflect externalities, governments often use taxes, subsidies, and regulations to discourage negative externalities and encourage positive externalities. For example, because education generates positive externalities (educated people can read road signs and have better paying options other than crime as sources of income), governments try to encourage education with free public schools, subsidized higher education, and keeping people in school until their 16th birthdays.

A More Equal Distribution of Income

As mentioned earlier, some people, because of poor education, mental or physical disabilities, or perhaps the need to care for small children, are unable to support themselves and their families. Because resource markets do not guarantee even a minimum level of income, transfer payments reflect society's attempt to provide a basic standard of living to all households. Nearly all citizens agree that government should redistribute income to the poor (note the normative nature of this statement). Opinions differ about how much should be redistributed, what form it should take, who should receive benefits, and how long benefits should last.

Full Employment, Price Stability, and Economic Growth

Perhaps the most important responsibility of government is fostering a healthy economy, which benefits just about everyone. The government—through its ability to tax, to spend, and to control the money supply—attempts to promote full employment, price stability, and economic growth. Pursuing these objectives by taxing and spending is called **fiscal policy.** Pursuing them by regulating the money supply is called **monetary policy.** Macroeconomics examines both policies.

Government's Structure and Objectives

The United States has a *federal system* of government, meaning that responsibilities are shared across levels of government. State governments grant some powers to local governments and surrender some powers to the national, or federal, government. As the system has evolved, the federal government has assumed primary responsibility for national security, economic stability, and market competition. State governments fund public higher education, prisons, and—with aid from the federal government—highways and welfare. Local governments provide primary and secondary education with aid from the state, plus police and fire protection. Here are some distinguishing features of government.

Difficulty in Defining Government Objectives

We assume that households try to maximize utility and firms try to maximize profit, but what about governments—or, more specifically, what about government decision makers?

EXTERNALITY

A cost or a benefit that falls on a third party and is therefore ignored by the two parties to the market transaction

The annual Economic Report of the President is an invaluable source of information on current economic policy. It also contains many useful data tables. You can find it online at http://w3. access.gpo.gov/eop/index.html.

FISCAL POLICY

The use of government purchases, transfer payments, taxes, and borrowing to influence economy-wide activity such as inflation, employment, and economic growth

MONETARY POLICY

Regulation of the money supply to influence economy-wide activity such as inflation, employment, and economic growth

What do they try to maximize? One problem is that our federal system consists of not one but many governments—more than 87,000 separate jurisdictions in all. What's more, because the federal government relies on offsetting, or countervailing, powers across the executive, legislative, and judicial branches, government does not act as a single, consistent decision maker. Even within the federal executive branch, there are so many agencies and bureaus that at times they seem to work at cross-purposes. For example, at the same time as the U.S. Surgeon General requires health warnings on cigarettes, the U.S. Department of Agriculture pursues policies to benefit tobacco growers. Given this thicket of jurisdictions, branches, and bureaus, one useful theory of government behavior is that elected officials try to maximize the number of votes they receive in the next election. So let's assume that elected officials try to maximize votes. In this theory, vote maximization guides the decisions of elected officials who, in turn, control government employees.

Voluntary Exchange Versus Coercion

Market exchange relies on the voluntary behavior of buyers and sellers. Don't like tofu? No problem—don't buy any. But in political markets, the situation is different. Any voting rule except unanimous consent must involve some government coercion. Public choices are enforced by the police power of the state. Those who fail to pay their taxes could go to jail, even though they may object to some programs those taxes support.

No Market Prices

Another distinguishing feature of governments is that the selling price of public output is usually either zero or below the cost. If you are now paying in-state tuition at a public college or university, your tuition probably covers only about half the state's cost of providing your education. Because the revenue side of the government budget is usually separate from the expenditure side, there is no necessary link between the cost and the benefit of a public program. In the private sector, the expected marginal benefit is at least as great as marginal cost; otherwise, market exchange would not occur.

The Size and Growth of Government

One way to track the impact of government over time is by measuring government outlays relative to the U.S. *gross domestic product,* or *GDP,* which is the total value of all final goods and services produced in the United States. In 1929, the year the Great Depression began, government outlays, mostly by state and local governments, totaled about 10 percent of GDP. At the time, the federal government played a minor role. In fact, during the nation's first 150 years, federal outlays, except during wars, never exceeded 3 percent relative to GDP.

The Great Depression, World War II, and a change in macroeconomic thinking boosted the share of government outlays to 36 percent of GDP in 2004, with about two-thirds of that by the federal government. In comparison, government outlays relative to GDP were 38 percent in Japan, 40 percent in Canada, 43 percent in the United Kingdom, 48 percent in Germany and Italy, and 54 percent in France. Government outlays by the 24 largest industrial economies averaged 40 percent of GDP in 2004.[1] Thus, government outlays in the United States represent a relatively small share of GDP compared to other advanced economies.

Let's look briefly at the composition of federal outlays. Since 1960, defense spending has declined from over half of federal outlays to one-fifth by 2004, as shown in Exhibit 3.

---

1. The Organization of Economic Cooperation and Development, *OECD Economic Outlook* (June 2004), Annex Table 26.

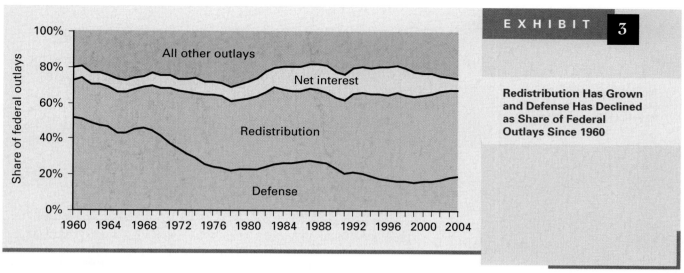

EXHIBIT 3

Redistribution Has Grown and Defense Has Declined as Share of Federal Outlays Since 1960

Source: Computed based on figures from the *Economic Report of the President*, February 2004, Table B-80. For the latest figures, go to http://w3.access.gpo.gov/eop.

Redistribution—Social Security, Medicare, and welfare programs—is the mirror image of defense spending, jumping from only about one-fifth of federal outlays in 1960 to nearly half by 2004.

Sources of Government Revenue

Taxes provide the bulk of revenue at all levels of government. The federal government relies primarily on the individual income tax, state governments rely on income and sales taxes, and local governments rely on the property tax. In addition to taxes, other revenue sources include user charges, such as highway tolls, and borrowing. To make money, some states monopolize certain markets, such as for lottery tickets and liquor.

Exhibit 4 focuses on the composition of federal revenue since 1960. The share made up by the individual income tax has remained relatively constant, ranging from a low of 42 percent in the mid-1960s to a high of 50 percent in 2000. The share from payroll taxes more than doubled from 15 percent in 1960 to 40 percent in 2004. *Payroll taxes* are deducted from paychecks to support Social Security and Medicare, which funds medical care for the elderly. Corporate taxes and revenue from other sources, such as excise (sales) taxes and user charges, have declined as a share of the total since 1960.

Tax Principles and Tax Incidence

The structure of a tax is often justified on the basis of one of two general principles. First, a tax could relate to the individual's ability to pay, so those with a greater ability pay more taxes. Income or property taxes often rely on this **ability-to-pay tax principle.** Alternatively, the **benefits-received tax principle** relates taxes to the benefits taxpayers receive from the government activity funded by the tax. For example, the tax on gasoline funds highway construction and maintenance, thereby linking tax payment to road use, since the more people drive, the more gas tax they pay.

Tax incidence indicates who actually bears the burden of the tax. One way to evaluate tax incidence is by measuring the tax as a percentage of income. Under **proportional taxation,** taxpayers at all income levels pay the same percentage of their income in taxes. A

ABILITY-TO-PAY TAX PRINCIPLE

Those with a greater ability to pay, such as those with a higher income or those who own more property, should pay more taxes

BENEFITS-RECEIVED TAX PRINCIPLE

Those who receive more benefits from the government program funded by a tax should pay more taxes

TAX INCIDENCE

The distribution of tax burden among taxpayers; who ultimately pays the tax

PROPORTIONAL TAXATION

The tax as a percentage of income remains constant as income increases; also called a flat tax

EXHIBIT 4

**Payroll Taxes Have Grown
as a Share of Federal
Revenue Since 1960**

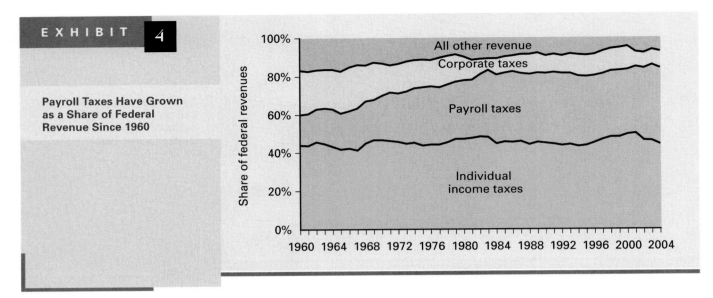

Source: Computed based on figures from the *Economic Report of the President*, February 2004, Tables B-81 and B-84. For the latest figures, go to http://w3.access.gpo.gov/eop.

PROGRESSIVE TAXATION

The tax as a percentage of income increases as income increases

MARGINAL TAX RATE

The percentage of each additional dollar of income that goes to the tax

REGRESSIVE TAXATION

The tax as a percentage of income decreases as income increases

proportional income tax is also called a flat tax, since the tax as a percentage of income remains constant, or flat, as income increases. Under **progressive taxation,** the percentage of income paid in taxes increases as income increases.

The **marginal tax rate** indicates the percentage of each additional dollar of income that goes to taxes. Because high marginal rates reduce the after-tax return from working or investing, they can reduce people's incentives to work and invest. As of 2004, the six marginal rates range from 10 to 35 percent, down from a range of 15 to 39.6 percent in 2000. The top marginal tax bracket each year during the history of the personal income tax is shown by Exhibit 5. Although the top marginal rate in 2004 was lower than it was during most other years, high income households still pay most of the federal income tax collected. For example, the top 1 percent of tax filers, based on income, pay about 33 percent of all income taxes collected. The bottom 50 percent pay less than 5 percent of all income taxes collected. So the U.S. income tax is progressive, and high-income filers pay the overwhelming share of the total.

Finally, under **regressive taxation,** the percentage of income paid in taxes decreases as income increases, so the marginal tax rate declines as income increases. Most U.S. *payroll taxes* are regressive, because they impose a flat rate up to a certain level of income, above which the marginal rate drops to zero. For example, Social Security taxes were levied on the first $87,900 of workers' pay in 2004. Half the 12.4 percent tax is paid by employers and half by employees (the self-employed pay the entire amount).

This discussion of revenue sources brings to a close, for now, our examination of the role of government in the U.S. economy. Government has a pervasive influence on the economy, and its role is discussed throughout the book.

The Rest of the World

So far, the focus has been on institutions within the United States—that is, on *domestic* households, firms, and governments. This focus is appropriate because our primary objective

HOMEWORK
Xpress!
*Ask the Instructor
Video*

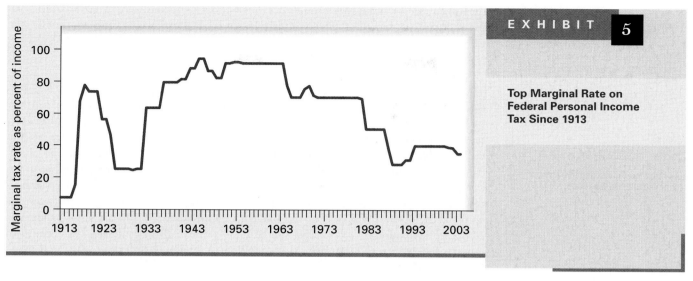

Source: U.S. Internal Revenue Service. For the latest figures on the personal income tax go to http://www.irs.gov/individuals/index.html.

is to understand the workings of the U.S. economy, by far the largest in the world. But the rest of the world affects what U.S. households consume and what U.S. firms produce. For example, Japan and China supply U.S. markets with all kinds of manufactured goods, thereby affecting U.S. prices, wages, and profits. Likewise, political events in the Persian Gulf can affect what Americans pay for oil. Foreign decision makers, therefore, have a significant effect on the U.S. economy—on what we consume and what we produce. The *rest of the world* consists of the households, firms, and governments in the two hundred or so sovereign nations throughout the world.

International Trade

Economics in the Movies

In the previous chapter, you learned about comparative advantage and the gains from specialization. These gains explain why householders stopped doing everything for themselves and began to specialize. International trade arises for the same reasons. *International trade occurs because the opportunity cost of producing specific goods differs across countries.* Americans import raw materials like crude oil, diamonds, and coffee beans and finished goods like cameras, DVD players, and automobiles. U.S. producers export sophisticated products like computer hardware and software, aircraft, and movies, as well as agricultural products like wheat and corn.

International trade between the United States and the rest of the world has increased in recent decades. In 1970, U.S. exports of goods and services amounted to only 6 percent of the gross domestic product. That percentage has since nearly doubled. Chief destinations for U.S. exports in order of importance are Canada, Japan, Mexico, the United Kingdom Germany, France, South Korea, and Taiwan.

The **merchandise trade balance** equals the value of exported goods minus the value of imported goods. Goods in this case are distinguished from services, which show up in another trade account. For the last two decades, the United States has imported more goods than it has exported, so there has been a merchandise trade deficit. Just as a household must pay for its spending, so too must a nation. The merchandise trade deficit must be offset by a

MERCHANDISE TRADE BALANCE

The value of a country's exported goods minus the value of its imported goods during a given period

BALANCE OF PAYMENTS

A record of all economic transactions between residents of one country and residents of the rest of the world during a given period

FOREIGN EXCHANGE

Foreign money needed to carry out international transactions

TARIFF

A tax on imports

QUOTA

A legal limit on the quantity of a particular product that can be imported or exported

surplus in one or more of the other *balance-of-payments* accounts. A nation's **balance of payments** is the record of all economic transactions between its residents and residents of the rest of the world.

Exchange Rates

The lack of a common currency complicates trade between countries. How many U.S. dollars buy a Porsche? An American buyer cares only about the dollar cost; the German carmaker cares only about the *euros* received (the common currency of 12 European countries). To facilitate trade when different currencies are involved, a market for foreign exchange has developed. **Foreign exchange** is foreign currency needed to carry out international transactions. The supply and demand for foreign exchange comes together in *foreign exchange markets* to determine the equilibrium exchange rate. The *exchange rate* measures the price of one currency in terms of another. For example, the exchange rate between the euro and the dollar might indicate that one euro exchanges for $1.10. At that exchange rate, a Porsche selling for 100,000 euros costs $110,000. The exchange rate affects the prices of imports and exports and thus helps shape the flow of foreign trade. The greater the demand for a particular foreign currency or the smaller the supply, the higher its exchange rate—that is, the more dollars it costs.

Trade Restrictions

Although there are clear gains from international specialization and exchange, nearly all nations restrict trade to some extent. These restrictions can take the form of (1) **tariffs,** which are taxes on imports; (2) **quotas,** which are limits on the quantity of a particular good that can be imported from a country; and (3) other trade restrictions. If specialization according to comparative advantage is so beneficial, why do most countries restrict trade? Restrictions benefit certain domestic producers that lobby their governments for these benefits. For example, U.S. textile manufacturers have benefited from legislation restricting textile imports, thereby raising U.S. textile prices. These higher prices hurt domestic consumers, but consumers are usually unaware of this harm. Trade restrictions interfere with the free flow of products across borders and tend to hurt the overall economy. International trade in the auto industry is discussed in the following case study.

Wheels of Fortune

The U.S. auto industry is huge, with annual sales of about $300 billion a year, an amount exceeding the gross domestic product of 90 percent of the world's economies. There are over 200 million motor vehicles in the United States alone, about two for every three people. In the decade following World War II, imports accounted for just 0.4 percent of U.S. auto sales. In 1973, however, the suddenly powerful Organization of Petroleum Exporting Countries (OPEC) more than tripled

© Stewart Cohen/Index Stock Imagery

oil prices. In response, Americans scrambled for more fuel-efficient cars, which at the time were primarily by foreign makers. As a result, imports jumped to 21 percent of U.S. auto sales by 1980.

In the early 1980s, at the urging of the so-called Big Three automakers (General Motors, Ford, and, at the time, Chrysler), the Reagan administration persuaded Japanese producers to adopt "voluntary" quotas limiting the number of automobiles they exported to the United States. The quotas, or supply restrictions, drove up the price of Japanese imports. U.S. automakers used this as an opportunity to raise their own prices. Experts estimate that reduced foreign competition cost U.S. consumers over $15 billion.

The quotas had two effects on Japanese producers. First, faced with a strict limit on the number of cars they could export to the United States, they began shipping more upscale models instead of subcompacts. Second, Japanese firms built factories in the United States. Making autos here also reduced complications caused by fluctuations in yen-dollar exchange rates. Japanese-owned auto plants in the United States now account for more than one-quarter of auto production in the United States. Imports still make up about one-quarter of U.S. car sales, with Japan accounting for most of that. Imports include cars produced abroad by foreign firms but sold under the names of U.S. firms. U.S. automakers also produce around the world. In fact, Ford is the largest automaker in Australia, the United Kingdom, Mexico, and Argentina.

In China, India, and Latin America, the potential car market is enormous. Here's something to consider: There are more people in China under age of 26 than the combined population of the United States, Japan, Germany, the United Kingdom, and Canada. For years private car ownership was banned in China by Chairman Mao. Now car ownership there is on a roll. Passenger car sales grew from 0.5 million in 1998 to 1.2 million in 2002, for an average annual growth of 24 percent. Because of high tariffs in China, less than 10 percent of cars sold are imports. As a condition for entry into the World Trade Organization, a group that streamlines world trade, China has agreed to reduce tariffs. So China's auto market should gradually open up.

Sources: "Ford to Triple China Production," *South China Morning Post,* 24 September 2003; "China Goes Car Crazy," *Fortune*, 8 September 2003; Micheline Maynard, "Foreign Automakers Unleash a New Wave of Luxury," *New York Times*, 27 September 2003; and Walter Adams and James Brock, "Automobiles," in *The Structure of American Industry*, 9th ed. (New York: Prentice-Hall, 1995), 65–92. For the latest in the auto industry, go to http://www.autocentral.com/.

Conclusion

This chapter examined the four economic decision makers: households, firms, governments, and the rest of the world. Domestic households are by far the most important, for they, along with foreign households, supply the resources and demand the goods and services produced. In recent years, the U.S. economy has come to depend more on the rest of the world as a market for U.S. goods and as a source of products.

If you were to stop reading right now, you would already know more economics than most people. But to understand market economies, you must learn how markets work. The next chapter introduces demand and supply.

SUMMARY

1. Most household income arises from the sale of labor, and most household income is spent on personal consumption, primarily services.

2. Household members once built their own homes, made their own clothes and furniture, grew their own food, and

supplied their own entertainment. Over time, however, the efficiency arising from comparative advantage resulted in a greater specialization among resource suppliers.

3. Firms bring together specialized resources and reduce the transaction costs of bargaining with all these resource

providers. Firms can be organized in three different ways: as sole proprietorships, partnerships, or corporations. Because corporations are typically large, they account for the bulk of sales.

4. When private markets yield undesirable results, government may intervene to address these market failures. Government programs are designed to (a) protect private property and enforce contracts; (b) promote competition; (c) regulate natural monopolies; (d) provide public goods; (e) discourage negative externalities and encourage positive externalities; (f) promote equality in the distribution of income; and (g) promote full employment, price stability, and economic growth.

5. In the United States, the federal government has primary responsibility for providing national defense, ensuring market competition, and promoting stability of the economy. State governments fund public higher education, prisons, and—with aid from the federal government—

highways and welfare. And local governments fund police and fire protection, and, with aid from the state, provide primary and secondary education.

6. The federal government relies primarily on the personal income tax, states rely on income and sales taxes, and localities rely on the property tax. A tax is often justified based on (a) the individual's ability to pay or (b) the benefits the taxpayer receives from the activities financed by the tax.

7. The rest of the world is also populated by households, firms, and governments. International trade creates gains that arise from comparative advantage. The balance of payments summarizes transactions between the residents of one country and the residents of the rest of the world. Despite the benefits from comparative advantage, nearly all countries impose trade restrictions to protect specific domestic industries.

QUESTIONS FOR REVIEW

1. *(Households as Demanders of Goods and Services)* Classify each of the following as a durable good, a nondurable good, or a service:

   a. A gallon of milk
   b. A lawn mower
   c. A DVD player
   d. A manicure
   e. A pair of shoes
   f. An eye exam
   g. A personal computer
   h. A neighborhood teenager mowing a lawn

2. (*Case* **Study**: The Electronic Cottage) How has the development of personal computer hardware and software reversed some of the trends brought on by the Industrial Revolution?

3. *(Evolution of the Firm)* Explain how production after the Industrial Revolution differed from production under the cottage industry system.

4. *(Household Production)* What factors does a householder consider when deciding whether to produce a good or service at home or buy it in the marketplace?

5. *(Corporations)* Why did the institution of the firm appear after the advent of the Industrial Revolution? What type of business organization existed before this?

6. *(Sole Proprietorships)* What are the disadvantages of the sole proprietorship form of business?

7. *(Government)* Often it is said that government is necessary when private markets fail to work effectively and fairly. Based on your reading of the text, discuss how private markets might break down.

8. *(Externalities)* Suppose there is an external cost associated with production of a certain good. What's wrong with letting the market determine how much of this good will be produced?

9. *(Government Revenue)* What are the sources of government revenue in the United States? Which types of taxes are most important at each level of government? Which two taxes provide the most revenue to the federal government?

10. *(Objectives of the Economic Decision Makers)* In economic analysis, what are the assumed objectives of households, firms, and the government?

11. *(International Trade)* Why does international trade occur? What does it mean to run a deficit in the merchandise trade balance?

12. *(International Trade)* Distinguish between a tariff and a quota. Who benefits from and who is harmed by such restrictions on imports?

13. (*Case* **Study**: Wheel of Fortune) What factors led Japanese auto producers to build factories in the United States?

PROBLEMS AND EXERCISES

14. *(Evolution of the Household)* Determine whether each of the following would increase or decrease the opportunity costs for mothers who choose not to work outside the home. Explain your answers.

    a. Higher levels of education for women
    b. Higher unemployment rates for women
    c. Higher average pay levels for women
    d. Lower demand for labor in industries that traditionally employ large numbers of women

15. *(Household Production)* Many households supplement their food budget by cultivating small vegetable gardens. Explain how each of the following might influence this kind of household production:

    a. Both husband and wife are professionals who earn high salaries.
    b. The household is located in a city rather than in a rural area.
    c. The household is located in a region where there is a high sales tax on food.
    d. The household is located in a region that has a high property tax rate.

16. *(Government)* Complete each of the following sentences:
    a. When the private operation of a market leads to overproduction or underproduction of some good, this is known as a(n) _____.
    b. Goods that are nonrival and nonexcludable are known as _____.
    c. _____ are cash or in-kind benefits given to individuals as outright grants from the government.
    d. A(n) _____ confers an external benefit on third parties that are not directly involved in a market transaction.
    e. _____ refers to the government's pursuit of full employment and price stability through variations in taxes and government spending.

17. *(Tax Rates)* Suppose taxes are related to income level as follows:

Income	Taxes
$1,000	$200
$2,000	$350
$3,000	$450

    a. What percentage of income is paid in taxes at each level?
    b. Is the tax rate progressive, proportional, or regressive?
    c. What is the marginal tax rate on the first $1,000 of income? The second $1,000? The third $1,000?

EXPERIENTIAL EXERCISES

18. *(The Evolution of the Firm)* Get a library copy of *The Wealth and Poverty of Nations,* by David Landes, and read pages 207–210. How would you interpret Landes's story about mechanization using the ideas developed in this chapter?

19. *(The Evolution of the Firm)* The Contracting and Organizations Research Institute at the University of Missouri maintains lots of interesting information about the evolution of the firm. Visit the institute's Web site at http://cori.missouri.edu/index.htm to familiarize yourself with the kinds of issues economists are studying.

20. *(International Trade)* Visit the McEachern Web site at http://mceachern.swlearning.com/ and click on Econ-Debate Online. Review the materials on "Does the U.S. economy benefit from foreign trade?" in the "International Trade" section. What are some of the benefits of international trade—not just to the United States, but to all nations?

21. *(Wall Street Journal)* The household is the most important decision-making unit in our economy. Look through the rotating columns (e.g., "Work and Family" and "Personal Technology") in the *Wall Street Journal* this week. Find a description of some technological change that might affect household production. Explain how production would be affected.

Demand and Supply Analysis

© Connie Coleman/Stone/Getty Images

W hy do roses cost more on Valentine's Day than during the rest of the year? Why do TV ads cost more during the Super Bowl ($2.3 million for 30 seconds in 2004) than during *Nick at Nite* reruns? Why do hotel rooms in Phoenix cost more in February than in August? Why do surgeons earn more than butchers? Why do pro basketball players earn more than pro hockey players? Why do economics majors earn more than most other majors? Answers to these and most economic questions boil down to the workings of demand and supply—the subject of this chapter.

This chapter introduces demand and supply and shows how they interact in competitive markets. *Demand and supply are the most fundamental and the most powerful of all economic tools*—important enough to warrant their own chapter. Indeed, some believe that if you program a computer to answer "demand and supply" to every economic question, you could put many economists out of work. An understanding of the two ideas will take you far in mastering the art and science of economic analysis. This chapter uses graphs, so you may need to review the Chapter 1 appendix as a refresher. Topics discussed include:

- Demand and quantity demanded
- Movement along a demand curve
- Shift of a demand curve
- Supply and quantity supplied
- Movement along a supply curve
- Shift of a supply curve
- Markets and equilibrium
- Disequilibrium

Demand

How many six packs of Pepsi will people buy each month if the price is $3? What if the price is $2? What if it's $4? The answers reveal the relationship between the price of Pepsi and the quantity purchased. Such a relationship is called the *demand* for Pepsi. **Demand** indicates how much of a good consumers are both *willing* and *able* to buy at each possible price during a given period, other things remaining constant. Because demand pertains to a specific period—a day, a week, a month—think of demand as the *planned rate of purchase per period* at each possible price. Also, notice the emphasis on *willing* and *able*. You may be *able* to buy a new Harley-Davidson for $5,000 because you can afford one, but you may not be *willing* to buy one if motorcycles don't interest you.

DEMAND

A relation between the price of a good and the quantity that consumers are willing and able to buy during a given period, other things constant

The Law of Demand

In 1962, Sam Walton opened his first store in Rogers, Arkansas, with a sign that read: "Wal-Mart Discount City. We sell for less." Wal-Mart now sells more than any other retailer in the world because its prices are among the lowest around. As a consumer, you understand why people buy more at a lower price. Sell for less, and the world will beat a path to your door. Wal-Mart, for example, sells on average over 20,000 pairs of shoes *an hour.* This relation between the price and the quantity demanded is an economic law. The **law of demand** says that quantity demanded varies inversely with price, other things constant. Thus, the higher the price, the smaller the quantity demanded; the lower the price, the greater the quantity demanded.

LAW OF DEMAND

The quantity of a good demanded during a given period relates inversely to its price, other things constant

Demand, Wants, and Needs

Consumer demand and consumer wants are not the same. As we have seen, wants are unlimited. You may want a new Mercedes SL600 convertible, but the $130,000 price tag is likely beyond your budget (that is, the quantity you demand at that price is zero). Nor is demand the same as need. You may need a new muffler for your car, but if the price is $200, you decide, "I am not going to pay a lot for this muffler." Apparently, you have better uses for your money. If, however, the price drops enough—say, to $100—then you become both willing and able to buy one.

The Substitution Effect of a Price Change

What explains the law of demand? Why, for example, is more demanded when the price is lower? The explanation begins with unlimited wants confronting scarce resources. Many goods and services could satisfy particular wants. For example, you can satisfy your hunger

Net Bookmark

The Inomics search engine at http://www.inomics.com/cgi/show is devoted solely to economics. Use it to investigate topics related to demand and supply and to other economic models.

with pizza, tacos, burgers, chicken, or hundreds of other goodies. Similarly, you can satisfy your desire for warmth in the winter with warm clothing, a home-heating system, a trip to Hawaii, or in many other ways. Clearly, some alternatives have more appeal than others (a trip to Hawaii is more fun than warm clothing). In a world without scarcity, everything would be free, so you would always choose the most attractive alternative. Scarcity, however, is a reality, and the degree of scarcity of one good relative to another helps determine each good's relative price.

Notice that the definition of *demand* includes the other-things-constant assumption. Among the "other things" assumed to remain constant are the prices of other goods. For example, if the price of pizza declines while other prices remain constant, pizza becomes relatively cheaper. Some consumers are more *willing* to purchase pizza when its relative price falls; they substitute pizza for other goods. This principle is called the **substitution effect of a price change**. On the other hand, an increase in the price of pizza, other things constant, causes some consumers to substitute other goods for the now higher-priced pizza, thus reducing their quantity of pizza demanded. Remember that *it is the change in the relative price—the price of one good relative to the prices of other goods—that causes the substitution effect*. If all prices changed by the same percentage, there would be no change in relative prices and no substitution effect.

The Income Effect of a Price Change

A fall in the price of a product increases the quantity demanded for a second reason. Suppose you clear $30 a week from a part-time job, so that's your money income. **Money income** is simply the number of dollars received per period, in this case, $30 per week. Suppose you spend all your income on pizza, buying three a week at $10 each. What if the price drops to $6? At the lower price you can now afford five pizzas a week. Your money income remains at $30 per week, but the decrease in the price has increased your **real income**— that is, your income measured in terms of what it can buy. The price reduction, other things constant, increases the purchasing power of your income, thereby increasing your ability to buy pizza. The quantity of pizza you demand will likely increase because of this **income effect of a price change**. You may not increase your quantity demanded to five pizzas, but you could. If you decide to purchase four pizzas a week when the price drops to $6, you have $6 remaining to buy other goods.

Thus, the income effect of a lower price increases your real income and thereby increases your ability to purchase all goods. Because of the income effect of a price decrease, other things constant, consumers typically increase their quantity demanded. Conversely, an increase in the price of a good, other things constant, reduces real income, thereby reducing the *ability* to purchase all goods. Because of the income effect of a price increase, consumers typically reduce their quantity demanded as price increases. Again, note that money income, not real income, is assumed to remain constant along a demand curve.

The Demand Schedule and Demand Curve

Demand can be expressed as a *demand schedule* or as a *demand curve*. Panel (a) of Exhibit 1 shows a hypothetical demand schedule for pizza. In describing demand, we must specify the units measured and the period considered. In our example, the unit is a 12-inch regular pizza and the period is a week. The schedule lists possible prices, along with the quantity demanded at each price. At a price of $15, for example, consumers demand 8 million pizzas per week. As you can see, the lower the price, other things constant, the greater the quantity demanded. Consumers substitute pizza for other foods. And as the price falls, real income

SUBSTITUTION EFFECT OF A PRICE CHANGE
When the price of a good falls, consumers substitute that good for other goods, which become relatively more expensive

MONEY INCOME
The number of dollars a person receives per period, such as $400 per week

REAL INCOME
Income measured in terms of the goods and services it can buy

INCOME EFFECT OF A PRICE CHANGE
A fall in the price of a good increases consumers' real income, making consumers more able to purchase goods; for a normal good, the quantity demanded increases

increases, causing consumers to increase the quantity of pizza they demand. If the price drops as low as $3, consumers demand 32 million per week.

The demand schedule in panel (a) appears as a **demand curve** in panel (b), with price on the vertical axis and the quantity demanded per week on the horizontal axis. Each price-quantity combination listed in the demand schedule in the left panel becomes a point in the right panel. Point *a*, for example, indicates that if the price is $15, consumers demand 8 million pizzas per week. These points connect to form the demand curve for pizza, labeled *D*. (By the way, some demand curves are straight lines, some are curved lines, and some are even jagged lines, but all are called demand *curves*.)

The demand curve slopes downward, reflecting the *law of demand:* Price and quantity demanded are inversely related, other things constant. Assumed constant along the demand curve are the prices of other goods. Thus, along the demand curve for pizza, the price of pizza changes *relative to the prices of other goods*. The demand curve shows the effect of a change in the *relative price* of pizza—that is, relative to other prices, which do not change.

Take care to distinguish between *demand* and *quantity demanded*. The *demand* for pizza is not a specific amount, but rather the *entire relationship* between price and quantity demanded—represented by the demand schedule or the demand curve. An individual point on the demand curve indicates the **quantity demanded** at a particular price. For example, at a price of $12, the quantity demanded is 14 million pizzas per week. If the price drops to, say, $9, this drop is shown in Exhibit 1 by *a movement along the demand curve*—in this case from point *b* to point *c*. Any movement along a demand curve reflects a *change in quantity demanded*, not a change in demand.

DEMAND CURVE

A curve showing the relation between the price of a good and the quantity demanded during a given period, other things constant

QUANTITY DEMANDED

The amount demanded at a particular price, as reflected by a point on a given demand curve

---

E X H I B I T   **1**

HOMEWORK
Xpress!
Graphing

The Demand Schedule and Demand Curve for Pizza
The market demand curve *D* shows the quantity of pizza demanded, at various prices, by all consumers. Price and quantity demanded are inversely related.

(a) Demand schedule

	Price per Pizza	Quantity Demanded per Week (millions)
a	$15	8
b	12	14
c	9	20
d	6	26
e	3	32

(b) Demand curve

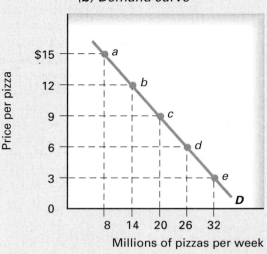

The law of demand applies to the millions of products sold in grocery stores, department stores, clothing stores, drugstores, music stores, bookstores, travel agencies, and restaurants, as well as through mail-order catalogs, the *Yellow Pages,* classified ads, Internet sites, stock markets, real estate markets, job markets, flea markets, and all other markets. The law of demand applies even to choices that seem more personal than economic, such as whether or not to own a pet. For example, after New York City passed an anti-dog-litter law, owners had to follow their dogs around the city with scoopers, plastic bags—whatever would do the job. Because the law raised the personal cost of owning a dog, the quantity demanded decreased. Some owners simply abandoned their dogs, raising the number of strays in the city. The number of dogs left at animal shelters doubled. The law of demand predicts this inverse relation between cost, or price, and quantity demanded.

It is useful to distinguish between **individual demand,** which is the demand of an individual consumer, and **market demand,** which is the sum of the individual demands of all consumers in the market. In most markets, there are many consumers, sometimes millions. Unless otherwise noted, when we talk about demand, we are referring to market demand, as in Exhibit 1.

Shifts of the Demand Curve

A demand curve isolates the relation between prices of a good and quantities demanded when other factors that could affect demand remain unchanged. What are those other factors, and how do changes in them affect demand? Variables that can affect market demand are (1) the money income of consumers, (2) prices of related goods, (3) consumer expectations, (4) the number or composition of consumers in the market, and (5) consumer tastes. How do changes in each affect demand?

Changes in Consumer Income

Exhibit 2 shows the market demand curve *D* for pizza. This demand curve assumes a given level of money income. Suppose consumer income increases. Some consumers will then be willing and able to buy more pizza at each price, so market demand increases. The demand curve shifts to the right from *D* to *D'*. For example, at a price of $12, the amount of pizza demanded increases from 14 million to 20 million per week, as indicated by the movement from point *b* on demand curve *D* to point *f* on demand curve *D'*. In short, *an increase in demand—that is, a rightward shift of the demand curve—means that consumers are willing and able to buy more pizza at each price.*

Goods are classified into two broad categories, depending on how demand responds to changes in money income. The demand for a **normal good** increases as money income increases. Because pizza is a normal good, its demand curve shifts rightward when consumer income increases. Most goods are normal. In contrast, demand for an **inferior good** actually decreases as money income increases, so the demand curve shifts leftward. Examples of inferior goods include bologna sandwiches, used furniture, and used clothing. As money income increases, consumers tend to switch from consuming these inferior goods to consuming normal goods (like roast beef sandwiches, new furniture, and new clothing).

Changes in the Prices of Related Goods

Again, the prices of other goods are assumed to remain constant along a given demand curve. Now let's bring these other prices into the picture. There are various ways of addressing any particular want. Consumers choose among substitutes based on relative prices. For example,

---

INDIVIDUAL DEMAND

The demand of an individual consumer

MARKET DEMAND

Sum of the individual demands of all consumers in the market

NORMAL GOOD

A good, such as new clothes, for which demand increases, or shifts rightward, as consumer incomes rise

INFERIOR GOOD

A good, such as used clothes, for which demand decreases, or shifts leftward, as consumer incomes rise

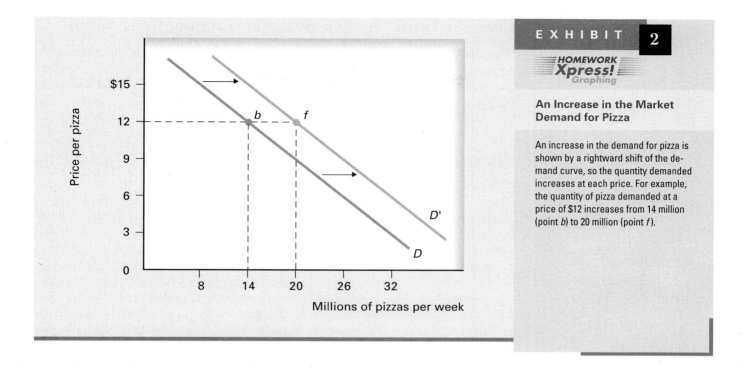

EXHIBIT 2

HOMEWORK
Xpress!
Graphing

An Increase in the Market Demand for Pizza

An increase in the demand for pizza is shown by a rightward shift of the demand curve, so the quantity demanded increases at each price. For example, the quantity of pizza demanded at a price of $12 increases from 14 million (point *b*) to 20 million (point *f*).

pizza and tacos are substitutes, though not perfect ones. An increase in the price of tacos, other things constant, reduces the quantity of tacos demanded along a given taco demand curve. An increase in the price of tacos also shifts the demand curve for pizza to the right. Two goods are considered **substitutes** if a price increase of one shifts the demand for the other rightward and, conversely, if a price decrease of one shifts demand for the other leftward.

Two goods used in combination are called *complements*. Examples include Coke and pizza, milk and cookies, computer software and hardware, and airline tickets and rental cars. Two goods are considered **complements** if a price increase of one shifts the demand for the other leftward. For example, an increase in the price of pizza shifts the demand curve for Coke leftward. But most pairs of goods selected at random are *unrelated*—for example, pizza and socks, or milk and gasoline.

Changes in Consumer Expectations

Another factor assumed constant along a given demand curve is consumer expectations about factors that influence demand, such as income or prices. A change in consumers' *income expectations* can shift the demand curve. For example, a consumer who learns about a pay raise might increase demand well before the raise takes effect. A college senior who lands that first real job may buy a new car even before graduation. Likewise, a change in consumers' *price expectations* can shift the demand curve. For example, if you expect the price of pizza to jump next week, you may buy an extra one today for the freezer, shifting this week's demand for pizza rightward. Or if consumers come to believe that home prices will climb next month, some will increase their demand for housing now, shifting this month's demand for housing rightward. On the other hand, if housing prices are expected to fall next month, some consumers will postpone purchases, thereby shifting this month's housing demand leftward.

SUBSTITUTES

Goods, such as Coke and Pepsi, that are related in such a way that an increase in the price of one shifts the demand for the other rightward

COMPLEMENTS

Goods, such as milk and cookies, that are related in such a way that an increase in the price of one shifts the demand for the other leftward

Changes in the Number or Composition of Consumers

As mentioned earlier, the market demand curve is the sum of the individual demand curves of all consumers in the market. If the number of consumers changes, the demand curve will shift. For example, if the population grows, the demand curve for pizza will shift rightward. Even if total population remains unchanged, demand could shift with a change in composition of the population. For example, a bulge in the teenage population could shift pizza demand rightward. A baby boom would shift rightward the demand for car seats and baby food.

Changes in Consumer Tastes

Do you like anchovies on your pizza or sauerkraut on your hot dog? Are you into tattoos and body piercings? Is music to your ears more likely to be rock, country, heavy metal, hip-hop, reggae, jazz, new age, or classical? Choices in food, body art, music, clothing, books, movies, TV—indeed, all consumer choices—are influenced by consumer tastes. **Tastes** are nothing more than your likes and dislikes as a consumer. What determines tastes? Your desires for food when hungry and drink when thirsty are largely biological. So is your desire for comfort, rest, shelter, friendship, love, status, personal safety, and a pleasant environment. Your family background affects some of your tastes—your taste in food, for example, has been shaped by years of home cooking. Other influences include the surrounding culture, peer influence, and religious convictions. So economists can say a little about the origin of tastes, but they claim no special expertise in understanding how tastes develop. Economists recognize, however, that tastes have an important impact on demand. For example, although pizza is popular, some people just don't like it and those who are lactose intolerant can't stomach the cheese topping. Thus, some people like pizza and some don't.

In our analysis of consumer demand, *we will assume that tastes are given and are relatively stable.* Tastes are assumed to remain constant along a demand curve. A change in the tastes for a particular good shifts the demand curve. For example, a discovery that the tomato sauce and cheese combination on pizza promotes overall health could change consumer tastes, shifting the demand curve for pizza to the right. But because a change in tastes is so difficult to isolate from other economic changes, we should be reluctant to attribute a shift of the demand curve to a change in tastes.

That wraps up our look at changes in demand. Before we turn to supply, you should remember the distinction between a **movement along a given demand curve** and a **shift of a demand curve.** A change in *price,* other things constant, causes a *movement along a demand curve,* changing the quantity demanded. A change in one of the determinants of demand other than price causes a *shift of a demand curve,* changing demand.

Supply

Just as demand is a relation between price and quantity demanded, supply is a relation between price and quantity supplied. **Supply** indicates how much producers are *willing* and *able* to offer for sale per period at each possible price, other things constant. The **law of supply** states that the quantity supplied is usually directly related to its price, other things constant. Thus, the lower the price, the smaller the quantity supplied; the higher the price, the greater the quantity supplied.

TASTES

Consumer preferences; likes and dislikes in consumption; assumed to be constant along a given demand curve

MOVEMENT ALONG A DEMAND CURVE

Change in quantity demanded resulting from a change in the price of the good, other things constant

SHIFT OF A DEMAND CURVE

Movement of a demand curve right or left resulting from a change in one of the determinants of demand other than the price of the good

SUPPLY

A relation between the price of a good and the quantity that producers are willing and able to sell during a given period, other things constant

LAW OF SUPPLY

The quantity of a good supplied during a given period is usually directly related to its price, other things constant

The Supply Schedule and Supply Curve

Exhibit 3 presents the market *supply schedule* and market **supply curve** S for pizza. Both show the quantities of pizza supplied per week at various possible prices by the thousands of pizza makers in the economy. As you can see, price and quantity supplied are directly, or positively, related. Producers offer more at a higher price than at a lower price, so the supply curve slopes upward.

There are two reasons producers offer more for sale when the price rises. First, as the price increases, other things constant, a producer becomes more *willing* to supply the good. Prices act as signals to existing and potential suppliers about the rewards for producing various goods. An increase in the price of pizza, with other prices constant, provides suppliers a profit incentive to shift some resources from producing other goods, for which the price is now relatively lower, and into pizza, for which the price is now relatively higher. *A higher pizza price attracts resources from lower-valued uses.*

Higher prices also increase the producer's *ability* to supply the good. The law of increasing opportunity cost, as noted in Chapter 2, states that the opportunity cost of producing more of a particular good rises as output increases—that is, the *marginal cost* of production increases as output increases. Because producers face a higher marginal cost for additional output, they must receive a higher price for that output to be *able* to increase the quantity supplied. *A higher price makes producers more able to increase quantity supplied.* As a case in point, a higher price for gasoline increases oil companies' ability to drill deeper and to explore in

SUPPLY CURVE

A curve showing the relation between price of a good and the quantity supplied during a given period, other things constant

---

E X H I B I T **3**

The Supply Schedule and Supply Curve for Pizza

Market supply curve *S* shows the quantity of pizza supplied, at various prices, by all pizza makers. Price and quantity supplied are directly related.

(a) Supply schedule

Price per Pizza	Quantity Supplied per Week (millions)
$15	28
12	24
9	20
6	16
3	12

(b) Supply curve

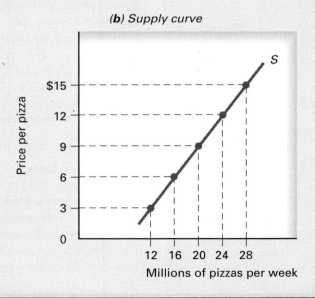

less accessible areas, such as the remote jungles of the Amazon, the stormy waters of the North Sea, and the frozen tundra above the Arctic Circle. On the other hand, the price of gold today is only half what it was decades ago so miners are less able to prospect for gold or to refine ore with lower gold content.

Thus, a higher price makes producers more *willing* and more *able* to increase quantity supplied. Producers are more *willing* because production becomes more profitable than the alternative uses of the resources involved. The higher price also *enables* producers to cover the higher marginal cost that typically results from a greater rate of output.

As with demand, we distinguish between *supply* and **quantity supplied.** *Supply* is the entire relationship between prices and quantities supplied, as reflected by the supply schedule or supply curve. *Quantity supplied* refers to a particular amount offered for sale at a particular price, as reflected by a point on a given supply curve. We also distinguish between **individual supply,** the supply of an individual producer, and **market supply,** the sum of individual supplies of all producers in the market. Unless otherwise noted the term supply refers to market supply.

Shifts of the Supply Curve

The supply curve isolates the relation between the price of a good and the quantity supplied, other things constant. Assumed constant along a supply curve are the determinants of supply other than the price of the good, including (1) the state of technology, (2) the prices of relevant resources, (3) the prices of alternative goods, (4) producer expectations, and (5) the number of producers in the market. Let's see how a change in each affects the supply curve.

Changes in Technology

Recall from Chapter 2 that the state of technology represents the economy's stock of knowledge about how to combine resources efficiently. Along a given supply curve, technology is assumed to remain unchanged. If a more efficient technology is discovered, production costs will fall; so suppliers will be more willing and more able to supply the good at each price. Consequently, supply will increase, as reflected by a rightward shift of the supply curve. For example, suppose a new high-tech oven bakes pizza in half the time. Such a breakthrough would shift the market supply curve rightward, as from S to S' in Exhibit 4, where more is supplied at each possible price. For example, if the price is $12, the amount supplied increases from 24 million to 28 million pizzas, as shown in Exhibit 4 by the movement from point *g* to point *h*. In short, *an increase in supply—that is, a rightward shift of the supply curve—means that producers are willing and able to sell more pizza at each price.*

Changes in the Prices of Relevant Resources

Relevant resources are those employed in the production of the good in question. For example, suppose the price of mozzarella cheese falls. This price decrease reduces the cost of pizza production, so producers are more willing and better able to supply pizza. The supply curve for pizza shifts rightward, as shown in Exhibit 4. On the other hand, an increase in the price of a relevant resource reduces supply, meaning a shift of the supply curve leftward. For example, a higher cheese price increases the cost of making pizzas. Higher production costs decrease supply, so pizza supply shifts leftward.

Changes in the Prices of Alternative Goods

Nearly all resources have alternative uses. The labor, building, machinery, ingredients, and knowledge needed to run a pizza business could produce other baked goods. **Alternative**

QUANTITY SUPPLIED

The amount offered for sale at a particular price, as reflected by a point on a given supply curve

INDIVIDUAL SUPPLY

The supply of an individual producer

MARKET SUPPLY

The sum of individual supplies of all producers in the market

RELEVANT RESOURCES

Resources used to produce the good in question

ALTERNATIVE GOODS

Other goods that use some or all of the same resources as the good in question

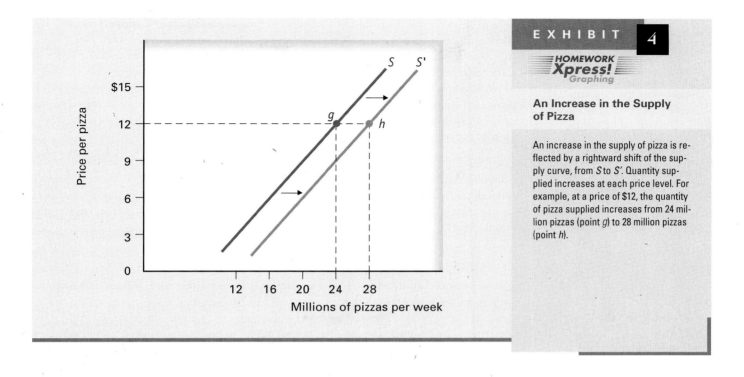

EXHIBIT 4

≡ *HOMEWORK* ≡
Xpress!
Graphing

**An Increase in the Supply
of Pizza**

An increase in the supply of pizza is reflected by a rightward shift of the supply curve, from *S* to *S'*. Quantity supplied increases at each price level. For
example, at a price of $12, the quantity
of pizza supplied increases from 24 million pizzas (point *g*) to 28 million pizzas
(point *h*).

goods are those that use some of the same resources employed to produce the good under
consideration. For example, a decrease in the price of Italian bread reduces the opportunity
cost of making pizza. As a result, some bread makers become pizza makers so the supply of
pizza increases, shifting the supply curve rightward as in Exhibit 3. On the other hand, if the
price of an alternative good, such as Italian bread, increases, supplying pizza becomes relatively less attractive compared to supplying Italian bread. As resources shift into bread making, the supply of pizza decreases, or shifts to the left.

Changes in Producer Expectations

Changes in producer expectations can shift the supply curve. For example, a pizza maker
expecting higher pizza prices in the future may expand his or her pizzeria now, thereby
shifting the supply of pizza rightward. When a good can be easily stored (crude oil, for example, can be left in the ground), expecting higher prices in the future might prompt some
producers to *reduce* their current supply while awaiting the higher price. Thus, an expectation of higher prices in the future could either increase or decrease current supply, depending on the good. More generally, any change expected to affect future profitability, such as a
change in business taxes, could shift the supply curve now.

Changes in the Number of Producers

Because market supply sums the amounts supplied at each price by all producers, market
supply depends on the number of producers in the market. If that number increases, supply
will increase, shifting supply to the right. If the number of producers decreases, supply will
decrease, shifting supply to the left. As an example of increased supply, the number of
gourmet coffee bars more than quadrupled in the United States during the last decade
(think Starbucks), shifting the supply curve of gourmet coffee to the right.

Finally, note again the distinction between a **movement along a supply curve** and a **shift of a supply curve.** A change in *price,* other things constant, causes *a movement along a supply curve,* changing the quantity supplied. A change in one of the determinants of supply other than price causes a *shift of a supply curve,* changing supply.

You are now ready to put demand and supply together.

Demand and Supply Create a Market

Demanders and suppliers have different views of price, because demanders pay the price and suppliers receive it. Thus, a higher price is bad news for consumers but good news for producers. As the price rises, consumers reduce their quantity demanded along the demand curve and producers increase their quantity supplied along the supply curve. How is this conflict between producers and consumers resolved?

Markets

A market sorts out differences between demanders and suppliers. A *market,* as you know from Chapter 1, includes all the arrangements used to buy and sell a particular good or service. Markets reduce **transaction costs**—the costs of time and information required for exchange. For example, suppose you are looking for a summer job. One approach might be to go from employer to employer looking for openings. But this would be time consuming and could have you running around for days. A more efficient strategy would be to pick up a copy of the local newspaper and read through the help-wanted ads or go online and look for openings. Classified ads and Web sites, which are elements of the job market, reduce the transaction costs of bringing workers and employers together.

The coordination that occurs through markets takes place not because of some central plan but because of Adam Smith's "invisible hand." For example, the auto dealers in your community tend to locate together, usually on the outskirts of town, where land is cheaper. The dealers congregate not because someone told them to or because they like one another's company but because together they become a more attractive destination for car buyers. Similarly, stores group together so that more shoppers will be drawn by the call of the mall. From Orlando theme parks to Broadway theaters to Las Vegas casinos, suppliers congregate to attract demanders. Some gatherings of suppliers can be quite specialized. For example, shops selling dress mannequins cluster along Austin Road in Hong Kong.

Market Equilibrium

To see how a market works, let's bring together market demand and supply. Exhibit 5 shows the market for pizza, using schedules in panel (a) and curves in panel (b). Suppose the price initially is $12. At that price, producers supply 24 million pizzas per week, but consumers demand only 14 million, resulting in an *excess quantity supplied,* or a **surplus,** of 10 million pizzas per week. Producers' desire to eliminate this surplus puts downward pressure on the price, as shown by the arrow pointing down in the graph. As the price falls, producers reduce their quantity supplied and consumers increase their quantity demanded. The price continues to fall as long as quantity supplied exceeds quantity demanded.

Alternatively, suppose the price initially is $6 per pizza. You can see from Exhibit 5 that at that price, consumers demand 26 million pizzas but producers supply only 16 million, resulting in an *excess quantity demanded,* or a **shortage,** of 10 million pizzas per week. Producers quickly notice that their quantity supplied has sold out and those customers still de-

---

MOVEMENT ALONG A SUPPLY CURVE

Change in quantity supplied resulting from a change in the price of the good, other things constant

SHIFT OF A SUPPLY CURVE

Movement of a supply curve left or right resulting from a change in one of the determinants of supply other than the price of the good

TRANSACTION COSTS

The costs of time and information required to carry out market exchange

SURPLUS

At a given price, the amount by which quantity supplied exceeds quantity demanded; a surplus usually forces the price down

SHORTAGE

At a given price, the amount by which quantity demanded exceeds quantity supplied; a shortage usually forces the price up

manding pizzas are grumbling. Profit-maximizing producers and frustrated consumers create market pressure for a higher price, as shown by the arrow pointing up in the graph. As the price rises, producers increase their quantity supplied and consumers reduce their quantity demanded. The price continues to rise as long as quantity demanded exceeds quantity supplied.

Thus, *a surplus creates downward pressure on the price, and a shortage creates upward pressure.* As long as quantity demanded differs from quantity supplied, this difference forces a price change. Note that a shortage or a surplus depends on the price. There is no such thing as a general shortage or a general surplus.

A market reaches equilibrium when the quantity demanded equals quantity supplied. In **equilibrium,** the independent plans of both buyers and sellers exactly match, so market forces exert no pressure to change price or quantity. In Exhibit 5, the demand and supply curves intersect at the *equilibrium point,* identified as point *c.* The *equilibrium price* is $9 per pizza, and the *equilibrium quantity* is 20 million per week. At that price and quantity,

EQUILIBRIUM

The condition that exists in a market when the plans of buyers match those of sellers, so quantity demanded equals quantity supplied and the market clears

(a) Market schedules

Millions of Pizzas per Week

Price per Pizza	Quantity Demanded	Quantity Supplied	Surplus or Shortage	Effect on Price
$15	8	28	Surplus of 20	Falls
12	14	24	Surplus of 10	Falls
9	20	20	Equilibrium	Remains the same
6	26	16	Shortage of 10	Rises
3	32	12	Shortage of 20	Rises

(b) Market curves

EXHIBIT 5

HOMEWORK
Xpress!
Graphing

Equilibrium in the Pizza Market

Market equilibrium occurs at the price where quantity demanded equals quantity supplied. This is shown at point *c.* Above the equilibrium price, quantity supplied exceeds quantity demanded. This creates a surplus, which puts downward pressure on the price. Below the equilibrium price, quantity demanded exceeds quantity supplied. The resulting shortage puts upward pressure on the price.

the market *clears*. Because there is no shortage or surplus, there is no pressure for a price change.

A market finds equilibrium through the independent actions of thousands, or even millions, of buyers and sellers. In one sense, the market is personal because each consumer and each producer makes a personal decision regarding how much to buy or sell at a given price. In another sense, the market is impersonal because it requires no conscious coordination among consumers or producers. *Impersonal market forces synchronize the personal and independent decisions of many individual buyers and sellers to achieve equilibrium price and quantity.*

Changes in Equilibrium Price and Quantity

Equilibrium is the combination of price and quantity at which the intentions of demanders and suppliers exactly match. Once a market reaches equilibrium, that price and quantity will prevail until one of the determinants of demand or supply changes. A change in any one of these determinants usually changes equilibrium price and quantity in a predictable way, as you'll see.

Shifts of the Demand Curve

In Exhibit 6, demand curve *D* and supply curve *S* intersect at point *c* to yield the initial equilibrium price of $9 and the initial equilibrium quantity of 20 million 12-inch regular pizzas per week. Now suppose that one of the determinants of demand changes in a way that increases demand, shifting the demand curve to the right from *D* to *D'*. Any of the following could shift the demand for pizza rightward: (1) an increase in the money income of consumers (because pizza is a normal good); (2) an increase in the price of a substitute, such as tacos, or a decrease in the price of a complement, such as Coke; (3) a change in consumer

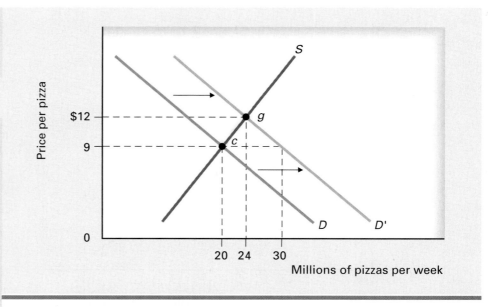

EXHIBIT   6

Graphing

Effects of an Increase in Demand

An increase in demand is shown by a shift of the demand curve rightward from *D* to *D'*. Quantity demanded exceeds quantity supplied at the original price of $9 per pizza, putting upward pressure on the price. As the price rises, quantity supplied increases along supply curve *S*, and quantity demanded decreases along demand curve *D'*. When the new equilibrium price of $12 is reached at point *g*, quantity demanded once again equals quantity supplied. Both price and quantity are higher following the rightward shift of the demand curve.

expectations that encourages them to demand more pizzas now; (4) a growth in the number of pizza consumers; or (5) a change in consumer tastes—based, for example, on a discovery that the tomato sauce on pizza has antioxidant properties that improve overall health.

After the demand curve shifts rightward to D' in Exhibit 6, the amount demanded at the initial price of $9 is 30 million pizzas, which exceeds the amount supplied of 20 million by 10 million pizzas. This shortage puts upward pressure on the price. As the price increases, the quantity demanded decreases along the new demand curve D', and the quantity supplied increases along the existing supply curve S until the two quantities are equal once again at equilibrium point g. The new equilibrium price is $12, and the new equilibrium quantity is 24 million pizzas per week. Thus, given an upward-sloping supply curve, an increase in demand, meaning a rightward shift of the demand curve, increases both equilibrium price and quantity. A decrease in demand, meaning a leftward shift of the demand curve, would lower both equilibrium price and quantity. These results can be summarized as follows: *Given an upward-sloping supply curve, a rightward shift of the demand curve increases both equilibrium price and quantity and a leftward shift of the demand curve decreases both equilibrium price and quantity.*

Shifts of the Supply Curve

Let's consider shifts of the supply curve. In Exhibit 7, as before, we begin with demand curve D and supply curve S intersecting at point c to yield an equilibrium price of $9 and an equilibrium quantity of 20 million pizzas per week. Suppose one of the determinants of supply changes, increasing supply from S to S'. Changes that could shift the supply curve rightward include (1) a technological breakthrough in pizza ovens; (2) a reduction in the price of a relevant resource, such as mozzarella cheese; (3) a decline in the price of an alternative good,

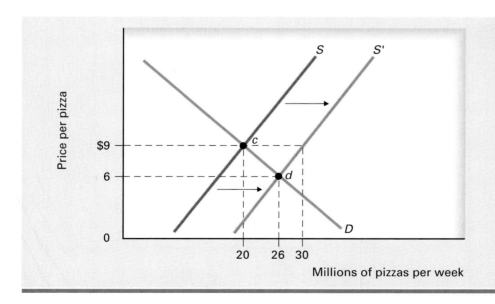

**Effects of an
Increase in Supply**

An increase in supply is shown by a shift of the supply curve rightward, from S to S'. Quantity supplied exceeds quantity demanded at the original price of $9 per pizza, putting downward pressure on the price. As the price falls, quantity supplied decreases along supply curve S', and quantity demanded increases along demand curve D. When the new equilibrium price of $6 is reached at point d, quantity demanded once again equals quantity supplied. At the new equilibrium, quantity is greater and the price is lower than before the increase in supply.

such as Italian bread; (4) a change in expectations that encourages pizza makers to expand production now; or (5) an increase in the number of pizzerias.

After the supply curve shifts rightward in Exhibit 7, the amount supplied at the initial price of $9 increases from 20 million to 30 million, so producers now supply 10 million more pizzas than consumers demand. This surplus forces the price down. As the price falls, the quantity supplied declines along the new supply curve and the quantity demanded increases along the existing demand curve until a new equilibrium point *d* is established. The new equilibrium price is $6, and the new equilibrium quantity is 26 million pizzas per week. In short, an increase in supply reduces the price and increases the quantity. On the other hand, a decrease in supply increases the price but decreases the quantity. Thus, *given a downward-sloping demand curve, a rightward shift of the supply curve decreases price but increases quantity, and a leftward shift increases price but decreases quantity.*

E X H I B I T   8

Indeterminate Effect of an Increase in Both Demand and Supply

When both demand and supply increase, the equilibrium quantity also increases. The effect on price depends on which curve shifts more. In panel (a), the demand curve shifts more, so the price rises. In panel (b), the supply curve shifts more, so the price falls.

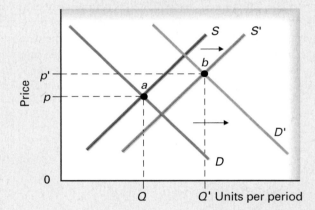

(a) **Shift of demand dominates**

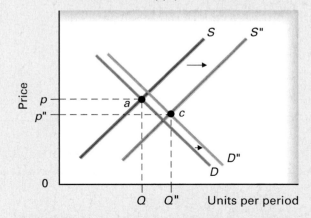

(b) **Shift of supply dominates**

Simultaneous Shifts of Demand and Supply Curves

As long as only one curve shifts, we can say for sure how equilibrium price and quantity will change. If both curves shift, however, the outcome is less obvious. For example, suppose both demand and supply increase, or shift rightward, as in Exhibit 8. Note that in panel (a), demand shifts more than supply, and in panel (b), supply shifts more than demand. In both panels, equilibrium quantity increases. The change in equilibrium price, however, depends on which curve shifts more. If demand shifts more, as in panel (a), equilibrium price increases. For example, in the last decade, the demand for housing has increased more than the supply, so both price and quantity have increased. But if supply shifts more, as in panel (b), equilibrium price decreases. For example, in the last decade, the supply of personal computers has increased more than the demand, so price has decreased and quantity increased.

Conversely, if both demand and supply decrease, or shift leftward, equilibrium quantity decreases. But, again, we cannot say what will happen to equilibrium price unless we examine relative shifts. (You can use Exhibit 8 to consider decreases in demand and supply by viewing *D'* and *S'* as the initial curves.) If demand shifts more, the price will fall. If supply shifts more, the price will rise.

If demand and supply shift in opposite directions, we can say what will happen to equilibrium price. Equilibrium price will increase if demand increases and supply decreases. Equilibrium price will decrease if demand decreases and supply increases. Without reference to particular shifts, however, we cannot say what will happen to equilibrium quantity.

These results are no doubt confusing, but Exhibit 9 summarizes the four possible combinations of changes. Using Exhibit 9 as a reference, please take the time right now to work through some changes in demand and supply to develop an intuitive understanding of the results. Then, in the following case study, evaluate changes in the market for professional basketball.

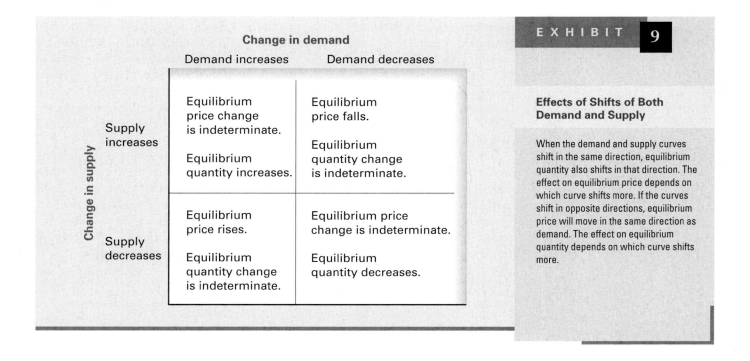

Change in demand

	Demand increases	**Demand decreases**
Supply increases	Equilibrium price change is indeterminate. Equilibrium quantity increases.	Equilibrium price falls. Equilibrium quantity change is indeterminate.
Supply decreases	Equilibrium price rises. Equilibrium quantity change is indeterminate.	Equilibrium price change is indeterminate. Equilibrium quantity decreases.

Change in supply (vertical axis label, left)

EXHIBIT 9

Effects of Shifts of Both Demand and Supply

When the demand and supply curves shift in the same direction, equilibrium quantity also shifts in that direction. The effect on equilibrium price depends on which curve shifts more. If the curves shift in opposite directions, equilibrium price will move in the same direction as demand. The effect on equilibrium quantity depends on which curve shifts more.

C a s e **S t u d y**

World of Business

*e*Activity
InsideHoops hosts a current salary list for top NBA players at http://www.insidehoops.com/nbasalaries.shtml.

The Market for Professional Basketball

Toward the end of the 1970s, the National Basketball Association (NBA) seemed on the verge of collapse. Attendance had sunk to little more than half capacity. Some teams were nearly bankrupt. Championship games didn't even get prime-time television coverage. But in the 1980s, three superstars turned things around. Michael Jordan, Larry Bird, and Magic Johnson attracted millions of new fans and breathed new life into the sagging league. Now a generation of new stars, including Allen Iverson, Tracy McGrady, and LeBron James, continue to fuel interest.

© Mike Cassese/Reuters/Corbis

Since 1980, game attendance has doubled, and the league expanded from 22 to 29 teams. New franchises sold for record amounts. More importantly, league revenue from broadcast rights jumped more than *40-fold* from $19 million per year during the 1978–1982 contract to $785 million per year during the 2002–2008 contract. Popularity also increased around the world as international players, such as Yao Ming, joined the league (basketball is now the most widely played team sport among young people in China). NBA rosters in 2003 included 80 international players from 36 countries. The NBA formed marketing alliances with global companies such as Coca-Cola and McDonald's, and league playoffs are now televised around the world.

What's the key resource in the production of NBA games? Talented players. Exhibit 10 shows the market for NBA players, with demand and supply in 1980 as D_{1980} and S_{1980}. The intersection of these two curves generated an average pay in 1980 of $170,000, or $0.17 million, for the 300 or so players in the league. Since 1980, the talent pool expanded somewhat, shifting the supply curve a bit rightward from S_{1980} to S_{2003} (almost by definition, the supply of the top few hundred players in the world is limited). But demand exploded from D_{1980} to D_{2003}. With supply relatively fixed, the greater demand boosted average pay to $4.1 million by 2003 for the 400 or so players in the league. Such pay attracts younger and younger players. For example, Kevin Garnett, whose $28 million annual salary topped the league in 2003, entered the NBA in 1995 right out of high school. LeBron James, the top pick in the 2003 NBA draft, and heir apparent to Michael Jordan, also had just graduated from high school.

But rare talent alone does not command high pay. For example, top rodeo riders, top bowlers, and top women basketball players also possess rare talent, but the demand for their talent is not enough to support pay anywhere near NBA levels. Demand is also critical. Some sports aren't even popular enough to support professional leagues (for example, the U.S. women's pro soccer league folded in 2003). NBA players are now the highest-paid team athletes in the world—earning 60 percent more than pro baseball's average and at least double that for pro football and pro hockey. Both demand *and* supply determine average pay.

Sources: Brian Straus, "Women's Pro Soccer League Forced to Fold," *Washington Post*, 16 September 2003; Allen Cheng, "Basketball Shoots to Top Sport for Young Chinese," *South China Morning Post*, 25 September 2003; "Salary Cap for 2003–04 Set at $43.8 million," http://www.nba.com/; "NBA TV Deal Moves to ABC, ESPN," http://espn.go.com/nba/news/2002/0122/1315389.html; and U.S. Census Bureau, *Statistical Abstract of the United States: 2003*, http://www.census.gov/prod/www/statistical-abstract-02.html.

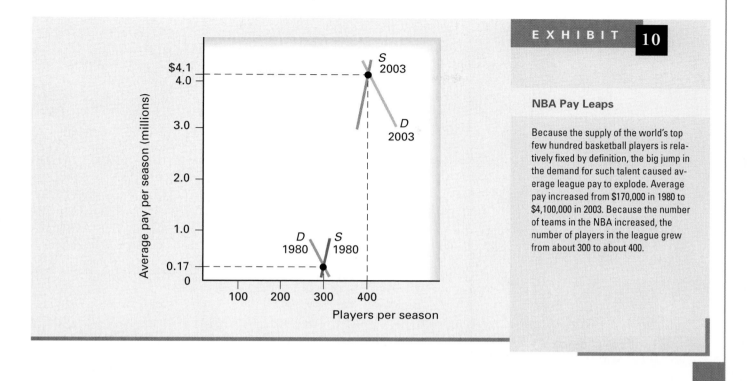

EXHIBIT 10

NBA Pay Leaps

Because the supply of the world's top few hundred basketball players is relatively fixed by definition, the big jump in the demand for such talent caused average league pay to explode. Average pay increased from $170,000 in 1980 to $4,100,000 in 2003. Because the number of teams in the NBA increased, the number of players in the league grew from about 300 to about 400.

Disequilibrium

A surplus exerts downward pressure on the price, and a shortage exerts upward pressure. Markets, however, do not always reach equilibrium quickly. During the time required to adjust, the market is said to be in disequilibrium. **Disequilibrium** is usually temporary as the market gropes for equilibrium. But sometimes, often as a result of government intervention, disequilibrium can last a while, as we will see next.

Price Floors

Sometimes public officials set prices above their equilibrium levels. For example, the federal government regulates some agriculture prices in an attempt to ensure farmers a higher and more stable income than they would otherwise earn. To achieve higher prices, the federal government sets a **price floor,** or a *minimum* selling price that is above the equilibrium price. Panel (a) of Exhibit 11 shows the effect of a $2.50 per gallon price floor for milk. At that price, farmers supply 24 million gallons per week, but consumers demand only 14 million gallons, yielding a surplus of 10 million gallons. This surplus milk will pile up on store shelves, eventually souring. To take it off the market, the government usually agrees to buy the surplus milk. The federal government, in fact, spends billions buying and storing surplus agricultural products. Note, to have an impact, a price floor must be set above the equilibrium price. A floor set below the equilibrium price would be irrelevant (how come?).

Price Ceilings

Sometimes public officials try to keep prices below their equilibrium levels by establishing a **price ceiling,** or a *maximum* selling price. For example, concern about the rising cost of

DISEQUILIBRIUM

The condition that exists in a market when the plans of buyers do not match those of sellers; a temporary mismatch between quantity supplied and quantity demanded as the market seeks equilibrium

PRICE FLOOR

A minimum legal price below which a good or service cannot be sold; to have an impact, a price floor must be set above the equilibrium price

PRICE CEILING

A maximum legal price above which a good or service cannot be sold; to have an impact, a price ceiling must be set below the equilibrium price

rental housing in some cities prompted city officials there to impose rent ceilings. Panel (b) of Exhibit 11 depicts the demand and supply of rental housing in a hypothetical city. The vertical axis shows monthly rent, and the horizontal axis shows the quantity of rental units. The equilibrium, or market-clearing, rent is $1,000 per month, and the equilibrium quantity is 50,000 housing units.

Suppose the government sets a maximum rent of $600 per month. At that ceiling price, 60,000 rental units are demanded, but only 40,000 supplied, resulting in a housing shortage of 20,000 units. Because of the price ceiling, the rental price no longer rations housing to those who value it the most. Other devices emerge to ration housing, such as long waiting lists, personal connections, and the willingness to make under-the-table payments, such as "key fees," "finder's fees," high security deposits, and the like. To have an impact, a price ceiling must be set below the equilibrium price. Price floors and ceilings distort markets.

Government intervention is not the only source of market disequilibrium. Sometimes, when new products are introduced or when demand suddenly changes, it takes a while to reach equilibrium. For example, popular toys, best-selling books, and chart-busting CDs sometimes sell out. On the other hand, some new products attract few customers and pile up unsold on store shelves, awaiting a "clearance sale." Disequilibrium is discussed in the following case study.

HOMEWORK
Xpress!
*Ask the Instructor
Video*

EXHIBIT   **11**   **Price Floors and Price Ceilings**

HOMEWORK
Xpress!
Graphing

A price floor set above the equilibrium price results in a surplus, as shown in panel (a). A price floor set at or below equilibrium price has no effect. A price ceiling set below the equilibrium price results in a shortage, as shown anel (b). A price ceiling set at or above the equilibrium price has no effect.

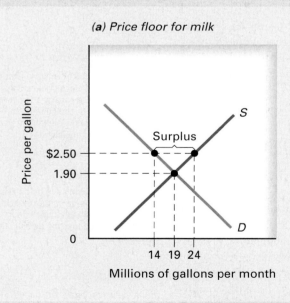

(a) Price floor for milk

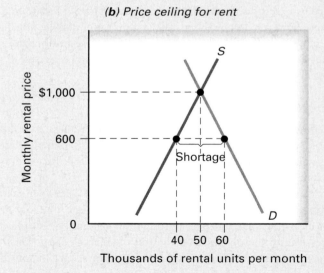

(b) Price ceiling for rent

The Toy Business Is Not Child's Play

U.S. toy sales exceeded $25 billion a year in 2003, but the business is not much fun for toy makers. Most toys don't make it from one season to the next, turning out to be costly duds. A few have staying power, like G.I. Joe, who could retire after 40 years of military service; Barbie, who is now over 40; and the Wiffle Ball, still a hit after 50 years. Because toy factories, which are mostly in China, need time to gear up, most retailers must order in February for Christmas delivery. Can you imagine the uncertainty of this market? Who, for example, could have anticipated the success of Chicken Dance Elmo, Beanie Babies, Teletubbies, FurReal Friends, or Yu-Gi-Oh trading cards?

© Photodisc/Getty Images

A few years ago, the Mighty Morphin Power Rangers were the rage. Within a year, the manufacturer increased production 10-fold, with 11 new factories churning out nearly $1 billion in Rangers. Still, at $13 each, quantity demanded exceeded quantity supplied. Why don't toy makers simply let the price find its equilibrium level? Suppose, for example, that the market-clearing price for Power Rangers was $26, twice the actual price. First, it's hard for toymakers to anticipate demand well enough to boost the price before supplies run out. Second, suppliers who hope to retain customers over the long haul may want to avoid appearing greedy. That may be why Home Depot doesn't raise the price of snow shovels after the first winter storm, why Wal-Mart doesn't boost air conditioner prices during the dog days of summer, and why DaimlerChrysler preferred long waiting lists to raising prices still higher for its Mercedes SUV.

To sum up, uncertainty abounds in the market for new products. Suppliers can only guess what the demand will be, so they must feel their way in deciding what price to charge and how much to produce. Eventually, markets do achieve equilibrium. For example, Daimler-Chrysler doubled production of its SUV, eventually erasing the shortage. Because finding the market-clearing price takes time, some markets are temporarily in disequilibrium. But even when hot toys are sold out at retailers, they are usually available on the Internet at a higher price. For example, just before one recent Christmas, the hot toy that year, Spider-Man Web Blaster, was sold out most everywhere. But the toy was still available on eBay for $135, or nine times its $15 retail price.

Sources: Alexander Coolidge, "Hot Toys Are Hard to Come By for Those Who Wait," *Sarasota Herald Tribune*, 21 December 2002; "Hot Toys," *BusinessWeek*, 9 December 2002; Raymond Gorman and James Kehr, "Fairness as a Constraint on Profit Seeking," *American Economic Review*, March 1992; the Official Yu-Gi-Oh site at http://www.yugiohkingofgames.com; and the Toy Industry Association site at http://www.toy-tia.org/.

Conclusion

Demand and supply are the building blocks of a market economy. Although a market usually involves the interaction of many buyers and sellers, few markets are consciously designed. Just as the law of gravity works whether or not we understand Newton's principles, market forces operate whether or not participants understand demand and supply. These forces arise naturally, much the way car dealers cluster on the outskirts of town.

Markets have their critics. Some observers may be troubled, for example, that NBA star Kevin Garnett's annual salary could fund a thousand new schoolteachers, or that U.S. consumers spend billions each year on pet food when some people lack enough to eat. On your next trip to the supermarket, notice how much shelf space goes to pet products—often an entire aisle. Petsmart, a chain store, sells over 12,000 pet items. Veterinarians offer cancer treatment, cataract removal, and root canals for pets. Kidney dialysis for a pet can cost $55,000 per year.

SUMMARY

1. Demand is a relationship between the price and the quantity consumers are willing and able to buy per period, other things constant. According to the law of demand, quantity demanded varies inversely with its price, so the demand curve slopes downward.

2. A demand curve slopes downward for two reasons. A price decrease makes consumers (a) more *willing* to substitute this good for other goods and (b) more *able* to buy the good because the lower price increases real income.

3. Assumed to be constant along a demand curve are (a) money income, (b) prices of related goods, (c) consumer expectations, (d) the number and composition of consumers in the market, and (e) consumer tastes. A change in any one of these will shift the demand curve.

4. Supply is a relationship between the price of a good and the quantity producers are willing and able to sell per period, other things constant. According to the law of supply, price and quantity supplied are usually directly related, so the supply curve typically slopes upward. The supply curve slopes upward because higher prices make producers (a) more *willing* to supply this good rather than supply other goods that use the same resources and (b) more *able* to cover the higher marginal cost associated with greater output rates.

5. Assumed to be constant along a supply curve are (a) the state of technology; (b) the prices of resources used to produce the good; (c) the prices of other goods that could be produced with these resources; (d) supplier expectations; and (e) the number of producers in this market. A change in any one of these will shift the supply curve.

6. Demand and supply come together in the market for the good. Markets provide information about the price, quan-

tity, and quality of the good. In doing so, markets reduce the transaction costs of exchange—the costs of time and information required for buyers and sellers to make a deal. The interaction of demand and supply guides resources and products to their highest-valued use.

7. Impersonal market forces reconcile the personal and independent intentions of buyers and sellers. Market equilibrium, once established, will continue unless there is a change in factor that shapes demand or supply. Disequilibrium is usually temporary while markets seek equilibrium, but sometimes disequilibrium lasts a while, such as when government regulates the price or when new products are introduced.

8. A price floor is the minimum legal price below which a particular good or service cannot be sold. The federal government imposes price floors on some agricultural products to help farmers achieve a higher and more stable income than would be possible with freer markets. If the floor price is set above the market clearing price, quantity supplied exceeds quantity demanded. Policy makers must figure out some way to prevent this surplus from pushing the price down.

9. A price ceiling is a maximum legal price above which a particular good or service cannot be sold. Governments impose price ceilings to reduce the price of some consumer goods such as rental housing. If the ceiling price is below the market clearing price, quantity demanded exceeds the quantity supplied, creating a shortage. Because the price system is not allowed to clear the market, other mechanisms arise to ration the product among demanders.

QUESTIONS FOR REVIEW

1. *(Law of Demand)* What is the law of demand? Give two examples of how you have observed the law of demand at work in the "real world." How is the law of demand related to the demand curve?

2. *(Changes in Demand)* What variables influence the demand for a normal good? Explain why a reduction in the price of a normal good does not increase the demand for that good.

3. *(Substitution and Income Effects)* Distinguish between the substitution effect and income effect of a price change. If a good's price increases, does each effect have a positive or a negative impact on the quantity demanded?

4. *(Demand)* Explain the effect of an increase in consumer income on the demand for a good.

5. *(Income Effects)* When moving along the demand curve, income must be assumed constant. Yet one factor that can cause a change in the quantity demanded is the "income effect." Reconcile these seemingly contradictory facts.

6. *(Demand)* If chocolate is found to have positive health benefits, would this lead to a shift of the demand curve or a movement along the demand curve?

7. *(Supply)* What is the law of supply? Give an example of how you have observed the law of supply at work. What is the relationship between the law of supply and the supply curve?

8. *(Changes in Supply)* What kinds of changes in underlying conditions can cause the supply curve to shift? Give some examples and explain the direction in which the curve shifts.

9. *(Supply)* If a severe frost destroys some of Florida's citrus crop, would this lead to a shift of the supply curve or a movement along the supply curve?

10. *(Markets)* How do markets coordinate the independent decisions of buyers and sellers?

11. (**C a s e S t u d y:** The Market for Professional Basketball) In what sense can we speak of a market for professional basketball? Who are the demanders and who are the suppliers? What are some examples of how changes in supply or demand conditions have affected this market?

PROBLEMS AND EXERCISES

12. *(Shifting Demand)* Using demand and supply curves, show the effect of each of the following on the market for cigarettes:

   a. A cure for lung cancer is found.
   b. The price of cigars increases.
   c. Wages increase substantially in states that grow tobacco.
   d. A fertilizer that increases the yield per acre of tobacco is discovered.
   e. There is a sharp increase in the price of matches, lighters, and lighter fluid.
   f. More states pass laws restricting smoking in public places.

13. *(Substitutes and Complements)* For each of the following pair of goods, determine whether the goods are substitutes, complements, or unrelated:

   a. Peanut butter and jelly
   b. Private and public transportation
   c. Coke and Pepsi
   d. Alarm clocks and automobiles
   e. Golf clubs and golf balls

14. *(Equilibrium)* "If a price is not an equilibrium price, there is a tendency for it to move to its equilibrium value. Regardless of whether the price is too high or too low to begin with, the adjustment process will increase the quantity of the good purchased." Explain, using a demand and supply diagram.

15. *(Market Equilibrium)* Determine whether each of the following statements is true, false, or uncertain. Then briefly explain each answer.

    a. In equilibrium, all sellers can find buyers.
    b. In equilibrium, there is no pressure on the market to produce or consume more than is being sold.
    c. At prices above equilibrium, the quantity exchanged exceeds the quantity demanded.
    d. At prices below equilibrium, the quantity exchanged is equal to the quantity supplied.

16. *(Equilibrium)* Assume the market for corn is depicted as in the table that appears below.
    a. Complete the table.
    b. What market pressure occurs when quantity demanded exceeds quantity supplied? Explain.
    c. What market pressure occurs when quantity supplied exceeds quantity demanded? Explain.
    d. What is the equilibrium price?
    e. What could change the equilibrium price?
    f. At each price in the first column of Exhibit 12, how much is sold?

17. *(Demand and Supply)* How do you think each of the following affected the world price of oil? (Use basic demand and supply analysis.)

    a. Tax credits were offered for expenditures on home insulation.
    b. The Alaskan oil pipeline was completed.
    c. The ceiling on the price of oil was removed.
    d. Oil was discovered in the North Sea.
    e. Sport utility vehicles and minivans became popular.
    f. The use of nuclear power decreased.

18. *(Demand and Supply)* What happens to the equilibrium price and quantity of ice cream in response to each of the following? Explain your answers.

    a. The price of dairy cow fodder increases.
    b. The price of beef decreases.
    c. Concerns arise about the fat content of ice cream. Simultaneously, the price of sugar (used to produce ice cream) increases.

19. *(Equilibrium)* Consider the following graph in which demand and supply are initially *D* and *S*, respectively. What are the equilibrium price and quantity? If demand increases to *D'*, what are the new equilibrium price and quantity? What happens if the government does not allow the price to change when demand increases?

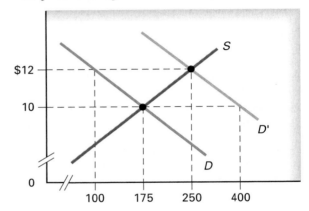

20. *(Changes in Equilibrium)* What are the effects on the equilibrium price and quantity of steel if the wages of steelworkers rise and, simultaneously, the price of aluminum rises?

Price per Bushel	Quantity Demanded (millions of bushels)	Quantity Supplied (millions of bushels)	Surplus/ Shortage	Will Price Rise or Fall?
$1.80	320	200	_____	_____
2.00	300	230	_____	_____
2.20	270	270	_____	_____
2.40	230	300	_____	_____
2.60	200	330	_____	_____
2.80	180	350	_____	_____

21. *(Price Floor)* There is considerable interest in whether the minimum wage rate contributes to teenage unemployment. Draw a demand and supply diagram for the unskilled labor market, and discuss the effects of a minimum wage. Who is helped and who is hurt by the minimum wage?

22. *(Price Ceilings)* Suppose the demand and supply curves for rental housing units have the typical shapes and that the rental housing market is in equilibrium. Then, government establishes a rent ceiling below the equilibrium level.

a. What happens to the quantity of housing consumed?
b. Who benefits from rent control?
c. Who loses from rent control?

23. *(Case Study: The Toy Business Is Not Child's Play)* Use a demand and supply graph to describe developments in the market for Mighty Morphin Power Rangers toys. Keep in mind the shortage at the $13 selling price, the development of new factories, and the continued shortage.

EXPERIENTIAL EXERCISES

24. *(Market Demand)* With some other students in your class, determine your market demand for gasoline. Make up a chart listing a variety of prices per gallon of gasoline— $1.00, $1.25, $1.50, $1.75, $2.00, $2.25. Ask each student—and yourself—how many gallons per week they would purchase at each possible price. Then:

a. Plot each student's demand curve. Check to see whether each student's responses are consistent with the law of demand.
b. Derive the "market" demand curve by adding the quantities demanded by all students at each possible price.
c. What do you think will happen to that market demand curve after your class graduates and your incomes rise?

25. *(Price Floors)* The minimum wage is a price floor in a market for labor. The government sets a minimum price per

hour of labor in certain markets, and no employer is permitted to pay a wage lower than that. Go to the Department of Labor's minimum wage Web page to learn more about the mechanics of the program: http://www.dol.gov/esa/whd/flsa. Then use a demand and supply diagram to illustrate the effect of imposing an above-equilibrium minimum wage on a particular labor market. What happens to quantity demanded and quantity supplied as a result of the minimum wage?

26. *(Wall Street Journal)* After reading this chapter, you have a basic understanding of how demand and supply determine market price and quantity. Find an article in the "first section" of today's *Wall Street Journal* and interpret the article, using a demand and supply diagram. Explain at least one case in which a curve shifts. What caused the shift, and how did it affect price and quantity?

HOMEWORK XPRESS! EXERCISES

*These exercises require access to McEachern Homework Xpress! If Homework Xpress! did not come with your book, visit **http://homeworkxpress.swlearning.com** to purchase.*

1. Ice cream sellers recognize that demand for ice cream is seasonal: high in the summer, lower in the winter. Draw a demand curve for ice cream in the winter months. Draw a demand curve for ice cream in the summer months.

2. The major ingredients in ice cream are dairy products derived from milk. This summer the price of milk is expected to rise significantly. Draw a supply curve for ice cream before the price increase in milk is known. Draw a supply curve for ice cream in the summer months following the increase in the price of milk.

3. The increasing popularity of sports utility vehicles, SUVs, has led auto dealers to keep a large quantity of them in stock. With the increase in the price of gasoline, however, demand has been falling. Draw demand and supply curves in the diagram for SUVs before the increase in the price of gasoline. Show the equilibrium price and quantity. Illustrate the effect of the increase in the price of gasoline in the market for SUVs. Indicate the effect of this on equilibrium price and quantity.

4. Innovations in materials engineering allow automakers to substitute lower cost materials in their production of sports utility vehicles, SUVs, without reducing the safety of the vehicles. Draw demand and supply curves in the diagram for SUVs before the innovations in materials and show the equilibrium price and quantity. Illustrate the effect of the cost reducing innovations in the market for SUVs. Indicate the effect of this on equilibrium price and quantity.

Elasticity of Demand and Supply

© Frank Siteman Studio

W hy did visits to Microsoft's online magazine, *Slate*, drop 95 percent when the access charge increased from zero to $20 a year? Why did total online usage explode when AOL switched from an hourly charge to a flat monthly fee? Why do higher cigarette taxes cut smoking by teenagers more than by other age groups? Why does a good harvest often spell trouble for farmers? Answers to these and other questions are explored in this chapter, which takes a closer look at demand and supply.

As you learned in Chapter 1, macroeconomics concentrates on aggregate markets—on the big picture. But the big picture is a mosaic pieced together from individual decisions made by households, firms, governments, and the rest of the world. To understand how a market economy works, you must take a closer look at these individual decisions, especially at the role of prices. In a market economy, prices inform producers and consumers about the relative scarcity of products and resources.

A downward-sloping demand curve and an upward-sloping supply curve combine to form a powerful analytical tool. But to use this tool, you must learn more about demand and supply curves. The more you know, the better you can predict the effects of a change in the price on quantity demanded and on quantity supplied. Decision makers are willing to pay dearly for such knowledge. For example, Taco Bell would like to know what happens to sales if taco prices change. Governments would like to know how cigarette taxes affect teenage smoking. Colleges would like to know how tuition increases affect enrollments. And subway officials would like to know how price changes affect ridership. To answer such questions, we must learn how responsive consumers and producers are to price changes. This chapter introduces the idea of *elasticity*, a measure of *responsiveness*. Topics discussed include:

- Price elasticity of demand
- Determinants of price elasticity
- Price elasticity and total revenue
- Price elasticity of supply
- Income elasticity of demand
- Cross-price elasticity of demand

Price Elasticity of Demand

To fill more seats just before a recent Thanksgiving weekend, Delta Airlines cut fares up to 50 percent. Was that a good idea? A firm's success or failure often depends on how much it knows about the demand for its product. For Delta's total revenue to increase, the gain in ticket sales would have to more than make up for the decline in ticket prices. Likewise, the operators of Taco Bell would like to know what happens to sales if its price drops, say, from $1.10 to $0.90 per taco. The law of demand says a lower price increases quantity demanded, but by how much? How sensitive is quantity demanded to a change in price? After all, if quantity demanded increases enough, a price cut could be a profitable move for Taco Bell.

Calculating Price Elasticity of Demand

Let's get more specific about how sensitive changes in quantity demanded are to changes in price. Take a look at the demand curve in Exhibit 1. At the initial price of $1.10 per taco, consumers demand 95,000 per day. If the price drops to $0.90, quantity demanded increases to 105,000. Is such a response a little or a lot? The *price elasticity of demand* measures in a standardized way how responsive consumers are to a change in price. *Elasticity* is another word for *responsiveness*. In simplest terms, the **price elasticity of demand** measures the percentage change in quantity demanded divided by the percentage change in price, or:

PRICE ELASTICITY OF DEMAND

Measures how responsive quantity demanded is to a price change; the percentage change in quantity demanded divided by the percentage change in price

$$\text{Price elasticity of demand} = \frac{\text{Percentage change in quantity demanded}}{\text{Percentage change in price}}$$

So what's the price elasticity of demand when the price of tacos falls from $1.10 to $0.90—that is, what's the price elasticity of demand between points *a* and *b* in Exhibit 1? For price elasticity to be a clear and reliable measure, we should come up with the same result between points *a* and *b* as we get between points *b* and *a*. To ensure that consistency, we must take the average of the initial price and the new price and use that as the base for computing the percentage change in price. For example, in Exhibit 1, the base used to calculate the percentage change in price is the average of $1.10 and $0.90, which is $1.00. The per-

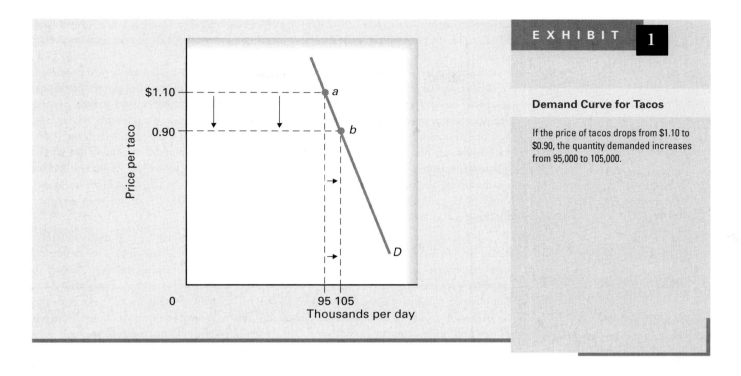

EXHIBIT 1

Demand Curve for Tacos

If the price of tacos drops from $1.10 to $0.90, the quantity demanded increases from 95,000 to 105,000.

centage change in price is therefore the change in price, –$0.20, divided by $1.00, which works out to be –20 percent.

The same holds for changes in quantity demanded. In Exhibit 1, the base used for computing the percentage change in quantity demanded is the average of 95,000 and 105,000, which is 100,000. So the percentage increase in quantity demanded is the change in quantity demanded, 10,000, divided by 100,000, which works out to be 10 percent. So the resulting price elasticity of demand between points *a* and *b* is the percentage increase in quantity demanded, 10 percent, divided by the percentage decrease in price, –20 percent, which is –0.5 (=10%/–20%).

Let's generalize the **price elasticity formula**. If the price changes from p to p', other things constant, the quantity demanded changes from q to q'. The change in price can be represented as Δp and the change in quantity as Δq. The formula for calculating the price elasticity of demand, E_D, between the two points is the percentage change in quantity demanded divided by the percentage change in price, or:

$$E_D = \frac{\Delta q}{(q + q')/2} \div \frac{\Delta p}{(p + p')/2}$$

PRICE ELASTICITY FORMULA

Percentage change in quantity demanded divided by the percentage change in price; the average quantity and the average price are used as bases for computing percentage changes in quantity and in price

Again, because the average quantity and average price are used as the bases for computing percentage change, the same elasticity results whether going from the higher price to the lower price or the other way around.

Elasticity expresses a relationship between two amounts: the percentage change in quantity demanded and the percentage change in price. Because the focus is on the *percentage change*, we need not be concerned with how output or price is measured. For example, suppose the good in question is apples. It makes no difference in the elasticity formula whether we measure apples in pounds, bushels, or even tons. All that matters is the percentage change in quantity demanded. Nor does it matter whether we measure price in U.S. dollars, Mexican pesos, French francs, or Zambian kwacha. All that matters is the percentage change in price.

Finally, the law of demand states that price and quantity demanded are inversely related, so the change in price and the change in quantity demanded move in opposite directions. In the elasticity formula, the numerator and the denominator have opposite signs, leaving the price elasticity of demand with a negative sign. Because constantly referring to elasticity as a negative number gets old fast, from here on we will discuss the price elasticity of demand as an absolute value, or as a positive number. For example, the absolute value of the elasticity measured in Exhibit 1 is 0.5. Still, from time to time, you will be reminded that we are discussing absolute values.

Categories of Price Elasticity of Demand

As you will see, the price elasticity of demand usually varies along a given demand curve. The price elasticity of demand can be divided into three general categories, depending on how responsive quantity demanded is to a change in price. If the percentage change in quantity demanded is smaller than the percentage change in price, the resulting price elasticity has an absolute value between 0 and 1.0. That portion of the demand curve is said to be **inelastic,** meaning that quantity demanded is relatively *unresponsive* to a change in price. For example, the elasticity derived in Exhibit 1 between points *a* and *b* was 0.5, so that portion of the demand curve was inelastic. If the percentage change in quantity demanded just equals the percentage change in price, the resulting price elasticity has an absolute value of 1.0, and that portion of a demand curve has **unit-elastic demand.** Finally, if the percentage change in quantity demanded exceeds the percentage change in price, the resulting price elasticity has an absolute value exceeding 1.0, and that portion of a demand curve is said to be **elastic.** In summary, *the price elasticity of demand is inelastic if its absolute value is between 0 and 1.0, unit elastic if equal to 1.0, and elastic if greater than 1.0.*

summary!

Elasticity and Total Revenue

Knowledge of price elasticity is especially valuable to producers, because it indicates the effect of a price change on total revenue. **Total revenue** (*TR*) is the price (*p*) multiplied by the quantity demanded (*q*) at that price, or $TR = p \times q$. What happens to total revenue when price decreases? Well, according to the law of demand, a lower price increases quantity demanded, which tends to increase total revenue. But, a lower price means producers get less for each unit sold, which tends to decrease total revenue. The overall impact of a lower price on total revenue depends on the net result of these opposite effects. *If the positive effect of greater quantity demanded more than offsets the negative effect of a lower price, then total revenue will rise.* More specifically, if demand is *elastic,* the percentage increase in quantity demanded exceeds the percentage decrease in price, so total revenue increases. If demand is *unit elastic,* the percentage increase in quantity demanded just equals the percentage decrease in price, so total revenue remains unchanged. Finally, if demand is *inelastic,* the percentage increase in quantity demanded is more than offset by the percentage decrease in price, so total revenue decreases.

Price Elasticity and the Linear Demand Curve

A look at elasticity along a particular type of demand curve, the linear demand curve, will tie together the ideas discussed so far. A **linear demand curve** is simply a straight-line demand curve, as in panel (a) of Exhibit 2. Panel (b) shows the total revenue generated by each

INELASTIC DEMAND

A change in price has relatively little effect on quantity demanded; the percentage change in quantity demanded is less than the percentage change in price; the resulting price elasticity has an absolute value less than 1.0

UNIT-ELASTIC DEMAND

The percentage change in quantity demanded equals the percentage change in price; the resulting price elasticity has an absolute value of 1.0

ELASTIC DEMAND

A change in price has a relatively large effect on quantity demanded; the percentage change in quantity demanded exceeds the percentage change in price; the resulting price elasticity has an absolute value exceeding 1.0

TOTAL REVENUE

Price multiplied by the quantity demanded at that price

LINEAR DEMAND CURVE

A straight-line demand curve; such a demand curve has a constant slope but usually has a varying price elasticity

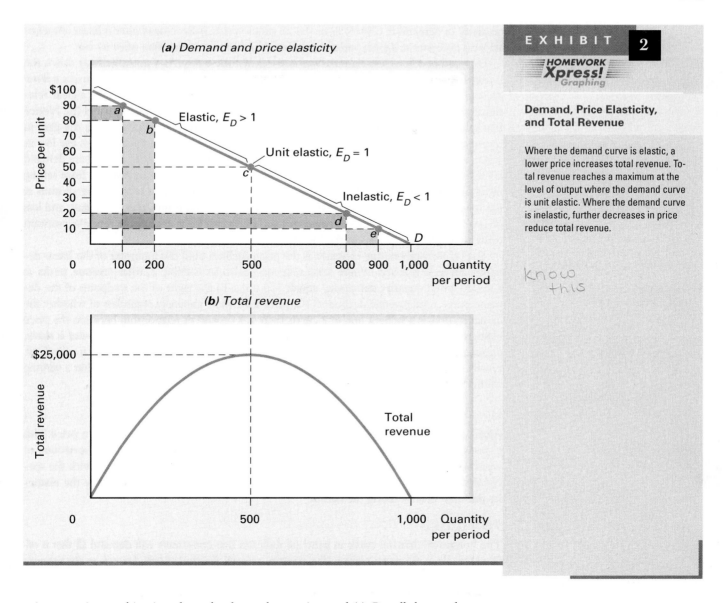

(a) Demand and price elasticity

Elastic, $E_D > 1$

Unit elastic, $E_D = 1$

Inelastic, $E_D < 1$

(b) Total revenue

Total revenue

Demand, Price Elasticity, and Total Revenue

Where the demand curve is elastic, a lower price increases total revenue. Total revenue reaches a maximum at the level of output where the demand curve is unit elastic. Where the demand curve is inelastic, further decreases in price reduce total revenue.

know this

price-quantity combination along the demand curve in panel (a). Recall that total revenue equals price times quantity.

Because the demand curve is linear, its slope is constant, so a given decrease in price always causes the same unit increase in quantity demanded. For example, along the demand curve in Exhibit 2, a $10 drop in price always increases quantity demanded by 100 units. But the price elasticity of demand is larger on the higher-price end of the demand curve than on the lower-price end. Here's why. Consider a movement from point *a* to point *b* on the upper end of the demand curve in Exhibit 2. The 100-unit increase in quantity demanded is a percentage change of 100/150, or 67 percent. The $10 price drop is a percentage change of 10/85, or 12 percent. Therefore, the price elasticity of demand between points *a* and *b* is 67%/12%, which equals 5.6. Between points *d* and *e* on the lower end, however, the 100-unit quantity increase is a percentage change of 100/850, or only 12 percent, and the $10 price decrease is a percentage change of 10/15, or 67 percent. The price

PERFECTLY ELASTIC DEMAND CURVE

A horizontal line reflecting a situation in which any price increase reduces quantity demanded to zero; the elasticity has an absolute value of infinity

elasticity of demand is 12%/67%, or 0.2. In other words, *if the demand curve is linear, consumers are more responsive to a given price change when the initial price is high than when it's low.*

Demand becomes less elastic as we move down the curve. At a point halfway down the linear demand curve in Exhibit 2, the elasticity equals 1.0. *This halfway point divides a linear demand curve into an elastic upper half and an inelastic lower half.* You can observe a clear relationship between the elasticity of demand in panel (a) and total revenue in panel (b). Notice that where demand is elastic, a decrease in price increases total revenue because the gain in revenue from selling more units (represented by the large blue rectangle) exceeds the loss in revenue from selling all units at the lower price (the small red rectangle). But where demand is inelastic, a price decrease reduces total revenue because the gain in revenue from selling more units (the small blue rectangle) is less than the loss in revenue from selling all units at the lower price (the large red rectangle). And where demand is unit elastic, the gain and loss of revenue exactly cancel each other out, so total revenue at that point remains constant (thus, total revenue "peaks" in the lower panel).

To review, total revenue increases as the price declines until the midpoint of the linear demand curve is reached, where total revenue peaks. In Exhibit 2, total revenue peaks at $25,000 when quantity demanded equals 500 units. To the right of the midpoint of the demand curve, total revenue declines as the price falls. More generally, regardless of whether the demand curve is a straight line or a curve, there is a consistent relationship between the price elasticity of demand and total revenue: *A price decline increases total revenue if demand is elastic, decreases total revenue if demand is inelastic, and has no effect on total revenue if demand is unit elastic.* Finally, note that a downward-sloping linear demand curve has a constant slope but a varying elasticity, so *the slope of a demand curve is not the same as the price elasticity of demand.*

Constant-Elasticity Demand Curves

Again, price elasticity measures the responsiveness of consumers to a change in price. This responsiveness varies along a linear demand curve unless the demand curve is horizontal or vertical, as in panels (a) and (b) of Exhibit 3. These two demand curves, along with the special demand curve in panel (c), are called *constant-elasticity demand curves* because the elasticity does not change along the curves.

Perfectly Elastic Demand Curve

The horizontal demand curve in panel (a) indicates that consumers will demand all that is offered for sale at the given price *p* (the quantity actually demanded will depend on the amount supplied at that price). If the price rises above *p,* however, quantity demanded drops to zero. It is a **perfectly elastic demand curve,** and its elasticity value is infinity, a number too large to be defined. You may think it is an odd sort of demand curve: Consumers, as a result of a small increase in price, go from demanding as much as is supplied to demanding none of the good. Consumers are so sensitive to price changes that they will tolerate no price increase. As you will see in a later chapter, this behavior reflects the demand for the output of any individual producer when many producers sell identical products. The shape of the demand curve for a firm's product is an important element in the pricing and output decision.

Perfectly Inelastic Demand Curve

Along the vertical demand curve in panel (b) of Exhibit 3, quantity demanded does not vary when the price changes. This demand curve expresses consumer sentiment when "price is no object." For example, if you are extremely rich and need insulin injections to survive, price would be no object. No matter how high the price, you would continue to demand whatever it takes. And if the price of insulin should drop, you would not increase your quan-

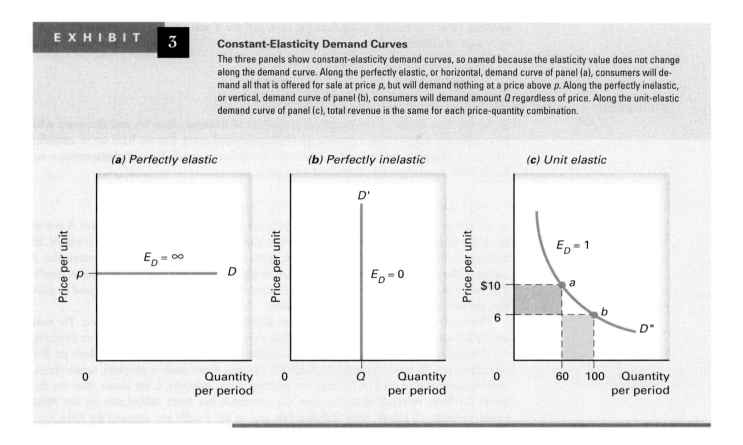

EXHIBIT 3

Constant-Elasticity Demand Curves

The three panels show constant-elasticity demand curves, so named because the elasticity value does not change along the demand curve. Along the perfectly elastic, or horizontal, demand curve of panel (a), consumers will demand all that is offered for sale at price *p*, but will demand nothing at a price above *p*. Along the perfectly inelastic, or vertical, demand curve of panel (b), consumers will demand amount *Q* regardless of price. Along the unit-elastic demand curve of panel (c), total revenue is the same for each price-quantity combination.

tity demanded. Because the percentage change in quantity demanded is zero for any given percentage change in price, the numerical value of the price elasticity is zero. A vertical demand curve is called a **perfectly inelastic demand curve** because price changes do not affect quantity demanded.

Unit-Elastic Demand Curve

Panel (c) in Exhibit 3 presents a demand curve that is unit elastic everywhere. Along a **unit-elastic demand curve,** any percentage change in price results in an identical and offsetting percentage change in quantity demanded. Because percentage changes in price and in quantity are equal and offsetting, total revenue remains constant for every price-quantity combination along the curve. For example, when the price falls from $10 to $6, the quantity demanded increases from 60 to 100 units. The pink shaded rectangle shows the loss in total revenue because units are sold at the lower price; the blue shaded rectangle shows the gain in total revenue because more units are sold when the price drops. Because the demand curve is unit elastic, the revenue gained from selling more units just equals the revenue lost from lowering the price on all units, so total revenue is unchanged at $600.

Each demand curve in Exhibit 3 is called a **constant-elasticity demand curve** because the elasticity is the same all along the curve. In contrast, the downward-sloping linear demand curve examined earlier had a different elasticity value at each point along the curve. Exhibit 4 lists the absolute values for the five categories of price elasticity we have discussed, summarizing the effects of a 10 percent price increase on quantity demanded and on total

PERFECTLY INELASTIC DEMAND CURVE

A vertical line reflecting a situation in which any price change has no effect on the quantity demanded; the elasticity value equals zero

UNIT-ELASTIC DEMAND CURVE

Everywhere along the demand curve, the percentage change in price causes an equal but offsetting percentage change in quantity demanded, so total revenue remains the same; the elasticity has an absolute value of 1.0

CONSTANT-ELASTICITY DEMAND CURVE

The type of demand that exists when price elasticity is the same everywhere along the curve; the elasticity value is constant

revenue. Give this exhibit some thought now, and see if you can draw a demand curve for each type of elasticity.

Determinants of the Price Elasticity of Demand

So far we have explored the technical properties of demand elasticity and discussed why price elasticity varies along a downward-sloping demand curve. But we have yet to consider why price elasticities of demand are different for different goods. Several characteristics influence the price elasticity of demand for a good.

Availability of Substitutes

As we saw in Chapter 4, your particular wants can be satisfied in a variety of ways. A rise in the price of pizza makes other food relatively cheaper. If close substitutes are available, an increase in the price of pizza will prompt some consumers to shift to substitutes. But if nothing else satisfies like pizza, the quantity of pizza demanded will not decline as much. *The greater the availability of substitutes and the more similar the substitutes are to the good in question, the greater the good's price elasticity of demand.*

The number and similarity of substitutes depend on how the good is defined. *The more broadly defined a good is, the fewer substitutes there are and the less elastic the demand.* For example, the demand for shoes is less elastic than the demand for running shoes because there are few substitutes for shoes but several substitutes for running shoes, such as sneakers, tennis shoes, cross-trainers, and so on. The demand for running shoes, however, is less elastic than the demand for Nike running shoes because the consumer has more substitutes for the Nike brand, including Reebok, New Balance, Fila, and so on. Finally, the demand for Nike running shoes is less elastic than the demand for a specific Nike model, because Nike has dozens of models.

E X H I B I T **4**   **Summary of Price Elasticity of Demand**

Effects of a 10 Percent Increase in Price

Absolute Value of Price Elasticity	Type of Demand	What Happens to Quantity Demanded	What Happens to Total Revenue
$E_D = 0$	Perfectly inelastic	No change	Increases by 10 percent
$0 < E_D < 1$	Inelastic	Drops by less than 10 percent	Increases by less than 10 percent
$E_D = 1$	Unit elastic	Drops by 10 percent	No change
$1 < E_D < \infty$	Elastic	Drops by more than 10 percent	Decreases
$E_D = \infty$	Perfectly elastic	Drops to 0	Drops to 0

Certain goods—some prescription drugs, for instance—have no close substitutes. The demand for such goods tends to be less elastic than for goods with close substitutes, such as Bayer aspirin. Much advertising is aimed at establishing in the consumer's mind the uniqueness of a particular product—an effort to convince consumers "to accept no substitutes." Why might a firm want to make the demand for its product less elastic?

As an example of the impact of substitutes on price elasticity, consider the pattern of commercial breaks during network TV movies. When the movie begins, viewers have several substitutes for it, including other shows and perhaps movies on other networks. To keep viewers from switching channels, the first movie segment is longer than usual, perhaps 20 or 25 minutes before a commercial break. But once viewers get interested in the movie, shows on other channels are no longer close substitutes, so broadcasters inject commercials with greater frequency without fear of losing many viewers.

Proportion of the Consumer's Budget Spent on the Good

Recall that a higher price reduces quantity demanded in part because a higher price reduces the real spending power of consumer income. Because spending on some goods claims a large share of the consumer's budget, a change in the price of such a good has a substantial impact on the consumer's *ability* to buy it. An increase in the price of housing, for example, reduces consumers' ability to buy housing. The income effect of a higher price reduces the quantity demanded. In contrast, the income effect of an increase in the price of, say, paper towels is trivial because paper towels represent such a tiny share of any budget. *The more important the item is as a share of the consumer's budget, other things constant, the greater is the income effect of a change in price, so the more price elastic is the demand for the item.* Hence, the quantity of housing demanded is more responsive to a given percentage change in price than is the quantity of paper towels demanded.

A Matter of Time

Consumers can substitute lower-priced goods for higher-priced goods, but finding substitutes usually takes time. Suppose your college announces a significant increase in room and board fees, effective next term. Some students will move off campus before the next term begins; others may wait until the next academic year. Over time, more incoming students will choose off-campus housing. The longer the adjustment period, the greater the consumers' ability to substitute away from relatively higher-priced products toward lower-priced substitutes. Thus, *the longer the period of adjustment, the more responsive the change in quantity demanded is to a given change in price.* Here's another example: Between 1973 and 1974, the OPEC cartel raised the price of oil sharply. The result was a 45 percent increase in the price of gasoline, but the quantity demanded decreased only 8 percent. As more time passed, however, people purchased smaller cars and made greater use of public transportation. Because the price of oil used to generate electricity and to heat homes increased as well, people bought more energy-efficient appliances and added more insulation to their homes. Again, the change in the amount of oil demanded was greater as consumers adjusted to the price hike.

Exhibit 5 demonstrates how demand becomes more elastic over time. Given an initial price of $1.00 at point *e*, let D_w be the demand curve one week after a price change; D_m, one month after; and D_y, one year after. Suppose the price increases to $1.25. The more time consumers have to respond to the price increase, the greater the reduction in quantity demanded. The demand curve D_w shows that one week after the price increase, the quantity demanded has not declined much—in this case, from 100 to 95 per day. The demand curve D_m indicates a reduction to 75 per day after one month, and demand curve D_y shows a re-

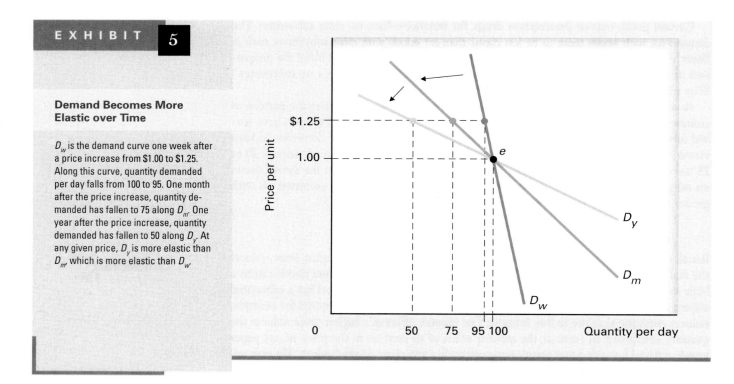

E X H I B I T   **5**

Demand Becomes More Elastic over Time

D_w is the demand curve one week after a price increase from $1.00 to $1.25. Along this curve, quantity demanded per day falls from 100 to 95. One month after the price increase, quantity demanded has fallen to 75 along D_m. One year after the price increase, quantity demanded has fallen to 50 along D_y. At any given price, D_y is more elastic than D_m, which is more elastic than D_w.

duction to 50 per day after one year. Notice that among these demand curves and over the range starting from point *e*, the flatter the demand curve, the more price elastic the demand. Here, elasticity seems linked to the slope because we begin from a common point—the same price-quantity combination.

Elasticity Estimates

WALL STREET JOURNAL

Reading It **Right**

What's the relevance of the following statement from the Wall Street Journal: "By selling directly via the Internet, catalogs, and the telephone, Dell maintains direct contact with customers and can regularly gauge their sensitivity to price changes."

Let's look at some estimates of the price elasticity of demand for particular goods and services. As we have noted, finding substitutes when the price increases takes time. Thus, when estimating price elasticity, economists often distinguish between a period during which consumers have little time to adjust—let's call it the *short run*—and a period during which consumers can more fully adjust to a price change—let's call it the *long run*. Exhibit 6 provides some short-run and long-run price elasticity estimates for selected products.

The price elasticity of demand is greater in the long run because consumers have more time to adjust. For example, if the price of electricity rose today, consumers in the short run might cut back a bit in their use of electrical appliances, and those in homes with electric heat might lower the thermostat in winter. Over time, however, consumers would switch to more energy-efficient appliances and might convert from electric heat to oil or natural gas. So the demand for electricity is more elastic in the long run than in the short run, as shown in Exhibit 6. In fact, in every instance where values for both the short run and the long run are listed, the long run is more elastic than the short run. Notice also that the long-run price elasticity of demand for Chevrolets exceeds that for automobiles in general. There are many more substitutes for Chevrolets than for automobiles in general. There are no close substitutes for cigarettes, even in the long run, so the demand for cigarettes among adults is price inelastic. Such elasticity measures are of more than just academic interest, as discussed in the following case study.

Product	Short Run	Long Run
Cigarettes (among adults)	—	0.4
Electricity (residential)	0.1	1.9
Air travel	0.1	2.4
Medical care and hospitalization	0.3	0.9
Gasoline	0.4	1.5
Milk	0.4	—
Fish (cod)	0.5	—
Wine	0.7	1.2
Movies	0.9	3.7
Natural gas (residential)	1.4	2.1
Automobiles	1.9	2.2
Chevrolets	—	4.0

Selected Price Elasticities of Demand (absolute values)

Sources: F. Chaloupka, "Rational Addictive Behavior and Cigarette Smoking," *Journal of Political Economy* (August 1991); Hsaing-tai Cheng and Oral Capps, Jr., "Demand for Fish," *American Journal of Agricultural Economics* (August 1998); J. Johnson et al., "Short-Run and Long-Run Elasticities for Canadian Consumption of Alcoholic Beverages," *Review of Economics and Statistics* (February 1992); Douglas Young, et al., "Alcohol Consumption, Measurement Error, and Beverage Prices," *Journal of Studies on Alcohol* (March 2003); J. Griffin, *Energy Conservation in the OECD, 1980–2000* (Cambridge, Mass.: Balinger, 1979); H. Houthakker and L. Taylor, *Consumer Demand in the United States: Analysis and Projections*, 2nd ed. (Cambridge, Mass.: Harvard University Press, 1970); and G. Lakshmanan and W. Anderson, "Residential Energy Demand in the United States," *Regional Science and Urban Economics* 10 (August 1980).

Deterring Young Smokers

As the U.S. Surgeon General warns on each pack of cigarettes, smoking can be hazardous to your health. Researchers estimate that smoking kills 440,000 Americans a year, ten times the deaths from traffic accidents. Lung cancer is now the top cancer killer among women, and 9 of 10 lung cancers are smoking related. Smoking is also the leading cause of heart disease, emphysema, and stroke.

According to the U.S. Centers for Disease Control and Prevention, each pack of cigarettes sold in the United States results in $7.18 in added health care costs and in lost worker productivity. The total cost exceeds $150 billion a year, divided roughly between health care and productivity losses. This amount works out to be about $3,400 per smoker per year. Health-related issues have created a growing public-policy concern about smoking, especially smoking by teenagers, which jumped by one-third during the 1990s. A federal study of 16,000 U.S. high school students found cigarette smoking rose from 27.5 percent of those surveyed in 1991 to 36.4 percent in 1997. Among black youths, the rate nearly doubled from 12.6 percent to 22.7 percent. Reasons behind these jumps include stable prices for cigarettes (prices didn't increase between 1992 and 1997), advertising aimed at young people (such as Joe Camel), and glamorization of smoking in movies and television (for exam-

C a s e **S t u d y**

Public Policy

*e*Activity

In 2003, only 1 in 5 high school students smoked. The CDC stated that anti-smoking efforts targeting high school teens have been successful—including TV ads, school campaigns, and higher cost per pack. Read more at http://166.70.44.66/2004/Jun/06182004/nation_w/176579.asp. Also read about the Mayo Clinic's smoking cessation study at http://www.mayoclinic.org/checkup-2003/march-teens.html, or visit the Web site of the CDC at http://www.cdc.gov for their studies and findings.

ple, in the hit movie of the decade, *Titanic*, the two young, attractive leading characters smoked cigarettes). In one study, teens indicated that they were more likely to try smoking if they saw their favorite characters smoke in movies. Each day, about 3,000 U.S. teens under 18 become regular smokers. Worldwide, an estimated 100,000 teens become regular smokers each day.

One way to reduce youth smoking is to prohibit the sale of cigarettes to minors. A second way is to raise the price through higher cigarette taxes. The amount by which a given price increase reduces teen smoking depends on the price elasticity of demand. This elasticity is higher for teens than for adults. Why are teenagers more sensitive to price changes than adults? First, recall that one of the factors affecting elasticity is the importance of the item in the consumer's budget. Because teen income is relatively low, the share spent on cigarettes usually exceeds the share for adult smokers. Second, peer pressure is more influential in a young person's decision to smoke than in an adult's decision to continue smoking (if anything, adults face negative peer pressure for smoking). The impact of a higher price gets multiplied among young smokers because it reduces smoking by peers. With fewer peers smoking, teens receive less pressure to smoke. And third, young people not yet hooked are more sensitive to price increases than are adult smokers, who are more likely to be addicted. The experience from other countries supports the effectiveness of higher prices in reducing teen smoking. For example, a large tax increase on cigarettes in Canada cut youth smoking by two-thirds.

Another way to reduce smoking is to change consumer tastes through health warnings on packages. The Canadian government has proposed putting pictures of cancerous tongues and lips on cigarette packs and publicizing the link between smoking and male impotence (so much for the Marlboro man). In California, a combination of higher cigarette taxes and an ambitious awareness program has contributed to a 5 percent decline in lung cancer among women there, even as it rose 13 percent in the rest of the country.

In a 1997 U.S. court settlement, tobacco companies agreed to pay $368 billion in health-related damages, tear down billboards, and retire Joe Camel. A federal study reported a slight decline in teenage smoking, dropping from 36.4 percent of those surveyed in 1997 to 34.8 percent in 1999.

Sources: "Annual Smoking-Attributable Mortality, Years of Potential Life Lost, and Economic Costs," Centers for Disease Control and Prevention, 12 April 2002; Hana Ross and Frank Chaloupka, "The Effects of Public Policies and Prices on Youth Smoking," *Southern Economic Journal* (April 2004); and Madeline Dalton, et al., "Effect of Viewing Smoking in Movies on Adolescent Smoking Initiative," *The Lancet*, Vol. 362, Issue 9380 (2003). For background on the tobacco settlement, go to http://www.pbs.org/wgbh/pages/frontline/shows/settlement/.

Price Elasticity of Supply

PRICE ELASTICITY OF SUPPLY

A measure of the responsiveness of quantity supplied to a price change; the percentage change in quantity supplied divided by the percentage change in price

Prices are signals to both sides of the market about the relative scarcity of products. Higher prices discourage consumption but encourage production. The price elasticity of demand measures how responsive consumers are to a price change. Likewise, the **price elasticity of supply** measures how responsive producers are to a price change. This elasticity is calculated in the same way as price elasticity of demand. In simplest terms, the price elasticity of supply equals the percentage change in quantity supplied divided by the percentage change in price. Because the higher price usually results in an increased quantity supplied, the percentage change in price and the percentage change in quantity supplied move in the same direction, so the price elasticity of supply is usually a positive number.

Exhibit 7 depicts a typical upward-sloping supply curve. As you can see, if the price increases from p to p', the quantity supplied increases from q to q'. Price and quantity supplied move in the same direction. Let's look at the elasticity formula for the supply curve. The price elasticity of supply is:

$$E_S = \frac{\Delta q}{(q + q')/2} \div \frac{\Delta p}{(p + p')/2}$$

where Δq is the change in quantity supplied and Δp is the change in price. This is the same formula used to compute the price elasticity of demand except that q here is quantity supplied, not quantity demanded. The terminology for supply elasticity is the same as for demand elasticity: If supply elasticity is less than 1.0, supply is **inelastic;** if it equals 1.0, supply is **unit elastic;** and if it exceeds 1.0, supply is **elastic.**

Constant Elasticity Supply Curves

Again, price elasticity of supply measures the responsiveness of producers to a change in price. This responsiveness varies along a linear supply curve unless it's horizontal or vertical, as in panels (a) and (b) of Exhibit 8, or passes through the origin, as in panel (c). These three supply curves are called *constant-elasticity supply curves* because the elasticity does not change along the curves.

Perfectly Elastic Supply Curve

At one extreme is the horizontal supply curve, such as supply curve *S* in panel (a) of Exhibit 8. In this case, producers will supply none of the good at a price below *p* but will supply any

INELASTIC SUPPLY

A change in price has relatively little effect on quantity supplied; the percentage change in quantity supplied is less than the percentage change in price; the price elasticity of supply has a value less than 1.0

UNIT-ELASTIC SUPPLY

The percentage change in quantity supplied equals the percentage change in price; the resulting price elasticity of supply equals 1.0

ELASTIC SUPPLY

A change in price has a relatively large effect on quantity supplied; the percentage change in quantity supplied exceeds the percentage change in price; the resulting price elasticity of supply exceeds 1.0

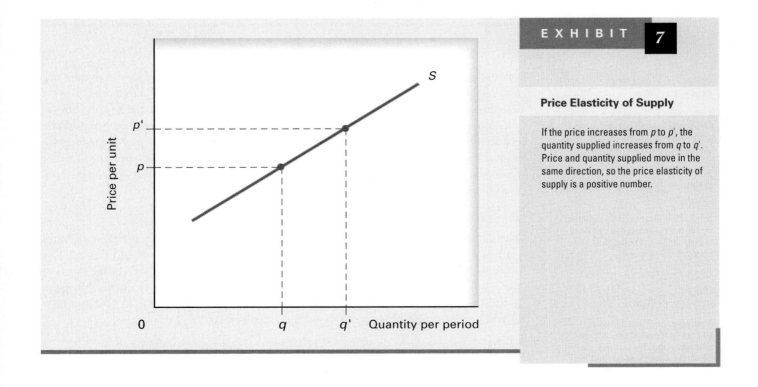

EXHIBIT 7

Price Elasticity of Supply

If the price increases from *p* to *p'*, the quantity supplied increases from *q* to *q'*. Price and quantity supplied move in the same direction, so the price elasticity of supply is a positive number.

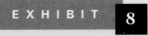

EXHIBIT   8

Constant-Elasticity Supply Curves

In each of the three panels is a constant-elasticity supply curve, so named because the elasticity value does not change along the curve. Supply curve *S* in panel (a) is perfectly elastic, or horizontal. Along *S*, firms will supply any amount of output demanded at price *p*, but will supply none at prices below *p*. Supply curve *S'* is perfectly inelastic, or vertical. *S'* shows that the quantity supplied is independent of the price. In panel (c), *S"*, a straight line from the origin, is a unit-elastic supply curve. Any percentage change in price results in the same percentage change in quantity supplied.

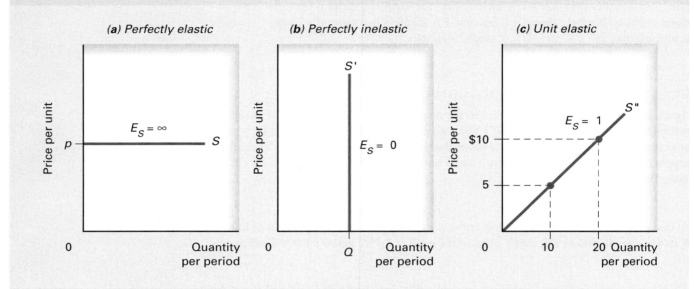

(a) Perfectly elastic   **(b) Perfectly inelastic**   **(c) Unit elastic**

PERFECTLY ELASTIC SUPPLY CURVE

A horizontal line reflecting a situation in which any price decrease drops the quantity supplied to zero; the elasticity value is infinity

PERFECTLY INELASTIC SUPPLY CURVE

A vertical line reflecting a situation in which a price change has no effect on the quantity supplied; the elasticity value is zero

UNIT-ELASTIC SUPPLY CURVE

A percentage change in price causes an identical percentage change in quantity supplied; depicted by a supply curve that is a straight line from the origin; the elasticity value equals 1.0

amount at price *p* (the quantity actually supplied at price *p* will depend on the amount demanded at that price). Because a tiny increase from a price just below *p* to a price of *p* results in an unlimited quantity supplied, this is called a **perfectly elastic supply curve,** which has a numerical value of infinity. As individual consumers, we typically face perfectly elastic supply curves. When we go to the supermarket, we usually can buy as much as we want at the prevailing price but none at a lower price. Obviously all consumers together could not buy an unlimited amount at the prevailing price (recall the fallacy of composition from Chapter 1).

Perfectly Inelastic Supply Curve

The most unresponsive relationship is where there is no change in the quantity supplied regardless of the price, as shown by the vertical supply curve *S'* in panel (b) of Exhibit 8. Because the percentage change in quantity supplied is zero, regardless of the change in price, the price elasticity of supply is zero. This is a **perfectly inelastic supply curve.** Any good in fixed supply, such as Picasso paintings, 1995 Dom Perignon champagne, or Cadillacs once owned by Elvis Presley, has a perfectly inelastic supply curve.

Unit-Elastic Supply Curve

Any supply curve that is a straight line from the origin—such as *S"* in panel (c) of Exhibit 8— is a **unit-elastic supply curve.** This means a percentage change in price will always generate an identical percentage change in quantity supplied. For example, along S'' a doubling of the price results in a doubling of the quantity supplied. Note that unit elasticity is based not on the slope of the line but on the fact that the linear supply curve emanates from the origin.

Determinants of Supply Elasticity

The elasticity of supply indicates how responsive producers are to a change in price. Their responsiveness depends on how easy it is to alter quantity supplied when the price changes. If the cost of supplying additional units rises sharply as output expands, then a higher price will elicit little increase in quantity supplied, so supply will tend to be inelastic. But if the marginal cost rises slowly as output expands, the lure of a higher price will prompt a large increase in quantity supplied. In this case, supply will be more elastic.

One determinant of supply elasticity is the length of the adjustment period under consideration. Just as demand becomes more elastic over time as consumers adjust to price changes, supply also becomes more elastic over time as producers adjust to price changes. The longer the time period under consideration, the more able producers are to adjust to changes in relative prices. Exhibit 9 presents a different supply curve for each of three periods. S_w is the supply curve when the period of adjustment is a week. As you can see, a higher price will not elicit much of a response in quantity supplied because firms have little time to adjust. This supply curve is inelastic if the price increases from $1.00 to $1.25.

S_m is the supply curve when the adjustment period under consideration is a month. Firms have a greater ability to vary output in a month than they do in a week. Thus, supply is more elastic when the adjustment period is a month than when it's a week. Supply is even more elastic when the adjustment period is a year, as is shown by S_y. So a given price increase elicits a greater quantity supplied as the adjustment period lengthens. For example, if

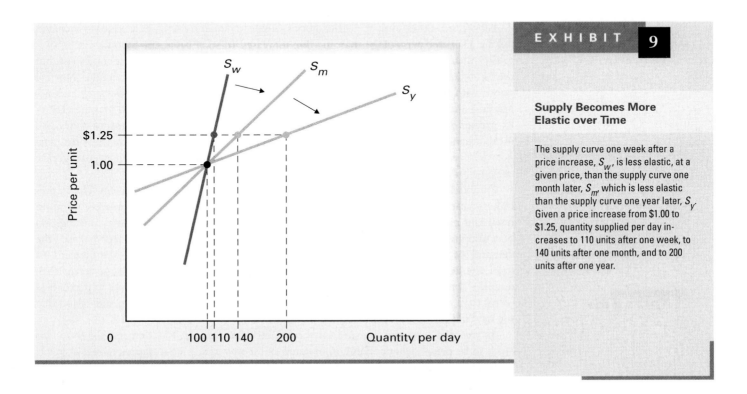

EXHIBIT 9

Supply Becomes More Elastic over Time

The supply curve one week after a price increase, S_w, is less elastic, at a given price, than the supply curve one month later, S_m, which is less elastic than the supply curve one year later, S_y. Given a price increase from $1.00 to $1.25, quantity supplied per day increases to 110 units after one week, to 140 units after one month, and to 200 units after one year.

the price of oil increases, oil producers in the short run can try to pump more from existing wells, but in the long run, a higher price stimulates more exploration. Research confirms the positive link between the price elasticity of supply and the length of the adjustment period. *The elasticity of supply is typically greater the longer the period of adjustment.*

The ease of increasing quantity supplied in response to a higher price differs across industries. The response time will be slower for producers of electricity, oil, and timber (where expansion may take years) than for window washing, lawn maintenance, and hot-dog vending (where expansion may take only days).

Other Elasticity Measures

Price elasticities of demand and supply are frequently used in economic analysis, but two other elasticity measures also provide useful information.

Income Elasticity of Demand

What happens to the demand for new cars, fresh vegetables, or computer software if consumer income increases by, say, 10 percent? The answer is of great interest to producers because it helps them predict the effect of changing consumer income on quantity sold and on total revenue. The **income elasticity of demand** measures how responsive demand is to a change in consumer income. Specifically, *the income elasticity of demand measures the percentage change in demand divided by the percentage change in income that caused it.*

As noted in Chapter 4, the demand for some products, such as used furniture and used clothing, actually declines, or shifts leftward, as income increases. Thus, the income elasticity of demand for such products is negative. Goods with income elasticities less than zero are called *inferior goods.* The demand for most goods increases, or shifts rightward, as income increases. These are called *normal goods* and have income elasticities greater than zero.

Let's take a closer look at normal goods. Suppose demand increases as income increases but by a smaller percentage than income increases. In such cases, the income elasticity is greater than 0 but less than 1. For example, people buy more food as their incomes rise, but the percentage increase in demand is less than the percentage increase in income. Normal goods with income elasticities less than 1 are called *income inelastic. Necessities* such as food, housing, and clothing often have income elasticities less than 1. Goods with income elasticity greater than 1 are called *income elastic. Luxuries* such as high-end cars, vintage wines, and meals at fancy restaurants have income elasticities greater than 1. By the way, the terms *inferior goods, necessities,* and *luxuries* are not value judgment about the merits of particular goods; these terms are simply convenient ways of classifying economic behavior.

Exhibit 10 presents income elasticity estimates for some goods and services. The figures indicate, for example, that as income increases, consumers spend proportionately more on restaurant meals, owner-occupied housing, and wine. Spending on food, rental housing, and beer also increases as income increases, but less than proportionately. So as income rises, the demand for restaurant meals increases more in percentage terms than does the demand for food, the demand for owner-occupied housing increases more in percentage terms than does the demand for rental housing, and the demand for wine increases more in percentage terms than does the demand for beer. Flour has negative income elasticity, indicating that the demand for flour declines as income increases.

As we have seen, the demand for food is income inelastic. The demand for food also tends to be price inelastic. This combination of income and price inelasticity creates special problems in agricultural markets, as discussed in the following case study.

**INCOME ELASTICITY
OF DEMAND**

The percentage change in demand divided by the percentage change in consumer income; the value is positive for normal goods and negative for inferior goods

| EXHIBIT 10 | Selected Income Elasticities of Demand |

Product	Income Elasticity	Product	Income Elasticity
Private education	2.46	Physicians' services	0.75
Automobiles	2.45	Coca-Cola	0.68
Wine	2.19	Beef	0.62
Owner-occupied housing	1.49	Food	0.51
Furniture	1.48	Coffee	0.51
Dental service	1.42	Cigarettes	0.50
Restaurant meals	1.40	Gasoline and oil	0.48
Shoes	1.10	Rental housing	0.43
Chicken	1.06	Beer	0.27
Spirits ("hard" liquor)	1.02	Pork	0.18
Clothing	0.92	Flour	−0.36

Sources: Ivan Bloor, "Food for Thought," *Economic Review* (September 1999); F. Gasmi et al., "Econometric Analysis of Collusive Behavior in a Soft-Drink Market," *Journal of Economics and Management Strategy* (Summer 1992); J. Johnson et al., "Short-Run and Long-Run Elasticities for Canadian Consumption of Alcoholic Beverages," *Review of Economics and Statistics* (February 1992); H. Houthakker and L. Taylor, *Consumer Demand in the United States: Analyses and Projections*, 2nd ed. (Cambridge, Mass.: Harvard University Press, 1970); C. Huang et al., "The Demand for Coffee in the United States, 1963–77," *Quarterly Review of Economics and Business* (Summer 1980); and G. Brester and M. Wohlgenant, "Estimating Interrelated Demands for Meats Using New Measures for Ground and Table Cut Beef," *American Journal of Agricultural Economics* (November 1991).

The Market for Food and "The Farm Problem"

Despite decades of federal support and billions of tax dollars spent on various farm-assistance programs, the number of American farmers continues its long slide, dropping from 10 million in 1950 to under 3 million today. The demise of the family farm can be traced to the price and income elasticities of demand for farm products and to technological breakthroughs that increased supply.

© Photodisc/Getty Images

Many of the forces that determine farm production are beyond a farmer's control. Temperature, rainfall, insects, and other natural forces affect crop size and quality. For example, favorable weather boosted crop production 16 percent in one recent year. Such jumps in production create special problems for farmers because the demand for most farm crops, such as milk, eggs, corn, potatoes, oats, sugar, and beef, is price inelastic.

The effect of inelastic demand on farm revenue is illustrated in Exhibit 11. Suppose that in a normal year, farmers supply 10 billion bushels of grain at a market price of $5 a bushel. Annual farm revenue, which is price times quantity, totals $50 billion in our example. What

C a s e **Study**

Public Policy

eActivity

What are the forces shaping U.S. agriculture today? The Economic Research Service of the U.S. Department of Agriculture provides some answers with its briefing book at http://www.ers.usda.gov/Emphases/Competitive/. Find out what the latest edition says about the current state of the American farm family. How have farm size and the number of family farms been changing? How does farm family income compare to average household income? What percent of farm income is a result of government farm support policies?

if favorable weather raises grain production to 11 billion bushels, an increase of 10 percent? Because demand is price inelastic, the average price in our example must fall by more than 10 percent to, say, $4 per bushel to sell the extra billion bushels. Thus, the 10 percent increase in farm production gets sold only if the price drops by 20 percent.

Because, in percentage terms, the drop in price exceeds the increase in quantity demanded, total revenue declines from $50 billion to $44 billion. So total revenue drops by over 10 percent, despite the 10 percent rise in production. *Because demand is price inelastic, total revenue falls when the price falls*. Of course, for farmers, the upside of inelastic demand is that a lower-than-normal crop results in a higher total revenue. For example, one recent drought sent corn prices up 50 percent, increasing farm revenue in the process. So weather-generated changes in farm production create year-to-year swings in farm revenue.

Fluctuations in farm revenue are compounded in the long run by the *income inelasticity* of demand for grain and, more generally, for food. As household incomes grow over time, spending on food may increase because consumers substitute prepared foods and restaurant meals for home cooking. But this switch has little effect on the total demand for farm products. Thus, as the economy grows over time and incomes rise, the demand for farm products tends to increase but by less than the increase in income. This modest increase in demand from *D* to *D'* is reflected in Exhibit 12.

Because of technological improvements in production, however, the supply of farm products has increased sharply. Farm output per hour of labor is about *eight times* greater now than in 1950 because of such developments as more sophisticated machines, better fertilizers, and healthier seed strains. For example, farmers can seed at night using a 32-row planter and global positioning satellites. With new strains of pest-resistant plants, farmers have cut insecticide applications from seven per season to one or none.

Exhibit 12 shows a big increase in the supply of grain from *S* to *S'*. Because the increase in supply exceeds the increase in demand, the price declines. And because the demand for

EXHIBIT **11**

The Demand for Grain

The demand for grain tends to be price inelastic. As the market price falls, so does total revenue.

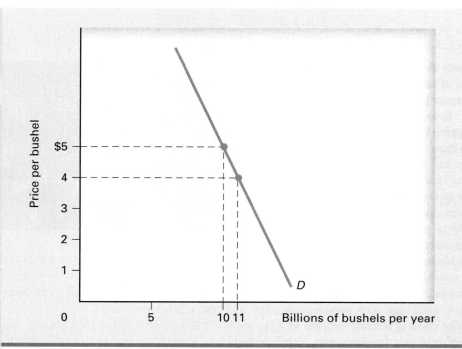

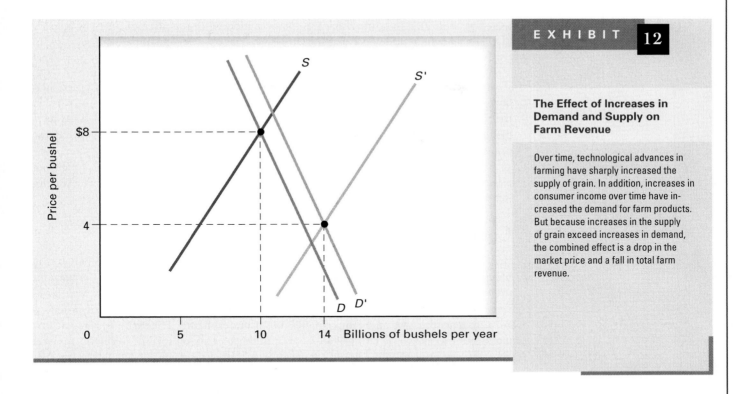

The Effect of Increases in Demand and Supply on Farm Revenue

Over time, technological advances in farming have sharply increased the supply of grain. In addition, increases in consumer income over time have increased the demand for farm products. But because increases in the supply of grain exceed increases in demand, the combined effect is a drop in the market price and a fall in total farm revenue.

grain is price inelastic, the percentage drop in price exceeds the percentage increase in output. The combined effect in our example is lower total revenue. In fact, net income (adjusted for inflation) to all U.S. farmers in 2003 was 20 percent below what it was in 1960.

Sources: Bruce L. Gardner, "Changing Economic Perspective on the Farm Problem," *Journal of Economic Literature* 30 (March 1992): 62–105; and *Economic Report of the President*, February 2004, Tables B-97 at http://www.gpoaccess.gov/eop/index.html. For current economic research at the U.S. Department of Agriculture, go to http://www.ers.usda.gov/.

Cross-Price Elasticity of Demand

Because a firm often produces an entire line of products, it has a special interest in how a change in the price of one product will affect the demand for another. For example, the Coca-Cola Company needs to know how changing the price of Lemon Coke will affect sales of Classic Coke. The company also needs to know the relationship between the price of Coke and the demand for Pepsi and vice versa. The responsiveness of the demand for one good to changes in the price of another good is called the **cross-price elasticity of demand.** It is defined as the percentage change in the demand of one good divided by the percentage change in the price of another good. Its numerical value can be positive, negative, or zero, depending on whether the two goods in question are substitutes, complements, or unrelated, respectively.

Substitutes

If an increase in the price of one good leads to an increase in the demand for another good, their cross-price elasticity is positive and the two goods are *substitutes*. For example, an increase in the price of Coke, other things constant, shifts the demand for Pepsi rightward, so the two are substitutes. The cross-price elasticity between Coke and Pepsi has been esti-

CROSS-PRICE ELASTICITY OF DEMAND

The percentage change in the demand of one good divided by the percentage change in the price of another good

mated at about 0.7, indicating that a 10 percent increase in the price of one will increase the demand for the other by 7 percent.[1]

Complements

If an increase in the price of one good leads to a decrease in the demand for another, their cross-price elasticity is negative and the goods are *complements*. For example, an increase in the price of gasoline, other things constant, shifts the demand for tires leftward because people drive less and replace their tires less frequently. Gasoline and tires have a negative cross-price elasticity and are complements.

In summary: *The cross-price elasticity of demand is positive for substitutes and negative for complements.* Most pairs of goods selected at random are *unrelated,* so their cross-price elasticity is zero.

Conclusion

Because this chapter has been more quantitative than earlier ones have, the mechanics may have overshadowed the intuitive appeal and neat simplicity of elasticity. *Elasticity measures the willingness and ability of buyers and sellers to alter their behavior in response to changes in their economic circumstances.* Firms try to estimate the price elasticity of demand for their products. Governments also have an ongoing interest in various elasticities. For example, state governments want to know the effect of an increase in the sales tax on total tax receipts, and local governments want to know how an increase in income will affect the demand for real estate and thus the revenue generated by a property tax. International groups are interested in elasticities; for example, the Organization of Petroleum Exporting Countries (OPEC) is concerned about the price elasticity of demand for oil—in the short run and in the long run. Because a corporation often produces an entire line of products, it also has a special interest in certain cross-price elasticities. Some corporate economists estimate elasticities for a living. The appendix to this chapter shows how price elasticities of demand and supply shed light on who ultimately pays a tax.

SUMMARY

1. The price elasticities of demand and supply show how responsive buyers and sellers are to changes in the price of a good. More elastic means more responsive.

2. When the percentage change in quantity demanded exceeds the percentage change in price, demand is price elastic. If demand is price elastic, a price increase reduces total revenue and a price decrease increases total revenue. When the percentage change in quantity demanded is less than the percentage change in price, demand is price inelastic. If demand is price inelastic, a higher price increases total revenue and a lower price reduces total revenue. When the percentage change in quantity demanded

equals the percentage change in price, demand is unit elastic; a price change does not affect total revenue.

3. Along a linear, or straight-line, downward-sloping demand curve, the elasticity of demand falls steadily as the price falls. But a constant-elasticity demand curve has the same elasticity everywhere.

4. Demand is more elastic (a) the greater the availability of substitutes and the more similar they are to the good in question; (b) the more narrowly the good is defined; (c) the larger the proportion of the consumer's budget spent on the good; and (d) the longer the time allowed for adjustment to a change in price.

---

1. F. Gasmi, J. Laffont, and Q. Vuong, "Econometric Analysis of Collusive Behavior in a Soft-Drink Market," *Journal of Economics and Management Strategy* (Summer 1992).

5. The price elasticity of supply uses a similar approach to the price elasticity of demand. Price elasticity of supply depends on how much the marginal cost of production changes as output changes. If marginal cost rises sharply as output expands, quantity supplied is less responsive to price increases and is thus less elastic. Also, the longer the time producers have to adjust to price changes, other things constant, the more elastic the supply.

6. Income elasticity of demand measures the responsiveness of demand to changes in consumer income. Income elasticity is positive for normal goods and negative for inferior goods.

7. The cross-price elasticity of demand measures the impact of a change in the price of one good on the demand for another good. Two goods are defined as substitutes, complements, or unrelated, depending on whether their cross-price elasticity of demand is positive, negative, or zero, respectively.

QUESTIONS FOR REVIEW

1. *(Categories of Price Elasticity of Demand)* For each of the following values of price elasticity of demand, indicate whether demand is elastic, inelastic, perfectly elastic, perfectly inelastic, or unit elastic. In addition, determine what would happen to total revenue if a firm raised its price in each elasticity range identified.

    a. $E_D = 2.5$
    b. $E_D = 1.0$
    c. $E_D = \infty$
    d. $E_D = 0.8$

2. *(Elasticity and Total Revenue)* Explain the relationship between the price elasticity of demand and total revenue.

3. *(Price Elasticity and the Linear Demand Curve)* How is it possible for many price elasticities to be associated with a single demand curve?

4. *(Determinants of Price Elasticity)* Why is the price elasticity of demand for Coca-Cola greater than the price elasticity of demand for soft drinks generally?

5. *(Determinants of Price Elasticity)* Would the price elasticity of demand for electricity be more elastic over a shorter or a longer period of time?

6. *(Determinants of Price Elasticity)* What factors help determine the price elasticity of demand? What factors help determine the price elasticity of supply?

7. *(Cross-Price Elasticity)* Using demand and supply curves, predict the impact on the price and quantity demanded of Good 1 of an increase in the price of Good 2 if the two goods are substitutes. What if the two goods are complements?

8. *(Other Elasticity Measures)* Complete each of the following sentences:

    a. The income elasticity of demand measures, for a given price, the _____ in quantity demanded divided by the _____ income from which it resulted.
    b. If a decrease in the price of one good causes a decrease in demand for another good, the two goods are _____.
    c. If the value of the cross-price elasticity of demand between two goods is approximately zero, they are considered _____.

PROBLEMS AND EXERCISES

9. *(Calculating Price Elasticity of Demand)* Suppose that 50 units of a good are demanded at a price of $1 per unit. A reduction in price to $0.20 results in an increase in quantity demanded to 70 units. Show that these data yield a price elasticity of 0.25. By what percentage would a 10 percent rise in the price reduce the quantity demanded, assuming price elasticity remains constant along the demand curve?

10. *(Price Elasticity and Total Revenue)* Fill in values for each price-quantity combination listed in the following table. What relationship have you depicted?

P	Q	Price Elasticity	Total Revenue
$8	2	_____	_____
7	3	_____	_____
6	4	_____	_____
5	5	_____	_____
4	6	_____	_____
3	7	_____	_____
2	8	_____	_____

11. *(Income Elasticity of Demand)* Calculate the income elasticity of demand for each of the following goods:

	Quantity Demanded When Income Is $10,000	Quantity Demanded When Income Is $20,000
Good 1	10	25
Good 2	4	5
Good 3	3	2

12. *(Price Elasticity of Supply)* Calculate the price elasticity of supply for each of the following combinations of price and quantity supplied. In each case, determine whether supply is elastic, inelastic, perfectly elastic, perfectly inelastic, or unit elastic.

   a. Price falls from $2.25 to $1.75; quantity supplied falls from 600 units to 400 units.
   b. Price falls from $2.25 to $1.75; quantity supplied falls from 600 units to 500 units.
   c. Price falls from $2.25 to $1.75; quantity supplied remains at 600 units.
   d. Price increases from $1.75 to $2.25; quantity supplied increases from 466.67 units to 600 units.

Use the following diagram to answer the next two questions.

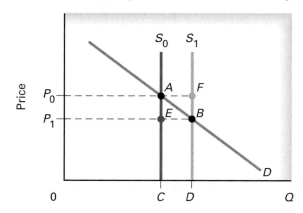

13. *(**C a s e S t u d y :** The Market for Food and "the Farm Problem")* Interpret this diagram as showing the market demand and supply curves for agricultural products. Suppose that demand is inelastic over the relevant range of prices and supply increased from S_0 to S_1. What areas in the figure would you use to illustrate the net change in farmers' total revenue as a result of the increase in supply?

14. *(**C a s e S t u d y :** The Market for Food and "the Farm Problem")* Again suppose that this diagram represents the market for agricultural products and that supply has increased from S_0 to S_1. To aid farmers, the federal government decides to stabilize the price at P_0 by buying up surplus farm products. Show on the diagram how much this would cost the government. By how much would farm income change compared to what it would have been without government intervention?

15. *(Cross-Price Elasticity)* Rank the following in order of increasing (from negative to positive) cross-price elasticity of demand with coffee. Explain your reasoning.

   Bleach

   Tea

   Cream

   Cola

EXPERIENTIAL EXERCISES

16. *(**C a s e S t u d y :** Deterring Young Smokers)* The Campaign for Tobacco Free Kids maintains a Web site with a page devoted to articles on the economics of tobacco policy at http://tobaccofreekids.org/campaign/global/worldconference.shtml. For additional background information in the form of the transcript of a five-part television series, check *The Tobacco Wars,* by Walter Adams and James Brock (Cincinnati, OH: South-Western College Publishing Co., 1999).

17. (*C a s e* **Study**: The Market for Food and "the Farm Problem") Farm problems are not unique to the United States. Alan Matthews at Trinity College, Dublin, has an interesting Web page devoted to "The Farm Problem and Farm Policy Objectives" at http://econserv2.bess.tcd.ie/amtthews/FoodCourse/LectureTopics/Topics.htm. Review the material presented there and determine to what extent agricultural issues in the European Union (EU) are similar to those experienced in the United States. What role does economics play in the analysis of EU farm policy?

18. *(Wall Street Journal)* In the computer industry, cross-elasticities of demand are quite important. For example, we know that computers and computer software are complements, and the cross-elasticity of demand would tell us how strong that relationship is. Read the "Personal Technology" column in Thursday's Wall Street Journal and find a story that describes pricing of computer hardware or software. Based on what you know about the relationships among different types of computers, among different types of software, and between computers and software, try to predict the effects of the price change. How will the change affect the quantity demanded of the item described? How will it affect the demand for substitutes and complements to that item?

HOMEWORK XPRESS! EXERCISES

These exercises require access to McEachern Homework Xpress! If Homework Xpress! did not come with your book, visit **http://homeworkxpress.swlearning.com** *to purchase.*

1. Sellers of personal computers, PCs, to households quickly notice changes in consumer sensitivity to price because most are made to order. Draw and label a demand curve for PCs that is relatively insensitive to changes in price. Identify an initial price as P, and the quantity that would be demanded at this price as Q. Identify a lower price as P1 and show the quantity that would be demanded as Q1.

   Illustrate the effect of an increase in consumer sensitivity to price by drawing in a new demand curve, D1, that passes through P but is more elastic than D at lower prices. Show the quantity that would be purchased along this demand curve if the price were to fall to P1. Label this as Q2.

2. Most PCs sold to households now come equipped with DVD players. When DVD players were first introduced several years ago, they were very expensive, so the supply of PCs with DVD players was very inelastic. Now that the cost of DVD players has fallen significantly, supply is much more elastic. Draw and label a supply curve for DVD-equipped PCs that is relatively insensitive to changes in price. Identify an initial price as P, and the quantity that would be supplied at this price as Q. Identify a higher price as P1 and show the quantity that would be supplied as Q1.

   Illustrate the effect of an increase in the elasticity of supply by drawing in a new supply curve, S1, that passes through P but is more elastic than S. Show the quantity that would be offered for sale along this supply curve if the price were to rise to P1. Label this as Q2.

3. Innovations in seed corn have dramatically increased the productivity of U.S. corn producers. Nonetheless, revenues for corn farmers do not seem to increase. Draw and label a demand and supply diagram for corn in which both curves are relatively inelastic before the innovations in seed. Show the equilibrium price and quantity. Illustrate the effect on supply of the innovations in corn seed, the effect of a small population increase on the demand for corn, and the resulting effects on equilibrium price and quantity.

4. Government officials are debating whether to impose a 50-cent per pound tax on coffee or carrots. They are wondering which would be more effective at raising revenue. Draw a supply curve that represents the quantity supplied per pound for coffee. Let this supply curve also represent the supply for carrots.

   Draw in a new supply curve representing supply for both with the tax.

   Draw in a relatively inelastic demand curve for coffee, D, and indicate the pretax price and quantity as P and Q.

   Draw in a relatively elastic demand curve, D1, for carrots so that the pretax price and quantity are identical.

   Illustrate the effects of the tax on the price and quantity of carrots, labeling the new values as P1 and Q1.

   Illustrate the effects of the tax on the price and quantity of coffee, labeling the new values as P2 and Q2.

Price Elasticity and Tax Incidence

A contributing factor to the Revolutionary War was a British tax on tea imported by the American Colonies. The tea tax led to the Boston Tea Party, during which colonists dumped tea leaves into Boston Harbor. There was confusion about who would ultimately pay such a tax: Would it be paid by suppliers, demanders, or both? As you will see, tax incidence—that is, who pays a tax—depends on the price elasticities of demand and supply.

Demand Elasticity and Tax Incidence

Panel (a) of Exhibit 13 depicts the market for tea leaves, with demand D and supply S. Before the tax is imposed, the intersection of demand and supply yields a market price of $1.00 per ounce and a market quantity of 10 million ounces per day. Now suppose a tax of $0.20 is imposed on each ounce sold. Recall that the supply curve represents the amount that producers are willing and able to supply at each

---

EXHIBIT **13**

Effects of Price Elasticity of Demand on Tax Incidence

The imposition of a $0.20-per-ounce tax on tea shifts the supply curve leftward from S to S_t. In panel (a), which has a less elastic demand curve, the market price rises from $1.00 to $1.15 per ounce and the market quantity falls from 10 million to 9 million ounces. In panel (b), which has a more elastic demand curve, the same tax leads to an increase in price from $1.00 to $1.05; market quantity falls from 10 million to 7 million ounces. The more elastic the demand curve, the more the tax is paid by producers in the form of a lower net-of-tax receipt.

(a) Less elastic demand

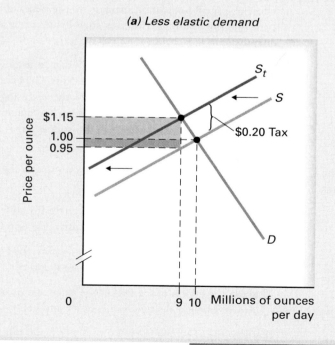

(b) More elastic demand

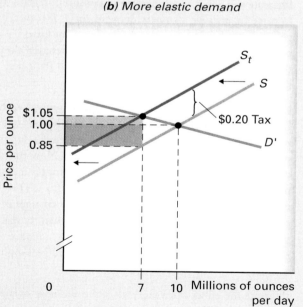

price. Because the government now gets $0.20 for each ounce sold, that amount must be added to the original supply curve to get a supply curve that includes the tax. Thus, the shift of the supply curve from S to S_t reflects the decrease in supply resulting from the tax. *The effect of a tax on tea is to decrease the supply by the amount of the tax.* The demand curve remains the same because nothing happened to demand; only the quantity demanded changes.

The result of the tax in panel (a) is to raise the equilibrium price from $1.00 to $1.15 and to decrease the equilibrium quantity from 10 million to 9 million ounces. As a result of the tax, consumers pay $1.15, or $0.15 more per ounce, and producers receive $0.95 after the tax, or $0.05 less per ounce. Thus, consumers pay $0.15 of the $0.20 tax as a higher price, and producers pay $0.05 as a lower receipt.

The shaded area of panel (a) shows the total tax collected, which equals the tax per ounce of $0.20 times the 9 million ounces sold, for a total of $1.8 million in tax revenue per day. You can see that the original price line at $1 divides the shaded area into two portions—an upper portion showing the tax paid by consumers through a higher price and a lower portion showing the tax paid by producers through a lower net-of-tax receipt.

The same situation is depicted in panel (b) of Exhibit 13, except that demand is more elastic than in the left panel. Consumers in panel (b) cut their quantity demanded more sharply in response to a price change, so producers cannot as easily pass the tax along as a higher price. The tax increases the price by $0.05, to $1.05, and the net-of-tax receipt to suppliers declines by $0.15 to $0.85. Total tax revenue equals $0.20 per ounce times 7 million ounces sold, or $1.4 million per day. Again, the upper rectangle of the shaded area shows the portion of the tax paid by consumers through a higher price, and the lower rectangle shows the portion paid by producers through a lower net-of-tax receipt. The tax is the difference between the amount consumers pay and the amount producers receive.

More generally, as long as the supply curve slopes upward, the more price elastic the demand, the more tax producers pay as a lower net-of-tax receipt and the less consumers bear as a higher price. Also notice that the amount sold decreases more in panel (b) than in panel (a): Other things constant, the total tax revenue declines more when demand is more elastic. Because tax revenue falls as the price elasticity of demand increases, governments around the world tend to tax products with inelastic demand, such as cigarettes, liquor, gasoline, gambling, coffee, tea, and salt.

Supply Elasticity and Tax Incidence

The effect of the elasticity of supply on tax incidence is shown in Exhibit 14. The same demand curve appears in both panels, but the supply curve is more elastic in panel (a). Again we begin with an equilibrium price of $1.00 per ounce and an equilibrium quantity of 10 million ounces of tea leaves per day. Once the sales tax of $0.20 per ounce is imposed, supply decreases in both panels to reflect the tax. Notice that in panel (a), the price rises to $1.15, or $0.15 above the pretax price of $1.00, while in panel (b), the price increases by only $0.05. Thus, more of the tax is passed on to consumers in panel (a), where supply is more elastic. The more easily suppliers can cut production in response to a newly imposed tax, the more of the tax consumers will pay. More generally, as long as the demand curve slopes downward, *the more elastic the supply, the less tax producers pay and the more consumers pay.*

We conclude that *the less elastic the demand and the more elastic the supply, the greater the share of the tax paid by consumers.* The side of the market that's more nimble (that is, more price elastic) in adjusting to a price increase is more able to stick the other side of the market with most of the tax.

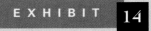

E X H I B I T 14

Effects of Price Elasticity of Supply on Tax Incidence

The imposition of a $0.20-per-ounce tax on tea shifts leftward both the more elastic supply curve in panel (a) and the less elastic curve of panel (b). In panel (a) the market price rises from $1.00 to $1.15 per ounce. In panel (b), the price rises only to $1.05 per ounce. Thus, the more elastic the supply curve, the more the tax is paid by consumers as a higher price.

(a) More elastic supply

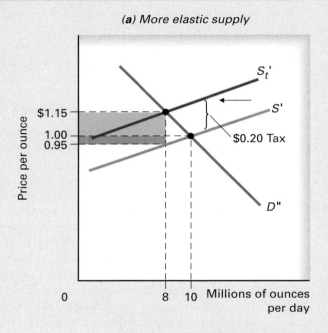

(b) Less elastic supply

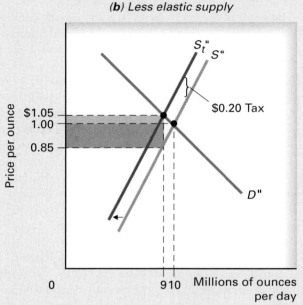

APPENDIX QUESTIONS

1. The claim is often made that a tax on a specific good will simply be passed on to consumers. Under what conditions of demand and supply elasticities will this occur? Under what conditions will little of the tax be passed on to consumers?

2. Suppose a tax is imposed on a good with a perfectly elastic supply curve.

   a. Who pays the tax?

   b. Using demand and supply curves, show how much tax is collected.

   c. How would this tax revenue change if the supply curve becomes less elastic?

3. During the 1980s, the U.S. Congress imposed a high sales tax on yachts, figuring that the rich could afford to pay for this luxury. But so many jobs were lost in the boat-building industry that the measure was finally repealed. What did Congress get wrong in imposing this luxury tax?

Consumer Choice and Demand

© Gary Houlder/Corbis

W hy are newspapers sold in vending machines that allow you to take more than one copy? How much do you eat when you can eat all you want? Why don't restaurants allow doggie bags with their all-you-can-eat specials? What's a cure for spring fever? Why is water cheaper than diamonds even though water is essential to life and diamonds are mere baubles? To answer these and other questions, we take a closer look at consumer demand, a key building block in economics.

You have already learned two reasons why demand curves slope downward. The first is the *substitution effect* of a price change. When the price of a good falls, consumers substitute that now-cheaper good for other goods. The second is the *income effect* of a price change. When the price of a good falls, real incomes increase, boosting consumers' ability to buy more.

Demand is so important that you must learn more about it. This chapter develops the law of demand based on the utility, or satisfaction, derived from consumption. As usual, the assumption is that you and other consumers try to maximize utility, or satisfaction. The point of this chapter is not to teach you how to maximize utility—that comes naturally. But understanding the theory behind your behavior will help you understand the implications of that behavior, making predictions more accurate. Topics discussed include:

- Total and marginal utility
- Law of diminishing marginal utility
- Measuring utility

- Utility-maximizing condition
- Consumer surplus
- Role of time in demand
- Time price of goods

Utility Analysis

Suppose you and a friend dine out together. After dinner, your friend asks how you liked your meal. You wouldn't say, "I liked mine twice as much as you liked yours." Nor would you say, "It deserves a rating of 86 on the U.S. Consumer Satisfaction Index." The utility, or satisfaction, you derive from that meal cannot be compared with another person's experience, nor can you measure your utility objectively. But you might say, "I liked it better than my last meal here" or "I liked it better than campus food." More generally, you can say whether one of your experiences was more satisfying than another. Even if you say nothing about your likes and dislikes, we can draw conclusions by observing your behavior. For example, we can conclude that you prefer apples to oranges if, when the two are priced the same, you always buy apples.

Tastes and Preferences

As was mentioned in Chapter 3, *utility* is the sense of pleasure, or satisfaction, that comes from consumption. Utility is subjective. The utility you derive from consuming a particular good depends on your *tastes*, which are your preferences for different goods and services—your likes and dislikes in consumption. Some goods are extremely appealing to you and others are not. You may not understand, for example, why someone would pay good money for sharks' fin soup, calves' brains, polka music, or martial arts movies. Why are nearly all baby carriages sold in the United States navy blue, whereas they are yellow in Italy and chartreuse in Germany? And why do Australians favor chicken-flavored potato chips and chicken-flavored salt?

Economics in the Movies

Economists actually have little to say about why tastes differ across individuals, across households, across regions, and across countries. *Economists assume simply that tastes are given and are relatively stable—that is, different people may have different tastes, but an individual's tastes are not constantly in flux.* To be sure, tastes for some products do change over time. Here are two examples: (1) during the last two decades, hiking and work boots replaced running shoes as everyday footwear among college students, and (2) Americans began consuming leaner cuts of beef after a 1982 report linked the fat in red meat to a greater risk of cancer. Still, economists believe tastes are stable enough to allow us to examine relationships such as that between price and quantity demanded. If tastes were not relatively stable, then we could not reasonably make the other-things-constant assumption in demand analysis. We could not even draw a demand curve.

The Law of Diminishing Marginal Utility

Suppose it's a hot summer day and you are extremely thirsty after jogging four miles. You pour yourself an eight-ounce glass of ice water. That first glass is wonderful, and it puts a serious dent in your thirst. The next glass is not quite as wonderful, but it is still pretty good. The third one is just fair; and the fourth glass you barely finish. Let's talk about the *utility,* or satisfaction, you get from water.

It's important to distinguish between total utility and marginal utility. **Total utility** is the total satisfaction you derive from consumption. For example, total utility is the total satisfaction you get from consuming four glasses of water. **Marginal utility** is the change in total utility resulting from a one-unit change in consumption of a good. For example, the marginal utility of a third glass of water is the change in total utility resulting from consuming that third glass of water.

Your experience with water reflects an economic law—the **law of diminishing marginal utility.** This law states that the more of a good a person consumes per period, other things constant, the smaller the increase in total utility from additional consumption—that is, the smaller the marginal utility of each additional unit consumed. The marginal utility you derive from each additional glass of water declines as your consumption increases. You enjoy the first glass a lot, but each additional glass provides less and less marginal utility. If forced to drink a fifth glass, you wouldn't enjoy it; your marginal utility would be negative. Diminishing marginal utility is a feature of all consumption. A second foot-long Subway sandwich at one meal, for most people, would provide little or no marginal utility. You might still enjoy a second movie on Friday night, but a third would probably be too much to take.

After a long winter, that first warm day of spring is something special and is the cause of "spring fever." The fever is "cured" by many warm days like the first. By the time August rolls around, you attach much less marginal utility to yet another warm day. For some goods, the drop in marginal utility with additional consumption is more pronounced. A second copy of the same daily newspaper would likely provide no marginal utility (in fact, the design of newspaper vending machines relies on the fact that people will take no more than one).[1] Likewise, a second viewing of the same movie at one sitting usually yields no additional utility. More generally, expressions such as "Been there, done that" and "Same old, same old" conveys the idea that, for many activities, things start to get old after the first time. Restaurants depend on the law of diminishing marginal utility when they hold all-you-can-eat specials—and no doggie bags allowed, because the deal is all you can eat now, not now and the next few days.

Measuring Utility

So far, the description of utility has used such words as *wonderful, good,* and *fair.* The analysis cannot be pushed very far with such subjective language. To predict consumption behavior, we must develop a consistent way of viewing utility.

Units of Utility

Let's go back to the water example. Although there really is no objective way of measuring utility, if pressed, you could be more specific about how much you enjoyed each glass of water. For example, you might say the second glass was half as good as the first, the third was half as good as the second, the fourth was half as good as the third, and you passed up a fifth

TOTAL UTILITY

The total satisfaction a consumer derives from consumption; it could refer to either the total utility of consuming a particular good or the total utility from all consumption

MARGINAL UTILITY

The change in total utility derived from a one-unit change in consumption of a good

LAW OF DIMINISHING MARGINAL UTILITY

The more of a good a person consumes per period, the smaller the increase in total utility from consuming one more unit, other things constant

HOMEWORK
Xpress!
*Ask the Instructor
Video*

glass because you expected no positive utility. To get a handle on this, let's assign arbitrary numbers to the amount of utility you derived from each quantity consumed, so the pattern of numbers reflects your expressed level of satisfaction. Let's say the first glass of water provides you with 40 units of utility, the second glass with 20, the third with 10, and the fourth with 5. A fifth glass, if you were forced to drink it, would yield negative utility, in this case, say, −2 units of utility. *Developing numerical values for utility allows us to be more specific about the utility derived from consumption.* If it would help, you could think of units of utility more playfully as thrills, kicks, or jollies—as in, getting your kicks from consumption.

By attaching a numerical measure to utility, we can compare the total utility a particular consumer gets from different goods as well as the marginal utility that consumer gets from additional consumption. Thus, we can employ units of utility to evaluate a consumer's preferences for additional units of a particular good or even additional units of different goods. Note, however, that we cannot compare utility levels across consumers. *Each person has a uniquely subjective utility scale.*

The first column of Exhibit 1 lists possible quantities of water you might consume after running 4 miles on a hot day. The second column presents the total utility derived from that consumption, and the third column shows the marginal utility of each additional glass of water consumed. Recall that marginal utility is the change in total utility from consuming an additional unit of the good. You can see from the second column that total utility increases with each of the first four glasses but by smaller and smaller amounts. The third column shows that the first glass of water yields 40 units of utility, the second glass yields an additional 20 units, and so on. Marginal utility declines after the first glass of water, becoming negative with the fifth glass. *At any level of consumption, marginal utilities sum to total utility.* Total utility is graphed in panel (a) of Exhibit 2. Again, because of diminishing marginal utility, each glass adds less to total utility, so total utility increases for the first four glasses but at a decreasing rate. Marginal utility appears in panel (b).

Utility Maximization in a World Without Scarcity

Economists assume that your purpose for drinking water, as with all consumption, is to *maximize your total utility.* So how much water do you consume? If the price of water is zero, you drink water as long as doing so increases total utility; so you consume four glasses of water. *If a good is free, you increase consumption as long as additional units add utility.* Let's extend the analysis to discuss the consumption of two goods—pizza and video rentals. We will continue to translate the satisfaction you receive from consumption into units of utility. Based on your tastes and preferences, suppose your total utility and marginal utility from con-

EXHIBIT 1	Units of Water Consumed (8-ounce glasses)	Total Utility	Marginal Utility
	0	0	—
	1	40	40
Utility You Derive from Water After Jogging Four Miles	2	60	20
	3	70	10
	4	75	5
	5	73	−2

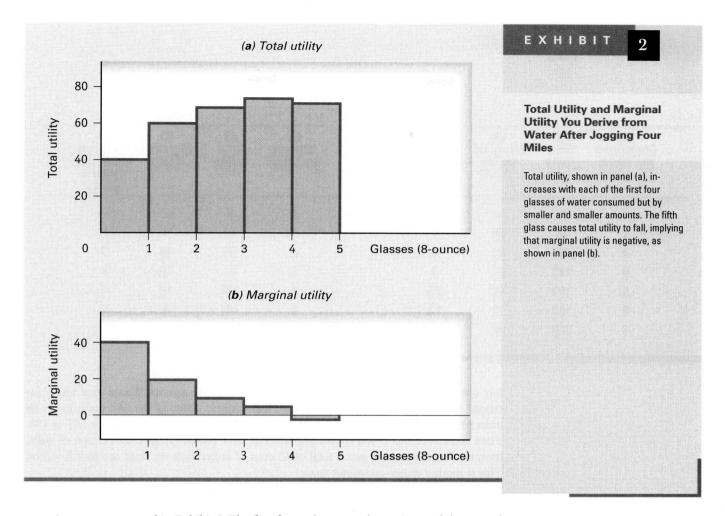

Total Utility and Marginal Utility You Derive from Water After Jogging Four Miles

Total utility, shown in panel (a), increases with each of the first four glasses of water consumed but by smaller and smaller amounts. The fifth glass causes total utility to fall, implying that marginal utility is negative, as shown in panel (b).

sumption are as presented in Exhibit 3. The first four columns apply to pizza and the second four to video rentals. Please take a little time right now with each column.

Notice from columns (3) and (7) that each good shows diminishing marginal utility. Given this set of preferences, how much of each good would you consume per week? At a zero price, you would increase consumption as long as marginal utility is positive. Thus, you would consume at least the first six pizzas and first six videos because the sixth unit of each good yields marginal utility. Did you ever go to a party where the food and drinks were free to you? How much did you eat and drink? You ate and drank until you didn't want any more—that is, until the marginal utility of each additional bite and each additional sip fell to zero. Your consumption was determined not by prices or income but simply by your tastes.

Utility Maximization in a World of Scarcity

Alas, goods are usually scarce, not free. Suppose the price of a pizza is $8, the rental price of a video is $4, and your after-tax income from a part-time job is $40 per week. Your utility is still based on your tastes, but you now must pay for the goods with your limited income. How do you allocate your income between the two goods to maximize utility? To get the ball rolling, suppose you start off spending your entire budget of $40 on pizza, purchasing five pizzas a week, which yields a total of 142 units of utility. You soon realize that if you

EXHIBIT **3**   **Total and Marginal Utilities from Pizza and Videos**

	Pizza				Video Rentals		
(1) Consumed per Week	(2) Total Utility	(3) Marginal Utility	(4) Marginal Utility per Dollar if $p = \$8$	(5) Viewed per Week	(6) Total Utility	(7) Marginal Utility	(8) Marginal Utility per Dollar if $p = \$4$
0	0	—	—	0	0	—	—
1	56	56	7	1	40	40	10
2	88	32	4	2	68	28	7
3	**112**	**24**	**3**	3	88	20	5
4	130	18	$2\frac{1}{4}$	**4**	**100**	**12**	**3**
5	142	12	$1\frac{1}{2}$	5	108	8	2
6	150	8	1	6	114	6	$1\frac{1}{2}$

buy one less pizza, you free up enough money to rent two movies. Would total utility increase? Sure. You give up 12 units of utility, the marginal utility of the fifth pizza, to get 68 units of utility from the first two videos. Total utility thereby increases from 142 to 198. Then you notice that if you reduce purchases to three pizzas, you give up 18 units of utility from the fourth pizza but gain a total of 32 units of utility from the third and fourth videos. This is another utility-increasing move.

Further reductions in pizza, however, would reduce your total utility because you would give up 24 units of utility from the third pizza but gain only 14 units from the fifth and sixth videos. Thus, you quickly find that the utility-maximizing equilibrium combination is three pizzas and four videos per week, for a total utility of 212. This combination involves an outlay of $24 on pizza and $16 on videos. *You are in equilibrium when consuming this combination because any affordable change would reduce your total utility.* Note that you demand fewer pizzas and videos now than when their price was zero.

Utility-Maximizing Conditions

Once equilibrium has been achieved, any change in your consumption pattern will decrease utility. *Once a consumer is in equilibrium, there is no way to increase utility by reallocating the budget.* But we can say more: *In equilibrium, the last dollar spent on each good yields the same marginal utility.* Let's see how this works. Column (4) shows the marginal utility of pizza divided by its price of $8. Column (8) shows the marginal utility of videos divided by its price of $4. The equilibrium choice of three pizzas and four videos exhausts the $40 budget and adds 3 units of utility for the last dollar spent on each good. **Consumer equilibrium** is achieved when the budget is completely spent and the last dollar spent on each good yields the same amount of marginal utility. In equilibrium, pizza's marginal utility divided by its price equals video's marginal utility divided by its price. In short, the consumer gets the same bang per last buck spent on each good. This equality can be expressed as:

CONSUMER EQUILIBRIUM

The condition in which an individual consumer's budget is spent and the last dollar spent on each good yields the same marginal utility; therefore, utility is maximized

$$\frac{MU_p}{p_p} = \frac{MU_v}{p_v}$$

where MU_p is the marginal utility of pizza, p_p is the price of pizza, MU_v is the marginal utility of videos, and p_v is the rental price. The consumer will reallocate spending until the last dollar spent on each product yields the same marginal utility. Although this example considers only two goods, the logic of utility maximization applies to any number of goods.

In equilibrium, higher-priced goods must yield more marginal utility than lower-priced goods—enough additional utility to compensate for their higher price. Because a pizza costs twice as much as a video rental, the marginal utility of the final pizza purchased must, in equilibrium, be twice that of the final video rented. Indeed, the marginal utility of the third pizza, 24, is twice that of the fourth video, 12. Economists do not claim that you consciously equate the ratios of marginal utility to price, but they do claim that you act as if you had made such calculations. *Thus, you decide how much of each good to purchase by considering your tastes, market prices, and your income. Consumers maximize utility by equalizing the marginal utility per dollar of expenditure across goods.* This approach resolved what had been an economic puzzle, as discussed in the following case study.

Water, Water, Everywhere

Centuries ago, economists puzzled over the price of diamonds relative to the price of water. Diamonds are mere baubles—certainly not a necessity of life in any sense. Water is essential to life and has hundreds of valuable uses. Yet diamonds are expensive, while water is cheap. For example, the $10,000 spent on a one-carat diamond could instead buy about 10,000 bottles of water or about 4 million gallons of municipally supplied water (which typically sells for about 25 cents per 100 gallons). However measured, diamonds are extremely expensive relative to water. For the price of a one-carat diamond, you could buy enough water to last a lifetime.

How can the price of something as useful as water be so much lower than something of such limited use as diamonds? In 1776, Adam Smith discussed what has come to be called the *diamonds-water paradox.* Because water is essential to life, the total utility derived from water greatly exceeds the total utility derived from diamonds. Yet the market value of a good is based not on its total utility but on what consumers are willing and able to pay for an additional unit—that is, on its marginal utility. Because water is so abundant in nature, we consume water to the point where the marginal utility of the last gallon purchased is relatively low. Because diamonds are relatively scarce compared to water, the marginal utility of the last diamond purchased is relatively high. Thus, water is cheap and diamonds expensive. As Ben Franklin said "We will only know the worth of water when the well is dry."

Speaking of water, sales of bottled water doubled in the United States between 1997 and 2002—growing faster than any other beverage category—creating an $8.5 billion industry. The United States offers the world's largest market for bottled water—importing water from places such as Italy, France, Sweden, Wales, even Fiji. "Water bars" in Boston, New York, and Los Angeles offer bottled water as the main attraction.

Bringing Theory to Life

*e*Activity

Almost any question you might have about water supply and use in the United States can be answered by visiting the U.S. Geological Survey's Water Q&A Web page at http://ga.water.usgs.gov/edu/mqanda.html. Various terms are linked to pages with additional information. What is the number one use of water in the United States? How does domestic use rate in importance? From which sources is most of the water in your state drawn—surface or groundwater supplies? How does water supply and use in the United States compare with the rest of the world? Find the answer in "Water: Critical Shortages Ahead?" from the World Resource Institute at http://www.wri.org/wr-98-99/water.htm.

Why would consumers pay a premium for bottled water when they can drink from the tap for virtually nothing? First, many people do not view the two as good substitutes. Some people have concerns about the safety of tap water, and they consider bottled water a healthy alternative (about half those surveyed in a Gallup Poll said they won't drink water straight from the tap). Second, even those who drink tap water find bottled water a convenient option away from home. According to the theory of utility maximization, people who buy bottled water apparently feel the additional benefit offsets the additional cost.

Bottled-water sales threaten the soft-drink industry. Fast food restaurants now offer bottled water as a healthy alternative to soft drinks. McDonald's, for example, is test marketing a "Go Active Happy Meal" that includes a bottle of water. But if you can't fight 'em, join 'em: Pepsi's Aquafina is the top-selling U.S. brand of bottled water, and Coke also has its own brand, Dasani.

Sources: "Bottled Water Continues Double-Digit Growth," *Beverage Aisle*, 15 August 2003; and "Wendy's Joins Rival Chains in Offering Healthier Foods," *Wall Street Journal*, 24 September 2003. The Definitive Bottled Water site is http://www.bottledwaterweb.com/ and the International Bottled Water Association site is http://www.bottledwater.org/.

The Law of Demand and Marginal Utility

How does utility analysis relate to your demand for pizza? The previous analysis yields a single point on your demand curve for pizza: At a price of $8, you demand three pizzas per week. This point is based on income of $40 per week, a price of $4 per video, and your tastes reflected by the utility tables in Exhibit 3. This single point, in itself, offers no clue about the shape of your demand curve for pizza. To generate another point, let's see what happens to quantity demanded if the price of pizza changes, while keeping other things constant (such as tastes, income, and the price of video rentals). Suppose the price of a pizza drops from $8 to $6.

Exhibit 4 is the same as Exhibit 3, except the price per pizza is $6. Your original choice was three pizzas and four video rentals. At that combination and with the price of pizza now $6, the marginal utility per dollar expended on the third pizza is 4, but the marginal utility per dollar on the fourth video remains at 3. The marginal utilities of the last dollar spent on each good are no longer equal. What's more, the original combination leaves $6 unspent. So you could still buy your original combination but have $6 to spend (this, incidentally, shows the income effect of a lower price of pizza). You can increase your utility by consuming a different bundle. Take a moment now to see if you can figure out what the new equilibrium should be.

In light of your utility schedules in Exhibit 4, you would increase your consumption to four pizzas per week. This strategy exhausts your budget and equates the marginal utilities of the last dollar expended on each good. Your video rentals remain the same (although they could have changed due to the income effect of the price change). But as your consumption increases to four pizzas, the marginal utility of the fourth pizza, 18, divided by the price of $6 yields 3 units of utility per dollar of expenditure, which is the same as for the fourth video. You are in equilibrium once again. Your total utility increases by the 18 units you derive from the fourth pizza. Thus, you are clearly better off as a result of the price decrease.

We now have a second point on your demand curve for pizza—if the price of pizza is $6, your quantity demanded is four pizzas. The two points are presented as *a* and *b* in Exhibit 5. We could continue to change the price of pizza and thereby generate additional points on the demand curve, but you can get some idea of the demand curve's downward slope from these two points. The shape of the demand curve for pizza conforms to our expectations based on the law of demand: Price and quantity demanded are inversely related.

EXHIBIT 4	Total and Marginal Utilities from Pizza and Videos After the Price of Pizza Decreases from $8 to $6 Each

Pizza					Video Rentals			
(1) Consumed per Week	(2) Total Utility	(3) Marginal Utility	(4) Marginal Utility per Dollar if *p* = $6		(5) Viewed per Week	(6) Total Utility	(7) Marginal Utility	(8) Marginal Utility per Dollar if *p* = $4
0	0	—	—		0	0	—	—
1	56	56	9⅓		1	40	40	10
2	88	32	5⅓		2	68	28	7
3	112	24	4		3	88	20	5
4	**130**	**18**	**3**		**4**	**100**	**12**	**3**
5	142	12	2		5	108	8	2
6	150	8	1⅓		6	114	6	1½

EXHIBIT 5

Demand for Pizza Generated from Marginal Utility

At a price of $8 per pizza, the consumer is in equilibrium when consuming three pizzas (point *a*). Marginal utility per dollar is the same for all goods consumed. If the price falls to $6, the consumer will increase consumption to four pizzas (point *b*). Points *a* and *b* are two points on this consumer's demand curve for pizza.

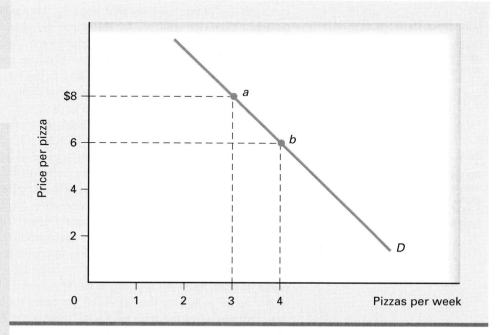

(Try estimating the price elasticity of demand between points *a* and *b*. Hint: What does total spending on pizza tell you?)

We have gone to some length to see how you (or any consumer) maximizes utility. Given prices and your income, your tastes and preferences naturally guide you to the most preferred bundle. You are not even conscious of your behavior. The urge to maximize utility is like the force of gravity—both work whether or not you understand them. Even animal behavior seems consistent with the law of demand. Wolves, for example, exhibit no territorial concerns when game is plentiful. But when game becomes scarce, wolves carefully mark their territory and defend it against intruders. Thus, wolves appear to value game more when it is scarce.

Now that you have some idea of utility, let's consider an application of utility analysis.

Consumer Surplus

In our earlier example, total utility increased when the price of pizza fell from $8 to $6. In this section, we take a closer look at how consumers benefit from a lower price. Suppose your demand for foot-long Subway sandwiches is as shown in Exhibit 6. Recall that in constructing an individual's demand curve, we hold tastes, income, and the prices of related goods constant. Only the price varies. At a price of $8 or above, you find that the marginal utility of other goods that you could buy for $8 is higher than the marginal utility of a Subway. Consequently, you buy no Subways. At a price of $7, you are willing and able to buy one per month, so the marginal utility of that first Subway exceeds the marginal utility you expected from spending that $7 on your best alternative—say, a movie ticket. A price of $6 prompts you to buy two Subways a month. The second is worth at least $6 to you. At a price of $5, you buy three Subways, and at $4, you buy four. *In each case, the value of the last Subway purchased must at least equal the price; otherwise, you wouldn't buy it.* Along the demand curve, therefore, the price reflects your **marginal valuation** of the good, or the dollar value of the marginal utility derived from consuming each additional unit.

MARGINAL VALUATION

The dollar value of the marginal utility derived from consuming each additional unit of a good

Notice that if the price is $4, you can purchase each of the four Subways for $4 each, even though you would have been willing to pay more than $4 for each of the first three Subways. The first sandwich provides marginal utility that you valued at $7; the second you valued at $6; and the third you valued at $5. In fact, if you had to, you would have been willing to pay $7 for the first, $6 for the second, and $5 for the third. The dollar value of the total utility of the first four sandwiches is $7 + $6 + $5 + $4 = $22 per month. But when the price is $4, you get all four for $16. Thus, a price of $4 confers a **consumer surplus,** or a consumer bonus, equal to the difference between the maximum amount you would have been willing to pay ($22) rather than go without Subways altogether and what you actually pay ($16). When the price is $4, your consumer surplus is $6, as approximated by the six darker shaded blocks in Exhibit 6. Consumer surplus equals the value of the total utility you receive from consuming the sandwiches minus your total spending on them. Consumer surplus is reflected by the area under the demand curve but above the price.

CONSUMER SURPLUS

The difference between the maximum amount that a consumer is willing to pay for a given quantity of a good and what the consumer actually pays

If the price falls to $3, you purchase five Subways a month. Apparently, you feel that the marginal utility from the fifth one is worth at least $3. The lower price means that you get all five for $3 each, even though all but the fifth are worth more to you than $3. Your consumer surplus when the price is $3 is the value of the total utility conferred by the first five, which is $7 + $6 + $5 + $4 + $3 = $25, minus your cost, which is $3 × 5 = $15. Thus, your consumer surplus totals $25 − $15 = $10, as indicated by both the dark and the light shaded blocks in Exhibit 6. So if the price declines to $3, your consumer surplus increases by $4, as reflected by the four lighter-shaded blocks in Exhibit 6. You can see how consumers benefit from lower prices.

EXHIBIT 6

Consumer Surplus from Subway Sandwiches

At a given quantity of Subway sandwiches, the height of the demand curve shows the value of the last one purchased. The area under the demand curve for a specific quantity shows the total value a consumer attaches to that quantity. At a price of $4, the consumer purchases four Subways. The first one is valued at $7, the second at $6, the third at $5, and the fourth at $4. The consumer values four at $22. Because the consumer pays $4 per Subway, all four can be purchased for $16. The difference between what the consumer would have been willing to pay ($22) and what the consumer actually pays ($16) is called consumer surplus. When the price is $4, the consumer surplus is $6, as represented by the dark shaded area under the demand curve above $4. When the price of Subways falls to $3, consumer surplus increases by $4, as reflected by the lighter shaded area.

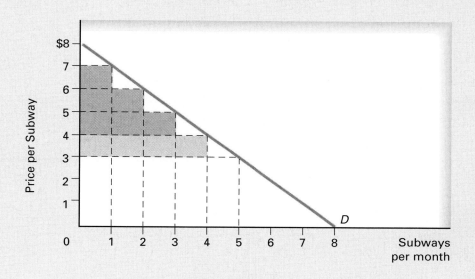

Market Demand and Consumer Surplus

Let's talk now about the market demand for a good, assuming the market consists of you and two other consumers. *The market demand curve is simply the horizontal sum of the individual demand curves for all consumers in the market.* Exhibit 7 shows how the demand curves for three consumers in the market for Subway sandwiches sum horizontally to yield the market demand. At a price of $4, for example, you demand four Subways per month, Brittany demands two, and Chris demands none. The market demand at a price of $4 is therefore six sandwiches. At a price of $2, you demand six per month, Brittany four, and Chris two, for a market demand of 12. *The market demand curve shows the total quantity demanded per period by all consumers at various prices.* Consumer surplus can be used to examine market demand as well as individual demand. *At a given price, consumer surplus for the market is the difference between the most consumers are willing to pay for that quantity and the total amount they do pay.*

Instead of just three consumers in the market, suppose there are many. Exhibit 8 presents market demand for a good with millions of consumers. If the price is $2 per unit, each person adjusts his or her quantity demanded until the marginal valuation of the last unit purchased equals $2. But each consumer gets to buy all other units for $2 each as well. In Exhibit 8, the dark shading, bounded above by the demand curve and below by the price of $2, depicts the consumer surplus when the price is $2. The light shading shows the increase

EXHIBIT 7

Summing Individual Demand Curves to Derive the Market Demand for Subway Sandwiches

At a price of $4 per Subway, you demand 4 per month, Brittany demands 2 , and Chris demands 0. Quantity demanded at a price of $4 is 4 + 2 + 0 = 6 Subways per month. At a lower price of $2, you demand 6, Brittany demands 4 , and Chris demands 2 . Quantity demanded at a price of $2 is 12 Subways. The market demand curve *D* is the horizontal sum of individual demand curves d_Y, d_B, and d_C.

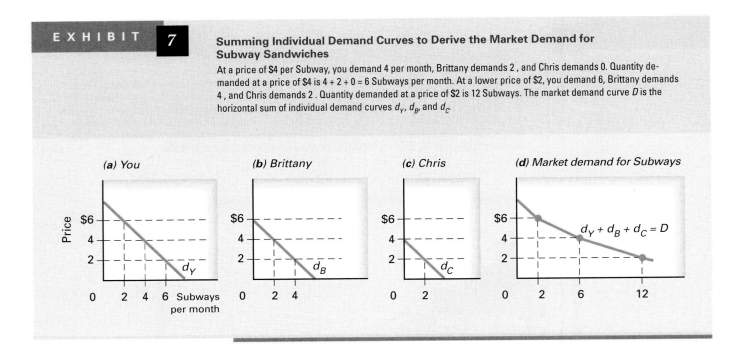

EXHIBIT 8

≡ **HOMEWORK** ≡
Xpress! ≡
Graphing

Market Demand and Consumer Surplus

Consumer surplus at a price of $2 is shown by the darker area. If the price falls to $1, consumer surplus increases to include the lighter area.

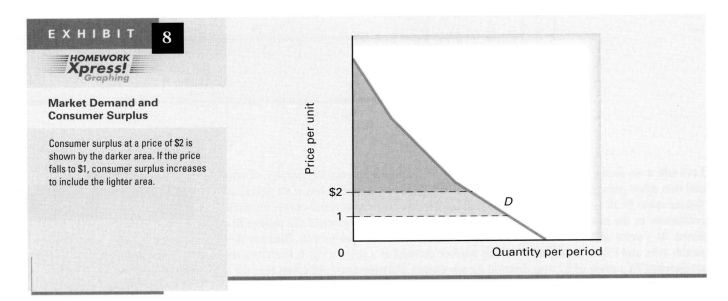

in consumer surplus if the price drops to $1. Notice that if this good were given away, the consumer surplus would not be significantly greater than when the price is $1.

Consumer surplus is the net benefit consumers get from market exchange. It can be used to measure economic welfare and to compare the effects of different market structures, different tax structures, and different public expenditure programs, such as for medical care, as discussed in the following case study.

The Marginal Value of Free Medical Care

Certain Americans, such as the elderly and those on welfare, receive government-subsidized medical care. State and federal taxpayers spend over $420 billion a year providing medical care to 75 million Medicare and Medicaid recipients, for an average annual cost of about $5,600 per beneficiary. The dollar cost to most beneficiaries is usually little or nothing. The problem with giving something away is that beneficiaries consume it to the point where their marginal valuation is zero, although the marginal cost to taxpayers can be sizeable.

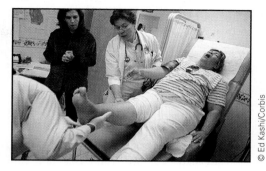
© Ed Kashi/Corbis

C a s e **S t u d y**

Public Policy

eActivity
This case study points out that patients have little incentive to monitor physician behavior when they do not pay the bill. In an attempt to control costs, Medicare reduces the reimbursement rate for services provided by physicians. How do you suppose physicians respond? Auditors with the Health Care Financing Administration (HCFA) examined physician behavior and found that they increase the volume and intensity of work in response to declining prices to maintain revenue. HCFA's easy-to-read report on physician response, which includes several real examples, can be found at http://www.cms.hhs.gov/statistics/actuary/physicianresponse/.

This is not to say that beneficiaries derive no benefit from free medical care. Although they may attach little or no value to the final unit, they likely derive a substantial consumer surplus from all the other units they consume. For example, suppose that Exhibit 8 represents the demand for medical care by Medicaid beneficiaries. Because the price to them is zero, they consume to the point where the demand curve intersects the horizontal axis, where their marginal valuation is zero. Their consumer surplus is the entire area under the demand curve.

One way to reduce the cost to taxpayers of such programs without significantly harming beneficiaries is to charge a small amount—say, $1 per physician visit. Beneficiaries would eliminate visits they value less than $1. This practice would yield significant savings to taxpayers but would still leave beneficiaries with excellent health care and a considerable consumer surplus (measured in Exhibit 8 as the area under the demand curve but above the $1 price). As a case in point, one Medicaid experiment in California required some beneficiaries to pay $1 per visit for their first two office visits per month (after two visits, the price of additional visits reverted to zero). A control group continued to receive free medical care. The $1 charge reduced office visits by 8 percent compared to the control group.

Medical care, like other goods and services, is also sensitive to its time cost (a topic discussed in the next section). For example, a 10 percent increase in the average travel time to a free outpatient clinic reduced visits by 10 percent. Similarly, when the relocation of a free clinic at one college campus increased students' walking time by 10 minutes, visits dropped 40 percent.

Another problem with giving something away is that beneficiaries are less vigilant about getting honest value, which may increase the possibility of fraud and abuse. According to a study by the U.S. General Accounting Office, about 1 in 7 Medicare dollars is wasted because of padded bills and fake claims that recipients would not tolerate if they paid their own bills. For example, in one case, the government was billed for round-the-clock cardiac monitoring when the patient was in fact monitored only 30 minutes a month.

These findings do not mean that certain groups do not deserve low-cost medical care. The point is that when something is free, people consume it until their marginal valuation is zero and they pay less attention to getting honest value. Some Medicare beneficiaries, for example, visit one or more medical specialists most days of the week. Does all this medical attention improve their health care? Maybe not. Researchers have found no apparent medical benefit from so many visits. As one doctor told the *New York Times*, "The system is broken. I'm not being a mean ogre, but when you give something away for free, there is nothing to keep utilization down."[2] Even a modest money cost or time cost would reduce utilization, yet would still leave beneficiaries with quality health care and a substantial consumer surplus.

Sources: Elliot Fisher, et al., "The Implications of Regional Variation in Medicare Spending," *Annals of Internal Medicine*, 18 February 2003; Gina Kolata, "Patients in Florida Lining Up for All That Medicare Covers," *New York Times*, 13 September 2003; and Steven Rhoads, "Marginalism," in *The Fortune Encyclopedia of Economics*, edited by D. R. Henderson (New York: Warner Books, 1993), pp. 31–33. For more on Medicare and Medicaid, go to the Centers for Medicare & Medicaid Services site at http://www.cms.hhs.gov/.

NetBookmark

Go to http://www.freechess.org, where you can play chess online with people around the world. (There are many other similar sites, just do a search in Yahoo! or Google.) Suppose you play 50 games of chess in the next two years in each of two settings. In setting X, you always play chess with the same person, and in setting Y, you always play each game with a different person. In which setting, X or Y, do you think the marginal utility of the 40th game of chess will be higher? What can you conclude about the marginal utility of playing chess?

The Role of Time in Demand

Because consumption does not occur instantaneously, time also plays an important role in demand analysis. Consumption takes time and, as Ben Franklin said, time is money—time has a positive value for most people. Consequently, the cost of consumption has two components: the *money price* of the good and the *time price* of the good. Goods are demanded because of the benefits they offer. Thus, you may be willing to pay more for medicine that works faster. Similarly, it is not the microwave oven, personal computer, or airline trip that you value but the benefits they provide. Other things constant, you are willing to pay more to get the same benefit in less time, as with faster ovens, computers, and airline trips. Likewise, you are willing to pay more for seedless grapes, seedless oranges, and seedless watermelon.

Your willingness to pay a premium for time-saving goods and services depends on the opportunity cost of your time. Differences in the value of time among consumers help explain differences in the consumption patterns observed in the economy. For example, a retired couple has more leisure time than a working couple and may clip coupons and search the newspapers for bargains, sometimes going from store to store for particular grocery items on sale that week. The working couple tends to ignore the coupons and sales and will eat out more often or buy more at convenience stores, where they pay extra for the "convenience." The retired couple will be more inclined to drive across the country on vacation, whereas the working couple will fly to a vacation destination.

Just inside the gates at Disneyland, Disney World, and Universal Studios are signs posting the waiting times of each attraction and ride. At that point, the dollar cost of admission has already been paid, so the marginal dollar cost of each ride and attraction is zero. The waiting times offer a menu of the marginal *time costs* of each ride or attraction. Incidentally, people who are willing to pay up to $55 an hour at Disney World and $60 an hour at Disneyland (plus the price of admission) until recently could take VIP tours that bypass the lines.[3] How much would you pay to avoid the lines?

Differences in the opportunity cost of time among consumers shape consumption patterns and add another dimension to our analysis of demand.

Conclusion

This chapter has analyzed consumer choice by focusing on utility, or satisfaction. We assumed that utility could be measured in some systematic way for a particular individual, even though utility could not be compared across individuals. The ultimate goal is to predict how consumer choice is affected by such variables as a change in price. We judge a theory not by the realism of its assumptions but by the accuracy of its predictions. Based on this criterion, the theory of consumer choice presented in this chapter has proven to be quite useful.

2. As reported by Gina Kolata, "Patients in Florida Lining Up for All That Medicare Covers," *New York Times*, 13 September 2003.

3. Nancy Keates, "Tourists Learn How to Mouse Around Disney's Long Lines," *Wall Street Journal*, 27 March 1998.

Again, to maximize utility, you or any other consumer need not understand the material presented in this chapter. Economists assume that rational consumers seek to maximize utility naturally and instinctively. In this chapter, we simply tried to analyze that process. A more general approach to consumer choice, one that does not require a specific measure of utility, is developed in the appendix to this chapter.

SUMMARY

1. Utility is the sense of pleasure or satisfaction that comes from consumption; it is the want-satisfying power of goods, services, and activities. The utility you receive from consuming a particular good depends on your tastes. The law of diminishing marginal utility says that the more of a particular good consumed per period, other things constant, the smaller the increase in total utility received from each additional unit consumed. The total utility derived from consuming a good is the sum of the marginal utilities derived from consuming each additional unit of the good.

2. Utility is subjective. Each consumer makes a personal assessment of the want-satisfying power of consumption. By translating an individual's subjective measure of satisfaction into units of utility, we can predict the quantity demanded at a given price as well as the effect of a change in price on quantity demanded.

3. The consumer's objective is to maximize utility within the limits imposed by income and prices. In a world without scarcity, utility is maximized by consuming each good until its marginal utility reaches zero. In the real world—a world shaped by scarcity as reflected by prices—utility is maximized when the budget is spent and the marginal utility for the final unit consumed divided by that good's price is identical for each different good.

4. Utility analysis can be used to construct an individual consumer's demand curve. By changing the price and observing the change in consumption, we can generate points along a demand curve.

5. When the price of a good declines, other things constant, a consumer is able to buy all units of the good at the lower price. Consumers typically receive a surplus, or a bonus, from consumption, and this surplus increases as the price declines. Consumer surplus is the difference between the maximum amount consumers would pay for a given quantity of the good and the amount they actually pay.

6. There are two components to the cost of consumption: the money price of the good and the time price of the good. People are willing to pay a higher money price for goods and services that save time.

QUESTIONS FOR REVIEW

1. *(Law of Diminishing Marginal Utility)* Some restaurants offer "all you can eat" meals. How is this practice related to diminishing marginal utility? What restrictions must the restaurant impose on the customer to make a profit?

2. *(Law of Diminishing Marginal Utility)* Complete each of the following sentences:

   a. Your tastes determine the _____ you derive from consuming a particular good.
   b. _____ utility is the change in _____ utility resulting from a _____ change in the consumption of a good.
   c. As long as marginal utility is positive, total utility is _____.

   d. The law of diminishing marginal utility states that as an individual consumes more of a good during a given time period, other things constant, total utility _____.

3. *(Marginal Utility)* Is it possible for marginal utility to be negative while total utility is positive? If yes, under what circumstances is it possible?

4. *(Utility-Maximizing Conditions)* For a particular consumer, the marginal utility of cookies equals the marginal utility of candy. If the price of a cookie is less than the price of candy, is the consumer in equilibrium? Why or why not? If not, what should the consumer do to attain equilibrium?

5. *(Utility-Maximizing Conditions)* Suppose that marginal utility of Good $X = 100$, the price of X is $10 per unit, and the price of Y is $5 per unit. Assuming that the consumer is in equilibrium and is consuming both X and Y, what must the marginal utility of Y be?

6. *(Utility-Maximizing Conditions)* Suppose that the price of X is twice the price of Y. You are a utility maximizer who allocates your budget between the two goods. What must be true about the equilibrium relationship between the marginal utility levels of the last unit consumed of each good? What must be true about the equilibrium relationship between the marginal utility levels of the last dollar spent on each good?

7. *(Consumer Surplus)* The height of the demand curve at a given quantity reflects the marginal valuation of the last unit of that good consumed. For a normal good, an increase in income shifts the demand curve to the right and therefore increases its height at any quantity. Does this mean that consumers get greater marginal utility from each unit of this good than they did before? Explain.

8. *(Consumer Surplus)* Suppose supply of a good is perfectly elastic at a price of $5. The market demand curve for this good is linear, with zero quantity demanded at a price of $25. Given that the slope of this linear demand curve is -0.25, draw a supply and demand graph to illustrate the consumer surplus that occurs when the market is in equilibrium.

9. *(**Case Study**: The Marginal Value of Free Medical Care)* Medicare recipients pay a monthly premium for coverage, must meet an annual deductible, and have a co-payment for doctors' office visits. President George W. Bush introduced some coverage of prescription medications (prior to that, there was none). What impact would an increase in the monthly premium have on their consumer surplus? What would be the impact of a reduction in co-payments? What is the impact on consumer surplus of offering some coverage for prescription medication?

10. *(Role of Time in Demand)* In many amusement parks, you pay an admission fee to the park but you do not need to pay for individual rides. How do people choose which rides to go on?

11. *(**Case Study**: Water, Water Everywhere)* What is the diamonds–water paradox, and how is it explained? Use the same reasoning to explain why bottled water costs so much more than tap water.

PROBLEMS AND EXERCISES

12. *(Utility Maximization)* The following tables illustrate Eileen's utilities from watching first-run movies in a theater and from renting movies from a video store. Suppose that she has a monthly movie budget of $36, each movie ticket costs $6, and each video rental costs $3.

Movies in a Theater

Q	TU	MU	MU/P
0	0	——	——
1	200	——	——
2	290	——	——
3	370	——	——
4	440	——	——
5	500	——	——
6	550	——	——
7	590	——	——

Movies from a Video Store

Q	TU	MU	MU/P
0	0	——	——
1	250	——	——
2	295	——	——
3	335	——	——
4	370	——	——
5	400	——	——
6	425	——	——
—	——	——	——

a. Complete the tables.
b. Do these tables show that Eileen's preferences obey the law of diminishing marginal utility? Explain your answer.
c. How much of each good will Eileen consume in equilibrium?

d. Suppose the prices of both types of movies drop to $1 while Eileen's movie budget shrinks to $10. How much of each good will she consume in equilibrium?

13. *(Utility Maximization)* Suppose that a consumer has a choice between two goods, X and Y. If the price of X is $2 and the price of Y is $3, how much of X and Y will the consumer purchase, given an income of $17? Use the following information about marginal utility:

Units	MU_X	MU_Y
1	10	5
2	8	4
3	2	3
4	2	2
5	1	2

14. *(The Law of Demand and Marginal Utility)* Daniel allocates his budget of $24 per week among three goods. Use the following table of marginal utilities for good A, good B, and good C to answer the questions below:

Q_A	MU_A	Q_B	MU_B	Q_C	MU_C
1	50	1	75	1	25
2	40	2	60	2	20
3	30	3	40	3	15
4	20	4	30	4	10
5	15	5	20	5	7.5

a. If the price of A is $2, the price of B is $3, and the price of C is $1, how much of each will Daniel purchase in equilibrium?

b. If the price of A rises to $4 while other prices and Daniel's budget remain unchanged, how much of each will he purchase in equilibrium?

c. Using the information from parts (a) and (b), draw the demand curve for good A. Be sure to indicate the price and quantity demanded for each point on the curve.

15. *(Consumer Surplus)* Suppose the linear demand curve for shirts slopes downward and that consumers buy 500 shirts per year when the price is $30 and 1,000 shirts per year when the price is $25.

a. Compared to the prices of $30 and $25, what can you say about the marginal valuation that consumers place on the 300th shirt, the 700th shirt, and the 1,200th shirt they might buy each year?

b. With diminishing marginal utility, are consumers deriving any consumer surplus if the price is $25 per shirt? Explain.

c. Use a market demand curve to illustrate the change in consumer surplus if the price drops from $30 to $25.

EXPERIENTIAL EXERCISES

16. *(Consumer Surplus)* Access a copy of "Creating Value and Destroying Profit? Three Measures of Information Technology's Contributions," by Loren Hitt and Erik Brynjolfsson at http://ccs.mit.edu/papers/CCSWP183.html. Use your browser's Edit/Find function to search for the words *consumer surplus* in this paper. How do Hitt and Brynjolfsson use the concept of consumer surplus to measure the value of information technology?

17. *(Case Study: The Marginal Value of Free Medical Care)* To learn more about economic issues related to health care, visit the McEachern Web page, http://mceachern.swlearning.com/, click on EconDebate Online, and find the debate "Is there a need for healthcare reform?" in the Government and the Economics section. What are some economic issues related to healthcare reform?

18. *(The Role of Time in Demand)* To learn more about the economics of consumption, read Jane Katz's "The Joy of Consumption: We Are What We Buy," in the Federal Reserve Bank of Boston's *Regional Review* at http://www.bos.frb.org/nerr/rr1997/winter/katz97_1/htm. What evidence does Katz cite about how the rising value of time has affected consumer spending patterns?

19. *(Wall Street Journal)* In this chapter, you learned that the cost of consumption involves both a money price and a time price. Turn to the Wednesday *Wall Street Journal* and find the "Work and Family" column. See if you can find some examples of changes in new goods, services, government policies, or institutional arrangements that work by reducing the time price of a product. How do you think that change will affect the demand for the product? Will demand for any related products be affected?

HOMEWORK XPRESS! EXERCISES

These exercises require access to McEachern Homework Xpress! If Homework Xpress! did not come with your book, visit **http://homeworkxpress.swlearning.com** *to purchase.*

1. Would another topping on a pizza always increase the utility derived from eating it? Consider Maria's total utility curve for pizza toppings as shown in the table. Find the marginal utility for each additional topping and draw a diagram indicating the corresponding marginal utility curve.

Number of toppings	Total utility
0	0
1	10
2	22
3	32
4	39
5	43
6	42

2. Demand curves for movie tickets per month for Rene, Eddie, and Mary are shown in the table. Sketch the market demand curves for movie tickets for each of them, labeling them as D1, D2, and D3, respectively. Find the market demand when the market consists only of these three people. Label the market demand curve D4.

Price per movie ticket	Rene	Eddie	Mary
$10	1	0	0
9	2	0	0
7	3	0	1
6	4	1	2
5	5	2	3

Indifference Curves and Utility Maximization

The approach used in the body of the chapter, marginal utility analysis, requires some numerical measure of utility to determine optimal consumption. Economists have developed another, more general, approach to consumer behavior, one that does not rely on a numerical measure of utility. All this new approach requires is that consumers be able to indicate their preferences for various combinations of goods. For example, the consumer should be able to say whether combination *A* is preferred to combination *B*, combination *B* is preferred to combination *A*, or both combinations are equally preferred. This approach is more general and more flexible than the one developed in the body of the chapter. But it's also a little more complicated.

Consumer Preferences

An **indifference curve** shows all combinations of goods that provide the consumer with the same satisfaction, or the same utility. Thus, the consumer finds all combinations on a curve equally preferred. Because each bundle of goods yields the same level of utility, the consumer is *indifferent* about which combination is actually consumed. We can best understand the use of indifference curves through the following example.

In reality, consumers choose among thousands of goods and services, but to keep the analysis manageable, suppose only two goods are available: pizzas and video rentals. In Exhibit 9, the horizontal axis measures the number of pizzas you buy per week, and the vertical axis measures the number of videos you rent per week. Point *a*, for example, consists of one pizza and eight video rentals. Suppose you are given a choice of combination *a* or some combination with more pizza. The question is: Holding your total utility constant, how many video rentals would you be willing to give up to get a second pizza? As you can see, in moving from point *a* to point *b*, you are willing to give up four videos to get a second pizza. Total utility is the same at points *a* and *b*. The marginal utility of that additional pizza per week is just sufficient to compensate you for the utility lost from decreasing your videos by four movies per week. Thus, at point *b*, you are eating two pizzas and watching four movies a week.

In moving from point *b* to point *c*, again total utility is constant; you are now willing to give up only one video for another pizza. At point *c*, your consumption bundle consists of three pizzas and three videos. Once at point *c*, you are willing to give up another video only if you get two more pizzas in return. Combination *d*, therefore, consists of five pizzas and two videos.

Points *a*, *b*, *c*, and *d* connect to form indifference curve *I*, which represents possible combinations of pizza and video rentals that would provide you the same level of total utility. Because points on the curve offer the same total utility, you are indifferent about which you choose—hence the name *indifference curve*. Note that we don't know, nor do we need to know, the value you attach to the utility reflected by the

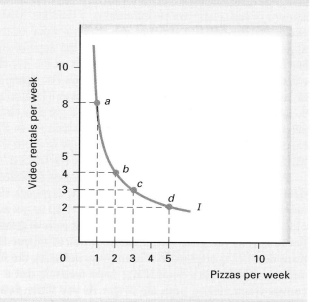

EXHIBIT   9   **An Indifference Curve**

An indifference curve, such as *I*, shows all combinations of two goods that provide a consumer with the same total utility. Points *a* through *d* depict four such combinations. Indifference curves have negative slopes and are convex to the origin.

indifference curve—that is, there is no particular number attached to the total utility along *I*. *Combinations of goods along an indifference curve reflect some constant, though unspecified, level of total utility.* So unlike the approach adopted in the body of the chapter, indifference curves need not be measured in units of utility.

For you to remain indifferent among consumption combinations, the increase in your utility from eating more pizza must just offset the decrease in your utility from watching fewer videos. Thus, along an indifference curve, there is an inverse relationship between the quantity of one good consumed and the quantity of another consumed. Because of this inverse relationship, *indifference curves slope downward.*

Indifference curves are also *convex to the origin,* which means they are bowed inward toward the origin. The curve gets flatter as you move down it. Here's why. Your willingness to substitute pizza for videos depends on how much of each you already consume. At combination *a,* for example, you watch eight videos and eat only one pizza a week. Because there are many videos relative to pizza, you are willing to give up four movies to get another pizza. Once you reach point *b,* your pizza consumption has doubled, so you are not quite so willing to give up movies to get a third pizza. In fact, you will forgo only one video to get one more pizza. This moves you from point *b* to point *c.*

The **marginal rate of substitution,** or **MRS,** between pizza and videos indicates the number of videos that you are willing to give up to get one more pizza, neither gaining nor losing utility in the process. Because the MRS measures your willingness to trade videos for pizza, it depends on the amount of each good you are consuming at the time. Mathematically, the MRS is equal to the absolute value of the slope of the indifference curve. Recall that the slope of any line is the vertical change between two points on the line divided by the corresponding horizontal change. For example, in moving from combination *a* to combination *b* in Exhibit 9, you are willing to give up four videos to get one more pizza; the slope between those two points equals −4, so the MRS is 4. In the move from *b* to *c,* the slope is −1, so the MRS is 1. And from *c* to *d,* the slope is −¹⁄₂?, so the MRS is ¹⁄₂.

The **law of diminishing marginal rate of substitution** says that as your consumption of pizza increases, the number of videos that you are willing to give up to get another pizza declines. This law applies to most pairs of goods. Because your marginal rate of substitution of videos for pizza declines as your pizza consumption increases, the indifference curve has a diminishing slope, meaning that it is convex when viewed from the origin. As you move down the indifference curve, your pizza consumption increases, so

the marginal utility of additional pizza decreases. Conversely, the number of movies you rent decreases, so the marginal utility of movies increases. Thus, in moving down the indifference curve, you require more pizza to offset the loss of each video.

We have focused on a single indifference curve, which indicates some constant but unspecified level of utility. We can use the same approach to generate a series of indifference curves, called an **indifference map.** An indifference map is a graphical representation of a consumer's tastes. Each curve reflects a different level of utility. Part of such a map is shown in Exhibit 10, where indifference curves for a particular consumer, in this case you, are labeled I_1, I_2, I_3, and I_4. Each consumer has a unique indifference map based on his or her preferences.

Because both goods yield marginal utility, you, the consumer, prefer more of each, rather than less. Curves farther from the origin represent greater consumption levels and, therefore, higher levels of utility. The utility level along I_2 is higher than that along I_1. I_3 reflects a higher level of utility

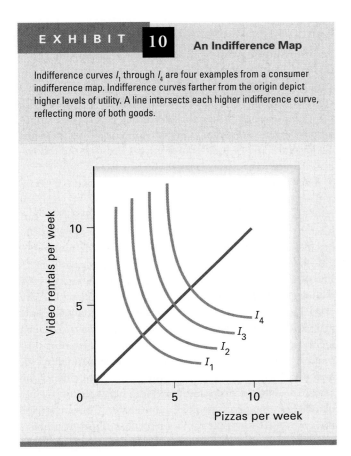

E X H I B I T   10   An Indifference Map

Indifference curves I_1 through I_4 are four examples from a consumer indifference map. Indifference curves farther from the origin depict higher levels of utility. A line intersects each higher indifference curve, reflecting more of both goods.

than I_2, and so on. We can show this best by drawing a line from the origin and following it to higher indifference curves. Such a line has been included in Exhibit 10. By following that line to higher and higher indifference curves, you can see that the combination on each successive indifference curve reflects greater amounts of *both* goods. Because you value both goods, the greater amounts of each reflected on higher indifference curves represent higher levels of utility.

Indifference curves in a consumer's indifference map do not intersect. Exhibit 11 shows why. If indifference curves did cross, as at point *i*, then every point on indifference curve *I* and every point on curve *I'* would have to reflect the same level of utility as at point *i*. But because point *k* in Exhibit 11 is a combination with more pizza and more videos than point *j*, it must represent a higher level of utility. This contradiction means that indifference curves cannot intersect.

Let's summarize the properties of indifference curves:

1. A particular indifference curve reflects a constant level of utility, so *the consumer is indifferent about all consumption combinations along a given curve.* Combinations are equally attractive.

2. If total utility is to remain constant, an increase in the consumption of one good must be offset by a decrease in the consumption of the other good, so *each indifference curve slopes downward.*

3. Because of the law of diminishing marginal rate of substitution, *indifference curves bow in toward the origin.*

4. Higher indifference curves represent higher levels of utility.

5. Indifference curves do not intersect.

An indifference map is a graphical representation of a consumer's tastes for the two goods. Given a consumer's indifference map, how much of each good will be consumed? To determine that, we must consider the relative prices of the goods and the consumer's income. In the next section, we focus on the consumer's budget.

The Budget Line

The **budget line** depicts all possible combinations of videos and pizzas, given their prices and your budget. Suppose videos rent for $4, pizza sells for $8, and your budget is $40 per week. If you spend the entire $40 on videos, you can afford 10 per week. Alternatively, if you spend the entire $40 on pizzas, you can afford 5 per week. In Exhibit 12, your budget line meets the vertical axis at 10 video rentals and meets the horizontal axis at 5 pizzas. We connect the intercepts to form the budget line. You can purchase any combi-

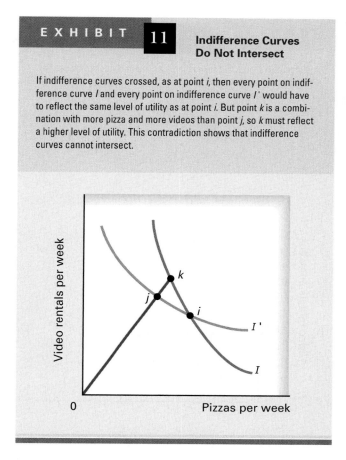

EXHIBIT 11 **Indifference Curves Do Not Intersect**

If indifference curves crossed, as at point *i*, then every point on indifference curve *I* and every point on indifference curve *I'* would have to reflect the same level of utility as at point *i*. But point *k* is a combination with more pizza and more videos than point *j*, so *k* must reflect a higher level of utility. This contradiction shows that indifference curves cannot intersect.

nation on your budget line, or your budget constraint. You might think of the budget line as your *consumption possibilities frontier.*

Let's find the slope of the budget line. At the point where the budget line meets the vertical axis, the maximum number of videos you can rent equals your income (I) divided by the video rental price (p_v), or I/p_v. At the point where the budget line meets the horizontal axis, the maximum quantity of pizzas that you can purchase equals your income divided by the price of a pizza (p_p), or I/p_p. The slope of the budget line between the vertical intercept in Exhibit 12 and the horizontal intercept equals the vertical change, or $-I/p_v$, divided by the horizontal change, or I/p_p:

$$\text{Slope of budget line} = -\frac{I/p_v}{I/p_p} = -\frac{p_p}{p_v}$$

Note that the income term cancels out, so the slope of a budget line depends only on relative prices, not on the level of income. In our example the slope is −$8/$4, which equals −2. The slope of the budget line indicates the cost of another

EXHIBIT   12   A Budget Line

A budget line shows all combinations of pizza and videos that can be purchased at fixed prices with a given amount of income. If all income is spent on videos, 10 can be purchased. If all income is spent on pizzas, 5 can be purchased. Points between the vertical intercept and the horizontal intercept show combinations of pizzas and videos. The slope of this budget line is –2, illustrating that the price of 1 pizza is 2 videos.

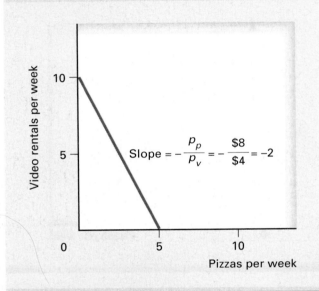

$$\text{Slope} = -\frac{p_p}{p_v} = -\frac{\$8}{\$4} = -2$$

pizza in terms of forgone videos. You must give up two videos for each additional pizza.

The indifference curve indicates what you are *willing* to buy. The budget line shows what you are *able* to buy. We must therefore bring together the indifference curve and the budget line to find out what quantities of each good you are both *willing* and *able* to buy.

Consumer Equilibrium at the Tangency

As always, the objective of consumption is to maximize utility. We know that indifference curves farther from the origin represent higher levels of utility. You, as a utility-maximizing consumer, will select a combination along the budget line in Exhibit 13 that lies on the highest attainable indifference curve. Given prices and income, you maximize utility at the combination of pizza and videos depicted by point *e* in Exhibit 13, where indifference curve I_2 just touches, or is *tangent to,* your budget line. At point *e*, you buy 3 pizzas at $8

each and rent 4 videos at $4 each, exhausting your budget of $40 per week. Other attainable combinations along the budget line reflect lower levels of utility. For example, point *a* is on the budget line, making it a combination you are *able* to purchase, but *a* is on a lower indifference curve, I_1. Other "better" indifference curves, such as I_3, lie completely above the budget line and are thus unattainable.

Because you maximize your utility at point *e*, that combination is an equilibrium outcome. Note that the indifference curve is tangent to the budget line at the equilibrium point, and at the point of tangency, the slope of a curve equals the slope of a line drawn tangent to that curve. At point *e*, the slope of the indifference curve equals the slope of the budget line. Recall that the absolute value of the slope of the indifference curve is your marginal rate of substitution, and the absolute value of the slope of the budget line equals the price ratio. In equilibrium, therefore, your marginal rate of substitution between videos and pizza, MRS, must equal the ratio of the price of pizza to the price of video rentals:

$$MRS = \frac{p_p}{p_v}$$

The marginal rate of substitution of pizza for video rentals can also be found from the marginal utilities of pizza and

EXHIBIT   13   Utility Maximization

A consumer's utility is maximized at point *e*, where indifference curve I_2 is just tangent to the budget line.

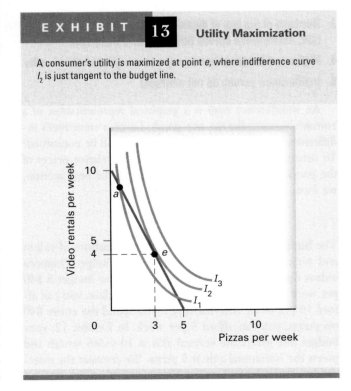

videos presented in the chapter. Exhibit 3 indicated that, at the consumer equilibrium, the marginal utility you derived from the third pizza was 24 and the marginal utility you derived by the fourth video was 12. Because the marginal utility of pizza (MU_p) is 24 and the marginal utility of videos (MU_v) is 12, in moving to that equilibrium, you were willing to give up two videos to get one more pizza. Thus, the marginal rate of substitution of pizza for videos equals the ratio of pizza's marginal utility (MU_p) to video's marginal utility (MU_v), or

$$MRS = \frac{MU_p}{MU_v}$$

In fact, the absolute value of the slope of the indifference curve equals MU_p/MU_v. Because the absolute value of the slope of the budget line equals p_p/p_v, the equilibrium condition for the indifference curve approach can be written as

$$\frac{MU_p}{p_p} = \frac{MU_v}{p_v}$$

This equation is the same equilibrium condition for utility maximization presented in the chapter using marginal utility analysis. The equality says that in equilibrium—that is, when the consumer maximizes utility—the last dollar spent on each good yields the same marginal utility. If this equality did not hold, the consumer could increase utility by adjusting consumption until the equality occurs.

Effects of a Change in Price

What happens to your equilibrium consumption when there is a change in price? The answer can be found by deriving the demand curve. We begin at point *e*, our initial equilibrium, in panel (a) of Exhibit 14. At point *e*, you eat 3 pizzas and watch 4 videos per week. Suppose that the price of pizzas falls from $8 to $6 per unit, other things constant. The price drop means that if the entire budget were devoted to pizza, you could purchase 6.67 pizzas (= $40/$6). Your money income remains at $40 per week, but your real income has increased because of the lower pizza price. Because the rental price of videos has not changed, however, 10 remains the maximum number you can rent. Thus, the budget line's vertical intercept remains fixed at 10 videos, but the lower end of the budget line rotates to the right from 5 to 6.67.

After the price of pizza changes, the new equilibrium occurs at *e"*, where pizza purchases increase from 3 to 4 and, as it happens, video rentals remains at 4. Thus, price and the quantity of pizza demanded are inversely related. The demand curve in panel (b) of Exhibit 14 shows how price and quan-

tity demanded are related. Specifically, if the price of pizza falls from $8 per unit to $6 per unit, other things constant, your quantity demanded increases from 3 to 4. Because you are on a higher indifference curve at *e"*, you are clearly better off after the price reduction (your consumer surplus has increased).

Income and Substitution Effects

The law of demand was initially explained in terms of an income effect and a substitution effect of a price change. You

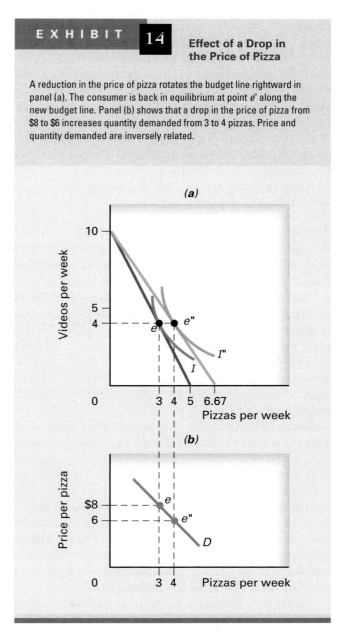

EXHIBIT 14

Effect of a Drop in the Price of Pizza

A reduction in the price of pizza rotates the budget line rightward in panel (a). The consumer is back in equilibrium at point *e"* along the new budget line. Panel (b) shows that a drop in the price of pizza from $8 to $6 increases quantity demanded from 3 to 4 pizzas. Price and quantity demanded are inversely related.

now have the tools to examine these two effects more precisely. Suppose the price of a pizza falls from $8 to $4, other things constant. You can now purchase a maximum of 10 pizzas with a budget of $40 per week. As shown in Exhibit 15, the budget-line intercept rotates out from 5 to 10 pizzas. After the price change, the quantity of pizzas demanded increases from 3 to 5. The increase in utility shows how you benefit from the price decrease.

The increase in the quantity of pizzas demanded can be broken down into the substitution effect and the income effect of a price change. When the price of pizza falls, the change in the ratio of the price of pizza to the price of video rentals shows up through the change in the slope of the budget line. To derive the substitution effect, let's initially assume that you must maintain the same level of utility after the price change as before. In other words, let's suppose your utility level has not yet changed, but the relative prices you face have changed. We want to learn how you would adjust to the price change. A new budget line reflecting just the change in relative prices, not a change in utility, is shown by the dashed line, *CF*, in Exhibit 15. Given the new set of relative prices, you would increase the quantity of pizza demanded to the point on indifference curve *I* where the indifference curve is just tangent to the dashed budget line. That tangency keeps utility at the initial level but reflects the new set of relative prices. Thus, we adjust your budget line to correspond to the new relative prices, but we adjust your income level so that your utility remains unchanged.

You move down along indifference curve *I* to point *e'*, renting fewer videos but buying more pizza. These changes in quantity demanded reflect the *substitution effect* of lower pizza prices. The substitution effect always increases the quantity demanded of the good whose price has dropped. Because consumption bundle *e'* represents the same level of utility as consumption bundle *e,* you are neither better off nor worse off at point *e'*.

But at point *e'*, you have not spent your full budget. The drop in the price of pizza has increased the quantity of pizza you can buy, as shown by the expanded budget line that runs from 10 video rentals to 10 pizzas. Your *real income* has increased because of the lower price of pizza. As a result, you are able to attain point *e** on indifference curve *I**. At this point, you buy 5 pizzas and rent 5 videos. Because prices remain constant during the move from *e'* to *e**, the change in consumption is due solely to a change in real income. Thus, the change in the quantity demanded from 4 to 5 pizzas reflects the *income effect* of the lower pizza price.

We can now distinguish between the substitution effect and the income effect of a drop in the price of pizza. The

EXHIBIT   15   **Substitution and Income Effects of a Drop in the Price of Pizza from $8 to $4**

A reduction in the price of pizza moves the consumer from point *e* to point *e**. This movement can be decomposed into a substitution effect and an income effect. The substitution effect, shown from *e* to *e'*, reflects the consumer's reaction to a change in relative prices along the original indifference curve. The income effect, shown from *e'* to *e**, moves the consumer to a higher indifference curve at the new relative price ratio.

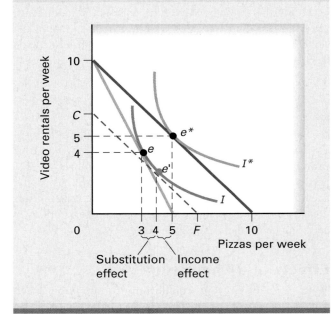

substitution effect is shown by the move from point *e* to point *e'* in response to a change in the relative price of pizza, with your utility held constant along *I*. The income effect is shown by the move from *e'* to *e** in response to an increase in your real income, with relative prices held constant.

The overall effect of a change in the price of pizza is the sum of the substitution effect and the income effect. In our example, the substitution effect accounts for a one-unit increase in the quantity of pizza demanded, as does the income effect. Thus, the income and substitution effects combine to increase the quantity of pizza demanded by two units when the price falls from $8 to $4. The income effect is not always positive. For inferior goods, the income effect is negative; so as the price falls, the income effect can cause consumption to fall, offsetting part or even all the substitution effect. Incidentally, notice that as a result of the increase in your real income, video rentals increase as well—from 4 to 5 rentals per week in our example, though it will not always be the case that the income effect is positive.

Conclusion

Indifference curve analysis does not require us to attach numerical values to particular levels of utility, as marginal util-

ity theory does. The results of indifference curve analysis confirm the conclusions drawn from our simpler models. Indifference curves provide a logical way of viewing consumer choice, but consumers need not be aware of this approach to make rational choices. The purpose of the analysis in this chapter is to predict consumer behavior—not to advise consumers how to maximize utility.

APPENDIX QUESTIONS

1. *(Consumer Preferences)* The absolute value of the slope of the indifference curve equals the marginal rate of substitution. If two goods were *perfect* substitutes, what would the indifference curves look like? Explain.

2. *(Effects of a Change in Price)* Chris has an income of $90 per month to allocate between Goods A and B. Initially the price of A is $3 and the price of B is $4.

    a. Draw Chris's budget line, indicating its slope if units of A are measured on the horizontal axis and units of B are on the vertical axis.
    b. Add an indifference curve to your graph and label the point of consumer equilibrium. Indicate Chris's

    consumption level of A and B. Explain why this is a consumer equilibrium. What can you say about Chris's total utility at this equilibrium?

    c. Now suppose the price of A rises to $4. Draw the new budget line, a new point of equilibrium, and the consumption level of Goods A and B. What is Chris's marginal rate of substitution at the new equilibrium point?
    d. Draw the demand curve for Good A, labeling the different price-quantity combinations determined in parts (b) and (c).

Production and Cost in the Firm

Why do too many cooks spoil the broth? Why do movie theaters have so many screens? Why don't they add even more? If you go into business for yourself, how much must you earn just to break even? Why might your grade average fall even though you improved from the previous term? Answers to these and other questions are discovered in this chapter, which introduces production and cost in the firm.

The previous chapter explored the consumer behavior shaping the demand curve. This chapter examines the producer behavior shaping the supply curve. A firm's operation is background for an analysis of supply. In the previous chapter, you were asked to think like a consumer, or demander. In this chapter, you must think like a producer, or supplier. You may feel more natural as a consumer (after all, you *are* one), but you already know more about producers than you may realize. You have been around them all your life—Wal-Mart, Blockbuster, Starbucks, Exxon, Barnes & Noble, Mc-Donald's, Pizza Hut, FedEx Kinko's, Ford, The Gap, and hundreds more. So you already have a crude idea how businesses operate. They all have the same goal—they try to maximize profit, which is revenue minus cost. This chapter introduces the cost side of the profit equation. Topics discussed include:

- Explicit and implicit costs
- Economic and normal profit
- Increasing and diminishing returns
- Short-run costs
- Long-run costs
- Economies and diseconomies of scale

Cost and Profit

With demand, we assume that consumers try to maximize utility, a goal that motivates their behavior. With supply, we assume that producers try to maximize *profit,* and this goal motivates their behavior. *Firms transform resources into products to earn a profit.* Over time, firms that survive and grow are those that are more profitable. Unprofitable firms eventually fail. Each year, millions of new firms enter the marketplace and almost as many leave. The firm's decision makers must choose what goods and services to produce and what resources to employ. They must make plans while confronting uncertainty about consumer demand, resource availability, and the intentions of other firms in the market. *The lure of profit is so strong, however, that eager entrepreneurs are always ready to pursue their dreams.*

Explicit and Implicit Costs

To hire a resource, a firm must pay at least the resource's *opportunity cost*—that is, at least what the resource could earn in its best alternative use. For most resources, a cash payment approximates the opportunity cost. For example, the $3 per pound that Domino's Pizza pays for cheese must at least equal the cheese producer's opportunity cost of supplying it. Some firms (or firm owners) own their resources, so they make no direct cash payments. For example, a firm pays no rent to operate in a company-owned building. Similarly, small-business owners usually don't pay themselves an hourly wage. Yet these resources are not free. *Whether hired in resource markets or owned by the firm, all resources have an opportunity cost.* Company-owned buildings can be rented or sold; small-business owners can find other jobs.

A firm's **explicit costs** are its actual cash payments for resources: wages, rent, interest, insurance, taxes, and the like. In addition to these direct cash outlays, or explicit costs, the firm also incurs **implicit costs,** which are the opportunity costs of using resources owned by the firm or provided by the firm's owners. Examples include the use of a company-owned building, use of company funds, or the time of the firm's owners. Like explicit costs, implicit costs are opportunity costs. But unlike explicit costs, implicit costs require no cash payment and no entry in the firm's *accounting statement,* which records its revenues, explicit costs, and accounting profit.

Alternative Measures of Profit

An example may help clarify the distinction between explicit and implicit costs. Wanda Wheeler earns $50,000 a year as an aeronautical engineer with the Skyhigh Aircraft Corporation. On her way home from work one day, she gets an idea for a rounder, more friction-resistant airplane wheel. She decides to quit her job and start a business, which she calls Wheeler Dealer. To buy the necessary machines and equipment, she withdraws $20,000

EXPLICIT COST

Opportunity cost of resources employed by a firm that takes the form of cash payments

IMPLICIT COST

A firm's opportunity cost of using its own resources or those provided by its owners without a corresponding cash payment

from her savings account, where it was earning interest of $1,000 a year. She hires an assistant and starts producing the wheel using the spare bay in her condominium's parking garage that she had been renting to a neighbor for $100 a month.

Sales are slow at first—people keep telling her she is just trying to reinvent the wheel—but her wheel eventually gets rolling. When Wanda and her accountant examine the firm's performance after the first year, they are quite pleased. As you can see in the top portion of Exhibit 1, company revenue in 2004 totaled $105,000. After paying her assistant and for materials and equipment, the firm shows an accounting profit of $64,000. **Accounting profit** equals total revenue minus explicit costs. Accountants use this profit to determine a firm's taxable income.

But accounting profit ignores the opportunity cost of Wanda's own resources used in the firm. First is the opportunity cost of her time. Remember, she quit a $50,000-a-year job to work full time on her business, thereby forgoing that salary. Second is the $1,000 annual interest she passes up by funding the operation with her own savings. And third, by using the spare bay in the garage for the business, she forgoes $1,200 per year in rental income. The forgone salary, interest, and rental income are implicit costs because she no longer earns income generated from their best alternative uses.

Economic profit equals total revenue minus all costs, both implicit and explicit; *economic profit takes into account the opportunity cost of all resources used in production.* In Exhibit 1, accounting profit of $64,000 less implicit costs of $52,200 equals economic profit of $11,800. What would happen to the accounting statement if Wanda decided to pay herself a salary of $50,000 per year? Explicit costs would increase by $50,000, and implicit costs would decrease by $50,000 (because her salary would no longer be forgone). Thus, accounting profit would decrease by $50,000, but economic profit would not change because it reflects both implicit and explicit costs.

There is one other profit measure to consider. The accounting profit just sufficient to ensure that *all* resources used by the firm earn their opportunity cost is called a **normal profit.** Wheeler Dealer earns a normal profit when accounting profit equals implicit costs—the sum of the salary Wanda gave up at her regular job ($50,000), the interest she gave up by using her own savings ($1,000), and the rent she gave up on her garage ($1,200). Thus, if the accounting profit is $52,200 per year—the opportunity cost of resources Wanda

---

ACCOUNTING PROFIT

A firm's total revenue minus its explicit costs

HOMEWORK Xpress!
Ask the Instructor
Video

ECONOMIC PROFIT

A firm's total revenue minus its explicit and implicit costs

NORMAL PROFIT

The accounting profit earned when all resources earn their opportunity cost

---

EXHIBIT 1		
Accounts of Wheeler Dealer, 2004	Total revenue		$105,000
	Less explicit costs:		
	Assistant's salary	–$21,000	
	Material and equipment	–$20,000	
	Equals accounting profit		$64,000
	Less implicit costs:		
	Wanda's forgone salary	–$50,000	
	Forgone interest on savings	–$1,000	
	Forgone garage rental	–$1,200	
	Equals economic profit		$11,800

supplies to the firm—the company earns a normal profit. *Any accounting profit in excess of a normal profit is economic profit.* If accounting profit is large enough, it can be divided into normal profit and economic profit. The $64,000 in accounting profit earned by Wanda's firm consists of (1) a normal profit of $52,200, which covers her implicit costs—the opportunity cost of resources she supplies the firm, and (2) an economic profit of $11,800, which is over and above what these resources, including Wanda's time, could earn in their best alternative use.

As long as economic profit is positive, Wanda is better off running her own firm than working for Skyhigh Aircraft. If total revenue had been only $50,000, an accounting profit of only $9,000 would cover less than one-fifth of her salary, to say nothing of her forgone rent and interest. Because Wanda would not have covered her implicit costs, she would not be earning even a normal profit and would be better off back in her old job.

To understand profit maximization, you must develop a feel for both revenue and cost. In this chapter, you will begin learning about the cost of production, starting with the relationship between inputs and outputs.

Production in the Short Run

We shift now from a discussion of profit, which is why firms exist, to a discussion of how firms operate. Suppose a new McDonald's has just opened in your neighborhood and business is booming far beyond expectations. The manager responds to the unexpected demand by quickly hiring more workers. But cars are still backed up into the street waiting for a parking space. The solution is to add a drive-through window, but such an expansion takes time.

Fixed and Variable Resources

Some resources, such as labor, are called **variable resources** because they can be varied quickly to change the output rate. But adjustments in some other resources take more time. Resources that cannot be altered easily—the size of the building, for example—are called **fixed resources.** When considering the time required to change the quantity of resources employed, economists distinguish between the short run and the long run. In the **short run,** at least one resource is fixed. In the **long run,** no resource is fixed.

Output can be changed in the short run by adjusting variable resources, but the size, or *scale,* of the firm is fixed in the short run. In the long run, all resources can be varied. The length of the long run differs from industry to industry because the nature of production differs. For example, the size of a McDonald's outlet can be increased more quickly than can the size of an auto plant. Thus, the long run for that McDonald's is shorter than the long run for an automaker.

The Law of Diminishing Marginal Returns

Let's focus on the short-run link between resource use and the rate of output by considering a hypothetical moving company called Smoother Mover. Suppose the company's fixed resources are already in place and consist of a warehouse, a moving van, and moving equipment. In this example, labor is the only variable resource. Exhibit 2 relates the amount of labor employed to the amount of output produced. Labor is measured in worker-days, which is one worker for one day, and output is measured in tons of furniture moved per day. The first column shows the amount of labor employed, which ranges from 0 to 8 worker-days. The second column shows the tons of furniture moved, or the **total product,** at each level of employment. The relationship between the amount of resources employed and total product is called the firm's **production function.** The third column shows the **marginal product** of each worker—that is, the amount by which the total product changes with each

VARIABLE RESOURCE
Any resource that can be varied in the short run to increase or decrease production

FIXED RESOURCE
Any resource that cannot be varied in the short run

SHORT RUN
A period during which at least one of a firm's resources is fixed

LONG RUN
A period during which all resources under the firm's control are variable

TOTAL PRODUCT
The total output produced by a firm

PRODUCTION FUNCTION
The relationship between the amount of resources employed and a firm's total product

MARGINAL PRODUCT
The change in total product that occurs when the use of a particular resource increases by one unit, all other resources constant

EXHIBIT **2**	Units of the Variable Resource (worker-days)	Total Product (tons moved per day)	Marginal Product (tons moved per day)
	0	0	—
The Short-Run Relationship Between Units of Labor and Tons of Furniture Moved	1	2	2
	2	5	3
	3	9	4
Marginal product increases as the firm hires the first three workers, reflecting increasing marginal returns. Then marginal product declines, reflecting diminishing marginal returns. Adding more workers may, at some point, actually reduce total product (as occurs here with an eighth worker) because workers start getting in each other's way.	4	12	3
	5	14	2
	6	15	1
	7	15	0
	8	14	−1

INCREASING MARGINAL RETURNS

The marginal product of a variable resource increases as each additional unit of that resource is employed

LAW OF DIMINISHING MARGINAL RETURNS

As more of a variable resource is added to a given amount of a fixed resource, marginal product eventually declines and could become negative

additional unit of labor, assuming other resources remain unchanged. Spend a little time now getting acquainted with each column.

Increasing Marginal Returns

Without labor, nothing gets moved, so total product is 0. If one worker is hired, that worker must do all the driving, packing, crating, and moving. Some of the larger items, such as couches and major appliances, cannot easily be moved by a single worker. Still, in our example one worker moves 2 tons of furniture per day. When a second worker is hired, some division of labor occurs, and two can move the big stuff more easily, so production more than doubles to 5 tons per day. The marginal product of the second worker is 3 tons per day. Adding a third worker allows for a finer division of labor. For example, one can pack fragile items while the other two do the heavy lifting. Total product is 9 tons per day, 4 tons more than with two workers. Because the marginal product increases, the firm experiences **increasing marginal returns** from labor as each of the first three workers is hired.

Diminishing Marginal Returns

A fourth worker's marginal product is less than that of a third worker. Hiring still more workers increases total product by successively smaller amounts, so the marginal product declines after three workers. With that fourth worker, the **law of diminishing marginal returns** takes hold. This law states that as more of a variable resource is combined with a given amount of a fixed resource, marginal product eventually declines. *The law of diminishing marginal returns is the most important feature of production in the short run.* As additional units of labor are added, marginal product could turn negative, so total product declines. For example, when Smoother Mover hires an eighth worker, workers start getting in each other's way, and workers take up valuable space in the moving van. As a result, the eighth worker actually subtracts from total output, yielding a negative marginal product. Likewise, a McDonald's outlet can hire only so many workers before congestion and confusion in the work area cut total product ("too many cooks spoil the broth").

The Total and Marginal Product Curves

Exhibit 3 illustrates the relationship between total product and marginal product, using data from Exhibit 2. Note that because of increasing marginal returns, marginal product in

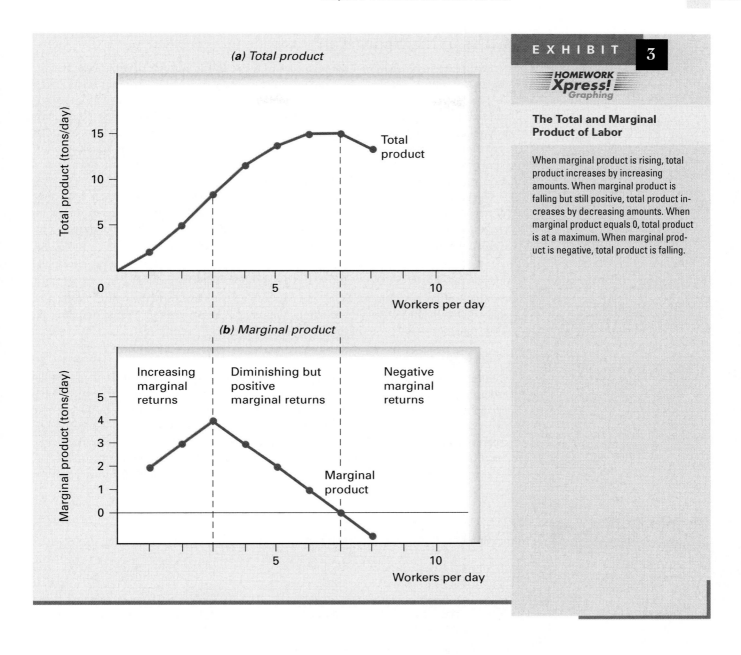

(a) Total product

(b) Marginal product

EXHIBIT 3

HOMEWORK
Xpress!
Graphing

The Total and Marginal Product of Labor

When marginal product is rising, total product increases by increasing amounts. When marginal product is falling but still positive, total product increases by decreasing amounts. When marginal product equals 0, total product is at a maximum. When marginal product is negative, total product is falling.

panel (b) increases with each of the first three workers. With marginal product increasing, total product in panel (a) increases at an increasing rate (although this is hard to see in Exhibit 3). But once decreasing marginal returns set in, which begins with the fourth worker, marginal product declines. Total product continues to increase but at a decreasing rate. As long as marginal product is positive, total product increases. Where marginal product turns negative, total product starts to fall. Exhibit 3 summarizes all this by sorting production into three ranges: (1) increasing marginal returns, (2) diminishing but positive marginal returns, and (3) negative marginal returns. These ranges for marginal product correspond with total product that (1) increases at an increasing rate, (2) increases at a decreasing rate, and (3) declines.

Costs in the Short Run

FIXED COST

Any production cost that is independent of the firm's rate of output

VARIABLE COST

Any production cost that changes as the rate of output changes

Now that we have examined the relationship between the amount of resources used and the rate of output, let's consider how the cost of production varies as output varies. There are two kinds of costs in the short run: fixed and variable. Fixed cost pays for fixed resources and variable cost pays for variable resources. A firm must pay a **fixed cost** even if no output is produced. Even if Smoother Mover hires no labor and moves no furniture, it incurs property taxes, insurance, vehicle registration, plus any opportunity cost for warehouse and equipment. By definition, fixed cost is just that: fixed—it does not vary with output in the short run. Suppose the firm's *fixed cost* is $200 per day.

Variable cost, as the name implies, is the cost of variable resources—in this case, labor. When no labor is employed, output is zero, as is variable cost. As workers are hired, output increases, as does variable cost. Variable cost depends on the amount of labor employed and the wage. If the wage is $100 per day, *variable cost* equals the number of workers hired times $100.

Total Cost and Marginal Cost in the Short Run

Exhibit 4 offers cost data for Smoother Mover. The table lists the daily cost of production associated with alternative rates of output. Column (1) shows possible rates of output in the short run, measured in tons of furniture moved per day.

Total Cost

Column (2) indicates the fixed cost (*FC*) at each rate of output. Note that fixed cost, by definition, remains constant at $200 per day regardless of output. Column (3) shows the labor needed to produce each output based on the productivity figures reported in the previous two exhibits. For example, moving 2 tons a day requires one worker, 5 tons requires two workers, and so on. Only the first six workers are listed because more contribute nothing to output. Column (4) lists variable cost (*VC*) per day, which equals $100 times the number of workers employed. For example, the variable cost of moving 9 tons of furniture per day is

---

E X H I B I T   4   Short-Run Cost Data for Smoother Mover

(1) Tons Moved per Day (q)	(2) Fixed Cost (FC)	(3) Workers per Day	(4) Variable Cost (VC)	(5) Total Cost ($TC = FC + VC$)	(6) Marginal Cost ($MC = \Delta TC / \Delta q$)
0	$200	0	0	$200	—
2	200	1	$100	300	$ 50.00
5	200	2	200	400	33.33
9	200	3	300	500	25.00
12	200	4	400	600	33.33
14	200	5	500	700	50.00
15	200	6	600	800	100.00

$300 because this output requires three workers. Column (5) lists the **total cost** (*TC*), the sum of fixed cost and variable cost: *TC = FC + VC*. As you can see, when output is zero, variable cost is zero, so total cost consists entirely of the fixed cost of $200. Incidentally, because total cost is the opportunity cost of all resources used by the firm, total cost includes a normal profit but not an economic profit. Think about that.

TOTAL COST

The sum of fixed cost and variable cost, or *TC = FC + VC*

Marginal Cost

Of special interest to the firm is how total cost changes as output changes. In particular, what is the marginal cost of producing another unit? The **marginal cost** (*MC*) of production listed in column (6) of Exhibit 4 is simply the change in total cost divided by the change in output, or *MC = ΔTC/Δq*, where Δ means "change in." For example, increasing output from 0 to 2 tons increases total cost by $100 (= $300 − $200). The marginal cost of each of the first 2 tons is the change in total cost, $100, divided by the change in output, 2 tons, or $100/2, which equals $50. The marginal cost of each of the next 3 tons is $100/3, or $33.33.

MARGINAL COST

The change in total cost resulting from a one-unit change in output; the change in total cost divided by the change in output, or *MC = ΔTC/Δq*

Notice in column (6) that marginal cost first decreases and then increases. *Changes in marginal cost reflect changes in the marginal productivity of the variable resource employed.* Because of increasing marginal returns, each of the first three workers produces more than the last. This greater productivity results in a falling marginal cost for the first 9 tons moved. Beginning with the fourth worker, the firm experiences diminishing marginal returns from labor, so the marginal cost of output increases. *When the firm experiences increasing marginal returns, the marginal cost of output falls; when the firm experiences diminishing marginal returns, the marginal cost of output increases.* Thus, marginal cost in Exhibit 4 first falls and then rises, because marginal returns from labor first increase and then diminish.

Total and Marginal Cost Curves

Exhibit 5 shows cost curves for the data in Exhibit 4. Because fixed cost does not vary with output, the fixed cost curve is a horizontal line at the $200 level in panel (a). Variable cost is zero when output is zero, so the *variable cost curve* starts from the origin. The *total cost curve* sums the fixed cost curve and the variable cost curve. Because a constant fixed cost is added to variable cost, the total cost curve is just the variable cost curve shifted vertically by the amount of fixed cost.

In panel (b) of Exhibit 5, marginal cost declines until the ninth unit of output and then increases, reflecting labor's increasing and then diminishing marginal returns. There is a relationship between the two panels because the change in total cost resulting from a one-unit change in production equals the marginal cost. With each successive unit of output, total cost increases by the marginal cost of that unit. Thus, *the slope of the total cost curve at each rate of output equals the marginal cost at that rate of output.* The total cost curve can be divided into two sections, based on what happens to marginal cost:

1. Because of increasing marginal returns from labor, marginal cost at first declines, so total cost initially increases by successively smaller amounts and the total cost curve becomes less steep.

2. Because of diminishing marginal returns from labor, marginal cost starts increasing after the ninth unit of output, leading to a steeper total cost curve.

Notice that the total cost curve has a backward S shape, the result of combining the two sections discussed above. Keep in mind that economic analysis is marginal analysis. Marginal cost is the key to economic decisions firms make. *Marginal cost indicates how much total cost will increase if one more unit is produced or how much total cost will drop if production declines by one unit.*

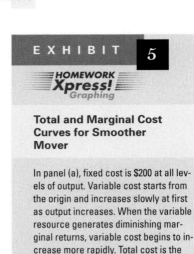

Total and Marginal Cost Curves for Smoother Mover

In panel (a), fixed cost is $200 at all levels of output. Variable cost starts from the origin and increases slowly at first as output increases. When the variable resource generates diminishing marginal returns, variable cost begins to increase more rapidly. Total cost is the vertical sum of fixed cost and variable cost. In panel (b), marginal cost first declines, reflecting increasing marginal returns, and then increases, reflecting diminishing marginal returns.

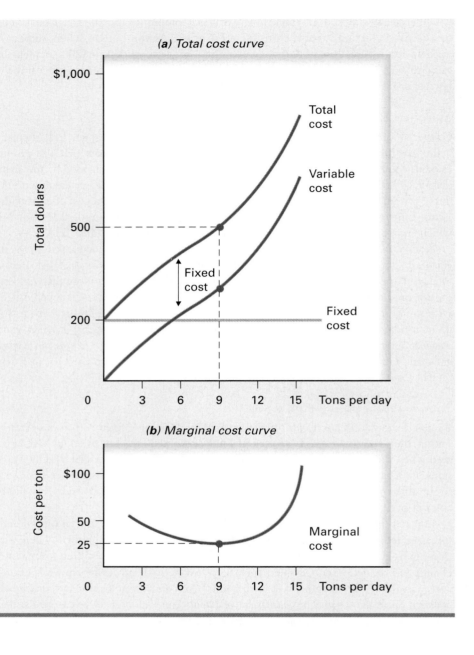

AVERAGE VARIABLE COST

Variable cost divided by output, or $AVC = VC/q$

AVERAGE TOTAL COST

Total cost divided by output, or $ATC = TC/q$; the sum of average fixed cost and average variable cost, or $ATC = AFC + AVC$

Average Cost in the Short Run

Although marginal cost is of most interest, the average cost per unit of output is also useful. Average cost measures correspond to variable cost and to total cost. These measures appear in columns (5) and (6) of Exhibit 6. Column (5) lists **average variable cost,** or AVC, which equals variable cost divided by output, or $AVC = VC/q$. The final column lists **average total cost,** or ATC, which equals total cost divided by output, or $ATC = TC/q$. Average cost first declines as output expands and then increases.

EXHIBIT 6	Short-Run Cost Data for Smoother Mover

Because of increasing marginal returns from labor, marginal cost at first declines, as shown in column (4). Because of diminishing marginal returns from labor, marginal cost starts increasing after the 9 tons are moved per day. Average costs first decline then increase, reflecting increasing and diminishing marginal returns.

(1) Tons Moved per Day (q)	(2) Variable Cost (VC)	(3) Total Cost ($TC = FC + VC$)	(4) Marginal Cost ($MC = \Delta TC / \Delta q$)	(5) Average Variable Cost ($AVC = VC/q$)	(6) Average Total Cost ($ATC = TC/q$)
0	$ 0	$200	0	—	∞
2	100	300	$50.00	$ 50.00	$150.00
5	200	400	33.33	40.00	80.00
9	300	500	25.00	33.33	55.55
12	400	600	33.33	33.33	50.00
14	500	700	50.00	35.71	50.00
15	600	800	100.00	40.00	53.33

The Relationship Between Marginal Cost and Average Cost

To understand the relationship between marginal cost and average cost, let's begin with an example of college grades. Think about how your grades each term affect your grade point average (GPA). Suppose you do well your first term, starting your college career with a 3.4. Your grades for the second term drop to 2.8, reducing your GPA to 3.1. You slip again in the third term to a 2.2, lowering your GPA to 2.8. Your fourth-term grades improve a bit to 2.4, but your GPA continues to slide to 2.7. In the fifth term, your grades improve to 2.7, leaving your GPA unchanged at 2.7. And in the sixth term, you get 3.3, pulling your GPA up to 2.8. Notice that when your term grades are below your GPA, your GPA falls. Even when your term performance improves, your GPA does not improve until your term grades *exceed* your GPA. Your term grades first pull down your GPA and then eventually pull it up.

Let's now take a look at the relationship between marginal cost and average cost. In Exhibit 6, marginal cost has the same relationship to average cost as your term grades have to your GPA. You can observe this marginal-average relationship in columns (4) and (5). Because of increasing marginal returns from the first three workers, the marginal cost falls for the first 9 tons of furniture moved. If marginal cost is below average cost, marginal cost pulls down average cost. Marginal cost and average cost are equal when output equals 12 tons, and marginal cost exceeds average cost when output exceeds 12 tons, so marginal cost pulls up average cost.

Exhibit 7 shows the same marginal cost curve first presented in Exhibit 5, along with average cost curves based on data in Exhibit 6. At low rates of output, marginal cost declines as output expands because of increasing marginal returns from labor. As long as marginal cost is below average cost, average cost falls as output expands. At higher rates of output, marginal cost increases because of diminishing marginal returns from labor. Once marginal cost exceeds average cost, marginal cost pulls up the average. The fact that marginal cost first pulls average cost down and then pulls it up explains why the average cost curves have a U shape. The shapes of the average variable cost curve and the average total cost curve are determined by the shape of the marginal cost curve, so each is shaped by increasing and diminishing marginal returns.

Average and Marginal Cost Curves for Smoother Mover

Average variable cost and average total cost curves first decline, reach low points, and then rise. Overall, they have U shapes. When marginal cost is below average variable cost, average variable cost is falling. When marginal cost equals average variable cost, average variable cost is at its minimum. When marginal cost is above average variable cost, average variable cost is increasing. The same relationship holds between marginal cost and average total cost.

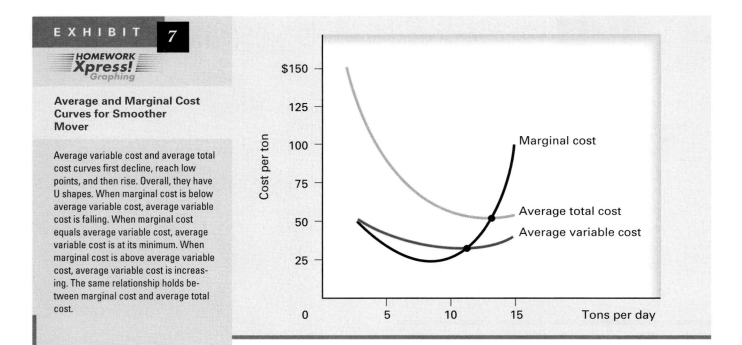

Notice also that the rising marginal cost curve intersects both the average variable cost curve and the average total cost curve where these average curves are at their minimum. This occurs because the marginal pulls down the average where the marginal is below the average and pulls up the average where the marginal is above the average. One more thing: The distance between the average variable cost curve and the average total cost curve is *average fixed cost,* which gets smaller as the rate of output increases. (Why does average fixed cost get smaller?)

The law of diminishing marginal returns determines the shapes of short-run cost curves. When the marginal product of labor increases, the marginal cost of output falls. Once diminishing marginal returns take hold, the marginal cost of output rises. Thus, marginal cost first falls and then rises. And the marginal cost curve dictates the shapes of the average cost curves. When marginal cost is less than average cost, average cost declines. When marginal cost is above average cost, average cost increases. Got it? If not, please reread this paragraph.

Costs in the Long Run

So far, the analysis has focused on how costs vary as the rate of output expands in the short run for a firm of a given size. In the long run, all inputs that are under the firm's control can be varied, so there is no fixed cost. The long run is not just a succession of short runs. The long run is best thought of as a *planning horizon*. In the long run, the choice of input combinations is flexible. But once the size of the plant has been selected and the concrete has been poured, the firm has fixed costs and is operating in the short run. Firms plan for the long run, but they produce in the short run. We turn now to long-run costs.

The Long-Run Average Cost Curve

Because of the special nature of technology in the industry, suppose a firm must choose from among three possible plant sizes: small, medium, and large. Exhibit 8 presents this simple case. The average cost curves for the three sizes are *SS'*, *MM'*, and *LL'*. Which size

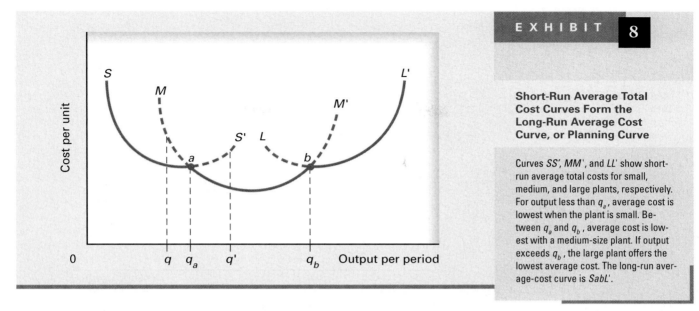

EXHIBIT 8

Short-Run Average Total Cost Curves Form the Long-Run Average Cost Curve, or Planning Curve

Curves *SS′*, *MM′*, and *LL′* show short-run average total costs for small, medium, and large plants, respectively. For output less than q_a, average cost is lowest when the plant is small. Between q_a and q_b, average cost is lowest with a medium-size plant. If output exceeds q_b, the large plant offers the lowest average cost. The long-run average-cost curve is *SabL′*.

should the firm build to minimize average cost? The appropriate size, *or scale,* for the firm depends on how much the firm wants to produce. For example, if *q* is the desired output, average cost will be lowest with a small plant size. If the desired output is *q′*, the medium plant size offers the lowest average cost.

More generally, for any output less than q_a, average cost is lowest when the plant is small. For output between q_a and q_b, average cost is lowest for the plant of medium size. And for output that exceeds q_b, average cost is lowest when the plant is large. The **long-run average cost curve,** sometimes called the firm's *planning curve,* connects portions of the three short-run average cost curves that are lowest for each output rate. In Exhibit 8, that curve consists of the line segments connecting *S, a, b,* and *L′*.

Now suppose there are many possible plant sizes. Exhibit 9 presents a sample of short-run cost curves shown in *pink.* The long-run average cost curve, shown in *red,* is formed by connecting the points on the various short-run average cost curves that represent the lowest per-unit cost for each rate of output. Each of the short-run average cost curves is tangent to the long-run average cost curve, or *planning curve.* If we could display enough short-run cost curves, we would have a different plant size for each rate of output. *These points of tangency represent the least-cost way of producing each particular rate of output, given the technology and resource prices.* For example, the short-run average total cost curve ATC_1 is tangent to the long-run average cost curve at point *a,* where $11 is the lowest average cost of producing output *q.* Note, however, that other output rates along ATC_1 have a lower average cost. For example, the average cost of producing *q′* is only $10, as identified at point *b.* Point *b* depicts the lowest average cost along ATC_1. So, while the point of tangency reflects the least-cost way of producing a particular rate of output, that tangency point does not reflect the minimum average cost for this particular plant size.

If the firm decides to produce *q′*, which size plant should it choose to minimize the average cost of production? Output rate *q′* could be produced at point *b,* which represents the minimum average cost along ATC_1. But average cost is lower with a larger plant. With the plant size associated with ATC_2, the average cost of producing *q′* would be minimized at $9 per unit at point *c. Each point of tangency between a short-run average cost curve and the long-run average cost curve represents the least-cost way of producing that particular rate of output.*

LONG-RUN AVERAGE COST CURVE

A curve that indicates the lowest average cost of production at each rate of output when the size, or scale, of the firm varies; also called the planning curve

EXHIBIT 9

Many Short-Run Average Total Cost Curves Form a Firm's Long-Run Average Cost Curve, or Planning Curve

With many possible plant sizes, the long-run average cost curve is the envelope of portions of the short-run average cost curves. Each short-run curve is tangent to the long-run average cost curve. Each point of tangency represents the least-cost way of producing that level of output.

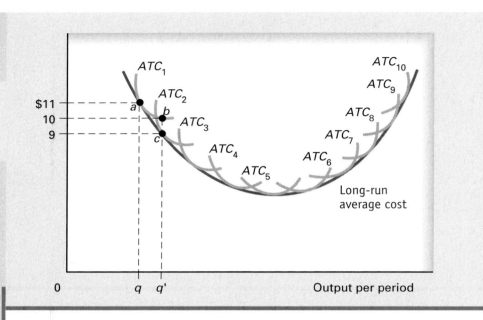

WALL STREET JOURNAL

Reading It **Right**

What's the relevance of the following statement from the Wall Street Journal: *"As with any new technology, the early OLED [organic light-emitting diode] display screens are expensive, perhaps six times more than liquid-crystal-display screens. But OLED backers say that problem will in part be addressed once mass production gears up and economies of scale are reached."*

ECONOMIES OF SCALE

Forces that reduce a firm's average cost as the scale of operation increases in the long run

DISECONOMIES OF SCALE

Forces that may eventually increase a firm's average cost as the scale of operation increases in the long run

Economies of Scale

Like short-run average cost curves, the long-run average cost curve is U-shaped. Recall that the shape of the short-run average total cost curve is determined primarily by increasing and diminishing marginal returns of the variable resource. A different principle shapes the long-run cost curve. If a firm experiences **economies of scale,** long-run average cost falls as output expands. Consider some sources of economies of scale. *A larger size often allows for larger, more specialized machines and greater specialization of labor.* For example, compare the household-size kitchen of a small restaurant with the kitchen at a McDonald's. At low rates of output, the smaller kitchen produces meals at a lower average cost than does McDonald's. But if production in the smaller kitchen increases beyond, say, 100 meals per day, a kitchen on the scale of McDonald's would produce at a lower average cost. Thus, because of economies of scale, the long-run average cost for a restaurant may fall as size increases.

A larger scale of operation allows a firm to use larger, more efficient machines and to assign workers to more specialized tasks. Production techniques such as the assembly line can be introduced only if the rate of output is great enough. Typically, as the scale of firm increases, capital substitutes for labor and complex machines substitute for simpler machines. As an extreme example of capital substituting for labor, some Japanese auto factories are automated enough to operate in the dark.

Diseconomies of Scale

Often another force, called **diseconomies of scale,** eventually takes over as a firm expands its plant size, increasing long-run average cost as output expands. As the amount and variety of resources employed increase, so does the *task of coordinating all these inputs.* As the workforce grows, additional layers of management are needed to monitor production. In the thicket of bureaucracy that develops, communications may get mangled. Top executives have more difficulty keeping in touch with the factory floor because information is distorted as it moves up and down the chain of command. Indeed, in very large organizations, rumors may become a primary source of information, reducing the efficiency of the organization and increasing average cost. Note that *diseconomies of scale result from a larger firm size, whereas diminishing marginal returns result from using more variable resources in a firm of a given size.*

In the long run, a firm can vary the inputs under its control. Some resources, however, are not under the firm's control, and the inability to vary them may contribute to diseconomies of scale. Let's look at economies and diseconomies of scale at movie theaters in the following case study.

At the Movies

Movie theaters experience both economies and diseconomies of scale. A theater with one screen needs someone to sell tickets, someone to sell popcorn (concession stand sales account for well over half the profit at most theaters), and someone to operate the projector. If another screen is added, the same staff can perform these tasks for both screens. Thus, the ticket seller becomes more productive by selling tickets to both movies. Furthermore, construction costs per screen are reduced be-

cause only one lobby and one set of rest rooms are required. The theater can run bigger, more noticeable newspaper ads and can spread the cost over more films. These are the reasons why we see theater owners adding more and more screens at the same location; they are taking advantage of economies of scale. From 1990 to 2000, the number of screens in the United States grew faster than the number of theaters, so the average number of screens per theater increased. Europe experienced similar growth.

But why stop at, say, 10 or even 20 screens per theater? Why not 30 screens, particularly in thickly populated areas with sufficient demand? One problem with expanding the number of screens is that the public roads leading to the theater are a resource the theater cannot control. The congestion around the theater grows with the number of screens at that location. Also, the supply of popular films may not be large enough to fill so many screens.

Finally, time itself is a resource that the firm cannot easily control. Only certain hours are popular with moviegoers. Scheduling becomes more difficult because the manager must space out starting and ending times to avoid the congestion that occurs when too many customers come and go at the same time. No more "prime time" can be created. Thus, theater owners lack control over such inputs as the public roads, the supply of films, and the amount of "prime time" in the day. These factors contribute to diseconomies of scale.

Sources: "Not-So-Special Effects," *Daily Variety*, 2 July 2003; "AMC Will Build Megaplex in Virginia," *Business Journal*, 14 May 2003; and *Statistical Abstract of the United States: 2002*, U.S. Census Bureau, http://www.census.gov/prod/www/statistical-abstract-us.html.

It is possible for average cost to neither increase nor decrease with changes in firm size. If neither economies of scale nor diseconomies of scale are apparent over some range of output, a firm experiences **constant long-run average cost.** Perhaps economies and diseconomies of scale exist simultaneously in the firm but have offsetting effects. Exhibit 10 presents a firm's long-run average cost curve, which is divided into output segments reflecting economies of scale, constant long-run average costs, and diseconomies of scale. Output

---

Case **Study**

World of Business

eActivity

With substantial economies of scale in the movie theater industry, a few chains now operate thousands of theaters. Their corporate Web sites provide information on current plans and include histories of how they grew to be so large. Browse through the following sites: AMC theatres at http://www.amctheatres.com/aboutamc/ourhistory.html and Regal Cinemas at http://www.uatc.com/corporate/about.html. Can you find the average number of screens per theater for each corporation? What is a megaplex? Where can megaplexes be found?

CONSTANT LONG-RUN AVERAGE COST

A cost that occurs when, over some range of output, long-run average cost neither increases nor decreases with changes in firm size

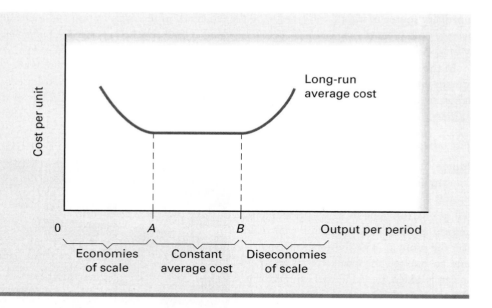

© Timothy O'Keefe /Index Stock Imagery

EXHIBIT **10**

A Firm's Long-Run Average Cost Curve

Up to output level *A*, long-run average cost falls as the firm experiences economies of scale. Output level *A* is the minimum efficient scale—the lowest rate of output at which the firm takes full advantage of economies of scale. Between *A* and *B*, the average cost is constant. Beyond output level *B*, long-run average cost increases as the firm experiences diseconomies of scale.

MINIMUM EFFICIENT SCALE

The lowest rate of output at which a firm takes full advantage of economies of scale

must reach quantity *A* for the firm to achieve the **minimum efficient scale,** which is the lowest rate of output at which long-run average cost is at a minimum.

Economies and Diseconomies of Scale at the Firm Level

Our discussion so far has referred to a particular plant—a movie theater or a restaurant, for example. But a firm could also be a collection of plants, such as the hundreds of movie theaters in a chain or the thousands of McDonald's restaurants. More generally, we can distinguish between economies and diseconomies of scale at the *plant level*—that is, at a particular location—and at the *firm level,* where the firm is a collection of plants. The following case study explores issues of multiplant scale economies and diseconomies.

Billions and Billions of Burgers

McDonald's experiences economies of scale at the plant, or restaurant, level because of its specialization of labor and machines, but it also benefits from economies of scale at the firm level. Experience gained from decades of selling hamburgers can be shared with new managers through centralized training programs. Costly research and efficient production techniques can also be shared across thousands of locations. For example, McDonald's took three years to decide on the exact temper-

ature of the holding cabinets for its hamburger patties and took seven years to develop Chicken McNuggets. What's more, the cost of advertising and promoting McDonald's through sponsorship of world events such as the Olympics can be spread across its 29,000 restaurants in 121 countries.

Some diseconomies may also arise in such large-scale operations. The fact that the menu must be reasonably uniform across thousands of locations means that if customers in some parts of the country or the world do not like a product, it may not get on the menu, even though it might be popular elsewhere. Another problem with a uniform menu is that the ingredients must be available around the world and cannot be subject to droughts or sharp swings in price. For example, one chain decided not to top its burgers with bacon strips because the price of bacon fluctuates too much.

Because McDonald's has moved aggressively overseas (10 percent of the beef sold in Japan is in McDonald's hamburgers, and McDonald's is the third largest corporate employer in Brazil), planning has grown increasingly complex. For example, McDonald's is kosher in Israel, closes five times a day for Muslim prayer in Saudi Arabia, and serves mutton burgers in India, where cows are worshiped, not eaten. Running a worldwide operation also opens the company to global risks, such as mad-cow disease in Europe and terrorism worldwide.

Change usually comes slowly in large corporations, but it does come. McDonald's recently reorganized its U.S. operation into five regions, allowing managers in each region more leeway in pricing and promotion. McDonald's has also become more flexible by putting mini-restaurants in airports, gas stations, and Wal-Marts. These so-called satellite restaurants recently accounted for half of the company's new U.S. openings. McDonald's has also begun closing unprofitable restaurants. This greater flexibility across regions and in restaurant structure is an effort by McDonald's to address diseconomies of scale.

Sources: Erin White and Shirley Leung, "McDonald's Germany: Little Mac?", *Wall Street Journal*, 23 September 2003; Pallavi Gogoi and Michael Arndt, "Hamburger Hell: McDonald's Aims to Save Itself by Going Back to Basics," *Business Week*, 3 March 2003; James L. Watson, ed., *Golden Arches East: McDonald's in East Asia* (Palo Alto, Calif.: Stanford University Press, 1998); and McDonald's Web site at http://www.mcdonalds.com/.

serves the Rhode Island McFeast Menu? If you can read a foreign language, try to find a McDonald's page for a country where it is spoken.

Other large firms do what they can to reduce diseconomies of scale at the firm level. For example, IBM undertook a massive restructuring program to decentralize into six smaller decision-making groups. Some big corporations have spun off parts of their operation to form new corporations. For example, Hewlett-Packard split off Agilent Technologies, and AT&T created Lucent Technologies.

Conclusion

By considering the relationship between production and cost, we have developed the foundation for a theory of firm behavior. Despite what may appear to be a tangle of short-run and long-run cost curves, *only two relationships between resources and output underlie all the curves. In the short run, it's increasing and diminishing returns from the variable resource. In the long run, it's economies and diseconomies of scale.* If you understand the sources of these two phenomena, you grasp the central ideas of the chapter. Our examination of production and cost in the short run and long run lays the groundwork for a firm's supply curve, to be covered in the next chapter. But before that, the appendix develops a more sophisticated approach to production and cost.

SUMMARY

1. Explicit costs are opportunity costs of resources employed by a firm that take the form of cash payments. Implicit costs are the opportunity costs of using resources owned by the firm. A firm earns a normal profit when total revenue covers all implicit and explicit costs. Economic profit equals total revenue minus both explicit and implicit costs.

2. Resources that can quickly be varied to increase or decrease output are called variable resources. In the short run, at least one resource is fixed. In the long run, all resources are variable.

3. A firm may initially experience increased marginal returns as it takes advantage of increased specialization of the variable resource. But the law of diminishing marginal returns indicates that the firm will eventually reach a point where additional units of the variable resource yield an ever-smaller marginal product.

4. The law of diminishing marginal returns from the variable resource is the most important feature of production in the short run and explains why marginal cost and average cost eventually increase as output expands.

5. In the long run, all inputs under the firm's control are variable, so there is no fixed cost. The firm's long-run average cost curve, also called its planning curve, is an envelope formed by a series of short-run average total cost curves. The long run is best thought of as a planning horizon.

6. In the long run, a firm selects the most efficient size for the desired rate of output. Once the firm's size is chosen, some resources become fixed, so the firm is back operating in the short run. Thus, the firm plans for the long run but produces in the short run.

7. A firm's long-run average cost curve, like its short-run average cost curves, is U-shaped. As output expands, average cost at first declines because of economies of scale—a larger plant size allows for bigger and more specialized machinery and a more extensive division of labor. Eventually, average cost stops falling. Average cost may be constant over some range. If output expands still further, the plant may encounter diseconomies of scale as the cost of coordinating resources grows. Economies and diseconomies of scale can occur at the plant level and at the firm level.

QUESTIONS FOR REVIEW

1. *(Explicit and Implicit Costs)* Amos McCoy is currently raising corn on his 100-acre farm and earning an accounting profit of $100 per acre. However, if he raised soybeans, he could earn $200 per acre. Is he currently earning an economic profit? Why or why not?

2. *(Explicit and Implicit Costs)* Determine whether each of the following is an explicit cost or an implicit cost:

   a. Payments for labor purchased in the labor market
   b. A firm's use of a warehouse that it owns and could rent to another firm
   c. Rent paid for the use of a warehouse not owned by the firm
   d. The wages that owners could earn if they did not work for themselves

3. *(Alternative Measures of Profit)* Calculate the accounting profit or loss as well as the economic profit or loss in each of the following situations:

   a. A firm with total revenues of $150 million, explicit costs of $90 million, and implicit costs of $40 million
   b. A firm with total revenues of $125 million, explicit costs of $100 million, and implicit costs of $30 million
   c. A firm with total revenues of $100 million, explicit costs of $90 million, and implicit costs of $20 million
   d. A firm with total revenues of $250,000, explicit costs of $275,000, and implicit costs of $50,000

4. *(Alternative Measures of Profit)* Why is it reasonable to think of normal profit as a type of cost to the firm?

5. *(Short Run Versus Long Run)* What distinguishes a firm's short-run period from its long-run period?

6. *(Law of Diminishing Marginal Returns)* As a farmer, you must decide how many times during the year you will plant a new crop. Also, you must decide how far apart to space the plants. Will diminishing returns be a factor in your decision making? If so, how will it affect your decisions?

7. *(Marginal Cost)* What is the difference between fixed cost and variable cost? Does each type of cost affect short-run marginal cost? If yes, explain how each affects marginal cost. If no, explain why each does or does not affect marginal cost.

8. *(Marginal Cost)* Explain why the marginal cost of production *must* increase if the marginal product of the variable resource is decreasing.

9. *(Costs in the Short Run)* What effect would each of the following have on a firm's short-run marginal cost curve and its total fixed cost curve?

   a. An increase in the wage rate
   b. A decrease in property taxes
   c. A rise in the purchase price of new capital
   d. A rise in energy prices

10. *(Costs in the Short Run)* Identify each of the curves in the following graph:

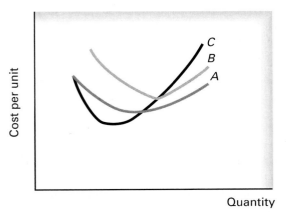

11. *(Marginal Cost and Average Cost)* Explain why the marginal cost curve must intersect the average total cost curve and the average variable cost curve at their minimum points. Why do the average total cost and average variable cost curves get closer to one another as output increases?

12. *(Marginal Cost and Average Cost)* In Exhibit 7 in this chapter, the output level where average total cost is at a minimum is greater than the output level where average variable cost is at a minimum. Why?

13. *(Long-Run Average Cost Curve)* What types of changes could shift the long-run average cost curve? How would these changes also affect the short-run average total cost curve?

14. *(Long-Run Average Cost Curve)* Explain the shape of the long-run average cost curve. What does "minimum efficient scale" mean?

15. (*Case* **Study**: At the Movies) The case study notes that the concession stand accounts for well over half the profits at most theaters. Given this, what are the benefits of the staggered movie times allowed by multiple screens? What is the benefit to a multiscreen theater of locating at a shopping mall?

16. (*Case* **Study**: Billions and Billions of Burgers) How does having a menu that is uniform around the country provide McDonald's with economies of scale? How is menu planning made more complex by expanding into other countries?

PROBLEMS AND EXERCISES

17. *(Production in the Short Run)* Complete the following table. At what point does diminishing marginal returns set in?

Units of the Variable Resource	Total Product	Marginal Product
0	0	—
1	10	_____
2	22	_____
3	_____	9
4	_____	4
5	34	_____

18. *(Total Cost and Marginal Cost)* Complete the following table, assuming that each unit of labor costs $75 per day.

Quantity of Labor per Day	Output per Day	Fixed Cost	Variable Cost	Total Cost	Marginal Cost
0	_____	$300	$_____	$_____	$_____
1	5	_____	75	_____	15
2	11	_____	150	450	12.5
3	15	_____	_____	525	_____
4	18	_____	300	600	25
5	20	_____	_____	_____	37.5

a. Graph the fixed cost, variable cost, and total cost curves for these data.

b. What is the marginal product of going from two to three units of labor?

c. What is average total cost when output is 18 units per day?

19. *(Total Cost and Marginal Cost)* Complete the following table, where L is units of labor, Q is units of output, and MP is the marginal product of labor.

L	Q	MP	VC	TC	MC	ATC
0	0	____	$ 0	$12	___	___
1	6	____	3	15	___	___
2	15	____	6		___	___
3	21	____	9		___	___
4	24	____	12		___	___
5	26	____	15		___	___

a. At what level of labor input do the marginal returns to labor begin to diminish?

b. What is the average variable cost when $Q = 24$?

c. What is this firm's fixed cost?

d. What is the wage rate per day?

20. *(Relationship Between Marginal Cost and Average Cost)* Assume that labor and capital are the only inputs used by a firm. Capital is fixed at 5 units, which cost $100 each. Workers can be hired for $200 each. Complete the following table to show average variable cost (AVC), average total cost (ATC), and marginal cost (MC).

Quantity of Labor	Total Output	AVC	ATC	MC
0	0	___	___	___
1	100	___	___	___
2	250	___	___	___
3	350	___	___	___
4	400	___	___	___
5	425	___	___	___

21. *(Long-Run Costs)* Suppose the firm has only three possible scales of production as shown below:

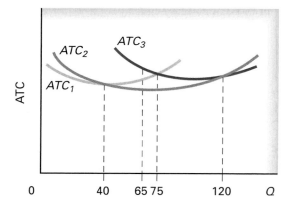

a. Which scale of production is most efficient when $Q = 65$?

b. Which scale of production is most efficient when $Q = 75$?

c. Trace out the long-run average cost curve on the diagram.

EXPERIENTIAL EXERCISES

22. *(Short- and Long-Run Costs)* The terms "diminishing returns" and "economies of scale" are often referred to in everyday discussions and in the popular press. Using an Internet search engine, search for diminishing returns or economies of scale. Check the first five sites you find and, in each case, decide whether the term is being used correctly or incorrectly. If the latter, see if you can determine the nature of the writer's confusion. For example, check "The Concepts of Increasing and Diminishing Returns" (http://www.useit.com/alertbox/increasingreturns.html), in which the author manages to compare a short-run concept—diminishing (marginal) returns—with a long-run concept—increasing returns (to scale).

23. *(Costs in the Long Run)* Find Erik Brynjolfsson and Shinkyu Yang's "Information Technology and Productivity: A Review of the Literature," available online at http://ccs.mit.edu/papers/ccswp202/. Using the concepts you learned in this chapter, try to explain the expected long-run impact of information technology on productivity and costs.

24. *(Wall Street Journal)* A firm's cost curves are based on the prices of the inputs it uses and on the firm's technology. Technology is the way the inputs are combined to produce a product. The "Technology" column in the Marketplace section of the *Wall Street Journal* describes many in-

teresting technological innovations. Pick one and see if you can determine how it might affect a firm's cost curves. Will it cause one resource to be substituted for another? Try to guess both the short-run and long-run effects.

HOMEWORK XPRESS! EXERCISES

These exercises require access to McEachern Homework Xpress! If Homework Xpress! did not come with your book, visit **http://homeworkxpress.swlearning.com** *to purchase.*

1. The total product of workers added to the production line at Charles Cobbler, maker of fine shoes, is shown in the table. Find the marginal product for each additional worker. Plot the points indicating increasing marginal returns and identify. Then plot the points representing diminishing but positive marginal returns and identify, and plot the points representing negative marginal returns and identify them. Include any border points in each section.

Workers per day	Total product
0	0
1	3
2	7
3	12
4	16
5	19
6	21
7	22
8	22
9	21

2. Charles Cobbler faces typical short-run cost functions. The firm's fixed costs are $200 per day, and workers cost $100 per day. Draw a line to represent fixed costs. Then draw in curves to represent variable cost and total cost.

3. Charles Cobbler, who continues to make fine shoes, faces typical short-run cost curves. Draw a curve that would represent marginal cost of production for this firm. Then draw in curves that would represent average total cost and average variable cost of production for this firm.

4. Industries in which small, medium, and large firms all compete are usually characterized by economies of scale initially, followed by a long range of constant returns to scale before eventually running into diseconomies of scale. In the diagram draw in a long-run average cost curve for such an industry where economies of scale are exhausted at a quantity of 100 and diseconomies of scale begin at quantities greater than 1,000.

A Closer Look at Production and Costs

This appendix develops a model for determining how a profit-maximizing firm will combine resources to produce a particular rate of output. The quantity of output that can be produced with a given amount of resources depends on the existing *state of technology,* which is the prevailing knowledge of how resources can be combined. Therefore, let's begin by considering the technological possibilities available to the firm.

The Production Function and Efficiency

The ways in which resources can be combined to produce output are summarized by a firm's production function. The *production function* identifies the maximum quantities of a particular good or service that can be produced per time period with various combinations of resources, for a given level of technology. The production function can be presented as an equation, a graph, or a table.

The production function summarized in Exhibit 11 reflects, for a hypothetical firm, the output resulting from particular combinations of resources. This firm uses only two resources: capital and labor. The amount of capital used is listed down the left side of the table, and the amount of labor employed is listed across the top. For example, if 1 unit of capital is combined with 7 units of labor, the firm can produce 290 units of output per month. The firm produces the maximum possible output given the combination of resources used; that same output could not be produced with fewer resources. Because the production function combines resources efficiently, 290 units are the most that can be produced with 7 units of labor and 1 unit of capital. Thus, we say that production is **technologically efficient.**

We can examine the effects of adding labor to an existing amount of capital by starting with any level of capital and reading across the table. For example, when the firm uses 1 unit of capital and 1 unit of labor, it produces 40 units of output per month. If the amount of labor increases by 1 unit and the amount of capital remains constant, output increases to 90 units, so the marginal product of labor is 50 units. If the amount of labor employed increases from 2 to 3 units, other things constant, output goes to 150 units, yielding a marginal product of 60 units. By reading across the table, you will discover that the marginal product of labor first

EXHIBIT 11 — A Firm's Production Function Using Labor and Capital: Production per Month

Units of Capital Employed per Month	Units of Labor Employed per Month						
	1	2	3	4	5	6	7
1	40	90	150	200	240	270	290
2	90	140	200	250	290	315	335
3	150	195	260	310	345	370	390
4	200	250	310	350	385	415	440
5	240	290	345	385	420	450	475
6	270	320	375	415	450	475	495
7	290	330	390	435	470	495	510

rises, showing increasing marginal returns from labor, and then declines, showing diminishing marginal returns. Similarly, by holding the amount of labor constant and following down the column, you will find that the marginal product of capital also reflects first increasing marginal returns and then diminishing marginal returns.

Isoquants

Notice from the tabular presentation of the production function in Exhibit 11 that different combinations of resources yield the same rate of output. For example, several combinations of labor and capital yield 290 units of output per month (try to find the four combinations). Some of the information provided in Exhibit 11 can be presented more clearly in graphical form. In Exhibit 12, labor is measured along the horizontal axis and capital along the vertical axis. Combinations that yield 290 units of output are presented in Exhibit 12 as points *a, b, c,* and *d.* These points can be connected to form an *isoquant,* Q_1, a curve that shows the possible combinations of the two resources that produce 290 units of output per month. Likewise, Q_2 shows combinations of inputs that yield 415 units of output, and Q_3, 475 units of output. (The isoquant colors match those of the corresponding entries in the production function table in Exhibit 11.)

An **isoquant,** such as Q_1 in Exhibit 12, is a curve that shows all the technologically efficient combinations of two resources, such as labor and capital, that produce a certain rate of output. *Iso* is from the Greek word meaning "equal," and *quant* is short for "quantity"; so *isoquant* means "equal quantity." Along a particular isoquant, such as Q_1, the rate of output produced remains constant—in this case, 290 units per month—but the combination of resources varies. To produce a particular rate of output, the firm can use resource combinations ranging from much capital and little labor to little capital and much labor. For example, a paving contractor can put in a new driveway with 10 workers using shovels, wheelbarrows, and hand rollers; the same job can also be done with only 2 workers, a road grader, and a paving machine. A charity car wash is labor intensive, involving many workers per car, plus buckets, sponges, and hose. In contrast, a professional car wash is fully automated, requiring only

one worker to turn on the machine and collect the money. An isoquant depicts alternative combinations of resources that produce the same rate of output. Although we have included only three isoquants in Exhibit 12, there is a different isoquant for every quantity of output listed in Exhibit 11. Indeed, there is a different isoquant for every output rate the firm could possibly produce. Let's consider some properties of isoquants:

1. Isoquants farther from the origin represent greater output rates.

2. *Isoquants have negative slopes* because along a given isoquant, the quantity of labor employed inversely relates to the quantity of capital employed.

3. *Isoquants do not intersect* because each isoquant refers to a specific rate of output. An intersection would indicate that the same combination of resources could, with equal efficiency, produce two different amounts of output.

4. *Isoquants are usually convex to the origin,* which means that any isoquant becomes flatter as you move down along the curve.

The slope of an isoquant measures the ability of additional units of one resource—in this case, labor—to substitute in production for another—in this case, capital. As noted already, the isoquant has a negative slope. The absolute value of the slope of the isoquant is the **marginal rate of technical substitution,** or **MRTS,** between two resources. The MRTS is the rate at which labor substitutes for capital without affecting output. When much capital and little labor are used, the marginal productivity of labor is relatively great and the marginal productivity of capital relatively small, so one unit of labor will substitute for a relatively large amount of capital. For example, in moving from point *a* to *b* along isoquant Q_1 in Exhibit 12, one unit of labor substitutes for two units of capital, so the MRTS between points *a* and *b* equals 2. But as more labor and less capital are employed, the marginal product of labor declines and the marginal product of capital increases, so it takes more labor to make up for a one-unit reduction in capital. For example, in moving from point *c* to point *d,* two units of labor substitute for one unit of capital; thus, the MRTS between points *c* and *d* equals $\frac{1}{2}$.

The extent to which one input substitutes for another, as measured by the marginal rate of technical substitution, is directly linked to the marginal productivity of each input. For example, between points *a* and *b,* one unit of labor replaces two units of capital, yet output remains constant. So labor's marginal product, MP_L—that is, the additional out-

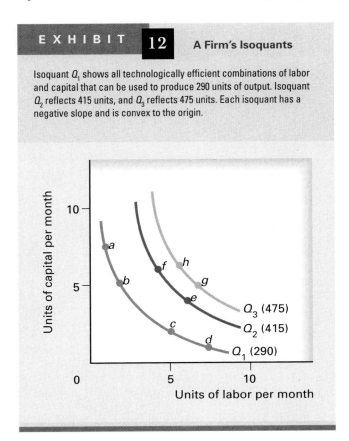

E X H I B I T   12   A Firm's Isoquants

Isoquant Q_1 shows all technologically efficient combinations of labor and capital that can be used to produce 290 units of output. Isoquant Q_2 reflects 415 units, and Q_3 reflects 475 units. Each isoquant has a negative slope and is convex to the origin.

put resulting from an additional unit of labor—must be twice as large as capital's marginal product, MP_C. In fact, *anywhere along the isoquant, the marginal rate of technical substitution of labor for capital equals the marginal product of labor divided by the marginal product of capital, which also equals the absolute value of the slope of the isoquant,* or:

$$|\text{Slope of isoquant}| = MRTS = MP_L/MP_C$$

where the vertical lines on either side of "Slope of isoquant" indicate the absolute value. For example, the slope between points *a* and *b* equals −2 and has an absolute value of 2, which equals both the marginal rate of substitution of labor for capital and the ratio of marginal productivities. Between points *b* and *c,* three units of labor substitute for three units of capital, while output is constant at 290. Thus, the slope between *b* and *c* is −3/3, for an absolute value of 1. Note that the absolute value of the isoquant's slope declines as we move down the curve because larger increases in labor are required to offset each one-unit decline in capital. Put another way, as less capital is employed, its marginal product increases, and as more labor is employed, its marginal product decreases.

If labor and capital were perfect substitutes in production, the rate at which labor substituted for capital would remain fixed along the isoquant, so the isoquant would be a downward-sloping straight line. Because most resources are *not* perfect substitutes, however, the rate at which one substitutes for another changes along an isoquant. As we move down along an isoquant, more labor is required to offset each one-unit decline in capital, so the isoquant becomes flatter and is convex to the origin.

Isocost Lines

Isoquants graphically illustrate a firm's production function for all quantities of output the firm could possibly produce. We turn now to the question of what combination of resources to employ to minimize the cost of producing a given rate of output. The answer, as we'll see, depends on the cost of resources.

Suppose a unit of labor costs the firm $1,500 per month, and a unit of capital costs $2,500 per month. The total cost (*TC*) of production per month is

$$TC = (w \times L) + (r \times C)$$
$$= \$1,500L + \$2,500C$$

where *w* is the monthly wage rate, *L* is the quantity of labor employed, *r* is the monthly cost of capital, and *C* is the quantity of capital employed. An **isocost line** identifies all combinations of capital and labor the firm can hire for a given total cost. Again, *iso* is Greek for "equal," so an isocost line is

a line representing resource combinations of equal cost. In Exhibit 13, for example, the line *TC* = $15,000 identifies all combinations of labor and capital that cost the firm $15,000 per month. The entire $15,000 could pay for either 6 units of capital or 10 units of labor per month. Or the firm could employ any other combination of resources along the isocost line.

Recall that the slope of any line is the vertical change between two points on the line divided by the corresponding horizontal change. At the point where the isocost line meets the vertical axis, the quantity of capital that can be purchased equals the total cost divided by the monthly cost of a unit of capital, or *TC/r.* At the point where the isocost line meets the horizontal axis, the quantity of labor that can be hired equals the firm's total cost divided by the monthly wage, or *TC/w.* The slope of any isocost line in Exhibit 13 can be calculated by considering a movement from the vertical intercept to the horizontal intercept. That is, we divide the vertical change (−*TC/r*) by the horizontal change (*TC/w*), as follows:

$$\text{Slope of isocost line} = -\frac{TC/r}{TC/w} = -\frac{w}{r}$$

EXHIBIT 13   **A Firm's Isocost Lines**

Each isocost line shows combinations of labor and capital that can be purchased for a given amount of total cost. The slope of each equals the negative of the monthly wage rate divided by the rental cost of capital per month. Higher costs are represented by isocost lines farther from the origin.

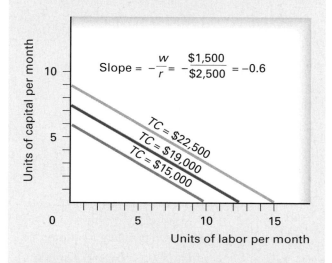

The slope of the isocost line is the negative of the price of labor divided by the price of capital, or $-w/r$, which indicates the relative prices of the inputs. In our example, the absolute value of the slope of the isocost line equals w/r, or

$$|\text{Slope of isocost line}| = w/r$$
$$= \$1,500/\$2,500$$
$$= 0.6$$

The monthly wage is 0.6, or six-tenths, of the monthly cost of a unit of capital, so hiring one more unit of labor, without changing total cost, implies that the firm must employ 0.6 fewer units of capital.

A firm is not confined to a particular isocost line. This is why Exhibit 13 includes three of them, each corresponding to a different total budget. In fact, there is a different isocost line for every possible budget. *These isocost lines are parallel because each reflects the same relative resource prices.* Resource prices in our example are assumed to be constant regardless of the amount of each resource the firm employs.

The Choice of Input Combinations

Exhibit 14 brings together the isoquants and the isocost lines. Suppose the firm has decided to produce 415 units of output and wants to minimize the cost of doing so. The firm could select point *f*, where 6 units of capital combine with 4 units of labor to produce 415 units. This combination, however, would cost $21,000 at prevailing prices. Because the profit-maximizing firm wants to produce its chosen output at the minimum cost, it tries to find the isocost line closest to the origin that still touches the isoquant. The isoquant for 415 units of output is tangent to the isocost line at point *e*. From that point of tangency, any movement in either direction along an isoquant increases the cost. So *the tangency between the isocost line and the isoquant shows the minimum cost required to produce a given output.*

Look at what's going on at the point of tangency. At point *e* in Exhibit 14, the isoquant and the isocost line have the same slope. As mentioned already, the absolute value of the slope of an isoquant equals the *marginal rate of technical substitution* between labor and capital, and the absolute value of the slope of the isocost line equals the *ratio of the input prices.* So when a firm produces output in the least costly way, the marginal rate of technical substitution must equal the ratio of the resource prices, or:

$$\text{MRTS} = w/r = \$1,500/\$2,500 = 0.6$$

This equality shows that the firm adjusts resource use so that the rate at which one input substitutes for another in production—that is, the marginal rate of technical substitution—equals the rate at

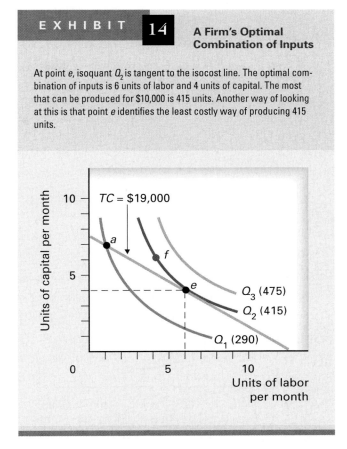

EXHIBIT 14 **A Firm's Optimal Combination of Inputs**

At point *e*, isoquant Q_2 is tangent to the isocost line. The optimal combination of inputs is 6 units of labor and 4 units of capital. The most that can be produced for $10,000 is 415 units. Another way of looking at this is that point *e* identifies the least costly way of producing 415 units.

which one resource exchanges for another in resource markets, which is w/r. If this equality does not hold, the firm could adjust its input mix to produce the same output for a lower cost.

The Expansion Path

Imagine a set of isoquants representing each possible rate of output. Given the relative cost of resources, we could then draw isocost lines to determine the optimal combination of resources for producing each rate of output. The points of tangency in Exhibit 15 show the least-cost input combinations for producing several output rates. For example, output rate Q_2 can be produced most cheaply using C units of capital and L units of labor. The line formed by connecting these tangency points is the firm's **expansion path.** The expansion path need not be a straight line, although it will generally slope upward, indicating that the firm will expand the use of both resources in the long run as output increases. Note that we have assumed that the prices of inputs remain constant as the firm varies output along the expansion path, so the isocost lines at the points of tangency are parallel—that is, they have the same slope.

Points of tangency between isoquants and isocost lines identify the least costly resource combination of producing each particular quantity of output. Connecting these tangency points traces out the firm's expansion path.

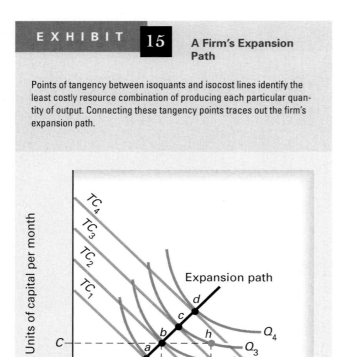

We can use Exhibit 15 to distinguish between short-run and long-run adjustments in output. Let's begin with the firm producing Q_2 at point b, which requires C units of capital and L units of labor. Now suppose that in the short run, the firm wants to increase output to Q_3. Because capital is fixed in the short run, the only way to produce Q_3 is by increasing the quantity of labor employed to L', which requires moving to point h in Exhibit 15. Point h is not the cheapest way to produce Q_3 in the long run because it is not a tangency point. In the long run, capital is variable, and if the firm wishes to produce Q_3, it should minimize total cost by adjusting from point h to point c.

One final point: If the relative prices of resources change, the least-cost resource combination will also change, so the firm's expansion path will change. For example, if the price of labor increases, capital becomes cheaper relative to labor. The efficient production of any given rate of output will therefore call for less labor and more capital. With the cost of labor higher, the firm's total cost for each rate of output rises. Such a cost increase would also be reflected by an upward shift of the average total cost curve.

Summary

A firm's *production function* specifies the relationship between resource use and output, given prevailing technology. An *isoquant* is a curve that illustrates the possible combinations of resources that will produce a particular rate of output. An *isocost* line presents the combinations of resources the firm can employ, given resource prices and the firm's total budget. For a given rate of output—that is, for a given isoquant—the firm minimizes total cost by choosing the lowest isocost line that just touches, or is tangent to, the isoquant. The least-cost combination of resources depends on the productivity of resources and their relative cost. Economists believe that although firm owners may not understand the material in this appendix, they must act as if they do to maximize profit.

The expansion path indicates the lowest long-run total cost for each rate of output. For example, the firm can produce output rate Q_2 for TC_2, output rate Q_3 for TC_3, and so on. Similarly, the firm's long-run average cost curve indicates, at each rate of output, the total cost divided by the rate of output. The firm's expansion path and the firm's long-run average cost curve represent alternative ways of portraying costs in the long run, given resource prices and technology.

APPENDIX QUESTIONS

1. *(Choice of Input Combinations)* Suppose that a firm's cost per unit of labor is $100 per day and its cost per unit of capital is $400 per day.

   a. Draw the isocost line for a total cost per day of $2,000. Label the axes.

   b. If the firm is producing efficiently, what is the mar-

   ginal rate of technical substitution between labor and capital?

   c. Demonstrate your answer to part (b) using isocost lines and isoquant curves.

2. *(The Expansion Path)* How are the expansion path and the long-run average cost curve related?

Perfect Competition

© Photodisc/Getty Images

W hat does a bushel of wheat have in common with a share of Microsoft stock? Why might a firm continue to operate even though it's losing money? Why do many firms fail to earn an economic profit? In what sense can it be said that the more competitive the industry, the less individual firms compete with each other? What's the difference between making stuff right and making the right stuff? And what's so perfect about perfect competition? To answer these and other questions, we examine our first market structure—perfect competition.

The previous chapter developed cost curves for an individual firm in the short run and in the long run. In light of these costs, how much should a firm produce and what price should it charge? To discover the firm's profit-maximizing output and price, we revisit an old friend—demand. Demand and supply, together, guide the firm to maximum economic profit. In the next few chapters, we will examine how firms respond to their economic environments in deciding what to supply, in what quantities, and at what price. We continue to assume that firms try to maximize profit. Topics discussed include:

- Market structure
- Price takers
- Marginal revenue
- Golden rule of profit maximization
- Loss minimization

- Short-run supply curve
- Long-run supply curve
- Competition and efficiency
- Producer surplus
- Gains from exchange

An Introduction to Perfect Competition

MARKET STRUCTURE

Important features of a market, such as the number of firms, product uniformity across firms, firms' ease of entry and exit, and forms of competition

Market structure describes the important features of a market, such as the number of suppliers (are there many or few?), the product's degree of uniformity (do firms in the market supply identical products, or are there differences across firms?), the ease of entry into the market (can new firms enter easily or is entry blocked?), and the forms of competition among firms (do firms compete only based on price, or do they also compete through advertising and product differences?). The various features will become clearer as we examine each market structure in the next few chapters. *A firm's decisions about how much to produce or what price to charge depend on the structure of the market.*

Before we get started, a few words about terminology. An *industry* consists of all firms that supply output to a particular *market*, such as the auto market, the shoe market, or the wheat market. The terms *industry* and *market* are used interchangeably throughout this chapter.

Perfectly Competitive Market Structure

PERFECT COMPETITION

A market structure with many fully informed buyers and sellers of a standardized product and no obstacles to entry or exit of firms in the long run

We begin with **perfect competition,** in some ways the most basic of market structures. A *perfectly competitive* market is characterized by (1) many buyers and sellers—so many that each buys or sells only a tiny fraction of the total amount exchanged in the market; (2) firms sell a **commodity,** which is a standardized product, such as a bushel of wheat or an ounce of gold; such a product does not differ across producers; (3) buyers and sellers that are fully informed about the price and availability of all resources and products; and (4) firms and resources that are freely mobile—that is, over time they can easily enter or leave the industry without facing obstacles like patents, licenses, high capital costs, or ignorance about available technology.

COMMODITY

A standardized product, a product that does not differ across producers, such as bushels of wheat or an ounce of gold

If these conditions exist in a market, an individual buyer or seller has no control over the price. Price is determined by market demand and supply. Once the market establishes the price, each firm is free to produce whatever quantity maximizes profit. *A perfectly competitive firm is so small relative to the size of the market that the firm's choice about how much to produce has no effect on the market price.* Examples of perfectly competitive markets include those for most agricultural products, such as wheat, corn, and livestock; markets for basic commodities, such as gold, silver, and copper; markets for widely traded stock, such as Microsoft, Citibank, and General Electric; and markets for foreign exchange, such as yen, euros, and pesos. Again, there are so many buyers and sellers that the actions of any one cannot influence the market price. For example, about 150,000 farmers in the United States raise hogs, and tens of millions of U.S. households buy pork products.

The model of perfect competition allows us to make a number of predictions that hold up well when compared to the real world. Perfect competition is also an important benchmark for evaluating the efficiency of other types of markets. Let's look at demand under perfect competition.

Demand Under Perfect Competition

Suppose the market in question is the world market for wheat and the firm in question is a wheat farm. In the world market for wheat, there are tens of thousands of farms, so any one supplies only a tiny fraction of market output. For example, the thousands of wheat farmers in Kansas together produce less than 3 percent of the world's supply of wheat. In Exhibit 1, the market price of wheat of $5 per bushel is determined in panel (a) by the intersection of the market demand curve *D* and the market supply curve *S*. Once the market determines the price, any farmer can sell all he or she wants to at that market price.

Each farm is so small relative to the market that each has no impact on the market price. Because all farmers produce an identical product—bushels of wheat, in this case—anyone who charges more than the market price sells no wheat. For example, a farmer charging $5.05 per bushel would find no buyers. Of course, any farmer is free to charge less than the market price, but why do that when all wheat can be sold at the market price? Farmers aren't stupid (or if they are, they don't last long). *The demand curve facing an individual farmer is, therefore, a horizontal line drawn at the market price.* In our example, the demand curve facing an individual farmer, identified as *d* in panel (b), is drawn at the market price of $5 per

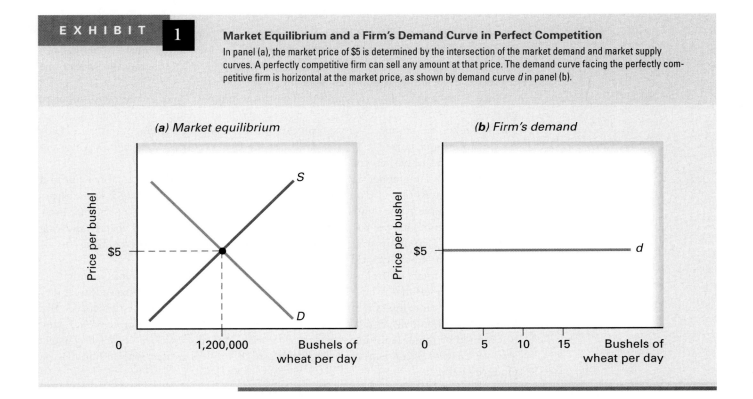

EXHIBIT 1

Market Equilibrium and a Firm's Demand Curve in Perfect Competition

In panel (a), the market price of $5 is determined by the intersection of the market demand and market supply curves. A perfectly competitive firm can sell any amount at that price. The demand curve facing the perfectly competitive firm is horizontal at the market price, as shown by demand curve *d* in panel (b).

(a) Market equilibrium

(b) Firm's demand

bushel. Thus, each farmer faces a horizontal, or a *perfectly elastic,* demand curve. A perfectly competitive firm is called a **price taker** because that firm must "take," or accept, the market price—as in "take it or leave it."

It has been said, "In perfect competition there is no competition." Ironically, two neighboring wheat farmers in perfect competition are not really rivals. They both can sell all they want at the market price. The amount one sells has no effect on the market price or amount the other can sell.

Short-Run Profit Maximization

Each firm tries to maximize economic profit. Firms that ignore this strategy don't survive. Economic profit equals total revenue minus total cost, including both explicit and implicit costs. Implicit cost, you will recall, is the opportunity cost of resources owned by the firm and includes a normal profit. Economic profit is any profit above normal profit. How do firms maximize profit? You have already learned that the perfectly competitive firm has no control over price. What the firm does control is the rate of output—the quantity. The question the wheat farmer asks boils down to: *How much should I produce to earn the most profit?*

Total Revenue Minus Total Cost

The firm maximizes economic profit by finding the quantity at which total revenue exceeds total cost by the greatest amount. The firm's total revenue is simply its output times the price per unit. Column (1) in Exhibit 2 shows an individual farmer's output possibilities measured in bushels of wheat per day. Column (2) shows the market price per bushel of $5, a price that does not vary with the farmer's output. Column (3) shows total revenue, which is output times price, or column (1) times column (2). And column (4) shows the total cost of production. Total cost already includes a normal profit, so total cost includes all opportunity costs. Although the table does not distinguish between fixed and variable costs, fixed cost must equal $15 per day, because total cost is $15 when output is zero. The presence of fixed cost tells us that at least one resource is fixed, so the farm must be operating in the short run.

Total revenue in column (3) minus total cost in column (4) yields the farmer's economic profit or economic loss in column (7). As you can see, total revenue exceeds total cost when 7 to 14 bushels are produced, so the farm earns an *economic profit* at those output rates. Economic profit is maximized at $12 per day when the farm produces 12 bushels of wheat per day (the $12 and 12 bushels combination is just a coincidence).

These results are graphed in panel (a) of Exhibit 3, which shows the total revenue and total cost curves. As output increases by 1 bushel, total revenue increases by $5, so the farm's total revenue curve is a straight line emanating from the origin, with a slope of 5. The short-run total cost curve has the backward S shape introduced in the previous chapter, showing increasing and then diminishing marginal returns from the variable resource. Total cost always increases as more output is produced.

Subtracting total cost from total revenue is one way to find the profit-maximizing output. For output less than 7 bushels and greater than 14 bushels, total cost exceeds total revenue. The economic loss is measured by the vertical distance between the two curves. Between 7 and 14 bushels per day, total revenue exceeds total cost. The economic profit, again, is measured by the distance between the two curves. *Profit is maximized at the rate of output where total revenue exceeds total cost by the greatest amount.* Profit is greatest when 12 bushels are produced per day.

(1) Bushels of Wheat per Day (q)	(2) Marginal Revenue (Price) (p)	(3) Total Revenue (TR = q x p)	(4) Total Cost (TC)	(5) Marginal Cost (MC = ΔTC/Δq)	(6) Average Total Cost (ATC = TC/q)	(7) Economic Profit or Loss = TR − TC
0	—	$ 0	$15.00	—	—	−$15.00
1	$5	5	19.75	$4.75	$19.75	−14.75
2	5	10	23.50	3.75	11.75	−13.50
3	5	15	26.50	3.00	8.83	−11.50
4	5	20	29.00	2.50	7.25	−9.00
5	5	25	31.00	2.00	6.20	−6.00
6	5	30	32.50	1.50	5.42	−2.50
7	5	35	33.75	1.25	4.82	1.25
8	5	40	35.25	1.50	4.41	4.75
9	5	45	37.25	2.00	4.14	7.75
10	5	50	40.00	2.75	4.00	10.00
11	5	55	43.25	3.25	3.93	11.75
12	**5**	**60**	**48.00**	**4.75**	**4.00**	**12.00**
13	5	65	54.50	6.50	4.19	10.50
14	5	70	64.00	9.50	4.57	6.00
15	5	75	77.50	13.50	5.17	−2.50
16	5	80	96.00	18.50	6.00	−16.00

EXHIBIT 2

Short-Run Costs and Revenues for a Perfectly Competitive Firm

Marginal Revenue Equals Marginal Cost

Another way to find the profit-maximizing rate of output is to focus on marginal revenue and marginal cost. **Marginal revenue,** or *MR,* is the change in total revenue from selling another unit of output. In perfect competition, each firm is a price taker, so selling one more unit increases total revenue by the market price. Thus, *in perfect competition, marginal revenue is the market price*—in this example, $5. Column (2) of Exhibit 2 presents the farm's marginal revenue for each bushel of wheat.

In the previous chapter, you learned that *marginal cost* is the change in total cost from producing another unit of output. Column (5) of Exhibit 2 shows the farm's marginal cost for each bushel of wheat. Marginal cost first declines, reflecting increasing marginal returns in the short run as more of the variable resource is employed. Marginal cost then increases, reflecting diminishing marginal returns from the variable resource.

The firm will increase production as long as each additional unit adds more to total revenue than to total cost—that is, as long as marginal revenue exceeds marginal cost. Comparing columns (2) and (5) in Exhibit 2, we see that marginal revenue exceeds marginal cost for each of the first 12 bushels of wheat. The marginal cost of bushel 13, however, is $6.50, compared with its marginal revenue of $5. Therefore, producing bushel 13 would reduce economic profit by $1.50. The farmer, as a profit maximizer, will limit output to 12 bushels per day. More

MARGINAL REVENUE

The change in total revenue from selling an additional unit; in perfect competition, marginal revenue is also the market price

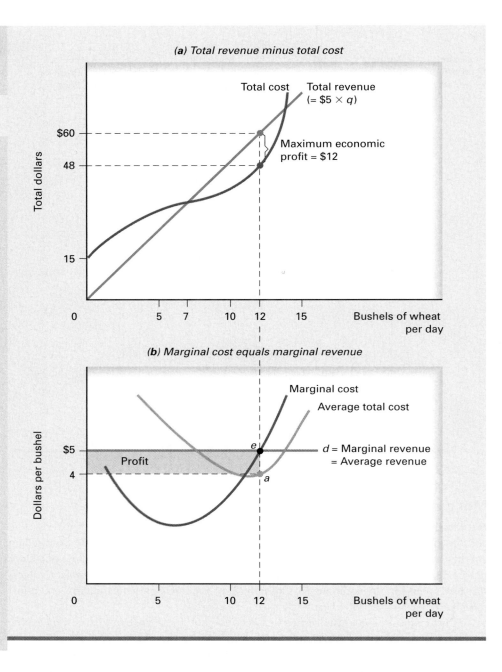

EXHIBIT 3

**Short-Run Profit
Maximization**

In panel (a), the total revenue curve for
a competitive firm is a straight line with
a slope of 5, the market price. Total cost
increases with output, first at a decreasing rate and then at an increasing
rate. Economic profit is maximized
where total revenue exceeds total cost
by the greatest amount, which occurs
at 12 bushels of wheat per day. In panel
(b), marginal revenue is a horizontal line
at the market price of $5. Economic
profit is maximized at 12 bushels of
wheat per day, where marginal revenue
equals marginal cost (point *e*). That
profit equals 12 bushels multiplied by
the amount by which the market price
of $5 exceeds the average total cost of
$4. Economic profit is identified by the
shaded rectangle.

(a) Total revenue minus total cost

(b) Marginal cost equals marginal revenue

**GOLDEN RULE OF PROFIT
MAXIMIZATION**

To maximize profit or minimize loss,
a firm should produce the quantity
at which marginal revenue equals
marginal cost; this rule holds for all
market structures

generally, a firm will expand output as long as marginal revenue exceeds marginal cost and
will stop expanding before marginal cost exceeds marginal revenue. A shorthand expression
for this approach is the **golden rule of profit maximization,** which says that a profit-
maximizing firm produces the quantity where *marginal revenue equals marginal cost.*

Economic Profit in the Short Run

Per-unit revenue and cost data from Exhibit 2 are graphed in panel (b) of Exhibit 3. Because marginal revenue in perfect competition equals the market price, the marginal revenue curve is a horizontal line at the market price of $5, which is also the perfectly competitive firm's demand curve. At any quantity measured along the demand curve, marginal revenue is the price. Because the perfectly competitive firm can sell any quantity for the same price per unit, marginal revenue is also **average revenue,** or *AR*. Average revenue equals total revenue divided by quantity, or $AR = TR/q$. Regardless of the output rate, therefore, the following equality holds along a perfectly competitive firm's demand curve:

AVERAGE REVENUE

Total revenue divided by output, or $AR = TR/q$; in all market structures, average revenue equals the market price

Market price = Marginal revenue = Average revenue

The marginal cost curve intersects the marginal revenue curve at point *e,* where output is about 12 bushels per day. At lower rates of output, marginal revenue exceeds marginal cost, so the farm could increase profit by expanding output. At higher rates of output, marginal cost exceeds marginal revenue, so the farm could increase profit by reducing output. Profit itself appears as the shaded rectangle. The height of that rectangle, *ae,* equals the price (or average revenue) of $5 minus the average total cost of $4. Price minus average total cost yields an average profit of $1 per bushel. Profit per day, $12, equals the average profit per bushel, $1 (denoted by *ae*), times the 12 bushels produced.

Note that with the total cost and total revenue curves, we measure economic profit by the vertical *distance* between the two curves, as shown in panel (a). But with the per-unit curves of panel (b), we measure economic profit by an *area*—that is, by multiplying the average profit of $1 per bushel times the 12 bushels sold.

Minimizing Short-Run Losses

An individual firm in perfect competition has no control over the market price. Sometimes that price may be so low that a firm loses money no matter how much it produces. Such a firm can either continue to produce at a loss or temporarily shut down. But even if the firm shuts down, it cannot, *in the short run,* go out of business or produce something else. The short run is by definition a period too short to allow existing firms to leave the industry. In a sense, firms are stuck in their industry in the short run.

Fixed Cost and Minimizing Losses

So should a firm produce at a loss or temporarily shut down? Intuition suggests the firm should shut down. But it's not that simple. Keep in mind that the firm faces two types of cost in the short run: fixed cost, such as property taxes and fire insurance, which must be paid in the short run even if the firm produces nothing, and variable cost, such as labor, which depends on the amount of output the firm wants to produce. A firm that shuts down in the short run must still pay its fixed cost. But, by producing, a firm's revenue may pay variable cost and also cover a portion of fixed cost. What this boils down to is that *a firm will produce rather than shut down if total revenue exceeds the variable cost of production.* After all, if total revenue exceeds variable cost, that excess can go toward covering at least a portion of fixed cost.

Let's look at the same cost data presented in Exhibit 2, but now suppose the market price of wheat is $3 a bushel, not $5. This new situation is presented in Exhibit 4. Because of the lower price, total revenue is less than total cost at all output rates. Each quantity thus results in a loss, as indicated by Column (8). If the firm produces nothing, it loses the fixed cost of $15 per day. But, by producing anywhere from 6 and 12 bushels, the firm can reduce that

E X H I B I T **4**   **Minimizing Short-Run Losses**

(1) Bushels of Wheat per Day (q)	(2) Marginal Revenue (Price) (p)	(3) Total Revenue (TR = q × p)	(4) Total Cost (TC)	(5) Marginal Cost (MC = ΔTC/Δq)	(6) Average Total Cost (ATC = TC/q)	(7) Average Variable Cost (AVC = VC/q)	(8) Economic Profit or Loss = TR − TC
0	—	$ 0	$15.00	—	—	—	−$15.00
1	$3	3	19.75	$4.75	$19.75	$4.75	−16.75
2	3	6	23.50	3.75	11.75	4.25	−17.50
3	3	9	26.50	3.00	8.83	3.83	−17.50
4	3	12	29.00	2.50	7.25	3.50	−17.00
5	3	15	31.00	2.00	6.20	3.20	−16.00
6	3	18	32.50	1.50	5.42	2.92	−14.50
7	3	21	33.75	1.25	4.82	2.68	−12.75
8	3	24	35.25	1.50	4.41	2.53	−11.25
9	3	27	37.25	2.00	4.14	2.47	−10.25
10	**3**	**30**	**40.00**	**2.75**	**4.00**	**2.50**	**−10.00**
11	3	33	43.25	3.25	3.93	2.57	−10.25
12	3	36	48.00	4.75	4.00	2.75	−12.00
13	3	39	54.50	6.50	4.19	3.04	−15.50
14	3	42	64.00	9.50	4.57	3.50	−22.00
15	3	45	77.50	13.50	5.17	4.17	−32.50
16	3	48	96.00	18.50	6.00	5.06	−48.00

loss. From column (8), you can see that the loss is minimized at $10 per day where 10 bushels are produced. Producing that amount adds $25 to total cost but adds $30 to total revenue. The net gain of $5 can pay some of the firm's fixed cost.

Panel (a) of Exhibit 5 presents the firm's total cost and total revenue curves for data in Exhibit 4. The total cost curve remains as before in Exhibit 3. Because the price is $3, the total revenue curve now has a slope of 3, so it's flatter than at a price of $5. The total revenue curve now lies below the total cost curve at all quantities. The vertical distance between the two curves measures the loss at each quantity. If the farmer produces nothing, the loss is the fixed cost of $15 per day. The vertical distance between the two curves is minimized at 10 bushels, where the loss is $10 per day.

Marginal Revenue Equals Marginal Cost

We get the same result using marginal analysis. The per-unit data from Exhibit 4 are presented in panel (b) of Exhibit 5. First we find the rate of output where marginal revenue

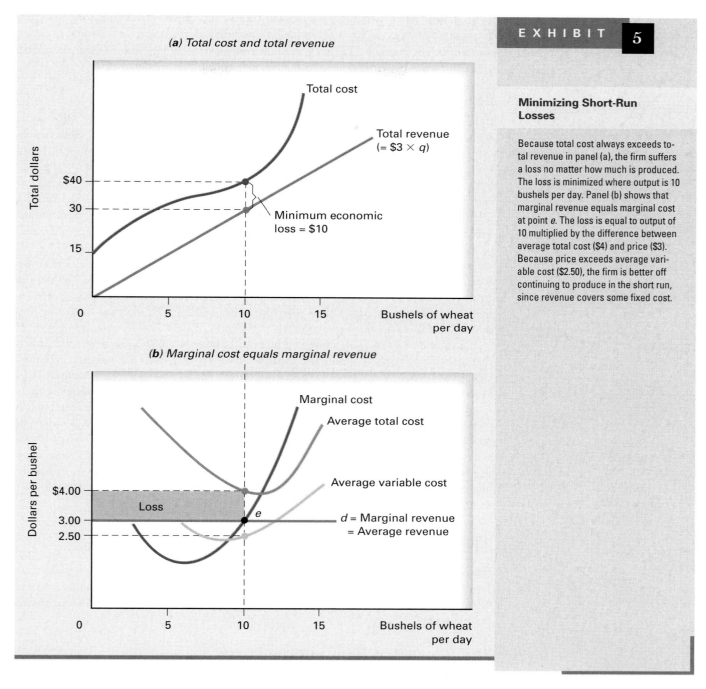

(a) Total cost and total revenue

(b) Marginal cost equals marginal revenue

Minimizing Short-Run Losses

Because total cost always exceeds to-tal revenue in panel (a), the firm suffers a loss no matter how much is produced. The loss is minimized where output is 10 bushels per day. Panel (b) shows that marginal revenue equals marginal cost at point *e*. The loss is equal to output of 10 multiplied by the difference between average total cost ($4) and price ($3). Because price exceeds average vari-able cost ($2.50), the firm is better off continuing to produce in the short run, since revenue covers some fixed cost.

equals marginal cost. Marginal revenue equals marginal cost at an output of 10 bushels per day. At that output, the market price of $3 exceeds the average variable cost of $2.50. Be-cause price exceeds average variable cost, total revenue covers variable cost plus a portion of fixed cost. Specifically, $2.50 of the price pays the average variable cost, and the remaining $0.50 helps pay some of average fixed cost (average fixed cost equals average total cost of $4.00 minus average variable cost of $2.50). This still leaves a loss of $1 per bushel, which when multiplied by 10 bushels yields an economic loss of $10 per day, identified in panel (b) by the shaded rectangle. *The bottom line is that the firm will produce rather than shut down if there is some rate of output where the price at least covers average variable cost.* (Why is the farmer in the short run better off operating at a loss rather than shutting down?)

Shutting Down in the Short Run

If the loss that results from producing is less than the shutdown loss, the farmer will produce in the short run. You may have read or heard of firms reporting a loss; most continue to operate. In fact, many new firms lose money during the first few years of operations because they expect to be profitable eventually (for example, the upstart TV network UPN lost $1 billion during its first five years[1]). But *if the average variable cost exceeds the price at all rates of output, the firm will shut down.* After all, why produce if doing so only increases the loss? For example, a wheat price of $2 would be below the average variable cost at all rates of output. Faced with such a low price, a farmer would shut down and lose just fixed cost, rather than produce and lose both fixed cost plus some variable cost.

From column (7) of Exhibit 4, you can also see that the lowest price at which the farmer would just cover average variable cost is $2.47 per bushel, when output is 9 bushels per day. At this price, the farmer is indifferent about producing or shutting down, because either way the loss is the $15 per day in fixed cost. Any price above $2.47 allows the farmer, by producing, to also cover some fixed cost.

Shutting down is not the same as going out of business. In the short run, even a firm that shuts down keeps its productive capacity intact—paying for rent, insurance, and property taxes, keeping water pipes from freezing in the winter, and so on. For example, Dairy Queen shuts down for the winter in cooler climates, a business serving a college community may close during term breaks, and an auto plant responds to slack sales by temporarily halting production. These firms do not escape fixed cost by shutting down. When demand picks up, production will resume. If the market outlook remains grim, the firm may decide to leave the market, but that's a long-run decision. The short run is defined as a period during which some costs are fixed, so a firm cannot escape those costs in the short run, no matter what it does. *Fixed cost is sunk cost in the short run, whether the firm produces or shuts down.*

The Firm and Industry Short-Run Supply Curves

If average variable cost exceeds price at all output rates, the firm will shut down in the short run. But if price exceeds average variable cost, the firm will produce the quantity at which marginal revenue equals marginal cost. As we'll see, a firm will alter quantity if the market price changes.

The Short-Run Firm Supply Curve

The relationship between price and quantity is summarized in Exhibit 6. Points 1, 2, 3, 4, and 5 identify where the marginal cost curve intersects various marginal revenue, or demand, curves. At a price as low as p_1, the firm will shut down rather than produce at point 1 because that price is below average variable cost. So the loss-minimizing output rate at price p_1 is zero, as identified by q_1. At price p_2, that price just equals average variable cost, so the

---

1. Joe Flint, "Will Viacom's Big Bet on 'Buffy' Become UPN's Savior or Slayer," *Wall Street Journal*, 12 July 2001.

firm will be indifferent about producing q_2 or shutting down; either way the firm loses fixed cost. Point 2 is called the *shutdown point*. If the price is p_3, the firm will produce q_3 to minimize its loss (see if you can identify that loss in the diagram). At p_4, the firm will produce q_4 to earn just a normal profit, because price equals average total cost. Point 4 is called the *break-even point*. If the price rises to p_5, the firm will earn short-run economic profit by producing q_5 (see if you can identify that economic profit).

As long as the price covers average variable cost, the firm will supply the quantity at which the upward-sloping marginal cost curve intersects the marginal revenue, or demand, curve. Thus, that portion of the firm's marginal cost curve that intersects and rises above the lowest point on its average variable cost curve becomes the **short-run firm supply curve**. In Exhibit 6, the short-run supply curve is the upward-sloping portion of the marginal cost curve, beginning at point 2, the shutdown point. The solid portion of the short-run supply curve indicates the quantity the firm offers for sale at each price. The quantity supplied when the price is p_2 or higher is determined by the intersection of the firm's marginal cost curve and its demand, or marginal revenue, curve. At prices below p_2, the firm shuts down in the short run.

The Short-Run Industry Supply Curve

Exhibit 7 presents examples of how supply curves for three firms with identical marginal cost curves can be summed *horizontally* to form the short-run industry supply curve (in perfect competition, there will be many more firms). The **short-run industry supply curve** is the horizontal sum of all firms' short-run supply curves. At a price below p, no

SHORT-RUN FIRM SUPPLY CURVE

A curve that shows the quantity a firm supplies at each price in the short run; in perfect competition, that portion of a firm's marginal cost curve that intersects and rises above the low point on its average variable cost curve

SHORT-RUN INDUSTRY SUPPLY CURVE

A curve that indicates the quantity supplied by the industry at each price in the short run; in perfect competition, the horizontal sum of each firm's short-run supply curve

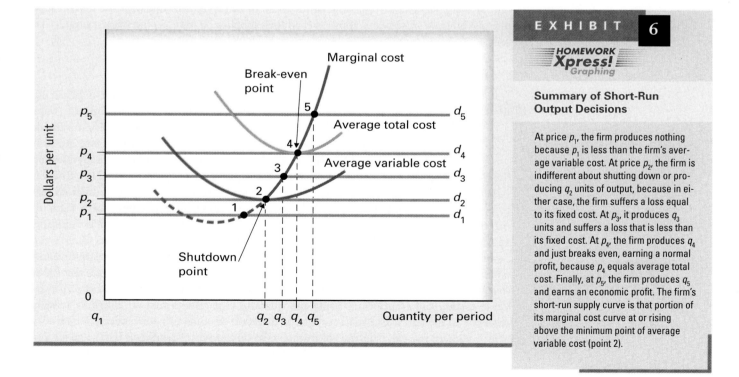

EXHIBIT 6

HOMEWORK Xpress! Graphing

Summary of Short-Run Output Decisions

At price p_1, the firm produces nothing because p_1 is less than the firm's average variable cost. At price p_2, the firm is indifferent about shutting down or producing q_2 units of output, because in either case, the firm suffers a loss equal to its fixed cost. At p_3, it produces q_3 units and suffers a loss that is less than its fixed cost. At p_4, the firm produces q_4 and just breaks even, earning a normal profit, because p_4 equals average total cost. Finally, at p_5, the firm produces q_5 and earns an economic profit. The firm's short-run supply curve is that portion of its marginal cost curve at or rising above the minimum point of average variable cost (point 2).

EXHIBIT

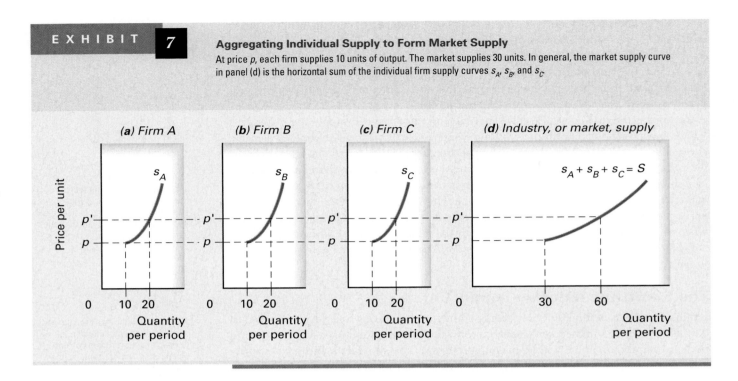

EXHIBIT **7**

Aggregating Individual Supply to Form Market Supply

At price p, each firm supplies 10 units of output. The market supplies 30 units. In general, the market supply curve in panel (d) is the horizontal sum of the individual firm supply curves s_A, s_B, and s_C

output is supplied. At price p, each of the three firms supplies 10 units, for the market supplies 30 units. At p', which is above p, each firm supplies 20 units, so the market supplies 60 units.

Firm Supply and Market Equilibrium

Exhibit 8 shows the relationship between the short-run profit-maximizing output of the individual firm and market equilibrium price and quantity. Suppose there are 100,000 identical wheat farmers in this industry. Their individual supply curves (represented by the portions of the marginal cost curve at or rising above the average variable cost) are summed horizontally to yield the market, or industry, supply curve. The market supply curve appears in panel (b), where it intersects the market demand curve to determine the market price of $5 per bushel. At that price, each farmer supplies 12 bushels per day, as shown in panel (a), which sums to 1,200,000 bushels for the market, as shown in panel (b). Each farmer in the short run earns an economic profit of $12 per day, represented by the shaded rectangle in panel (a).

In summary: *A perfectly competitive firm supplies the short-run quantity that maximizes profit or minimizes loss. When confronting a loss, a firm either supplies an output that minimizes that loss or shuts down temporarily.* Given the conditions for perfect competition, the market will converge toward the equilibrium price and quantity. But how is that equilibrium actually reached? In the real world, markets operate based on customs and conventions, which vary across markets. For example, the rules acceptable on the New York Stock Exchange are not the same as those followed in the market for fresh fish. The following case study discusses one mechanism for reaching equilibrium—auctions.

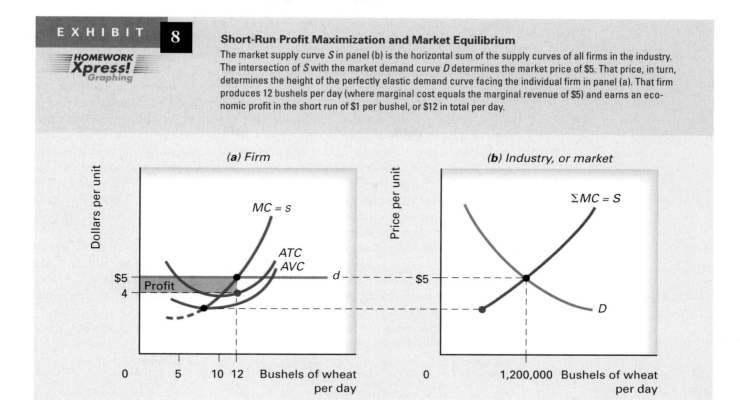

EXHIBIT 8

≡HOMEWORK≡
Xpress!
Graphing

Short-Run Profit Maximization and Market Equilibrium

The market supply curve *S* in panel (b) is the horizontal sum of the supply curves of all firms in the industry. The intersection of *S* with the market demand curve *D* determines the market price of $5. That price, in turn, determines the height of the perfectly elastic demand curve facing the individual firm in panel (a). That firm produces 12 bushels per day (where marginal cost equals the marginal revenue of $5) and earns an economic profit in the short run of $1 per bushel, or $12 in total per day.

(a) Firm

Dollars per unit

MC = s

ATC
AVC

$5
4
Profit
d

0   5   10 12   Bushels of wheat per day

(b) Industry, or market

Price per unit

ΣMC = S

$5

D

0   1,200,000   Bushels of wheat per day

Auction Markets

Five days a week, in a huge building 10 miles outside Amsterdam, some 2,500 buyers gather to participate in Flower Auction Holland, the largest auction of its kind in the world. Over 14 million flowers from 5,600 growers around the globe are auctioned off each day in the world's largest commercial building, spread across the equivalent of 100 football fields. Flowers are grouped and auctioned off by type—long-stemmed roses, tulips, and so on. Hundreds of buyers are seated in theater settings with their fingers on buttons. Once the flowers are presented, a clock-like instrument starts ticking off descending prices until a buyer pushes a button. The winning bidder gets to choose how many and which items to take. The clock starts again until another buyer stops it, and so on, until all flowers are sold. Buyers can also bid from remote locations over the Internet. Auctions occur rapidly—on average a transaction occurs every 4 seconds.

This is an example of a *Dutch auction,* which starts at a high price and works down. Dutch auctions are more common when selling multiple lots of similar, though not identical, items, such as flowers in Amsterdam, tobacco in Canada, and fish in seaports around the world. Because there is some difference among the products for sale in a given market—for

© Richard Glover/Corbis

C a s e **S t u d y**

World of Business

eActivity
Are you fast enough to compete in the Dutch Flower Auction Simulation? Try your hand in a computer simulation at http://research.haifa.ac.il/~avinoy/auction/dutch/. How often did a winning bid appear before the price fell to the point where you could earn a profit? Did you lose out on any profitable opportunities? Were you tempted to bid faster and too high after losing out a few times? If so, you can return to the entry page to choose a slower clock speed. If you think you can go faster, try increasing the speed.

example, some flower lots are in better condition than others—this is not quite perfect competition because perfectly competitive markets sell identical products.

More common than the Dutch auction is the *English open outcry auction,* where bidding starts at a low price and moves up until only one buyer remains. Products sold this way include stocks, bonds, wine, art (think Sotheby's and Christie's), antiques, and livestock. For example, on markets, such as the Chicago Board of Trade, prices for commodities such as wheat, gold, and coffee beans are continuously determined in the trading pits using variations of an open outcry auction.

The birth of the Internet has breathed new life into auctions. Web sites such as eBay, Ubid, Yahoo!, and hundreds more hold online auctions for old maps, used computers, wine, airline tickets, antiques, military memorabilia, comic books, paperweights—you name it. The largest online site, eBay, offers over 2,000 categories in a forum that mimics a live auction. Internet auctions allow specialized sellers to reach a world of customers. A listing on eBay, for example, could reach millions of people in more than one hundred countries.

Computers are taking over markets in other ways. In New York, Chicago, Philadelphia, London, and Frankfurt, hand-waving traders in what seem like mosh pits are being replaced by electronic trading. The Nasdaq is the world's first virtual stock market. There is no Nasdaq trading floor as with the New York Stock Exchange. On the Matif, the French futures exchange, after electronic trading was added as an option to the open-outcry system, electronic trading dominated within a matter of months. Computers reduce the transaction costs of market exchange.

Sources: Nick Wingfield, "eBay's Results Keep a Strong Pace," *Wall Street Journal*, 17 October 2003; Michelle Slatalla, "At a Virtual Garage Sale, It Frequently Pays to Wait," *New York Times*, 2 November 2000; "We Have Lift-Off," *Economist*, 3 February 2001. The Web site for eBay is http://www.ebay.com/; Nasdaq's is http://nasdaq.com/; and the French trading exchange, Matif, is at http://www.matif.com/indexE4.htm.

Perfect Competition in the Long Run

In the short run, the quantity of variable resources can change, but other resources, which mostly determine firm size, are fixed. In the long run, however, firms have time to enter and leave and to adjust their size—that is, to adjust the *scale* of their operations. In the long run, there is no distinction between fixed and variable cost because all resources under the firm's control are variable.

Short-run economic profit will, in the long run, encourage new firms to enter the market and may prompt existing firms to get bigger. Economic profit will attract resources from industries where firms are losing money or earning only a normal profit. This expansion in the number and size of firms will shift the industry supply curve rightward in the long run, driving down the price. New firms will continue to enter a profitable industry and existing firms will continue to expand as long as economic profit is greater than zero. Entry and expansion will stop only when the resulting increase in supply drives down the price enough to erase economic profit. In the case of wheat farming, economic profit attracts new wheat farmers and may encourage existing wheat farmers to expand their scale of operation. *Short-run economic profit attracts new entrants in the long run and may cause existing firms to expand. Market supply thereby increases, driving down the market price until economic profit disappears.*

On the other hand, a short-run loss will, in the long run, force some firms to leave the industry or to reduce their scale of operation. In the long run, departures and reductions in scale shift the market supply curve to the left, thereby increasing the market price until remaining firms just break even—that is, earn a normal profit.

Zero Economic Profit in the Long Run

In the long run, firms in perfect competition earn just a normal profit, which means zero economic profit. Exhibit 9 shows a firm and the market in long-run equilibrium. In the long run, market supply adjusts as firms enter or leave or change their size. *This long-run adjustment continues until the market supply curve intersects the market demand curve at a price that corresponds to the lowest point on each firm's long-run average cost curve, or LRAC curve.* Because the long run is a period during which all resources under a firm's control can be varied, a *firm in the long run will be forced by competition to adjust its scale until its average cost of production is minimized.* A firm that fails to minimize cost will not survive in the long run. At point *e* in panel (a) of Exhibit 9, the firm is in equilibrium, producing *q* units and earning just a normal profit. At point *e*, price, marginal cost, short-run average total cost, and long-run average cost are all equal. No firm in the market has any reason to change its output rate, and no outside firm has any incentive to enter this industry, because firms in this market are earning normal, but not economic, profit.

The Long-Run Adjustment to a Change in Demand

To explore the long-run adjustment process, let's consider how a firm and an industry respond to an increase in market demand. Suppose that the costs facing each firm do not depend on the number of firms in the industry (this assumption will be explained soon).

Effects of an Increase in Demand

Exhibit 10 shows a perfectly competitive firm and industry in long-run equilibrium, with the market supply curve intersecting the market demand curve at point *a* in panel (b). The

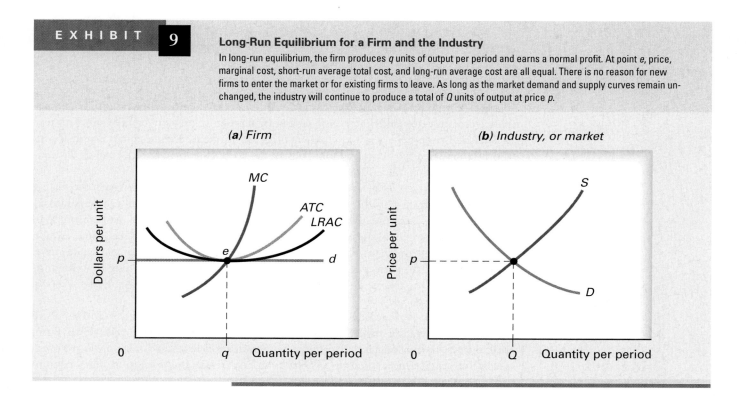

EXHIBIT	9

Long-Run Equilibrium for a Firm and the Industry

In long-run equilibrium, the firm produces *q* units of output per period and earns a normal profit. At point *e*, price, marginal cost, short-run average total cost, and long-run average cost are all equal. There is no reason for new firms to enter the market or for existing firms to leave. As long as the market demand and supply curves remain unchanged, the industry will continue to produce a total of *Q* units of output at price *p*.

(a) Firm

(b) Industry, or market

EXHIBIT 10

Long-Run Adjustment to an Increase in Demand

An increase in market demand from *D* to *D'* in panel (b) moves the short-run market equilibrium from *a* to *b*. Output rises to Q_b, and price increases to *p'*. The price increase corresponds to the rise of the firm's demand curve from *d* to *d'* in panel (a). The firm responds to the higher price by increasing output to *q'* and earns economic profit, identified by the shaded rectangle. Economic profit attracts new firms to the industry in the long run. Market supply shifts right to *S'* in panel (b), pushing the market price back down to *p*. In panel (a), the firm's demand curve shifts back down to *d*, eliminating economic profit. The short-run adjustment is from point *a* to point *b* in panel (b), but the long-run adjustment is from point *a* to point *c*.

(a) Firm

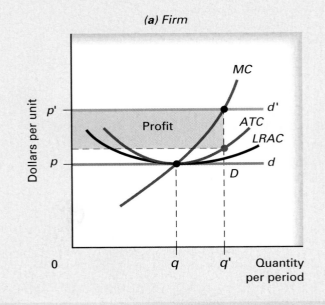

(b) Industry, or market

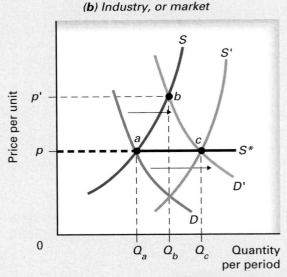

market-clearing price is *p*, and the market quantity is Q_a. The firm, shown in panel (a), supplies *q* units at that market price, earning a normal profit in long-run equilibrium. This representative firm produces at a level where price, or marginal revenue, equals marginal cost, short-run average total cost, and long-run average cost. (Remember, a normal profit is included in the firm's average total cost curve.)

Now suppose market demand increases, as reflected by a shift to the right in the market demand curve, from *D* to *D'*, causing the market price to increase in the short run to *p'*. Each firm responds to the higher price by expanding output along its short-run supply, or marginal cost, curve until the quantity supplied increases to *q'*, shown in panel (a) of Exhibit 10. At that output, the firm's marginal cost curve intersects the new marginal revenue curve, which is also the firm's new demand curve, *d'*. Because all firms expand, industry output increases to Q_b. Note that in the short run, each firm now earns an economic profit, shown by the shaded rectangle.

Economic profit attracts new firms in the long run. Their entry adds additional supply to the market, shifting the market supply curve to the right and pushing the price down. Firms continue to enter as long as they can earn economic profit. The market supply curve eventually shifts to *S'*, where it intersects *D'* at point *c*, returning the price to its initial equilibrium level, *p*. The firm's demand curve drops from *d'* back down to *d*. As a result, each firm reduces output from *q'* back to *q*, and once again, each earns just a normal profit. Notice that although industry output increases from Q_a to Q_c, each firm's output returns to *q*. In this example, the additional output comes entirely from new firms drawn to the industry rather than from more output by existing firms (existing firms don't expand in this example because an increase in scale would increase average cost).

New firms are attracted to the industry by short-run economic profits resulting from the increase in demand. But this new entry increases market supply, pushing the price down until economic profit disappears. In panel (b) of Exhibit 10, the short-run adjustment to increased demand is from point *a* to point *b*; the long-run adjustment moves to point *c*.

Effects of a Decrease in Demand

Next, let's consider the effect of a decrease in demand on the long-run market adjustment process. The initial long-run equilibrium situation in Exhibit 11 is the same as in Exhibit 10. Market demand and supply curves intersect at point *a* in panel (b), yielding the equilibrium price *p* and an equilibrium quantity Q_a. As shown in panel (a), the firm earns a normal profit in the long run by producing output rate *q*, where price, or marginal revenue, equals marginal cost, short-run average total cost, and long-run average cost.

EXHIBIT 11

Long-Run Adjustment to a Decrease in Demand

A decrease in demand to *D"* in panel (b) disturbs the long-run equilibrium at point *a*. The price is driven down to *p"* in the short run; output falls to Q_f. In panel (a), the firm's demand curve shifts down to *d"*. Each firm reduces its output to *q"* and suffers a loss. As firms leave the industry in the long run, the market supply curve shifts left to *S"*. Market price rises to *p* as output falls further to Q_g. At price *p*, the firms once again earn a normal profit. Thus, the short-run adjustment is from point *a* to point *f* in panel (b); the long-run adjustment is from point *a* to point *g*.

(a) *Firm*

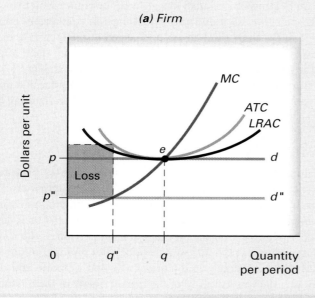

(b) *Industry or market*

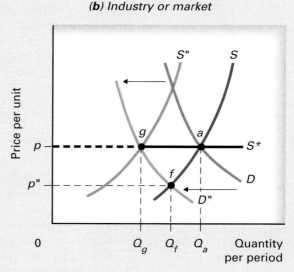

Now suppose that the demand for this product declines, as reflected by a leftward shift of the market demand curve, from D back to D''. In the short run, this reduces the market price to p''. As a result, the demand curve facing each individual firm drops from d to d''. Each firm responds in the short run by cutting its output to q'', where marginal cost equals the now-lower marginal revenue, or price. Market output falls to Q_f. Because the lower market price is below short-run average total cost, each firm operates at a loss. This loss is shown by the shaded rectangle. Note, the price must still be above the average variable cost, because the firm's short-run supply curve, *MC,* is defined as that portion of the firm's marginal cost curve at or above its average variable cost curve.

A short-run loss, if it continues, will in the long run force some firms out of business. As firms exit, market supply decreases, so the price increases. Firms continue to leave until the market supply curve decreases to S'', where it intersects D'' at point *g*. Market output has fallen to Q_g, and price has returned to p. With the price back up to p, remaining firms once again earn a normal profit. When the dust settles, each firm produces q, the initial equilibrium quantity. But, because some firms have left the industry, market output has fallen from Q_a to Q_g. Again, note that the adjustment involves the departure of firms from the industry rather than a reduction in the scale of firms, as a reduction in scale would increase each firm's long-run average cost.

The Long-Run Industry Supply Curve

Thus far, we have looked at a firm's and industry's response to changes in demand, distinguishing between a short-run adjustment and a long-run adjustment. In the short run, a firm alters quantity supplied by moving up or down its marginal cost curves (that portion at or above average variable cost) until marginal cost equals marginal revenue, or price. If price is too low to cover minimum average variable cost, a firm shuts down in the short run. An economic profit (or loss) will, in the long run, prompt some firms to enter (or leave) the industry or to adjust firm size until remaining firms earn a normal profit.

In Exhibits 10 and 11, we began with an initial long-run equilibrium point; then, in response to a shift of the demand curve, we found two more long-run equilibrium points. In each case, the price changed in the short run but was unchanged in the long run. Industry output increased in Exhibit 10 and decreased in Exhibit 11. Connecting these long-run equilibrium points yields the *long-run industry supply curve,* labeled $S^\star$ in Exhibits 10 and 11. The **long-run industry supply curve** shows the relationship between price and quantity supplied once firms fully adjust to any short-term economic profit or loss resulting from a change in demand.

Constant-Cost Industries

The industry we have examined thus far is called **constant-cost industry** because each firm's long-run average cost curve does not shift up or down as industry output changes. In a constant-cost industry, each firm's per-unit costs are independent of the number of firms in the industry. *The long-run supply curve for a constant-cost industry is horizontal,* as is depicted in Exhibits 10 and 11. A constant-cost industry uses such a small portion of the resources available that increasing output does not bid up resource prices. For example, output in the pencil industry can expand without bidding up the prices of wood, graphite, and rubber, because the pencil industry uses such a small share of the market supply of these resources.

LONG-RUN INDUSTRY SUPPLY CURVE

A curve that shows the relationship between price and quantity supplied by the industry once firms adjust fully to any change in market demand

CONSTANT-COST INDUSTRY

An industry that can expand or contract without affecting the long-run per-unit cost of production; the long-run industry supply curve is horizontal

Increasing-Cost Industries

The firms in some industries encounter higher average costs as industry output expands in the long run. Firms in these **increasing-cost industries** find that expanding output bids up the prices of some resources or otherwise increases per-unit production costs, and these higher costs shift up each firm's cost curves. For example, a market expansion of oil production could bid up the price of drilling rigs and the wages of petroleum engineers and geologists, raising per-unit production costs for each oil firm. Likewise, more housing construction could bid up what developers must pay for land, carpenters, lumber, and other building materials.

INCREASING-COST INDUSTRY

An industry that faces higher per-unit production costs as industry output expands in the long run; the long-run industry supply curve slopes upward

To illustrate the equilibrium adjustment process for an increasing-cost industry, we begin again in long-run equilibrium in Exhibit 12, with the firm shown in panel (a) and the industry in panel (b). Market demand curve D in panel (b) intersects short-run market supply curve S at equilibrium point a to yield market price p_a and market quantity Q_a. When the price is p_a, the demand (and marginal revenue) curve facing each firm is d_a, as shown in panel (a). The firm produces the quantity q, where the price, or marginal revenue, equals marginal cost. At that output, average total cost equals the price, so the firm earns no economic profit in this long-run equilibrium.

Suppose an increase in the demand for this product shifts the market demand curve in panel (b) to the right from D to D'. The new demand curve intersects the short-run market supply curve S at point b, yielding the price p_b and market quantity Q_b. With an increase in the market price, each firm's demand curve shifts from d_a up to d_b. The new short-run equilibrium occurs at point b in panel (a), where the marginal cost curve intersects the new demand curve, which is also the marginal revenue curve. Each firm produces output q_b. In the short run, each firm earns an economic profit equal to q_b times the difference between price p_b and the average total cost at that rate of output. So far, the sequence of events is the same as for a constant-cost industry.

Economic profit attracts new firms. Because this is an increasing-cost industry, new entrants drive up the cost of production, raising each firm's marginal and average cost curves. In panel (a) of Exhibit 12, MC and ATC shift up to MC' and ATC'. (We assume for simplicity that new average cost curves are vertical shifts of the initial ones, so the minimum efficient plant size remains the same.)

The entry of new firms also shifts the short-run industry supply curve to the right in panel (b), thus reducing the market price. *New firms enter the industry until the combination of a higher production cost and a lower price squeezes economic profit to zero.* This long-run equilibrium occurs when the entry of new firms has shifted the short-run industry supply curve out to S', which lowers the price until it equals the minimum on each firm's new average total cost curve. The market price does not fall back to the initial equilibrium level because each firm's average total cost curve has increased, or shifted up, with the expansion of industry output. The intersection of the new short-run market supply curve, S', and the new market demand curve, D', determines the new long-run market equilibrium point, c. Points a and c in panel (b) are on the *upward-sloping* long-run supply curve, S^*, for this increasing-cost industry.

In constant-cost industries, each firm's costs depend simply on the scale of its plant and its rate of output. For increasing-cost industries, each firm's costs depend also on the number of firms in the market. By bidding up the price of resources, long-run expansion in an increasing-cost industry increases each firm's marginal and average costs. The long-run supply curve slopes upward, like S^* in Exhibit 12.

An Increasing-Cost Industry

An increase in demand to *D'* in panel (b) disturbs the initial equilibrium at point *a*. Short-run equilibrium is established at point *b*, where *D'* intersects the short-run market supply curve *S*. At the higher price p_b, the firm's demand curve shifts up to d_b, and its output increases to q_b in panel (a). At point *b*, the firm is now earning economic profit, which attracts new firms. As new firms enter, input prices get bid up, so each firm's marginal and average cost curves rise. New firms increase the short-run market supply curve from *S* to *S'*. The intersection of the new market supply curve, *S'*, with *D'* determines the market price, p_c. At p_c, individual firms are earning a normal profit. Point *c* shows the long-run equilibrium combination of price and quantity. By connecting long-run equilibrium points *a* and *c* in panel (b), we obtain the upward-sloping long-run market supply curve *S** for this increasing-cost industry.

(a) Firm

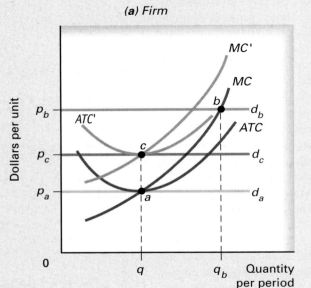

(b) Industry, or market

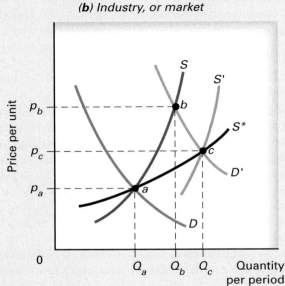

To review: Firms in perfect competition can earn an economic profit, a normal profit, or an economic loss in the short run. But in the long run, the entry or exit of firms and adjustments in firm scale force economic profit to zero, so firms earn only a normal profit. This is true whether the industry in question exhibits constant costs or increasing costs in the long run. Notice that, regardless of the nature of costs in the industry, the market supply curve is more elastic in the long run than in the short run. In the long run, firms can adjust all their resources, so they are better able to respond to changes in price. One final point: Firms in an industry could theoretically experience a lower average cost as output expands in the long run, resulting in a downward-sloping long-run industry supply curve. But such an outcome is considered so rare that we have not examined it.

As mentioned at the outset, perfect competition provides a useful benchmark for evaluating the efficiency of markets. Let's examine the qualities of perfect competition that make it so useful.

Perfect Competition and Efficiency

Economics in
the Movies

How does perfect competition stack up as an efficient user of resources? Two concepts of efficiency are used to judge market performance. The first, called *productive efficiency,* refers to producing output at the least possible cost. The second, called *allocative efficiency,* refers to producing the output that consumers value the most. Perfect competition guarantees both productive efficiency and allocative efficiency in the long run.

Productive Efficiency: Making Stuff Right

Productive efficiency occurs when the firm produces at the minimum point on its long-run average cost curve, so the market price equals the minimum average cost. The entry and exit of firms and any adjustment in the scale of each firm ensure that each firm produces at the minimum point on its long-run average cost curve. Firms that do not reach minimum long-run average cost must, to avoid continued losses, either adjust their scale or leave the industry. Thus, *perfect competition produces output at minimum average cost in the long run.*

Allocative Efficiency: Making the Right Stuff

Just because *production* occurs at the least possible cost does not mean that the *allocation* of resources is the most efficient one possible. The goods being produced may not be the ones consumers want. This situation is akin to that of the airline pilot who informs passengers that there's good news and bad news: "The good news is that we're making record time. The bad news is that we're lost!" Likewise, firms may be producing goods efficiently but producing the wrong goods—that is, making stuff right but making the wrong stuff.

   Allocative efficiency occurs when firms produce the output that is most valued by consumers. How do we know that perfect competition guarantees allocative efficiency? The answer lies with the market demand and supply curves. Recall that the demand curve reflects the marginal value that consumers attach to each unit of the good, so the market price is the amount people are willing and able to pay for the final unit they consume. We also know that, in both the short run and the long run, the equilibrium price in perfect competition equals the marginal cost of supplying the last unit sold. Marginal cost measures the opportunity cost of all resources employed to produce that last unit sold. Thus, the demand and supply curves intersect at the combination of price and quantity at which *the marginal value, or the marginal benefit that consumers attach to the final unit purchased, just equals the opportunity cost of the resources employed to produce that unit.*

   As long as marginal benefit equals marginal cost, the last unit produced is valued as much as, or more than, any other good those resources could have produced. There is no way to reallocate resources to increase the total value of output. Thus, there is no way to reallocate resources to increase the total utility or total benefit consumers reap from production. *When the marginal benefit that consumers derive from a good equals the marginal cost of producing that good, that market is said to be allocatively efficient.*

Marginal benefit = Marginal cost

Firms not only are making stuff right, they are making the right stuff.

What's So Perfect About Perfect Competition?

If the marginal cost of supplying a good just equals the marginal benefit to consumers, does this mean that market exchange confers no net benefits to participants? No. Market

PRODUCTIVE EFFICIENCY

The condition that exists when market output is produced using the least-cost combination of inputs; minimum average cost in the long run

ALLOCATIVE EFFICIENCY

The condition that exists when firms produce the output most preferred by consumers; marginal benefit equals marginal cost

exchange usually benefits both consumers and producers. Recall that consumers enjoy a surplus from market exchange because the maximum amount they would be willing and able to pay for each unit of the good exceeds the amount they actually do pay. Exhibit 13 depicts a market in short-run equilibrium. The *consumer surplus* in this exhibit is represented by blue shading, which is the area below the demand curve but above the market-clearing price of $10.

Producers in the short run also usually derive a net benefit, or a surplus, from market exchange, because the amount they receive for their output exceeds the minimum amount they would require to supply that amount in the short run. Recall that the short-run market supply curve is the sum of that portion of each firm's marginal cost curve at or above the minimum point on its average variable cost curve. Point *m* in Exhibit 13 is the minimum point on the market supply curve; it indicates that at a price of $5, firms are willing to supply 100,000 units. At prices below $5, quantity supplied is zero because firms could not cover variable costs and would shut down. At point *m*, firms in this industry gain no net benefit from production over shutting down in the short run. At a price of $5, each firm's total revenue just covers the firm's variable cost.

If the price rises to $6, firms increase their quantity supplied until their marginal cost equals $6. Market output increases from 100,000 to 120,000 units, and total market revenue increases from $500,000 to $720,000. Part of the increased revenue covers the higher marginal cost of production. But the rest provides a bonus to producers, who would have been willing to supply the first 100,000 units for only $5 each. If the price is $6, they get to sell

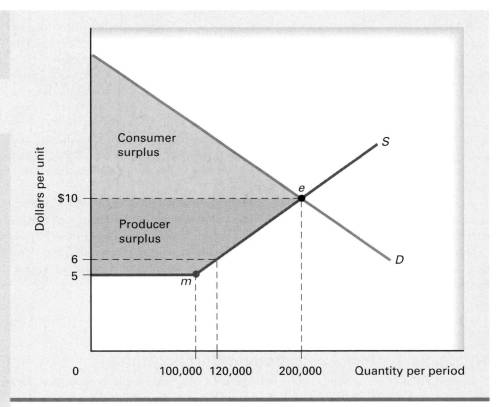

EXHIBIT 13

Consumer Surplus and Producer Surplus for a Competitive Market

Consumer surplus is represented by the area above the market-clearing price of $10 per unit and below the demand curve; it appears as the blue triangle. Producer surplus is represented by the area above the short-run market supply curve and below the market-clearing price of $10 per unit; it appears as the gold area. At a price of $5 per unit, there would be no producer surplus. At a price of $6 per unit, producer surplus would be the gold shaded area between $5 and $6.

these 100,000 units for $6 each rather than $5 each. Producer surplus at a price of $6 is the shaded area between $5 and $6.

In the short run, **producer surplus** is the total revenue producers are paid minus their variable cost of production. In Exhibit 13, the market-clearing price is $10 per unit, and producer surplus is depicted by the gold-shaded area under the price but above the market supply curve. That area represents the market price minus the marginal cost of each unit produced. The most the firm can lose in the short run is to shut down. Any price that exceeds average variable cost will reduce that short-run loss, and a high enough price could yield economic profit.

The combination of consumer surplus and producer surplus shows the gains from voluntary exchange. Productive and allocative efficiency in the short run occurs at equilibrium point *e,* which also is the combination of price and quantity that maximizes the sum of consumer surplus and producer surplus, thus maximizing social welfare. **Social welfare** is the overall well-being of people in the economy. Even though marginal cost equals marginal benefit for the final unit produced and consumed, both producers and consumers usually derive a surplus, or a bonus, from market exchange.

The gains from market exchange have been examined in an experimental setting, as discussed in the following case study.

Experimental Economics

Economists have limited opportunities to carry out the kind of controlled experiments available in the physical and biological sciences. But about four decades ago, Professor Vernon Smith, now at the George Mason University in Virginia, began some experiments to see how quickly and efficiently a group of test subjects could achieve market equilibrium. His original experiment involved 22 students, 11 of whom were designated as "buyers" and 11 as "sellers." Each buyer was given a card indicating the value of purchasing one unit of a hypothetical commodity; these values ranged from $3.25 down to $0.75, forming a downward-sloping demand curve. Each seller was given a card indicating the cost of supplying one unit of that commodity; these costs ranged from $0.75 up to $3.25, forming an upward-sloping supply curve. Each buyer and seller knew only what was on his or her own card.

© Stewart Cohen/Index Stock Imagery

To provide market incentives, participants were told they would receive a cash bonus at the end of the experiment based on the difference between the price they negotiated in the market and their value (for buyers) or their cost (for sellers). As a way of trading, Smith employed a system in which any buyer or seller could announce a bid or an offer to the entire group—a system called a *double-continuous auction*—based on rules similar to those governing stock markets and commodity exchanges. A transaction occurred whenever any buyer accepted an offer to sell or when any seller accepted an offer to buy. *Smith found that the price quickly moved to the market-clearing level,* which in his experiment was $2.00.

Economists have since performed thousands of experiments to test the properties of markets. These show that under most circumstances, markets are extremely efficient in moving goods from producers with the lowest costs to consumers who place the highest value on the goods. This movement maximizes the sum of consumer and producer surplus and thus maximizes social welfare. One surprising finding is how few participants are required

---

PRODUCER SURPLUS

A bonus for producers in the short run; the amount by which total revenue from production exceeds variable cost

SOCIAL WELFARE

The overall well-being of people in the economy; maximized when the marginal cost of production equals the marginal benefit to consumers

C a s e S t u d y

The Information Economy

eActivity

Market.Econ brings "experimental economics to the Internet" at http://market.econ.arizona.edu/. By supplying your email address, you can receive a password and play one of their games online. Be sure to read through any rules carefully. Rules and results of a variety of other games are available at http://eeps.caltech.edu/ from Caltech's Laboratory for Experimental Economics and Political Science. The director is Professor Charles Plott, an early innovator of experimental economics. Be sure to check out the *Jaws* animation, a QuickTime video presentation of changing equilibrium prices. Charles Holt of the University of Virginia, an innovator in using games in the classroom, maintains a Web site with instructions and game sheets for some experiments at http://www.people.virginia.edu/~cah2k/programs.html.

to establish a market price. Market experiments sometimes use only four buyers and four sellers, each capable of trading several units. Some experiments use only two sellers, yet the competitive equilibrium model performs quite well under double-continuous auction rules. Professor Smith won the Nobel Prize in 2002 for his work in experimental economics.

Incidentally, most U.S. retail markets, such as supermarkets and department stores, use *posted-offer pricing*—that is, the price is marked, not negotiated. Experiments show that posted pricing does not adjust to changing market conditions as quickly as does a double-continuous auction. Despite their slow response time, posted prices may be the choice for large, relatively stable markets, because posted prices involve low transaction costs—that is, buyer and seller don't have to haggle over each purchase. In contrast, double-continuous-auction pricing involves high transaction costs and, in the case of stock and commodity markets, requires thousands of people in full-time negotiations to maintain prices at their equilibrium levels (although, as discussed in the previous case study, the Internet is reducing these transaction costs).

Experiments have provided empirical support for economic theory and have yielded insights about how market rules affect market outcomes. They have also helped shape markets that did not exist before, such as the market for pollution rights or for broadcast spectrum rights—markets to be discussed in later chapters. Experiments also offer a safe and inexpensive way for people in emerging market economies to learn how markets work. The rapid development of online auctions has opened up a world of data for experimentalists.

Experimental economics is now a hot area for research and industry. For example, the number of papers published in the field jumped from fewer than 20 a year in the 1970s to more than ten times that. Most top U.S. business schools employ experimental economists. And some top corporations, such as Hewlett-Packard and IBM, have opened experimental-economics labs.

Sources: Vernon Smith, "Experimental Methods in Economics," *The New Palgrave Dictionary of Economics*, Vol. 2, edited by J. Eatwell et al. (Hampshire, England: Stockton Press, 1987), pp. 241–249; T. C. Bergstrom and J. H. Miller, *Experiments with Economic Principles*, Second Edition (New York: McGraw-Hill, 1999); Vernon Smith and Lynne Kiesling, "Socket to California," *Wall Street Journal*, 10 November 2003; and the University of Arizona's Economic Science Laboratory at http://www.econlab.arizona.edu/.

Conclusion

Let's review the assumptions of a perfectly competitive market and see how each relates to ideas developed in this chapter. *First,* there are many buyers and many sellers. This assumption ensures that no individual buyer or seller can influence the price (although recent experiments show that competition occurs even when there are few buyers and sellers). *Second,* firms produce a commodity, or a uniform product. If consumers could distinguish between the products of different suppliers, they might prefer one firm's product even at a higher price, so different producers could sell at different prices. In that case, not every firm would be a price taker—that is, each firm's demand curve would no longer be horizontal. *Third,* market participants have full information about all prices and all production processes. Otherwise, some producers could charge more than the market price, and some uninformed consumers would pay that higher price. Also, through ignorance, some firms might select outdated technology or fail to recognize opportunities for short-run economic profits. *Fourth,* all resources are mobile in the long run, with nothing preventing firms in the long run from entering profitable markets or leaving losing markets. If firms couldn't enter profitable markets, then some firms already in that market could earn economic profit in the long run.

Perfect competition is not the most common market structure observed in the real world. The markets for agricultural products, commodities such as gold and silver, widely traded stocks, and foreign exchange come close to being perfect. But even if not a single industry could be found, the model would still be useful for analyzing market behavior. As you will see in the next two chapters, perfect competition provides a valuable benchmark for evaluating the efficiency of other market structures.

SUMMARY

1. Market structures describe important features of the economic environment in which firms operate. These features include the number of buyers and sellers in the market, the ease or difficulty of entering the market, differences in the product across firms, and the forms of competition among firms.

2. Perfectly competitive markets are characterized by (a) a large number of buyers and sellers, each too small to influence market prices; (b) firms in the market produce a commodity, or undifferentiated product; (c) buyers and sellers possess full information about the availability and prices of all resources, goods, and technologies; and (d) firms and resources are freely mobile in the long run. Firms in perfect competition are said to be price takers because no firm can influence the market price. Each firm can vary only the amount it supplies at that price.

3. The market price in perfect competition is determined by the intersection of the market demand and market supply curves. Each firm then faces a demand curve that is a horizontal line at the market price. The firm's demand curve also shows the average revenue and marginal revenue received at each rate of output.

4. For a firm to produce in the short run, the market price must at least equal the firm's average variable cost. If price is below average variable cost, the firm will shut down. That portion of the marginal cost curve at or rising above the average variable cost curve becomes the perfectly competitive firm's short-run supply curve. The horizontal sum of all firms' supply curves forms the market supply curve. Each perfectly competitive firm maximizes profit or minimizes loss by producing where marginal revenue equals marginal cost.

5. Because firms are not free to enter or leave the market in the short run, economic profit or loss is possible. In the long run, however, some firms may adjust their scale of operation and other firms enter or leave the market until any economic profit or loss is eliminated.

6. Each firm in the long run will produce at the lowest point on its long-run average cost curve. At this rate of output, marginal revenue equals marginal cost and also equals the price and average cost. Firms that fail to produce at this least-cost combination will not survive in the long run.

7. In the short run, a firm alters the quantity supplied in response to a change in market demand by moving up or down its marginal cost, or supply, curve. The long-run adjustment to a change in market demand involves firms entering or leaving the market and perhaps existing firms changing their scale of operation until firms still in the industry earn just a normal profit. As the industry expands or contracts in the long run, the long-run industry supply curve has a shape that reflects either constant costs or increasing costs.

8. Perfectly competitive markets exhibit both productive efficiency (because output is produced using the most efficient combination of resources available) and allocative efficiency (because the goods produced are those most valued by consumers). In equilibrium, a perfectly competitive market allocates goods so that the marginal cost of the final unit produced equals the marginal value that consumers attach to that final unit. In the long run, market pressure minimizes the average cost of production. Voluntary exchange in competitive markets maximizes the sum of consumer surplus and producer surplus, thus maximizing social welfare.

QUESTIONS FOR REVIEW

1. *(Market Structure)* Define *market structure.* What factors are considered in determining the market structure of a particular industry?

2. *(Demand Under Perfect Competition)* What type of demand curve does a perfectly competitive firm face? Why?

3. *(Total Revenue)* Look back at Exhibit 3, panel (a) in this chapter. Explain why the total revenue curve is a straight line from the origin, whereas the slope of the total cost curve changes.

4. *(Profit in the Short Run)* Look back at Exhibit 3, panel (b), in this chapter. Why doesn't the firm choose the output that maximizes average profit (i.e., the output where average cost is the lowest)?

5. *(The Short-Run Firm Supply Curve)* An individual competitive firm's short-run supply curve is the portion of its marginal cost curve that equals or rises above the average variable cost. Explain why.

6. *(C a s e* **S t u d y :** Auction Markets) Which of the characteristics of the perfectly competitive market structure are found in the Flower Auction Holland?

7. *(Long-Run Industry Supply)* Why does the long-run industry supply curve for an increasing-cost industry slope upward? What causes the increasing costs in an increasing-cost industry?

8. *(Perfect Competition and Efficiency)* Define productive efficiency and allocative efficiency. What conditions must be met to achieve them?

9. *(C a s e* **S t u d y :** Experimental Economics) In Professor Vernon Smith's experiment, which "buyers" ended up with a surplus at the market-clearing price of $2? Which "sellers" had a surplus? Which "buyers" or "sellers" did not engage in transactions?

PROBLEMS AND EXERCISES

10. *(Short-Run Profit Maximization)* A perfectly competitive firm has the following fixed and variable costs in the short run. The market price for the firm's product is $150.

Output	FC	VC	TC	TR	Profit/ Loss
0	$100	$ 0	___	___	___
1	100	100	___	___	___
2	100	180	___	___	___
3	100	300	___	___	___
4	100	440	___	___	___
5	100	600	___	___	___
6	100	780	___	___	___

a. Complete the table.

b. At what output rate does the firm maximize profit or minimize loss?

c. What is the firm's marginal revenue at each positive level of output? Its average revenue?

d. What can you say about the relationship between marginal revenue and marginal cost for output rates below the profit-maximizing (or loss-minimizing) rate? For output rates above the profit-maximizing (or loss-minimizing) rate?

11. *(The Short-Run Firm Supply Curve)* Use the following data to answer the questions below:

Q	VC	MC	AVC
1	$10	___	___
2	16	___	___
3	20	___	___
4	25	___	___
5	31	___	___
6	38	___	___
7	46	___	___
8	55	___	___
9	65	___	___

a. Calculate the marginal cost and average variable cost for each level of production.
b. How much would the firm produce if it could sell its product for $5? For $7? For $10?
c. Explain your answers.
d. Assuming that its fixed cost is $3, calculate the firm's profit at each of the production levels determined in part (b).

12. *(The Short-Run Firm Supply Curve)* Each of the following situations could exist for a firm in the short run. In each case, indicate whether the firm should produce in the short run or shut down in the short run, or whether additional information is needed to determine what it should do in the short run.

a. Total cost exceeds total revenue at all output levels.
b. Total variable cost exceeds total revenue at all output levels.
c. Total revenue exceeds total fixed cost at all output levels.
d. Marginal revenue exceeds marginal cost at the current output level.
e. Price exceeds average total cost at all output levels.
f. Average variable cost exceeds price at all output levels.
g. Average total cost exceeds price at all output levels.

13. *(Perfect Competition in the Long Run)* Draw the short- and long-run cost curves of a competitive firm in long-run equilibrium. Indicate the long-run equilibrium price and quantity.

a. Discuss the firm's short-run response to a reduction in the price of a variable resource.
b. Assuming that this is a constant-cost industry, describe the process by which the industry returns to long-run equilibrium following a change in market demand.

14. *(The Long-Run Industry Supply Curve)* A normal good is being produced in a constant-cost, perfectly competitive industry. Initially, each firm is in long-run equilibrium.

a. Graphically illustrate and explain the short-run adjustments of the market and the firm to a decrease in consumer incomes. Be sure to discuss any changes in output levels, prices, profits, and the number of firms.
b. Next, show on your graph and explain the long-run adjustment to the income change. Be sure to discuss any changes in output levels, prices, profits, and the number of firms.

15. *(The Long-Run Industry Supply Curve)* The following graph shows possible long-run market supply curves for a perfectly competitive industry. Determine which supply curve indicates a constant-cost industry and which an increasing-cost industry.

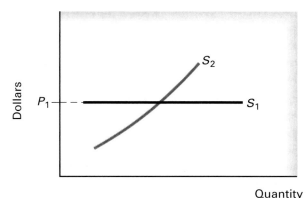

a. Explain the difference between a constant-cost industry and an increasing-cost industry.
b. Distinguish between the long-run impact of an increase in market demand in a constant-cost industry and the impact in an increasing-cost industry.

16. *(What's So Perfect About Perfect Competition)* Use the following data to answer the questions.

Quantity	Marginal Cost	Marginal Benefit
0	—	—
1	$ 2	$10
2	3	9
3	4	8
4	5	7
5	6	6
6	8	5
7	10	4
8	12	3

a. For the product shown, assume that the minimum point of each firm's average variable cost curve is at $2. Construct a demand and supply diagram for the product and indicate the equilibrium price and quantity.
b. On the graph, label the area of consumer surplus as *f*. Label the area of producer surplus as *g*.
c. If the equilibrium price were $2, what would be the amount of producer surplus?

EXPERIENTIAL EXERCISES

17. The National Council of Economic Education's EconEd-Link has an interesting module on the economics of Internet access at http://www.econedlink.org/lessons/index.cfm?lesson=NN10. Review the materials provided (including the video, if you have the right software available). Is provision of Internet access a competitive industry? How would you use the tools of demand and supply to model recent developments in Internet pricing?

18. (*C a s e* **S t u d y :** Auction Markets) Rent the movie *Trading Places,* starring Eddie Murphy and Dan Ackroyd. Enjoy the movie and pay special attention to the scene near the end when Billy Ray and Louis participate in an auction of orange-juice futures. How does the arrival of new information affect the price of those futures contracts? Try to model the situation, using demand and supply curves.

19. *(Wall Street Journal)* Financial markets are quintessential examples of perfectly competitive markets. And, of course, the *Wall Street Journal* features in-depth coverage of these markets. Turn to the Money and Investing section of today's *Wall Street Journal*, and choose one or two articles that seem interesting to you. Then, try to determine how financial markets contribute to productive and allocative efficiency in the U.S. economy.

20. *(Wall Street Journal)* Commodities often trade in markets that are examples of perfect competition. Look in the Money and Investing section of the *Wall Street Journal*. In the index, locate commodities and turn to the page where commodities are covered. Find a commodity that you believe trades in a perfectly competitive market. Describe why you believe this is so.

HOMEWORK XPRESS! EXERCISES

These exercises require access to McEachern Homework Xpress! If Homework Xpress! did not come with your book, visit **http://homeworkxpress.swlearning.com** *to purchase.*

Charles Cobbler, maker of fine shoes, sells in a competitive market and must decide how to respond to any particular market price.

1. At the current price P the firm is earning above normal profits. Draw typical marginal cost, average cost, and average cost curves that would illustrate the firm's situation. Identify the quantity the firm would choose to produce at this price.

2. Draw a marginal revenue curve for a price at which the firm would suffer losses but continue to operate in the short-run given the marginal cost, average total cost, and average variable costs in the diagram. Identify the price as P and the quantity the firm would choose to produce. Identify the average total cost per unit at this quantity as C.

3. Draw a marginal revenue curve for a price at which the firm would suffer such severe losses that it would choose to shut down in the short run given the marginal cost, average total cost, and average variable costs in the diagram.

4. Supply schedules for three firms, A, B, and C that sell identical products in a competitive market are given in the table below. Each firm has slightly different costs. Draw supply curves for each, labeling them S_A, S_B, and S_C, accordingly. Use the data in the table to derive and draw the industry supply curve. Label this curve as S.

Price	Firm A	Firm B	Firm C
$ 2	1	2	3
4	2	3	4
6	3	4	5

Monopoly

© Tim Wright/Corbis

How can a firm monopolize a market? Why aren't most markets monopolized? Why don't most monopolies last? Why don't monopolies charge the
highest possible price? Why do some firms offer discounts to students, senior citizens, and other groups? Why are some airfares lower with a weekend stay? These and
other questions are answered in this chapter, which looks at our second market
structure—monopoly.

Monopoly is from the Greek, meaning "one seller." In some parts of the United
States, monopolists sell electricity, cable TV service, and local phone service. Monopolists also sell postage stamps, hot dogs at sports arenas, some patented products,
and other goods and services with no close substitutes. You have probably heard

BARRIER TO ENTRY

Any impediment that prevents new firms from entering an industry and competing on an equal basis with existing firms

PATENT

A legal barrier to entry that grants its holder the exclusive right to sell a product for 20 years from the date the patent application is filed

INNOVATION

The process of turning an invention into a marketable product

about the evils of monopoly. You may have even played the board game *Monopoly* on a rainy day. Now we will sort out fact from fiction.

Like perfect competition, pure monopoly is not as common as other market structures. But by understanding monopoly, you will grow more familiar with market structures that lie between the extremes of perfect competition and pure monopoly. This chapter examines the sources of monopoly power, how a monopolist maximizes profit, differences between monopoly and perfect competition, and why a monopolist sometimes charges different prices for the same product. Topics include:

- Barriers to entry
- Price elasticity and marginal revenue
- Profit maximization and loss minimization

- Monopoly and resource allocation
- Welfare cost of monopoly
- Price discrimination
- The monopolist's dream

Barriers to Entry

As noted in Chapter 3, a *monopoly* is the sole supplier of a product with no close substitutes. Why do some markets come to be dominated by a single supplier? A monopolized market is characterized by **barriers to entry**, which are restrictions on the entry of new firms into an industry. Because of barriers, new firms cannot profitably enter that market. Let's examine three types of entry barriers: legal restrictions, economies of scale, and the monopolist's control of an essential resource.

Legal Restrictions

One way to prevent new firms from entering a market is to make entry illegal. Patents, licenses, and other legal restrictions imposed by the government provide some producers with legal protection against competition.

Patents and Invention Incentives

In the United States, a **patent** awards an inventor the exclusive right to produce a good or service for 20 years from the date the patent is filed with the patent office. Originally enacted in 1790, patent laws encourage inventors to invest the time and money required to discover and develop new products and processes. If others could simply copy successful products, inventors would have less incentive to incur the up-front costs of invention. Patents also provide the stimulus to turn inventions into marketable products, a process called **innovation.**

Licenses and Other Entry Restrictions

Governments often confer monopoly status by awarding a single firm the exclusive right to supply a particular good or service. Federal licenses give certain firms the right to broadcast radio and TV signals. State licenses authorize suppliers of medical care, haircuts, and legal advice. A license may not grant a monopoly, but it does block entry and often confers the power to charge a price above the competitive level. Thus, a license can serve as an effective barrier against new competitors. Governments also grant monopoly rights to sell hot dogs at civic auditoriums, collect garbage, provide bus and taxi service, and supply services ranging from electricity to cable TV. The government itself may claim that right by outlawing competitors. For example, many states sell liquor and lottery tickets, and the U.S. Postal Service has the exclusive right to deliver first-class mail to your mailbox.

Economies of Scale

A monopoly sometimes occurs naturally when a firm experiences *economies of scale,* as reflected by the downward-sloping, long-run average cost curve shown in Exhibit 1. In such instances, a single firm can supply market demand at a lower average cost per unit than could two or more firms each producing less. Put another way, market demand is not great enough to allow more than one firm to achieve sufficient economies of scale. Thus, a single firm will emerge from the competitive process as the only supplier in the market. For example, even though the *production* of electricity has become more competitive, the *transmission* of electricity still exhibits economies of scale. Once wires are run throughout a community, the marginal cost of linking additional households to the power grid is relatively small. Consequently, the average cost of delivering electricity declines as more and more households are wired into the system.

A monopoly that emerges from the nature of costs is called a *natural monopoly,* to distinguish it from the artificial monopolies created by government patents, licenses, and other legal barriers to entry. A new entrant cannot sell enough to enjoy the economies of scale enjoyed by an established natural monopolist, so market entry is naturally blocked. A later chapter will discuss the regulation of natural monopolies.

Control of Essential Resources

Economics in the Movies

Sometimes the source of monopoly power is a firm's control over some resource critical to production. Here are four examples: (1) Alcoa was the sole

HOMEWORK
Xpress!
econ-apps news

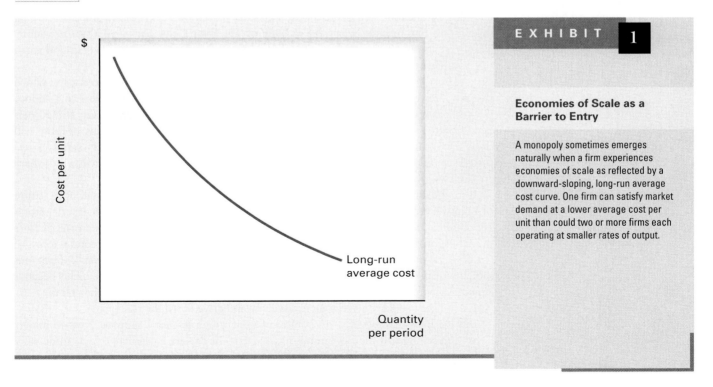

EXHIBIT 1

Economies of Scale as a Barrier to Entry

A monopoly sometimes emerges naturally when a firm experiences economies of scale as reflected by a downward-sloping, long-run average cost curve. One firm can satisfy market demand at a lower average cost per unit than could two or more firms each operating at smaller rates of output.

U.S. maker of aluminum from the late 19th century until World War II. Its monopoly power initially stemmed from production patents that expired in 1909, but for the next three decades, it controlled the supply of bauxite, the key raw material. (2) Professional sports leagues try to block the formation of competing leagues by signing the best athletes to long-term contracts and by seeking the exclusive use of sports stadiums and arenas. (3) China is a monopoly supplier of pandas to the world's zoos. The National Zoo in Washington, D.C., for example, rents its pair of pandas from China for $1 million a year. As a way of controlling the panda supply, China stipulates that any offspring from the pair becomes China's property.[1] Finally, (4) since the 1930s, the world's diamond trade has been controlled primarily by De Beers Consolidated Mines, which mines diamonds and also buys most of the world's supply of rough diamonds, as discussed in the following case study.

Is a Diamond Forever?

© Peter Kaskons/Index Stock Imagery

In 1866, a child walking along the Orange River in South Africa picked up an odd pebble that turned out to be a 21-carat diamond. That discovery on a farm owned by Johannes De Beers sparked the largest diamond mine in history. Ever since the Great Depression caused a slump in diamond prices, De Beers Consolidated Mines has tried to control the world supply of uncut diamonds. The company has kept prices high by carefully limiting supply and by advertising. For example, De Beers spent $183 million in 2003 trying to convince people that diamonds are scarce, valuable, and perfect reflections of love. One promotional coup was to persuade *Baywatch,* a TV show now seen in reruns around the world, to devote an episode to a diamond engagement ring. The story played up the De Beers line that the ring should cost two months' salary. An episode of *The Drew Carey Show* had a similar theme. The latest attempt to boost the demand for diamonds is the "spirit ring," a diamond worn on a woman's right hand as a sign of independence.

De Beers limits the supply of rough diamonds reaching the market. The company, which is sometimes called "The Syndicate," invites about one hundred wholesalers to London, where each is offered a box of uncut diamonds for a set price—no negotiating. If De Beers needs to prop up the price of a certain size and quality of diamond, then few of those will show up in the boxes, thus restricting their supply. The company's actions violate U.S. antitrust laws (De Beers executives could be arrested if they traveled to America). But there are no laws prohibiting U.S. wholesalers from buying from De Beers.

It might surprise you that, as gems go, diamonds are not especially rare, either in nature or in jewelry stores. Diamonds may be the most common natural gemstone. Jewelry stores sell more diamonds than any other gem. Jewelers are willing to hold large inventories because they are confident that De Beers will keep prices up. De Beers' slogan, "A diamond is forever," sends several messages, including (1) a diamond lasts forever, and so should love; (2) diamonds should remain in the family and not be sold; and (3) diamonds retain their value. This slogan is aimed at keeping secondhand diamonds, which are good substitutes for new ones, off the market, where they could otherwise increase supply and drive down the price.

But De Beers has recently lost control of some rough diamond supplies. Russian miners have been selling half their diamonds to independent dealers. Australia's Argyle mine, now

1. Francis Clines, "Capital Exults Over Pandas," *New York Times,* 7 December 2000.

the world's largest, stopped selling to De Beers in 1996. And Yellowknife, a huge Canadian mine, began operations in 1998, but De Beers is guaranteed only about one-third of its output. As a result of all this erosion, DeBeers' share of the world's uncut diamond supply slipped from nearly 90 percent in the mid-1980s to about 62 percent in 2002. Worse still for De Beers, newly developed synthetic diamonds are starting to appear on the market. To counter that threat, De Beers is supplying precision equipment to jewelers so they can spot synthetic diamonds.

A monopoly that relies on the control of a key resource, as De Beers does, loses its power once that control slips away. In a reversal of policy, De Beers now says it will abandon efforts to control the world diamond supply and will instead become the "supplier of choice" by promoting the DeBeers brand of diamonds. But as of 2004 there are only a few DeBeers retail stores worldwide, in London and in Tokyo. De Beers is now trying to settle U.S. antitrust charges so it can open stores in the states. (Americans account for only 5 percent of the world's population but for half the world's diamond purchases.) In an effort to differentiate its diamonds, De Beers is etching the company name and an individual security number on some diamonds. Whether this branding effort will work remains to be seen.

Sources: Phyllis Berman and Lea Goldman, "The Billionaire Who Cracked De Beers," *Forbes*, 15 September 2003; Rob Walker, "The Right-Hand Diamond Ring," *New York Times*, 4 January 2004; Joshua Davis, "The New Diamond Age," *Wired Magazine*, September 2003; John Wilke, "De Beers Is in Talks to Settle Charges of Price Fixing," *Wall Street Journal*, 24 February 2004; and the De Beers home page at http://www.adiamondisforever.com/.

Local monopolies are more common than national or international monopolies. In rural areas, monopolies may include the only grocery store, movie theater, or restaurant for miles around. These are natural monopolies for products sold in local markets. But long-lasting monopolies are rare because, as we will see, a profitable monopoly attracts competitors. Also, over time, technological change tends to break down barriers to entry. For example, the development of wireless transmission of long-distance calls created competitors to AT&T. Wireless transmission will soon erase the monopoly held by local cable TV providers and even local phone service. Likewise, fax machines, email, the Internet, and firms such as FedEx now compete with the U.S. Postal Service's monopoly, as we will see in a later case study.

Revenue for the Monopolist

Because a monopoly, by definition, supplies the entire market, the demand for goods or services produced by a monopolist is also the market demand. The demand curve for the monopolist's output therefore slopes downward, reflecting the law of demand—price and quantity demanded are inversely related. Let's look at demand, average revenue, and marginal revenue.

Demand, Average Revenue, and Marginal Revenue

Suppose De Beers controls the entire diamond market. Exhibit 2 shows the demand curve for 1-carat diamonds. De Beers, for example, can sell three diamonds a day at $7,000 each. That price-quantity combination yields total revenue of $21,000 (=$7,000 × 3). Total revenue divided by quantity is the *average revenue per diamond,* which also is $7,000. Thus, the monopolist's price equals the average revenue per unit. To sell a fourth diamond, De Beers must drop the price to $6,750. Total revenue for four diamonds is $27,000 (=$6,750 × 4) and average revenue is $6,750. All along the demand curve, price equals average revenue. Therefore, *the demand curve is also the monopolist's average revenue curve,* just as the perfectly competitive firm's demand curve is that firm's average revenue curve.

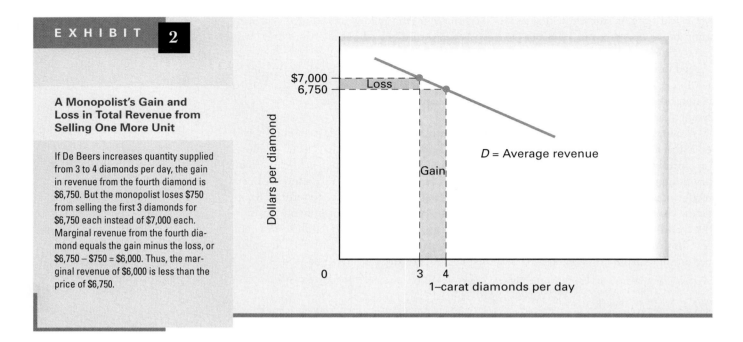

EXHIBIT   **2**

A Monopolist's Gain and Loss in Total Revenue from Selling One More Unit

If De Beers increases quantity supplied from 3 to 4 diamonds per day, the gain in revenue from the fourth diamond is $6,750. But the monopolist loses $750 from selling the first 3 diamonds for $6,750 each instead of $7,000 each. Marginal revenue from the fourth diamond equals the gain minus the loss, or $6,750 − $750 = $6,000. Thus, the marginal revenue of $6,000 is less than the price of $6,750.

What's the monopolist's marginal revenue from selling a fourth diamond? When De Beers drops the price from $7,000 to $6,750, total revenue goes from $21,000 to $27,000. Thus, *marginal revenue*—the change in total revenue from selling one more diamond—is $6,000, which is less than the price, or average revenue, of $6,750. *For a monopolist, marginal revenue is less than the price, or average revenue.* Recall that for a perfectly competitive firm, marginal revenue equals the price, or average revenue, because that firm can sell all it wants to at the market price.

The Gains and Loss from Selling One More Unit

A closer look at Exhibit 2 reveals why a monopolist's marginal revenue is less than the price. By selling another diamond, De Beers gains the revenue from that sale. For example, De Beers gets $6,750 from the fourth diamond, as shown by the blue-shaded vertical rectangle marked "Gain." But to sell that fourth unit, De Beers must sell all four diamonds for $6,750 each. Thus, to sell a fourth diamond, De Beers must sacrifice $250 on each of the first three diamonds, which could have been sold for $7,000 each. This loss in revenue from the first three units totals $750 (=$250 × 3) and is identified in Exhibit 2 by the pink-shaded horizontal rectangle marked "Loss." The net change in total revenue from selling the fourth diamond—that is, the marginal revenue from the fourth diamond—equals the *gain* minus the *loss,* which equals $6,750 minus $750, or $6,000. So marginal revenue equals the gain minus the loss, or the price minus the revenue forgone by selling all units for a lower price. Because a monopolist's marginal revenue equals the price minus the loss, you can see why the price exceeds marginal revenue.

Incidentally, this analysis assumes that all units of the good are sold at the market price; for example, the four diamonds are sold for $6,750 each. Although this is usually true, later in the chapter you will learn how some monopolists try to increase profit by charging different customers different prices.

(1) 1-Carat Diamonds per Day (*Q*)	(2) Price (average revenue) (*p*)	(3) Total Revenue (*TR* = *p* × *Q*)	(4) Marginal Revenue (*MR* = Δ*TR*/Δ*Q*)
0	$7,750	0	—
1	7,500	$ 7,500	$7,500
2	7,250	14,500	7,000
3	7,000	21,000	6,500
4	6,750	27,000	6,000
5	6,500	32,500	5,500
6	6,250	37,500	5,000
7	6,000	42,000	4,500
8	5,750	46,000	4,000
9	5,500	49,500	3,500
10	5,250	52,500	3,000
11	5,000	55,000	2,500
12	4,750	57,000	2,000
13	4,500	58,500	1,500
14	4,250	59,500	1,000
15	4,000	60,000	500
16	3,750	60,000	0
17	3,500	59,500	−500

EXHIBIT 3

Revenue for De Beers, a Monopolist

To sell more, the monopolist must lower the price on all units sold. Because the revenue lost from selling all units at a lower price must be subtracted from the revenue gained by selling another unit, marginal revenue is less than the price. At some point, marginal revenue turns negative, as shown here when the price is reduced to $3,500.

Revenue Schedules

Let's flesh out more fully the revenue schedules behind the demand curve of Exhibit 2. Column (1) of Exhibit 3 lists the quantity of diamonds demanded per day, and column (2) lists the corresponding price, or average revenue. The two columns together are the demand schedule facing De Beers for 1-carat diamonds. The price in column (2) times the quantity in column (1) yields the monopolist's *total revenue*, shown in column (3). So *TR* = *p* × *Q*. As De Beers expands output, total revenue increases until quantity reaches 15 diamonds.

Marginal revenue, the change in total revenue from selling one more diamond, appears in column (4). In shorthand, *MR* = Δ*TR*/Δ*Q*, or the change in total revenue divided by the change in quantity. Note in Exhibit 3 that after the first unit, marginal revenue is less than price. As the price declines, the gap between price and marginal revenue widens because the *loss* from selling all diamonds for less increases (because quantity increases) and the gain from selling another diamond decreases (because the price falls).

Revenue Curves

The data in Exhibit 3 are graphed in Exhibit 4, which shows the demand and marginal revenue curves in panel (a) and the total revenue curve in panel (b). Recall that total revenue equals price times quantity. Note that *the marginal revenue curve is below the demand curve and*

**Monopoly Demand and
Marginal Total Revenue**

Where demand is price elastic, marginal revenue is positive, so total revenue increases as the price falls.
Where demand is price inelastic, marginal revenue is negative, so total revenue decreases as the price falls.
Where demand is unit elastic, marginal
revenue is zero, so total revenue is at
a maximum, neither increasing nor
decreasing.

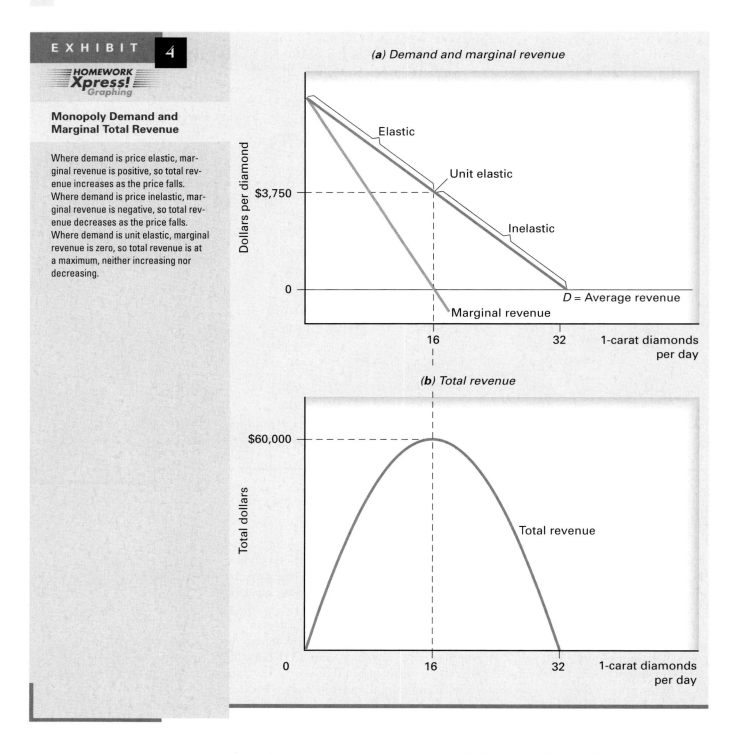

(a) Demand and marginal revenue

Elastic

Unit elastic

Inelastic

$3,750

0

D = Average revenue

Marginal revenue

16   32   1-carat diamonds
per day

(b) Total revenue

$60,000

Total revenue

0   16   32   1-carat diamonds
per day

that total revenue reaches a maximum when marginal revenue reaches zero. Take a minute now to
study these relationships—they are important.

Again, at any level of sales, price equals average revenue, so the demand curve is also the
monopolist's average revenue curve. In Chapter 5 you learned that the price elasticity for a

straight-line demand curve decreases as you move down the curve. When demand is elastic—that is, when the percentage increase in quantity demanded more than offsets the percentage decrease in price—a decrease in price increases total revenue. Therefore, *where demand is elastic, marginal revenue is positive, and total revenue increases as the price falls.* On the other hand, where demand is inelastic—that is, where the percentage increase in quantity demanded is less than the percentage decrease in price—a decrease in price reduces total revenue. In other words, the loss in revenue from selling all diamonds for the lower price overwhelms the gain in revenue from selling more diamonds. Therefore, *where demand is inelastic, marginal revenue is negative, and total revenue decreases as the price falls.*

From Exhibit 4, you can see that marginal revenue turns negative if the price drops below $3,750, indicating inelastic demand below that price. *A profit-maximizing monopolist would never willingly expand output to where demand is inelastic because doing so would reduce total revenue.* It would make no sense to sell more just to see total revenue drop. Also note that demand is unit elastic at the price of $3,750. At that price, marginal revenue is zero and total revenue reaches a maximum.

The Firm's Costs and Profit Maximization

In the case of perfect competition, each firm's choice is confined to *quantity* because the market already determines the price. The perfect competitor is a *price taker.* The monopolist, however, can choose either the price or the quantity, but choosing one determines the other—they come in pairs. For example, if De Beers decides to sell 10 diamonds a day, consumers would buy that many only at a price of $5,250. Alternatively, if De Beers decides to sell diamonds for $6,000 each, consumers would buy 7 a day at that price. Because the monopolist can select the price that maximizes profit, we say the monopolist is a *price maker.* More generally, any firm that has some control over what price to charge is a **price maker.**

PRICE MAKER

A firm that must find the profit-maximizing price when the demand curve for its output slopes downward

Profit Maximization

Exhibit 5 repeats the revenue data from Exhibits 3 and 4 and also includes short-run cost data reflecting costs similar to those already introduced in the two previous chapters. Take a little time now to become familiar with this table. Then ask yourself, which price-quantity combination should De Beers select to maximize profit? As was the case with perfect competition, the monopolist can approach profit maximization in two ways—the total approach and the marginal approach.

Total Revenue Minus Total Cost

The profit-maximizing monopolist employs the same decision rule as the competitive firm. *The monopolist produces the quantity at which total revenue exceeds total cost by the greatest amount.* Economic profit appears in column (8) of Exhibit 5. As you can see, the maximum profit is $12,500 per day, which occurs when output is 10 diamonds per day and the price is $5,250 per diamond. At that quantity, total revenue is $52,500 and total cost is $40,000.

Marginal Revenue Equals Marginal Cost

De Beers, as a profit-maximizing monopolist, increases output as long as selling more diamonds adds more to total revenue than to total cost. So De Beers expands output as long as marginal revenue, shown in column (4) of Exhibit 5, exceeds marginal cost, shown in column (6). But De Beers will stop short of where marginal cost exceeds marginal revenue. Again, profit is maximized at $12,500 when output is 10 diamonds per day. For the 10th diamond, marginal revenue is $3,000 and marginal cost is $2,750. As you can see, if output

EXHIBIT 5 **Short-Run Costs and Revenue for a Monopolist**

(1) Diamonds per Day (Q)	(2) Price (p)	(3) Total Revenue (TR = p × Q)	(4) Marginal Revenue (MR = ΔTR/ΔQ)	(5) Total Cost (TC)	(6) Marginal Cost (MC = ΔTC/ΔQ)	(7) Average Total Cost (ATC = TC/Q)	(8) Total Profit or Loss (= TR − TC)
0	$7,750	0	——	$15,000	——	——	−$15,000
1	7,500	$7,500	$7,500	19,750	$4,750	$19,750	−12,250
2	7,250	14,500	7,000	23,500	3,750	11,750	−9,000
3	7,000	21,000	6,500	26,500	3,000	8,833	−5,500
4	6,750	27,000	6,000	29,000	2,500	7,750	−2,000
5	6,500	32,500	5,500	31,000	2,000	6,200	1,500
6	6,250	37,500	5,000	32,500	1,500	5,417	5,000
7	6,000	42,000	4,500	33,750	1,250	4,821	8,250
8	5,750	46,000	4,000	35,250	1,500	4,406	10,750
9	5,500	49,500	3,500	37,250	2,000	4,139	12,250
10	**5,250**	**52,500**	**3,000**	**40,000**	**2,750**	**4,000**	**12,500**
11	5,000	55,000	2,500	43,250	3,250	3,932	11,750
12	4,750	57,000	2,000	48,000	4,750	4,000	9,000
13	4,500	58,500	1,500	54,500	6,500	4,192	4,000
14	4,250	59,500	1,000	64,000	9,500	4,571	−4,500
15	4,000	60,000	500	77,500	13,500	5,167	−17,500
16	3,750	60,000	0	96,000	18,500	6,000	−36,000
17	3,500	59,500	−500	121,000	25,000	7,117	−61,500

exceeds 10 diamonds per day, marginal cost exceeds marginal revenue. An 11th diamond's marginal cost of $3,250 exceeds its marginal revenue of $2,500. For simplicity, we say that *the profit-maximizing output occurs where marginal revenue equals marginal cost,* which, you will recall, is the golden rule of profit maximization.

Graphical Solution

The cost and revenue data in Exhibit 5 are graphed in Exhibit 6, with per-unit cost and revenue curves in panel (a) and total cost and revenue curves in panel (b). The intersection of the two marginal curves at point *e* in panel (a) indicates that profit is maximized when 10 diamonds are sold. At that quantity, we move up to the demand curve to find the profit-maximizing price of $5,250. The average total cost of $4,000 is identified by point *b*. The average profit per diamond equals the price of $5,250 minus the average total cost of $4,000. Economic profit is the average profit per unit of $1,250 multiplied by the 10 diamonds sold, for a total profit of $12,500 per day, as identified by the shaded rectangle. *So the profit-maximizing rate of output is found where the rising marginal cost curve intersects the marginal revenue curve.*

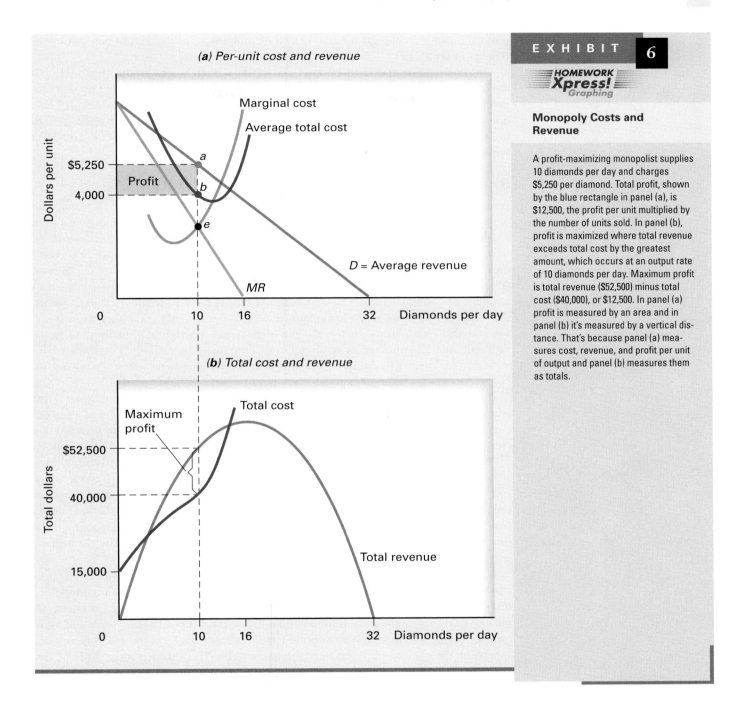

(a) Per-unit cost and revenue

Dollars per unit

Marginal cost

Average total cost

$5,250 — — — — — — *a*

Profit   *b*

4,000 — — — —

                          e

                                              D = Average revenue

                    MR

0   10   16   32   Diamonds per day

(b) Total cost and revenue

Total dollars

Maximum
profit

Total cost

$52,500 — — — — —

40,000 — — — —

                                        Total revenue

15,000 —

0   10   16   32   Diamonds per day

EXHIBIT 6

HOMEWORK
Xpress!
Graphing

**Monopoly Costs and
Revenue**

A profit-maximizing monopolist supplies
10 diamonds per day and charges
$5,250 per diamond. Total profit, shown
by the blue rectangle in panel (a), is
$12,500, the profit per unit multiplied by
the number of units sold. In panel (b),
profit is maximized where total revenue
exceeds total cost by the greatest
amount, which occurs at an output rate
of 10 diamonds per day. Maximum profit
is total revenue ($52,500) minus total
cost ($40,000), or $12,500. In panel (a)
profit is measured by an area and in
panel (b) it's measured by a vertical distance. That's because panel (a) measures cost, revenue, and profit per unit
of output and panel (b) measures them
as totals.

In panel (b), the firm's profit or loss is measured by the vertical distance between the total revenue and total cost curves. De Beers will expand output as long as the increase in total revenue from selling one more diamond exceeds the increase in total cost. *The profit-maximizing firm will produce where total revenue exceeds total cost by the greatest amount.* Again, profit
is maximized where De Beers sells 10 diamonds per day. Note again that in panel (b), total
profit is measured by the *vertical distance* between the two total curves, and in panel (a), total

profit is measure by the shaded *area* formed by multiplying average profit per unit by the number of units sold.

One common myth about monopolies is that they charge the highest price possible. But the monopolist is interested in maximizing profit, not price. The monopolist's price is limited by consumer demand. De Beers, for example, could charge $7,500 but would sell only one diamond at that price and would lose money. Indeed, De Beers could charge $7,750 or more but would sell no diamonds. So charging the highest possible price is not consistent with maximizing profit.

Short-Run Losses and the Shutdown Decision

A monopolist is not assured a profit. Although a monopolist is the sole supplier of a good with no close substitutes, the demand for that good may not generate economic profit in either the short run or the long run. After all, many new products are protected from direct competition by patents, yet most patents never turn into a profitable product. And even a monopolist that is initially profitable may eventually suffer losses because of rising costs, falling demand, or market entry of similar products. For example, Coleco, the original mass producer of Cabbage Patch dolls, went bankrupt after that craze died down. And Cuisinart, the company that introduced the food processor in the early 1980s, soon faced many imitators and filed for bankruptcy before the end of the decade (though its name lives on). In the short run, the loss-minimizing monopolist, like the loss-minimizing perfect competitor, must decide whether to produce or to shut down. *If the price covers average variable cost, the firm will produce. If not, the firm will shut down, at least in the short run.*

Exhibit 7 brings average variable cost back into the picture. Recall from Chapter 7 that average variable cost and average fixed cost sum to average total cost. Loss minimization occurs in Exhibit 7 at point *e,* where the marginal revenue curve intersects the marginal cost curve. At the equilibrium rate of output, Q, price *p* is found on the demand curve at point *b.* That price exceeds average variable cost, at point *c,* but is below average total cost, at point *a.* Because price covers average variable cost and makes some contribution to average fixed cost, this monopolist loses less by producing Q than by shutting down. The average loss per unit, measured by *ab,* is average total cost minus average revenue, or price. The loss, identified by the shaded rectangle, is the average loss per unit, *ab,* times the quantity sold, Q. The firm will shut down in the short run if the average variable cost curve is above the demand curve, or average revenue curve, at all output rates.

Recall that a perfectly competitive firm's supply curve is that portion of the marginal cost curve at or above the average variable cost curve. The intersection of a monopolist's marginal revenue and marginal cost curves identifies the profit-maximizing (or loss-minimizing) quantity, but the price is found up on the demand curve. Because the equilibrium quantity can be found along a monopolist's marginal cost curve, but the equilibrium price appears on the demand curve, no single curve shows both price and quantity supplied. Because no curve reflects combinations of price and quantity supplied, *there is no monopolist supply curve.*

Long-Run Profit Maximization

For perfectly competitive firms, the distinction between the short run and the long run is important because entry and exit of firms can occur in the long run, erasing any economic profit or loss. For the monopolist, the distinction between the short run and long run is less important. *If a monopoly is insulated from competition by high barriers that block new entry, economic profit can persist in the long run.* Yet short-run profit is no guarantee of long-run profit.

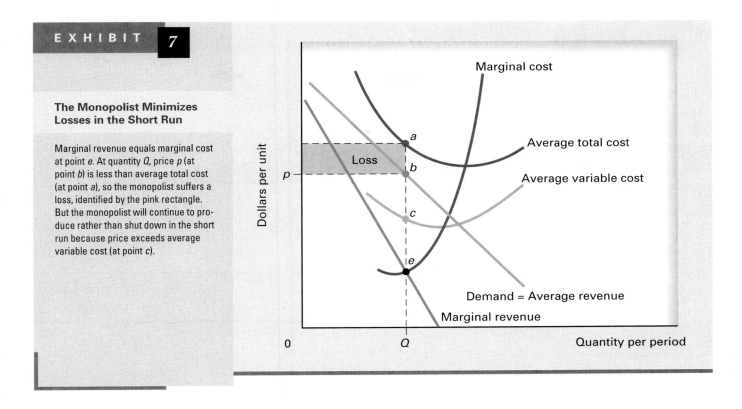

EXHIBIT   7

The Monopolist Minimizes Losses in the Short Run

Marginal revenue equals marginal cost at point *e*. At quantity *Q*, price *p* (at point *b*) is less than average total cost (at point *a*), so the monopolist suffers a loss, identified by the pink rectangle. But the monopolist will continue to produce rather than shut down in the short run because price exceeds average variable cost (at point *c*).

For example, suppose the monopoly relies on a patent. Patents last only so long and even while its product is under patent, the monopolist often must defend it in court (patent litigation has increased more than half in the last decade). On the other hand, a monopolist may be able to erase a loss (most start-up firms lose money initially) or increase profit in the long run by adjusting the scale of the firm or by advertising to increase demand. A monopolist unable to erase a loss will leave the market.

Monopoly and the Allocation of Resources

If monopolists are no greedier than perfect competitors (because both maximize profit), if monopolists do not charge the highest possible price, and if monopolists are not guaranteed a profit, then what's the problem with monopoly? To get a handle on the problem, let's compare monopoly with the benchmark established in the previous chapter—perfect competition.

Price and Output Under Perfect Competition

Let's begin with the long-run equilibrium price and output for a perfectly competitive market. Suppose the long-run market supply curve in perfect competition is horizontal, as shown by S_c in Exhibit 8. Because this is a constant-cost industry, the horizontal long-run supply curve also shows marginal cost and average total cost at each quantity. Equilibrium occurs at point *c*, where market demand and market supply curves intersect to yield price p_c and quantity Q_c. Remember, the demand curve reflects the marginal benefit of each unit purchased. In competitive equilibrium, the marginal benefit equals the marginal cost to

Perfect Competition and Monopoly

A perfectly competitive industry would produce output Q_c, determined by the intersection of the market demand curve *D* and the market supply curve S_c. The price would be p_c. A monopoly that could produce output at the same minimum average cost as a perfectly competitive industry would produce output Q_m, determined at point *b*, where marginal cost and marginal revenue intersect. The monopolist would charge price p_m. Thus, given the same costs, output is lower and price is higher under monopoly than under perfect competition.

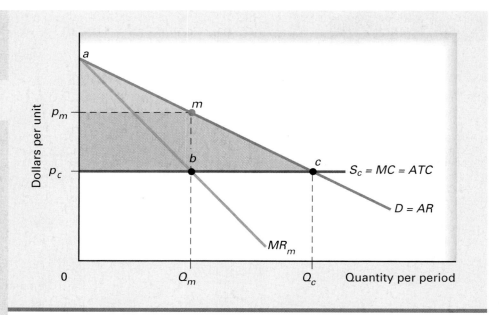

society of producing the final unit sold. As noted in the previous chapter, when the marginal benefit that consumers derive from a good equals the marginal cost of producing that good, that market is said to be allocatively efficient and to maximize social welfare. There is no way of reallocating resources to increase the total value of output or to increase social welfare. Because consumers are able to purchase Q_c units at price p_c, they enjoy a net benefit from consumption, or a consumer surplus, measured by the entire shaded triangle, acp_c.

Price and Output Under Monopoly

When there is only one firm in the industry, the industry demand curve becomes the monopolist's demand curve, so the price the monopolist charges determines how much gets sold. Because the monopolist's demand curve slopes downward, the marginal revenue curve also slopes downward and is beneath the demand curve, as is indicated by MR_m in Exhibit 8. Suppose the monopolist can produce at the same constant cost in the long run as can the competitive industry. The monopolist maximizes profit by equating marginal revenue with marginal cost, which occurs at point *b*, yielding equilibrium price p_m and output Q_m. Again, the price shows the consumers' marginal benefit for unit Q_m. This marginal benefit, identified at point *m*, exceeds the monopolist's marginal cost, identified at point *b*. Because marginal benefit exceeds marginal cost, society would be better off if output were expanded beyond Q_m. The monopolist restricts quantity below what would maximize social welfare. Even though the monopolist restricts output, consumers still derive some benefit; consumer surplus is shown by the smaller triangle, amp_m.

Allocative and Distributive Effects

Consider the allocative and distributive effects of monopoly versus perfect competition. In Exhibit 8, consumer surplus under perfect competition was the large triangle, acp_c. Under monopoly, consumer surplus shrinks to the smaller triangle amp_m, which in this example is only one-fourth as large. The monopolist earns economic profit equal to the shaded rectangle. By comparing the situation under monopoly with that under perfect competition, you can see that the monopolist's economic profit comes entirely from what was consumer surplus under perfect competition. Because the profit rectangle reflects a transfer from consumer surplus to monopoly profit, this amount is not lost to society and so is not considered a welfare loss.

Notice, however, that consumer surplus has been reduced by more than the profit rectangle. Consumers have also lost the triangle *mcb*, which was part of the consumer surplus under perfect competition. The *mcb* triangle is called the **deadweight loss of monopoly** because it is a loss to consumers but a gain to nobody. This loss results from the *allocative inefficiency arising from the higher price and reduced output of monopoly*. Again, society would be better off if output exceeded the monopolist's profit-maximizing quantity, because the marginal benefit of more output exceeds its marginal cost. Under monopoly, the price, or marginal benefit, always exceeds marginal cost. Empirical estimates of the annual deadweight loss of monopoly in the United States range from about 1 percent to about 5 percent of national income. Applied to national income data for 2004, these estimates imply a deadweight loss ranging from about $400 to $2,000 per capita, not a trivial amount.

Problems Estimating the Deadweight Loss of Monopoly

The actual cost of monopoly could differ from the deadweight loss described above. These costs could be lower or higher. Here's the reasoning.

Why the Deadweight Loss of Monopoly Might Be Lower

If economies of scale are substantial enough, a monopolist might be able to produce output at a lower cost per unit than could competitive firms. Therefore, the price, or at least the cost of production, could be lower under monopoly than under competition. The deadweight loss shown in Exhibit 8 may also overstate the true cost of monopoly because monopolists might, in response to public scrutiny and political pressure, keep prices below what the market could bear. Although monopolists would like to earn as much profit as possible, they realize that if the public outcry over high prices and high profit grows loud enough, some sort of government intervention could reduce or even erase that profit. For example, the prices and profit of drug companies, which individually are monopoly suppliers of patented medicines, come under scrutiny from time to time by federal legislators who want to regulate drug prices. Drug firms might try to avoid such treatment by keeping prices below the level that would maximize profit. Finally, a monopolist might keep the price below the profit-maximizing level to avoid attracting new competitors to the market. For example, some observers claim that Alcoa, when it was the only U.S. producer of aluminum, kept prices low enough to discourage new entry.

Why the Deadweight Loss Might Be Higher

Another line of reasoning suggests that the deadweight loss of monopoly might, in fact, be greater than shown in our simple diagram. *If resources must be devoted to securing and maintaining a monopoly position, monopolies may involve more of a welfare loss than simple models suggest.* For example, radio and TV broadcasting rights confer on the recipient the use a particular band of the scarce broadcast spectrum. In the past, these rights have been given away by government agencies to the applicants deemed most deserving. Because these rights are so valuable, numerous applicants spend millions on lawyers' fees, lobbying expenses, and other costs associated with making themselves appear the most deserving. The efforts devoted to securing and maintaining a monopoly position are largely a social waste because they use up scarce resources but add not one unit to output. Activities undertaken by individuals or firms to influence public policy in a way that will directly or indirectly redistribute income to them are referred to as **rent seeking.**

The monopolist, insulated from the rigors of competition in the marketplace, might also grow fat and lazy—and become inefficient. Because some monopolies could still earn an economic profit even if the firm is inefficient, corporate executives might waste resources creating a more comfortable life for themselves. Long lunches, afternoon golf, plush offices, corporate jets, and extensive employee benefits might make company life more pleasant, but they increase the cost of production and raise the price.

Monopolists have also been criticized for being slow to adopt the latest production techniques, being reluctant to develop new products, and generally lacking innovation. Because monopolists are largely insulated from the rigors of competition, they might take it easy. It's been said "The best of all monopoly profits is a quiet life."

The following case study discusses the performance of one of the nation's oldest monopolies, the U.S. Postal Service.

RENT SEEKING

Activities undertaken by individuals or firms to influence public policy in a way that will increase their incomes

C a s e **Study**

Public Policy

eActivity

How has the U.S. Postal Service dealt with competition and change? A chapter in its online history, at http://www.usps.com/history/his3_5. htm, describes the reforms made in the 1990s to compete with for-profit firms and email. How does the Postal Service set rates now that it is no longer a monopoly? The process is described at http://www.usps.com/ratecase/ how_rates.htm. What role do forces of competition play in rate setting? Online cost calculators are provided by both USPS at http://postcalc.usps.gov/ and UPS (United Parcel Service) at http://wwwapps.ups.com/QCC WebApp/request. Try finding the cost of sending a letter to Uruguay. Which is cheaper—USPS or UPS? Why?

The Mail Monopoly

The U.S. Post Office was granted a monopoly in 1775 and has operated under federal protection ever since. In 1971, Congress converted the Post Office Department into a semi-independent agency called the U.S. Postal Service, or USPS, with total revenue of about $70 billion in 2003. About 800,000 USPS employees handle more than half a billion pieces of mail a day—over 40 percent of the world's total. USPS pays no taxes and is exempt from local zoning laws. It has a legal monopoly in delivering regular, first-class letters and has the exclusive right to use the space inside your mailbox. Outfits like FedEx or UPS cannot deliver to mail boxes or post office boxes.

© Frank Siteman Studio

The USPS monopoly has suffered in recent years because of rising costs and stiff competition from new technologies. The price of a first-class stamp climbed from 6 cents in 1970 to 37 cents by 2003—a growth rate double that of inflation. Long-distance phone service, one possible substitute for first-class mail, has become cheaper since 1970. New technologies such as fax machines and email also compete with USPS (email messages now greatly outnumber first-class letters). Because the monopoly applies only to regular first-class mail, USPS has lost chunks of other business to private firms offering lower rates and better service. The United Parcel Service (UPS) is more mechanized and more containerized than the USPS and thus has lower costs and less breakage. The USPS has tried to emulate UPS but with only limited success. Postal employees are paid more on average than those at UPS or other private-sector delivery services, such as FedEx.

When the Postal Service raised third-class ("junk" mail) rates, businesses substituted other forms of advertising, including cable TV and telemarketing. UPS and other rivals now account for 75 percent of the ground-shipped packages. Even USPS's first-class monopoly is being threatened, because FedEx and others have captured 90 percent of the overnight mail business. Thus, USPS is losing business because of competition from overnight mail and from new technologies.

USPS has been fighting back, trying to leverage its monopoly power while increasing efficiency. On the electronic front, USPS tried to offer online postage purchases, online bill-paying service, and secure online document transmission service. But by December 2003, these new products had been scrapped as failures. In more successful efforts, USPS has partnered with eBay to confirm delivery of auctioned items and expedite payments. USPS also provides some local delivery service—the so-called "last mile"—for several major shippers including DHL, Emery, and FedEx. Despite these efforts, changing technology and competition are eroding the government-granted monopoly power.

Sources: Rick Brooks, "New UPS Service Sends Packages Through the Post Office," *Wall Street Journal*, 6 November 2003; Angela Kean, "Modernizing USPS," *Traffic World*, 9 June 2003; Mark Fitzgerald, "USPS' Snail-Mail Spam," *Editor & Publisher*, 14 April 2003; Rick Brooks, "Postal Service to Discontinue Online Bill-Payment Service," *Wall Street Journal*, 14 November 2003; and the USPS home page at http://www.usps.com.

Not all economists believe that monopolies, especially private monopolies, manage their resources with any less vigilance than perfect competitors do. Some argue that because monopolists are protected from rivals, they are in a good position to capture the fruits of any innovation and therefore will be more innovative than competitive firms are. Others believe that if a private monopolist strays from the path of profit maximization, its share price will drop enough to attract someone who will buy controlling interest and shape up the company. This market for corporate control is said to keep monopolists on their toes.

Price Discrimination

In the model developed so far, a monopolist, to sell more output, must lower the price. In reality, a monopolist can sometimes increase profit by charging higher prices to those who value the product more. This practice of charging different prices to different groups of consumers is called **price discrimination.** For example, children, students, and senior citizens often pay lower admission prices to ball games, movies, plays, and other events. Firms offer certain groups reduced prices because doing so boosts profits. Let's see how and why.

PRICE DISCRIMINATION

Increasing profit by charging different groups of consumers different prices when the price differences are not justified by differences in production costs

Conditions for Price Discrimination

To practice price discrimination, a firm's product must meet certain conditions. First, the demand curve for the firm's product must slope downward, indicating that the firm is a price maker—the producer has some market power, some control over the price. Second, there must be at least two groups of consumers for the product, each with a different price elasticity of demand. Third, the firm must be able, at little cost, to charge each group a different price for essentially the same product. Finally, the firm must be able to prevent those who pay the lower price from reselling the product to those who pay the higher price.

A Model of Price Discrimination

Exhibit 9 shows the effects of price discrimination. Consumers are sorted into two groups with different demand elasticities. For simplicity, we assume that the firm produces at a constant long-run average and marginal cost of $1.00. *At a given price,* the price elasticity of demand in panel (b) is greater than that in panel (a). Think of panel (b) as reflecting the demand of college students, senior citizens, or some other group more sensitive to the price. *This firm maximizes profit by finding the price in each market that equates marginal revenue with marginal cost.* For example, consumers with a lower price elasticity pay $3.00, and those with a higher price elasticity pay $1.50. Profit maximization results in charging a lower price to the group with the more elastic demand. Despite the price difference, the firm gets the same marginal revenue from the last unit sold to each group. Note that charging both groups $3.00 would eliminate any profit from that right-hand group of consumers, who would be priced out of the market. Charging both groups $1.50 would lead to negative marginal revenue from the left-hand group, which would reduce profit. No single price could generate the profit achieved through price discrimination.

Examples of Price Discrimination

Let's look at some examples of price discrimination. Because businesspeople face unpredictable yet urgent demands for travel and communication, and because their employers pay such expenses, businesspeople are less sensitive to price than are householders. In other words, businesspeople have a less elastic demand for business travel and long-distance phone use than do householders, so airlines and telephone services try to maximize profits by charging business customers higher rates than residential customers.

But how do firms distinguish between customer groups? Telephone companies are able to sort out customers by charging different rates based on the time of day. Long-distance rates are often higher during normal *business* hours than during evenings and weekends, when householders, who have a higher price elasticity of demand, make social calls. Airlines distinguish between business and household customers based on the terms under which tickets are purchased. Householders usually plan their trips well in advance and often spend the weekend. But business travel is more unpredictable, more urgent, and seldom involves a

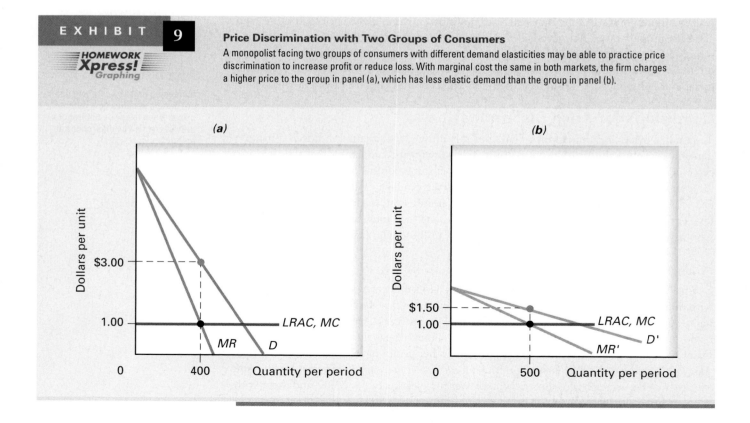

EXHIBIT 9

HOMEWORK
Xpress!
Graphing

Price Discrimination with Two Groups of Consumers

A monopolist facing two groups of consumers with different demand elasticities may be able to practice price discrimination to increase profit or reduce loss. With marginal cost the same in both markets, the firm charges a higher price to the group in panel (a), which has less elastic demand than the group in panel (b).

weekend stay. The airlines sort out the two groups by limiting discount fares to travelers who buy tickets well in advance and who stay over Saturday night. Airline tickets for business class costs much more than for coach class.

Here's another example of price discrimination: IBM wanted to charge business users of its laser printer more than home users. To distinguish between the two groups, IBM decided to slow down the home printer to 5 pages a minute (versus 10 for the business model). To do this, they added an extra chip that inserted pauses between pages.[2] Thus, IBM could sell the home model for less than the business model without cutting into sales of its business model.

Here's a final example. Major amusement parks, such as Disney World and Universal Studios, distinguish between local residents and out-of-towners when it comes to the price of admission. Out-of-towners typically spend a substantial amount on airlines and lodging just to be there, so they are less sensitive to the admission price than are local residents. The problem is how to charge a lower price to locals. The parks do this by making discount coupons available at local businesses, such as dry cleaners, which vacationers are less likely to visit.

Perfect Price Discrimination: The Monopolist's Dream

The demand curve shows the marginal value of each unit consumed, which is also the maximum amount consumers would pay for each unit. If the monopolist could charge a different price for each unit sold—a price reflected by the height of the demand curve—the firm's marginal revenue from selling one more unit would equal the price of that unit. Thus, the demand curve would become the firm's marginal revenue curve. A **perfectly discriminating monopolist** would charge a different price for each unit sold.

In Exhibit 10, again for simplicity, the monopolist is assumed to produce at a constant average and marginal cost in the long run. A perfectly discriminating monopolist, like any producer, would maximize profit by producing the quantity at which marginal revenue equals marginal cost. Because the demand curve is now the marginal revenue curve, the profit-maximizing quantity occurs where the demand, or marginal revenue, curve intersects the marginal cost curve, identified at point *e* in Exhibit 10. Price discrimination is a way of increasing profit. The area of the shaded triangle *aec* defines the perfectly discriminating monopolist's economic profit.

By charging a different price for each unit sold, the perfectly discriminating monopolist is able to convert every dollar of consumer surplus into economic profit. Although this practice may seem unfair to consumers, perfect price discrimination gets high marks based on allocative efficiency. Because such a monopolist does not have to lower the price to all customers to sell more, there is no reason to restrict output. In fact, because this is a constant-cost industry, Q is the same quantity produced in perfect competition (though in perfect competition, the triangle *aec* would be consumer surplus, not economic profit). As in the perfectly competitive outcome, the marginal benefit of the final unit produced and consumed just equals its marginal cost. And although perfect price discrimination yields no consumer surplus, the total benefits consumers derive just equal the total amount they pay for the good. Note also that because the monopolist does not restrict output, there is no deadweight loss. Thus, perfect price discrimination enhances social welfare when compared with monopoly output in the absence of price discrimination. But the monopolist reaps all net gains from production, while consumers just break even on the deal because their total benefit equals their total cost.

PERFECTLY DISCRIMINATING MONOPOLIST

A monopolist who charges a different price for each unit sold; also called the monopolist's dream

WALL STREET JOURNAL
Reading It **Right**

What's the relevance of the following statement from the Wall Street Journal: "Any merchant would love to sell a product at the highest price each customer will pay."

2. Carl Shapiro and Hal Varian, *Information Rules: A Strategic Guide to the Network Economy* (Boston: Harvard Business School Press, 1999), p. 59.

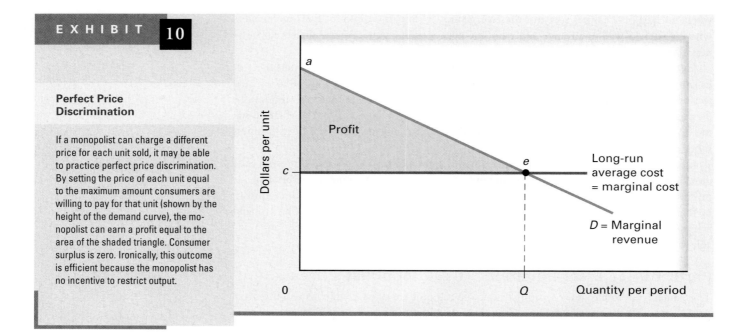

E X H I B I T 10

Perfect Price Discrimination

If a monopolist can charge a different price for each unit sold, it may be able to practice perfect price discrimination. By setting the price of each unit equal to the maximum amount consumers are willing to pay for that unit (shown by the height of the demand curve), the monopolist can earn a profit equal to the area of the shaded triangle. Consumer surplus is zero. Ironically, this outcome is efficient because the monopolist has no incentive to restrict output.

Examples of attempts to capture consumer surplus include pricing schemes for Internet service, cable television, and cellular phone service. For example, a cellular phone service offers several pricing alternatives, such as (1) price per minute with no basic fee, (2) a flat rate for the month plus a price per minute, and (3) a flat rate for unlimited calls. These alternatives allow the company to charge those who use fewer minutes more per minute than those who call more frequently. Such suppliers are trying to convert some consumer surplus into profit.

Conclusion

Pure monopoly, like perfect competition, is not that common. Perhaps the best examples are firms producing patented items with unique characteristics, such as certain prescription drugs. Some firms may have monopoly power in the short run, but the lure of economic profit encourages rivals to hurdle seemingly high entry barriers in the long run. Changing technology also works against monopoly in the long run. For example, the railroad monopoly was erased by the interstate highway system. AT&T's monopoly on long-distance phone service crumbled as microwave technology replaced copper wire. The U.S. Postal Service's monopoly on first-class mail is being eroded by overnight delivery, fax machines, and email. De Beers is losing its grip on the diamond market. And cable TV service is losing its local monopoly to technological breakthroughs in fiber-optics technology, wireless broadband, and the Internet.

Although perfect competition and pure monopoly are relatively rare, our examination of them yields a framework to help understand market structures that lie between the two extremes. As we will see, many firms have some degree of monopoly power—that is, they face downward-sloping demand curves. In the next chapter, we will consider the two market structures that lie in the gray region between perfect competition and monopoly.

S U M M A R Y

1. A monopolist sells a product with no close substitutes. Short-run economic profit earned by a monopolist can persist in the long run only if the entry of new firms is blocked. Three barriers to entry are (a) legal restrictions, such as patents and operating licenses; (b) economies of scale over a broad range of output; and (c) control over a key resource.

2. Because a monopolist is the sole supplier of a product with no close substitutes, its demand curve is also the market demand curve. Because a monopolist that does not price discriminate can sell more only by lowering the price for all units, marginal revenue is less than the price. Where demand is price elastic, marginal revenue is positive and total revenue increases as the price falls. Where demand is price inelastic, marginal revenue is negative and total revenue decreases as the price falls. A monopolist will never voluntarily produce where demand is inelastic because charging a higher price would increase total revenue.

3. If the monopolist can at least cover variable cost, profit is maximized or loss is minimized in the short run by finding the output rate that equates marginal revenue with marginal cost. At the profit-maximizing quantity, the price is found on the demand curve.

4. In the short run, a monopolist, like a perfect competitor, can earn economic profit but will shut down unless price at least covers average variable cost. In the long run, a monopolist, unlike a perfect competitor, can continue to earn economic profit as long as entry of other firms is blocked.

5. Resources are usually allocated less efficiently under monopoly than under perfect competition. If costs are similar, the monopolist will charge a higher price and supply less output than will a perfectly competitive industry. Monopoly usually results in a deadweight loss when compared with perfect competition because the loss of consumer surplus exceeds the gains in monopoly profit.

6. To increase profit through price discrimination, the monopolist must have at least two identifiable groups of customers, each with a different price elasticity of demand at a given price, and must be able to prevent customers charged the lower price from reselling to those charged the higher price.

7. A perfect price discriminator charges a different price for each unit of the good sold, thereby converting all consumer surplus into economic profit. Perfect price discrimination seems unfair because the monopolist "cleans up," but this approach is as efficient as perfect competition because the monopolist has no incentive to restrict output.

Q U E S T I O N S   F O R   R E V I E W

1. *(Barriers to Entry)* Complete each of the following sentences:

   a. A U.S. _____ awards inventors the exclusive right to production for 20 years.
   b. Patents and licenses are examples of government-imposed _____ that prevent entry into an industry.
   c. When economies of scale make it possible for a single firm to satisfy market demand at a lower cost per unit than could two or more firms, the single firm is considered a _____.
   d. A potential barrier to entry is a firm's control of a(n) _____ critical to production in the industry.

2. *(Barriers to Entry)* Explain how economies of scale can be a barrier to entry.

3. *(C a s e **Study:** Is a Diamond Forever?)* How did the De Beers cartel try to maintain control of the price in the diamond market? How has this control been threatened?

4. *(Revenue for the Monopolist)* How does the demand curve faced by a monopolist differ from the demand curve faced by a perfectly competitive firm?

5. *(Revenue for the Monopolist)* Why is it impossible for a profit-maximizing monopolist to choose any price *and* any quantity it wishes?

6. *(Revenue Schedules)* Explain why the marginal revenue curve for a monopolist lies below its demand curve, rather than coinciding with the demand curve, as is the case for a perfectly competitive firm. Is it ever possible for a monop-

olist's marginal revenue curve to coincide with its demand curve?

7. *(Revenue Curves)* Why would a monopoly firm never knowingly produce on the inelastic portion of its demand curve?

8. *(Profit Maximization)* Review the following graph showing the short-run situation of a monopolist. What output level will the firm choose in the short run? Why?

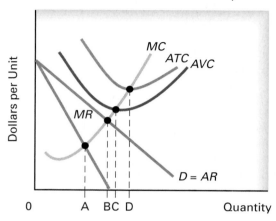

9. *(Allocative and Distributive Effects)* Why is society worse off under monopoly than under perfect competition, even if both market structures face the same constant long-run average cost curve?

10. *(Welfare Cost of Monopoly)* Explain why the welfare loss of a monopoly may be smaller or larger than the loss shown in Exhibit 8 in this chapter.

11. (*C a s e* **S t u d y :** The Mail Monopoly) Can the U.S. Postal Service be considered a monopoly in first-class mail? Why or why not? What has happened to the price elasticity of demand for first-class mail in recent years?

12. *(Conditions for Price Discrimination)* What four conditions must be met for a monopolist to price discriminate successfully?

13. *(Price Discrimination)* Explain how it may be profitable for South Korean manufacturers to sell new autos at a lower price in the United States than in South Korea, even with transportation costs included.

14. *(Perfect Price Discrimination)* Why is the perfectly discriminating monopolist's marginal revenue curve identical to the demand curve it faces?

PROBLEMS AND EXERCISES

15. *(Short-Run Profit Maximization)* Answer the following questions on the basis of the monopolist's situation illustrated in the following graph.

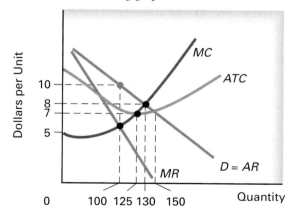

a. At what output rate and price will the monopolist operate?

b. In equilibrium, approximately what will be the firm's total cost and total revenue?

c. What will be the firm's profit or loss in equilibrium?

16. *(Monopoly)* Suppose that a certain manufacturer has a monopoly on the sorority and fraternity ring business (a constant-cost industry) because it has persuaded the "Greeks" to give it exclusive rights to their insignia.

a. Using demand and cost curves, draw a diagram depicting the firm's profit-maximizing price and output level.

b. Why is marginal revenue less than price for this firm?

c. On your diagram, show the deadweight loss that occurs because the output level is determined by a monopoly rather than by a competitive market.

d. What would happen if the Greeks decided to charge the manufacturer a royalty fee of $3 per ring?

EXPERIENTIAL EXERCISES

17. *(The Welfare Cost of Monopoly)* In many larger U.S. cities, monopoly owners of sports franchises have been lobbying local governments for new publicly financed sports stadiums. Is this a form of rent seeking? Go to Heartland Institute's Web site at http://www.heartland.org/Index.cfm, conduct a search for sports stadiums, and look at one of the documents collected there. Is there convincing evidence of rent seeking? If so, how does that relate to the welfare cost of monopoly?

18. *(Price Discrimination)* The Robinson–Patman Act is a federal statute that outlaws certain forms of price discrimination. Review the main provisions of the Act as outlined by RPAMall at http://www.lawmall.com/rpa/. Then visit a local supermarket and look for evidence of price discrimination. Are the conditions for price discrimination, as outlined in this chapter, met there? Do you think the forms of price discrimination you found are legal under the Robinson–Patman Act?

19. *(Wall Street Journal)* The Legal Beat column, found in the Marketplace section of the Wall Street Journal, chronicles court decisions and legal trends that affect American businesses. In the legal arena, firms and the government often struggle over monopoly power. Find an article describing a firm seeking to restrict competition or a government action aimed at reducing monopoly power. See if you can use the monopoly model to understand the issues involved.

20. *(Wall Street Journal)* Look at the Travel page in the Weekend section of Friday's Wall Street Journal. Find the section displaying airfares. You will find that there are often a number of different fares between identical locations. Do these price differences necessarily represent the use of price discrimination? Why or Why not?

HOMEWORK XPRESS! EXERCISES

These exercises require access to McEachern Homework Xpress! If Homework Xpress! did not come with your book, visit **http://homeworkxpress.swlearning.com** *to purchase.*

Sal's Sandals has obtained a patent for its innovative footwear. Sal's estimate of demand for the firm's sandals is shown in the table.

1. Use Sal's values to plot the demand curve and to find and plot the marginal revenue curve for his sandals.

Quantity of sandals per period	Price
0	$ 50
10	45
20	40
30	35
40	30
50	25
60	20

2. Sal's estimates of demand and marginal revenue are as from Problem 1. Add a marginal cost curve so that the profit maximizing quantity is 30. Identify the price Sal would charge. Add an average total cost curve so that the average cost per unit is $30. Create a shaded box illustrating profits.

3. Sal's estimates of demand and marginal revenue are as from Problem 1. Draw typically shaped marginal cost, average total cost, and average variable cost curves to illustrate when Sal might choose to operate at a loss in the short run. Identify the quantity he would produce and the price he would charge. Create a shaded box illustrating his loss.

4. Red River Valley Electric Power has a monopoly in the supply of electric power in its region. Draw a diagram with a downward sloping demand curve and the corresponding marginal revenue curve. Add a constant average cost curve and identify the quantity produced and price charged when Red River exercises its monopoly power.

   However, the industry is soon to be opened to competition. Identify the price and quantity that would be expected in a competitive market for electric power. Shade in the area that represents the deadweight loss eliminated when the market is opened to competition.

Monopolistic Competition and Oligopoly

© Andrew Winning/Reuters/Corbis

Why is Perrier water sold in green, tear-shaped bottles? Why are some shampoos sold only in salons? Why do some pizza makers deliver? Why do airlines engage in airfare warfare? Why was the oil cartel, OPEC, created, and why has it met with only spotty success? Why is there a witness protection program? To answer these and other questions, we turn in this chapter to the vast gray area that lies between perfect competition and monopoly.

Perfect competition and monopoly are extreme market structures. Under perfect competition, many suppliers offer an identical product and, in the long run, can enter or leave the industry with ease. A monopolist supplies a product with no close substitutes in a market where natural and artificial barriers keep out would-be competitors. These polar market structures are logically appealing and offer a useful description of some industries observed in the economy.

But most firms fit into neither market structure. Some markets have many sellers producing goods that vary slightly, such as the many convenience stores that abound. Other markets consist of just a few sellers that in some industries produce commodities (such as oil) and in other industries produce differentiated goods (such as automobiles). This chapter examines the two remaining market structures that together include most firms in the economy. Topics discussed include:

- Monopolistic competition
- Product differentiation
- Excess capacity

- Oligopoly
- Collusion
- Prisoner's dilemma

Monopolistic Competition

During the 1920s and 1930s, economists began formulating models that fit between perfect competition and monopoly. Two models of *monopolistic competition* were developed independently. In 1933 Edward Chamberlin of Harvard University published *The Theory of Monopolistic Competition*. Across the Atlantic that same year, Joan Robinson of Cambridge University published *The Economics of Imperfect Competition*. Although the theories differed, their underlying principles were similar. We will discuss Chamberlin's approach.

Characteristics of Monopolistic Competition

As the expression **monopolistic competition** suggests, this market structure contains elements of both monopoly and competition. Chamberlin used the term to describe a market in which many producers offer products that are substitutes but are not viewed as identical by consumers. Because the products of different suppliers differ slightly—for example, some convenience stores are closer to you than others—the demand curve for each is not horizontal but slopes downward. Each supplier has some power over the price it can charge. Thus, the firms that populate this market are not *price takers,* as they would be under perfect competition, but are *price makers.*

Because barriers to entry are low, firms in monopolistic competition can, in the long run, enter or leave the market with ease. Consequently, there are enough sellers that they behave competitively. There are also enough sellers that each tends to get lost in the crowd. For example, in a large metropolitan area, an individual restaurant, gas station, drugstore, video store, dry cleaner, or convenience store tends to act *independently.* In other market structures, there may be only two or three sellers in each market, so they keep an eye on one another; they act *interdependently.* You will understand the relevance of this distinction later in the chapter.

Product Differentiation

In perfect competition, the product is a commodity, meaning it's identical across producers, such as a bushel of wheat. In monopolistic competition, the product differs somewhat among sellers, as with the difference between one rock radio station and another. Sellers differentiate their products in four basic ways.

Physical Differences

The most obvious way products differ is in their physical appearance and their qualities. Packaging is also designed to make a product stand out in a crowded field, such as a distinctive bottle of water (Perrier) and instant soup in a cup (Cup O' Soup®). Physical differences

MONOPOLISTIC COMPETITION

A market structure with many firms selling products that are substitutes but different enough that each firm's demand curve slopes downward; firm entry is relatively easy

are seemingly endless: size, weight, color, taste, texture, and so on. Shampoos, for example, differ in color, scent, thickness, lathering ability, and bottle design. Particular brands aim at consumers with dandruff and those with normal, dry, or oily hair.

Location

The number and variety of locations where a product is available are other ways of differentiation—*spatial differentiation*. Some products seem to be available everywhere, including the Internet; finding other products requires some search and travel. If you live in a metropolitan area, you are no doubt accustomed to the many convenience stores that populate the region. Each wants to be closest to you when you need that gallon of milk or loaf of bread—thus, the proliferation of stores. As the name says, these mini grocery stores are selling *convenience*. Their prices are higher and selections more limited than those of regular grocery stores, but they are likely to be nearer customers, they don't have long lines, and some are open all night.

Services

Products also differ in terms of their accompanying services. For example, some pizza sellers, like Domino's, and some booksellers, like Amazon.com, deliver; others don't. Some retailers offer product demonstrations by a well-trained staff; others are mostly self-service. Some products include online support and toll-free numbers; others provide no help at all. Some offer money-back guarantees; others say "no returns." The quality and range of service often differentiate otherwise close substitutes.

Product Image

A final way products differ is in the image the producer tries to foster in the consumer's mind. For example, suppliers of sportswear, clothing, watches, and cosmetics often pay for endorsements from athletes, models, and other celebrities. Some producers try to demonstrate high quality based on where products are sold, such as shampoo sold only in hair salons. Some products tout their all-natural ingredients, such as Ben & Jerry's ice cream and Tom's of Maine toothpaste, or appeal to environmental concerns by focusing on recycled packaging, such as the Starbucks coffee cup insulating sleeve "made from 60% post-consumer recycled fiber." Producers try to create and maintain brand loyalty through product promotion and advertising.

Short-Run Profit Maximization or Loss Minimization

Because each monopolistic competitor offers a product that differs somewhat from what others supply, each has some control over the price charged. This *market power* means that each firm's demand curve slopes downward. Because many firms are selling substitutes, any firm that raises its price can expect to lose some customers, but not all, to rivals. By way of comparison, a price hike would cost a monopolist fewer customers but would cost a perfect competitor *all* customers. Therefore, a monopolistic competitor faces a demand curve that tends to be more elastic than a monopolist's but less elastic than a perfect competitor's.

Recall that the availability of substitutes for a given product affects its price elasticity of demand. The price elasticity of the monopolistic competitor's demand depends on (1) the number of rival firms that produce similar products and (2) the firm's ability to differentiate its product from those of its rivals. *A firm's demand curve will be more elastic the more substitutes there are and the less differentiated its product is.*

Marginal Revenue Equals Marginal Cost

From our study of monopoly, we know that the downward-sloping demand curve means the marginal revenue curve also slopes downward and lies beneath the demand curve. Exhibit 1 depicts demand and marginal revenue curves for a monopolistic competitor. The exhibit also presents average and marginal cost curves. Remember that the forces that determine the cost of production are largely independent of the forces that shape demand, so there is nothing special about a monopolistic competitor's cost curves. In the short run, a firm that can at least cover its variable cost will increase output as long as marginal revenue exceeds marginal cost. A monopolistic competitor maximizes profit just as a monopolist does: *the profit-maximizing quantity occurs where marginal revenue equals marginal cost; the profit-maximizing price for that quantity is found up on the demand curve.* Exhibit 1 shows the price and quantity combinations that maximize short-run profit in panel (a), and minimize short-run loss in panel (b). In each panel, the marginal cost and marginal revenue curves intersect at point *e*, yielding equilibrium output *q*, equilibrium price *p*, and average total cost *c*.

Maximizing Profit or Minimizing Loss in the Short Run

Recall that the short run is a period too brief to allow firms to enter or leave the market. The demand and cost conditions shown in panel (a) of Exhibit 1 indicate that this firm will earn economic profit in the short run. At the firm's profit-maximizing quantity, average total

EXHIBIT 1

Monopolistic Competitor in the Short Run

The monopolistically competitive firm produces the level of output at which marginal revenue equals marginal cost (point *e*) and charges the price indicated by point *b* on the downward-sloping demand curve. In panel (a), the firm produces *q* units, sells them at price *p*, and earns a short-run economic profit equal to (*p* – *c*) multiplied by *q*, shown by the blue rectangle. In panel (b), the average total cost exceeds the price at the output where marginal revenue equals marginal cost. Thus, the firm suffers a short-run loss equal to (*c* – *p*) multiplied by *q*, shown by the pink rectangle.

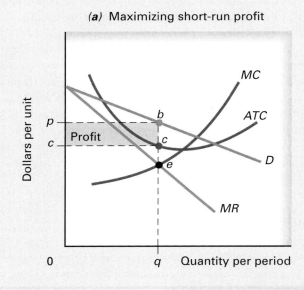

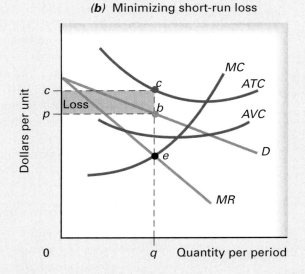

EXHIBIT 2

Long-Run Equilibrium in Monopolistic Competition

If existing firms earn economic profits, new firms will enter the industry in the long run. This entry reduces the demand facing each firm. In the long run, the demand curve shifts leftward until marginal revenue equals marginal cost (point *a*) and the demand curve is tangent to the average total cost curve (point *b*). Economic profit is zero at output *q*. With zero economic profit, no more firms will enter, so the industry is in long-run equilibrium. The same long-run outcome will occur if firms suffer a short-run loss. Firms will leave until remaining firms earn just a normal profit.

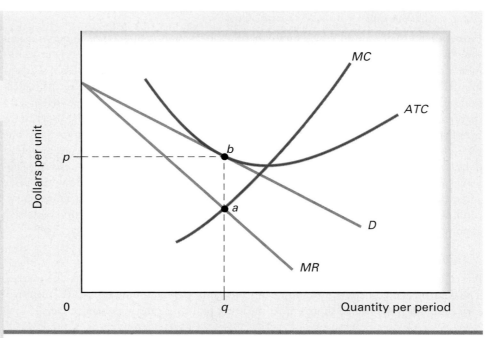

cost, c , is below the price, p. Price minus average total cost is the firm's profit per unit, which, when multiplied by the quantity, yields economic profit, shown by the shaded rectangle. Again, the profit-maximizing quantity is found where marginal revenue equals marginal cost; price is found up on the demand curve at that quantity. Thus, a monopolistic competitor, like a monopolist, has no supply curve—that is, *there is no curve that uniquely relates alternative prices and corresponding quantities supplied*.

The monopolistic competitor, like other firms, has no guarantee of economic profit. The firm's demand and cost curves could be as shown in panel (b), where the average total cost curve lies entirely above the demand curve, so no quantity would allow the firm to break even. In such a situation, the firm must decide whether to produce or to shut down temporarily. The rule here is the same as with perfect competition and monopoly: as long as the price exceeds average variable cost, the firm in the short run will lose less by producing than by shutting down. If no price covers average variable cost, the firm will shut down. Recall that the halt in production may be only temporary; shutting down is not the same as going out of business. Firms that expect economic losses to persist may, in the long run, leave the industry.

Short-run profit maximization in monopolistic competition is quite similar to that under monopoly. But the stories differ in the long run, as we'll see next.

Zero Economic Profit in the Long Run

Low barriers to entry in monopolistic competition mean that short-run economic profit will attract new entrants in the long run. Because new entrants offer products that are similar to those offered by existing firms, they draw customers away from existing firms, thereby reducing the demand facing each firm. Entry will continue in the long run until economic profit disappears. *Because of the ease of entry to the market, monopolistically competitive firms earn zero economic profit in the long run.*

If they continue to suffer short-run losses, some monopolistic competitors will leave the industry in the long run, redirecting their resources to products expected to earn at least a normal profit. As firms leave, their customers will switch to the remaining firms, increasing the demand for those products. Firms will continue to leave in the long run until the remaining firms have sufficient customers to earn normal profit, but not economic profit.

Exhibit 2 shows long-run equilibrium for a typical monopolistic competitor. In the long run, entry and exit will alter each firm's demand curve until economic profit disappears—that is, until price equals average total cost. In Exhibit 2, the marginal revenue curve intersects the marginal cost curve at point *a*. At the equilibrium quantity, *q*, the average total cost curve at point *b* is tangent to the demand curve. Because average total cost equals the price, the firm earns no economic profit but does earn a normal profit. At all other rates of output, the firm's average total cost is above the demand curve, so the firm would lose money if it reduced or expanded its output.

Thus, because entry is easy in monopolistic competition, short-run economic profit will draw new entrants into the industry in the long run. The demand curve facing each monopolistic competitor shifts left until economic profit disappears. A short-run economic loss will prompt some firms to leave the industry in the long run until remaining firms earn just a normal profit. In summary: *Monopolistic competition is like monopoly in the sense that firms in each industry face demand curves that slope downward. Monopolistic competition is like perfect competition in the sense that easy entry and exit eliminate economic profit or economic loss in the long run.*

One way to understand how firm entry erases short-run economic profit is to consider the evolution of an industry, as is discussed in the following case study.

Fast Forward

The introduction of videocassette recorders, or VCRs, fueled demand for videotaped movies. The initial surge in demand was magnified by rentals of older movies that consumers had missed at theaters. The first wave of outlets charged about $5 per day, required security deposits for tapes, and imposed membership fees of up to $100. In the late 1970s and early 1980s, most rental stores faced little competition and many earned short-run economic profits. But because entry was relatively easy, this profit attracted competitors. Convenience stores, grocery stores, bookstores, even drugstores began renting videos as a sideline. Between 1982 and 1987, the number of video outlets quadrupled, growing faster than the demand for VCRs. Once consumers caught up with the backlog of older movies, demand focused primarily on new releases.

World of Business

eActivity

Movielink, LLC, at http://www.movielink.com, is a joint venture of Metro-Goldwyn-Mayer Studios, Paramount Pictures, Sony Pictures Entertainment, Universal Studios, and Warner Bros. Studios. Movielink provides downloadable movies from a wide selection of listings, including independent films. Visit its site and read about the company and its management. What problems provided the catalyst for this company's creation? Is the company practicing monopolistic competition? Or something else?

Thus, the supply of rental outlets increased faster than the demand. The 1990s brought more bad news for the industry, when hundreds of cable channels and pay-per-view options offered substitutes for video rentals. The greater supply of rentals along with the increased availability of substitutes had the predictable effect on market prices. Rental rates crashed to as little as $0.99. Membership fees and tape deposits disappeared. Rental stores that could not survive folded. So many failed that a market developed to buy and resell their tape inventories.

The video rental business grew little during the 1990s. The industry "shakeout" is still going on. Even after the addition of DVDs and video games, rental revenue per store declined in 2003. Blockbuster has grown to more than 6,000 U.S. stores, and now accounts for more than a third of the U.S. market, four times the share of second-ranked Hollywood Video. Blockbuster is transforming the rental industry from monopolistic competition to *oligopoly*, a market structure to be examined later in the chapter. But Blockbuster faces its own growing pains, including an "excess inventory" of tapes and a failed effort to sell books, magazines, and snacks at its rental stores.

The latest threat to the rental business is on-demand movies delivered by broadband cable. With a remote control and a digital cable box, customers can rent, rewind, pause, and replay movies, all without leaving the couch. Five of the largest Hollywood studios launched an Internet service called Movielink to supply downloaded movies. Blockbuster is trying to get into the broadband business, but success there could cannibalize its rental business. With an inventory of over 12,000 tapes and DVDs per store, Blockbuster would get stuck with more than 75 million tapes nationwide. Such is the dynamic nature of market evolution— out with the old and in with the new, in a competitive process that has been aptly called *creative destruction*.

Sources: "VHS and DVD Rental Spending," *Video Business*, 5 April 2004; Janet Whitman, "Blockbuster's Poor Sales Results Cast Shadow Over Rise in Net," *Wall Street Journal*, 22 October 2003; and "Movie Mayhem with Video-on-Demand," *Retail Merchandiser*, January 2003. Blockbuster's home page is http://www.blockbuster.com/.

Monopolistic Competition and Perfect Competition Compared

How does monopolistic competition compare with perfect competition in terms of efficiency? In the long run, neither can earn economic profit, so what's the difference? The difference arises because of the different demand curves facing individual firms in each of the two market structures. Exhibit 3 presents the long-run equilibrium price and quantity for a typical firm in each market structure, assuming each firm has identical cost curves. In each case, the marginal cost curve intersects the marginal revenue curve at the quantity where the average total cost curve is tangent to the firm's demand curve.

A perfect competitor's demand curve is a horizontal line drawn at the market price, as shown in panel (a). This demand curve is tangent to the lowest point of the long-run average total cost curve. Thus, a perfect competitor in the long run produces at the lowest possible average cost. In panel (b), a monopolistic competitor faces a downward-sloping demand curve because its product differs somewhat from those of other suppliers. In the long run, the monopolistic competitor produces less than required to achieve the lowest possible average cost. Thus, the price and average cost under monopolistic competition, identified as p' in panel (b), exceed the price and average cost under perfect competition, identified as p in panel (a). *If firms have the same cost curves, the monopolistic competitor produces less and charges more than the perfect competitor does in the long run, but neither earns economic profit.*

Firms in monopolistic competition are not producing at minimum average cost. They are said to have **excess capacity**, because production falls short of the quantity that would achieve the lowest average cost. Excess capacity means that each producer could easily serve more customers and in the process would lower average cost. *The marginal value of increased output would exceed its marginal cost, so greater output would increase social welfare.* Such excess

capacity exists with gas stations, drugstores, convenience stores, restaurants, motels, book-stores, flower shops, and firms in other monopolistic competitive industries. A specific example is the funeral business. Industry analysts argue that the nation's 22,000 funeral directors could efficiently handle 4 million funerals a year, but only about 2.3 million people die. So the industry operates at less than 60 percent of capacity, resulting in a higher average cost per funeral because valuable resources remain idle much of the time.

One other difference between perfect competition and monopolistic competition does not show up in Exhibit 3. Although the cost curves drawn in each panel of the exhibit are identical, firms in monopolistic competition advertise more to differentiate their products than do firms in perfect competition. These higher advertising costs shift up their average cost curves.

Some economists have argued that monopolistic competition results in too many suppliers and artificial product differentiation. The counterargument is that consumers are willing to pay a higher price for a wider selection. According to this latter view, consumers benefit from more choice among gas stations, restaurants, convenience stores, clothing stores, video

---

EXHIBIT 3

Perfect Competition Versus Monopolistic Competition in Long-Run Equilibrium

Cost curves are assumed to be the same in each panel. The perfectly competitive firm of panel (a) faces a demand curve that is horizontal at market price *p*. Long-run equilibrium occurs at output *q*, where the demand curve is tangent to the average total cost curve at its lowest point. The monopolistically competitive firm of panel (b) is in long-run equilibrium at output *q'*, where demand is tangent to average total cost. Because the demand curve slopes downward in panel (b), however, the tangency does not occur at the minimum point of average total cost. Thus, the monopolistically competitive firm produces less output and charges a higher price than does a perfectly competitive firm with the same cost curves. Neither firm earns economic profit in the long run.

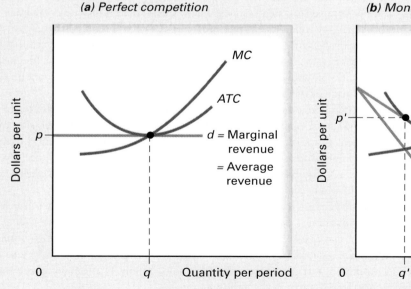

(a) Perfect competition

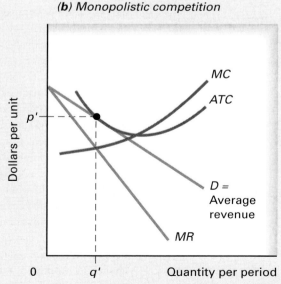

(b) Monopolistic competition

stores, drugstores, textbooks, hiking boots, and many other goods and services. For example, what if half of the restaurants in your area were to close just so the remaining ones could reduce their excess capacity? Some consumers, including you, might be disappointed if a favorite closed.

Perfect competitors and monopolistic competitors are so numerous in their respective markets that an action by any one of them has little or no effect on the behavior of others in the market. Another important market structure on the continuum between perfect competition and monopoly has just a few firms. We explore this market structure in the balance of the chapter.

An Introduction to Oligopoly

The final market structure we examine is *oligopoly,* a Greek word meaning "few sellers." When you think of "big business," you are thinking of **oligopoly,** a market dominated by just a few firms. Perhaps three or four account for more than half the market supply. Many industries, including steel, automobiles, oil, breakfast cereals, cigarettes, personal computers, and operating systems software, are *oligopolistic.* Because an oligopoly has only a few firms, each must consider the effect of its own actions on competitors' behavior. Oligopolists are therefore said to be *interdependent.*

Varieties of Oligopoly

In some oligopolies, such as steel or oil, the product is identical, or undifferentiated, across producers. Thus, an **undifferentiated oligopoly** sells a commodity, such as an ingot of steel or a barrel of oil. But in other oligopolies, such as automobiles or breakfast cereals, the product is differentiated across producers. A **differentiated oligopoly** sells products that differ across producers, such as a Toyota Camry versus a Ford Taurus or General Mills's Wheaties versus Kellogg's Corn Flakes.

The more similar the products, the greater the interdependence among firms in the industry. For example, because steel ingots are essentially identical, steel producers are quite sensitive to each other's prices. A small rise in one producer's price will send customers to rivals. But with differentiated oligopoly, such as the auto industry, producers are not quite as sensitive about each other's prices. As with monopolistic competitors, oligopolists differentiate their products through (1) physical qualities, (2) sales locations, (3) services provided with the product, and (4) the image of the product established in the consumer's mind.

Because of interdependence, the behavior of any particular firm is difficult to predict. *Each firm knows that any changes in its product's quality, price, output, or advertising policy may prompt a reaction from its rivals. And each firm may react if another firm alters any of these features.* Monopolistic competition is like a professional golf tournament, where each player strives for a personal best. Oligopoly is more like a tennis match, where each player's actions depend on how and where the opponent hits the ball.

Why have some industries evolved into oligopolies, dominated by only a few firms? Although the reasons are not always clear, *an oligopoly can often be traced to some form of barrier to entry, such as economies of scale, legal restrictions, brand names built up by years of advertising, or control over an essential resource.* In the previous chapter, we examined barriers to entry as they applied to monopoly. The same principles apply to oligopoly. The following case study considers some barriers to entry in the airline industry.

OLIGOPOLY

A market structure characterized by a few firms whose behavior is interdependent

UNDIFFERENTIATED OLIGOPOLY

An oligopoly that sells a commodity, or a product that does not differ across suppliers, such as an ingot of steel or a barrel of oil

DIFFERENTIATED OLIGOPOLY

An oligopoly that sells products that differ across suppliers, such as automobiles or breakfast cereal

The Unfriendly Skies

At one time, airline routes were straight lines from one city to another. Now they radiate like the spokes of a wagon wheel from a "hub" city. From about 30 hub airports across the country, the airlines send out planes along the spokes to about 400 commercial airports and then quickly bring them back to the hubs. Major airlines dominate hub airports. For example, half the passengers at Dallas–Fort Worth airport fly United Airlines. A new airline trying to enter the industry must secure a hub airport as well as landing slots at crowded airports around the country—not an easy task because hubs are crowded and landing slots are scarce. Hubs and landing slots create the first barrier to entry in the airline industry. Research shows that ticket prices at airports dominated by a single airline are higher than at more competitive airports.

© George Hall/Corbis

A second barrier to entry is frequent-flyer mileage programs. The biggest airlines fly more national and international routes, so they offer more opportunities both to accumulate frequent-flyer miles and to use them. Thus, the biggest airlines have the most attractive programs. A third barrier to entry is federal restrictions that prevent foreign ownership of U.S. airlines and block foreign airlines from offering connecting service between U.S. cities. Thus, scarce hubs and gates, frequent-flier programs, and restrictions against foreign competition create barriers to entry in the airline industry. Seven airlines account for over 80 percent of all passenger service.

But the entry of low-cost carriers is now challenging the top airlines. Upstart Jet Blue and Southwest Airlines were among the few to earn a profit in recent years. Both airlines fill a higher proportion of their seats than does the industry on average. So the entry barriers discussed above apparently have not blocked all entry.

Sources: "Low Cost Airlines: Crowded Skies," *The Economist;* 24 April 2004; "Southwest's Entry Shakes Up Airline Competition at Philadelphia Airport," *Philadelphia Inquirer,* 29 October 2003; Nick Pachetti, "Jet Blue Skies," *Money,* 1 April 2003; and Steven Morrison and Clifford Winston, *The Evolution of the Airline Industry* (Washington, D.C.: Brookings Institution, 1995). The travel site formed by the world's major airlines is http://www.orbitz.com/.

Case Study

World of Business

eActivity
The Government Accounting Office (GAO) prepares reports on competition in the domestic airline industry. For example, read "Domestic Aviation: Barriers to Entry Continue to Limit Benefits of Airline Deregulation" at http://ntl.bts.gov/card_view.cfm?docid=485. This report includes data on the concentration of ownership of landing slots at the major U.S. airports. What particular barriers to entry does GAO cite? Current statistics on air travel are available in the *Economic Report of the Air Transport Association* at http://www.airlines.org/econ/econ.aspx. Try clicking through the series of graphs showing recent trends in the airline industry. What trends do you find in prices, number of passengers, and percentage of Americans who have never flown?

Economies of Scale

Perhaps the most important barrier to entry is economies of scale. Recall that the minimum efficient scale is the lowest output at which the firm takes full advantage of economies of scale. If a firm's minimum efficient scale is relatively large compared to industry output, then only a few firms are needed to satisfy industry demand. For example, an automobile plant of minimum efficient scale could make enough cars to supply nearly 10 percent of the U.S. market. If there were 100 auto plants, each would supply such a tiny portion of the market that the average cost per car would be higher than if only 10 plants manufacture autos. In the automobile industry, economies of scale create a barrier to entry. To compete with existing producers, a new entrant must sell enough automobiles to reach a competitive scale of operation.

Exhibit 4 presents the long-run average cost curve for a typical firm in the industry. If a new entrant sells only S cars, the average cost per unit, c_a, far exceeds the average cost, c_b, of a manufacturer that sells enough cars to reach the minimum efficient size, M. If autos sell for less than c_a, a potential entrant can expect to lose money, and this prospect will discour-

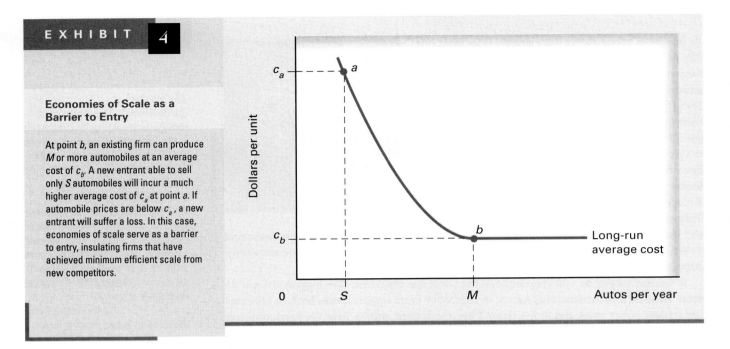

EXHIBIT 4

Economies of Scale as a Barrier to Entry

At point *b*, an existing firm can produce *M* or more automobiles at an average cost of c_b. A new entrant able to sell only *S* automobiles will incur a much higher average cost of c_a at point *a*. If automobile prices are below c_a, a new entrant will suffer a loss. In this case, economies of scale serve as a barrier to entry, insulating firms that have achieved minimum efficient scale from new competitors.

age entry. For example, John Delorean tried to break into the auto industry in the early 1980s with a modern design featured in the movie *Back to the Future*. But his company built only 8,583 Deloreans before going bankrupt.

The High Cost of Entry

Potential entrants into oligopolistic industries may face another problem. The total investment needed to reach the minimum efficient size is often gigantic. A new auto plant or new semiconductor plant can cost over $2 billion. The average cost of developing and testing a new drug exceeds $500 million. Advertising a new product enough to compete with established brands may also require enormous outlays.

High start-up costs and established brand names create substantial barriers to entry, especially because the market for new products is so uncertain (four out of every five new consumer products don't survive). An unsuccessful product could cripple an upstart firm. The prospect of such losses discourages many potential entrants. Most new products come from established firms, which can better withstand the possible losses. For example, Colgate-Palmolive spent $100 million introducing Total toothpaste, as did McDonald's in its failed attempt to sell the Arch Deluxe. Unilever lost $160 million when its new detergent, Power, washed out.

Firms often spend millions and sometimes billions trying to differentiate their products. Some of these outlays offer consumers valuable information and wider choice. But some spending seems to offer neither. For example, Pepsi and Coke spend billions on messages such "Joy of Pepsi" or "Life is Good." Regardless, *product differentiation expenditures create a barrier to entry*.

Crowding Out the Competition

Oligopolies compete with existing rivals and try to block new entry by offering a variety of products. Entrenched producers may flood the market with new products in part to crowd out any new entrants. For example, a few cereal makers offer more than a dozen products each. Many of these variations offer little that is new. One study of 25,500 new products introduced one year found only 7 percent offered new or added benefits.[1] *Multiple products from the same brand dominate shelf space and attempt to crowd out new entrants.*

Models of Oligopoly

Because oligopolists are interdependent, analyzing their behavior is complicated. No single model or single approach explains oligopoly behavior completely. At one extreme, oligopolists may try to coordinate their behavior so they act collectively as a single monopolist, forming a cartel, such as the Organization of Petroleum Exporting Countries (OPEC). At the other extreme, oligopolists may compete so fiercely that price wars erupt, such as those that break out among airlines, tobacco companies, computer chip makers, and wireless service providers.

Many theories have been developed to explain oligopoly behavior. We will study three of the better-known approaches: collusion, price leadership, and game theory. As you will see, each approach has some relevance in explaining observed behavior, although none is entirely satisfactory as a general theory of oligopoly. Thus, *there is no general theory of oligopoly but rather a set of theories, each based on the diversity of observed behavior in an interdependent market.*

Collusion and Cartels

In an oligopolistic market, there are just a few firms so, to decrease competition and increase profits, they may try to *collude,* or conspire to rig the market. **Collusion** is an agreement among firms in the industry to divide the market and fix the price. A **cartel** is a group of firms that agree to collude so they can act as a monopoly to increase economic profit. Cartels are more likely among sellers of a commodity, like oil or steel. Colluding firms, compared with competing firms, usually produce less, charge more, block new firms, and earn more profit. Consumers pay higher prices, and potential entrants are denied the opportunity to compete.

Collusion and cartels are illegal in the United States. Still, monopoly profit can be so tempting that some U.S. firms break the law. For example, top executives at Archer Daniels Midland were convicted in 1998 of conspiring with four Asian competitors to rig the $650 million world market for lysine, an amino acid used in animal feed. Some other countries are more tolerant of cartels and a few even promote cartels, as with the 11 member-nations of OPEC. But if OPEC ever met in the United States, its representatives could be arrested for price fixing. Cartels can operate worldwide because there are no international laws against them.

Suppose all firms in an industry formed a cartel. The market demand curve, *D,* appears in Exhibit 5. What price will maximize the cartel's profit, and how will output be allocated among participating firms? The first task of the cartel is to determine its marginal cost of production. Because a cartel acts like a monopoly that is operating many plants, the marginal cost curve in Exhibit 5 is the horizontal sum of each firm's marginal cost curve. The cartel's marginal cost curve intersects the market's marginal revenue curve to determine output that maximizes the cartel's profit. This intersection yields quantity *Q.* The cartel's price, *p,* is read off the demand curve at that quantity.

COLLUSION

An agreement among firms to increase economic profit by dividing the market or fixing the price

CARTEL

A group of firms that agree to coordinate their production and pricing decisions to act like a monopolist

---

1. The study was carried out by Market Intelligence Service and was reported in "Market Makers," *The Economist,* 14 March 1998.

EXHIBIT   5

Cartel as a Monopolist

A cartel acts like a monopolist. Here, *D* is the market demand curve, *MR* the associated marginal revenue curve, and *MC* the horizontal sum of the marginal cost curves of cartel members (assuming all firms in the market join the cartel). Cartel profits are maximized when the industry produces quantity *Q* and charges price *p*.

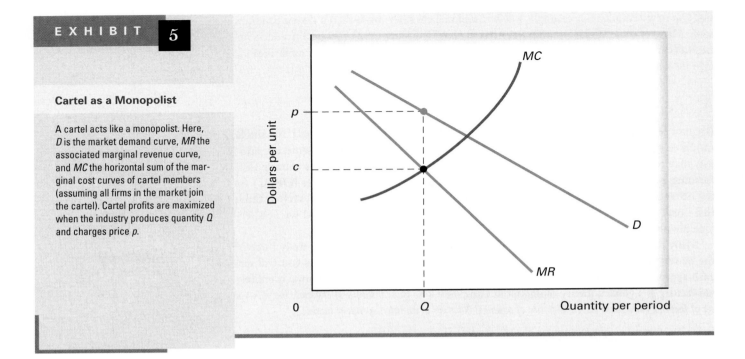

So far, so good. To maximize cartel profit, output Q must be allocated among cartel members so that each member's marginal cost equals c. Any other allocation would lower cartel profit. Thus, *for cartel profit to be maximized, output must be allocated so that the marginal cost for the final unit produced by each firm is identical.* Let's look at why this is easier said than done.

Differences in Average Cost

If all firms have identical average cost curves, output and profit would be easily allocated across firms (each firm would produce the same amount), but if costs differ, as they usually do, problems arise. The greater the difference in average costs across firms, the greater the differences in economic profits among firms. If cartel members try to equalize each firm's total profit, a high-cost firm would need to sell more than would a low-cost firm. But this allocation scheme would violate the cartel's profit-maximizing condition. Thus, *if average costs differ across firms, the output allocation that maximizes cartel profit will yield unequal profit across cartel members.* Firms that earn less profit could drop out of the cartel, thereby undermining it. Usually, the allocation of output is the result of haggling among cartel members. Firms that are more influential or more adept at bargaining get a larger share of output and profit. Allocation schemes are sometimes based on geography or on the historical division of output among firms. OPEC, for example, allocates output in proportion to each member country's share of estimated oil reserves.

Number of Firms in the Cartel

The more firms in an industry, the more difficult it is to negotiate an acceptable allocation of output among them. *Consensus becomes harder to achieve as the number of firms grows.* And the more firms in the industry, the more likely that some will become dissatisfied and bolt from the cartel.

New Entry into the Industry

If a cartel can't prevent new entry into the market, new firms will eventually force prices down, squeeze economic profit, and disrupt the cartel. The profit of the cartel attracts entry, entry increases market supply, and increased supply forces the price down. A cartel's success therefore depends on barriers that block the entry of new firms.

Cheating

Perhaps the biggest problem in keeping the cartel together is the powerful temptation to cheat on the agreement. Because oligopolists usually operate with excess capacity, some cheat on the established price. By offering a price slightly below the established price, any cartel member can usually increase sales and profit. Even if cartel members keep an eagle eye on each firm's price, one firm can increase sales by offering extra services, secret rebates, or other concessions. Cartels collapse if cheating becomes widespread.

OPEC's Spotty History

The problems of establishing and maintaining a cartel are reflected in the spotty history of OPEC. Many members are poor countries that rely on oil as their major source of revenue, so they argue over the price and their market share. OPEC members also cheat on the cartel. In 1980, the price of oil reached $80 a barrel (measured in 2004 dollars). For the last decade, the price has averaged around $32 a barrel, and it has been as low as $10 a barrel. Like other cartels, OPEC has also experienced difficulty with new entrants. The high prices resulting from OPEC's early success attracted new oil supplies from the North Sea, Mexico, and Siberia. Over 60 percent of the world's oil now comes from non–OPEC countries. Efforts to cartelize the world supply of a number of products, including bauxite, copper, and coffee, have failed so far.

In summary: Establishing and maintaining an effective cartel is more difficult if (1) the product is differentiated among firms, (2) average costs differ among firms, (3) there are many firms in the industry, (4) entry barriers are low, or (5) cheating on the cartel agreement becomes widespread.

Price Leadership

An informal, or *tacit,* form of collusion occurs if there is a **price leader** who sets the price for the rest of the industry. Typically, a dominant firm sets the market price, and other firms follow that lead, thereby avoiding price competition. The price leader also initiates any price changes, and, again, others follow. The steel industry was an example of the price-leadership form of oligopoly. Typically, U.S. Steel, the largest firm in the industry, would set the price for various products. Public pressure on U.S. Steel not to raise prices shifted the price-leadership role onto less prominent producers, resulting in a rotation of leadership among firms. Although the rotating price leadership reduced price conformity, price leadership kept prices high.

Like other forms of collusion, price leadership faces obstacles. Most importantly, the practice violates U.S. antitrust laws. Second, the greater the product differentiation among sellers, the less effective price leadership will be as a means of collusion. Third, there is no guarantee that other firms will follow the leader. Firms that fail to follow a price increase take business away from firms that do. Fourth, unless there are barriers to entry, a profitable price will attract new entrants, which could destabilize the price-leadership agreement. And finally, as with formal cartels, some firms are tempted to cheat on the agreement to boost sales and profits.

PRICE LEADER

A firm whose price is adopted by other firms in the industry

Game Theory

How will firms act when they recognize their interdependence but either cannot or do not collude? Because oligopoly involves interdependence among a few firms, we can think of interacting firms as players in a game. **Game theory** examines oligopolistic behavior as a series of strategic moves and countermoves among rival firms. It analyzes the behavior of decision makers, or players, whose choices affect one another. Game theory is not really a separate model of oligopoly but a general approach, an approach that can focus on each player's incentives to cooperate—say, through cartels or price leaders—or to compete, in ways to be discussed now.

To get some feel for game theory, let's work through the **prisoner's dilemma,** the most widely examined game. The game originally considered a situation in which two thieves, let's call them Ben and Jerry, are caught near the crime scene and brought to police headquarters, where they are interrogated in separate rooms. The police know the two guys did it but can't prove it, so they need a confession. Each faces a choice of confessing, thereby "squealing" on the other, or "clamming up," thereby denying any knowledge of the crime. If one confesses, turning state's evidence, he is granted immunity from prosecution and goes free, while the other guy is put away for 10 years. If both clam up, each gets only a 1-year sentence on a technicality. If both confess, each gets 5 years.

What will Ben and Jerry do? The answer depends on the assumptions about their behavior—that is, what *strategy* each pursues. A **strategy** reflects a player's game plan. In this game, suppose each player tries to save his own skin—each tries to minimize his time in jail, regardless of what happens to the other (after all, there is no honor among thieves). Exhibit 6 shows the *payoff matrix* for the prisoner's dilemma. A **payoff matrix** is a table listing the rewards (or, in this case, the penalties) that Ben and Jerry can expect based on the strategy each pursues.

Ben's choices are shown down the left margin and Jerry's across the top. Each prisoner can either confess or clam up. The numbers in the matrix indicate the prison time in years each can expect based on the corresponding strategies. Ben's numbers are in red and Jerry's in blue. Take a moment now to see how the matrix works. Notice that the sentence each player receives depends on the strategy he chooses *and* on the strategy the other player chooses.

What strategies are rational assuming that each player tries to minimize jail time? For example, put yourself in Ben's shoes. You know that Jerry, who is being questioned in another room, will either confess or clam up. If Jerry confesses, the left column of Exhibit 6 shows the penalties. If you confess too, you both get 5 years in jail, but if you clam up, you get 10 years and Jerry "walks." So, if you think Jerry will confess, you should too.

What if you believe Jerry will clam up? The right-hand column shows the two possible outcomes. If you confess, you do no time, but if you clam up too, you each get 1 year in jail. Thus, if you think Jerry will clam up, you're better off confessing. In short, whatever Jerry does, Ben is better off confessing. The same holds for Jerry. He is better off confessing, regardless of what Ben does. So each has an incentive to confess and both get 5 years in jail. This is called the **dominant-strategy equilibrium** of the game because each player's action does not depend on what he thinks the other player will do.

But notice that if each crook could just hang tough and clam up, both would be better off. After all, if both confess, each gets 5 years, but if both clam up, the police can't prove otherwise, so each gets only 1 year in jail. If each could trust the other to clam up, they both would be better off. But there is no way for the two to communicate or to coordinate their actions. That's why police investigators keep suspects apart, that's why organized crime

---

Economics in the Movies

GAME THEORY

An approach that analyzes oligopolistic behavior as a series of strategic moves and counter-moves by rival firms

PRISONER'S DILEMMA

A game that shows why players have difficulty cooperating even though they would benefit from cooperation

STRATEGY

In game theory, the operational plan pursued by a player

PAYOFF MATRIX

In game theory, a table listing the payoffs that each player can expect based on the actions of the other player

DOMINANT-STRATEGY EQUILIBRIUM

In game theory, the outcome achieved when each player's choice does not depend on what the other player does

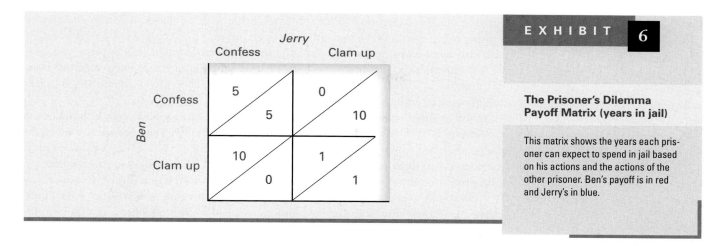

EXHIBIT 6

The Prisoner's Dilemma Payoff Matrix (years in jail)

This matrix shows the years each prisoner can expect to spend in jail based on his actions and the actions of the other prisoner. Ben's payoff is in red and Jerry's in blue.

threatens "squealers" with death, and that's why the witness protection program tries to shield "squealers."

Price-Setting Game

The prisoner's dilemma applies to a broad range of economic phenomena including pricing policy and advertising strategy. For example, consider the market for gasoline in a rural community with only two gas stations, Texaco and Exxon. Here the oligopoly consists of two sellers, or a **duopoly.** Suppose customers are indifferent between the brands and focus only on the price. Each station sets its daily price early in the morning before knowing the price set by the other. To keep it simple, suppose only two prices are possible—a low price or a high price. If both charge the low price, they split the market and each earns a profit of $500 per day. If both charge the high price, they also split the market, but profit jumps to $700 each. If one charges the high price but the other the low one, the low-price station gets most of the business, earning a profit of $1,000, leaving the high-price station with only $200.

Exhibit 7 shows the payoff matrix, with Texaco's strategy down the left margin and Exxon's across the top. Texaco's profit appears in red, and Exxon's in blue. Suppose you are

DUOPOLY

A market with only two producers; a type of oligopoly market structure

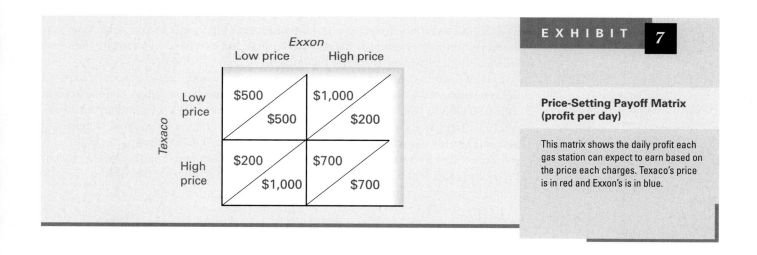

EXHIBIT 7

Price-Setting Payoff Matrix (profit per day)

This matrix shows the daily profit each gas station can expect to earn based on the price each charges. Texaco's price is in red and Exxon's is in blue.

running the Texaco station and are trying to decide what to charge. If Exxon charges the low price, you earn $500 charging the low price but only $200 charging the high price. So you earn more charging the low price. If, instead, Exxon charges the high price, you earn $1,000 charging the low price and $700 charging the high price. Again, you earn more charging the low price. Exxon faces the same incentives. Thus, each charges the low price, regardless of what the other does.

In this prisoner's dilemma, each charges the low price, earning $500 a day, although each would earn $700 charging the high price. Think of yourself as a member of the oil cartel discussed earlier, where the cartel determines the price and sets production quotas for each member. If you think other firms in the cartel will stick with their quotas, you can increase your profit by cutting your price and increasing quantity sold. If you think the other firms will cheat and overproduce, then you should too—otherwise, you will get your clock cleaned by those cheaters. Either way, your incentive as a cartel member is to cheat on the quota. All members have an incentive to cheat, although all would earn more by sticking with the agreement that maximizes joint profit.

This incentive to cut prices suggests why price wars sometimes break out among oligopolists. For example, in recent years automakers have aggressively matched and exceeded one another's price cuts and rebate programs, cutting auto prices sharply. In 2003, for example, the Cadillac DeVille with a sticker price of $48,000 sold for under $35,000. General Motors managed a profit in the third quarter of 2003 of just $15 on each car and truck sold, and Ford lost money on each vehicle.[2] A bitter price war with Dell in 2003 cut Hewlett-Packard's earnings on each $500 personal computer sold to a razor-thin $1.75.[3] And just before a recent Thanksgiving weekend, a price war erupted in airfares. American Airlines first announced holiday discounts. Delta responded with cuts of up to 50 percent. Within hours, American, United, and other major carriers said they would match Delta's reductions. All these airlines were losing money at the time. So go the price wars.

Cola War Game

As a final example of a prisoner's dilemma, consider the marketing strategies of Coke and Pepsi. Suppose each is putting together a promotional budget for the coming year, not knowing the other's plans. The choice boils down to adopting either a moderate budget or a big budget that involves multiple Super Bowl ads, showy in-store displays, and other efforts aimed mostly at attracting customers from each other. If each adopts a big budget, their costly efforts will, for the most part, cancel each other out and limit each company's profit to $2 billion a year. If each adopts a moderate promotional budget, the money saved boosts profit for each to $3 billion a year. And if one adopts a big budget but the other does not, the heavy promoter captures a bigger market share and earns $4 billion, while the other loses market share and earns only $1 billion. What to do, what to do?

Exhibit 8 shows the payoff matrix for the two strategies, with Pepsi's choices listed down the left margin and Coke's across the top. In each cell of the matrix, Pepsi's profit appears in red, and Coke's in blue. Let's look at Pepsi's decision. If Coke adopts a big promotional budget, Pepsi earns $2 billion by doing the same but only $1 billion by adopting a moderate budget. Thus, if Coke adopts a big budget, so should Pepsi. If Coke adopts a moderate budget, Pepsi earns $4 billion with a big budget and $3 billion with a moderate one. Again, Pepsi earns more with a big budget. Coke faces the same incentives, so both adopt big bud-

2. Micheline Maynard, "Car Sticker Prices Mask Some Big Bargains," *New York Times,* 29 October 2003.
3. David Bank, "H-P Posts 10% Increase in Revenue," *Wall Street Journal,* 20 November 2003.

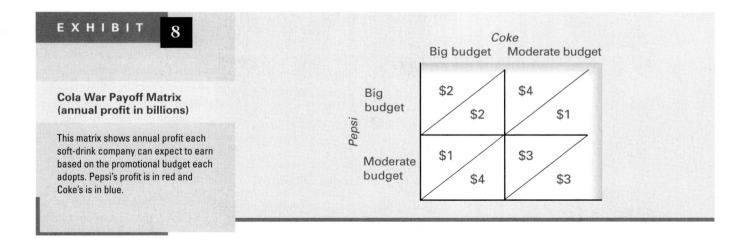

EXHIBIT 8

Cola War Payoff Matrix (annual profit in billions)

This matrix shows annual profit each soft-drink company can expect to earn based on the promotional budget each adopts. Pepsi's profit is in red and Coke's is in blue.

gets, earning $2 billion each in profit, even though each would have earned $3 billion with a moderate budget.

One-Shot Versus Repeated Games

The outcome of a game often depends on whether it is a *one-shot game* or a *repeated game.* The classic prisoner's dilemma is a one-shot game. If the game is to be played just once, the strategy of confessing makes you better off regardless of what the other player does. Your choice won't influence the other player's behavior. But if the same players repeat the prisoner's dilemma, as would likely occur with the price-setting game, the cola war game, and the OPEC cartel, other possibilities unfold. In a repeated-game setting, each player has a chance to establish a reputation for cooperation and thereby can encourage other players to do the same. After all, the cooperative solution—whether that involves clamming up, maintaining a high price, or adopting a moderate promotional budget—makes both players better off than if both fail to cooperate.

Experiments have shown that the strategy with the highest payoff in repeated games turns out to be the simplest—**tit-for-tat.** You begin by cooperating in the first round. On every round thereafter, you cooperate if the other player cooperated in the previous round, and you cheat if your opponent cheated in the previous round. In short, in any given round, you do whatever your opponent did in the previous round. The tit-for-tat strategy offers the other player an immediate punishment for cheating and an immediate reward for cooperation. Some cartels seem to employ tit-for-tat strategies.

Our discussion has given you some idea of game theory by focusing on the prisoner's dilemma. Other games can be more complicated and involve more strategic interaction. Because firms are interdependent, oligopoly gives rise to all kinds of behavior and many approaches. Each approach helps explain certain phenomena observed in oligopolistic markets. The *cartel,* or *collusion,* model shows why oligopolists might want to cooperate to set the market price; that model also explains why a cartel is hard to establish and maintain. The *price-leadership* model explains why and how firms may charge the same price without actually establishing a formal cartel. Finally, *game theory,* expressed here by the prisoner's dilemma, shows how difficult a cooperative solution might be even though players benefit from cooperation. Game theory is more of an approach than a distinct model.

TIT-FOR-TAT

In game theory, a strategy in repeated games when a player in one round of the game mimics the other player's behavior in the previous round; an optimal strategy for encouraging the other player to cooperate

Comparison of Oligopoly and Perfect Competition

As we have seen, each approach explains a piece of the oligopoly puzzle. But each has limitations, and none provides a complete picture of oligopoly behavior. Because there is no typical, or representative, model of oligopoly, "the" oligopoly model cannot be compared with the competitive model. We might, however, imagine an experiment in which we took the many firms that populate a competitive industry and, through a series of giant mergers, combined them to form, say, four firms. We would thereby transform the industry from perfect competition to oligopoly. How would firms in this industry behave before and after the massive merger?

Price Is Usually Higher Under Oligopoly

With fewer competitors after the merger, remaining firms would become more interdependent. Oligopoly models presented in this chapter suggest why firms may try to coordinate their pricing policies. *If oligopolists engaged in some sort of implicit or explicit collusion, industry output would be smaller and the price would be higher than under perfect competition.* Even if oligopolists did not collude but simply operated with excess capacity, the price would be higher and the quantity lower with oligopoly than with perfect competition. The price could become lower under oligopoly compared with perfect competition only if a price war broke out among oligopolists. Behavior will also depend on whether there are barriers to entry. The lower the barriers to entry into the oligopoly, the more oligopolists will act like perfect competitors.

Higher Profits Under Oligopoly

In the long run, easy entry prevents perfect competitors from earning more than a normal profit. With oligopoly, however, there may be barriers to entry, such as economies of scale or brand names, which allow firms in the industry to earn long-run economic profit. *If there are barriers to entry, we should expect profit in the long run to be higher under oligopoly than under perfect competition.* Profit rates do in fact appear to be higher in industries where a few firms account for a high proportion of industry sales. Some economists view these higher profit rates as troubling evidence of market power. But not all economists share this view. Some note that the largest firms in oligopolistic industries tend to earn the highest rate of profit. Thus, the higher profit rates observed in oligopolistic industries do not necessarily stem from market power per se. Rather, these higher profit rates stem from the greater efficiency arising from economies of scale in these large firms. Many of these issues will be revisited later, when we explore the government's role in promoting market competition.

Conclusion

This chapter has moved us from the extremes of perfect competition and monopoly to the gray area inhabited by most firms. Exhibit 9 compares features and examples of the four market structures. Please take a moment now to review these key distinctions.

Firms in monopolistic competition and in oligopoly face a downward-sloping demand curve for their products. With monopolistic competition, there are so many firms in the market that each tends to get lost in the crowd. Each behaves independently. But with oligopoly, there are so few firms in the market that each must consider the impact its pricing, output, and marketing decisions will have on other firms. Each oligopolist behaves interdependently, and this makes oligopoly difficult to analyze. As a result, there are different models and approaches to oligopoly, three of which were discussed in this chapter.

EXHIBIT 9	Comparison of Market Structures			
	Perfect Competition	Monopoly	Monopolistic Competition	Oligopoly
Number of firms	Most	One	Many	Few
Control over price	None	Complete	Limited	Some
Product differences	None	None	Some	None or some
Barriers to entry	None	Insurmountable	Low	Substantial
Examples	Wheat	Local electricity	Convenience stores	Automobiles

The analytical results derived in this chapter are not as clear-cut as for the polar cases of perfect competition and monopoly. Still, we can draw some general conclusions, using perfect competition as a guide. In the long run, perfect competitors operate at minimum average cost, while other types of firms usually operate with excess capacity. Therefore, given identical cost curves, monopolists, monopolistic competitors, and oligopolists tend to charge higher prices than perfect competitors do, especially in the long run. In the long run, monopolistic competitors, like perfect competitors, earn only a normal profit because entry barriers are low. Monopolists and oligopolists can earn economic profit in the long run if new entry is restricted. In a later chapter, we will examine government policies aimed at increasing competition. *Regardless of the market structure, however, profit maximization prompts firms to produce where marginal revenue equals marginal cost.*

SUMMARY

1. Whereas the output of a monopolist has no substitutes, a monopolistic competitor must contend with many rivals. But because of differences among the products offered by different firms, each monopolistic competitor faces a downward-sloping demand curve.

2. Sellers in monopolistic competition and in oligopoly differentiate their products through (a) physical qualities, (b) sales locations, (c) services provided with the product, and (d) the product image.

3. In the short run, monopolistic competitors that can at least cover their average variable costs will maximize profits or minimize losses by producing where marginal revenue equals marginal cost. In the long run, easy entry and exit of firms ensures that monopolistic competitors earn

only a normal profit, which occurs where the average total cost curve is tangent to a firm's downward-sloping demand curve.

4. An oligopoly is an industry dominated by a few sellers, some of which are large enough relative to the market to influence the price. In undifferentiated oligopolies, such as steel or oil, the product is a commodity. In differentiated oligopolies, such as automobiles or breakfast cereals, the product differs across firms.

5. Because an oligopoly consists of just a few firms, each may react to another firm's changes in quality, price, output, services, or advertising. Because of this interdependence, the behavior of oligopolists is difficult to analyze. No single approach characterizes all oligopolistic markets.

6. In this chapter, we considered three approaches of oligopoly behavior: (a) collusion, in which firms form a cartel to act collectively like a monopolist; (b) price leadership, in which one firm, usually the biggest one, sets the price for the industry and other firms follow the leaders; and (c) game theory, which analyzes oligopolistic behavior as a series of strategic moves by rival firms.

QUESTIONS FOR REVIEW

1. *(Characteristics of Monopolistic Competition)* Why does the demand curve facing a monopolistically competitive firm slope downward in the long run, even after the entry of new firms?

2. *(Product Differentiation)* What are four ways in which a firm can differentiate its product? What role can advertising play in product differentiation? How can advertising become a barrier to entry?

3. *(Zero Economic Profit in the Long Run)* In the long run, a monopolistically competitive firm earns zero economic profit, which is exactly what would occur if the industry were perfectly competitive. Assuming that the cost curves for each firm are the same whether the industry is perfectly or monopolistically competitive, answer the following questions.

   a. Why don't perfectly and monopolistically competitive industries produce the same equilibrium quantity in the long run?
   b. Why is a monopolistically competitive industry said to be economically inefficient?
   c. What benefits might cause us to prefer the monopolistically competitive result to the perfectly competitive result?

4. *(Varieties of Oligopoly)* Do the firms in an oligopoly act independently or interdependently? Explain your answer.

5. *(Case Study: The Unfriendly Skies)* One complaint frequently heard about airfares is that flying from an airline's hub city airport is more expensive than flying from a nearby city that is not a hub. How might this reflect a different level of competition in hub city airports?

6. *(Collusion and Cartels)* Why would each of the following induce some members of OPEC to cheat on their cartel agreement?

   a. Newly joined cartel members are less-developed countries.
   b. The number of cartel members doubles from 10 to 20.
   c. International debts of some members grow.
   d. Expectations grow that some members will cheat.

7. *(Price Leadership)* Why might a price-leadership model of oligopoly not be an effective means of collusion in an oligopoly?

8. *(Market Structures)* Determine whether each of the following is a characteristic of perfect competition, monopolistic competition, oligopoly, and/or monopoly:

   a. A large number of sellers
   b. Product is a commodity
   c. Advertising by firms
   d. Barriers to entry
   e. Firms are price makers

PROBLEMS AND EXERCISES

9. *(Short-Run Profit Maximization)* A monopolistically competitive firm faces the following demand and cost structure in the short run:

Output	Price	FC	VC	TC	TR	Profit/Loss
0	$100	$100	$0	___	___	___
1	90	___	50	___	___	___
2	80	___	90	___	___	___
3	70	___	150	___	___	___
4	60	___	230	___	___	___
5	50	___	330	___	___	___
6	40	___	450	___	___	___
7	30	___	590	___	___	___

a. Complete the table.
b. What is the best profit or loss available to this firm?
c. Should the firm operate or shut down in the short run? Why?
d. What is the relationship between marginal revenue and marginal cost as the firm increases output?

10. *(Case Study: Fast Forward)* Use a cost-and-revenue graph to illustrate and explain the short-run profits in the video rental business. Then, use a second graph to illustrate the long-run situation. Explain fully.

11. *(Monopolistic Competition and Perfect Competition Compared)* Illustrated below are the marginal cost and average total cost curves for a small firm that is in long-run equilibrium.

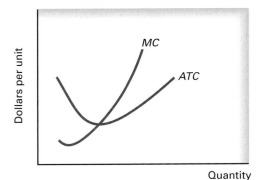

a. Locate the long-run equilibrium price and quantity if the firm is perfectly competitive.
b. Label the price and quantity p_1 and q_1.
c. Draw in a demand and marginal revenue curve to illustrate long-run equilibrium if the firm is monopolistically competitive. Label the price and quantity p_2 and q_2.

d. How do the monopolistically competitive firm's price and output compare to those of the perfectly competitive firm?
e. How do long-run profits compare for the two types of firms?

12. *(Collusion and Cartels)* Use revenue and cost curves to illustrate and explain the sense in which a cartel behaves like a monopolist.

13. *(Game Theory)* Suppose there are only two automobile companies, Ford and Chevrolet. Ford believes that Chevrolet will match any price it sets. Use the following price and profit data to answer the following questions.

Ford's Selling Price	Chevrolet's Selling Price	Ford's Profits (millions)	Chevrolet's Profits (millions)
$ 4,000	$4,000	$8	$8
4,000	8,000	12	6
4,000	12,000	14	2
8,000	4,000	6	12
8,000	8,000	10	10
8,000	12,000	12	6
12,000	4,000	2	14
12,000	8,000	6	12
12,000	12,000	7	7

a. What price will Ford charge?
b. What price will Chevrolet charge?
c. What is Ford's profit after Chevrolet's response?
d. If the two firms collaborated to maximize joint profits, what prices would they set?
e. Given your answer to part (d), how could undetected cheating on price cause the cheating firm's profit to rise?

14. *(Game Theory)* While grading a final exam, an economics professor discovers that two students have virtually identical answers. She is convinced the two cheated but cannot prove it. The professor speaks with each student separately and offers the following deal: Sign a statement admitting to cheating. If both students sign the statement, each will receive an "F" for the course. If only one signs, he is allowed to withdraw from the course while the other student is expelled. If neither signs, both receive a "C" because the professor does not have sufficient evidence to prove cheating.

a. Draw the payoff matrix.
b. Which outcome do you expect? Why?

EXPERIENTIAL EXERCISES

15. *(Product Differentiation)* One important way monopolistic competitors differentiate their products is by location. Review John Campbell's article, "Time to Shop: The Geography of Retailing," from the Federal Reserve Bank of Boston's Regional Review at http://www.bos.frb.org/economic/nerr/rr1996/summer/rgrv96_3.htm. What locational strategies are retailers using? What does the theory of monopolistic competition predict about the success of such strategies in the short run and in the long run?

16. *(OPEC)* OPEC is the economist's favorite cartel to study. That is partly because it had such a spectacular short-run success and partly because oligopoly theory could be used to predict how OPEC pricing actually evolved. Take a look at the U.S. Department of Energy's OPEC Fact Sheet at http://www.eia.doe.gov/emeu/cabs/opec.html. What are some recent developments in petroleum pricing? How relevant are the factors listed in this chapter as affecting the difficulty of maintaining a cartel?

17. *(Wall Street Journal)* If you look carefully, you can often find evidence of price leadership. For example, the *Wall Street Journal* frequently runs stories about airfares. Typically, one airline will raise its fares—on certain routes or across the board—and other airlines will match those changes within a day or two. As you read through the *Wall Street Journal* this week, be on the lookout for such stories. They are typically reported on the front page—in the "What's News" column. When you find such a story, check back over the next few days. Did other airlines match the leader, or was the leader forced to back off its price changes?

18. *(Wall Street Journal)* Read the *Wall Street Journal* and look for articles that discuss firms that have successfully utilized product differentiation to create competitive advantage. Describe the actions of a firm that has been successful. Was advertising important?

HOMEWORK XPRESS! EXERCISES

These exercises require access to McEachern Homework Xpress! If Homework Xpress! did not come with your book, visit **http://homeworkxpress.swlearning.com** *to purchase.*

1. Giorgio's Brick Oven Pizza is the only pizzeria with a brick oven in town. It is not the only pizza seller so it faces a downward-sloping demand curve. The demand schedule is:

Quantity of Pizzas	Price
0	$20
10	16
20	12
30	8
40	4
50	0

Draw the demand curve and the corresponding marginal revenue curve. Add a marginal cost curve so that the profit-maximizing price of a Giorgio's pizza will be $14. Add an average total cost curve so that the profit on each pizza is two dollars. Illustrate total profits.

2. Draw a downward-sloping demand curve and the corresponding marginal revenue curve for a monopolistically competitive firm. Add a marginal cost curve and an average total cost curve so that the firm is in long-run equilibrium. Identify the price it would set and the quantity it would choose to produce.

3. Draw a downward-sloping demand curve and the corresponding marginal revenue curve for a monopolistically competitive firm. Add a marginal cost curve and an average total cost curve so that the firm is in long-run equilibrium. Identify the price it would set and the quantity it would choose to produce. Add a demand curve the firm would face if it is in a perfectly competitive market and earning zero economic profits. Identify the price it faces and the quantity it would choose to produce.

4. Draw a world demand curve for bananas. A cartel, OBEC, the Organization of Banana Exporting Countries, is founded in an attempt to drive up the world price of bananas. Add a marginal revenue curve corresponding to the demand curve and a marginal cost curve representing the sum of the marginal cost curves of the cartel members. Identify the quantity that would maximize profits for the industry and the price the cartel would charge.

Resource Markets

© Eyewire/Fonts.com

W hy do surgeons earn twice as much as general practitioners? Why do truck drivers in the United States earn at least 20 times more than rickshaw drivers in India? Why does prime Iowa corn acreage cost more than scrubland in the high plains of Montana? Why are buildings taller in downtown Chicago than those in the suburbs? To answer these and other questions, we turn to the demand and supply of resources.

You say you've been through this demand-and-supply drill already? True. But your earlier focus was on the product market—that is, on the market for final goods and services. Goods and services are produced by resources—labor, capital, natural resources, and entrepreneurial ability. Demand and supply in resource markets determine the price and quantity of resources. And the ownership of resources determines the distribution of income throughout the economy.

Because your earnings depend on the market value of your resources, you should find resource markets particularly relevant to your future. Certainly one consideration in your career decision will be the expected income associated with alternative careers. The next three chapters examine how demand and supply interact to establish market prices for various resources. Topics discussed include:

- Demand and supply of resources
- Opportunity cost and economic rent
- Marginal revenue product
- Marginal resource cost
- Changes in resource demand

The Once-Over

Just to prove you already know more about resource markets than you may think, try answering the questions that arise in the following examples of resource demand and supply.

Resource Demand

Let's begin with the demand for labor. The manager of Wal-Mart estimates that hiring another sales clerk would increase total revenue by $500 per week and increase total cost by $400 per week. Should another sales clerk be hired? Sure, because Wal-Mart's profit would increase by $100 per week. *As long as the additional revenue from employing another worker exceeds the additional cost, the firm should hire that worker.*

What about capital? Suppose that you operate a lawn service during the summer, earning an average of $40 per lawn. You mow about 15 lawns a week, for total revenue of $600. You are thinking of upgrading to a larger, faster mower called the Lawn Monster, but it would cost you an extra $400 per week. The bigger mower would cut your time per lawn in half, enabling you to mow 30 lawns per week, so your total revenue would double to $1,200. Should you make the switch? Because the additional revenue of $600 exceeds the additional cost of $400, you should move up to the Monster.

What about natural resources? A neighbor offers Farmer Jones the chance to lease 100 acres of farmland. Jones figures that farming the extra land would cost $70 per acre but would yield $60 per acre in additional revenue. Should Jones lease the extra land? What do you think? Because the additional cost of farming that land would exceed the additional revenue, the answer is no.

These examples show that a *producer demands another unit of a resource as long as its marginal revenue exceeds its marginal cost.*

Resource Supply

You likely also understand the economic logic behind resource supply. Suppose you are trying to decide between two jobs that are identical except that one pays more than the other. Is there any question which job you'll take? If the working conditions are equally attractive, you would choose the higher-paying job. Now let's say your choice is between two jobs that pay the same. One has normal 9-to-5 hours, but the other starts at 5 A.M., an hour when your body tends to reject conscious activity. Which would you choose? You would pick one that suits your tastes.

People will supply their resources to the highest-paying alternative, other things constant. Because other things are not always constant, people must be paid more for jobs less suited to their

N e t B o o k m a r k

What makes a good job good? Working for a good employer might be one factor. Each year, *Fortune* magazine lists the 100 best employers at http://www.fortune.com/fortune/bestcompanies. What factors other than compensation are cited in the report as creating a favorable work environment? What are the best and worst jobs? Search the Web for news and reviews of *the National Business Employment Weekly's* Jobs Rated Almanac; it ranks 250 jobs. Web site managers come out on top. Fishing ranks 248, yet most fishing grounds are overfished. Why do so many people want to fish for a living, when others consider this to be one of the worst jobs?

tastes. Your utility depends on both monetary and nonmonetary aspects of the job. Generally, people must be paid more for jobs that are dirty, dangerous, dull, exhausting, illegal, low status, have no future, have no benefits, and involve inconvenient hours than for jobs that are clean, safe, interesting, energizing, legal, high status, have bright prospects, have good benefits, and involve convenient hours.

The Demand and Supply of Resources

In the market for goods and services—that is, in the product market—households are the demanders and firms are suppliers. Households demand the goods and services that maximize utility, and firms supply the goods and services that maximize profit. In the resource market, roles are reversed: Firms are demanders and households are suppliers. Firms demand resources to maximize profit, and households supply resources to maximize utility. *Any differences between the profit-maximizing goals of firms and the utility-maximizing goals of households are reconciled through voluntary exchange in markets.*

Exhibit 1 presents the market for a particular resource—in this case, carpenters. As you can see, the demand curve slopes downward and the supply curve slopes upward. *Like the demand and supply for final goods and services, the demand and supply for resources depend on the willingness and ability of buyers and sellers to engage in market exchange.* This market will converge to the equilibrium wage, or the market price, for this type of labor.

The Market Demand for Resources

Why do firms employ resources? Resources produce goods and services, which firms try to sell for a profit. A firm values not the resource itself but the resource's ability to produce goods and services. Because the value of any resource depends on the value of what it produces, the demand for a resource is said to be a **derived demand**—arising from the

DERIVED DEMAND

Demand that arises from the demand for the product the resource produces

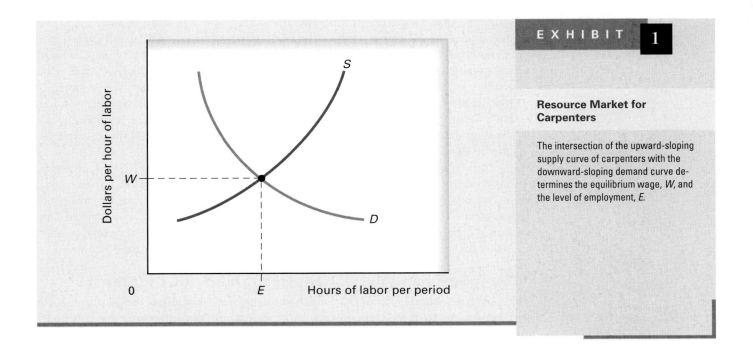

EXHIBIT 1

Resource Market for Carpenters

The intersection of the upward-sloping supply curve of carpenters with the downward-sloping demand curve determines the equilibrium wage, *W*, and the level of employment, *E*.

demand for the final product. For example, a carpenter's pay derives from the demand for the carpenter's output, such as a cabinet or a new deck. A professional baseball player's pay derives from the demand for ballgames. A truck driver's pay derives from the demand for transporting goods. The derived nature of resource demand helps explain why professional baseball players usually earn more than professional hockey players, why brain surgeons earn more than tree surgeons, and why drivers of big rigs earn more than drivers of delivery vans.

The market demand for a particular resource is the sum of demands for that resource in all its different uses. For example, the market demand for carpenters adds together the demands for carpenters in residential and commercial construction, remodeling, cabinetmaking, and so on. Similarly, the market demand for the resource, timber, sums the demand for timber as lumber, railway ties, firewood, furniture, pencils, toothpicks, paper products, and so on. The demand curve for a resource, like the demand curves for the goods produced by that resource, slopes downward, as depicted in Exhibit 1.

As the price of a resource falls, producers are more willing and able to employ that resource. Consider first the producer's greater *willingness* to hire resources as the resource price falls. In developing the demand curve for a particular resource, we assume the prices of other resources remain constant. So if the price of a particular resource falls, it becomes relatively cheaper compared with other resources the firm could use to produce the same output. Firms therefore are more willing to hire this resource rather than hire other, now relatively more costly, resources. Thus, we observe *substitution in production*—carpenters for masons, coal for oil, security alarms for security guards, and backhoes for grave diggers, as the relative prices of carpenters, coal, security alarms, and backhoes fall.

A lower price for a resource also increases a producer's *ability* to hire that resource. For example, if the wage of carpenters falls, home builders can hire more carpenters for the same total cost. The lower resource price means the firm is *more able* to buy the resource.

The Market Supply of Resources

The market supply curve for a resource sums all the individual supply curves for that resource. Resource suppliers are more *willing* and more *able* to increase quantity supplied as the resource price increases, so the market supply curve slopes upward, as in Exhibit 1. Resource suppliers are more *willing* because a higher resource price, other things constant, means more goods and services can be purchased with the earnings from each unit of the resource supplied. Resource prices are signals about the rewards for supplying resources. A high resource price tells the resource owner, "The market will pay more for what you supply." Higher prices draw resources from lower-valued uses, including leisure. For example, as the wage for carpenters increases, the quantity of labor supplied increases. Some carpenters give up leisure to work more hours.

The second reason a resource supply curve slopes upward is that resource owners are more *able* to increase the quantity supply as the resource price increases. For example, a higher carpenter's wage means more apprentices can undergo extensive training to become carpenters. A higher wage *enables* resource suppliers to increase their quantity supplied. Similarly, a higher timber price enables loggers to harvest trees in more remote regions, and a higher oil price enables producers to drill deeper and explore remote parts of the world.

Temporary and Permanent Resource Price Differences

People have a strong interest in selling their resources where they are valued the most. *Resources tend to flow to their highest-valued use.* If, for example, carpenters can earn more building homes than making furniture, they will shift into home building until wages in the two

uses are equal. Because resource owners seek the highest pay, *other things constant,* the prices paid for identical resources should tend toward equality. For example, suppose carpenters who build homes earn $25 per hour, which is $5 more than carpenters who make furniture. This difference is shown in Exhibit 2 by an initial wage of $25 per hour in panel (a) and an initial wage of $20 per hour in panel (b). This gap will encourage some carpenters to move from furniture making to home building, pulling up the wage in furniture making and driving down the wage in home building. Carpenters will move into home building until wages equalize. In Exhibit 2, supply shifts leftward for furniture making and rightward for home building until the wage reaches $24 in both markets. Note that 2,000 hours of labor per day shift from furniture making to home building. *As long as the nonmonetary benefits of supplying resources to alternative uses are identical and as long as resources are freely mobile, resources will adjust across uses until they earn the same in different uses.*

Sometimes earnings appear to differ between seemingly similar resources. For example, corporate economists on average earn more than academic economists, and land in the city

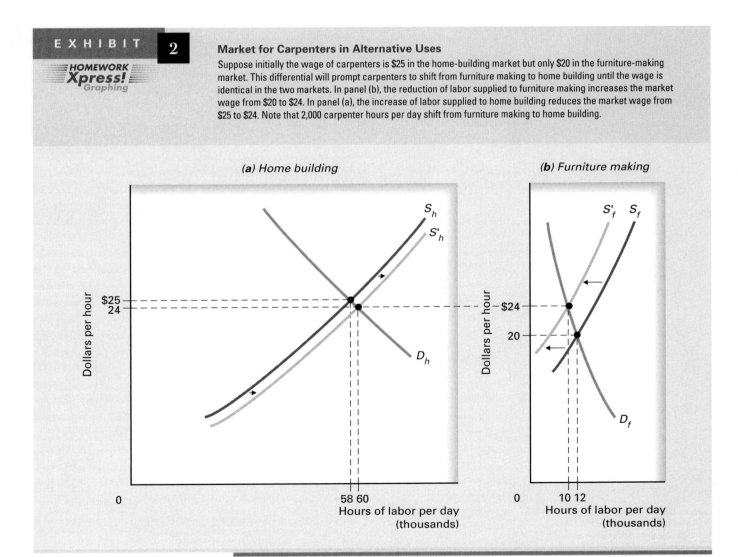

EXHIBIT 2

HOMEWORK
Xpress!
Graphing

Market for Carpenters in Alternative Uses

Suppose initially the wage of carpenters is $25 in the home-building market but only $20 in the furniture-making market. This differential will prompt carpenters to shift from furniture making to home building until the wage is identical in the two markets. In panel (b), the reduction of labor supplied to furniture making increases the market wage from $20 to $24. In panel (a), the increase of labor supplied to home building reduces the market wage from $25 to $24. Note that 2,000 carpenter hours per day shift from furniture making to home building.

(a) Home building

(b) Furniture making

costs more than land in the country. As you will now see, these differences also reflect the workings of demand and supply.

Temporary Differences in Resource Prices

Resource prices might differ temporarily across markets because adjustment takes time. For example, sometimes wage differences occur among workers who appear equally qualified. As you have seen, however, a difference between the prices of similar resources prompts resource owners and firms to make adjustments that drive resource prices toward equality, as with the carpenters in Exhibit 2. The process may take years, but when resource markets are free to adjust, price differences trigger the reallocation of resources, which equalizes earnings for similar resources.

Permanent Differences in Resource Prices

Not all resource price differences cause reallocation. For example, land along New York's Fifth Avenue sells for as much as $36,000 a *square yard!* For that amount, you could buy several acres in Upstate New York. Yet such a difference does not prompt upstate landowners to supply their land to New York City—obviously that's impossible. Likewise, the price of farmland itself varies widely, reflecting differences in the land's productivity and location. Such differences do not trigger shifts in resource supply. Similarly, certain wage differentials stem in part from the different costs of acquiring the education and training required to perform particular tasks. This difference explains why brain surgeons earn more than tree surgeons, why ophthalmologists earn more than optometrists, and why airline pilots earn more than truck drivers.

Differences in the nonmonetary aspects of similar jobs also lead to pay differences. For example, other things constant, most people require more pay to work in a grimy factory than in a pleasant office. Similarly, academic economists earn less than corporate economists, in part because academic economists typically have more freedom in their daily schedules, their attire, their choices of research topics, and even in their public statements.

Some price differences are temporary because they spark shifts of resource supply away from lower-paid uses and toward higher-paid uses. Other price differences cause no such shifts and are permanent. Permanent price differences are explained by *a lack of resource mobility* (urban land versus rural land), *differences in the inherent quality of the resource* (fertile land versus scrubland), *differences in the time and money involved in developing the necessary skills* (certified public accountant versus file clerk), or *differences in nonmonetary aspects of the job* (lifeguard at Malibu Beach versus prison guard at San Quentin).

Opportunity Cost and Economic Rent

Shaquille O'Neal earned about $30 million in 2004 playing basketball plus at least $10 million more from product endorsements. But he would probably have been willing to play basketball and endorse products for less. The question is, how much less? What is his best alternative? Suppose his best alternative is to become a full-time rap artist, something he now does in his spare time (as of 2004, he had released six rap albums). Suppose, as a full-time rapper, he could earn $1 million a year, including endorsements. And suppose, aside from the pay gap, he's indifferent between basketball and rap, so the nonmonetary aspects of the two jobs even out. Thus, he must be paid at least $1 million to remain in basketball, and this amount represents his opportunity cost. *Opportunity cost is what that resource could earn in its best alternative use.*

The amount O'Neal earns in excess of his opportunity cost is called *economic rent.* **Economic rent** is that portion of a resource's earnings that is not necessary to keep

ECONOMIC RENT

Portion of a resource's total earnings that exceeds its opportunity cost; earnings greater than the amount required to keep the resource in its present use the resource in its present use. Economic rent is, as the saying goes, "pure gravy." In O'Neal's case, economic rent is at least $39 million. Economic rent is producer surplus earned by resource suppliers. The *division* of earnings between opportunity cost and economic rent depends on the resource owner's elasticity of supply. *In general, the less elastic the resource supply, the greater the economic rent as a proportion of total earnings.* To develop a feel for the difference between opportunity cost and economic rent, let's go over three cases.

Case A: All Earnings Are Economic Rent

If the supply of a resource to a particular market is perfectly inelastic, that resource has no alternative use. Thus, there is no opportunity cost, and all earnings are economic rent. For example, scrubland in the high plains of Montana has no use other than for grazing cattle. The supply of this land is depicted by the red vertical line in panel (a) of Exhibit 3, which indicates that the 10 million acres have no alternative use. Because supply is fixed, the amount paid to rent this land for grazing has no effect on the quantity supplied. *The land's opportunity cost is zero, so all earnings are economic rent, shown by the blue-shaded area.* Here, fixed supply determines the equilibrium quantity of the resource, but demand determines the equilibrium price.

Case B: All Earnings Are Opportunity Costs

At the other extreme is the case in which a resource can earn as much in its best alternative use as in its present use. This situation is illustrated by the perfectly elastic supply curve in panel (b) of Exhibit 3, which shows the market for janitors in the local school system. Here, janitors earn $10 an hour to supply 1,000 hours of labor per day. If the school system paid less than $10 per hour, janitors would find jobs elsewhere, perhaps in nearby factories, where the wage is $10 per hour. *Janitors earn their opportunity costs.* In this case, the horizontal supply curve determines the equilibrium wage, but demand determines the equilibrium quantity.

Case C: Earnings Include Both Economic Rent and Opportunity Costs

If the supply curve slopes upward, most resource suppliers earn economic rent in addition to their opportunity cost. For example, if the market wage for unskilled work in your college community increases from $5 to $10 per hour, the quantity of labor supplied would increase, as would the economic rent earned by these workers. This situation occurs in panel (c) of Exhibit 3, where the pink shading identifies opportunity costs and the blue shading, economic rent. If the wage increases from $5 to $10 per hour, the quantity supplied will increase by 5,000 hours. For those who were willing to work for $5 per hour, the difference between $5 and $10 is economic rent. *When supply slopes upward, as it usually does, earnings consist of both opportunity cost and economic rent.* In the case of an upward-sloping supply curve and a downward-sloping demand curve, both demand and supply determine equilibrium price and quantity.

Note that specialized resources tend to earn a higher proportion of economic rent than do resources with many alternative uses. Thus, Shaquille O'Neal earns a greater *proportion* of his income as economic rent than does the janitor who cleans the Miami Heat's locker room. O'Neal would take a huge pay cut if he didn't play professional basketball, but the Heat's janitor could probably find another semiskilled job that would pay nearly as much.

To review: Given a resource demand curve that slopes downward, when the resource supply curve is vertical (perfectly inelastic), all earnings are economic rent; when that supply curve is horizontal (perfectly elastic), all earnings are opportunity cost; and when that supply curve slopes upward (an elasticity greater than zero but less than infinity), earnings divide between opportunity cost and economic rent. Remember, *the opportunity cost of a*

HOMEWORK
Xpress!
Ask the Instructor
Video

EXHIBIT 3

Opportunity Cost and Economic Rent

In panel (a), the resource supply curve is vertical, indicating that the resource has no alternative use. The price is demand determined, and all earnings are economic rent. In panel (b), the resource supply curve is horizontal at $10 per hour, indicating that the resource can also earn that much in its best alternative use. Employment is demand determined, and all earnings are opportunity costs. Panel (c) shows an upward-sloping resource supply curve. Earnings are partly opportunity costs and partly economic rent. Both demand and supply determine the equilibrium price and quantity.

(a) All resource earnings are economic rent

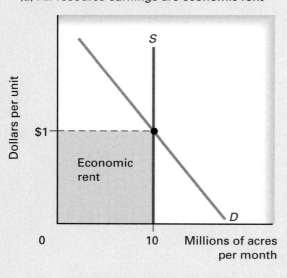

(b) All resource earnings are opportunity costs

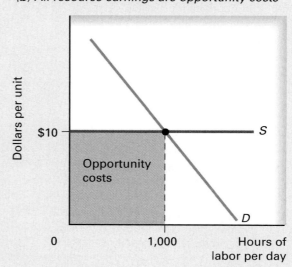

(c) Resource earnings are divided between economic rent and opportunity cost

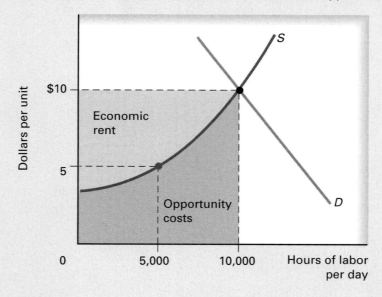

resource is what that resource could earn in its best alternative use. Economic rent is earnings in excess of opportunity cost.

This completes our introduction to resource supply. In the balance of this chapter, we take a closer look at resource demand. The determinants of the demand for a resource are largely the same whether we are talking about labor, capital, or natural resources. The supply of different resources, however, has certain peculiarities depending on the resource, so the supply of resources will be taken up in the next chapter.

A Closer Look at Resource Demand

Although production usually involves many resources, we will cut the analysis down to size by focusing on a single resource, assuming that the quantities of other resources employed remain constant. As usual, we will assume that firms try to maximize profit and households try to maximize utility.

The Firm's Demand for a Resource

You may recall that when the firm's costs were first introduced, we considered a moving company, where labor was the only variable resource in the short run. We examined the relationship between the quantity of labor employed and the amount of furniture moved per day. We use the same approach in Exhibit 4, where only one resource varies. Column (1) in the table lists possible employment levels of the variable resource, here measured as workers per day. Column (2) lists the amount produced, or total product, and column (3) lists the marginal product. The *marginal product* of labor is the change in total product from employing one more unit of labor.

When one worker is employed, total product is 10 units and so is the marginal product. The marginal product of adding the second worker is 9 units. As the firm hires more

(1) Workers per Day	(2) Total Product	(3) Marginal Product	(4) Product Price	(5) Total Revenue (5) = (2) × (4)	(6) Marginal Revenue Product (6) = (3) × (4)
0	0	—	$20	$ 0	—
1	10	10	20	200	$200
2	19	9	20	380	180
3	27	8	20	540	160
4	34	7	20	680	140
5	40	6	20	800	120
6	45	5	20	900	100
7	49	4	20	980	80
8	52	3	20	1040	60

EXHIBIT 4

Marginal Revenue Product When a Firm Sells in a Competitive Market

Because of diminishing marginal returns, the marginal product of labor declines as more labor is employed, as shown in column (3). Because this firm sells in a competitive market, it can sell all it wants at the market price of $20 per unit of output, as shown in column (4). The marginal product of labor in column (3) times the product price of $20 in column (4) yields the marginal revenue product of labor in column (6). Labor's marginal revenue product is the change in total revenue as a result of hiring another unit of labor.

workers, the marginal product of labor declines, reflecting the law of diminishing marginal returns. Notice in this example that diminishing marginal returns set in immediately—that is, right after the first worker.

Although labor is the variable resource here, we could examine the marginal product of any resource. For example, we could consider how many lawns could be cut per week by varying the quantity of capital employed. We might start off with very little capital—imagine cutting grass with a pair of scissors—and then move up to a push mower, a power mower, and the Lawn Monster. By holding labor constant and varying the quantity of capital employed, we could compute the marginal product of capital. Likewise, we could compute the marginal product of natural resources by examining crop production for varying amounts of farmland, holding other inputs constant.

Marginal Revenue Product

MARGINAL REVENUE PRODUCT

The change in total revenue when an additional unit of a resource is hired, other things constant

The important question is: what happens to the firm's *revenue* when additional workers are hired? The first three columns of Exhibit 4 show output as the firm hires more workers. The *marginal revenue product* of labor indicates how much total revenue changes as more labor is employed, other things constant. The **marginal revenue product** of any resource is the change in the firm's total revenue resulting from employing an additional unit of the resource, other things constant. You could think of the marginal revenue product as the firm's "marginal benefit" from hiring one more unit of the resource. *A resource's marginal revenue product depends on how much additional output the resource produces and the price at which output is sold.*

Selling Output in Competitive Markets

The calculation of marginal revenue product is simplest when the firm sells in a perfectly competitive market, which is the assumption underlying Exhibit 4. An individual firm in perfect competition can sell as much as it wants at the market price. The marginal revenue product, listed in column (6) of Exhibit 4, is the change in total revenue that results from changing input usage by one unit. For the perfectly competitive firm, the marginal revenue product is simply the marginal product of the resource multiplied by the product price of $20. Notice that because of diminishing returns, the marginal revenue product falls steadily as the firm uses more of the resource.

Selling Output with Some Market Power

If the firm has some market power in the product market—that is, some ability to set the price—the demand curve for that firm's output slopes downward. To sell more, the firm must lower its price. Exhibit 5 reproduces the first two columns of Exhibit 4. Column (3) now shows the price at which that output can be sold. Total output multiplied by the price yields the firm's total revenue, which appears in column (4).

The marginal revenue product of labor, which is the change in total revenue resulting from a 1-unit change in the quantity of labor employed, appears in column (5). For example, the first worker produced 10 units per day, which sell for $40 each, yielding total revenue of $400. Hiring the second worker adds 9 more units to total product, but to sell 9 more units, the firm must lower the price of each unit from $40 to $35.20. Total revenue increases to $668.80, which means the marginal revenue product from hiring a second worker is $268.80. For firms selling with some market power, the marginal revenue product curve slopes downward both because of diminishing marginal returns and because additional output can be sold only if the price falls.

(1) Workers per day	(2) Total Product	(3) Product Price	(4) Total Revenue (4) = (2) × (3)	(5) Marginal Revenue Product
0	0	—	—	—
1	10	$40.00	$400.00	$400.00
2	19	35.20	668.80	268.80
3	27	31.40	847.80	179.00
4	34	27.80	945.20	97.40
5	40	25.00	1000.00	54.80
6	45	22.50	1012.50	12.50
7	49	20.50	1004.50	−8.00
8	52	19.00	988.00	−16.50

EXHIBIT 5

The Marginal Revenue Product When a Firm Sells with Market Power

To sell more, this firm must lower the price, as indicated in column (3). Total revenue in column (4) equals total product in column (2) times the product price in column (3). Labor's marginal revenue product in column (5) equals the change in total revenue from hiring another worker. The marginal revenue product declines both because of diminishing marginal returns from labor and because the product price must fall to sell more.

Again, *the marginal revenue product is the additional revenue that results from employing each additional worker.* The profit-maximizing firm should be willing and able to pay as much as the marginal revenue product for an additional unit of the resource. Thus, *the marginal revenue product curve can be thought of as the firm's demand curve for that resource.* You could think of the marginal revenue product curve as the marginal benefit to the firm of hiring each additional unit of the resource.

To review: Whether a firm sells its product in a competitive market or sells with some market power, the marginal revenue product of a resource is the change in total revenue resulting from a 1-unit change in that resource, other things constant. The marginal revenue product curve of a resource is the demand curve for that resource—it shows the most a firm would be willing and able to pay for each additional unit of the resource. For firms selling in competitive markets, the marginal revenue product curve slopes downward only because of diminishing marginal returns to the resource. For firms selling with some market power, the marginal revenue product curve slopes downward both because of diminishing marginal returns and because additional output can be sold only if the price falls. *For all types of firms, the marginal revenue product is the change in total revenue resulting from hiring an additional unit of the resource.*

Marginal Resource Cost

If we know a firm's marginal revenue product, can we determine how much labor that firm should employ to maximize profit? Not yet, because we must also know how much labor costs the firm. Specifically, what is the **marginal resource cost**—what does another unit of labor cost the firm? The typical firm hires such a tiny fraction of the available resource that its hiring decision has no effect on the market price of the resource. Thus, each firm usually faces a given market price for the resource and decides only on how much to hire at that price.

For example, panel (a) of Exhibit 6 shows the market for factory workers, measured as workers per day. The intersection of market demand and market supply determines the

MARGINAL RESOURCE COST

The change in total cost when an additional unit of a resource is hired, other things constant

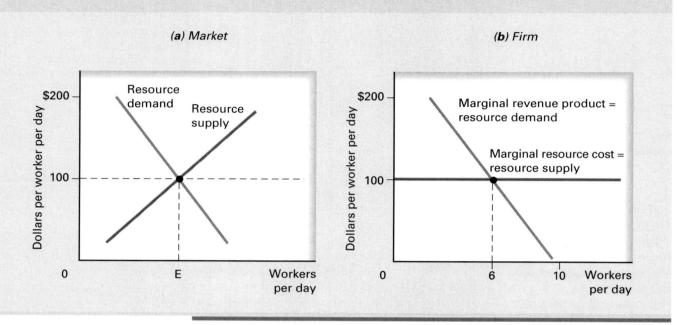

EXHIBIT 6

Market Equilibrium for a Resource and the Firm's Employment Decision
Market demand and supply of a resource, in panel (a), determine that resource's market price and quantity. In panel (b), an individual firm can employ as much as it wants at the market price, so price becomes the firm's marginal resource cost. The marginal resource cost curve also is the supply curve of that resource to the firm. In panel (b), a resource's marginal revenue product is the firm's demand curve for that resource. The firm maximizes profit (or minimizes its loss) by hiring a resource up to the point where the marginal revenue product equals the marginal resource cost, which is six workers per day in this example.

(a) Market

(b) Firm

market wage of $100 dollars per day. Panel (b) shows the situation for the firm. The market wage becomes the marginal resource cost of labor to the firm. The *marginal resource cost* curve is shown by the horizontal line drawn at the $100 level in panel (b); this is the labor supply curve to the firm. Panel (b) also shows the marginal revenue product curve, or resource demand curve, based on the schedule presented in Exhibit 4. The marginal revenue product curve indicates the additional revenue the firm receives as a result of employing another unit of labor.

Given a marginal resource cost of $100 per worker per day, how much labor will the firm employ to maximize profit? *The firm will hire more labor as long as doing so adds more to revenue than to cost—that is, as long as the marginal revenue product exceeds the marginal resource cost. The firm will stop hiring labor only when the two are equal.* If marginal resource cost is a constant $100 per worker, the firm will hire six workers per day because the marginal revenue product from hiring a sixth worker equals $100. Thus, the firm hires additional resources up to the level at which

$$\text{Marginal revenue product} = \text{Marginal resource cost}$$

This equality holds for all resources employed, whether the firm sells in competitive markets or has some market power. Profit maximization occurs where labor's marginal revenue product equals the market wage. Based on data presented so far, we can't yet determine the firm's actual profit because we don't yet know the firm's other costs. We do know, however, that in Exhibit 6, a seventh worker would add $100 to cost but would add less than that to revenue, so hiring a seventh worker would reduce the firm's profit (or increase its loss).

Whether a firm sells in competitive markets or with some market power, the profit-maximizing level of employment occurs where the marginal revenue product of labor equals its marginal resource cost. Similarly, profit-maximizing employment of other resources, such as natural resources and capital, occurs where their respective marginal revenue products equal their marginal resource costs. Each resource must "pull its own weight"—it must yield additional revenue that at least equals the additional cost.

In earlier chapters, you learned how to find the profit-maximizing level of output. Maximum profit (or minimum loss) occurs where the marginal revenue from *output* equals its marginal cost. Likewise, maximum profit (or minimum loss) occurs where the marginal revenue from an *input* equals its marginal resource cost. Although the first rule focuses on output and the second on input, the two are equivalent ways of deriving the same principle of profit maximization. For example, in Exhibit 6, the firm maximizes profit by hiring six workers when the market wage is $100 per day. Exhibit 4 indicates that a sixth worker adds five units to output, which sell for $20 each, yielding labor's marginal revenue product of $100. The *marginal revenue* of that output is the change in total revenue from selling another unit of output, which is $20. The *marginal cost* of that output is the change in total cost, $100, divided by the change in output, 5 units; so the marginal cost of output is $100/5, or $20. Thus, *in equilibrium, the marginal revenue of output equals its marginal cost.* Now that you have some idea of how to derive the demand for a resource, let's discuss what could shift resource demand.

Shifts of the Demand for Resources

As we have seen, a resource's marginal revenue product consists of two components: the resource's marginal product and the price at which that product is sold. Two factors can change a resource's marginal product: a change in the amount of other resources employed and a change in technology. One factor can change the price of the product: a change in demand for the product. Let's first consider changes that could affect marginal product, then changes that could affect demand for the product.

Change in the Price of Other Resources

Although our analysis so far has focused on a single input, in reality the marginal product of any resource depends on the quantity and quality of other resources used in production. Sometimes resources are *substitutes.* For example, coal substitutes for oil in generating electricity. And automatic teller machines, or ATMs, substitute for tellers in handling bank transactions. If two resources are **substitutes,** an increase in the price of one increases the demand for the other. An increase in the price of oil increases the demand for coal, and an increase in the wage of tellers increases the demand for ATMs.

Sometimes resources are *complements*—trucks and truck drivers, for example. If two resources are **complements,** a decrease in the price of one leads to an increase in the demand for the other. If the price of tractor-trailers decreases, the quantity demanded increases, which increases the demand for truck drivers. More generally, any increase in the quantity and quality of a complementary resource, such as trucks, hikes the marginal productivity of the resource in question, such as truck drivers, and so increases the demand for that resource. A bigger and better truck makes the driver more productive. One reason a truck driver in the United States earns much more than a rickshaw driver in India is the truck.

RESOURCE SUBSTITUTES

Resources that substitute in production; an increase in the price of one resource increases the demand for the other

RESOURCE COMPLEMENTS

Resources that enhance one another's productivity; an increase in the price of one resource decreases the demand for the other

Changes in Technology

Technological improvements can boost the productivity of some resources but can make others obsolete. The introduction of computer-controlled machines increased the demand for computer-trained machinists but decreased the demand for machinists without computer skills. The development of synthetic fibers, such as rayon and Orlon, increased the demand for acrylics and polyesters but reduced the demand for natural fibers, such as cotton and wool. Breakthroughs in fiber-optic and satellite telecommunication increased the demand for fiberglass and satellites and reduced the demand for copper wire.

Computer programs are changing job prospects in fields such as law, medicine, and accounting. For example, Quicken's WillMaker software has written more wills than any lawyer alive. In medicine, software such as Iliad helps doctors diagnose more than a thousand diseases. And in accounting, software such as TurboTax completes tax forms with ease. As software and hardware get cheaper, better, and more accessible, the demand for some professional services declines and the demand for others increases.

Changes in the Demand for the Final Product

Because the demand for a resource is *derived* from the demand for the final output, any change in the demand for output affects resource demand. For example, an increase in the demand for automobiles increases their market price and thereby increases the marginal revenue product of autoworkers. Let's look at the derived demand for architects in the following case study.

The Derived Demand for Architects

Architects design mostly buildings, particularly nonresidential structures such as offices, shopping centers, schools, and health-care facilities. After a boom in the 1980s, construction in the 1990s cooled significantly because of slower workforce growth and increased telecommuting. These changes reduced the demand for architects. In New York City, for example, the number of classified ads for architectural positions fell from 5,000 in 1987 to 500 in 1991. Similar drops occurred in other major U.S. cities. Employment at one national architectural firm shrank from 1,600 in 1988 to 700 in 1992.

© Photodisc/Getty Images

Among new architects, job losses were compounded by better architectural software. Drafting jobs long represented the entry-level positions for architects, but computer-aided design and drafting (CADD) software coupled with cheaper and more powerful computers reduced the demand for young architects. Programs such as 3D Manager helped configure all aspects of a structure and create plans that could be manipulated in three-dimensional space, something impossible with traditional drawings. Design software such as 3D Home Architect came with online support for amateurs. Whereas construction-grade blueprints drafted by an architect cost about $550 a set, do-it-yourself CDs sold for $40 to $70. Thus, software substituted for entry-level architectural positions.

The recession of 2001 and job losses that continued over the next two years also cut into the demand for architects. Those who couldn't find jobs struggled on their own. About one in four architects are now self-employed, which is about three times the self-employment rate of similar professionals.

The declining demand for architects had a predictable effect on the demand for higher education, which itself is a derived demand. Enrollment in undergraduate architecture classes declined as entry-level positions disappeared. Enrollment in graduate courses, however, remained relatively stable. Apparently, many out-of-work architects decided to pursue graduate study, because the poor job market reduced their opportunity cost. The exception that proves the rule about derived demand is that those architectural firms that specialized in the health-care industry flourished because health care is the fastest-growing sector of the economy.

Sources: Reed Abelson, "Generous Medicare Payments Spur Specialty Hospital Boom," *New York Times*, 26 October 2003; D. W. Dunlap, "Recession Is Ravaging Architects' Firms," *New York Times*, 17 May 1992; Alex Frangos, "More Women Design Their Way to the Top," *Wall Street Journal*, 5 November 2003; and http://autodesk.com/siteselect.htm.

In summary: The demand for a resource depends on its marginal revenue product, which is the change in total revenue resulting from employing one more unit of the resource. Any change that increases a resource's marginal revenue product will increase resource demand.

The Optimal Use of More Than One Resource

As long as the marginal revenue product exceeds the marginal resource cost, a firm can increase profit or reduce a loss by employing more of that resource. Again, the firm will hire more of a resource until the marginal revenue product just equals the marginal resource cost. This principle holds for each resource employed. The opening paragraph asked why buildings in downtown Chicago are taller than those in the suburbs. Land and capital, to a large extent, substitute in the production of building space. Because land is more expensive downtown than in the suburbs, builders there substitute capital for land, building up instead of out. Hence, buildings are taller when they are closer to the center of the city and are tallest in cities where land is most expensive. Buildings in Chicago and New York City are taller than those in Salt Lake City and Tucson, for example.

The high price of land in metropolitan areas has other implications for the efficient employment of resources. For example, in New York City, as in many large cities, sidewalk vending carts sell everything from hot dogs to ice cream. Why are these carts so popular, with over 3,000 in New York City alone? Consider the resources used to supply hot dogs: land, labor, capital, entrepreneurial ability, plus intermediate goods such as hot dogs, buns, and other ingredients. Which of these do you suppose is most expensive in New York City? Retail space along Madison Avenue rents for an average of $550 a year per square foot. Because operating a hot dog cart requires about 4 square yards, it could cost as much as $20,000 a year to rent that much commercial space. Aside from the necessary public permits, however, space on the public sidewalk is free to vendors. Profit-maximizing street vendors substitute public sidewalks for costly commercial space. (Incidentally, does this free space mean sidewalk vendors earn long-run economic profit?)

Government policy can affect resource allocation in other ways, as discussed in this closing case study.

The McMinimum Wage

In March 2000, Congress sent to President Clinton a measure to increase the minimum wage by $1.00 to $6.15 over two years; the legislation was vetoed because it was tied to a tax cut for businesses. Ever since a federal minimum wage of 25 cents was established in 1938, economists have been debating the benefits and costs of the law. The law initially covered only 43 percent of the workforce—primarily workers in large firms involved in

eActivity
The U.S. Department of Labor maintains a Minimum Wage page at http://www.dol.gov/esa/minwage/q-a.htm with questions and answers about the legal aspects and history of the minimum wage. A continually updated chart can be found at the Employment Policies Institute Web site at: http://www.epionline.org/mw_statistics_annual.cfm. The site also provides links to Questions and Answers about the economic impact of the minimum wage, living wage, and other labor issues. There are also links to several research reports on the impacts of minimum-wage laws. The liberal view can be found at the Economic Policy Institute's Web page on labor markets at http://epinet.org/subjectpages/labor.html.

WALL STREET JOURNAL

Reading It **Right**

What's the relevance of the following statement from the Wall Street Journal: *"'I'm afraid you are going to unemploy more people,' Sen. Don Nickles, R-Okla., said of what would happen if a minimum wage increase is included."*

interstate commerce. Over the years, the minimum wage has been raised and the coverage has been broadened. By 2003, coverage doubled to about 86 percent of the workforce (groups still not covered include those in small retail establishments and small restaurants). In 2003 only 3 percent of workers earned the minimum wage or less; this number is down from 15 percent in 1980.

When the 2000 legislation was vetoed, about 7 percent of the workforce earned between $5.15 and $6.15 an hour and thus could have been affected by an increase. This group included mostly young workers, the majority working part time, primarily in service and sales occupations. For example, 8 of 10 working teenagers earned less than a dollar above the minimum wage. Eleven states and the District of Columbia have a minimum wage exceeding the federal level. As of 2004, Washington had the highest state minimum at $7.16 per hour. In addition, at least 110 municipalities across the nation have so-called *living-wage laws* that exceed federal and state minimums. Among the highest is in Santa Monica, California's, where the minimum is $12.25 per hour for jobs without health-care benefits (this is three times the minimum wage *per day* in nearby Mexico).

Advocates of minimum-wage legislation argue that it can increase the income of the poorest workers. Critics claim that it can encourage employers either to cut nonwage compensation or to scale back employment. Dozens of studies have examined the effects of the minimum wage on employment. A few found a small positive effect on employment, but most found either no effect or a negative effect, particularly among teenage workers. One reason a higher minimum wage may not reduce total employment is that employers often respond by substituting part-time jobs for full-time jobs, by substituting more-qualified minimum-wage workers (such as college students) for less-qualified workers (such as high school dropouts), and by adjusting nonwage components of the job to reduce costs or increase worker productivity.

Here are some of nonwage adjustments an employer could impose on workers in response to a higher minimum wage: less convenient work hours, greater expected work effort, less on-the-job training, less time for meals and breaks, less extra pay for night shifts, less paid vacation, fewer paid holidays, less sick leave, fewer health-care benefits, stricter tardiness policy, and so on. For example, one researcher found that restaurants responded to a higher minimum wage by reducing vacation time and night-shift premiums.

Of most concern to economists is a possible reduction in on-the-job training of young workers, especially those with little education. A higher minimum wage also raises the opportunity cost of staying in school. According to one study, a higher minimum wage encouraged some 16- to 19-year-olds to quit school and look for work, though many failed to find jobs. Thus, an increase in the minimum wage may have the unintended consequence of cutting school enrollment. And those who had already dropped out were more likely to become unemployed.

A survey of 193 labor economists found that 87 percent believed "a minimum wage increases unemployment among young and unskilled workers." Minimum-wage increases, however, have broad public support. In one poll, the highest support, 81 percent, came from those aged 18 to 29, the group most likely to be affected by a hike in the minimum wage.

Sources: Robert Whaples, "Is There Consensus Among American Labor Economists?" *Journal of Labor Research* 27 (Fall 1996): 725–734; David Francis, "New Efforts Surface to Raise Minimum Wage," *Christian Science Monitor*, 15 September 2003; William Alpert, *The Minimum Wage in the Restaurant Industry* (New York: Praeger, 1986); and William Carrington and Bruce Fallick, "Do Some Workers Have Minimum Wage Careers?" *Monthly Labor Review* (May 2001): 7–26, which can also be found online at http://www.bls.gov/opub/mlr/mlrhome.htm.

Conclusion

A firm hires each resource until the marginal revenue product of that resource equals its marginal cost. The objective of profit maximization ensures that to produce any given level of output, firms will employ the least-cost combination of resources and thereby will use the economy's resources most efficiently. Although our focus has been on the marginal productivity of each resource, we should keep in mind that an orchestra of resources combine to produce output, so the marginal productivity of a particular resource depends in part on the amount and quality of other resources employed.

SUMMARY

1. Firms demand resources to maximize profits. Households supply resources to maximize utility. The profit-maximizing goals of firms and the utility-maximizing goals of households are reconciled through voluntary exchange in resource markets.

2. Because the value of any resource depends on what it produces, the demand for a resource is a derived demand—arising from the demand for the final product. Resource demand curves slope downward because firms are more willing and able to increase quantity demanded as the price of a resource declines. Resource supply curves slope upward because resource owners are more willing and able to increase quantity supplied as their reward for doing so increases.

3. Some differences in the market prices of similar resources trigger the reallocation of resources to equalize those prices. Other price differences do not cause a shift of resources among uses because of a lack of resource mobility, differences in the inherent quality of the resources, differences in the time and money involved in developing necessary skills, and differences in nonmonetary aspects of jobs.

4. Resource earnings divide between (a) earnings that reflect the resource's opportunity cost and (b) economic rent—that portion of earnings that exceeds opportunity cost. If a

resource has no alternative use, earnings consist entirely of economic rent; if a resource has other uses that pay as well, earnings consist entirely of opportunity cost. Most resources earn both opportunity cost and rent.

5. A firm's demand curve for a resource is the resource's marginal revenue product curve, which shows the change in total revenue from employing one more unit of the resource, other things constant. If a firm sells output in a competitive market, the marginal revenue product curve slopes downward because of diminishing marginal returns. If a firm has some market power in the product market, the marginal revenue product curve slopes downward both because of diminishing marginal returns and because the product price must fall to sell more output.

6. The demand curve for a resource shifts to the right if there is an increase either in its marginal productivity or in the price of the output. The demand curve for a resource also shifts to the right with an increase in the price of a substitute resource or a decrease in the price of a complement resource.

7. Marginal resource cost is the change in total cost resulting from employing one more unit of a resource, other things constant. A firm maximizes profit by employing each resource up to the point where its marginal revenue product equals its marginal resource cost.

QUESTIONS FOR REVIEW

1. *(Resource Demand and Supply)* Answer each of the following questions about the labor market:

   a. Which economic decision makers determine the demand for labor? What is their goal, and what decision criteria do they use in trying to reach that goal?

   b. Which economic decision makers determine the supply of labor? What is their goal and what decision criteria do they use in trying to reach that goal?

   c. In what sense is the demand for labor a derived demand?

2. *(Market Supply for Resources)* Explain why the market supply curve of a resource slopes upward.

3. *(Resource Price Differences)* Distinguish between how the market reacts to a temporary difference in prices for the same resource and how the market reacts to a permanent difference. Why do the reactions differ?

4. *(Opportunity Cost and Economic Rent)* On-the-job experience typically enhances a person's productivity in that particular job. If the person's salary increases to reflect increased experience but the additional experience has no relevance for other jobs, does this higher salary reflect an increase in opportunity cost or in economic rent?

5. *(Firm's Demand for a Resource)* How does the law of diminishing marginal returns affect a firm's demand for labor?

6. *(Shifts of Resource Demand)* Many countries are predominantly agricultural. How would changes in the supply of fertilizer affect the marginal product, and thus the income, of farmers in such countries?

7. *(Optimal Use of More Than One Resource)* Explain the rule for determining optimal resource use when a firm employs more than one resource.

PROBLEMS AND EXERCISES

8. *(Opportunity Cost and Economic Rent)* Define economic rent. In the graph below, assume that the market demand curve for labor is initially D_1.

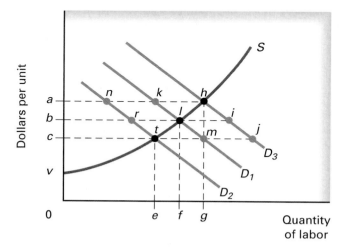

   a. What are the equilibrium wage rate and employment level? What is the economic rent?

   b. Next assume that the price of a substitute resource increases, other things constant. What happens to demand for labor? What are the new equilibrium wage rate and employment level? What happens to economic rent?

   c. Suppose instead that demand for the final product drops, other things constant. Using labor demand curve D_1 as your starting point, what happens to the demand for labor? What are the new equilibrium wage rate and employment level? Does the amount of economic rent change?

9. *(Firm's Demand for a Resource)* Use the following data to answer the questions below. Assume a perfectly competitive product market.

Units of Labor	Units of Output
0	0
1	7
2	13
3	18
4	22
5	25

   a. Calculate the marginal revenue product for each additional unit of labor if output sells for $3 per unit.

   b. Draw the demand curve for labor based on the above data and the $3-per-unit product price.

c. If the wage rate is $15 per hour, how much labor will be hired?

d. Using your answer to part (c), compare the firm's total revenue to the total amount paid for labor. Who gets the difference?

e. What would happen to your answers to parts (b) and (c) if the price of output increased to $5 per unit, other things constant?

10. *(Selling Output as a Price Taker)* If a competitive firm hires another full-time worker, total output will increase from 100 units to 110 units per week. Suppose the market price of output is $25 per unit. What is the maximum weekly wage at which the firm would hire that additional worker?

11. *(Shifts in Resource Demand)* A local pizzeria hires college students to make pizza, wait on tables, take phone orders,

and deliver pizzas. For each situation described, determine whether the demand for student employees by the restaurant would increase, decrease, or remain unchanged. Explain each answer.

a. The demand for pizza increases.

b. Another pizzeria opens up next door.

c. An increase in the minimum wage raises the cost of hiring student employees.

d. The restaurant buys a computer system for taking phone orders.

12. *(C a s e **S t u d y**:* The Derived Demand for Architects) Use a demand-and-supply diagram to illustrate the change in the market for entry-level architects as described in the case study. Explain your conclusions.

EXPERIENTIAL EXERCISES

13. *(Resource Demand)* The *Occupational Outlook Handbook* (OOH) is a U.S. Department of Labor publication that projects employment trends. Using the search feature available at the OOH Web site at http://www.bls.gov/oco/, search several occupations. What factors seem to be affecting employment prospects in those fields? What role does derived demand play? How about technological change?

14. A table from the Department of Labor with the real minimum wage in the United States can be found at: http://www.dol.gov/ILAB/media/reports/oiea/wagestudy/FS-UnitedStates.htm. A better alternative, however, is a continually updated chart with nominal and real mini-

mum wage that can be found at the Employment Policy Institute Web site at: http://www.epionline.org/mw_statistics_annual.cfm.

15. *(Wall Street Journal)* Review the "Work Week" column on the front page of Tuesday's *Wall Street Journal*. Choose an interesting article, read it, and then try to interpret it using the tools developed in this chapter. Did labor supply, labor demand, or both change? Was only a single labor market affected, or were the effects felt in several markets simultaneously? Be sure that your explanation accounts for what happened to both the wage rate and the level of employment.

HOMEWORK XPRESS! EXERCISES

These exercises require access to McEachern Homework Xpress! If Homework Xpress! did not come with your book, visit **http://homeworkxpress.swlearning.com** *to purchase.*

1. Every summer, pool managers and park directors hire lifeguards. Many of the workers are high school and college students looking for summer jobs. In the diagram, draw a demand curve for lifeguards that illustrates how those making the employment decisions will choose to be open

for fewer hours and hire fewer guards, the higher the wage that is paid. Draw a supply curve that illustrates how students would be willing to sacrifice more hours of summer leisure the higher the wage rate. Identify the market equilibrium wage and hours of labor.

2. Many of the skills required for life-guarding are also required for guiding whitewater rafting trips. Word gets around among students who usually work as lifeguards that outfitters hiring guides are paying $5 per hour more than the average for life-guarding at pools and beaches. Use the diagram from Problem 11–1 to illustrate the effects of this wage differential in the market for lifeguards.

3. Commercial fishing is often the lowest rated occupation on lists ranking the attractiveness of various jobs. For people living in and wanting to remain in small coastal communities, other job opportunities are few and the wage rate needed to attract them would be low. However, if there are few such workers, higher wage rates will have to be offered to attract more fishers. Use the demand-and-supply diagram for labor in commercial fishing to identify the equilibrium wage rate and quantity of labor. Use the diagram to illustrate the economic rent earned by workers who would fish at wage rates below the market equilibrium by shading in the appropriate area.

4. On a lobster boat, the more hands working, the more traps that can be checked per day, and the more lobsters landed. The relationship between workers per day and total product for a typical boat are as shown in the table. Find the marginal revenue product for workers per day and plot this as the demand curve for labor in the diagram, given a price of $10 per lobster landed. Add a marginal resource cost curve at $30 per day per worker and identify the number of workers employed per day on a typical boat.

Workers per day	Total Product
0	0
1	5
2	9
3	12
4	14
5	15

Labor Markets and Labor Unions

© Robert Galbraith/Reuters/Corbis

How do you divide your time between work and leisure? Why do many people work *less* if the wage increases enough? For example, why do unknown rock bands play for hours for peanuts, while famous bands play much less for much more? Why are butchers more likely than surgeons to mow their own lawns? What determines the wage structure in the economy? What else besides the wage affects your labor supply? This chapter digs deeper into wage determination.

You can be sure of one thing: demand and supply play a central role in the wage structure. You have already examined the demand for resources. Demand depends on a resource's marginal revenue product. The first half of this chapter focuses on the supply of labor, and then brings demand and supply together to arrive at the market wage. The second half considers the role of labor unions. We examine the economic impact of unions and review recent trends in union membership. Topics discussed include:

- Theory of time allocation
- Backward-bending labor supply curve
- Nonwage factors in labor supply

- Why wages differ
- Unions and collective bargaining
- Union wages and employment
- Trends in union membership

Labor Supply

As a resource supplier, you have a labor supply curve for each of the many possible uses of your labor. To some markets, your quantity supplied is zero over the realistic range of wages. The qualifier "over the realistic range" is added because, for a high enough wage (say, $1 million per hour), you might supply labor to just about *any* activity. In most labor markets, your quantity supplied may be zero either because you are *willing* but *unable* to perform the job (professional golfer, airline pilot, novelist) or because you are *able* but *unwilling* to do so (soldier of fortune, prison guard, P.E. instructor).

So you have as many individual supply curves as there are labor markets, just as you have as many individual demand curves as there are markets for goods and services. Your labor supply to each market depends, among other things, on your abilities, your taste for the job, and the opportunity cost of your time. Your supply to a particular labor market assumes that wages in other markets are constant, just as your demand for a particular product assumes that other prices are constant.

Labor Supply and Utility Maximization

Recall the definition of economics: *the study of how people use their scarce resources in an attempt to satisfy their unlimited wants*—that is, how individuals attempt to use their scarce resources to maximize their utility. Two sources of utility are of special interest to us in this chapter: the consumption of goods and services and the enjoyment of leisure. The utility derived from consuming goods and services serves as the foundation for consumer demand. Another valuable source of utility is leisure—time spent relaxing with friends, sleeping, eating, watching TV, and other recreation. Leisure is a normal good that, like other goods, is subject to the law of diminishing marginal utility. Thus, the more leisure time you have, the less you value an additional hour of it. Sometimes you may have so much leisure that you "have time on your hands" and are "just killing time." As that sage of the comic page Garfield the cat once lamented, "Spare time would be more fun if I had less to spare." Or as Shakespeare wrote, "If all the year were playing holidays, to sport would be as tedious as to work." Leisure's diminishing marginal utility explains why some of the idle rich grow bored in their idleness.

Three Uses of Time

Some of you are at a point in your careers when you have few resources other than your time. Time is the raw material of life. You can use your time in three ways. First, you can undertake **market work**—selling your time in the labor market in return for income. When you supply labor, you usually surrender control of your time to the employer in return for a wage. Second, you can undertake **nonmarket work**—using time to produce your own goods and services. Nonmarket work includes the time you spend doing your laundry,

MARKET WORK

Time sold as labor

NONMARKET WORK

Time spent getting an education or producing goods and services for personal consumption

making a sandwich, or cleaning up after yourself. Nonmarket work also includes the time spent acquiring skills and education to enhance your productivity. Although studying and attending class may provide little immediate payoff, you are betting that the knowledge and perspective so gained will enrich your future. Third, you can spend time as **leisure**—using your time in nonwork pursuits.

LEISURE

Time spent on nonwork activities

Work and Utility

Unless you are one of the fortunate few, work is not a pure source of utility, as it often generates some boredom, discomfort, and aggravation. In short, time spent working can be "a real pain," a source of *disutility*—the opposite of utility. And work is subject *to increasing marginal disutility*—the more you work, the greater the marginal disutility of working another hour. You may work nonetheless, because your earnings buy goods and services. You expect the utility from these products to more than offset the disutility of work. Thus, the *net utility of work*—the utility of the consumption made possible through earnings minus the disutility of the work itself—usually makes some amount of work an attractive use of your time. In the case of market work, your income buys goods and services. In the case of nonmarket work, either you produce goods and services directly, as in making yourself a sandwich, or you invest your time in education with an expectation of higher future earnings and higher future consumption. The additional utility you expect from the sandwich and higher future consumption possibilities resulting from education are the marginal benefits of nonmarket work.

Utility Maximization

Within the limits of a 24-hour day, seven days a week, you balance your time among market work, nonmarket work, and leisure to maximize utility. As a rational consumer, *you attempt to maximize utility by allocating your time so that the expected marginal utility of the last unit of time spent in each activity is identical.* Thus, in the course of a week or a month, the expected marginal utility of the last hour of leisure equals the expected net marginal utility of the last hour of market work, which equals the expected net marginal utility of the last hour of nonmarket work. In the case of time devoted to acquiring more human capital, you must consider the marginal utility expected from the future increase in earnings that will result from your enhanced productivity.

Maybe at this point you are saying, "Wait a minute. I don't know what you're talking about. I don't allocate my time like that. I just sort of bump along, doing what feels good." Economists do not claim that you are even aware of making these marginal calculations. But as a rational decision maker, you allocate your scarce time trying to satisfy your unlimited wants, or trying to maximize utility. And utility maximization, or "doing what feels good," implies that you act *as if* you allocated your time to derive the same expected net marginal utility from the last unit of time spent in each alternative use.

You probably have settled into a rough plan for meals, work, entertainment, study, sleep, and so on—a plan that fits your immediate objectives. This plan is probably in constant flux as you make expected and unexpected adjustments in your use of time. For example, last weekend you may have failed to crack a book, despite good intentions. This morning you may have slept later than you planned because you were up late. Over a week, a month, or a year, however, your use of time is roughly in line with an allocation that maximizes utility as you perceive it at the time. Put another way, if you could alter your use of time to increase your utility, you would do so. Nobody's stopping you! You may emphasize immediate gratification over long-term goals, but, hey, that's your choice and you bear the consequences. *This time-allocation process ensures that at the margin, the expected net utilities from the last unit of time spent in each activity are equal.*

Because information is costly and because the future is uncertain, you sometimes make mistakes. You don't always get what you expect. Some mistakes are minor, such as going to a movie that turns out to be a waste of time. But other mistakes can be costly. For example, some people are now studying for a field that will grow crowded by the time they graduate, or some people may be acquiring skills that new technology will make obsolete.

Implications

The theory of time allocation described thus far has several implications for individual choice. First, consider the choices of market work, nonmarket work, and leisure. The higher your market wage, other things constant, the higher your opportunity cost of leisure and nonmarket work. For example, those who earn a high wage will spend less time in nonmarket work, other things constant. Surgeons are less likely to mow their lawns than are butchers. And among those earning the same wage, those more productive in nonmarket work—handy around the house, good cooks—will do more for themselves. Conversely, those who are all thumbs around the house and have trouble boiling water will hire more household services and eat out more frequently.

By the same logic, the higher the expected earnings right out of high school, other things constant, the higher the opportunity cost of attending college. Most young, successful movie stars do not go to college, and some even drop out of high school, as noted earlier. Promising athletes often turn pro right after high school or before completing college. But the vast majority of people, including female basketball stars, do not face such a high opportunity cost of higher education. As one poor soul lamented, "Since my wife left me, my kids joined a cult, my job is history, and my dog died, I think now might be a good time to go back for an MBA."

Wages and Individual Labor Supply

To breathe life into the time-allocation problem, consider your choices for the summer. If you can afford to, you can take the summer off, spending it entirely on leisure, perhaps as a fitting reward for a rough academic year. Or you can supply your time to market work. Or you can undertake nonmarket work, such as cleaning the garage, painting the house, or attending summer school. As a rational decision maker, you will select the combination of leisure, market work, and nonmarket work that you expect will maximize your utility. And the optimal combination is likely to involve allocating time to each activity. For example, even if you work, you might still take one or two summer courses.

Suppose the only summer job available is some form of unskilled labor, such as working in a fast-food restaurant or for the municipal parks department. For simplicity, let's assume that you view all such jobs as equally attractive (or unattractive) in terms of their nonmonetary aspects, such as working conditions, working hours, and so on. (These nonmonetary aspects are discussed in the next section.) If there is no difference among these unskilled jobs, the most important question for you in deciding how much market labor to supply is: What's the market wage?

Suppose the wage is $6 per hour. Rather than working at a wage that low, you might decide to work around the house, attend summer school full time, take a really long nap, travel across the country to find yourself, or perhaps pursue some combination of these. In any case, you supply no market labor at such a low wage. The market wage must rise to $7 before you supply any market labor. Suppose at a wage of $7, you supply 20 hours per week, perhaps taking fewer summer courses and shorter naps.

As the wage increases, your opportunity cost of time spent in other activities rises, so you substitute market work for other uses of your time. You decide to work 30 hours per week

at a wage of $8 per hour, 40 hours at $9, 48 hours at $10, and 55 hours at $11. At a wage of $12 you go to 60 hours per week; you are starting to earn serious money—$720 a week. If the wage hits $13 per hour, you decide to cut back to 58 hours per week. Despite the cutback, your pay rises to $754, which is more than when the wage was $12. Finally, if the wage hits $14, you cut back to 55 per week, earning $770. To explain why you may eventually reduce the quantity of labor supplied, let's consider the impact of wage increases on your time allocation.

Substitution and Income Effects

An increase in the wage has two effects on your use of time. First, because each hour of work now buys more goods and services, a higher wage makes you want to work more. A higher wage increases the opportunity cost of leisure and nonmarket work. Thus, as the wage increases, you substitute market work for other activities; this is the **substitution effect of a wage increase.** But a higher wage means a higher income for the same number of hours. A higher income increases your demand for all normal goods. Because leisure is a normal good, a higher income increases your demand for leisure, thereby reducing your allocation of time to market work. This **income effect of a wage increase** tends to reduce the quantity of labor supplied to market work.

As the wage increases, the substitution effect causes you to work more, but the income effect causes you to work less and demand more leisure. In our example, the substitution effect exceeds the income effect for wages up to $12 per hour, resulting in more labor supplied as the wage increases. When the wage reaches $13, however, the income effect exceeds the substitution effect, causing you to reduce the quantity of labor supplied.

Backward-Bending Labor Supply Curve

The labor supply curve just described appears in Exhibit 1. As you can see, this slopes upward until a wage of $12 per hour is reached; then it bends backward. The **backward-bending supply curve** gets its shape because the income effect of a higher wage eventually dominates the substitution effect, reducing the quantity of labor supplied as the wage increases. We see evidence of a backward-bending supply curve particularly among high-wage individuals, who reduce their work and consume more leisure as their wage increases. For example, entertainers typically perform less as they become more successful. Unknown musicians will play for hours for hardly any money; famous musicians play much less for much more. The income effect of rising real wages helps explain the decline in the U.S. workweek from an average of 60 hours in 1900 to less than 40 hours today.

Flexibility of Hours Worked

The model we have been discussing assumes that workers have some control over the number of hours they work. Opportunities for part-time work and overtime allow workers to put together their preferred quantity of hours. Workers also have some control over the timing and length of their vacations. More generally, individuals can control how long to stay in school, when to enter or leave the workforce, and when to retire. Thus, they actually have more control over the number of hours worked than you might think if you focused simply on the benchmark of, say, a 40-hour work week.

Nonwage Determinants of Labor Supply

The supply of labor to a particular market depends on a variety of factors other than the wage, just as the demand for a particular good depends on factors other than the price. As we have already seen, the supply of labor to a particular market depends on wages in other

SUBSTITUTION EFFECT OF A WAGE INCREASE

A higher wage encourages more work because other activities now have a higher opportunity cost

INCOME EFFECT OF A WAGE INCREASE

A higher wage increases a worker's income, increasing the demand for all normal goods, including leisure, so the quantity of labor supplied to market work decreases

BACKWARD-BENDING SUPPLY CURVE OF LABOR

As the wage rises, the quantity of labor supplied may eventually decline; the income effect of a higher wage increases the demand for leisure, which reduces the quantity of labor supplied enough to more than offset the substitution effect of a higher wage

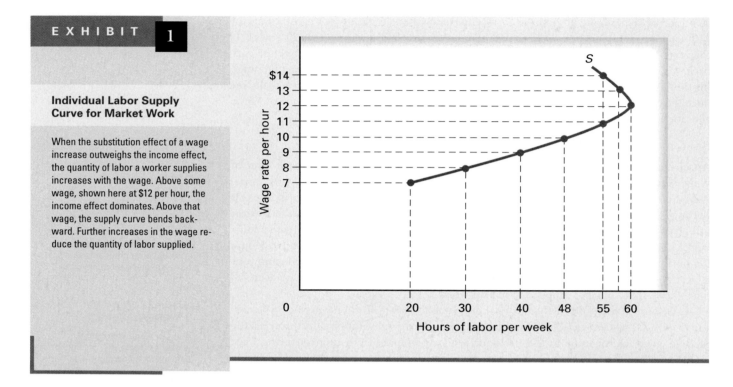

EXHIBIT 1

Individual Labor Supply Curve for Market Work

When the substitution effect of a wage increase outweighs the income effect, the quantity of labor a worker supplies increases with the wage. Above some wage, shown here at $12 per hour, the income effect dominates. Above that wage, the supply curve bends backward. Further increases in the wage reduce the quantity of labor supplied.

labor markets. But what are the nonwage factors that shape a college student's labor supply for the summer?

Other Sources of Income

Although some jobs are rewarding in a variety of nonmonetary ways, the main reason people work is to earn money. Thus, the willingness to supply time to a labor market depends on income from other sources, including from prior savings, borrowing, family, and scholarships. A student who receives a generous scholarship, for example, faces less pressure for summer earnings. More generally, wealthy people have less incentive to work. For example, multimillion-dollar lottery winners often quit their jobs.

Nonmonetary Factors

Labor is a special kind of resource. Unlike capital and natural resources, which can be supplied regardless of the whereabouts of the resource owner, the supplier of labor must be in the same place the work is performed. Because individuals must usually be physically present to supply labor, such *nonmonetary factors* as the difficulty of the job, the quality of the work environment, and the status of the position become important in labor supply. For example, deckhands on fishing boats in the Bering Sea off Alaska earn over $3,000 for five days' work, but the winter temperature seldom exceeds zero and daily shifts allow only three hours for sleep.

Consider the different working conditions you might encounter. A campus job that lets you study on the job is more attractive than one with no study time. Some jobs have flexible hours; others have rigid schedules. Is the workplace air-conditioned, or do you have to sweat it out? The more attractive the working conditions, the more labor you supply to that market, other things constant. Finally, some jobs convey more status than others. For example, the president of the United States earns less than one-tenth the average pay of corporate heads, but there is no shortage of presidential candidates. Similarly, U.S. Supreme Court justices typically take a huge pay cut to accept the job.

The Value of Job Experience

All else equal, you are more inclined to take a job that provides valuable experience. Serving as the assistant treasurer for a local business during the summer provides better job experience and looks better on a résumé than serving mystery meat at the college cafeteria. Some people are willing to accept relatively low wages now for the promise of higher wages in the future. For example, new lawyers are eager to fill clerkships for judges, though the pay is low and the hours long, because these positions offer experience and contacts future employers value. Likewise, athletes who play in the minor leagues for little pay believe that experience will help them get to the major leagues. Thus, *the more a job enhances future earning possibilities, the greater the supply of labor to that occupation, other things constant.* Consequently, the pay is usually lower than for jobs that impart less valuable experience. Sometimes the pay is zero, as with some internships.

Taste for Work

Just as the tastes for goods and services differ among consumers, the tastes for work also differ among labor suppliers. Some people prefer physical labor and hate office work. Some become surgeons; others can't stand the sight of blood. Some become airline pilots; others are afraid to fly. Teenagers prefer jobs at Starbucks and Gap to those at McDonald's and Burger King.[1] Many struggling writers, artists, actors, and dancers could earn more elsewhere, but prefer the creative process and the chance, albeit slim, of becoming rich and famous in the arts (for example, members of the Screen Actors Guild average less than $20,000 a year). Some people have such strong preferences for certain jobs that they work for free, such as auxiliary police officers or volunteer firefighters.

As with the taste for goods and services, economists do not try to explain the origin of tastes for work. They simply argue that your tastes are relatively stable and you supply more labor to jobs you like. Based on tastes, workers seek jobs in a way that tends to minimize the disutility of work. This is not to say that everyone will end up in his or her most preferred position. The transaction costs of job information and of changing jobs may prevent some matchups that might otherwise seem desirable. But in the long run, people tend to find jobs that suit them. We are not likely to find tour guides who hate to travel, zookeepers who are allergic to animals, or garage mechanics who hate getting their hands dirty.

Market Supply of Labor

In the previous section, we considered those factors, both monetary and nonmonetary, that influence individual labor supply. *The supply of labor to a particular* market *is the horizontal sum of all the individual supply curves.* The horizontal sum is found by adding the quantities supplied by each worker at each particular wage. If an individual supply curve of labor bends backward, does this mean that the market supply curve for labor also bends backward? Not necessarily. Because different individuals have different opportunity costs and different tastes for work, the bend in the supply curve occurs at different wages for different individuals. And, for some individuals, the labor supply curve may not bend backward over the realistic range of wages. Exhibit 2 shows how just three individual labor supply curves sum to yield a market supply curve that slopes upward.

---

1. Dirk Johnson, "For Teenagers, Fast Food Is a Snack, Not a Job," *New York Times*, 8 January 2001.

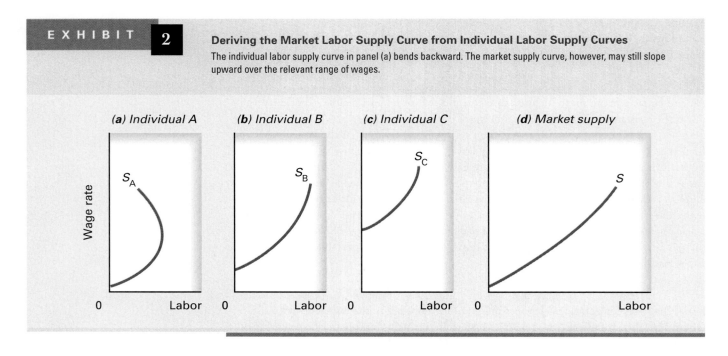

EXHIBIT 2

Deriving the Market Labor Supply Curve from Individual Labor Supply Curves

The individual labor supply curve in panel (a) bends backward. The market supply curve, however, may still slope upward over the relevant range of wages.

(a) *Individual A*   **(b)** *Individual B*   **(c)** *Individual C*   **(d)** *Market supply*

Why Wages Differ

Just as both blades of scissors contribute equally to cutting paper, both labor demand and labor supply determine the market wage. Exhibit 3 shows average hourly wages for the 128 million U.S. workers. Workers are sorted into 22 occupations from the highest to the lowest average wage. Management earns the highest wage, at $34 an hour. The lowest is the $8 an hour averaged by workers preparing and serving food. Wage differences across labor markets trace to differences in labor demand and in labor supply, as you will see. In the previous chapter, we discussed the elements that influence the demand for resources and examined labor in particular. In brief, *a profit-maximizing firm hires labor up to the point where labor's marginal revenue product equals its marginal resource cost*—that is, where the last unit employed increases total revenue enough to cover the added cost. Because we have already discussed what affects the demand for labor—namely, labor's marginal revenue product—let's focus more on labor supply.

Differences in Training, Education, Age, and Experience

Some jobs pay more because they require a long and expensive training period, which reduces market supply because few are willing to incur the time and expense required. But such training increases labor productivity, thereby increasing demand for the skills. Reduced supply and increased demand both raise the market wage. For example, certified public accountants (CPAs) earn more than file clerks because the extensive training of CPAs limits the supply to this field and because this training increases the productivity of CPAs compared to file clerks.

Exhibit 4 shows how education and experience affect earnings. Age groups are indicated on the horizontal axis and average annual earnings on the vertical axis. To standardize things, pay figures are for the highest level of education achieved. The relationship between income and education is clear. At every age, those with more education earn more. For example, among the three age groups between 35 and 64, those with professional degrees averaged *five times* more pay than those with less than a ninth-grade education.

E X H I B I T   **3**   **Average Hourly Wage by Occupation**

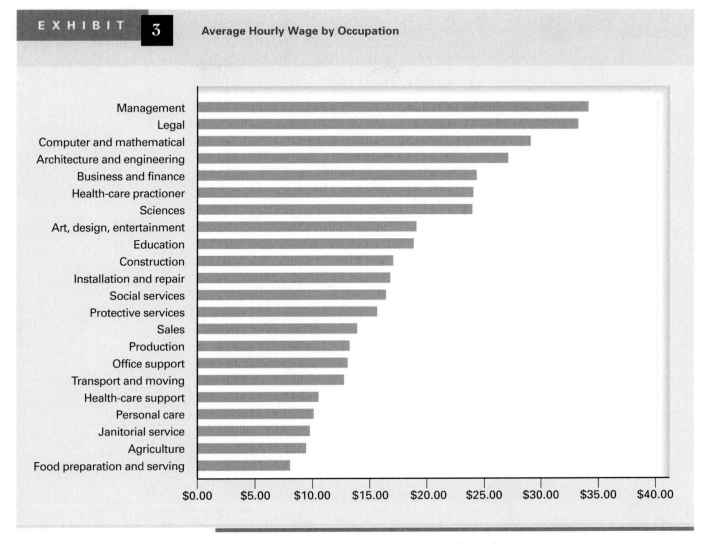

Source: U.S. Bureau of Labor Statistics. Figures are for 2001. For the latest figures, go to http://www.bls.gov/bls/blswage.htm.

Age itself also has an important effect on income. Earnings tend to increase as workers acquire job experience and get promoted. Among educated workers, experience pays more. For example, among those with a professional degree, workers in the 45–54 age group earned on average 86 percent more than those in the 25–34 age group. But among those with less than a ninth-grade education, workers in the 45–54 age group earned on average only 8 percent more than those in the 25–34 age group. Differences in earnings reflect the normal workings of resource markets, whereby workers are rewarded according to their marginal productivity.

Differences in Ability

Because they are more able and talented, some individuals earn more than others with the same training and education. For example, two lawyers may have identical educations, but

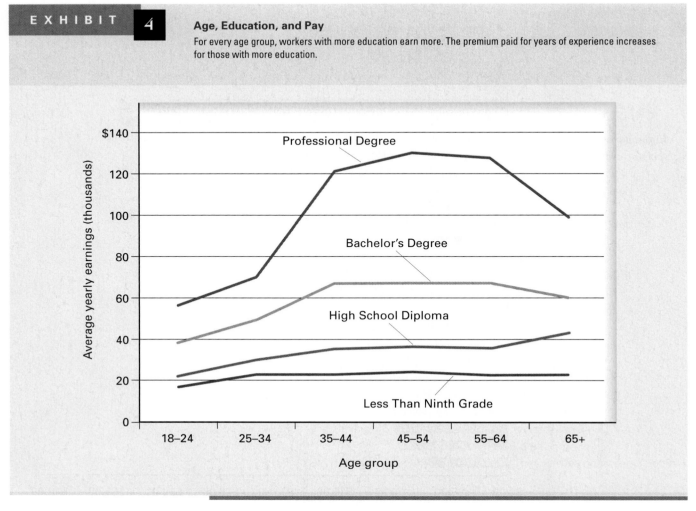

EXHIBIT 4

Age, Education, and Pay
For every age group, workers with more education earn more. The premium paid for years of experience increases for those with more education.

Source: U.S. Census Bureau. Figures are average earnings for all full-time, year-round workers in 2001.

WINNER-TAKE-ALL LABOR MARKETS

Markets in which a few key employees critical to the overall success of an enterprise are richly rewarded

Case **Study**

World of Business

*e*Activity
For current news stories about executive compensation, visit *Forbes* maga-

one earns more because of differences in underlying ability. Most executives have extensive training and business experience, but only a few get to head large corporations. In professional sports such as basketball and baseball, some players earn up to 50 times more than others. From lawyers to executives to professional athletes, pay differences reflect differing abilities and different marginal productivities. The following case study examines why the premium awarded greater marginal productivity has grown in recent decades.

Winner–Take–All Labor Markets

Each year *Forbes* magazine lists the multimillion-dollar earnings of top entertainers and professional athletes. Entertainment and pro sports have come to be called **winner-take-all labor markets** because a few key people critical to the overall success of an enterprise are richly rewarded. For example, the credits at the end of a movie list a hundred or more people directly involved in the production. Hundreds, sometimes thousands, more work behind the scenes. Despite a huge cast and crew, the difference between a movie's financial success and failure depends primarily on the performance of just a few critical people—the screenwriter, the director, and the lead actors. The same happens in sports. Although thousands compete each year in professional tennis, the value of television time, ticket sales, and endorsements is based on the drawing power of just the top few players. In professional golf tournaments, attendance and TV ratings have been significantly higher with Tiger Woods in the mix. Thus, top performers generate a high marginal revenue product.

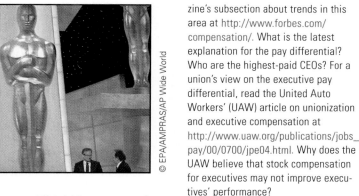

But high marginal productivity alone is not enough. To be paid anywhere near their marginal revenue product, there must be an open competition for top performers. This bids up pay, such as the $20 million per movie garnered by top stars—more than 1,000 times the average annual earnings of Screen Actors Guild members. In professional sports, before the free-agency rule was introduced (which allows players to seek the highest bidder), top players couldn't move on their own from team to team. They were stuck with the team that drafted them, earning only a fraction of their marginal revenue product.

Relatively high pay in entertainment and sports is not new. What is new is the spread of winner-take-all to other U.S. markets. The "star" treatment now extends to such fields as management, law, banking, finance, even academia. Consider, for example, corporate pay. In 1974, the chief executive officers (CEOs) of the 200 largest U.S. corporations earned about 35 times more than the average production worker. By 2000, this multiple topped 150. Comparable multiples were lower in Germany and Japan. Why the big U.S. jump?

First, the U.S. economy has grown sharply in recent decades and is by far the largest in the world—with output equaling that of the next three economies combined. So U.S. businesses serve a wider market, making the CEO potentially more productive and more valuable. Second, breakthroughs in communications, production, and transportation mean that a well-run U.S. company can now sell a valued product around the world. Third, wider competition for the top people has increased their pay. For example, in the 1970s, U.S. businesses usually hired CEOs from company ranks, promoting mainly from within (a practice still common today in Germany and Japan). Because other firms were not trying to bid away the most talented executives, companies were able to retain them for just a fraction of the pay that now prevails in a more competitive market. Today top executives are often drawn from outside the firm—even outside the industry and the country. One final reason why top CEO pay has increased in America is that high salaries are more socially acceptable here than they once were. High salaries are still frowned on in some countries, such as Japan and Germany.

Sources: Stefan Fatsis, "Thanks to Tiger's Roar, PGA Tour Signs Record TV Deal Through 2007," *Wall Street Journal*, 17 July 2001; "Making Companies Work," *Economist*, 25 October 2003; Barbara Whitaker, "Producers and Actors Reach Accord," *New York Times*, 5 July 2001; and *Economic Report of the President*, February 2004, at http://www.gpoaccess.gov/eop/index.html.

zine's subsection about trends in this area at http://www.forbes.com/compensation/. What is the latest explanation for the pay differential? Who are the highest-paid CEOs? For a union's view on the executive pay differential, read the United Auto Workers' (UAW) article on unionization and executive compensation at http://www.uaw.org/publications/jobs_pay/00/0700/jpe04.html. Why does the UAW believe that stock compensation for executives may not improve executives' performance?

Differences in Risk

Research indicates that jobs with a higher probability of injury or death, such as coal mining, pay more, other things constant. Russians working at the partially disabled nuclear power plant, Chernobyl, earned 10 times the national average. Truck drivers for American contractors in Iraq earn over $100,000 a year, but the job is dangerous. Workers also earn more, other things constant, in seasonal jobs such as construction, where the risk of unemployment is greater.

Geographic Differences

People have a strong incentive to sell their resources in the market where they earn the most. For example, the National Basketball Association attracts talent from around the world. About 20 percent of NBA players in 2004 came from 36 other countries. Likewise, thousands of foreign-trained physicians migrate here each year for the high pay. The flow of labor is not all one way: Some Americans seek their fortune abroad, with American basketball players going to Europe and baseball players going to Japan. Workers often face migration hurdles. Any reduction in these hurdles would reduce wage differentials across countries.

Job Discrimination

Sometimes wage differences stem from racial or gender discrimination in the job market. Although such discrimination is illegal, history shows that certain groups—including African Americans, Hispanics, and women—have systematically earned less than others of equal ability.

Union Membership

Other things equal, members of organized labor earn more than nonmembers. The balance of this chapter discusses the effects of unions on the market for labor.

Unions and Collective Bargaining

Economics in the Movies

Few aspects of the labor market make the news more often than the activities of labor unions. Labor negotiations, strikes, picket lines, confrontations between workers and employers—all fit TV's "action news" format. Despite media attention, only about one in seven U.S. workers is a union member and the overwhelming share of union agreements are reached without a strike. Let's examine the tools that unions use to seek higher pay and better benefits for their members.

Types of Unions

A **labor union** is a group of workers who join together to improve their terms of employment. Labor unions in the United States date back to the early days of national independence, when workers in various crafts—such as carpenters, shoemakers, and printers—formed local groups to seek higher wages and shorter work hours. A **craft union** was confined to people with a particular skill, or craft. Craft unions eventually formed their own national organization, the *American Federation of Labor (AFL)*. The AFL, founded in 1886 under the direction of Samuel Gompers, a cigar maker, was not a union itself but rather an organization of national unions, each retaining its autonomy.

By the beginning of World War I, the AFL, still under Gompers, was viewed as the voice of labor. The Clayton Act of 1914 exempted labor unions from antitrust laws, meaning that *unions at competing companies could legally join forces.* Unions were also tax exempt. Membership jumped during World War I but fell by half between 1920 and 1933, as the government retreated from its support of union efforts.

The *Congress of Industrial Organizations (CIO)* was formed in 1935 to serve as a national organization of unions in mass-production industries, such as autos and steel. Whereas the AFL organized workers in particular crafts, such as plumbers and carpenters, the CIO consisted of unions whose membership embraced all workers in a particular industry. These **industrial unions** included unskilled, semiskilled, and skilled workers in an industry, such as all autoworkers or all steelworkers.

LABOR UNION

A group of workers who organize to improve their terms of employment

CRAFT UNION

A union whose members have a particular skill or work at a particular craft, such as plumbers or carpenters

INDUSTRIAL UNION

A union of both skilled and unskilled workers from a particular industry, such as autoworkers or steelworkers

Collective Bargaining

Collective bargaining is the process by which representatives of union and management negotiate a mutually agreeable contract specifying wages, employee benefits, and working conditions. A tentative agreement, once reached, goes before the membership for a vote. If the agreement is rejected, the union can strike or can continue negotiations.

Mediation and Arbitration

If negotiations reach an impasse and the public interest is involved, government officials may ask an independent mediator to step in. A **mediator** is an impartial observer who listens to each side separately and then suggests a resolution. If each side still remains open to a settlement, the mediator brings them together to work out a contract, but the mediator has no power to impose a settlement. In certain critical sectors, such as police and fire protection, where a strike could harm the public interest, differences are sometimes settled through **binding arbitration.** A neutral third party evaluates each position and issues a ruling that both sides must accept. Some disputes skip the mediation and arbitration steps and go directly from impasse to strike.

The Strike

A major source of union power is a **strike,** which is a union's attempt to withhold labor to stop production, thereby hoping the firm will accept the union's position. But strikes are also risky for workers, who earn no pay or benefits during the strike and could lose their jobs. Union funds and, in some states, unemployment benefits, may aid strikers, but incomes still fall substantially. *Although neither party usually wants a strike, both sides, rather than concede on key points, usually act as if they could endure one.* Unions usually picket to prevent or discourage so-called strikebreakers, or "scabs," from crossing the picket lines to work. But the targeted firm, by hiring temporary workers and nonstriking union workers, can sometimes continue production.

Union Wages and Employment

Samuel Gompers, the AFL's long-time head, was once asked what unions want. "More," he roared. Union members, like everyone else, have unlimited wants. But because resources are scarce, choices must be made. A menu of union desires includes higher wages, more benefits, greater job security, better working conditions, and so on. To keep the analysis manageable, let's focus on a single objective, higher wages, and consider three ways unions might increase wages: (1) by forming an inclusive, or industrial, union; (2) by forming an exclusive, or craft, union; and (3) by increasing the demand for union labor.

Inclusive, or Industrial, Unions: Negotiating a Higher Industry Wage

With the *inclusive, or industrial,* approach, the union tries to negotiate an industry-wide wage for each class of labor. The market demand and supply curves for a particular type of labor are labeled *D* and *S* in panel (a) of Exhibit 5. In the absence of a union, the market wage is *W* and employment is *E*. At the market wage, each firm faces a horizontal, or perfectly elastic, supply of labor, as depicted by *s* in panel (b) of Exhibit 5. Thus, each firm can hire as much labor as it wants at the market wage of *W.* The firm hires up to the point where labor's marginal revenue product equals its marginal resource cost, resulting in *e* units of labor in panel (b). As we saw earlier, in equilibrium, labor is paid a wage just equal to its marginal revenue product.

COLLECTIVE BARGAINING
The process by which union and management negotiate a labor agreement

MEDIATOR
An impartial observer who helps resolve differences between union and management

BINDING ARBITRATION
Negotiation in which union and management must accept an impartial observer's resolution of a dispute

STRIKE
A union's attempt to withhold labor from a firm to stop production

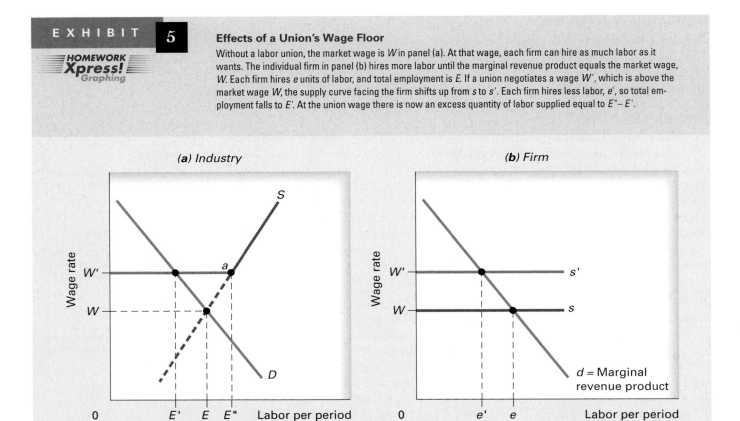

EXHIBIT 5

HOMEWORK Xpress!
Graphing

Effects of a Union's Wage Floor

Without a labor union, the market wage is *W* in panel (a). At that wage, each firm can hire as much labor as it wants. The individual firm in panel (b) hires more labor until the marginal revenue product equals the market wage, *W.* Each firm hires *e* units of labor, and total employment is *E.* If a union negotiates a wage *W'*, which is above the market wage *W*, the supply curve facing the firm shifts up from *s* to *s'*. Each firm hires less labor, *e'*, so total employment falls to *E'*. At the union wage there is now an excess quantity of labor supplied equal to *E"* – *E'*.

Now suppose the union negotiates a wage above the market-clearing level. Specifically, suppose the wage negotiated is *W'* in panel (a), meaning that no labor will be supplied at a lower wage. In effect, the market supply of labor is perfectly elastic at the union wage out to point *a.* Beyond point *a,* however, the wage floor no longer applies; *aS* becomes the relevant portion of the labor supply curve. For an industry facing a wage floor of *W'*, the entire labor supply curve becomes *W'aS,* which has a kink where the wage floor joins the upward-sloping portion of the original labor supply curve.

Once this wage floor is established, each firm faces a horizontal supply curve of labor at the collectively bargained wage, *W'.* Because the wage is now higher than the market-clearing wage, each firm hires less labor. Consequently, the higher wage leads to a reduction in total employment; the quantity demanded by the industry drops from *E* to *E'* in panel (a). At wage *W'* workers in the industry would like to supply, *E",* which exceeds the labor demanded, *E'.* Ordinarily this excess quantity supplied would force the wage down. But because union members agree *collectively* to the union wage, individual workers can't work for less, nor can employers hire them for less. *With the inclusive, or industrial, union, which negotiates with the entire industry, the wage is higher and employment lower than they would be in the absence of a union.*

The union must somehow ration the limited jobs available, such as by awarding them based on worker seniority or personal connections within the union. Those who can't find

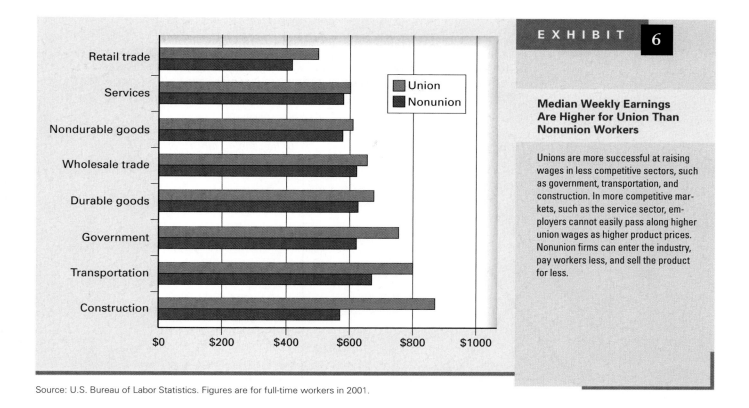

Source: U.S. Bureau of Labor Statistics. Figures are for full-time workers in 2001.

union jobs turn to the nonunion sector. *This increases the supply of labor in the nonunion sector, which drives down the nonunion wage.* So wages are relatively higher in the union sector first, because unions bargain for a wage that exceeds the market–clearing wage, and second, because those unable to find union jobs crowd into the nonunion sector. Studies show that union wages average about 15 percent above the wages of similarly qualified nonunion workers. Exhibit 6 compares median weekly earnings of union and nonunion workers. Note that unions are more successful at raising wages in less-competitive sectors. For example, unions have less impact on service industries, where product markets tend to be competitive. Unions have greater impact on wages in government, transportation, and construction, which tend to be less competitive. When there is more competition in the product market, employers cannot easily pass along higher union wages as higher product prices. New, nonunion, firms can enter the industry, pay lower wages, and sell the product for less.

Exclusive, or Craft, Unions: Reducing Labor Supply

One way to increase wages while avoiding an excess quantity of labor supplied is to somehow reduce the supply of labor, shown as a leftward shift of the labor supply curve in panel (a) of Exhibit 7. This supply reduction increases the wage and reduces employment. Successful supply restrictions of this type require that the union first limit its membership and second force all employers in the industry to hire only union members. The union can restrict membership with high initiation fees, long apprenticeship periods, tough qualification exams, restrictive licensing requirements, and other devices aimed at slowing down or

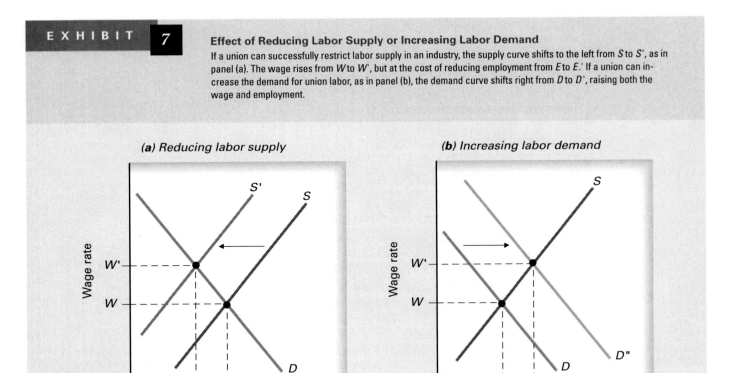

EXHIBIT 7

Effect of Reducing Labor Supply or Increasing Labor Demand

If a union can successfully restrict labor supply in an industry, the supply curve shifts to the left from S to S', as in panel (a). The wage rises from W to W', but at the cost of reducing employment from E to E'. If a union can increase the demand for union labor, as in panel (b), the demand curve shifts right from D to D', raising both the wage and employment.

(a) *Reducing labor supply*

(b) *Increasing labor demand*

discouraging new membership. But even if unions restrict membership, they still have difficulty unionizing all firms in the industry.

Whereas wage setting is more typical of industrial unions, restricting supply is more typical of craft unions, such as unions of carpenters, plumbers, or bricklayers. Professional groups—doctors, lawyers, and accountants, for instance—also impose entry restrictions through education and examination standards. These restrictions, usually defended as protecting the public, are often little more than self-serving attempts to increase wages by restricting labor supply.

Increasing Demand for Union Labor

A third way to increase the wage is to increase the demand for union labor by somehow shifting the labor demand curve outward as from D to D'' in panel (b) of Exhibit 7. This is an attractive alternative *because it increases both the wage and employment*, so there is no need to restrict labor supply or to ration jobs among union members. Here are some ways unions try to increase the demand for union labor.

Increase Demand for Union-Made Goods

The demand for union labor may be increased through a direct appeal to consumers to buy only union-made products. Because the demand for labor is a derived demand, increasing the demand for union-made products increases the demand for union labor.

Restrict Supply of Nonunion-Made Goods

Another way to increase the demand for union labor is to restrict the supply of products that compete with union-made products. Again, this approach relies on the derived nature of labor demand. The United Auto Workers (UAW), for example, supports restrictions on imported cars. Fewer imported cars means greater demand for cars produced by U.S. workers, who are mostly union members.

Increase Productivity of Union Labor

Some observers claim union representation improves labor-management relations. According to this theory, unions increase worker productivity by minimizing conflicts, resolving differences, and at times even straightening out workers who are goofing off. In the absence of a union, a dissatisfied worker may simply quit, causing job turnover. Turnover is costly to the firm because the departing worker leaves with company-specific, on-the-job training that increases workers' productivity. With a union, however, workers can resolve dissatisfactions through union channels. Quit rates are in fact significantly lower among union workers (although this could also be due to the higher pay). If unions increase the productivity of workers, the demand for union labor will increase.

Featherbedding

Yet another way unions try to increase the demand for union labor is by **featherbedding,** which makes employers hire more labor than they want or need. For example, union rules require that each Broadway theater have a permanent "house" carpenter, electrician, and property manager. Once the play run begins, these workers show up only on payday. The box office must be staffed by three people. The musicians' union requires that from 9 to 22 musicians be employed at each theater staging a musical, even if the show calls for just a piano player.

FEATHERBEDDING

Union efforts to force employers to hire more workers than wanted or needed

Featherbedding does not create a true increase in demand, in the sense of shifting the demand curve to the right. Instead, it forces the firm to a point to the right of its true labor demand curve. For example, changing one light bulb for the Broadway play *The Iceman Cometh* required a three-person crew, each earning $43.36 an hour.[2] The union tries to limit a firm to an all-or-none choice: Either hire so many workers for the job, or we'll strike. Thus, with featherbedding, *the union attempts to dictate not only the wage but also the quantity that must be hired at that wage, thereby moving employers to the right of their labor demand curve.*

To review: We have examined three ways in which unions try to raise members' wages: (1) by negotiating a wage floor above the equilibrium wage for the industry and somehow rationing the limited jobs among union members, (2) by restricting the supply of labor, and (3) by increasing the demand for union labor. Unions try to increase the demand for union labor in four ways: (1) through a direct public appeal to buy only union-made products, (2) by restricting the supply of products made by nonunion labor, (3) by reducing labor turnover and thereby increasing labor's marginal productivity, and (4) through featherbedding, which forces employers to hire more union labor than they want or need.

Recent Trends in Union Membership

In 1955, about one-third of U.S. workers belonged to unions. Union membership as a fraction of the workforce has since declined. Now, only one in seven U.S. workers belongs to a union. Government workers, who account for just one in six U.S. workers, now make up nearly half of all union members. A typical union member is a schoolteacher. Compared

2. Jesse McKinley, "$100 Tickets? Here's Why," *New York Times*, 8 April 1999.

WALL STREET JOURNAL

Reading It **Right**

What's the relevance of the following statement from the Wall Street Journal*: "The United Auto Workers lost its bid to represent 4,800 workers at Nissan Motor Co.'s auto factory in Smyrna, Tenn. . . . the latest in a string of failed efforts."*

RIGHT-TO-WORK STATES

States where workers in unionized companies do not have to join the union or pay union dues

with other industrialized countries, the United States ranks relatively low in the extent of unionization, though rates abroad are also declining.

The bar graph in Exhibit 8 indicates U.S. union membership rates by age and gender. The rates for men, shown by the green bars, are higher than the rates for women, in part because men are in manufacturing and women work more in the service sector, where union membership is lower. The highest membership rates are for middle-aged males. Although the exhibit does not show it, black employees have a higher union membership rate than their white counterparts (17 percent versus 13 percent), in part because black people are employed more by government and by heavy industries such as autos and steel, where union representation is higher. Union membership among those of Hispanic origin, who can be of any race, averaged only 11 percent.

Union membership rates also vary across states. New York had the highest unionization rate at 26.7 percent and North Carolina has the lowest at 3.7 percent. Unionization rates in right-to-work states average only half the rates in other states. In **right-to-work states**, workers in unionized companies do not have to join the union or pay union dues. Over the years, the number of right-to-work states has increased and this has hurt the union movement. The decline in membership rates is also due partly to structural changes in the U.S. economy. Unions have long been more important in the industrial sector than in the service sector. But employment in the industrial sector, which includes manufacturing, mining, and construction, has declined in recent decades as a share of all jobs. Another factor in the decline of the union movement is a growth in market competition, particularly from

EXHIBIT 8

Unionization Rates by Age and Gender

Unionization rates for men, shown by the green bars, are higher than the rates for women, in part because men are in manufacturing and women work more in the service sector, where union membership is lower. The highest membership rates are for middle-aged males.

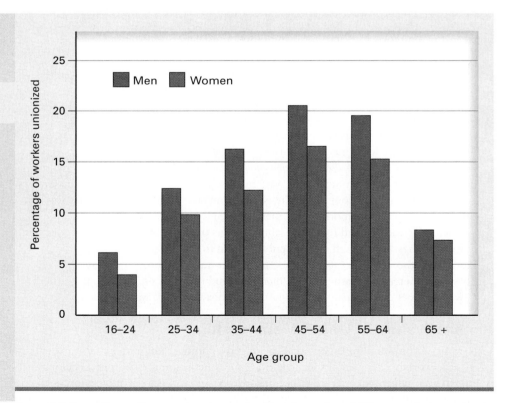

Source: U.S. Census Bureau. Figures are for union membership and percentage of U.S. wage and salary workers for 2002. For the latest figures go to http://www.bls.gov/.

imports. Increased competition from nonunion employers, both foreign and domestic, has reduced the ability of unionized firms to pass on higher labor costs as higher prices. And fewer union members mean fewer voters who belong to unions, so unions have lost political clout.

Finally, the near disappearance of the strike has cut union power. During the 1970s, there were about 300 strikes a year in the United States involving 1,000 or more workers. Such strikes now average only one-tenth that rate. Many recent strikes ended badly for union workers; companies such as Caterpillar, Phelps Dodge Copper, Continental Airlines, and Hormel Foods hired replacement workers. Union members are less inclined to strike because of the increased willingness of employers to hire strikebreakers and the increased willingness of workers—both union and nonunion—to cross picket lines. Strikes also cut company profits, which hurts workers who share in profits, thus dampening the incentive to strike. For example, a recent strike against General Motors cut each worker's average profit share to just $200 from more than $6,000 the year before. Because the strike and the threat of a strike have become less important, the power of unions has diminished.

The final case study examines why unions have achieved only limited success in organizing the fastest growing job sector—that for information technology workers.

Unionizing Information Technology Workers

Despite the demise of many online ventures and the outsourcing of software-related work overseas, information technology (IT) workers still make up a growing sector of the U.S. labor force. The U.S. Bureau of Labor Statistics predicts that job growth in computer and data processing will exceed that of most other fields during the next decade. Because labor unions want to grow, why don't they focus on IT jobs? Well, unions have tried to organize IT workers, but this group poses some special challenges for union organizers.

Case Study

The Information Economy

*e*Activity

How successful has the Communications Workers of America (CWA) union been in organizing information technology workers? Check out the union's list of new CWA workplaces at http://www.cwa-union.org/news/articles.asp?category=New+CWA+Work places to find the latest on its successes. How many of the latest organizing victories are IT firms? For general news about the labor movement's progress in the IT industry go to *Industry Week*'s Web site at http://www.industryweek.com/ and conduct a search for news on union organizing.

Compared to traditional union members, such as blue-collar and government workers, IT workers tend to be younger and comprise a motley crew of regular workers, telecommuters, part-timers, temporary workers, freelancers, and a growing number of foreigners on short-term work visas. Unions have a hard time even communicating with such a fragmented, independent bunch. IT firms are also more dynamic than traditional labor strongholds, such as autos, steel, and public schools. By the time a union has targeted an IT firm for organizing, that firm may have already moved, merged with another firm, or folded.

The only union with a significant presence among IT workers is the Communications Workers of America (CWA), which began decades ago with the then regulated phone monopoly, AT&T. The breakup of that monopoly in the early 1980s coupled with technological breakthroughs such as fiberglass and wireless transmission turned telecommunications into a hot, high-tech industry. Thus, CWA was in the right place at the right time. But the union has had difficulty moving into other IT industries. For example, since 1996 it has tried to organize Microsoft's 55,000 workers but has signed up few members. At Silicon Valley firms such as Intel and Hewlett-Packard, unions have successfully organized janitors but not IT workers. Worse yet for CWA, traditional telephone systems are losing ground to Internet-based technologies supplied by companies with no union members, such as Cisco. To keep from falling too far behind, CWA has even hired Cisco to help retrain some CWA members.

The Internet has reduced the transaction costs of having software development and maintenance carried out overseas. As a result, firms also are outsourcing more IT work overseas to places like India and Ireland, putting that labor out of reach of union organizers. Thus, American IT workers now see their job security threatened by foreign workers on temporary visas and by outsourcing IT work overseas. This trend could motivate some U.S. workers to unionize.

In summary, IT workers are an independent bunch, not easily organized by unions. Trying to organize IT workers has been like trying to herd cats. But the loss of IT jobs to foreign workers could spur greater unionization as American workers seek greater job security.

Sources: Jeff Nachtigal, "Tech Workers, Unions Protest Offshore Outsourcing Conference," *WashTech News*, 17 September 2003; Aliza Earnshaw, "Portland Techies Look for Union Label," *Portland Business Journal*, 27 October 2003; Scott Thurm, "Cisco Systems Helps to Train Union Workers in Web's Ways," *Wall Street Journal*, 3 July 2001; and the CWA Web site at http://www.cwa-union.org/.

Finally, some observers argue that unions have been in decline because employers have discouraged organizing efforts. Although federal law bars employers from firing or penalizing workers for supporting a union, a federal study estimates that employers punished or fired over 125,000 workers between 1992 and 1997 for trying to establish a union.[3] This amount seems like a lot, but it works out to be only about one in a thousand workers during the six-year period. Others say that unions have failed to grow not so much because of what employers do but because of the larger forces in the economy already discussed—right-to-work laws at the state level, growing global competition, the economy's shift from manufacturing to services, the increased reluctance to strike, and the inability to unionize IT workers.

Conclusion

The first half of this chapter focused on labor supply and explained why wages differ across occupations and among individuals within an occupation. The interaction of labor demand and supply determines wages and employment. The second half of the chapter explored the effect of unions on the labor market. At one time unions dominated some key industries. But as global competition intensifies, employers have a harder time passing higher union labor costs along to consumers. Both in the United States and in other industrial economies, union members represent a dwindling segment of the labor force.

SUMMARY

1. The demand for labor curve shows the relationship between the wage and the quantity of labor producers are willing and able to hire, other things constant. The supply of labor curve shows the relationship between the wage and the quantity of labor workers are willing and able to supply, other things constant. The intersection of labor demand and labor supply curves determines the market wage and market employment.

2. People allocate their time to maximize utility. There are three uses of time: market work, nonmarket work, and leisure. A person attempts to maximize utility by allocating time so that the expected marginal utility of the last unit of time spent in each activity is identical.

3. The higher the wage, other things constant, the more goods and services can be purchased with that wage, so a higher wage encourages labor suppliers to substitute

3. The National Labor Relations Board study was discussed in Steven Greenhouse, "Report Faults Law for Slowing Growth of Unions," *New York Times*, 24 October 2000.

market work for other uses of their time. But a higher wage also increases income, increasing the demand for all normal goods, including leisure. The net effect of a higher wage on the quantity of labor supplied depends on both the substitution effect and the income effect.

4. The supply of labor depends on factors other than the wage, including (a) other sources of income, (b) job amenities, (c) the value of job experience, and (d) worker tastes.

5. Market wages differ because of (a) differences in training and education; (b) differences in the skill and ability of workers; (c) risk differences, both in terms of the workers' safety and the chances of getting laid off; (d) geographic differences; (e) racial and gender discrimination; and (f) union membership.

6. Unions and employers try to negotiate a labor contract through collective bargaining. A major source of union power has been the threat of a strike, which is an attempt to withhold labor from the firm.

7. Inclusive, or industrial, unions attempt to establish a wage floor that exceeds the competitive, or market-clearing, wage. But a wage above the market-clearing level creates an excess quantity of labor supplied, so the union must somehow ration the limited jobs among its members. Exclusive, or craft, unions try to raise the wage by restricting the supply of labor. Another way to raise union wages is to increase the demand for union labor.

8. Union membership as a percentage of the labor force has been falling for decades. Today, only one in seven workers is a union member, compared to one in three in 1955. Reasons for the decline include right-to-work laws, greater global competition, a shift in employment from goods to services, a greater willingness to hire replacements for striking workers, a greater willingness of union members and others to cross picket lines, less political support for the labor movement, and difficulty signing up IT workers.

QUESTIONS FOR REVIEW

1. *(Uses of Time)* Describe the three possible uses of an individual's time, and give an example of each.

2. *(Work and Utility)* Explain the concept of the "net utility of work." How is it useful in developing the labor supply curve?

3. *(Utility Maximization)* How does a rational consumer allocate time among competing uses?

4. *(Substitution and Income Effects)* Suppose that the substitution effect of an increase in the wage rate exactly offsets the income effect as the hourly wage increases from $12 to $13. What would the supply of labor curve look like over this range of wages? Why?

5. *(Substitution and Income Effects)* Suppose that the cost of living increases, thereby reducing the purchasing power of your income. If your money wage doesn't increase, you may work *more* hours because of this cost-of-living increase. Is this response predominantly an income effect or a substitution effect? Explain.

6. *(Nonwage Determinants of Labor Supply)* Suppose that two jobs are exactly the same except that one is performed in an air-conditioned workplace. How could you measure the value workers attach to such a job amenity?

7. *(Why Wages Differ)* Why might permanent wage differences occur between different markets for labor or within the same labor market?

8. *(Mediation and Arbitration)* Distinguish between mediation and binding arbitration. Under what circumstances do firms and unions use these tools? What is the role of a strike in the bargaining process?

9. *(The Strike)* Why might firms in industries with high fixed costs be inclined to prevent strikes or end strikes quickly?

10. *(Industrial Unions)* Why are unions more effective at raising wages in oligopolistic industries than in competitive industries?

11. *(Craft Unions)* Both industrial unions and craft unions attempt to raise their members' wages, but each goes about it differently. Explain the difference in approaches and describe the impact these differences have on excess quantity of labor supplied.

12. (*Case Study*: Unionizing Information Technology Workers) Why haven't unions been more successful in organizing IT workers? Graduate and research assistants at New York University in 2000 were granted the right to join unions, but a federal body reversed that decision in 2004. Do you think the unions would have been more successful in organizing this group than IT workers? Why or why not?

PROBLEMS AND EXERCISES

13. (*Market Supply of Labor*) The following table shows the hours per week supplied to a particular market by three individuals at various wage rates. Calculate the total hours per week (Q_T) supplied to the market.

Hourly Wage	Hours per Week			
	Q_1	Q_2	Q_3	Q_T
$ 5	20	0	0	____
6	25	0	0	____
7	35	10	0	____
8	45	25	10	____
9	42	40	30	____
10	38	37	45	____

Which individuals, if any, have backward-bending supply curves in the wage range shown? Does the market supply curve bend backward in the wage range shown in the table?

14. (*Industrial Unions*) Review the logic underlying Exhibit 5. Then determine the effect, on the industry and a typical firm, of an increase in the demand for industry output. Show your conclusions on a graph. Does the magnitude of the increase in demand make a difference?

EXPERIENTIAL EXERCISES

15. (*Wall Street Journal*) On Tuesday the *Wall Street Journal* includes articles and information on careers in the Marketplace section. Turn to the Career Opportunities section where employment opportunities are detailed. Read several position descriptions for jobs that are of interest to you. Identify the education and skill requirements of the positions.

16. (*Wages and Labor Supply*) Interview five of your classmates to determine the nature of their labor supply curves for a summer job. Ask each of them how many hours of work he or she would be willing to supply at wage rates of $10, $15, $20, $25, and $30 per hour. Plot the results on a labor supply diagram. Do any of these individuals exhibit a backward-bending labor supply curve? Is the market supply curve for these five individuals backward bending?

17. (*Case Study*: Winner-Take-All Labor Markets) Robert Frank's "Talent and the Winner-Take-All-Society" appeared in *The American Prospect* (21 March, 1994) at http://www.prospect.org/print/V5/17/frank-r.html. Read this nontechnical article. What are some of the problems that Frank identifies?

18. (*Unions and Collective Bargaining*) Visit the AFL-CIO Executive Council Actions page at http://www.aflcio.org/aboutaflcio/ecouncil/ and look at some recent actions. Choose one and depict its intended effects, using the models developed in this chapter.

19. (*Wall Street Journal*) It shouldn't be too hard to find a *Wall Street Journal* story dealing with labor unions. Check the Economy page in the First Section, the Work Week report on the front page of the Tuesday *Journal,* or the "Legal Beat" column inside the Marketplace section. What's going on in the world of organized labor? Is the example you found consistent with the trends described in this chapter?

HOMEWORK XPRESS! EXERCISES

These exercises require access to McEachern Homework Xpress! If Homework Xpress! did not come with your book, visit **http://homeworkxpress.swlearning.com** *to purchase.*

1. Kelly is willing to work 20 hours per week if she's paid $10 per hour. She will work up to 45 hours per week if the wage rate is $20 per hour. However, for each additional dollar per hour, she would cut back on work by one hour per week. In the diagram, sketch both parts of Kelly's labor supply curve.

2. Labor supply schedules for three individuals A, B, and C who work in the same labor market are given in the table below. Each individual has different preferences with respect to how many hours to work for the given set of hourly wages. Draw labor supply curves for each, labeling them S_a, S_b, and S_c accordingly. Use the data in the table to derive and draw the market supply curve.

Wage Rate	Individual A	Individual B	Individual C
$ 0	0	0	0
10	0	20	0
15	0	30	0
20	40	40	0
25	35	50	30

3. New England shoe manufacturers hired workers in a competitive labor market. Use demand and supply curves for labor to illustrate how a wage rate was determined in the market for shoemakers. Shoemakers later formed a union and negotiated a higher wage with all shoe manufacturers. Show the effects of a union wage rate that is higher than the market wage rate. Be sure to identify the quantity of labor that would be demanded and the quantity of labor workers would like to supply.

4. Broadway theater producers must either hire at least nine musicians for each show they stage requiring even one musician or face picket lines of protesting musicians outside their theater doors that keep theatergoers away. Illustrate the effect in the market for musicians when the musicians are successful in having their demands met.

CHAPTER 13

Capital, Interest, and Corporate Finance

W hy can first-run movie theaters charge more than other theaters? Why do you burn your mouth eating pizza? What's seed money and why can't Farmer Jones grow anything without it? What's the big deal with pirated software and music? Why are state lottery jackpots worth much less than the advertised millions? These and other questions are answered in this chapter, which examines capital and investment.

So far, our discussion of resources has focused primarily on labor markets. This emphasis is appropriate because labor generates most income—more than two-thirds of the total. The rewards to labor, however, depend in part on the amount and quality of the other resources employed, particularly capital. A farmer plowing a field with a tractor is more productive than one scraping the soil with a stick. This

HOMEWORK Xpress!

Use Homework Xpress! for economic application, graphing, videos, and more.

chapter looks at the role of capital in production—its cost and its expected return. You will learn about the optimal use of capital and how firms finance their investments. Topics include:

- Production, saving, and time
- Consumption, saving, and time
- Optimal investment
- Loanable funds market
- Present value and discounting
- Corporate finance
- Stocks, bonds, and retained earnings

The Role of Time in Production and Consumption

Time is important in both production and consumption. In this section, we first consider the role of time on the production decision, and then show why firms borrow household savings. Next, we consider the role of time in the consumption decision and show why households are rewarded to save, or to defer present consumption. By bringing together borrowers and savers, we find the market interest rate.

Production, Saving, and Time

Suppose Jones is a primitive farmer in a simple economy. Isolated from any neighbors or markets, he literally scratches out a living on a plot of land, using only crude sticks. While his crop is growing, none of it is available for current consumption. Because production takes time, to survive, Jones must rely on food saved from prior harvests. The longer the growing season, the more Jones must save. Thus, even in this simple example, it is clear that *production cannot occur without prior saving.*

Suppose that with his current resources, consisting of land, labor, seed corn, fertilizer, and some crude sticks, Jones grows about 200 bushels of corn a year. He soon realizes that if he had a plow—a type of investment good, or capital—his productivity would increase. Making a plow in such a primitive setting, however, is time consuming and would keep him away from his fields for a year. Thus, the plow has an opportunity cost of 200 bushels of corn. He could not survive this drop in production without enough saving from previous harvests.

The question is: should he invest his time in the plow? The answer depends on the costs and benefits of the plow. We already know that the plow's opportunity cost is 200 bushels—the forgone output. The benefit depends on how much the plow will increase crop production and how long it will last. Jones figures that the plow would boost his annual yield by 100 bushels and would last his lifetime. In making the investment decision, he compares current costs to future benefits. Suppose he decides that adding 100 bushels a year outweighs the one-time cost of 200 bushels sacrificed to make the plow.

In making the plow, Jones engages in *roundabout production.* Rather than working the soil with his crude sticks, he produces capital to increase his productivity. More roundabout production in an economy means more capital, so more goods can be produced in the future. Advanced industrial economies are characterized by much roundabout production and thus abundant capital accumulation.

You can see why production cannot occur without prior saving. *Production requires saving because both direct and roundabout production require time—time during which goods and services are not available from current production.* Now let's modernize the example by introducing the ability to borrow. Many farmers visit the bank each spring to borrow enough "seed money" to get by until their crops come in. Likewise, other businesses often borrow at least a portion of the start-up funds needed to get going. Thus, in a modern economy, producers need not rely on their own prior saving. Banks and other financial institutions serve as *intermediaries* between savers and borrowers. As you will see toward the end of the chapter, financial markets for stocks and bonds also help channel savings to producers. Let's take a look at the incentive to save.

Consumption, Saving, and Time

Did you ever burn the roof of your mouth eating a slice of pizza that hadn't sufficiently cooled? Have you done this more than once? Why do you persist in such self-mutilation? You persist because that bite of pizza is worth more to you now than the same bite two minutes from now. In fact, you are willing to risk burning your mouth rather than wait until the pizza has lost its destructive properties. In a small way, this phenomenon reflects the fact that you and other consumers value *present* consumption more than *future* consumption. You and other consumers are said to have a **positive rate of time preference.**

Because you value present consumption more than future consumption, you are willing to pay more to consume now rather than wait. And prices often reflect this greater willingness to pay. Consider the movies. You pay more at a first-run theater than at other theaters. If you are patient, you can wait to rent the DVD. The same is true for books. By waiting for the paperback, you can save more than half the hardback price. Photo developers, dry cleaners, fast-food restaurants, convenience stores, cable news networks, and other suppliers tout the speed of their services, knowing that consumers prefer earlier availability. Thus, *impatience* is one explanation for a positive rate of time preference. Another is *uncertainty*. If you wait, something might prevent you from consuming the good. A T-shirt slogan captures this point best: "Life is uncertain. Eat dessert first."

Because people value present consumption more than future consumption, they must be rewarded to postpone consumption. Interest is the reward for postponing consumption. By saving a portion of their incomes in financial institutions such as banks, people forgo present consumption for a greater ability to consume in the future. The **interest rate** is the annual reward for saving as a percentage of the amount saved. For example, if the interest rate is 5 percent, the reward, or interest, is $5 per year for each $100 saved. The higher the interest rate, other things constant, the more consumers are rewarded for saving, so the more they save. You will learn more about this later in the chapter.

Optimal Investment

In a market economy characterized by specialization and exchange, Farmer Jones no longer needs to produce his own capital, nor must he rely on his own saving. He can purchase capital using borrowed funds. Suppose he wants to buy some farm equipment. He estimates how each piece of equipment will affect his productivity. Column (1) in panel (a) of Exhibit 1 identifies six pieces of farm machinery that Jones has ranked from most to least productive. The total product of the equipment is listed in column (2), and the marginal product of each piece is listed in column (3). Note that other resources are assumed to be constant.

With just his crude sticks, Jones can grow 200 bushels of corn per year. He figures that a tractor-tiller would boost the harvest to 1,200 bushels. Thus, the tractor-tiller would yield a marginal product of 1,000 bushels per year. The addition of a combine would increase total output to 2,000 bushels, yielding a marginal product of 800 bushels. Note that in this example, diminishing marginal returns from capital set in immediately. Marginal product continues to decrease as more capital is added, dropping to zero for a post-hole digger, which Jones has no use for.

Suppose Jones sells corn in a perfectly competitive market, so he can sell all he wants at the market price of $4 a bushel. The marginal product from column (3) multiplied by $4 yields capital's *marginal revenue product* listed in column (4). The marginal revenue product of

POSITIVE RATE OF TIME PREFERENCE

Consumers value present consumption more than future consumption

INTEREST RATE

Interest per year as a percentage of the amount saved or borrowed

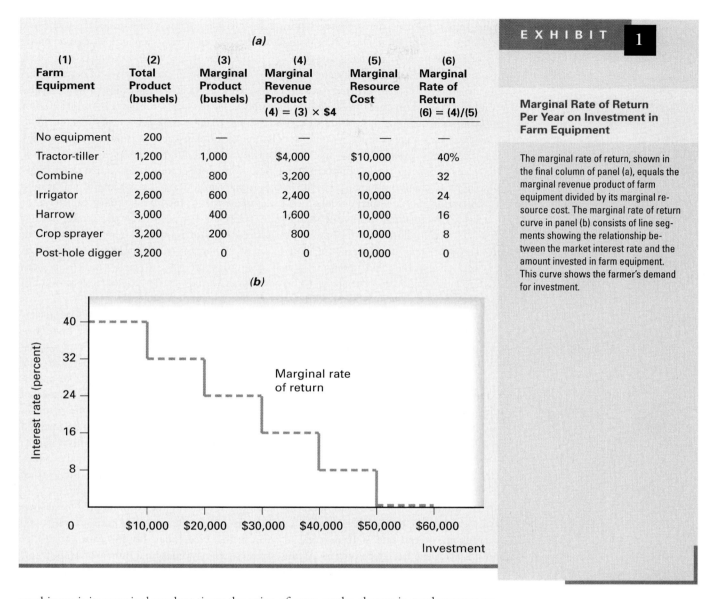

(a)

(1) Farm Equipment	(2) Total Product (bushels)	(3) Marginal Product (bushels)	(4) Marginal Revenue Product (4) = (3) × \$4	(5) Marginal Resource Cost	(6) Marginal Rate of Return (6) = (4)/(5)
No equipment	200	—	—	—	—
Tractor-tiller	1,200	1,000	\$4,000	\$10,000	40%
Combine	2,000	800	3,200	10,000	32
Irrigator	2,600	600	2,400	10,000	24
Harrow	3,000	400	1,600	10,000	16
Crop sprayer	3,200	200	800	10,000	8
Post-hole digger	3,200	0	0	10,000	0

(b)

Marginal rate of return

Interest rate (percent): 40, 32, 24, 16, 8, 0

Investment: \$10,000 \$20,000 \$30,000 \$40,000 \$50,000 \$60,000

EXHIBIT 1

Marginal Rate of Return Per Year on Investment in Farm Equipment

The marginal rate of return, shown in the final column of panel (a), equals the marginal revenue product of farm equipment divided by its marginal resource cost. The marginal rate of return curve in panel (b) consists of line segments showing the relationship between the market interest rate and the amount invested in farm equipment. This curve shows the farmer's demand for investment.

machinery is its marginal product times the price of corn, or the change in total revenue resulting from adding another piece of farm equipment.

For simplicity, suppose each piece of farm equipment costs \$10,000. Thus, the marginal resource cost is \$10,000, as listed in column (5). Suppose also that the equipment is so durable that it is expected to last indefinitely, that operating expenses are negligible, and that the price of corn is expected to remain at \$4 per bushel in the future. This farm equipment will increase revenue not only in the first year but every year into the future. The optimal investment decision requires Jones to take *time* into account. He can't simply equate marginal resource cost with marginal revenue product, because the marginal cost is an outlay this year, whereas the marginal product is an annual amount this year and each year in the future. As we will see, *markets bridge time with the interest rate.*

Jones must decide how much to invest in farm equipment. His first task is to compute the *marginal rate of return* he would earn each year by investing in farm machinery. The

**MARGINAL RATE OF RETURN
ON INVESTMENT**

The marginal revenue product of
capital expressed as a percentage
of its marginal cost

marginal rate of return on investment is capital's marginal revenue product as a percentage of its marginal resource cost. For example, the tractor-tiller yields a marginal revenue product of $4,000 per year and has a one-time marginal resource cost of $10,000. The rate of return Jones could earn on this investment is $4,000/$10,000, or 40 percent per year. Therefore, this investment yields a *marginal rate of return* of 40 percent per year, as shown in column (6). The combine yields a marginal revenue product of $3,200 per year and has a marginal cost of $10,000, so its marginal rate of return equals $3,200/$10,000, or 32 percent per year. Dividing the marginal revenue product of capital in column (4) by the marginal resource cost of that capital in column (5) yields the marginal rate of return in column (6) for each piece of equipment.

Given the marginal rate of return, how much should Jones invest to maximize profit? Suppose he borrows the money, paying the *market interest rate*. Jones will buy more capital as long as its marginal rate of return exceeds the market interest rate. He will stop before capital's marginal rate of return falls below the market rate of interest. For example, if the market interest rate is 20 percent, Jones will invest $30,000 in three pieces of equipment. The marginal rate of return on the final item purchased, an irrigator, is 24 percent. Investing another $10,000 to buy a harrow would yield a marginal return of only 16 percent, a rate below his cost of borrowing. At a market interest rate of 10 percent, Jones would invest in the harrow as well. An interest rate of 6 percent would lead Jones to also invest in the crop sprayer.

Farmer Jones should increase his investment as long as the marginal rate of return on that investment exceeds the market rate of interest. The marginal rate of return is the marginal benefit of the investment, and the market interest rate is the marginal cost, so Jones is simply maximizing profit (or minimizing loss) by investing until marginal benefit equals the marginal cost. The data in column (6) are depicted in panel (b) of Exhibit 1 as a step-like graph, where the solid lines reflect the amount Jones will invest at each interest rate. For example, if the market interest rate is between 32 percent and 40 percent, Jones should invest in the tractor-tiller. Because the marginal rate of return shows how much should be invested at each interest rate, this step-like graph represents the farmer's demand for investment. This is a derived demand, based on each additional piece of equipment's marginal productivity. The demand curve steps down to reflect the diminishing marginal productivity of capital.

Would the example change if Jones has saved enough to buy the equipment? Not as long as he can save at the market interest rate. For example, suppose Jones has saved $50,000 earning an interest rate of 10 percent per year. In that case, Jones should invest $40,000 in capital, with the last piece purchased, the harrow, earning a marginal return of 16 percent. The 10 percent interest Jones earns on his remaining savings of $10,000 exceeds the 8 percent he could earn by investing that amount in the crop sprayer. Thus, as long as he can borrow and save at the same interest rate, Jones ends up with the same equipment whether he borrows funds or draws down his own savings. *Whether Jones borrows the money or uses savings on hand, the market interest rate represents his opportunity cost of investing.*

Let's review the steps to determine the optimal amount of investment. First, compute the marginal revenue product of capital. Next, divide the marginal revenue product by the marginal resource cost to determine the marginal rate of return. The marginal rate of return curve becomes a firm's demand curve for investment—that is, it shows the amount a firm is willing and able to invest at each interest rate. The market interest rate is the opportunity cost of investing either borrowed funds or savings, and can be thought of as the supply of investment funds to the firm. A firm should invest more as long as the marginal rate of return on capital exceeds the market rate of interest.

We have now discussed investing in physical capital. Let's shift gears and turn to a less tangible form of capital in the following case study, intellectual property.

The Value of a Good Idea—Intellectual Property

One potentially valuable capital asset is information, or so-called *intellectual property*. But the market for information is unusual. On the demand side, consumers are uncertain about the value of information until they acquire it. But they can't acquire it until they pay for it. So there is a circularity problem. There is also a problem on the supply side. Information is costly to produce, but, once produced, it can be supplied at low cost. For example, the first copy of a new software program may cost over a $100 million to produce, but each additional copy can be streamed over the Internet for virtually nothing.

© Royalty-Free/Corbis

Because of these demand and supply problems, producers of information may have difficulty getting paid for their product. As soon as the producer sells information, that first customer becomes a potential supplier of that information. (Do you have any pirated software?) The original producer has difficulty controlling distribution of the product. To address these problems, laws grant property rights to the creators of new ideas and new inventions. Originators are thereby better able to benefit from their creations. A *patent* establishes property rights to an invention or other technical advances. A *copyright* confers property rights to an original expression of an author, artist, composer, or programmer. And a *trademark* establishes property rights in unique commercial marks and symbols, such as McDonald's golden arches or Nike's swoosh.

Granting property rights is one thing; enforcing them is quite another. Much of the software, music CDs, and movie videos sold around the world, particularly in Vietnam, China, and Russia, are pirated editions of products developed in the United States. In fact, some movies are available on the black market as DVDs before they appear in U.S. theaters. Enforcement of property rights is costly, which diminishes the incentive to create new products and new ideas. Even within the United States, the music industry has been devastated by the ease with which music can shared over the Internet through services such as Napster. Sharing music files online is not a victimless crime: between 1999 and 2003, more than one-fifth of music industry workers lost their jobs as sales declined.

Pirated videos, music, computer games, and software bring no royalties to the artists, no wages to industry workers, no profits to the producers or programmers, and no taxes to the government. For example, Microsoft's XP Professional, which retails for about $400 in the United States, sells in pirated form for only $1.50 in Vietnam. In Russia alone, pirated software costs U.S. producers about $500 million a year in lost revenue. It was concern about piracy that prompted Warner Brothers to release *The Matrix Revolutions* in more than 100 countries simultaneously—an effort to show the movie before it became available on the black market.

The ability to exchange files online now extends beyond music to movies and other forms of intellectual property. Some digital gurus argue that the ease of duplicating data on the Internet dooms copyright protection. They say that anything that can be reduced to bits can be copied. The courts are currently sorting this out. Intellectual property is a capital asset that fuels the information economy. How society nurtures incentives to create new ideas, inventions, and artistic creations will affect economic development around the globe this century.

Sources: Mark McDonald, "Piracy, Counterfeiting on the Rise in Russia," *Knight Ridder Newspapers*, 15 October 2003; Bruce Orwall, "New 'Matrix' Posts Ticket Sales Below the Previous Release," *Wall Street Journal*, 10 November 2003; Ethan Smith, "Music Industry's Woes Deepen with New Job Cuts at Universal," *Wall Street Journal*, 16 October 2003; and the World Intellectual Property Organization at http://www.wipo.int/.

The Market for Loanable Funds

You earlier learned why producers are willing to pay interest to borrow money: *Money provides a command over resources, making both direct production and roundabout production possible.* The simple principles developed for Farmer Jones can be generalized to other producers. The major demanders of loans are firms that borrow to start firms and to invest in physical capital, such as machines, trucks, and buildings, and in intellectual capital, such as patents, copyrights, and trademarks. At any time, a firm has a variety of investment opportunities. The firm ranks its opportunities from highest to lowest, based on the expected marginal rates of return. The firm will increase its investment until the expected marginal rate of return just equals the market interest rate. With other inputs held constant, as they were on the farm, the demand curve for investment slopes downward.

But firms are not the only demanders of loans. As we have seen, households value present consumption more than future consumption; they are often willing to pay extra to consume now rather than later. One way to ensure that goods and services are available now is to borrow for present consumption. Some people also borrow to invest in their human capital. Home mortgages, car loans, credit-card purchases, and college loans are examples of household borrowing. The household's demand curve for loans, like the firm's demand for loans, slopes downward, reflecting consumers' greater willingness and ability to borrow at lower interest rates, other things constant. The government sector and the rest of the world are also demanders of loans.

Banks are willing to pay interest on savings because they can, in turn, lend these savings to those who need credit, such as farmers, home buyers, college students, and entrepreneurs looking to start a new business or buy new capital. Banks play the role of *financial intermediaries* in what is known as the market for loanable funds. The **loanable funds market** brings together savers, or suppliers of loanable funds, and borrowers, or demanders of loanable funds, to determine the market interest rate.

The higher the interest rate, other things constant, the greater the reward for saving. As people save more, the quantity of loanable funds increases. The **supply of loanable funds** curve shows the positive relationship between the market interest rate and the quantity of savings supplied, other things constant, as reflected by the usual upward-sloping supply curve shown as *S* in Exhibit 2.

For the economy as a whole, if the amount of other resources and the level of technology are fixed, diminishing marginal productivity causes the marginal rate of return curve, which is the demand curve for investment, to slope downward. The **demand for loanable funds** curve is based on the expected marginal rate of return these borrowed funds yield when invested in capital. Each firm has a downward-sloping demand curve for loanable funds, reflecting a declining marginal rate of return on investment. With some qualifications, the demand for loanable funds by each firm can be summed horizontally to yield the market demand for loanable funds, shown as *D* in Exhibit 2. Factors assumed constant along this demand curve include the prices of other resources, the level of technology, and the tax laws.

The demand and supply of loanable funds together, as in Exhibit 2, determine the market interest rate. In this case, the equilibrium interest rate of 8 percent is the only one that exactly matches the wishes of borrowers and savers. The equilibrium quantity of loanable funds is $100 billion per year. Any change in the demand or supply of loanable funds will change the market interest rate. For example, a major technological breakthrough that increases the productivity of capital will increase its marginal rate of return and shift the demand curve for loanable funds rightward, as shown in the movement from *D* to *D'*. Such an increase in the demand for loanable funds would raise the equilibrium interest rate to 9 percent and increase the market quantity of loanable funds to $115 billion per year.

LOANABLE FUNDS MARKET

The market in which savers (suppliers of loanable funds) and borrowers (demanders of loanable funds) come together to determine the market interest rate and the quantity of loanable funds exchanged

SUPPLY OF LOANABLE FUNDS

The relationship between the market interest rate and the quantity of loanable funds supplied, other things constant

DEMAND FOR LOANABLE FUNDS

The relationship between the market interest rate and the quantity of loanable funds demanded, other things constant

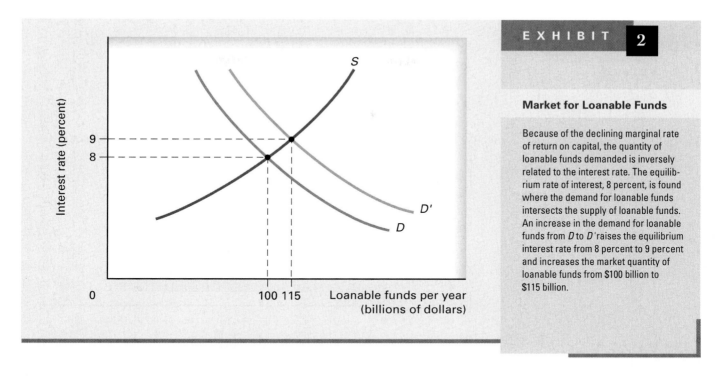

EXHIBIT 2

Market for Loanable Funds

Because of the declining marginal rate of return on capital, the quantity of loanable funds demanded is inversely related to the interest rate. The equilibrium rate of interest, 8 percent, is found where the demand for loanable funds intersects the supply of loanable funds. An increase in the demand for loanable funds from *D* to *D'* raises the equilibrium interest rate from 8 percent to 9 percent and increases the market quantity of loanable funds from $100 billion to $115 billion.

Why Interest Rates Differ

So far, we have been talking about *the* market interest rate, implying that only one rate prevails in the loanable funds market. At any particular time, however, a range of interest rates coexist in the economy. Exhibit 3 shows interest rates for loans in various markets. The lowest is the so-called **prime rate**, the interest rate lenders charge their most trustworthy business borrower. The highest is the rate charged on credit card balances, which is triple the prime rate. Let's see why interest rates differ.

Risk

Some borrowers are more likely than others to *default* on their loans—that is, not to pay them back. Before a bank lends money, it usually requires that a borrower put up **collateral**, which is an asset pledged by the borrower that can be sold to pay off the loan in the event of a default. With business loans, any valuable assets owned by the firm can serve as collateral. With a home mortgage, the home itself becomes collateral. And with car loans, the car becomes collateral. The more valuable the collateral backing up the loan, other things constant, the lower the interest rate changed on that loan. For example, the interest rate charged on car loans is usually higher than on home loans. A car loses its value more quickly than a home does, and a car can be driven away by a defaulting borrower, whereas a home usually increases in value and stays put. So a car offers worse collateral than a home. Interest rates are higher still for personal loans and credit cards, because such borrowers usually offer no collateral.

Duration of the Loan

The future is uncertain, and the further into the future a loan is to be repaid, the more uncertain that repayment becomes. Thus, as the duration of a loan increases, lenders become less willing to supply funds and require a higher interest rate to compensate for the greater

HOMEWORK
Xpress!
Ask the Instructor
Video

PRIME RATE

The interest rate lenders charge their most trustworthy business borrowers

COLLATERAL

An asset pledged by the borrower that can be sold to pay off the loan in the event the loan is not repaid

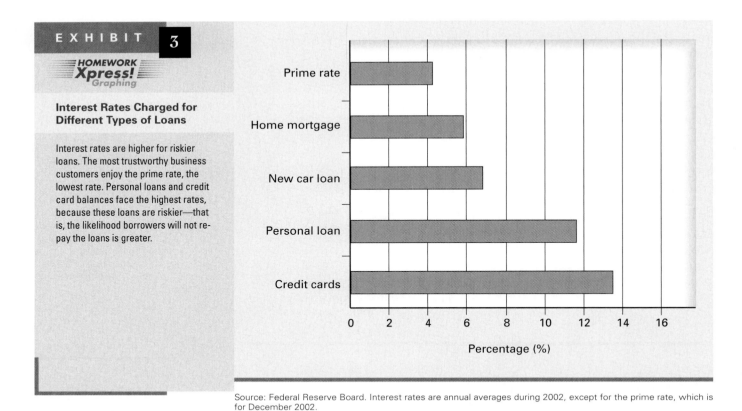

Interest Rates Charged for Different Types of Loans

Interest rates are higher for riskier loans. The most trustworthy business customers enjoy the prime rate, the lowest rate. Personal loans and credit card balances face the highest rates, because these loans are riskier—that is, the likelihood borrowers will not re-pay the loans is greater.

Source: Federal Reserve Board. Interest rates are annual averages during 2002, except for the prime rate, which is for December 2002.

TERM STRUCTURE OF INTEREST RATES

The relationship between the duration of a loan and the interest rate charged; typically interest rates increase with the duration of the loan

risk. The **term structure of interest rates** is the relationship between the duration of a loan and the interest rate charged. *The interest rate usually increases with the duration of the loan, other things constant.*

Cost of Administration

The costs of executing the loan agreement, monitoring the loan, and collecting payments are called the *administration costs* of the loan. These costs, as a proportion of the loan, decrease as the size of the loan increases. For example, the cost of administering a $100,000 loan will be less than 10 times the cost of administering a $10,000 loan. Consequently, that portion of the interest charge reflecting administration costs becomes smaller as the size of the loan increases, other things constant, thus reducing the interest rate for larger loans.

Tax Treatment

Differences in the tax treatment of different types of loans will also affect the interest rate charged. For example, the interest earned on loans to state and local governments is not subject to federal income taxes. Because lenders focus on their after-tax rate of interest, state and local governments can pay a lower interest rate than other borrowers pay.

Present Value and Discounting

Because present consumption is valued more than future consumption, present and future consumption cannot be directly compared. A way of standardizing the discussion is to measure all consumption in terms of its present value. **Present value** is the current value of a payment or payments that will be received in the future. For example, how much would you pay now to receive $100 one year from now? Put another way, what is the *present value* to you of receiving $100 one year from now?

Present Value of Payment One Year Hence

Suppose the market interest rate is 10 percent, so you can either lend or borrow at that rate. One way to determine how much you would pay for the opportunity to receive $100 one year from now is to ask how much you would have to save now, at the market interest rate, to end up with $100 one year from now. Here's the problem we are trying to solve: What amount of money, if saved at a rate of, say, 10 percent, would accumulate to $100 one year from now? We can calculate the answer with a simple formula:

$$\text{Present value} \times 1.10 = \$100$$

or:

$$\text{Present value} = \frac{\$100}{1.10} = \$90.91$$

Thus, if the interest rate is 10 percent, $90.91 is the present value of receiving $100 one year from now; it is the most you would be willing to pay today to receive $100 one year from now. Rather than pay more than $90.91, you could simply deposit your $90.91 at the market interest rate and end up with $100 a year from now (ignoring taxes). The procedure of dividing the future payment by 1 plus the prevailing interest rate to express it in today's dollars is called **discounting.**

The present value of $100 to be received one year from now depends on the interest rate. The more that present consumption is preferred to future consumption, the higher the interest rate that must be offered savers to defer consumption. *The higher the interest rate, the more the future payment is discounted and the lower its present value.* Put another way, the higher the interest rate, the less you need to save now to yield a given amount in the future. For example, if the interest rate is 15 percent, the present value of receiving $100 one year from now is $100/1.15, which equals $86.96.

Conversely, the less present consumption is preferred to future consumption, the less savers need to be paid to defer consumption so the lower the interest rate. The lower the interest rate, the less the future income is discounted and the greater its present value. A lower interest rate means that you must save more now to yield a given amount in the future. As a general rule, the present value of receiving an amount one year from now is:

$$\text{Present value} = \frac{\text{Amount received one year from now}}{1 + \text{interest rate}}$$

For example, when the interest rate is 5 percent, the present value of receiving $100 one year from now is:

$$\text{Present value} = \frac{\$100}{1 + 0.05} = \frac{\$100}{1.05} = \$95.24$$

Present Value for Payments in Later Years

Now consider the present value of receiving $100 two years from now. What amount of money, if deposited at the market interest rate of 5 percent, would yield $100 two years from now? At the end of the first year, the value would be the present value times 1.05, which would then earn the market interest rate during the second year. At the end of the second year, the deposit would have accumulated to the present value times 1.05 times 1.05. Thus, we have the equation:

$$\text{Present value} \times 1.05 \times 1.05 = \text{Present value} \times (1.05)^2 = \$100$$

Solving for the present value yields:

$$\text{Present value} = \frac{\$100}{(1.05)^2} = \frac{\$100}{1.1025} = \$90.70$$

If the $100 were to be received three years from now, we would discount the payment over three years:

$$\text{Present value} = \frac{\$100}{(1.05)^3} = \$86.38$$

If the interest rate is i, the present value of M dollars t years from now is:

$$\text{Present value} = \frac{M}{(1 + i)^t}$$

Because $(1 + i)$ is greater than 1, the more times it is multiplied by itself (as determined by t), the bigger the denominator and the smaller the present value. Thus, *the present value of a given payment will be smaller the further into the future that payment is to be received.*

Present Value of an Income Stream

The previous method is used to compute the present value of a single sum to be paid at some date in the future. Most investments, however, yield a stream of income over time. In cases where the income is received for a period of years, the present value of each receipt can be computed individually and the results summed to yield the present value of the entire income stream. For example, the present value of receiving $100 next year and $150 the year after is simply the present value of the first year's receipt plus the present value of the second year's receipt. If the interest rate is 5 percent:

$$\text{Present value} = \frac{\$100}{1.05} = \frac{\$150}{(1.05)^2} = \$231.29$$

Present Value of an Annuity

A given sum of money received each year for a specified number of years is called an **annuity.** Such an income stream is called a *perpetuity* if it continues indefinitely into the future, as it would with the indestructible farm machinery. The present value of receiving a certain amount forever seems like it should be a very large sum indeed. But because future income is valued less the more distant into the future it is to be received, the present value of receiving a particular amount forever is not much more than that of receiving it for, say, 20 years.

To determine the present value of receiving $100 a year forever, we need only ask how much money must be deposited in a savings account to yield $100 in interest each year. If the interest rate is 10 percent, a deposit of $1,000 will earn $100 per year. Thus, the present value of receiving $100 a year indefinitely when the interest rate is 10 percent is $1,000. More generally, the present value of receiving a sum forever equals the amount received each year divided by the interest rate.

The concept of present value is useful in making investment decisions. Farmer Jones, by investing $10,000 in the crop sprayer, expected to earn $800 more per year. So his marginal rate of return was 8 percent. At a market interest rate of 8 percent, the present value of a cash flow of $800 per year discounted at that rate would be $800/0.08, which equals $10,000. Thus, *Jones was willing to invest capital until, at the margin, his investment yields a cash stream with a present value just equal to the marginal cost of the investment.*

What about your decision to invest in human capital—to go to college? A chart in the previous chapter showed that those with at least a college degree earned twice as much as those with just a high school education. We could compute the present value of an education by discounting earnings based on that level of education, then summing total earnings over your working life. Even without carrying out those calculations, we can say with reasonable certainty that the present value of at least a college education will be more than twice that of just a high school education. You also learned way back in Chapter 1 that some college majors earn more than others. For example, among people 35 to 44 years old with a college degree as their highest degree, males who majored in economics had median earnings 55 percent higher than those who majored in philosophy. Among females, that advantage was 91 percent for the same majors. If such an advantage prevailed throughout all working years, the present value of a degree in economics would be 55 percent higher than the present value of a degree in philosophy for males and 91 percent higher for females.

To develop a hands-on appreciation for present value and discounting, let's put the payoff from state lotteries in perspective.

The Million-Dollar Lottery?

Since 1963, when New Hampshire introduced the first modern state-run lottery, 38 states and the District of Columbia have followed suit, generating profits of over $12 billion a year. Publicity photos usually show the winner receiving an oversized check for $1 million or more. But winners get paid in annual installments, so the present value of the prize is much less than the advertised millions. For example, a million-dollar prizewinner usually gets $50,000 a year for 20 years. To put this in perspective, keep in mind that at an interest rate of 10 percent, the $50,000 received in the 20th year has a present value of only $7,432. If today you deposited $7,432 in an account earning 10 percent interest, you would wind up with $50,000 in 20 years (if we ignore taxes).

Ask the Instructor
Video

© Aneal Vohra/Index Stock Imagery

Case **Study**

Bringing
Theory to Life

eActivity
Virginia has two big cash prize lotteries: Mega Millions and Lotto South. Winners in either can get a lump sum or payments over time. Visit the Web site at http://www.valottery.com to find out how each works. Note that the prizes are not awarded similarly. How is the value of the jackpot determined in each case? What interest rate is used?

If the interest rate is 10 percent, the present value of a $50,000 annuity for the next 20 years is $425,700. Thus the present value of actual payments is less than half of the promised million, which is why lottery officials pay in installments. The Multistate-Powerball lottery pays out over 25 years, so it's worth even less. Incidentally, we might consider the present value of receiving $50,000 a year forever. Using the formula for an annuity discussed earlier, the present value with an interest rate of 10 percent is $50,000/0.10 = $500,000. Because the present value of receiving $50,000 for 20 years is $425,700, continuing the $50,000 annual payment *forever* adds only $74,300 to the present value. This example shows the dramatic effect of discounting.

In some states, lottery winners can sell their jackpots. Winners typically receive only 40 cents on the dollar for the 20-year annuity. So a million-dollar pot, if sold by the winner, would fetch only $400,000. At tax rates prevailing in 2004, federal income taxes on $400,000 for a single tax filer amount to about $125,000. State and local income taxes could whack another $40,000, depending on the state. Because of time and taxes, the much-touted million could shrink to about $235,000 in after-tax income—less than one-fourth the advertised million.

Among all the forms of legal gambling, state lotteries offer the smallest payout—only $0.55 of every dollar wagered on average goes to winners. Still, lotteries apparently seem like a good bet to some people, especially to the 5 percent of the population who buys half of all the lottery tickets sold.

Sources: "State Lottery Scandals Are Multiplying," *United Press International*, 9 February 2004; Tedra DeSue, "Tennessee Governor Giving Nod to New State Lottery, *The Bond Buyer*, 11 June 2003; Phil Kabler, "West Virginia Lawmakers Fear State Lottery Is Peaking," *Charleston Gazette*, 5 February 2004; and an index of lottery sites found at http://www.state.wv.us/lottery/links.htm.

This discussion of present value and discounting concludes our treatment of capital and interest. We now have the tools to consider how firms, especially corporations, are financed.

Corporate Finance

During the Industrial Revolution, labor-saving machinery made large-scale production more profitable, but building huge factories filled with heavy machinery required substantial investments. The corporate structure became the easiest way to finance such outlays, and by 1920, corporations accounted for most employment and output in the U.S. economy. Way back in Chapter 3, you learned about the pros and cons of the corporate form of business. Thus far, however, little has been said about corporate finance. As noted in Chapter 3, a corporation is a legal entity, distinct from its shareholders. The corporation may own property, earn a profit, sue or be sued, and incur debt. Stockholders, the owners of the corporation, are liable only to the extent of their investment in the firm. Use of the abbreviation Inc. or Corp. in the company name serves as a warning to potential creditors that stockholders will not accept personal liability for the debts the company incurs.

Corporate Stock and Retained Earnings

Corporations acquire funds for investment in three ways: by issuing stock, by retaining some of their profits, and by borrowing. Corporations issue and sell stock to raise money for operations and for new plants and equipment. Suppose you have developed a recipe for a hot, spicy chili that your friends have convinced you will be a best-seller. You start a company called Six-Alarm Chili. As the founder, you are that firm's entrepreneur. An **entrepreneur** is a profit-seeking decision maker who organizes an enterprise and assumes the risk of operation. An entrepreneur pays resource owners for the opportunity to use their resources in the firm. The entrepreneur need not actually manage the firm's resources as long as he or she has the power to hire and fire the manager—that is, as long as the entrepreneur controls the manager.

Your company meets with early success, but you find that to remain competitive, you need to grow faster. To fund that growth, you decide to incorporate. The newly incorporated company issues 1,000,000 shares of stock. You take 100,000 shares yourself as your *owner's equity* in the corporation. The rest are sold to the public for $10 per share, which raises $9 million for the company. You, in effect, pay for your shares with the "sweat equity" required to found the company and get it rolling. The initial sale of stock to the public is called an **initial public offering,** or **IPO.** A *share* of **corporate stock** represents a claim on the net income and assets of a corporation, as well as the right to vote on corporate directors and on other important matters. A person who buys 1 percent of the 1,000,000 shares issued thereby owns 1 percent of the corporation, is entitled to 1 percent of any profit, and gets to cast 1 percent of the votes.

ENTREPRENEUR

A profit-seeking decision maker who organizes an enterprise and assumes the risk of its operation

INITIAL PUBLIC OFFERING (IPO)

The initial sale of corporate stock to the public

CORPORATE STOCK

Certificate reflecting part ownership of a corporation

Corporations must pay corporate income taxes on any profit. After-tax profit is either paid as **dividends** to shareholders or reinvested in the corporation. Reinvested profit, or **retained earnings,** helps the firm finance expansion. Stockholders usually expect dividends, but the corporation is not required to pay dividends. Once shares are issued, their price tends to fluctuate directly with the firm's profit prospects. People buy stock because of the dividends and because they hope the share price will appreciate, or increase.

Corporate Bonds

Again, your corporation can acquire funds by issuing stock, by retaining earnings, or by borrowing. To borrow money, the corporation can go to a bank for a loan or it can issue and sell bonds. A **bond** is the corporation's promise to pay back the holder a fixed sum of money on the designated *maturity date* plus make interest payments until that date. For example, a corporation might sell for $1,000 a bond that promises to make an annual interest payment of, say, $100 and to repay the $1,000 at the end of 20 years.

The payment stream for bonds is more predictable than that for stocks. Unless this corporation goes bankrupt, it must pay bondholders the promised amounts. In contrast, stockholders are last in line when resource suppliers get paid, so bondholders get paid before stockholders. Investors usually consider bonds less risky than stocks, although bonds involve risks as well. Risks include corporate bankruptcy and higher market interest rates. For example, suppose you buy bonds that pay 6 percent interest. After that purchase, the market interest rate increases, so newly issued bonds pay 8 percent interest. Your 6 percent bonds are less attractive than the new bonds, so the market value of your bonds will decline.

Securities Exchanges

Once stocks and bonds have been issued and sold, owners of these securities are free to resell them on *securities exchanges.* In the United States, there are seven securities exchanges registered with the *Securities and Exchange Commission (SEC),* the federal body that regulates securities markets. The largest is the New York Stock Exchange, which trades the securities of about 2,800 major corporations, including about 500 non-U.S. companies. Altogether about 10,000 corporations trade on various U.S. exchanges.

Nearly all the securities traded each business day are *secondhand securities* in the sense that they have already been issued by the corporation. So the bulk of daily transactions do not finance firms in need of investment funds. Most money from daily trading goes from a securities buyer to a securities seller. *Institutional investors,* such as banks, insurance companies, and mutual funds, account for over half the trading volume on major exchanges. By providing a *secondary market* for securities, exchanges enhance the *liquidity* of these securities—that is, the exchanges make the securities more readily sold for cash and thus more attractive to own.

The secondary markets for stocks also determine the current market value of the corporation. The market value of a firm at any given time can be found by multiplying the share price by the number of shares issued. Because the share price changes throughout the trading day, so does the value of the corporation. In theory, the share price reflects the present value of the discounted stream of expected profit. Just to give you some idea, General Electric, the top-valued U.S. firm, had a market value of $346.2 billion at the end of the trading day on September 1, 2004. The 2,300 U.S. corporations traded on the New York Stock Exchange had a combined value of about $12 trillion.

Securities prices give the firm's management some indication of the wisdom of raising investment funds through retained earnings, new stock issues, or new bond issues. The

greater a corporation's expected profit, other things constant, the higher the value of shares on the stock market and the lower the interest rate that would have to be paid on new bond issues. Securities markets usually promote the survival of the fittest by allocating investment funds to those firms that seem able to make the most profitable use of those funds. *Thus, securities markets allocate funds more readily to successful firms than to firms in financial difficulty.* Some firms may be in such poor shape that they can't issue new securities.

One final point: When economists talk about investing, they have in mind purchases of new capital, such as new machines and new buildings. When the media talk about investing, they usually mean buying stocks and bonds. To an economist, Farmer Jones is investing only when he buys new farm machinery, not when he buys stocks. As noted already, the overwhelming share of stock transactions are in secondary markets, so the money goes from buyers to sellers, and does not go toward new capital purchases.

Conclusion

This chapter introduced you to capital, interest, and corporate finance. Capital is a more complicated resource than this chapter has conveyed. For example, the demand curve for investment is a moving target, not the stable relationship drawn in Exhibit 1. An accurate depiction of the investment demand curve calls for knowledge of the marginal product of capital and the price of output in the future. But capital's marginal productivity changes with breakthroughs in technology and with changes in the employment of other resources. The future price of the product can also vary widely. Consider, for example, the dilemma of a firm contemplating an investment in oil-drilling rigs in recent years, when the price of crude oil fluctuated between $10 and more than $50 per barrel, as it has since 1998.

SUMMARY

1. Production cannot occur without savings, because both direct production and roundabout production require time—time during which the resources required for production must be paid. Because people value present consumption more than future consumption, they must be rewarded to defer consumption. Interest is the reward to savers for forgoing present consumption and the cost to borrowers for being able to spend now.

2. Choosing the profit-maximizing level of capital is complicated because capital purchased today yields a stream of benefit for years into the future. The marginal rate of return on capital equals the marginal revenue product of that capital as a percent of its marginal resource cost. The profit-maximizing firm invests up to the point where its marginal rate of return on capital equals the market rate

of interest. The market interest rate is the opportunity cost of investment.

3. The demand and supply of loanable funds determine the market interest rate. At any given time, interest rates may differ because of differences in risk, maturity, administrative costs, and tax treatment.

4. Corporations secure investment funding from three sources: new stock issues, retained earnings, and borrowing (either directly from a bank or by issuing bonds). Once new stocks and bonds are issued, they are then bought and sold on securities markets. The value of corporate stocks and bonds tends to vary directly with the firm's profit prospects. More profitable firms have more ready access to funds needed for expansion.

QUESTIONS FOR REVIEW

1. *(Role of Time)* Complete the following sentences with a word or a phrase:

   a. If Bryan values current consumption more than future consumption, he has a _____.
   b. The reward to households for forgoing current consumption is _____.
   c. Producing capital goods rather than producing final goods is known as _____.

2. *(Consumption, Saving, and Time)* Explain why the supply of loanable funds curve slopes upward to the right.

3. *(Why Interest Rates Differ)* At any given time, a range of interest rates prevails in the economy. What are some factors that contribute to differences among interest rates?

4. *(Present Value of an Annuity)* Why is $10,000 a close approximation of the price of an annuity that pays $1,000 each year for 30 years at 10 percent annual interest?

5. *(Present Value of an Annuity)* Suppose you are hired by your state government to determine the profitability of a lottery offering a grand prize of $10 million paid out in equal annual installments over 20 years. Show *how* to calculate the cost to the state of paying out such a prize. Assume payments are made at the end of each year.

6. (*Case* **Study:** The Million-Dollar Lottery?) In many states with lotteries, people can take their winnings in a single, discounted, lump–sum payment or in a series of annual payments for 20 years. What factors should a winner consider in determining how to take the money?

7. *(Corporate Finance)* Describe the three ways in which corporations acquire funds for investment.

8. *(Securities Exchanges)* What role do securities exchanges play in financing corporations?

PROBLEMS AND EXERCISES

9. *(Optimal Investment)* Look back at Exhibit 1 in this chapter. If the marginal resource cost rose to $24,000 what would be the optimal investment at a market interest rate of 10 percent? If the interest rate then rose to 16.6 percent, what would be the optimal level of investment?

10. *(Market for Loanable Funds)* Using the demand–supply for loanable funds diagram, show the effect on the market interest rate of each of the following:

    a. An increase in the marginal resource cost of capital
    b. An increase in the marginal productivity of capital
    c. A shift in preferences toward present consumption and away from future consumption

11. *(Present Value)* Calculate the present value of each of the following future payments. (For some of these problems you may wish to use the online calculator available at http://www.moneychimp.com/articles/finworks/fmpresval.htm.)

    a. A $10,000 lump sum received 1 year from now if the market interest rate is 8 percent
    b. A $10,000 lump sum received 2 years from now if the market interest rate is 10 percent
    c. A $1,000 lump sum received 3 years from now if the market interest rate is 5 percent
    d. A $25,000 lump sum received 1 year from now if the market interest rate is 12 percent
    e. A $25,000 lump sum received 1 year from now if the market interest rate is 10 percent
    f. A perpetuity of $500 per year if the market interest rate is 6 percent

12. *(Present Value of an Income Stream)* Suppose the market interest rate is 10 percent. Would you be willing to lend $10,000 if you were guaranteed to receive $1,000 at the end of each of the next 12 years plus a $5,000 payment 15 years from now? Why or why not?

EXPERIENTIAL EXERCISES

13. (*C a s e* **S t u d y**: The Value of a Good Idea—Intellectual Property) MIT's Michael Kremer has suggested an interesting way to encourage innovation in drug development. The basic idea is explained in a nontechnical article in the 15 June 1996 issue of *The Economist* at http://rider.wharton.upenn.edu/~faulhabe/790/patent_cure-all.html. Take a look at the article and determine how Kremer places a value on an innovation.

14. (*Corporate Finance*) Read Jane Katz, "Who Should Be in Charge," in the Federal Reserve Bank of Boston's *Regional Review* at http://www.bos.frb.org/economic/nerr/rr1997/fall/katz97_4.htm.. What are some of the current issues in corporate finance outlined by Katz?

15. (*Wall Street Journal*) Each day, the *Wall Street Journal* highlights a key interest rate in a graph in the left column of the first page of the Money and Investing section. Compare the graphs over several days and you will see the movements in rates for different securities. How have interest rates changed over the past year? Compare the graphs for several different securities. Have the rates on the various securities moved identically?

HOMEWORK XPRESS! EXERCISES

These exercises require access to McEachern Homework Xpress! If Homework Xpress! did not come with your book, visit **http://homeworkxpress.swlearning.com** *to purchase.*

1. Medical Receptionists, Inc. (MRI), handles the paperwork for filing of medical insurance claims. The work can be done entirely by hand, but by investing in computers the company can process more forms in the same amount of time. The relationship between the number of computers in which MRI invests and the total product—number of claims processed—is shown in the table below. MRI receives $20 per claim processed. Each computer would require an investment of $2,000. Given this information find the marginal rate of return on each computer and plot the data in the diagram.

Number of Computers	Total product
0	100
1	600
2	1,000
3	1,300
4	1,500
5	1,600
6	1,600

2. In the graph, draw a supply of loanable funds. Add a demand for loanable funds such that the equilibrium interest rate is 5 percent and the quantity of funds loaned is $100 billion per year. Show how an increase in demand for loanable funds arising from newfound optimism in the business community about future economic growth could increase the interest rate to 7 percent, while the amount of lending increases to $120 billion per year.

3. In the graph, draw a demand for loanable funds. Add a supply of loanable funds that are available for home mortgages and identify the market rate of interest for mortgages and the quantity of funds lent. Lenders are less willing to lend for new car loans than for homes, so draw a second supply curve representing the supply of loanable funds for new car loans. Identify the rate of interest and quantity of funds lent for purchasing new cars.

Transaction Costs, Imperfect Information, and Market Behavior

© Ken Osborn/Index Stock Imagery

Geneneral Motors offers car loans and issues credit cards, so why don't some credit card companies make automobiles? Why do some firms, such as Domino's Pizza, specialize in a single product, while other firms, such as General Electric, make hundreds of different products? Why stop at hundreds? Why not thousands? In fact, why isn't there a giant firm that makes everything? Why is proper spelling important on your résumé? Why is buying a used car so dicey? Why do some winners of online auctions end up losers? Answers to these and other seemingly unrelated questions are addressed in this chapter, which digs deeper into assumptions about firms and the availability information in the market.

In the first half of this chapter, we will step inside the firm to reconsider some simplifying assumptions about how firms work. We ask: Why do firms exist? How do they decide what to make and what to buy from other firms? These steps toward realism move us beyond the simple depiction of the firm employed to this point. In the second half of this chapter, we challenge some simplifying assumptions about the information available to market participants. We ask: How does the lack of certain information affect the behavior and shape market outcomes? Overall, this chapter should help you develop a more realistic view of how markets work. Topics discussed include:

- Transaction costs
- Vertical integration
- Economies of scope
- Optimal search
- Winner's curse

- Asymmetric information
- Adverse selection
- Principal-agent problem
- Moral hazard
- Signaling and screening

Rationale for the Firm and Its Scope of Operation

The competitive model assumes that all participants in the market know everything they need to about the price and availability of all inputs, outputs, and production processes. The firm is assumed to be headed by a brilliant decision maker with a computer-like ability to calculate all the relevant marginal products. This individual knows everything necessary to solve complex production and pricing problems. The irony is that if the marginal products of all inputs could be measured easily and if prices for all inputs could be determined without cost, there would be little reason for production to take place in firms. In a world characterized by perfect competition, perfect information, constant returns to scale, and costless exchange, the consumer could bypass the firm to deal directly with resource suppliers, purchasing inputs in the appropriate amounts. Someone who wanted a table could buy timber, have it milled, contract with a carpenter, contract with a painter, and end up with a finished product. The consumer could carry out transactions directly with each resource supplier.

The Firm Reduces Transaction Costs

So why is production carried out within firms? Nearly 70 years ago, in a classic article entitled "The Nature of the Firm," Nobel Prize winner Ronald Coase asked the question, "Why do firms exist?"[1] Why do people organize in the hierarchical structure of the firm and coordinate their decisions through a manager rather than simply rely on market exchange? His answer would not surprise today's students of economics: *Organizing activities through the hierarchy of the firm is usually more efficient than market exchange because production requires the coordination of many transactions among many resource suppliers.* In short, firms are superior to markets when production is complicated.

Consider again the example of purchasing a table by contracting directly with all the different resource suppliers—from the timber logger to the painter who applied the finishing varnish. Using resource markets directly involves (1) the cost of determining what inputs are needed and how they should be combined and (2) the cost of reaching an agreement with each resource supplier *over and above* the direct costs of the timber, nails, machinery, paint, and labor required to make the table. Where inputs are easily identified, measured, priced, and hired, production can be carried out through a price-guided "do it yourself" approach using the market. For example, getting your house painted is a relatively simple

---

1. *Economica* 4 (November 1937): 386–405.

task: You can buy the paint and brushes and hire painters by the hour. You become your own painting contractor, hiring inputs in the market and combining them to do the job.

Where the costs of identifying the appropriate inputs and negotiating for each specific contribution are high, the consumer minimizes transaction costs by purchasing the finished product from a firm. For example, although some people serve as their own contractor when painting a house, fewer do so when building a house; most buy a home already built or hire a building contractor. *The more complicated the task, the greater the ability to economize on transaction costs through specialization and centralized control.* For example, attempting to buy a car by contracting with the thousands of suppliers required to assemble one would be time consuming, costly, and impossible for most anyone. What type of skilled labor should be hired and at what wages? How much steel, aluminum, plastic, glass, paint, and other materials should be purchased? How should resources be combined and in what proportions? Anyone without detailed knowledge of auto production couldn't do it. (General Motors and Ford, for example, deal with some 30,000 suppliers.) That's why consumers buy assembled cars rather than contract separately with each resource supplier.

At the margin, some activities could go either way, with some consumers using firms and some hiring resources directly in markets. The choice depends on each consumer's skill and opportunity cost of time. For example, some people may not want to be troubled with hiring all the inputs to get their house painted. Instead, they simply hire a firm for an agreed-on price—they hire a painting contractor. As you will see later in the chapter, however, hiring a contractor may give rise to other problems of quality control.

The Boundaries of the Firm

So far, the chapter has explained why firms exist: *Firms minimize the transaction costs and the production costs of economic activity.* The next question is: What are the efficient boundaries of the firm? The theory of the firm described in earlier chapters is largely silent on the boundaries of the firm—that is, on the appropriate degree of vertical integration. **Vertical integration** is the expansion of a firm into stages of production earlier or later than those in which it specializes. For example, a steel company may decide (1) to integrate backward to mine iron ore or even mine the coal used to smelt iron ore (U.S. Steel owns coal mines) or (2) to integrate forward to fashion raw steel into various components. A large manufacturer employs an amazing variety of production processes, but on average about half of the cost of production goes to purchase inputs from other firms. For example, General Motors and Ford each spend over $80 billion a year on parts, materials, and services. The combined total exceeds the annual output of most economies of the world.

How does the firm determine which activities to undertake and which to purchase from other firms? Should IBM manufacture its own computer chips or buy them from another firm? The answer depends on the benefits and costs of internal production versus market purchases. The point bears repeating: *Internal production and market purchases are alternative ways of organizing transactions.* The choice will depend on which is a more efficient way of carrying out the transaction in question. Keep in mind that market prices coordinate transactions *between* firms, whereas managers coordinate activities *within* firms. The market coordinates resources by meshing the independent plans of separate decision makers, but a firm coordinates resources through the conscious direction of the manager.

The usual assumption is that transactions will be organized by market exchange unless markets pose problems. Market exchange allows each firm to benefit from specialization and comparative advantage. For example, IBM can specialize in making computers and buy chips from Intel, a specialist. Computer chips are a standard product, but sometimes the input is not standardized or the exact performance requirements are hard to specify. For

VERTICAL INTEGRATION

The expansion of a firm into stages of production earlier or later than those in which it specializes, such as a steel maker that also mines iron ore

example, suppose one firm wants to hire another firm to supply research and development services. The uncertainty involved in such a nonspecific service makes it difficult to write, execute, and enforce a purchase agreement covering all possible contingencies that could arise. What if the R&D supplier, in the course of fulfilling the agreement, makes a valuable discovery for a different application? Who has the right to that discovery—the firm that paid for the R&D service or the firm that came up with it? And who determines if the application is different? Because incomplete contracts create potentially troublesome situations, conducting research and development *within the firm* often involves a lower transaction cost than purchasing it in the market.

At this point, it might be useful to discuss specific criteria the firm considers when deciding whether to purchase a particular input from the market, thereby benefiting from another producer's comparative advantage, or to produce that input internally.

Bounded Rationality of the Manager

To direct and coordinate activity in a conscious way in the firm, a manager must understand how all the pieces of the puzzle fit together. As the firm takes on more and more activities, however, the manager may start losing track of details, so the quality of managerial decisions suffers. The more tasks the firm takes on, the longer the lines of communication between the manager and the production workers who must implement the decision. One constraint on vertical integration is the manager's **bounded rationality,** which limits the amount of information a manager can comprehend about the firm's operation. As the firm takes on more and more functions, coordination and communication become more difficult. The firm can experience diseconomies similar to those it experiences when it expands output beyond the efficient scale of production. The solution is for the firm to reduce its functions to those it does best. Such cutbacks occurred when automakers increased the proportion of parts they purchased from other firms.

Minimum Efficient Scale

As noted when firm costs were first discussed, the *minimum efficient scale* is the minimum level of output at which economies of scale are fully exploited. For example, suppose that minimum efficient scale in the production of personal computers is 1 million per year, as shown by the long-run average cost curve in panel (a) of Exhibit 1. Suppose this turns out to be the amount the firm needs to produce to maximize profit. Because the computer chip is an important component in a personal computer, should the PC maker integrate backward into chip production? What if the minimum efficient scale in chip production is 5 million per year? As you can see in panel (b) of Exhibit 1, the average cost of producing 1 million chips is much higher than the average cost at the minimum efficient scale of chip production. The PC manufacturer therefore minimizes costs by buying chips from a chip maker of optimal size. More generally, *other things constant, a firm should buy an input if the market price is below what it would cost the firm to make.*

Easily Observable Quality

If an input is well defined and its quality is easily determined at the time of purchase, that input is more likely to be purchased in the market than produced internally, other things constant. For example, a flourmill will typically buy wheat in the market rather than grow its own, as the quality of the wheat can be easily assessed on inspection. In contrast, the quality of certain inputs can be determined only as they are produced. Firms whose reputations depend on the operation of a key component are likely to produce the component, especially if the quality varies widely across producers over time and can't be easily observed by

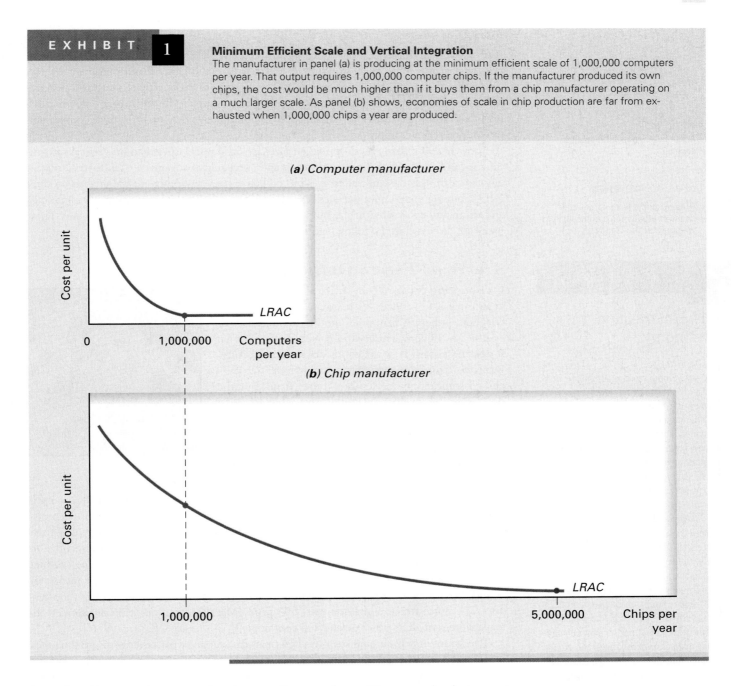

EXHIBIT 1

Minimum Efficient Scale and Vertical Integration
The manufacturer in panel (a) is producing at the minimum efficient scale of 1,000,000 computers per year. That output requires 1,000,000 computer chips. If the manufacturer produced its own chips, the cost would be much higher than if it buys them from a chip manufacturer operating on a much larger scale. As panel (b) shows, economies of scale in chip production are far from exhausted when 1,000,000 chips a year are produced.

(a) Computer manufacturer

Cost per unit

LRAC

0   1,000,000   Computers per year

(b) Chip manufacturer

Cost per unit

LRAC

0   1,000,000   5,000,000   Chips per year

inspection. For example, suppose that the manufacturer of a sensitive measuring instrument requires a crucial gauge, the quality of which can be observed only as the gauge is assembled. If the firm produces the gauge itself, it can closely monitor quality.

Producers sometimes integrate backward so they can offer consumers a guarantee about the quality of the components or ingredients in a product. For example, some chicken suppliers such as Tyson and Purdue can advertise the upbringing of their chickens because they raise their own. KFC, however, omits this family background because the company makes no claim about raising them.

OUTSOURCING

A firm buys inputs from outside suppliers

CORE COMPETENCY

Area of specialty; the product or phase of production a firm supplies with greatest efficiency

The Information Economy

*e*Activity

Want to learn more about outsourcing? Visit the Outsourcing FAQ at http://www.outsourcing-faq.com/. Should a firm hire an outside consultant to help manage its outsourcing? There are now firms that specialize in helping other firms with outsourcing. For example, Everest provides outsourcing management services at http://www.everestgrp.com/. Look under Our Knowledge and browse through White Papers and Articles to read some of its reports, such as "The Changing Face of the Outsourcing Marketplace." The Outsourcing Institute (http://www.outsourcing.com/content.asp?page=01i/index.html) provides an Internet B2B ("B2B" is short for "business to business.") meeting place for outsourcing managers, consultants, and others. Go to Outsourcing Intelligence and review some of the articles available free to the public to learn more about how outsourcing is evolving.

Many Suppliers

A firm wants an uninterrupted source of components. If there are many suppliers of a component, a firm is more likely to purchase that input in the market than to produce it internally, other things constant. Not only does the existence of many suppliers ensure a dependable source of components, competition among these suppliers keeps the price down. But a firm that cannot rely on a consistent supply of components may make its own components to ensure a reliable supply.

To review: If a firm relies on market purchases of inputs rather than on vertical integration, it can benefit from the specialization and comparative advantage of individual suppliers. Other things constant, the firm is more likely to buy a component rather than produce it if (1) buying the component is cheaper than making it, (2) the component is well defined and its quality easily observable, and (3) there are many suppliers of the component. These issues are discussed in the following case study.

The Trend Toward Outsourcing

Outsourcing occurs when a firm buys products, such as auto parts, or services, such as data processing, from outside suppliers. A firm relies on the division of labor and the law of comparative advantage to focus on what it does best, what it considers its **core competency**. Firms, particularly manufacturing firms, have long purchased some components from other firms, but the outsourcing movement extends this practice to a broader range of products and activities that typically had been produced internally. Japanese firms pioneered outsourcing to reduce production costs and enhance quality. In the United States, outsourcing blossomed in manufacturing during the 1980s and spread to virtually every industry.

© Brian Lee/Corbis

For example, DuPont, which produces hundreds of products from chemicals to carpeting, outsources the shipping of all imports and exports. Dell Computer, the world's largest online, phone, and mail-order seller of personal computers, also turns over shipping to an outside firm. Many computer firms outsource computer assembly. Even Microsoft outsources some software development. About a dozen wine makers outsource grape crushing to the Napa Wine Company. And in what may be the largest outsourcing contract on record, Merrill Lynch is paying $1 billion for IT support provided by a team of outside vendors. The outsourcing contract runs 1,500 pages. Merrill Lynch has even outsourced the management of all its other outsourced contracts.

The boom in outsourcing has benefited firms that supply what other firms no longer do for themselves. IBM's major business has shifted from selling hardware and software to servicing firms that have outsourced their information technology needs. As noted in a previous chapter, firms in India have sprung up to offer IT services to major U.S. corporations, usually supplying these services over the Internet. Many U.S. corporations have outsourced customer-service call centers to India and the Philippines. For example, Microsoft customers now get their email and phone call queries answered from India.

Perhaps the poster child of outsourcing is Stone Mountain Accessories. Not long ago the company had 500 employees scattered across three manufacturing and distribution plants in Georgia. But Stone Mountain was losing money and would have failed had it not outsourced most functions and trimmed down to a 12-person marketing and design firm. Outsourcing allowed the company to lower its price enough to quadruple handbags sales and become profitable.

One problem with outsourcing is the loss of control. For example, when Compaq outsourced some laptop production to a Japanese manufacturer, problems mushroomed in design, cost, and quality. Compaq now has a management team that oversees outsourced activities. Some companies fear that outsourcing can weaken customer ties. For example, several automakers had to recall 8 million vehicles because of faulty seat belts from a Japanese supplier. Customers blamed the auto companies for the recall, not the subcontractor. But in general, outsourcing allows a firm to focus on what it does best and turn over everything else to other firms that focus on what they do best. The law of comparative advantage reduces the cost of production and benefits consumers.

Sources: Todd Datz, "IT Outsourcing: Merrill Lynch's $1 Billion Bet," *CIO Magazine*, 15 September 2003; Lisa Fickenscher, "Handbag Maker Plays China Card," *Crain's New York Business*, 19 January 2004, http://www. crainsny.com; James Hookway, "At 2 A.M. in Manila, It's Time to Break for a Midday Snack," *Wall Street Journal*, 20 October 2003; "Microsoft's India Outsourcing Raises Protests," *CNET Asia*, 3 July 2003, http://asia.cnet. com; *Outsourcing Journal*, http://www.outsourcing-journal.com/; and the Outsourcing Institute at http://www. outsourcing.com/.

Economies of Scope

So far we have considered issues affecting the optimal degree of vertical integration in producing a particular product. Even with outsourcing, the focus is on how best to produce a particular product, such as an automobile or a computer. But some firms branch into product lines that do not have a vertical relationship. **Economies of scope** exist when it's cheaper to produce two or more different items in one firm than to produce them in separate firms. For example, General Electric produces hundreds of different products ranging from light bulbs to jet engines to NBC Universal. By spreading outlays for research and development and marketing ("Imagination at work") over different products, GE can reduce those costs. Or consider economies of scope on the farm. A farmer often grows a variety of crops and raises different farm animals—animals that recycle damaged crops and food scraps into useful fertilizer. With economies of *scale,* the average cost per unit of output falls as the *scale* of the firm increases; *with economies of scope, average costs per unit fall as the firm supplies more types of products—that is, as the scope of the firm increases.* The cost of some fixed resources, such as specialized knowledge, can be spread across product lines.

Some combinations don't work out. For example, in 1994, Quaker Oats paid $1.7 billion for the Snapple drink business. After Snapple sales dropped, Quaker Oats sold that business in 1997 for $300 million, less than one-fifth the purchase price. In 1991 AT&T bought NCR, which provides hardware and software for customer transactions. AT&T paid $7.5 billion and after spending another $2 billion trying to make the marriage work, it sold NCR in 1997 for $3.4 billion—taking a $6.1 billion haircut on the deal. Some mergers don't yield the expected economies of scope.

Our focus has been on why firms exist, why they often integrate vertically, why they outsource, and why they sometimes produce a range of products. These steps toward realism move us beyond the simple picture of the firm created earlier. The rest of the chapter challenges some simplifying assumptions about the amount of information available to market participants.

Market Behavior with Imperfect Information

For the most part, our analysis of market behavior has assumed that market participants have full information about products and resources. For consumers, full information involves

ECONOMIES OF SCOPE

Average costs decline as a firm makes different products rather than just one

knowledge about a product's price, quality, and availability. For firms, full information includes knowledge about the marginal productivity of various resources, about the appropriate technology for combining them, and about the demand for the firm's product. In reality, *reliable information is often costly for both consumers and producers.* This section examines the impact of less-than-perfect information on market behavior.

Optimal Search with Imperfect Information

Suppose you want to buy a new computer. You need information about the quality and features of each model and the prices at various retail outlets, mail-order firms, and online sites. To learn more about your choices, you may talk with friends and experts, read promotional brochures and computer publications, and visit online sites. Once you narrow your choice to one or two models, you may visit the mall, or let your fingers do the walking through the *Yellow Pages,* computer catalogs, Internet search engines, newspaper ads, and the like. Searching for the lowest price for a particular model involves a cost, primarily the opportunity cost of your time. This cost will obviously vary from individual to individual and from item to item. Some people actually enjoy shopping, but this "shop 'til you drop" approach does not necessarily carry over to all items. *For most of us, the process of gathering consumer information can be considered nonmarket work.*

Marginal Cost of Search

In your quest for product information, you gather the easy and obvious information first. You may check on the price and availability at the few computer stores at the mall. But as your search widens, the *marginal cost* of information increases, both because you may have to travel greater distances to check prices and services and because the opportunity cost of your time increases as you spend more time acquiring information. Consequently, the marginal cost curve for information slopes upward, as is shown in Exhibit 2. Note that a certain amount of information, I_f, is common knowledge and is freely available, so its marginal cost is zero.

Marginal Benefit of Search

The *marginal benefit* from acquiring additional information is a better quality for a given price or a lower price for a given quality. The marginal benefit is relatively large at first, but as you gather more information and grow more acquainted with the market, additional information yields less and less marginal benefit. For example, the likelihood of uncovering valuable information, such as an attractive feature or a lower price, at the second store or Web site visited is greater than the likelihood of finding this information at the twentieth store or Web site visited. Thus, the marginal benefit curve for additional information slopes downward, as is shown in Exhibit 2.

Optimal Search

Market participants will continue to gather information as long as the marginal benefit of additional information exceeds its marginal cost. *Optimal search occurs where the marginal benefit just equals the marginal cost,* which in Exhibit 2 occurs where the two marginal curves intersect. Notice that at search levels exceeding the equilibrium amount, the marginal benefit of additional information is still positive, but it's below the marginal cost. Notice also that at some point the value of additional information reaches zero, as identified by I_p on the horizontal axis. This level of information could be identified as *full information.* The high marginal cost of acquiring I_p, however, makes it impractical to become fully informed. Thus, firms and consumers, by gathering the optimal amount of information, I^*, have less-than-perfect information about the price, availability, and quality of products and resources.

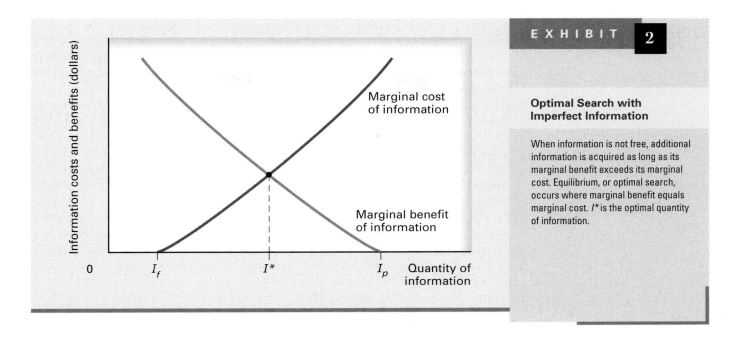

E X H I B I T 2

Optimal Search with Imperfect Information

When information is not free, additional information is acquired as long as its marginal benefit exceeds its marginal cost. Equilibrium, or optimal search, occurs where marginal benefit equals marginal cost. I^* is the optimal quantity of information.

Implications

The search model we have described was developed by Nobel laureate George Stigler, who showed that the price of a product can differ among sellers because some consumers are unaware of lower prices offered by some sellers.[2] Thus, *search costs result in price dispersion, or different prices, for the same product.* Some sellers call attention to price dispersions by claiming to have the lowest prices around and by promising to match any competitor's price (Gateway Computers does this). *Search costs also lead to quality differences across sellers, even for identically priced products, because consumers find it too costly to shop for the highest quality product.* There are other implications of Stigler's search model. The more expensive the item, the greater the price dispersion in dollar terms, so the greater the incentive to shop around. You are more likely to shop around for a new car than for a new comb. Also, as earnings increase, so does the opportunity cost of time, resulting in less searching and more price dispersion. On the other hand, any technological change that reduces the marginal cost of information will lower the marginal cost curve in Exhibit 1, increasing the optimal amount of information and reducing price dispersion. For example, some Internet sites, like mySimon.com, identify the lowest prices for books, airfares, automobiles, computers, and dozens of other products. And some Internet sellers, like Buy.com, maintain the lowest prices on the Web as a way of attracting customers who undertake such searches. Thus, by reducing search costs, the Internet reduces price dispersion.

The Winner's Curse

In 1996, the federal government auctioned off leases to valuable space on the scarce radio spectrum. The space was to be used for cell phones, wireless networks, and portable fax machines. The bidding was carried out in the face of much uncertainty about these new markets. Thus, bidders had little experience with the potential value of such leases. At the time,

---

2. George Stigler, "The Economics of Information," *Journal of Political Economy* (June 1961): 213–225.

89 companies made winning bids for 493 licenses totaling $10.2 billion. But by 1998, it became clear that many of the winning bidders couldn't pay, and many went bankrupt.[3] The auction eventually raised only half the amount of the winning bids. In auctions for products of uncertain value, such as wireless communications licenses, why do so many "winners" end up losers?

The actual value of space on the radio spectrum was unknown and could only be estimated. Suppose the average bid for a license was $10 million, with some higher and others lower. Suppose also that the winning bid was $20 million. The winning bid was not the average bid, which may have been the most reliable estimate of the true value, but the highest bid, which was the most optimistic estimate. Winners of such bids are said to experience the **winner's curse** because they often lose money after winning the bid, the price of being overly optimistic.

The winner's curse applies to all cases of bidding in which the true value is unknown at the outset. For example, movie companies often bid up the price of screenplays to what many argue are unrealistic levels (only about one in twenty screenplays purchased by studios ever become movies). Likewise, publishers get into bidding wars over book manuscripts and even book proposals that are little more than titles. Team owners bid and often overpay for athletes who become free agents. CBS lost money on the 1998 Winter Olympics. And NBC may have overbid by offering $2.3 billion for the rights to broadcast the Olympics in 2002, 2006, and 2008; at the time of the bid, Olympic cities had not even been selected. Online auctions, like eBay, often sell items of unknown value. With perfect information about market value, potential buyers would never bid more than that market value. But *when competitive bidding is coupled with imperfect information, the winning bidder often ends up an overly optimistic loser.*

Asymmetric Information in Product Markets

Economics in the Movies

We have considered the effects of costly information and limited information on market behavior. But the issue becomes more complicated when one side of the market knows more than the other side does, a situation in which there is **asymmetric information.** There are two types of information that a market participant may want but lack: information about a product's *characteristics* and information about *actions* taken by the other party to the transaction. This section examines several examples of asymmetric information in the product market and the effect on market efficiency.

Hidden Characteristics: Adverse Selection

When one side of the market knows more than the other side about important product characteristics, the asymmetric information problem involves **hidden characteristics.** For example, the seller of a used car normally has abundant personal experience with important *characteristics* of that car: accidents, breakdowns, gas mileage, maintenance record, performance in bad weather, and so on. A prospective buyer can only guess at these characteristics based on the car's appearance and perhaps a test drive. The buyer cannot really know how good the car is without driving it for several months under varying traffic and weather conditions.

To simplify the problem, suppose there are only two types of used cars for sale: good ones and bad ones, or "lemons." A buyer who is certain about a car's type would be willing to pay $10,000 for a good used car but only $4,000 for a lemon. Again, only the seller knows

WINNER'S CURSE

The plight of the winning bidder who overestimates an asset's true value

ASYMMETRIC INFORMATION

One side of the market has more reliable information about the product than does the other side

HIDDEN CHARACTERISTICS

One side of the market knows more than the other side about product characteristics that are important to the other side

3. Scott Ritter, "FCC Says Several Bidders to Return Wireless Licenses," *Wall Street Journal,* 18 June 1998.

which type is for sale. A buyer who believes that half the used cars on the market are good ones and half are lemons would be willing to pay, say, $7,000 for a car of unknown quality (the average perceived value of cars on the market). Would $7,000 be the equilibrium price of used cars?

So far, the analysis has ignored the actions of potential sellers, who know which type of car they have. Because sellers of good cars can get only $7,000 for cars they know to be worth $10,000 on average, many will keep their cars or will sell them only to friends or relatives. But sellers of lemons will find $7,000 an attractive price because they know their cars are worth only $4,000. As a result, the proportion of good cars on the market will fall and the proportion of lemons will rise, reducing the average value of used cars on the market. As buyers come to realize that the mix has shifted toward lemons, they will reduce what they are willing to pay for cars of unknown quality. As the market price of used cars falls, potential sellers of good cars become even more reluctant to sell at such a low price, so the proportion of lemons increases, leading to still lower prices. The process could continue until very few good cars are sold on the open market. More generally, *when sellers have better information about a product's quality than buyers do, lower-quality products dominate the market.*

When those on the informed side of the market self-select in a way that harms the uninformed side of the market, the problem is one of **adverse selection.** In our example, car sellers, the informed side, self-select—that is, they decide whether or not to offer their cars for sale—in a way that increases the proportion of lemons for sale. Because of adverse selection, those still willing to buy on the open market often get stuck with lemons.

Hidden Actions: The Principal-Agent Problem

A second type of problem occurs when one side of a transaction can pursue an unobservable *action* that affects the other side. Whenever one side of an economic relationship can take a relevant action that the other side cannot observe, the situation is described as one of **hidden actions.** In this age of specialization, there are many tasks we do not perform for ourselves because others do them better and because others have a lower opportunity cost of time. Suppose your car needs a repair that you can't do yourself. The mechanic you hire may have other objectives, such as maximizing on-the-job leisure or maximizing the garage's profit. But the mechanic's actions are hidden from you. Although your car's problem may be only a loose electrical wire, the mechanic could inflate the bill by charging you for work not needed or not performed. This asymmetric information problem occurs because one side of a transaction can pursue *hidden actions* that affect the other side. When buyers have difficulty monitoring and evaluating the quality of goods or services purchased, some suppliers may substitute poor-quality resources or exercise less diligence in providing the service.

The problem that arises from hidden actions is called the **principal-agent problem,** which describes a relationship in which one party, known as the **principal,** contracts with another party, known as the **agent,** in the expectation that the agent will act on behalf of the principal. *The problem arises when the goals of the agent are incompatible with those of the principal and when the agent can pursue hidden actions.* You could confront a principal-agent problem when you deal with a doctor, lawyer, auto mechanic, or stockbroker, to name a few. Any employer-employee relationship could become a principal-agent problem. Again, the problem arises because the agent's objectives are not the same as the principal's *and* because the agent's actions are hidden. Not all principal-agent relationships pose a problem. For example, when you hire someone to mow your lawn or cut your hair, there are no hidden actions and you can judge the results for yourself.

HOMEWORK
Xpress!
Ask the Instructor Video

ADVERSE SELECTION

Those on the informed side of the market self-select in a way that harms those on the uninformed side of the market

HIDDEN ACTIONS

One side of an economic relationship can do something that the other side cannot observe

PRINCIPAL-AGENT PROBLEM

The agent's objectives differ from those of the principal's, and one side can pursue hidden actions

PRINCIPAL

A person or firm who hires an agent to act on behalf of that person or firm

AGENT

A person or firm who is supposed to act on behalf of the principal

Asymmetric Information in Insurance Markets

Asymmetric information also creates problems in insurance markets. For example, from an insurer's point of view, ideal candidates for health insurance are those who lead long, healthy lives and then die peacefully in their sleep. But many people are poor risks for health insurers because of hidden characteristics (bad genes) or hidden actions (smoking and drinking excessively, getting exercise only on trips to the refrigerator, and thinking of a seven-course meal as beef jerky and a six-pack of beer). In the insurance market, it is the buyers, not the sellers, who have more information about the characteristics and actions that predict their likely need for insurance in the future.

If the insurance company has no way of distinguishing among applicants, it must charge those who are good health risks the same price as those who are poor ones. This price is attractive to poor health risks but not to good health risks, some of whom will not buy insurance. Because some healthy people opt out, the insured group becomes less healthy on average, so rates must rise, making insurance even less attractive to healthy people. *Because of adverse selection, insurance buyers tend to be less healthy than the population as a whole.* Adverse selection has been used as an argument for national health insurance.

The insurance problem is compounded by the fact that once people buy insurance, their behavior may change in a way that increases the probability that a claim will be made. For example, those with health insurance may take less care of their health, those with theft insurance may take less care of insured valuables, and those with fire insurance may take less care in fire prevention. This incentive problem is referred to as *moral hazard*. **Moral hazard** occurs when an individual's behavior changes in a way that increases the likelihood of an unfavorable outcome. More generally, *moral hazard is a principal-agent problem because it occurs when those on one side of a transaction have an incentive to shirk their responsibilities because the other side is unable to observe them.* The responsibility could be to repair a car, maintain one's health, or safeguard one's valuables. Both the mechanic and the policy buyer may take advantage of the ignorant party. In the car-repair example, the mechanic is the agent; in the insurance example, the policy buyer is the principal. Thus, moral hazard arises when someone can undertake hidden action; this could be either the agent or the principal, depending on the situation.

MORAL HAZARD

A situation in which one party, as a result of a contract, has an incentive to alter their behavior in a way that harms the other party to the contract

Coping with Asymmetric Information

There are ways of reducing the consequences of asymmetric information. An incentive structure or an information-revealing system can be developed to reduce the problems associated with the lopsided availability of information. For example, some states have "lemon laws" that offer compensation to buyers of new or used cars that turn out to be lemons. Used-car dealers may offer warranties to reduce the buyer's risk of getting stuck with a lemon. Most auto-repair garages provide written estimates before a job is done, and some return the defective parts to the customer as evidence that the repair was necessary and was carried out. Consumers often get multiple estimates for major repairs.

Health insurance companies deal with adverse selection and moral hazard in a variety of ways. Most require applicants to take a physical exam and to answer questions about their medical histories and lifestyles. To avoid adverse selection, an insurer often covers all those in a group, such as all company employees, not just those who would otherwise self-select. Insurers reduce moral hazard by making the policyholder pay, say, the first $250 of a claim as a "deductible" or by requiring the policyholder to co-pay a percentage of a claim. Also, if more claims are filed on a policy, the premiums go up and the policy may be canceled. Property insurers reduce rates to those who install security systems, smoke alarms, sprinkler systems, and who undertake other safety precautions.

HOMEWORK **Xpress!** *Ask the Instructor Video*

Asymmetric Information in Labor Markets

Our market analysis for particular kinds of labor typically assumes that workers are more or less interchangeable. In equilibrium, each worker in a particular labor market is assumed to be paid the same wage, a wage equal to the marginal revenue product of the last unit of labor hired. But what if ability differs across workers? Differences in ability present no particular problem as long as these differences can be readily observed by the employer. If the productivity of each worker is easily quantified through a measure such as the quantity of oranges picked, the number of garments sewn, or the number of cars sold, that measure itself can and does serve as the basis for pay. And such per-unit incentives seem to affect output. For example, when the British National Health Service changed the way dentists were paid from "contact hours" with patients to the number of cavities filled, dentists found more cavities and filled them in only a third of the time they took under the contact-hour pay scheme.[4]

But because production often occurs through the coordinated efforts of several workers, the employer may not be able to attribute specific outputs to particular workers. Because information about each worker's marginal productivity may be hard to come by, employers usually pay workers by the hour rather than try to keep track of each worker's contribution to total output. Sometimes the pay combines an hourly rate and incentive pay linked to a measure of productivity. For example, a sales representative typically receives a base salary plus a commission tied to sales. At times, the task of evaluating performance is left to the consumer. Workers who provide personal services, such as waiters, barbers, beauticians, pizza deliverers, and bellhops, are paid partly in tips. These services are "personal" and visible, so customers are usually in the best position to judge the quality and timeliness of service and to tip accordingly.

Adverse Selection in Labor Markets

Suppose an employer wants to hire a program coordinator for a new project, a job that calls for imagination, organizational skills, and the ability to work independently. The employer would like to attract the most qualified person in the market, but the qualities demanded are not directly observable. The employer offers the going wage for such a position. Individual workers are able to evaluate this market wage in light of their own abilities and opportunities. Talented people will find the wage too low and will be less inclined to apply for the job. Less-talented people, however, will find this wage attractive and will be more inclined to seek the position. Because of this adverse selection, the employer ends up with a pool of applicants of below-average ability.

Before being hired, a worker's true abilities—motivation, work habits, skills, ability to get along with others, and the like—are, to a large extent, *hidden characteristics*. In a labor market with hidden characteristics, employers might be better off offering a higher wage. The higher the wage, the more attractive the job is to more-qualified workers. Paying a higher wage also encourages workers not to goof off or otherwise do anything that would risk losing an attractive job. Paying a higher wage to attract and retain more-productive workers is called paying **efficiency wages.**

Signaling and Screening

The person on the side of the market with hidden characteristics and hidden actions has an incentive to say the right thing. For example, a job applicant might say, "Hire me because I am hardworking, reliable, prompt, highly motivated, and just an all-around great employee." Or a

EFFICIENCY WAGE THEORY

The idea that offering high wages attracts a more talented labor pool, making it easier for firms to hire and retain more-productive workers

4. John Pencavel, "Piecework and On-the-Job Screening," *Working Paper,* Stanford University, June 1975.

producer might say, "At Ford, quality is job one." But such claims appear self-serving and thus are not necessarily believable. To cut through this fog, both sides of the market have an incentive to develop credible ways of communicating reliable information about qualifications.

Signaling is the attempt by the informed side of the market to communicate information that the other side would find valuable. Consider signaling in the job market. Because some jobs require abilities that are unobservable on a résumé or in an interview, job applicants offer proxy measures, such as years of education, college grades, and letters of recommendation. A proxy measure is called a *signal,* which is an observable indicator of some hidden characteristic. A signal is sent by the informed side of the market to the uninformed side and will be useful as long as less-qualified applicants face more difficulty sending the same signal.

To identify the best workers, employers try to *screen* applicants. **Screening** is the attempt by the uninformed side of the market to uncover the relevant but hidden characteristics of the informed party. An initial screen might check each résumé for spelling and typographical errors. Although not important in themselves, such errors suggest a lack of attention to detail—which would reduce labor productivity. The uninformed party must detect signals that less-productive individuals will have more difficulty sending. A signal that can be sent with equal ease by all workers, regardless of their productivity, does not provide a useful way of screening applicants. But if, for example, more-productive workers find it easier to graduate from college than do less-productive workers, a college degree is a measure worth using to screen workers. In this case, education may be valuable, not so much because of its direct effect on a worker's productivity, but simply because it enables employers to distinguish among types of workers. Indeed, the actual pay increase resulting from a fourth year of college that results in graduation is several times the pay increase from just a third year of college. This finding is consistent with the screening theory of education.

To summarize: Because the potential productivity of job applicants cannot be measured directly, an employer must rely on proxy measures to screen applicants. *The most valuable proxy is a signal that can be sent more easily by more-productive workers and also is a good predictor of future productivity.* The problems of adverse selection, signaling, and screening are discussed in the following case study of how McDonald's chooses franchisees.

SIGNALING

Using a proxy measure to communicate information about unobservable characteristics; the signal is more effective if more-productive workers find it easier to send than do less-productive workers

SCREENING

The process used by employers to select the most qualified workers based on readily observable characteristics, such as a job applicant's level of education and course grades

---

World of Business

eActivity

McDonald's maintains a Web site devoted to information about obtaining a franchise at http://www.mcdonalds.com/corp/franchise.html. Look over the FAQ file. How much cash does a potential franchisee currently need to qualify? How many partners can be involved in a franchise? Who selects the sites and who constructs the building?

The Reputation of a Big Mac

McDonald's has 29,000 restaurants and nearly 500,000 employees in more than 121 countries. The secret to their success is that more than 40 million customers served around the world each day can count on product consistency whether they buy a Big Mac in Anchorage, Moscow, or Hong Kong. McDonald's has grown because it has attracted competent and reliable franchise owners and has provided these owners with appropriate incentives and constraints to offer a product of consistent quality.

To avoid adverse selection, McDonald's seldom advertises for franchisees but still has plenty of applicants for each new restaurant. Even to be granted an interview, applicants must show substantial financial resources and good business experience. Those who pass the initial screening must come up with a security deposit and complete the nine-month training program. A franchise costs anywhere from $460,000 to $800,000, depending on the size and location, plus an opening fee of $45,000. Of that amount, the new franchisee must come up with a minimum of $175,000 in cash; this money can't come from friends or relatives. Having so much saved is used by McDonald's as a signal of the individual's business sense and ability to manage money. The balance can be borrowed from a bank, so McDonald's, in effect, uses the bank's loan officers to screen the applicant's creditworthiness. Those selected as franchisees must also divest themselves of any other business interests.

McDonald's Hamburger University trains thousands each year (offering simultaneous translations in more than 27 different languages). During this training period, the applicant is paid nothing, not even expenses. Some who complete the training are rejected for a franchise. Once the restaurant opens, a franchisee must work full time.

Thus, the franchisee has a clear financial stake in the success of the operation. As a further incentive, successful owners may get additional restaurants. If all goes well, the franchise is valid for 20 years and renewable after that, but it can be canceled *at any time* if the restaurant fails the company's standards of quality, pricing, cleanliness, hours of operation, and so on. The franchisee is bound to the company by highly specific investments of money and time, such as time learning McDonald's operating system. The loss of a franchise would represent a huge financial blow. In selecting and monitoring franchisees, McDonald's has successfully addressed problems stemming from hidden characteristics and hidden actions.

Through its franchise policies, McDonald's is trying to protect its most valuable asset—the reputation of its brand name. McDonald's is the second most recognized symbol of any kind in the world (the Olympic rings rank first). To leverage that brand recognition, the company is experimenting with other products such as McDonald's ketchup in Germany, Golden Arch Hotels in Switzerland, and McCafé coffee bars around the world. The company also will put its McKids brand on a range of products, including toys, bicycles, jungle gyms, apparel, and interactive DVDs. Extending the brand involves some risk. For example, the company could get a black eye if one of these branded products turns out to be defective.

Source: Richard Gibson, "McDonald's Plans to Make 'McKids' a Multifaceted Brand," *Wall Street Journal*, 13 November 2003; "McD's 'I'm Lovin' It' Breaks in U.S.," *Adweek*, 28 September 2003; D. L. Noren, "The Economics of the Golden Arches," *American Economist* (Fall 1990); and "McDonald's Corporate Franchising" at http://www.mcdonalds.com/corp/franchise/faqs.html.

Conclusion

The firm has evolved through a natural selection process as the form of organization that minimizes both transaction and production costs. Ways of organizing production that are efficient will be selected by the economic system for survival. Attributes that yield an economic profit will thrive, and those that do not will fall away. The form of organization selected may not be optimal in the sense that it cannot be improved, but it will be the most efficient of those that have been tried. If there is a way to organize production that is more efficient, some entrepreneur will stumble on it one day and will be rewarded with greater profit. The improvement may not always be the result of any conscious design. Once a more efficient way of organizing production is uncovered, others will imitate it.

In conventional demand-and-supply analysis, trades occur in impersonal markets, and the buyer has no special concern about who is on the sell side. But with asymmetric information, the mix and characteristics of the other side of the market become important. When the problem of adverse selection is severe enough, some markets may cease to function. Market participants try to overcome the limitations of asymmetric information by signaling, screening, and trying to be quite explicit and transparent about the terms of the transaction.

SUMMARY

1. According to Ronald Coase, firms arise when production is more efficient using the hierarchy of the firm than using market transactions. Because production requires elaborate coordination of many resources, all this activity can usually be carried out more efficiently under the direction of a firm's manager than by having a consumer negotiate detailed performance contracts with many resource suppliers.

2. The extent to which a firm integrates vertically will depend on both the transaction and the production costs of economic activity. Other things constant, the firm is more likely to buy a component rather than produce it if (a) it's cheaper to buy it than make it, (b) the item is well defined and its quality easily observable, and (c) there are many suppliers of the item. Economies of scope exist when it is cheaper to produce two or more different products in one firm than to produce them in separate firms.

3. A buyer searches for product information as long as the marginal benefit of search exceeds its marginal cost. Because information is costly, product prices may differ across suppliers.

4. Asymmetric information occurs when one side of the market is better informed about a product than the other side is. The uninformed side may not know about hidden characteristics or about hidden actions. Because of adverse selection, those on the uninformed side of the market may find they are dealing with exactly the wrong people.

5. When the productivity of job applicants is not directly observable, an employer may try to screen them based on some signal that more-productive workers can send more easily than can less-productive workers.

QUESTIONS FOR REVIEW

1. *(Rationale for the Firm)* Explain Ronald Coase's theory of why firms exist. Why isn't all production consolidated in one large firm?

2. *(Bounds of the Firm)* Define vertical integration. What factors should a firm consider when determining what degree of vertical integration to undertake?

3. *(Bounds of the Firm)* Ashland Oil buys its crude oil in the market. Larger oil refiners, such as Texaco, drill for their own crude oil. Why do some oil companies drill for their own crude oil and others buy crude oil in the market?

4. (*Case* **Study:** The Trend Toward Outsourcing) In the movement to downsize government, advocates often recommend turning over some government services to private firms hired by the government. What are the potential benefits and costs of such outsourcing? Prepare your answer by reviewing The Outsourcing Institute's "Top 10 Reasons Companies Outsource" at http://www.horizontech.net/toptenreasons.htm.

5. *(Economies of Scope)* Distinguish between economies of scale and economies of scope. Why do some firms produce multiple product lines, while others produce only one?

6. *(Search with Imperfect Information)* Fifty years ago, people shopped by mail using catalogs from large mail-order houses. In the last few years, catalog shopping has again become a widely used method of buying. Online shopping is also growing. What reasons can you suggest for the growth in these forms of shopping?

7. *(Asymmetric Information)* Define asymmetric information. Distinguish between hidden characteristics and hidden actions. Which type of asymmetric information contributes to the principal-agent problem?

8. *(The Principal-Agent Problem)* Discuss the nature of the principal-agent problem. Determine which is the principal and which is the agent in each of the following relationships:

   a. A firm that produces export goods and the export management company that helps market its goods
   b. The management of a firm and its stockholders
   c. A homeowner and the plumber hired to make repairs
   d. A dentist and a patient
   e. An employee-pension management firm and the company using its services

9. *(Adverse Selection and Moral Hazard)* Describe the problems faced by health insurance companies as a result of adverse selection and moral hazard. How do insurance companies try to reduce these problems?

10. *(Signaling)* Give an example of signaling in each of the following situations:

 a. Choosing a doctor
 b. Applying to graduate school
 c. Filling out a form for a dating service

11. *(Signaling and Screening)* What roles do signaling and screening play in a labor market with asymmetric information?

12. (*C a s e* **S t u d y** : The Reputation of a Big Mac) Explain how the time and financial requirements involved in obtaining a McDonald's franchise relate to the hidden-characteristics problem. Why would existing franchise owners have an interest in the maintenance of high application standards for new franchise owners?

PROBLEMS AND EXERCISES

13. *(Search with Imperfect Information)* The following questions concern the accompanying graph.

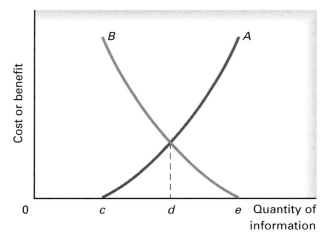

 a. Identify the two curves shown on the graph, and explain their upward or downward slopes.
 b. Why does curve *A* intersect the horizontal axis?
 c. What is the significance of quantity *d*?
 d. What does *e* represent?
 e. How would the optimal quantity of information change if the marginal benefit of information increased—that is, if the marginal benefit curve shifted upward?

14. *(Search with Imperfect Information)* Determine the effect of each of the following on the optimal level of search.

 a. The consumer's wage increases.
 b. One seller guarantees to offer the lowest price on the market.
 c. The technology of gathering and transmitting market information improves.

EXPERIENTIAL EXERCISES

15. *(Market Behavior with Imperfect Information)* Kenneth Arrow, a Nobel laureate, has contributed many important ideas in the economics of information. Read the interview with Arrow in *The Region* at http://woodrow.mpls.frb.fed. us/pubs/region/95-12/int9512.cfm. What does he think are the policy implications that arise because of imperfect information?

16. *(Adverse Selection)* Adverse selection is a serious problem for health insurers. As an example, read the brief analysis

in "Medical Savings Accounts for Medicare" at http://www.ncpa.org/ba/ba183.html. What is the mechanism by which adverse selection can make health insurance unprofitable for private insurers to provide?

17. *(Wall Street Journal)* Once you learn about the economics of asymmetric information, you begin to see examples all around you. To demonstrate this point, check today's *Wall Street Journal*. It should not be too hard to find a story that describes some new development that is a response to an

asymmetric information problem. Look on the Economy page in the First Section or in the Marketplace section. When you've found an article, try to analyze it using the ideas developed in this chapter.

18. (*Wall Street Journal*) Many firms utilize both the concepts of outsourcing and economies of scope. Find an example of a firm using one of these concepts in the *Wall Street Journal* (try the lead stories, or Industry/Corporate Focus, which appear daily, or the Monday Outlook sections). Analyze the firm's decision in the context of the theories developed in this chapter.

HOMEWORK XPRESS! EXERCISES

These exercises require access to McEachern Homework Xpress! If Homework Xpress! did not come with your book, visit **http://homeworkxpress.swlearning.com** *to purchase.*

1. Charles Cobbler, Inc., maker of fine shoes, could tan the 1,000 units of leather needed for use in its shoes or it could purchase leather from a tannery that produces 10,000 units of leather and supplies numerous shoe producers. Draw a long-run average cost curve and illustrate how economies of scale would enable Charles Cobbler to purchase the leather at a lower cost, C', than if it produces its own at cost C.

2. Ashley is considering purchasing a new car. To obtain quotes on prices from dealers, she plans to visit the dealers' showrooms. One dealer is within walking distance of her home, but others are farther away. The cost of each additional quote therefore rises, as she has to travel farther to get to the showroom. The marginal cost of each is shown in the table. Plot this information in the diagram. Add a downward-sloping marginal benefit of information curve such that the optimal number of quotes is 4.

Quantity of Information	Marginal Cost of Information
1	$ 0
2	1
3	3
4	6
5	10
6	15

3. Anthony and Linda are considering buying their own home. They intend to begin the process by conducting an online search of real estate listings. The value of their time in reviewing each listing is $5. The first five listings that appear as a result of their search most closely match their stated preferences and therefore are the most valuable. Each additional five are less likely to match what they are looking for and therefore are less valuable. The marginal benefits of additional sets of listings are as shown in the table. In the diagram, draw a marginal cost curve illustrating the cost of their time for searching and reviewing each listing. Add the marginal benefit data. Identify the optimal number of listings to review.

Quantity of Information	Marginal Benefit of Information
5	$ 25
10	17
15	11
20	5
25	0

CHAPTER

15

Economic Regulation and Antitrust Policy

© Richard T. Nowitz/Corbis

I f the "invisible hand" of competition yields such desirable results for the economy, why does the government need to regulate business? Is a monopoly ever better than competition? Who benefits the most when government regulates monopoly? Why did the government haul Microsoft into court? Is the U.S. economy getting more competitive or less competitive? Answers to these and other questions are addressed in this chapter, which discusses government regulation of business.

Businesspeople praise competition but they love monopoly. They praise competition because it harnesses the diverse and often conflicting objectives of various market participants and channels them into the efficient production of goods and services. Competition does this as if by "an invisible hand." Businesspeople love monopoly because it provides the surest path to economic profit in the long run—

and, after all, profit is the name of the game. The fruits of monopoly are so tempting that a firm might try to eliminate competitors or conspire with them. As Adam Smith remarked more than two centuries ago, "People of the same trade seldom meet together, even for merriment or diversion, but the conversation ends in a conspiracy against the public, or in some contrivance to raise prices."

The tendency of firms to seek monopolistic advantage is understandable, but monopoly usually harms consumers. Public policy can play a role by promoting competition in those markets where competition seems desirable and by reducing the harmful effects of monopoly in those markets where the output can be most efficiently produced by one or a few firms. Topics discussed include:

- Regulating natural monopolies
- Theories of economic regulation
- Deregulation
- Antitrust policy

- Per se illegality
- Rule of reason
- Merger waves
- Competitive trends

Business Behavior, Public Policy, and Government Regulation

You'll recall that a monopolist supplies a product with no close substitutes, so a monopolist can charge a higher price than would prevail with more competition. When a few firms account for most of the sales in a market, those firms are sometimes able to coordinate their actions, either explicitly or implicitly, to act like a monopolist. The ability of a firm to raise its price without losing all its sales to rivals is called **market power.** Any firm facing a downward-sloping demand curve has some control over the price and thus some market power. The presumption is that a monopoly, or a group of firms acting as a monopoly, restricts output to charge a higher price than competing firms would charge. With output restricted, the marginal benefit of the final unit produced exceeds its marginal cost, so expanding output would increase social welfare. By failing to expand output to the point where marginal benefit equals marginal cost, firms with market power produce too little of the good than would be socially optimal.

Other distortions have also been associated with monopolies. For example, some critics argue that because a monopoly is insulated from competition, it is not as innovative as aggressive competitors would be. Worse still, because of their size and economic importance, monopolies may influence political outcomes, which they use to protect and enhance their monopoly power.

Three kinds of government policies are designed to alter or control firm behavior: social regulation, economic regulation, and antitrust policy. **Social regulation** tries to improve health and safety, such as control over unsafe working conditions and dangerous products. Social regulation has economic consequences, but we will not discuss social regulation in this chapter. **Economic regulation** controls the price, output, the entry of new firms, and the quality of service *in industries in which monopoly appears inevitable or even desirable.* Government controls over *natural monopolies,* such as local electricity transmission, local phone service, and a subway system, are examples of economic regulation. Several other industries, such as land and air transportation, have also been regulated in the past. Federal, state, and local governments carry out economic regulation. **Antitrust policy** outlaws attempts to monopolize, or cartelize, markets in which competition is desirable. Antitrust policy is pursued in the courts by government attorneys and by individual firms that charge other firms with violating antitrust laws. Economic regulation and antitrust policy will be examined in this chapter.

MARKET POWER

The ability of a firm to raise its price without losing all its customers to rival firms

SOCIAL REGULATION

Government regulations aimed at improving health and safety

ECONOMIC REGULATION

Government regulation of natural monopoly, where, because of economies of scale, average production cost is lowest when a single firm supplies the market

ANTITRUST POLICY

Government regulation aimed at preventing monopoly and fostering competition in markets where competition is desirable

Let's turn first to economic regulation—specifically, the regulation of natural monopolies.

Regulating Natural Monopolies

Because of economies of scale, natural monopolies have a long-run average cost curve that slopes downward over the range of market demand. This means that the lowest average cost is achieved when one firm serves the entire market. For example, a subway system is a natural monopoly. If two competing subway systems tunnel parallel routes throughout a city, the average cost per trip would be higher than if a single system provided this service.

Unregulated Profit Maximization

Exhibit 1 shows the demand and cost conditions for a natural monopoly, in this case a metropolitan subway system. A natural monopoly usually faces huge initial capital costs, such as those associated with digging a subway system, building a natural gas pipeline, or wiring a city for electricity. Because of the heavy capital outlays, once capital is in place, average cost falls as output increases, so the average cost curve slopes downward over a broad range of output. In this situation, average cost is lowest when a single firm supplies the market.

An unregulated monopolist will choose the price-quantity combination that maximizes profit. In Exhibit 1, the monopolist—in this case, the operator of a subway system—maximizes profit by producing where marginal revenue equals marginal cost, which occurs at 50 million riders per month paying $4 per trip. The monopolist will reap the profit identified by the blue-shaded rectangle. The *abc* triangle, which is below the demand curve and above the $4 price, measures the consumer surplus, a measure of consumers' net gain from riding the subway. The problem with letting the monopolist maximize profit is that the resulting price-output combination is inefficient in terms of social welfare. Consumers pay a price that far exceeds the marginal cost of providing the service. The marginal value of additional output exceeds its marginal cost, so social welfare would increase if output expanded.

One option for government is to allow the monopolist to maximize profit. But government can increase social welfare by forcing the monopolist to expand output and lower price. To accomplish this, government can either operate the monopoly itself, as with most urban transit systems, or can *regulate* a privately owned monopoly, as it does with some urban transit systems, local phone services, and electricity transmission. Government-owned or government-regulated monopolies are called **public utilities.** Here we focus on government regulation, though the issues discussed are similar if the government chose to own and operate the monopoly.

PUBLIC UTILITIES

Government-owned or government-regulated monopolies

Setting Price Equal to Marginal Cost

Many facets of a natural monopoly have been regulated, but the price-output combination gets the most attention. Suppose government regulators require the monopolist to produce the level of output that is efficient—that is, where the price, which also measures the marginal benefit to consumers, equals the marginal cost of the good. This price-output combination is depicted in Exhibit 1 as point *e*, where the demand curve, or the marginal benefit curve, intersects the marginal cost curve, yielding a price of $0.50 per trip and quantity of 105 million trips per month. Consumers will clearly prefer this price to the $4 charged by the unregulated monopolist. The consumer surplus from riding the subway increases from triangle *abc* without regulation to triangle *aef* with regulation.

Notice, however, that the monopolist now has a problem. The average cost of supplying 105 million trips per month is $1.25, identified by point *g* on the average cost curve. This amount is more than double the regulated price of $0.50. Rather than earning a profit, the monopolist suffers a loss—in this case, $0.75 per trip, for a total loss of about $80 million a month, identified by the pink-shaded rectangle. *Forcing a natural monopolist to produce where price, or marginal benefit, equals marginal cost results in an economic loss to the monopolist.* In the long run, the monopolist would go out of business rather than endure such a loss.

Subsidizing the Natural Monopolist

How can regulators encourage the monopolist to stay in business yet still produce where price equals marginal cost? The government can cover the loss—*subsidize* the firm so it earns a normal profit. Bus and subway fares are typically set below the average cost of providing the service, with the difference made up by a government subsidy. For example, the Washington, D.C., Metro subway system gets over $200 million per year in federal subsidies. Amtrak requires a federal subsidy of at least $1.5 billion per year. One drawback with

---

EXHIBIT **1**

Regulating a Natural Monopoly

With a natural monopoly, the long-run average cost curve slopes downward where it intersects with the demand curve. The unregulated firm maximizes profit by producing where marginal revenue equals marginal cost, in this case, 50 million trips per month at a price of $4.00 per trip. This outcome is inefficient because price, or marginal benefit, exceeds marginal cost. To achieve the efficient level of output, regulators could set the price at $0.50 per trip. The subway would sell 105 million trips per month, which would be an efficient outcome. But at that price, the subway would lose money and would require a subsidy to keep going. As an alternative, regulators could set the price at $1.50 per trip. The subway would sell 90 million trips per month and would break even (because price equals average cost). Although the subway would earn a normal profit, social welfare could still be increased by expanding output as long as the price, or marginal benefit, exceeds marginal cost, but that would result in an economic loss, requiring a subsidy.

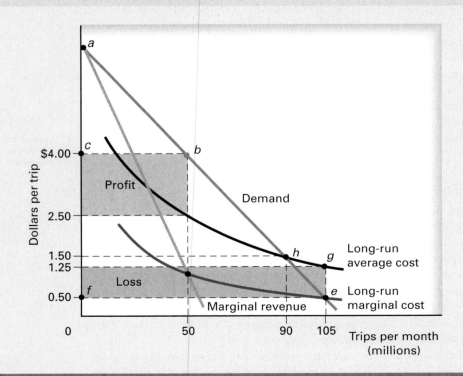

the subsidy solution is that, to provide the subsidy, the government must raise taxes or forgo public spending in some other area. Thus, the subsidy has an opportunity cost and could easily result in inefficiencies elsewhere in the economy.

Setting Price Equal to Average Cost

Although some public utilities are subsidized, most are not. Instead, regulators try to establish a price that will provide the monopolist with a "fair return." Recall that the average cost curve includes a normal profit. Thus, *setting price equal to average cost* provides a normal, or "fair," profit for the monopolist. In Exhibit 1, the demand curve intersects the average cost curve at point *h,* yielding a price of $1.50 and a quantity of 90 million trips a month. This price-output combination will allow the monopolist to stay in business without a subsidy.

Setting price equal to average total cost enhances social welfare compared to the unregulated situation. The monopolist would prefer an economic profit but will accept a normal profit to stay in business. After all, a normal profit is the best this firm could expect if resources were redirected to their best alternative uses. But note that the marginal benefit of the 90 millionth trip exceeds its marginal cost. Therefore, expanding output beyond 90 million trips per month would increase social welfare.

The Regulatory Dilemma

Setting price equal to marginal cost yields the *socially optimal* allocation of resources because *the consumers' marginal benefit from the last unit sold equals the marginal cost of producing that last unit.* In our example, setting the price at $0.50 equates marginal benefit and marginal cost, but the monopolist will face losses unless government provides a subsidy. These losses disappear if price equals average cost, which in our example is $1.50. The higher price ensures a normal profit, but the output is 15 million trips below the socially optimal level.

Thus, the dilemma facing the regulator is whether to set price equal to marginal cost, which is socially optimal but requires a government subsidy, or to set a break-even price even though output falls short of the socially optimal level. There is no right answer. Compared with the unregulated profit-maximizing price of $4, both reduce the price, increase output, erase economic profit, increase consumer surplus, and increase social welfare. Although Exhibit 1 lays out the options neatly, regulators usually face a cloudier picture. Demand and cost curves can only be estimated, and the regulated firm may withhold or distort information. For example, a utility may overstate its costs so it can charge more.

Alternative Theories of Economic Regulation

Why do governments regulate certain industries? Why not let market forces allocate resources? There are two views of government regulation. The first has been implicit in the discussion so far—namely, economic regulation is in the *public interest.* Economic regulation promotes social welfare by keeping prices down when one or just a few firms serve a market. A second, darker, view is that economic regulation is not in the public interest but is in the *special interest* of producers. According to this view, *well-organized producer groups expect to profit from economic regulation and persuade public officials to impose restrictions that existing producers find attractive, such as limiting entry into the industry or preventing competition among existing firms.* Individual producers have more to gain or to lose from regulation than do individual consumers. Producers typically are also better organized and more focused than consumers and are therefore better able to bring about regulations that favor producers.

Producers' Special Interest in Economic Regulation

To understand how and why producer interests could influence public regulation, think back to the last time you had your hair cut. Most states regulate the training and licensing of barbers and beauticians. If any new regulation affecting the profession is proposed, such as longer training requirements, who do you suppose has more interest in that legislation, you or those who cut hair for a living? *Producers have a strong interest in matters that affect their livelihood, so they play a disproportionately large role in trying to influence such legislation.* If there are public hearings on haircut regulations, the industry will provide self-serving testimony, while consumers will largely ignore the whole thing.

As a consumer, you do not specialize in getting haircuts. You purchase haircuts, cold cuts, hardware, software, underwear, and thousands of other goods and services. You have no *special interest* in haircuts. Some critics argue that because consumers fail to focus on such matters, business regulations often favor producer interests. Well-organized producer groups, as squeaky wheels in the legislative machinery, get the most grease in the form of favorable regulations. Such regulations are usually introduced under the guise of advancing consumer interests. Producer groups may argue that unbridled competition in their industry would hurt consumers. For example, the alleged problem of "cutthroat" competition among cab drivers has led to regulations that eliminate price competition and restrict the number of cabs in most large metropolitan areas. New York City has 10,000 fewer cabs now than it did 70 years ago. As a result, cabs there are harder to find and fares are more expensive. To operate a cab in New York City, someone must purchase a "medallion." The purchase price reflects the market value to cab owners of regulations that restrict entry and fix cab fares above the competitive level. The average price of a cab medallion increased from $27,000 in 1968 to $225,000 in 2003.[1] Regulation gives medallion owners an abiding interest in blocking new entry. If market entry and cab fares were deregulated, cabs would become more plentiful, fares would fall, and medallions would become worthless.

Regulation may be introduced under the guise of quality control, such as keeping unlicensed "quacks" from certain professions. But these supply restrictions usually reduce competition and increase the price. The special-interest theory may be valid even when the initial intent of the legislation was in the consumer interest. Over time, the regulatory machinery may shift toward the special interests of producers, who, in effect, "capture" the regulating agency. This **capture theory of regulation** was discussed by George Stigler, the Nobel laureate mentioned in the previous chapter. He argued that "as a general rule, regulation is acquired by the industry and is designed and operated for its benefit."[2]

Perhaps it would be useful at this point to discuss the regulation and, more recently, deregulation of a particular industry—airlines.

Airline Regulation and Deregulation

The Civil Aeronautics Board (CAB), established in 1938, once tightly regulated interstate airlines. Anyone trying to enter a particular airline market had to first persuade the CAB that the route needed another airline. During the 40 years prior to deregulation, potential entrants submitted more than 150 applications for long-distance routes, *but not a single new interstate airline was authorized.* The CAB also enforced strict compliance with regulated prices. In effect, the CAB had created a cartel that fixed prices among the 10 major airlines

---

1. These numbers were noted by Michael Luo, "46 Years in Cab, Recalling That Tip from Marylyn," *New York Times*, 7 December 2003.
2. George Stigler, "The Theory of Economic Regulation," *Bell Journal of Economics and Management Science* (Spring 1971): 3.

CAPTURE THEORY OF REGULATION

Producers' political power and strong stake in the regulatory outcome lead them, in effect, to "capture" the regulating agency and prevail on it to serve producer interests

Case **Study**

Public Policy

*e*Activity

A review of airline deregulation from a conservative viewpoint is available online from the Heritage Foundation's magazine at http://www.heritage.org/Research/Regulation/BG1173es.cfm. What actions was the Department of

and blocked new entry. This was a perfect example of the capture theory of regulation.

Regulation had insulated the industry from price competition, allowing labor unions to secure higher wages than they could in a more competitive setting. For working less than two weeks a month, airline pilots in 1978 earned more than $300,000 a year on average (in 2004 dollars). Some had so much free time they pursued second careers. Just how attractive a pilot's job was became apparent after deregulation. America West, a nonunion airline that sprouted from deregulation, paid its pilots $64,000 a year (in 2004 dollars) and required them to work 40 hours a week, performing other duties when they were not flying. Yet the company received more than 4,000 applications for its 29 pilot openings.

© Peter Schulz/Index Stock Imagery

Transportation considering at the time this review was written? What nonregulatory alternatives does the author suggest? The concerns of airline pilots about employment security and getting what they see as their fair share of industry revenues are presented through the Air Line Pilots' Association Web site at http://www.alpa.org/. What particular issues related to industry structure are of current concern to the pilots?

Although the CAB prohibited price competition, *nonprice competition flourished.* Airlines competed based on the frequency of flights, the quality of meals, the width of the seats, even the friendliness of the staff. For example, American Airlines put pianos in their jumbo jets. United Airlines countered with guitars and wine tastings. Such competition increased operating costs until firms earned only a normal rate of return. Thus, *airfares set above competitive levels coupled with entry restrictions were no guarantee of economic profit as long as airlines were free to compete in other ways, such as in the frequency of flights.*

The CAB had no regulatory power over airlines that flew only *intrastate* routes—flights between Los Angeles and San Francisco, for instance. The record shows that fares on intrastate airlines were only half those on identical routes flown by regulated airlines.

Airline Deregulation. Despite opposition from the existing airlines and labor unions, Congress passed the Airline Deregulation Act in 1978, which allowed price competition and new entry. By 2000, airfares in inflation-adjusted dollars averaged 27 percent below regulated prices. The airlines could afford to lower fares because they became more productive by filling a greater percentage of seats. The hub-and-spoke system developed under deregulation also allowed airlines to route planes more efficiently. Airline routes used to be straight lines from one city to another. Now they radiate like the spokes of a wagon wheel from a "hub" airport. From 30 hubs across the country, airlines send out planes along the spokes to over 400 commercial airports and then quickly bring them back to the hubs. Passenger miles flown nearly tripled since deregulation, and the net benefits to passengers now exceed $20 billion a year, or about $75 per U.S. resident.

Critics of deregulation worried that quality and safety would deteriorate. But the Federal Aviation Administration still regulates quality and safety. Since deregulation, accident rates have declined by anywhere from 10 to 45 percent, depending on the specific measure used. Also, because of lower fares, more people fly now rather than drive, thereby saving thousands of lives that would have been lost driving (per passenger mile, flying is about 20 times safer than driving).

Another concern with deregulation was that small communities would lose service. Because of the hub-and-spoke system, however, the number of scheduled departures from small cities and rural communities has increased more than one-third. The latest development in air travel is regional jets that bypass the hub-and-spoke system to fly 40 to 70 passengers from, say, Hartford, Connecticut, to Rochester, New York. The demand for air travel has increased enough to make such point-to-point service profitable.

Airport Capacity Limits Competition. Although airline traffic has more than doubled since deregulation, the air traffic control system has not expanded, and only one major new airport, Denver's, has opened. Airports and the air traffic control system are owned and operated by government agencies. *The government did not follow up deregulation with an expansion of airport capacity.* Revenue from taxes on airline tickets goes elsewhere. Departure gates, landing rights, and hub airports became the scarce resources in the industry. The major airlines may not have pushed for airport expansions because additional capacity could encourage more entry, which would increase competition.

Some passengers complain that the quality of food has declined in recent years, but that's because many consumers apparently prefer the lower fares of no-frills airlines. Most consumers view air travel as a commodity, and consider airlines as interchangeable. Thus, consumers seek the lowest fare. Low-cost, no-frills carriers such as Southwest Airlines and Jet Blue are grabbing market share and forcing down fares wherever they fly. Competition has been fierce and several airlines have disappeared or filed for bankruptcy. But, on the whole, deregulation has benefited consumers.

Sources: Steven Morrison and Clifford Winston, "The Remaining Role for Government Policy in the Deregulated Airline Industry," in *Deregulation of Network Industries: What's Next*; Sam Peltzman and Clifford Winston, eds. Brookings Institution, 2000, pp. 1–40; Scott McCartney, "AMR Is Challenging Jet Blue with Free Ticket Promotion," *Wall Street Journal*, 7 January 2004; and http://flyaow.com/, with links to nearly 500 airlines worldwide.

The course of regulation and deregulation raises some interesting questions about the true objectives of regulation. Recall the alternative views of regulation: one holds that regulation is in the public, or consumer, interest; the other holds that regulation is in the special, or producer, interest. In the airline industry, regulation appeared more in accord with producer interests, and producer groups fought deregulation, which benefited consumers.

This concludes our discussion of economic regulation, which tries to reduce the harmful consequences of monopolistic behavior in those markets where the output can be most efficiently supplied by one or a few firms. We now turn to antitrust policy, which tries to promote competition in those markets where competition seems desirable.

Antitrust Law and Enforcement

Although competition typically ensures the most efficient use of the nation's resources, an individual competitor would prefer to operate as a monopolist. If left alone, a firm might try to create a monopoly by driving competitors out of business, by merging with competitors, or by colluding with competitors. *Antitrust policy* is the government's attempt to reduce anticompetitive behavior and promote a market structure that will lead to greater competition. *Antitrust policy attempts to promote socially desirable market performance.*

Origins of Antitrust Policy

Economic developments in the last half of the 19th century created bigger firms serving wider markets. Perhaps the two most important developments were (1) technological breakthroughs that led to a larger optimal plant size in manufacturing and (2) the rise of the railroad from 9,000 miles of track in 1850 to 167,000 miles by 1890, which reduced transport costs. *Economies of scale and cheaper transport costs extended the geographical size of markets,* so firms grew larger and served a wider geographical market.

Sharp declines in the national economy in 1873 and in 1883, however, panicked large manufacturers. Because their heavy fixed costs required large-scale production, they cut prices in an attempt to stimulate sales. Price wars erupted, creating economic turmoil. Firms desperately sought ways to stabilize their markets. One solution was for each firm to form a *trust* by transferring their voting stock to a single board of trustees, which would vote in the interest of the industry. Early trusts were formed in the sugar, tobacco, and oil industries. Although the impact of these early trusts is still debated today, they allegedly pursued anticompetitive practices to develop and maintain a monopoly advantage. Gradually the word **trust** came to represent any firm or group of firms that tried to monopolize a market.

Trusts provoked widespread criticism and their creators were called "robber barons." Most farmers, especially, were hurt by these early trusts, for while farm prices were pushed down by technological change in agriculture, the prices farmers had to pay for supplies were higher because of trusts. At the time, farmers accounted for 40 percent of the U.S. workforce and thus had political clout. Some states, primarily agricultural, enacted *antitrust* laws in the 1880s, prohibiting trusts. But these laws were largely ineffective because a trust could simply move to a state without such restrictions.

Sherman Antitrust Act of 1890

In the presidential election of 1888, the major political parties put antitrust planks in their platforms. This consensus culminated in the **Sherman Antitrust Act of 1890,** the first national legislation in the world against monopoly. The law prohibited trusts, restraint of trade, and monopolization, but the law's vague language allowed much anticompetitive activity to slip by.

Clayton Act of 1914

The **Clayton Act of 1914** was passed to outlaw certain practices not prohibited by the Sherman Act and to help government stop a monopoly before it develops. For example, the Clayton Act outlaws price discrimination when this practice creates a monopoly. You'll recall that *price discrimination* is charging different customers different prices for the same good. The act also prohibits *tying contracts* and *exclusive dealing* if they substantially lessen competition. **Tying contracts** require the buyer of one good to purchase another good as part of the deal. For example, a seller of a patented machine might require customers to buy other supplies. **Exclusive dealing** occurs when a producer will sell a product only if the buyer agrees not to buy from other suppliers of the product. For example, a manufacturer might sell computer chips to a computer maker only if the computer maker agrees not to buy any chips elsewhere. Another prohibition of the act is **interlocking directorates,** whereby the same individual serves on the boards of directors of competing firms. Finally, acquiring of the corporate stock of a competing firm is outlawed if this would substantially lessen competition.

Federal Trade Commission Act of 1914

The **Federal Trade Commission (FTC) Act of 1914** established a federal body to help enforce antitrust laws. The president appoints the five commissioners, who are assisted by a staff of economists and lawyers. The Sherman, Clayton, and FTC acts provide the framework for antitrust laws. Subsequent amendments and court decisions have clarified and embellished these laws. A loophole in the Clayton Act was closed in 1950 with the passage of the *Celler-Kefauver Anti-Merger Act,* which prevents one firm from buying the *physical assets* of another firm if the effect is to reduce competition. This law can block both **horizontal mergers,** or the merging of firms that produce the same product, such as Coke and Pepsi, and **vertical mergers,** or the merging of firms where one supplies inputs to the other or demands output from the other, such as Microsoft and Dell.

TRUST
Any firm or group of firms that tries to monopolize a market

SHERMAN ANTITRUST ACT OF 1890
First national legislation in the world against monopoly; prohibited trusts, restraint of trade, and monopolization, but the law was vague and, by itself, ineffective

CLAYTON ACT OF 1914
Beefed up the Sherman Act; outlawed certain anticompetitive practices not prohibited by the Sherman Act, including price discrimination, tying contracts, exclusive dealing, interlocking directorates, and buying the corporate stock of a competitor

TYING CONTRACT
A seller of one good requires a buyer to purchase other goods as part of the deal

EXCLUSIVE DEALING
A supplier prohibits customers from buying from other suppliers of the product

INTERLOCKING DIRECTORATE
A person serves on the boards of directors of two or more competing firms

FEDERAL TRADE COMMISSION (FTC) ACT OF 1914
Established a federal body to help enforce antitrust laws; run by commissioners assisted by economists and lawyers

HORIZONTAL MERGER
A merger in which one firm combines with another that produces the same product

VERTICAL MERGER
A merger in which one firm combines with another from which it had purchased inputs or to which it had sold output

Antitrust Law Enforcement

Any law's effectiveness depends on the vigor and vigilance of enforcement. The pattern of antitrust enforcement goes something like this. Either the Antitrust Division of the U.S. Justice Department or the FTC charges a firm or group of firms with breaking the law. Federal agencies are often acting on a complaint by a customer or a competitor. At that point, those charged with the wrongdoing may be able, without admitting guilt, to sign a **consent decree,** whereby they agree not to continue doing what they had been charged with. If the accused contests the charges, evidence from both sides is presented in a court trial, and a judge renders a decision. Some decisions may be appealed all the way to the Supreme Court, and in such cases the courts may render new interpretations of existing laws.

Per Se Illegality and the Rule of Reason

The courts have interpreted antitrust laws in essentially two different ways. One set of practices has been declared **per se illegal**—that is, illegal regardless of the economic rationale or consequences. For example, under the Sherman Act, all formal agreements among competing firms to fix prices, restrict output, or otherwise restrain competition are viewed as per se illegal. To prove guilt under a per se rule, the government need only show that the offending practice took place. Thus, the government need only examine the firm's *behavior.*

Another set of practices falls under the **rule of reason.** Here the courts engage in a broader inquiry into the facts surrounding the particular offense—namely, the reasons why the offending practice was adopted and its effect on competition. The rule of reason was first set forth in 1911, when the Supreme Court held that Standard Oil had illegally monopolized the petroleum refining industry. Standard Oil allegedly had come to dominate 90 percent of the market by acquiring more than 120 former rivals and by practicing **predatory pricing** to drive remaining rivals out of business—for example, by temporarily selling below marginal cost or dropping the price only in certain markets. In finding Standard Oil guilty, the Court focused on both the company's *behavior* and the *market structure* that resulted from that behavior. Based on this approach, the Court found that the company had behaved *unreasonably* and ruled that the monopoly should be broken up.

But in 1920, the rule of reason led the Supreme Court to find U.S. Steel not guilty of monopolization. In that case, the Court ruled that not every contract or combination in restraint of trade is illegal—only those that "unreasonably" restrained trade violated antitrust laws. The Court said that *mere size is not an offense.* Although U.S. Steel clearly possessed market power, the company, in the Court's view, had not violated antitrust laws because it had not unreasonably used that power. The Court switched positions in 1945, ruling that although Alcoa's conduct might be reasonable and legal, its mere possession of market power—Alcoa controlled 90 percent of the aluminum ingot market—violated antitrust laws. Here the Court was using *market structure* rather than firm *behavior* as the test of legality.

Mergers and Public Policy

Some firms have pursued rapid growth by merging with other firms or by acquiring other firms. Much of what the Antitrust Division in the U.S. Justice Department and the FTC's Bureau of Competition do is approve or deny proposed mergers and acquisitions. In determining possible harmful effects that a merger might have on competition, one important consideration is its impact on the share of sales accounted for by the largest firms in the industry. If a few firms account for a relatively large share of sales, the industry is said to be *concentrated.* As a measure of sales concentration, the Justice Department uses the **Herfindahl-Hirschman Index,** or **HHI,** which is found by squaring the percentage of market share

---

CONSENT DECREE

The accused party, without admitting guilt, agrees to stop the alleged activity if the government drops the charges

PER SE ILLEGAL

In antitrust law, business practices that are deemed illegal regardless of their economic rationale or their consequences

RULE OF REASON

Before ruling on the legality of certain business practices, a court examines why they were undertaken and what effect they have on market competition

PREDATORY PRICING

Pricing tactics employed by a dominant firm to drive competitors out of business, such as temporarily selling below marginal cost or dropping the price only in certain markets

HERFINDAHL-HIRSCHMAN INDEX, OR HHI

A measure of market concentration that squares each firm's percentage share of the market then sums these squares

Firm	Industry I Market Share (percent)	Industry I Market Share Squared	Industry II Market Share (percent)	Industry II Market Share Squared	Industry III Market Share (percent)	Industry III Market Share Squared
A	23	529	15	225	57	3,249
B	18	324	15	225	1	1
C	13	169	15	225	1	1
D	6	36	15	225	1	1
Remaining 40 firms	1 each	40	1 each	40	1 each	40
HHI		1,098		940		3,292

EXHIBIT 2

Herfindahl-Hirschman Index (HHI) Based on Market Share in Three Industries

Each of the three industries shown has 44 firms. The HHI is found by squaring each firm's market share then summing the squares. Under each industry, each firm's market share is shown in the left column and the square of the market share is shown in the right column. For ease of exposition, only the market share of the top four firms differs across industries. The remaining 40 firms have 1 percent market share each. The HHI for Industry III is nearly triple that for each of the other two industries.

of each firm in the market and then summing those squares. For example, if the industry consists of 100 firms of equal size, the HHI is 100 [= 100 × (1)²]. If the industry is a monopoly, its index is 10,000 [= (100)²], the largest possible value. The more firms there are in the industry and the more equal their size, the smaller the HHI. This index gives greater weight to firms with larger market shares, as can be seen for the three examples presented in Exhibit 2. Each industry has 44 firms, but, for ease of exposition, only the market share of the top 4 firms differs across industries. Note that the index for Industry III is nearly triple that for each of the two other industries. Take a minute now to work through the logic of the exhibit.

The Justice Department's guidelines sort all mergers into one of two categories: *horizontal mergers,* which involve firms in the same market, and *nonhorizontal mergers,* which include all other types of mergers. Of greatest interest for antitrust purposes are horizontal mergers, such as a merger between competing oil companies like Mobil and Exxon. The Justice Department generally challenges any merger in an industry that meets two conditions: (1) the post-merger HHI exceeds 1,800 and (2) the merger increases the index by more than 100 points. Mergers in an industry that would have a post-merger index of less than 1,000 are seldom challenged.[3] Other factors, such as the ease of entry into the market and gains in efficiency, are considered for indexes between 1,000 and 1,800.

Merger Waves

There have been four merger waves in this country over the last century, as outlined in Exhibit 3. Between 1887 and 1904 some of today's largest firms, including U.S. Steel and Standard Oil, were formed. Mergers during this first wave tended to be horizontal. For example, the firm that is today U.S. Steel was created in 1901 through a billion-dollar merger that involved dozens of individual steel producers and two-thirds of the industry's production

3. Merger guidelines are laid out by the U.S. Department of Justice at http://www.usdoj.gov/atr/public/guidelines/horiz_book/hmg1.html.

Wave	Years	Dominant Type of Merger	Examples	Stimulus
First	1887–1904	Horizontal	U.S. Steel, Standard Oil	Span national markets
Second	1916–1929	Vertical	Copper refiner with fabricator	Stock market boom
Third	1948–1969	Conglomerate	Litton Industries	Diversification
Fourth	1982– present	Horizontal and vertical	Banking, tele-communications, health services, insurance	Span national and global markets, stock market boom

EXHIBIT 3

U.S. Merger Waves in the Past Century

HOMEWORK
Xpress!
Ask the Instructor Video

CONGLOMERATE MERGER

A merger of firms in different industries

capacity. This merger wave was a reaction to technological progress in transportation, communication, and manufacturing. Simply put, it became easier and cheaper to run a corporation that stretched across the nation, so firms merged to achieve national size. During this first wave, similar merger waves occurred in Canada, Great Britain, and elsewhere, creating dominant firms, some of which still exist today. The U.S. merger wave cooled with the severe national recession of 1904 and with the first stirrings of antitrust laws with real bite.

Because antitrust laws began to restrain *horizontal* mergers, *vertical* mergers became more common during the second merger wave, which occurred between 1916 and 1929. A vertical merger is one between a firm that either supplies the other firm inputs or demands the other firm's outputs—the merger of firms at different stages of the production process. For example, a copper refiner merges with a copper fabricator. The stock market boom of the 1920s fueled this second wave, and the stock market crash stopped it cold in 1929.

The Great Depression and World War II cooled mergers for two decades, but the third merger wave got under way after the war. More than 200 of the 1,000 largest firms in 1950 disappeared by the early 1960s as a result of the third merger wave, which occurred between 1948 and 1969. In that span, many large firms were absorbed by other, usually larger, firms. The third merger wave peaked during 1964 to 1969, when **conglomerate mergers,** which join firms in different industries, accounted for four-fifths of all mergers. For example, Litton Industries combined firms that made calculators, appliances, electrical equipment, and machine tools. Merging firms were looking to diversify their product mix and perhaps achieve some *economies of scope*—meaning, to reduce average costs by producing a variety of goods.

The fourth merger wave began in 1982 and involved both horizontal and vertical mergers. Some large conglomerate mergers from the third wave were dissolved during the fourth wave, as the core firm sold off unrelated operations. About one-third of mergers in the 1980s resulted from *hostile takeovers,* where one firm would buy control of another against the wishes of the target firm's management. Hostile takeovers dwindled to less than one-tenth of mergers during the 1990s.

Merger activity gained momentum during the latter half of the 1990s, with the dollar value of each new merger topping the previous record. Most mergers during this period were financed by the exchange of corporate stock and were spurred on by a booming stock market (like the mergers of the 1920s). The dissolution of the Soviet Union ended the Cold War and boosted capitalism around the world. Companies merged to achieve a stronger competitive position in global markets. The largest mergers in history were proposed during the late 1990s, with the biggest action in banking, radio and television, insurance, telecommunications, and health services.

In recent years, there have been fewer objections to mergers on antitrust grounds either from academics or regulatory officials. The government shifted from rules that restrict big mergers to a more flexible approach that allows big companies to merge. For example, the government approved Boeing's $15 billion acquisition of McDonnell Douglas, the commercial aircraft manufacturer, because the airlines said it made no difference to them whether or not the two combined. Boeing still competes fiercely with Airbus, its European rival, in the world market for aircraft. Antitrust officials ask "will the merger hurt competition?"[4] Most apparently do not. Regulators ultimately challenged only about 2 percent of all mergers proposed in recent years, though just the threat of a legal challenge has deterred countless potentially anticompetitive mergers and acquisitions.

Competitive Trends in the U.S. Economy

For years, there has been concern about the sheer size of some firms because of the real or potential power they might exercise in economic and political arenas. One way to measure the power of the largest corporations is to calculate the share of the nation's corporate assets controlled by the 100 largest firms. The 100 largest manufacturers now control about half of all manufacturing assets in the United States, up from a 40 percent share after World War II. We should recognize, however, that size alone is not synonymous with market power. A very big firm, such as a large automaker, may face stiff competition from other large automakers both foreign and domestic. On the other hand, the only movie theater in an isolated community may be able to raise its price with less concern about competition.

Market Competition over Time

More important than the size of the largest firms in the nation is the market structure of each industry. Various studies have examined the level of competition by industry and changes in competition over the years. All have begun with some measure of market share, such as the HHI. Among the most comprehensive is the research of William G. Shepherd, who relied on many sources to determine the competitiveness of each industry in the U.S. economy.[5] He sorted industries into four groups: (1) pure monopoly, in which a single firm controlled the entire market and was able to block entry; (2) dominant firm, in which a single firm had more than half the market share and had no close rival; (3) tight oligopoly, in which the top four firms supplied more than 60 percent of market output, with stable market shares and evidence of cooperation; and (4) effective competition, in which firms in the industry exhibited low concentration, low entry barriers, and little or no collusion.

Exhibit 4 presents Shepherd's breakdown of U.S. industries into the four categories for 1939, 1958, and 1988. Between 1939 and 1958, the table shows a modest trend toward increased competition, with the share of those industries rated as "effectively competitive"

4. "Prepared Remarks of Timothy J. Muris, Chairman, Federal Trade Commission," 17 February 2004 at http://www.ftc.gov/speeches/muris/040217hmgwksp.htm#N_4_.
5. William G. Shepherd, "Causes of Increased Competition in the U.S. Economy, 1939–1980," *Review of Economics and Statistics* 64 (November 1982); and William G. Shepherd, *The Economics of Industrial Organization*, 3rd ed. (Englewood Cliffs, N.J.: Prentice Hall, 1990), 15.

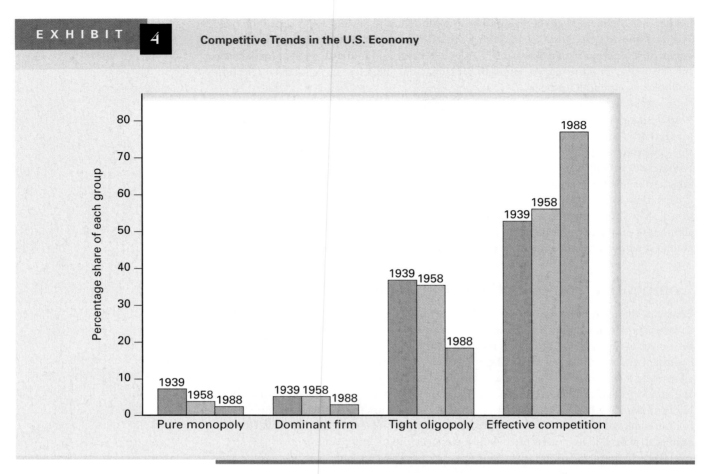

EXHIBIT **4**   **Competitive Trends in the U.S. Economy**

Sources: William G. Shepherd, "Causes of Increased Competition in the U.S. Economy, 1939–1980," *Review of Economics and Statistics* 64 (November 1982); and William G. Shepherd, *The Economics of Industrial Organization*, 3rd ed. (Englewood Cliffs, N.J.: Prentice Hall, 1997), 15.

growing from 52 percent to 56 percent of all industries. Between 1958 and 1988, however, there was a sharp rise in competitiveness in the economy, with the share of effectively competitive industries jumping from 56 percent to 77 percent.

According to Shepherd, the growth in competition from 1958 to 1988 can be traced to three sources: (1) *competition from imports,* (2) *deregulation,* and (3) *antitrust policy.* Foreign imports between 1958 and 1988 increased competition in 13 major industries, including autos, tires, and steel. The growth in imports accounted for one-sixth of the overall increase in competition. Imports were attractive to consumers because of their superior quality and lower price. Finding themselves at a cost and technological disadvantage, U.S. producers initially sought protection from foreign competitors through trade barriers, such as quotas and tariffs.

Shepherd argues that deregulation accounted for one-fifth of the increase in competition. Trucking, airlines, securities trading, banking, and telecommunications were among the industries deregulated between 1958 and 1988. We have already discussed some of the effects of deregulation in airlines, particularly in reducing barriers to entry and in eliminating

HOMEWORK
Xpress!
Ask the Instructor Video

uniform pricing schedules. With regard to telecommunications, in 1982, AT&T was forced to sell its 22 subsidiaries, which provided most of the country's local phone service. Since 1984, AT&T's share of the long-distance market declined from 88 percent to less than 40 percent today. This enhanced competition reduced long-distance rates.

Although it is difficult to attribute an increase in competition to specific antitrust cases, Shepherd credits antitrust policy with two-fifths of the growth in competition between 1958 and 1988. To summarize: According to Shepherd, the three primary reasons for increased competition were international trade, deregulation, and antitrust policy. One-sixth of the growth in competition between 1958 and 1988 came from imports, one-fifth from deregulation, and two-fifths, the largest share, from antitrust policy. In light of the important role that Shepherd accords antitrust policy, let's look at the most significant antitrust case in the last decade.

Microsoft on Trial

Microsoft released its long-awaited Windows 98 operating system in June 1998 under a cloud. The U.S. Justice Department and 20 state attorneys general had filed lawsuits a month earlier alleging that Microsoft tried to protect its operating-system monopoly and to extend that monopoly into Internet software. At the time, Windows software was used on 90 percent of the nation's desktop computers. The government charged that Microsoft's integration of its browser, Internet Explorer, into Windows 98 was not, as the company claimed, solely to make life easier for customers, but was aimed at boosting Explorer's market share. Controlling the gateway to the Internet would be a first step toward controlling Internet traffic and commerce. Government officials wanted Windows customers to have a choice of browsers. Microsoft disputed the charges and said the government was interfering with its right to create new products that benefit consumers.

© Jeff Christensen/AFP/Getty Images

Prior to any judicial ruling, Microsoft's choices were: (1) to separate its Internet browser from Windows 98, a task the company claimed would take "months if not years"; (2) to ship its major rival's browser, Netscape Navigator, as well as its own browser with Windows 98—a task Microsoft head Bill Gates likened to "requiring Coke to include three cans of Pepsi in every six-pack it sells"; or (3) to ship Windows 98 with Microsoft's browser bundled in the software. Microsoft chose the third alternative, which involved some risk because the practice could ultimately be deemed illegal.

The trial began in October 1998. The government argued that Microsoft engaged in predatory practices aimed at winning the browser war and harming competitors (the company's behavior would be considered illegal only if Microsoft was found to possess monopoly power). The government, by focusing on Microsoft's anticompetitive *behavior,* was using a rule-of-reason approach. Microsoft, for its part, characterized itself as an aggressive but legal player in a fiercely competitive industry. Microsoft's lawyers said that the company would not hold such a huge market share if it failed to improve quality and value with each new version. They argued that the high market share "does not begin to reflect the intense competitive dynamic in the software industry." Even such a market share, they said, was "susceptible to rapid deterioration should the market leader fail to innovate at a rapid and competitive pace."

After 78 days of testimony and months of deliberation, Judge Thomas Penfield Jackson ruled that Microsoft maintained a monopoly in operating-system software by anticompetitive means and attempted to monopolize the Web browser market by unlawfully "tying" Internet Explorer with Windows. He called Microsoft "an untrustworthy monopoly that refuses to abandon illegal business practices that crush competitors and harm consumers." As a remedy, he proposed restricting Microsoft's business practices and dividing the firm into a Windows-based operating-system company and an applications-software company.

Microsoft appealed the decision, arguing that it did not hold a monopoly and had not engaged in anticompetitive practices. Microsoft also charged that Judge Jackson showed bias in his ruling. In June 2001, the U.S. Court of Appeals upheld unanimously the finding that Microsoft violated antitrust laws and acted illegally in maintaining a monopoly in its operating system. But the appeals court also found that Judge Jackson had engaged in "serious judicial misconduct" in making derogatory comments about Microsoft to the media, so a new judge was chosen to decide on the punishment.

In November 2001, Microsoft reached a settlement with the Justice Department and with most of the state attorneys general. The settlement gives personal-computer makers greater freedom to install non-Microsoft software on new machines and to remove access to competing Microsoft features, such as Internet browsers. It also bans retaliation against companies that take advantage of these freedoms, prohibits exclusive contracts, and requires Microsoft to disclose design information to hardware and software makers so they can build competing products that will run smoothly with Windows. The court approved this settlement but that decision was appealed. By early 2004, Massachusetts remained the only state that had failed to settle with Microsoft. In July 2004, the U.S. Court of Appeals rejected that state's appeal, likely ending the court case in the United States. But Microsoft still faced charges brought by the European Union's antitrust authorities, who allege the company tried to extend monopoly power to its Windows Media Player. Fines, legal expenses, and dispute settlements cost Microsoft at least $2.5 billion in 2004. Still, Microsoft remains a huge company, with projected revenue in 2005 of $38 billion and a projected profit of $16 billion.

Sources: Brandon Mitchener and Matthew Newman, "Microsoft, EU Regulators Face More Pressure to Settle," *Wall Street Journal*, 24 November 2003; John Wilke and Ted Bridis, "Justice Department Says It Won't Seek Court-Ordered Breakup of Microsoft," *Wall Street Journal*, 7 September 2001; "Windows of Opportunity," *Economist*, 15 November 2003; and Brier Dudley, "Microsoft's Antitrust Settlement Upheld," *Seattle Times*, 1 July 2004.

Recent Competitive Trends

Shepherd's analysis of competition extended only to 1988. What has been the trend since then? Growing world trade has increased competition in the U.S. economy. For example, the share of the U.S. market controlled by the three major automakers fell from 80 percent in 1970 to 60 percent by 2000. And federal action to deregulate international phone service forced down the average price of international phone calls from $0.88 a minute in 1997 to well under $0.20 a minute by 2004. In an effort to reduce international phone rates, federal officials subpoenaed Filipino phone executives who were attending a conference in Hawaii, alleging they colluded on phone rates to the United States.[6]

Technological change is boosting competition in many markets. For example, the prime-time audience share of the three major television networks (NBC, CBS, and ABC) dropped from 90 percent in 1980 to under 40 percent in 2004 as satellite and cable tech-

6. Raissa Robles, "FBI Swoop Sparks Manila-U.S. Row," *South China Morning Post*, 15 January 2004.

nology delivered many more networks and channels. Despite Microsoft's dominance in operating systems, the software market barely existed in 1980 but now flourishes in a technology-rich environment populated by nearly 10,000 producers. And the Internet has opened far-ranging possibilities for greater competition in a number of industries, from online stock trading to all manner of electronic commerce.

Problems with Antitrust Policy

Despite the publicity and hoopla surrounding the Microsoft antitrust case (there was even a thinly disguised movie about Microsoft called *Antitrust*), there is growing doubt about the economic value of the lengthy antitrust cases pursued in the past. A case against Exxon, for example, was in the courts for 17 years before the company was cleared of charges in 1992. Another case began in 1969 when IBM, with nearly 70 percent of domestic sales of electronic data-processing equipment, was accused of monopolizing that market. IBM responded that its large market share was based on its innovative products and on its economies of scale. The trial began in 1975, the government took nearly three years to present its case; litigation dragged on for four more years. In the meantime, many other computer makers emerged both in this country and abroad to challenge IBM's dominance. In 1982, the government dropped the case, noting that the threat of monopoly had diminished enough that the case was "without merit." As noted already, the U.S. case against Microsoft took nearly six years to resolve.

Too Much Emphasis on the Competitive Model

Joseph Schumpeter argued half a century ago that competition should be viewed as a dynamic process, one of "creative destruction." Firms are continually in flux—introducing new products, phasing out old ones, trying to compete for the consumer's dollar in a variety of ways. In light of this, antitrust policy should not necessarily aim at increasing the *number* of firms in each industry. In some cases, firms will grow large because they are more efficient than rivals at offering what consumers want. Accordingly, firm size should not be the primary concern. Moreover, as noted in the chapter on perfect competition, economists have shown through market experiments that most of the desirable properties of perfect competition can be achieved with relatively few firms.[7] For example, the two leading chip makers, Intel and Advanced Micro Devices, have been locked in a price war for years, as each fights for market share. Likewise, Boeing is the only U.S. maker of commercial jets but it competes fiercely with Europe's Airbus for every new contract.

Abuse of Antitrust

Parties that can show injury from firms that violate antitrust laws can sue the offending company and recover three times the amount of the damages sustained. These so-called *treble damage* suits increased after World War II. More than 1,000 are filed each year. Courts have been relatively generous to those claiming to have been wronged. Even foreign firms have started suing in U.S. courts. But studies show that such suits can be used to intimidate an aggressive competitor or to convert a contract dispute between, say, a firm and its supplier into treble damage payoffs. The result can have a chilling effect on competition. Many economists now believe that the anticompetitive costs from this abuse of treble damage suits may exceed any competitive benefits of these laws.

---

7. See, for example, Vernon Smith, "Markets as Economizers of Information: Experimental Examinations of the 'Hayek Hypothesis,'" *Economic Inquiry* 20 (1982); and Douglas Davis and Charles Holt, *Experimental Economics* (Princeton, N.J.: Princeton University Press, 1993).

Growing Importance of International Markets

Finally, a standard approach to measuring the market power of a firm is its share of the market. With greater international trade, however, the local or even national market share becomes less relevant. General Motors may dominate U.S. auto manufacturing, accounting for half of national sales by U.S. firms. But when Japanese and European producers are included, GM's share of the U.S. auto market falls to only 28 percent. GM's share of world production has declined steadily since the mid-1950s. *Where markets are open to foreign competition, antitrust enforcement that focuses on domestic producers makes less economic sense.* In response to the global nature of markets, antitrust policy is starting to take an international approach. The U.S. government has signed cooperative agreements with some other governments, including Japan and the European Union, to promote antitrust enforcement and reduce conflicting decisions. For example, on February 12, 2003, antitrust investigators from the United States, the European Union, Japan, and Canada simultaneously raided 14 companies in 5 countries in a price fixing probe of the polyvinyl chloride market.

Conclusion

Competition has been growing in recent decades because of changing technology, greater international trade, industry deregulation, and antitrust policy. Federal Reserve Chairman Alan Greenspan, testifying before Congress, expressed skepticism about some antitrust intervention, arguing that changes in market conditions and in technologies tend to undermine monopolies over time. He called for "a higher degree of humility when enforcers make . . . projections" about the lasting effects of monopoly power. But, Joel Klein, then the antitrust chief for the Justice Department, said "we reject categorically the notion that markets will self-correct and we should sit back and watch."[8] So goes the debate about antitrust policy.

SUMMARY

1. In this chapter, we examined two forms of government regulation of business: (a) economic regulation, such as the regulation of natural monopolies, and (b) antitrust policy, which promotes competition and prohibits efforts to monopolize, or to cartelize, an industry.

2. Governments regulate natural monopolies so that output is greater and prices lower than if the monopolist was allowed to maximize profits. One problem with regulation is that the price that maximizes social welfare results in an economic loss, whereas the price that allows the firm to earn a normal profit does not maximize social welfare.

3. There are two views of economic regulation. The first is that economic regulation is in the public, or consumer,

interest because it controls natural monopolies where production by one or just a few firms is most efficient. A second view is that regulation is not in the public, or consumer, interest, but is more in the special interest of producers that use regulations to fix the price and block entry.

4. Regulations in effect for 50 years in the airline industry restricted entry and fixed prices. Deregulation in 1978 stimulated new entry, unleashed price competition, and reduced prices overall. Price wars in the industry are now common, and consumers have benefited.

5. Antitrust laws are aimed at promoting competition and prohibiting efforts to cartelize, or monopolize, an industry.

8. As quoted in John R. Wilke, "Greenspan Questions Government's Antitrust-Enforcement Campaigns," *Wall Street Journal,* 17 June 1998.

The Sherman, Clayton, and FTC acts provide the legal and institutional framework for antitrust enforcement, a framework that subsequent amendments and court cases have clarified and embellished.

6. Competition in U.S. industries has been increasing since World War II. Four sources of growing competition are greater international trade, deregulation, antitrust policy, and technological change.

QUESTIONS FOR REVIEW

1. *(Business Behavior and Public Policy)* Define market power, and then discuss the rationale for government regulation of firms with market power.

2. *(Government Regulation)* What three types of government policies are used to alter or control firm behavior? Determine which type of regulation is used for each of the following:

   a. Preventing a merger that the government believes would lessen competition
   b. The activities of the Food and Drug Administration
   c. Regulation of fares charged by a municipal bus company
   d. Occupational safety and health regulations that affect working conditions

3. *(Regulating Natural Monopolies)* What is the "regulatory dilemma?" That is, what trade-offs do regulators have to consider when deciding how to control a natural monopoly?

4. *(Theories of Regulation)* Why do producers have more interest in government regulations than consumers do?

   a. Compare and contrast the public-interest and special-interest theories of economic regulation. What is the capture theory of regulation?

   b. Which of these theories best describes the case of airline deregulation? Which best explains the government's case against Microsoft?

5. (*C a s e* **S t u d y**: Airline Regulation and Deregulation) Consumers now treat air travel like a commodity and meals on some airlines are nonexistent. Does this mean that consumers have suffered because of airline deregulation?

6. *(Antitrust Law and Enforcement)* Discuss the difference between per se illegality and the rule of reason.

7. *(Antitrust Activity)* "The existence of only two or three big U.S. auto manufacturers is evidence that the market structure is anticompetitive and that antitrust laws are being broken." Evaluate this assertion.

8. *(Mergers and Public Policy)* Under what circumstances, and why, would the government be opposed to a merger of two firms? How does the Justice Department decide which mergers to challenge?

9. *(Competitive Trends in the U.S. Economy)* William Shepherd's study of U.S. industries showed a clear increase in competition in the U.S. economy between 1958 and 1988. How did Shepherd explain this trend?

PROBLEMS AND EXERCISES

10. *(Regulating Natural Monopolies)* The following graph represents a natural monopoly.

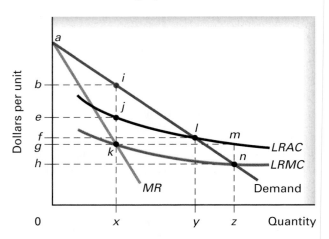

a. Why is this firm considered a natural monopoly?

b. If the firm is unregulated, what price and output would maximize its profit? What would be its profit or loss?

c. If a regulatory commission establishes a price with the goal of achieving allocative efficiency, what would be the price and output? What would be the firm's profit or loss?

d. If a regulatory commission establishes a price with the goal of allowing the firm a "fair return," what would be the price and output? What would be the firm's profit or loss?

e. Which one of the prices in parts b, c, and d maximizes consumer surplus? What problem, if any, occurs at this price?

11. *(Origins of Antitrust Policy)* Identify the type of anticompetitive behavior illustrated by each of the following:

a. A university requires buyers of season tickets for its basketball games to buy season tickets for its football games as well.

b. Dairies that bid on contracts to supply milk to school districts collude to increase what they charge.

c. The same individual serves on the boards of directors of General Motors and Ford.

d. A large retailer sells merchandise below cost in certain regions to drive competitors out of business.

e. A producer of carbonated soft drinks sells to a retailer only if the retailer agrees not to buy from the producer's major competitor.

12. *(Mergers and Public Policy)* Calculate the Herfindahl-Hirschman Index (HHI) for each of the following industries. Which industry is the most concentrated?

a. An industry with five firms that have the following market shares: 50 percent, 30 percent, 10 percent, 5 percent, and 5 percent

b. An industry with five firms that have the following market shares: 60 percent, 20 percent, 10 percent, 5 percent, and 5 percent

c. An industry with five firms, each of which has a 20 percent market share

EXPERIENTIAL EXERCISES

13. *(Mergers and Public Policy)* Find the Department of Justice and Federal Trade Commission merger guidelines at http://www.usdoj.gov/atr/public/guidelines/horiz_book/toc.html. How does the government use the Herfindahl-Hirschman Index to determine which proposed mergers to allow and which to challenge? Do these guidelines indicate that the Justice Department is using the per-se-illegality or rule-of-reason approach to antitrust enforcement?

14. (**C a s e S t u d y**: Microsoft on Trial) The latest information on the Justice Department's case against Microsoft is available at http://www.usdoj.gov/atr/cases/ms_index.htm. To get the other side of the story, check Microsoft's PressPass page at http://microsoft.com/presspass/legalnews.asp. What has happened with the case in Europe since this textbook went to press?

15. (*Wall Street Journal*) The best place for finding late-breaking information about antitrust activity is in the "Legal Beat" column of the *Wall Street Journal*. You can find it inside the Marketplace section. Try to find at least one relevant article and determine the basis for the antitrust action. Were the Justice Department guidelines and the Herfindahl-Hirschman index mentioned in the article?

16. *(Regulatory Policy)* Research a recent antitrust case at the Department of Justice Web site (http://www.usdoj. gov/atr). Summarize the case including: the parties involved, the legal basis for the case, and the current status.

HOMEWORK XPRESS! EXERCISES

These exercises require access to McEachern Homework Xpress! If Homework Xpress! did not come with your book, visit **http://homeworkxpress.swlearning.com** *to purchase.*

York Local Phone Company, Inc. (YLPC) has a natural monopoly in the supply of land lines in Yorktown. Information about the demand, marginal revenue, long-run average cost, and long-run marginal cost are given in the table below. Plot all four in a diagram.

Quantity (10,000)	Price	Marginal Revenue	Long-Run Average Cost	Long-Run Marginal Cost
0	$60	$60	—	—
10	50	40	$37	$30
20	40	20	30	20
30	30	0	24	15
40	20		20	11
50	10		15	10
60	0		12	9

1. Identify the price YLPC would charge and the quantity of land lines that would be demanded at this price if left unregulated. Create a shaded box to illustrate its profit or loss.

2. Identify the price YLPC would charge and the quantity of land lines that would be demanded if a regulatory commission sets the price it can charge with the goal of achieving allocative efficiency. Create a shaded box to illustrate its profit or loss.

3. Identify the price YLPC would charge and the quantity of land lines that would be demanded at this price if a regulatory commission sets the price it can charge with the goal of allowing the firm a fair rate of return.

CHAPTER

16

Public Goods and Public Choice

How do public goods differ from private goods? Why do most people remain largely ignorant about what's happening in the public sector? Why is voter turnout so low? Why do politicians talk about their concern for the middle class, while they are acting on the concerns of special interests? Why are elected officials more likely than challengers to support campaign spending limits? Answers to these and related questions are discussed in this chapter, which focuses on the public sector—both the rationale for public goods and public choices about those goods.

The effects of government are all around us. Stitched into the clothes you donned this morning are government-required labels providing washing instructions. Prices of the milk and sugar you put on your Cheerios are propped up by government price supports as are the oats in the Cheerios. Governments regulate the motor

HOMEWORK Xpress!

Use Homework Xpress! for economic application, graphing, videos, and more.

vehicle that provided your transportation as well the speed and the sobriety of the driver. Your education is subsidized by taxpayers in a variety of ways. Yes, government plays a major role in the economy. The federal government alone spends each year more than $2,400,000,000,000.00—more than $2.4 *trillion*—including $1 million on paper clips. State and local governments tax and spend more than $1 trillion on their own.

The role of government has been discussed throughout this book. For the most part, we assumed that government makes optimal adjustments to the shortcomings of the private sector; that is, when confronted with market failure, government adopts and implements the appropriate program to address the problem. But, just as there are limits to the market's effectiveness, there are limits to government's effectiveness. In this chapter, we look at the pros and cons of government activity. We begin with public goods, discuss the decision-making process, and then examine the limitations of that process. Topics discussed include:

- Private versus public goods
- Representative democracy
- Rational ignorance
- Special-interest legislation
- Rent seeking
- The underground economy
- Bureaucratic behavior
- Private versus public production

NetBookmark

Common Cause, a nonpartisan lobbying group promoting accountable government, provides information on special interest groups that donated to political campaigns at http://www.commoncause.org/laundromat. See the list of profiles of the largest soft money donors in past elections. You can visit http://www.policyalmanac.org/government/campaign_finance.shtml for a summary of the new law.

Public Goods

Throughout most of this book, we have been talking about *private goods*, such as pizzas and haircuts. As noted in Chapter 3, private goods have two important features. First, they are *rival* in consumption, meaning that the amount consumed by one person is unavailable for others to consume. For example, when you and friends share a pizza, each slice others eat is one less available for you (which is why you usually eat a little faster when sharing). A second key feature of private goods is that suppliers can easily *exclude* those who don't pay. Only paying customers get pizzas. Thus, private goods are said to be *rival* and *exclusive*.

Private Goods, Public Goods, and In Between

In contrast to private goods, *public goods*, such as national defense, the national weather service, the Centers for Disease Control, or a local mosquito-control program, are *nonrival* in consumption. One person's consumption does not diminish the amount available to others. Once produced, such goods are available to all in equal amount; the marginal cost of supplying the good to an additional consumer is zero. But once a public good is produced, suppliers cannot easily deny it to those who fail to pay. There are no vending machines for public goods. For example, if a firm sprays a neighborhood for mosquitoes, all households in the neighborhood benefit. The firm can't easily exclude those who fail to pay. Thus, the mosquito spraying is *nonexclusive*—it benefits all those in the neighborhood. Some people figure, "Since I can enjoy the benefits without paying, why bother paying?" As a consequence, for-profit firms can't profitably sell public goods. In this case of market failure, the government comes to the rescue by providing public goods and paying for them through enforced taxation. Sometimes nonprofit agencies also provide public goods, funding them through contributions and other revenue sources.

But the economy consists of more than just private and public goods. Some goods are *nonrival* but *exclusive*. For example, additional households can tune in a TV show without affecting the reception of other viewers. It's not as if there is only so much TV signal to go around. Television signals are nonrival in consumption. Yet the program's producers, should they choose to, could charge each household for reception, as with cable TV, so the TV

QUASI-PUBLIC GOOD

A good that is nonrival in consumption but exclusive, such as cable TV

signal is nonrival but exclusive. A good that is nonrival but exclusive is called a **quasi-public good.** Along the same lines, short of the point of congestion, additional people can benefit from a golf course, swimming pool, rock concert, or highway without diminishing the benefit to other users. These goods, when not congested, are nonrival. Yet producers can, with relative ease, exclude those who don't pay the greens fee, pool admission, ticket price, or road toll. These uncongested goods are both nonrival and exclusive and are therefore quasi-public goods. Once congestion sets in, however, these goods become rival—space is scarce on a backed-up golf course, in a crowded swimming pool, at a jam-packed concert, or on a traffic-clogged highway. Once congestion sets in, these quasi-public goods become private goods—both rival and exclusive.

OPEN-ACCESS GOOD

A good that is rival in consumption but nonexclusive, such as ocean fish

Some other goods are *rival* but *nonexclusive*. The fish in the ocean are rival in the sense that every fish caught is not available for others to catch; the same goes for migratory game, like geese. But ocean fish and migratory game are nonexclusive in that it would be costly or impossible for a private firm to prevent access to these goods. A good that is rival but nonexclusive is called an **open-access good** because it would be difficult and costly to prevent individuals from consuming the good. Problems that arise with open-access goods will be examined in the next chapter.

Exhibit 1 sorts out the four categories of goods. Across the top, goods are either *rival* or *nonrival,* and along the left margin, goods are either *exclusive* or *nonexclusive*. Private goods are usually provided by the private sector. Quasi-public goods are sometimes provided by the private sector, as with a private golf course, and sometimes provided by government, as with a municipal golf course. Open-access goods are usually regulated by government, as you will see in the next chapter. And public goods are usually provided by the government.

Optimal Provision of Public Goods

Because private goods are rival in consumption, the market demand for a private good is the sum of the quantities demanded by each consumer. For example, the market quantity of

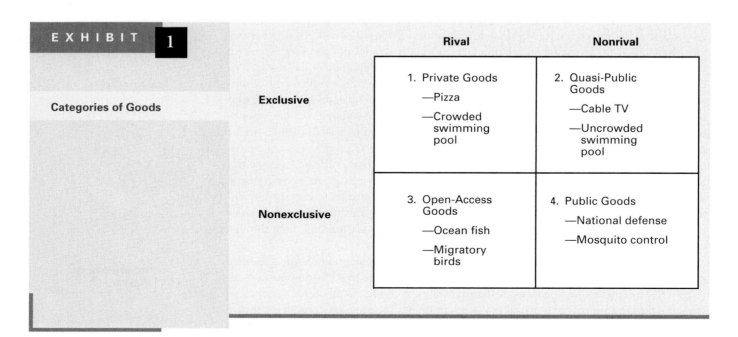

E X H I B I T   1

Categories of Goods

	Rival	Nonrival
Exclusive	1. Private Goods —Pizza —Crowded swimming pool	2. Quasi-Public Goods —Cable TV —Uncrowded swimming pool
Nonexclusive	3. Open-Access Goods —Ocean fish —Migratory birds	4. Public Goods —National defense —Mosquito control

pizza demanded when the price is $10 is the quantity demanded by Alan plus the quantity demanded by Maria plus the quantity demanded by all other consumers in the market. The market demand curve for a private good is the *horizontal* sum of individual demand curves, an idea developed in Exhibit 7 of Chapter 6. The efficient quantity of a private good occurs where the market demand curve intersects the market supply curve.

But a public good is nonrival in consumption, so that good, once produced, is available to all consumers. For example, the market demand for a given level of mosquito control reflects the marginal benefit that Alan gets from that amount of the good plus the marginal benefit that Maria gets from that amount plus the marginal benefit that all others in the community get from that amount of the good. Therefore, the market demand curve for a public good is the *vertical* sum of each consumer's demand for the public good. To arrive at the efficient level of the public good, we find where the market demand curve intersects the marginal cost curve—that is, where the sum of the marginal valuations equals the marginal cost.

Suppose the public good in question is mosquito control in a neighborhood, which, for simplicity, has only two households, one headed by Alan and the other by Maria. Alan spends more time in the yard than does Maria and thus values a mosquito-free environment more than she does. Their individual demand curves are shown in Exhibit 2 as D_a and D_m, reflecting the marginal benefits that Alan and Maria enjoy at each rate of output. Quantity is measured here as hours of mosquito spraying per week. By vertically summing marginal valuations at each rate of output, we derive the neighborhood demand curve, D, for mosquito spraying. For example, when the town sprays two hours a week, Maria values the second hour at $5 and Alan values it at $10. To get the market demand for two hours of spraying, we simply add each resident's marginal benefit to get $15, as identified by point e.

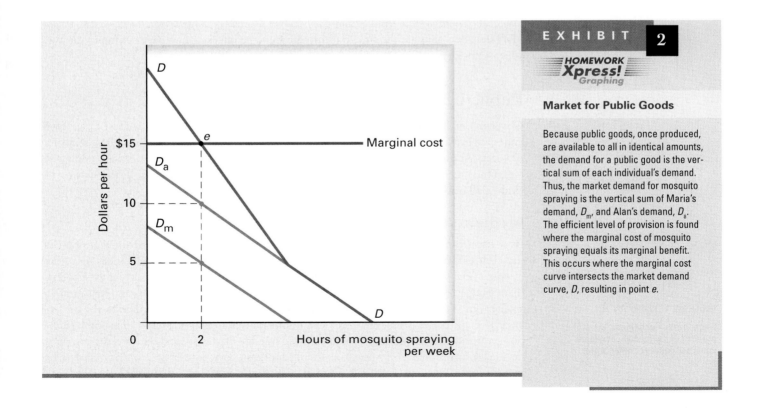

EXHIBIT 2

HOMEWORK **Xpress!** *Graphing*

Market for Public Goods

Because public goods, once produced, are available to all in identical amounts, the demand for a public good is the vertical sum of each individual's demand. Thus, the market demand for mosquito spraying is the vertical sum of Maria's demand, D_m, and Alan's demand, D_a. The efficient level of provision is found where the marginal cost of mosquito spraying equals its marginal benefit. This occurs where the marginal cost curve intersects the market demand curve, D, resulting in point e.

FREE-RIDER PROBLEM

Because a public good is nonexclusive, people may try to reap the benefits of the good without paying for it

How much mosquito spraying should the government provide? Suppose the marginal cost of spraying is a constant $15 an hour, as shown in Exhibit 2. The efficient level of output is found where the marginal benefit to the neighborhood equals the marginal cost, which occurs where the neighborhood demand curve intersects the marginal cost curve. In our example, these curves intersect where quantity is two hours per week.

Paying for Public Goods

The government pays for the mosquito spray through taxes, user fees, or some combination of the two. The efficient approach would be to impose a tax on each resident equal to his or her marginal valuation. Simple enough, but there are at least two problems with this. First, once people realize their taxes are based on how much the government thinks they value the good, people tend to understate their true valuation. Why admit you really value the good if, as a result, you get socked with a higher tax bill? So taxpayers are reluctant to offer information about their true valuation of public goods. This creates the **free-rider problem,** which occurs because people try to benefit from the public good without paying for it. For example, they can enjoy mosquito abatement whether or not they pay. But even if the government has accurate information about marginal valuations, some households have a greater ability to pay taxes than others. In our example, Alan values mosquito control more because he spends more time in the yard than does Maria. What if Alan is around more because he can't find a job? Should his taxes be double those of Maria, who, say, has a high-paying job? *Taxing people according to their marginal valuations of the public good may be efficient, but it may not be fair if incomes differ.*

Once the public good is produced, only that quantity is available, such as two hours of mosquito spraying per week. With private goods, each consumer can purchase any quantity he or she prefers and each can purchase a different amount. Thus, *public goods are more complicated than private goods in terms of what goods should be provided, in what quantities, and who should pay.* These decisions are thrashed out through public choices, which we examine in the balance of this chapter.

Public Choice in a Representative Democracy

Government decisions about the provision of public goods and the collection of tax revenues are *public choices.* In a democracy, public choices usually require approval by a majority of voters. About 60 percent of the world's two hundred independent nations are democracies. Thus, issues raised in this section about majority rule apply to most of the world, including all of Western Europe and nearly all of the Americas.

Median Voter Model

MEDIAN VOTER MODEL

Under certain conditions, the preferences of the median, or middle, voter will dominate other preferences

As it turns out, we can usually explain the outcome of majority rule by focusing on the preferences of the median voter. The *median voter* is the one whose preferences lie in the middle of the set of all voters' preferences. For example, if the issue is the size of the government budget, half the voters prefer a larger budget than the median voter and half prefer a smaller one. The **median voter model** predicts that under certain conditions, the preference of the median, or middle, voter will dominate other choices. Here's an example. Suppose you and two roommates have just moved into an apartment, and the three of you must decide on furnishings. You agree to share the common costs equally and to make choices by majority rule. The issue at hand is whether to buy a TV and, if so, of what size. But you each have a different preference. Your studious roommate considers a TV an annoying distraction and would rather go without; otherwise, the smaller, the better. Your other roommate, a real TV fan, prefers a 48-inch screen but would settle for a smaller one rather than go without. A 27-inch screen is your first choice, but you would accept the 48-inch screen rather than go without. What to do, what to do?

You all agree to make the decision by voting on two alternatives at a time, then pairing the winner against the remaining alternative until one dominates the others. When the 27-inch set is paired with the no-TV option, the 27-inch gets both your vote and the TV fan's vote. When the 27-inch screen is then paired with the 48-inch screen, the 27-inch screen wins again, this time because your studious roommate sides with you rather than voting for the super screen.

Majority voting in effect delegates the public choice to the person whose preference is the median for the group. As the median voter in this example, you get your way. You have the votes for any choice between no TV and a 48 incher. Similarly, *the median voter in an electorate often determines public choices. Political candidates try to get elected by appealing to the median voter.* This is why candidates focus their rhetoric on "hard-working Americans," "middle America," or "American families." They are targeting the median voter. This is one reason why candidates often seem so much alike. Note that under majority rule, only the median voter gets his or her way. Other voters must go along with the median choice. Thus, other voters usually end up paying for what they consider to be either too much or too little of the public good. In private markets people get whatever they are willing and able to buy.

People vote directly on issues at New England town meetings and on the occasional referendum, but *direct democracy* is not the most common means of public choice. When you consider the thousands of choices made in the public sector—from the number of teachers to hire to what software to use for municipal records—it becomes clear that direct democracy for all public choices through referenda would be unwieldy and impractical. Rather than make decisions by direct referenda, voters elect *representatives,* who, at least in theory, make public choices that reflect their constituents' views. Under certain conditions, the resulting public choices reflect the preferences of the median voter. Some complications of making public choices through representative democracy are explored next.

Special Interest and Rational Ignorance

We assume that consumers maximize utility and firms maximize profit, but what about governments? As noted in Chapter 3, there is no common agreement about what, if anything, governments try to maximize or, more precisely, what elected officials try to maximize. One theory that parallels the rational self-interest assumption employed in private choices is that elected officials attempt to *maximize their political support.*

Elected officials may cater to special interests rather than serve the interest of the public. The possibility arises because of the asymmetry between special interest and public interest, an idea introduced in the previous chapter. Consider only one of the thousands of decisions that are made each year by elected representatives: funding an obscure federal program that subsidizes U.S. wool production. Under the wool-subsidy program, the federal government guarantees that a floor price is paid to sheep farmers for each pound of wool they produce, a subsidy that costs taxpayers over $75 million per year. During deliberations to renew the program, the only person to testify before Congress was a representative of the National Wool Growers Association, who claimed that the subsidy was vital to the nation's economic welfare. Why didn't a single taxpayer challenge the subsidy? Why were sheep farmers able to pull the wool over taxpayers' eyes?

Households consume so many different public and private goods and services that they have neither the time nor the incentive to understand the effects of public choices on every product. What's more, voters realize that each of them has only a tiny possibility of influencing public choices. And even if an individual voter is somehow able to affect the outcome, the impact on that voter is likely to be small. For example, if a taxpayer could successfully stage a grassroots campaign to eliminate the wool subsidy, the taxpayer would save, on average, less than $0.55 per year in federal income taxes (based on about 135 million tax filers in 2004). Therefore, unless voters have a *special* interest in the legislation, they adopt a stance of **rational ignorance,** which means that they remain largely oblivious to most public choices. The cost to the typical voter of acquiring information about each public choice and acting on it usually exceeds any expected benefit. It's not easy to interest the public in the public interest.

In contrast, consumers have much more incentive to gather and act on information about decisions they make in private markets because they benefit directly from such information. *Because information and the time required to acquire and digest it are scarce, consumers concentrate on private choices rather than public choices. The payoff in making better private choices is usually more immediate, more direct, and more substantial.* For example, a consumer in the market for a new car has an incentive to examine the performance records of different models, test-drive a few, and check prices at dealerships and on the Internet. That same individual has less incentive to examine the performance records of candidates for public office because that single voter has virtually no chance of deciding the election. What's more, because candidates aim to please the median voter anyway, they often take positions that are similar.

Distribution of Benefits and Costs

Let's turn now to a different topic—how the costs and benefits of public choices are spread across the population. Depending on the issue, the benefits of particular legislation may affect only a small group or much of the population. Likewise, the costs of that legislation may be imposed either narrowly or widely over the population. The possible combinations of benefits and costs yield four categories of distributions: (1) widespread benefits and widespread costs, (2) concentrated benefits and widespread costs, (3) widespread benefits and concentrated costs, and (4) concentrated costs and concentrated benefits.

Traditional public-goods legislation, such as for national defense or a system of justice, have widespread benefits and widespread costs—nearly everyone benefits and nearly everyone pays. Traditional public-goods legislation usually has a positive impact on the economy because total benefits exceed total costs.

With **special-interest legislation,** benefits are concentrated but costs widespread. For example, as you'll see shortly, price supports for dairy products benefit dairy farmers with higher prices. The program's costs are spread across nearly all consumers and taxpayers. Legislation that caters to special interests usually harms the economy, on net, because total costs often exceed total benefits. Special-interest legislation of narrow geographical interest is called **pork-barrel spending.** For example, a recent federal budget appropriated $50,000 for a tattoo removal program in San Luis Obispo, California; $150,000 to restore the Augusta Historic Theater in Georgia; and $2 million for a statue of a Roman god in Birmingham, Alabama.[1] To boost their reelection prospects, members of Congress "bring home the bacon" by delivering pork-barrel programs for their constituents.

RATIONAL IGNORANCE

A stance adopted by voters when they find that the cost of understanding and voting on a particular issue exceeds the benefit expected from doing so

TRADITIONAL PUBLIC-GOODS LEGISLATION

Legislation that involves widespread costs and widespread benefits—nearly everyone pays and nearly everyone benefits

SPECIAL-INTEREST LEGISLATION

Legislation with concentrated benefits but widespread costs

PORK-BARREL SPENDING

Special-interest legislation with narrow geographical benefits but funded by all taxpayers

---

1. Dan Morgan and Helen Dewar, "GOP Dishes Out Pork in Growing Portions," *Washington Post,* 24 November 2003.

Populist legislation involves widespread benefits but concentrated costs. Populist legislation usually has a tough time getting approved because the widespread group that benefits typically remains rationally ignorant of the proposed legislation, so these voters provide little political support. But the concentrated group getting whacked will object strenuously. Most economists agree that tort-reform legislation, for example, would benefit the economy as a whole by limiting product liability lawsuits, reducing insurance costs, and bringing some goods to the market that, because of liability suits, have all but disappeared, such as personal aircraft. But trial lawyers, the group that would be most harmed by such limits, have successfully blocked reforms for years. Because the small group that bears the cost is savvy about the impact of the proposed legislation but those who would reap the benefits remain rationally ignorant, populist legislation has little chance of approval, unless elected officials can somehow get the issue on the voter's radar screen.

Finally, **competing-interest legislation** involves both concentrated benefits and concentrated costs, such as legislation affecting the power of labor unions in their dealings with employers, or legislation affecting steel makers versus steel-using industries. These are the fiercest political issues because both sides have a heavy stake in the outcome.

Exhibit 3 arrays the four categories of distributions. Across the top, benefits of legislation are either *widespread* or *concentrated,* and along the left margin, costs are either *widespread* or *concentrated.* Box 1 shows *traditional public-goods legislation,* such as national defense, with both widespread benefits and widespread costs. Box 2 shows *special-interest legislation,* such as farm subsidies, with concentrated benefits but widespread costs. Box 3 shows *populist legislation,* such as tort reform, with widespread benefits but concentrated costs. And Box 4 shows *competing-interest legislation,* such as labor union issues, with both concentrated benefits and concentrated costs.

The following case study considers a special-interest program—milk price supports.

POPULIST LEGISLATION

Legislation with widespread benefits but concentrated costs

COMPETING-INTEREST LEGISLATION

Legislation that confers concentrated benefits on one group by imposing concentrated costs on another group

---

EXHIBIT 3

Categories of Legislation Based on the Distribution of Costs and Benefits

	Distribution of Benefits	
	Widespread	**Concentrated**
Widespread	1. Traditional Public Goods —National defense	2. Special Interest —Farm subsidies
Concentrated	3. Populist —Tort reform	4. Competing Interest —Labor union issues

Distribution of Costs

Case **Study**

Public Policy

eActivity

"Provisions of the Federal Agriculture Improvement and Reform Act of 1996," available at http://www.ers.usda.gov/publications/aib729/, describes legislation aimed at reducing farmers' reliance on price support programs. You can learn about its impact on the dairy sector by reading the summary of "Structure of Dairy Markets: Past, Present, Future" at http://www.ers.usda.gov/publications/aer757. Which type of firm buys most of the fluid milk produced by dairy farmers? What does the future hold for dairy markets?

Farm Subsidies

The Agricultural Marketing Agreement Act became law in 1937 to prevent what was viewed as "ruinous competition" among farmers. In the years since, the government introduced a variety of policies that set floor prices for a wide range of farm products. Farm subsidies will cost U.S. taxpayers at least $20 billion a year for the next decade. In much of the country, milk prices are the most regulated of farm products. Explaining the intricacies of the price support program for milk takes up three volumes of the *Code of Federal Regulations,* and administering the regulations employs hundreds of people at the U.S. Department of Agriculture—more than oversee the entire federal budget in the Office of Management and Budget.

Let's see how price supports work in the dairy industry, using a hypothetical example. Exhibit 4 simplifies the market for milk. Without government intervention, suppose the market price of milk would average $1.50 per gallon for 100 million gallons per month. In long-run equilibrium, dairy farmers would earn a normal profit in this competitive industry. Consumer surplus is shown by the blue-shaded area. Recall that consumer surplus is the difference between the most that consumers would be willing to pay for that quantity and the amount they actually pay.

But suppose the dairy lobby persuades Congress that the market price is too low, so legislation establishes a price floor for milk of, say, $2.50 per gallon. The higher price encourages farmers to increase the quantity supplied to 150 million gallons per month. Consumers, however, reduce their quantity demanded to 75 million gallons per month. To make

EXHIBIT 4

Effects of Milk Price Supports

In the absence of government intervention, the market price of milk is $1.50 per gallon, and 100 million gallons are sold per month. If government establishes a floor price of $2.50 per gallon, then the quantity supplied will increase and the quantity demanded will decrease. To maintain the higher price, the government must buy the excess quantity at $2.50 per gallon.

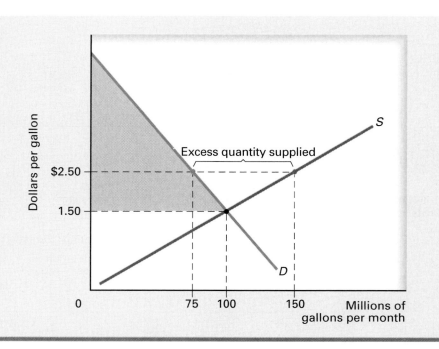

the higher price stick, the government must buy the 75 million gallons of surplus milk generated by the floor price or somehow get dairy farmers to restrict their output to 75 million gallons per month. For example, to reduce production, the government could buy cows from farmers (as occurred in the 1980s).

Consumers end up paying dearly to subsidize farmers. First, the price consumers pay increases by $1 per gallon. Second, as taxpayers, consumers must also buy the surplus milk or otherwise pay farmers not to supply that milk. And third, if the government buys the surplus, taxpayers must then pay for storage. So consumers pay $2.50 for each gallon they buy on the market, another $2.50 for each surplus gallon the government buys, plus, say, an extra $0.50 per gallon to convert surplus milk into powder and to store it. Instead of paying a free-market price of just $1.50 per gallon, the typical consumer-taxpayer in effect pays $5.50 (=$2.50 + $2.50 + $0.50), or nearly four times that, for each gallon actually consumed.

How do farmers make out? Each receives an extra $1 per gallon in revenue compared to the free-market price. As farmers increase their output, however, their marginal cost of production increases. At the margin, the higher price just offsets the higher marginal cost of production. The subsidy also increases the value of specialized resources, such as cows and especially grazing land. Farmers who own these resources when the subsidy is introduced will benefit. Farmers who purchase them after that (and, hence, after resource prices have increased) earn only a normal rate of return on their investment. Because farm subsidies were originally introduced more than half a century ago, most farmers today earn just a normal return on their investment, despite the billions spent annually on subsidies.

If the extra $1 per gallon that farmers receive for milk were pure profit, farm profits would increase by $150 million per month. But consumer-taxpayer costs increase by $300 million per month ($75 million for milk consumed, plus $187.5 million in higher taxes to pay for the 75 million surplus gallons purchased by the government, plus $37.5 million to store the 75 million surplus gallons). Thus, costs to consumer-taxpayers are double the farmers' maximum possible gain of $150 million. Like other special-interest legislation, farm subsidies have a negative impact on the economy, as the losses outweigh the gains. The only winners are those who owned specialized resources when the subsidy was first introduced. New farmers must pay more to get in a position to reap the subsidies. About half the nation's agricultural land is rented out by landlords who likely purchased the land after the subsidy program went into effect, and thus already paid to get in on the subsidy. Farmers who lease that land pay higher land rent because of the subsidy. Ironically, subsidies aimed at preserving the family farm raise the costs of becoming a farmer.

The dairy industry is supported in other ways. Some states ensure even higher price floors. Foreign imports of liquid milk are tightly restricted. Other laws promote the consumption of dairy products more generally. For example, some states prohibit restaurants from serving margarine instead of butter unless the customer specifically requests margarine.

The profound long-run problem for dairy farmers is that technological breakthroughs, such as genetically engineered hormones that stimulate milk production, have increased the milk yield per cow, making each farmer far more productive. Yet, despite the widely advertised "Got milk?" and milk-mustache campaigns, milk consumption remains flat. The combination of increased supply and stagnant demand creates excess quantity supplied.

Sources: "The Farmland Bubble," *New York Times*, 26 December 2003; "U.S. Dairy Farmers Seek Government Help to Slow Milk Product Imports," *Dow Jones Newswire*, 13 December 2003; Scott Kilman, "Dairy Aisle's Secret: Milk Is a Cash Cow," *Wall Street Journal*, 28 July 2003; "Ditching the Peace," *Economist*, 1 January 2004; and the U.S. Department of Agriculture's dairy products site at http://www.ams.usda.gov/dairy/index.htm.

Rent Seeking

An important feature of representative democracy is the incentive and political power it offers participants to employ legislation to increase their wealth, either through direct transfers or through favorable public expenditures and regulations. Special-interest groups, such
as dairy farmers and trial lawyers, try to persuade elected officials to provide the special interest with some market advantage or some outright transfer or subsidy. Such benefits are
often called *rents*. The term in this context means that the government transfer or subsidy
constitutes a payment to the resource owner that exceeds the earnings necessary to call forth
that resource—*a payment exceeding opportunity cost*. The activity that interest groups undertake to secure these special favors from government is called *rent seeking*, a term already
introduced.

The government frequently bestows some special advantage on a producer or group of
producers, and abundant resources are expended to acquire these rights. For example, *political action committees*, known more popularly as *PACs*, contribute millions to congressional
campaigns. About 4,000 PACs try to shape federal legislation. The top contributors recently
included the tobacco lobby and the American Trial Lawyers Association. Tobacco interests
would like to influence cigarette legislation, and lawyers fear reforms that would limit liability lawsuits.

To the extent that special-interest groups engage in rent seeking, they shift resources
from productive endeavors that create output and income to activities that focus more on
transferring income to their special interests. *Resources employed to persuade government to redistribute income and wealth are unproductive because they do nothing to increase total output and
usually end up reducing it*. Often many firms compete for the same government advantage,
thereby wasting still more resources. If the advantage conferred by government on some
special-interest group requires higher income taxes, the net return individuals expect from
working and investing will fall, so they may work less and invest less. If this happens, productive activity declines.

As a firm's profitability becomes more and more dependent on decisions made in Washington, resources are diverted from productive activity to rent seeking, or lobbying efforts,
to gain special advantage. One firm may thrive because it secured some special government
advantage at a critical time; another firm may fail because its managers were more concerned with productive efficiency than with rent seeking.

Think of the economy's output in a particular period as depicted by a pie. The pie represents the total value of goods and services produced. In answering the what, how, and for
whom questions introduced in Chapter 2, policy makers have three alternatives: (1) they
can introduce changes that increase the size of the pie (that is, positive-sum changes);
(2) they can decide simply to carve up the existing pie differently (redistribute income); or
(3) they can start fighting over how the pie is carved up, causing some of it to end up on
the floor (negative-sum changes).

Special-interest groups have little incentive to make the economy more efficient. In fact,
they will usually support legislation that transfers wealth to them even if the economy's
overall efficiency declines. For example, suppose that the American Trial Lawyers Association is able to revise product liability laws in a way that boosts lawyers' annual incomes by a
total of $1 billion, or about $1,900 for each lawyer in private practice. Suppose, too, that this
measure drives up insurance premiums, raising the total cost of production by, say, $2 billion
per year. Lawyers themselves will have to bear part of this higher cost, but because they account for only about 1 percent of the spending in the economy, they will bear only about

1 percent of the $2 billion in higher costs, or about $20 million. This amounts to about $40 per lawyer per year. Thus, the legislation is a good deal for lawyers because their annual incomes grow about $1,900 each but their annual costs increase only about $40 each, resulting in the net average gain of $1,860 per lawyer. Much special-interest legislation leads to a net reduction in social welfare. For example, some of the nation's best minds are occupied with devising schemes to avoid taxes or divert income to favored groups at the expense of market efficiency.

There are hundreds of special-interest groups representing farmers, physicians, lawyers, teachers, manufacturers, barbers, and so on. One way special interests try to gain access to the political process is through campaign contributions. The tricky issue of campaign finance reform is discussed in the following case study.

Campaign Finance Reform

Critics have long argued that American politics is awash in special-interest money. Most Americans seem to agree. Two-thirds of those surveyed in a recent poll support public financing of campaigns if it eliminates funding from large private donations and organized interest groups. Since the 1970s, presidential campaigns have been in part publicly funded, but not congressional races. Candidates who accept public funds must abide by campaign spending limits. But, by rejecting public funds in the primary, as John Kerry and George W. Bush did in the 2004 presidential primaries, candidates can ignore spending limits.

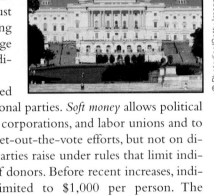

© Photodisc/Getty Images

Senators John McCain and Russ Feingold proposed a ban on so-called soft-money contributions to national parties. *Soft money* allows political parties to raise unlimited amounts from individuals, corporations, and labor unions and to spend it freely on party-building activities, such as get-out-the-vote efforts, but not on direct support for candidates. *Hard money* is the cash parties raise under rules that limit individual contributions and require public disclosure of donors. Before recent increases, individual contributions to candidates had been limited to $1,000 per person. The McCain-Feingold measure was approved as the Bipartisan Campaign Reform Act of 2002. The act bans the solicitation of soft money by federal candidates and prohibits political advertising by special interest groups in the weeks just before an election. The contribution limit was raised from $1,000 to $2,000.

Limits on special-interest contributions may reduce their influence in the political process, but such limits heighten the current advantage of incumbents. About 95 percent of congressional incumbents are reelected. Incumbents benefit from a taxpayer-funded staff and free mailing privileges; these mailings often amount to campaign literature masquerading as official communications. Limits on campaign spending also magnify the advantages of incumbency by reducing a challenger's ability to appeal directly to voters. Some liberal *and* conservative thinkers agree that the supply of political money should be increased, not decreased. As Curtis Gans, director of the Committee for the Study of the American Electorate argued, "The overwhelming body of scholarly research . . . indicates that low spending limits will undermine political competition by enhancing the existing advantages of incumbency." *Money matters more to challengers than to incumbents* because the public knows less about challengers than about incumbents. Challengers must be able to spend enough

C a s e **S t u d y**

Public Policy

eActivity
Common Cause, a nonpartisan lobbying group promoting accountable government, provides information on special interest groups that donated to political campaigns at http://www.commoncause.org/laundromat. See the list of profiles of the largest soft money donors in past elections. You can visit http://www.policyalmanac.org/government/campaign_finance.shtml for a summary of the new law.

to get their message out. One study found a positive relationship between spending by challengers and their election success but found no relationship between spending by incumbents and their reelection success. So campaign spending limits favor incumbents.

According to Common Cause, national party groups took in a total of $441 million in soft money for the 2000 election, with $225 million raised by Republicans and $216 million by Democrats. That money was used to fund presidential and congressional races across the country. Nearly half a billion dollars sounds like a lot of money, but Coke spent over four times that on advertising in 2000. The point is that legislation often has unintended consequences. Efforts to limit campaign spending may or may not reduce the influence of special-interest groups, but *a limit reduces a challenger's ability to reach the voters and thereby increase the advantage of incumbency, thus reducing political competition.*

Sources: David Stout, "Divided Court Says Government Can Ban 'Soft Money,'" *New York Times*; 10 December 2003; Jeanne Cummings et al., "Supreme Court Upholds Key Parts of New Campaign-Finance Law," *Wall Street Journal*, 11 December 2003; the Federal Election Commission at http://www.fec.gov/; and Common Cause at http://www.commoncause.org.

The Underground Economy

A per-unit government subsidy promotes production, as we saw in the case study on milk price supports. Conversely, a per-unit tax discourages production. Perhaps it would be more accurate to say that when government taxes productive activity, less production gets *reported*. If you ever worked as a waitress or waiter, did you faithfully report all your tip income to the Internal Revenue Service? If you didn't, your unreported income became part of the underground economy. The **underground economy** is a term used for all market activity that goes unreported either to avoid taxes or because the activity itself is illegal. Income arising in the underground economy ranges from unreported tips to the earnings of drug dealers.

The introduction of a tax on productive activity has two effects. First, resource owners may supply less of the taxed resource because the after-tax wage declines. Second, to evade taxes, some people will shift from the formal, reported economy to an underground, "off the books" economy. Thus, when the government taxes market exchange or the income it generates, less market activity gets reported.

We should take care to distinguish between tax *avoidance* and tax *evasion*. Tax avoidance is a *legal* attempt to arrange one's economic affairs to pay the least tax possible, such as buying municipal bonds because they yield interest free of federal income taxes. Tax evasion, on the other hand, is *illegal;* it takes the form of either failing to file a tax return or filing a fraudulent return by understating income or overstating deductions. Research around the world indicates that the underground economy grows more when (1) government regulations increase, (2) tax rates increase, and (3) government corruption is more widespread.[2]

The U.S. Commerce Department estimates that official figures capture only about 90 percent of U.S. income. An Internal Revenue Service survey estimates that only about 90 percent of taxable income gets reported on tax returns. These studies suggest an underground economy of about $1 trillion in 2004.

Those who pursue rent-seeking activity and those involved in the underground economy view government from opposite sides. Rent seekers want government to become actively involved in transferring wealth to them, but those in the underground economy want to avoid government contact. *Subsidies and other advantages bestowed by government draw some groups closer to government; taxes drive others underground.*

UNDERGROUND ECONOMY

An expression used to describe market activity that goes unreported either because it is illegal or because those involved want to evade taxes

HOMEWORK
Xpress!
Ask the Instructor
Video

2. For a summary of these studies, see Simon Johnson et al., "Regulatory Discretion and the Unofficial Economy," *American Economic Review* 88 (May 1998): 387–392.

Bureaucracy and Representative Democracy

Elected representatives approve legislation, but the task of implementing that legislation is typically left to **bureaus,** which are government departments and agencies whose activities are financed by appropriations from legislative bodies.

BUREAUS

Government agencies charged with implementing legislation and financed by appropriations from legislative bodies

Ownership and Funding of Bureaus

We can get a better feel for government bureaus by comparing them to corporations. Ownership of a corporation is based on the shares owned by stockholders. Stockholders share any profit or loss arising from the firm's operations. Stockholders also get to vote on important corporate matters based on the number of shares owned. Ownership in a corporation is *transferable:* the shares can be bought and sold in the stock market. Taxpayers are in a sense the "owners" of government bureaus. If the bureau earns a "profit," taxes may decline; if the bureau operates at a "loss," as most do, this loss must be made up by taxes. Each taxpayer has just one vote, regardless of the taxes he or she pays. Ownership in the bureau is surrendered only if the taxpayer dies or moves out of the jurisdiction; ownership is not transferable—it cannot be bought or sold directly.

Whereas firms receive their revenue when customers voluntarily purchase their products, bureaus are typically financed by a budget appropriation from the legislature. Most of this budget comes from taxpayers. Some bureaus earn revenue through user charges, such as admission fees to state parks or tuition at state colleges, but supplementary funds for these activities often come from taxpayers. Because of these differences in the forms of ownership and in the sources of revenue, bureaus have different incentives than do for-profit firms, so they are likely to behave differently.

Ownership and Organizational Behavior

A central assumption of economics is that people behave rationally and respond to economic incentives. The more tightly compensation is linked to individual incentives, the more people will behave in accordance with those incentives. For example, if a letter carrier's pay is based on customer satisfaction, the carrier will make a greater effort to deliver mail promptly and intact.

A private firm receives a steady stream of consumer feedback. If the price is too high or too low to clear the market, surpluses or shortages become obvious. Not only is consumer feedback abundant, but the firm's owners have a profit incentive to act on that information to satisfy consumer wants. The promise of profits also creates incentives to produce output at minimum cost. Thus, the firm's owners stand to gain from any improvement in customer satisfaction or any reduction in cost.

Because public goods and services are not sold in markets, government bureaus receive less consumer feedback and have less incentive to act on any feedback they do receive. There are usually no prices and no obvious shortages or surpluses. For example, how would you know whether there was a shortage or a surplus of police protection in your community? (Would gangs of police officers hanging around Dunkin' Donuts indicate a surplus?) Not only do bureaus receive less consumer feedback than firms do, they also have less incentive to act on the information available. Because any "profit" or "loss" arising in the bureau is spread among all taxpayers, and because there is no transferability of ownership, bureaus have less incentive to satisfy customers or to produce their output using the least-cost combination of resources. (Laws prevent bureaucrats from taking home any "profit.")

Some pressure for customer satisfaction and cost minimization may be communicated by voters to their elected representatives and thereby to the bureaus. But this discipline is not very precise, particularly because any gains or losses in efficiency are spread across taxpayers. For example, suppose that you are one of a million taxpayers in a city and you learn that by having FedEx Kinko's do all public copying, the city could save $1 million a year. If, through letters to the editor and calls to local officials, you somehow convince the city to adopt this cost-saving measure, you, as a typical taxpayer, would save yourself about a dollar a year in taxes.

Voters can leave a jurisdiction if they believe government is inefficient. This mechanism, whereby people "vote with their feet," does promote some efficiency and consumer satisfaction at the state and local levels, but it's rather crude. What if you like some public programs but not others? Moreover, voters dissatisfied with the biggest spender, the federal government, cannot easily vote with their feet. Even if you move abroad, you, as a U.S. citizen, must still pay U.S. federal taxes on your worldwide income (some other countries, such as Canada, tax only domestic income).

Because of differences between public and private organizations—in the owners' ability both to transfer ownership and to appropriate profits—we expect bureaus to be less concerned with satisfying consumer demand and with minimizing costs than private firms are. A variety of empirical studies compares costs for products that are provided by both public bureaus and private firms, such as garbage collection. Of those studies that show a difference, most find private firms to be more efficient.

Bureaucratic Objectives

Assuming that bureaus are not simply at the beck and call of the legislature—that is, assuming that bureaucrats have some autonomy—what sort of objectives will *they* pursue? The traditional view is that bureaucrats are "public servants," who try to serve the public as best they can. No doubt many public employees do just that, but is this a realistic assumption for bureaucrats more generally? Why should we assume self-sacrificing behavior by public-sector employees when we make no such assumption about private-sector employees?

One widely discussed theory of bureaucratic behavior claims that bureaus try to *maximize their budget,* for along with a bigger budget come size, prestige, amenities, staff, and pay—all features that are valued by bureaucrats.[3] According to this view, bureaus are monopoly suppliers of their output to the legislature. Rather than charge a price per unit, bureaus offer the legislature the entire amount as a package deal in return for the requested appropriation. This theory assumes that the legislature has only limited ability to dig into the budget and cut particular items. If the legislature does try to cut the bureau's budget, the bureau will threaten to make those cuts as painful to the legislature and constituents as possible. For example, if city officials attempt to reduce the school budget, school bureaucrats, rather than increase teaching loads, may threaten to eliminate kindergarten, abolish the high school football team, disband the school band, or cut textbook purchases. If such threats force the legislature to back off, the government budget turns out to be larger than most taxpayers would prefer. *Budget maximization results in a larger budget than that desired by the median voter.* The key to this argument is that bureaus are monopoly suppliers of the product and elected officials have only limited ability to cut that budget. If taxpayers have alternatives in the private sector, the monopoly power of the bureau is diminished.

3. William A. Niskanen Jr., in *Bureaucracy and Representative Government* (New York: Aldine-Atherton, 1971).

Private Versus Public Production

Simply because some goods and services are financed by the government does not mean that they must be produced by the government. Elected officials may contract directly with private firms to produce public output. For example, city officials may contract with a private firm to handle garbage collection for the city. Profit-making firms now provide everything from fire protection to prisons in some jurisdictions. Elected officials may also use some combination of bureaus and firms to produce the desired output. For example, the Pentagon, a giant bureau, hires and trains military personnel, yet contracts with private firms to develop and produce various weapon systems. State governments typically hire private contractors to build roads but employ state workers to maintain them. The mix of firms and bureaus varies over time and across jurisdictions, but the trend is toward increased *privatization,* or production by the private sector, of public goods and services.

When governments produce public goods and services, they are using *the internal organization of the government*—the bureaucracy—to supply the product. When governments contract with private firms to produce public goods and services, they are using *the market* to supply the product. While private firms have more incentives to be efficient than bureaus do, legislators sometimes prefer dealing with bureaus. In situations where it would be difficult to specify a contract for the public good in question, a bureau may be more responsive to the legislature's concerns than a for-profit firm would be. For example, suppose the service provided by social workers is put out for bid. The firm that wins the bid may be tempted to skimp on quality, particularly if quality can be determined only by direct observation at the time the service is provided. The governments would have difficulty monitoring the service quality provided by a private contractor. The services of social workers might be better provided by a government bureau. Because profit is not its goal, a bureau may be less inclined to minimize cost by reducing quality.

Conclusion

Governments attempt to address market failures in the private economy. But simply turning problems of perceived market failure over to government may not always be the best solution, because government has limitations and failings of its own. Participation in markets is based on voluntary exchange. Governments, however, have the legal power to enforce public choices. We should employ at least as high a standard in judging the performance of government, where allocations have the force of law, as we do in judging the private market, where allocations are decided by voluntary exchange between consenting parties. In other words, we should scrutinize a system that is compulsory at least as much as we scrutinize a system that is voluntary. After all, nobody is forcing you to buy tofu, but you can be forced to pay taxes for programs you may not like.

SUMMARY

1. Private goods are rival and exclusive, such as a pizza. Public goods are nonrival and nonexclusive, such as national defense. Goods that are in between public and private goods include quasi-public goods, which are nonrival but exclusive, such as cable TV, and open-access goods, which are rival but nonexclusive, such as ocean fish. Because private-sector producers cannot easily exclude nonpayers from consuming a public good, public goods are typically provided by government, which has the power to collect taxes.

2. Public choice based on majority rule usually reflects the preferences of the median voter. Other voters often must "buy" either more or less of the public good than they would prefer.

3. Producers have an abiding interest in any legislation that affects their livelihood. Consumers, however, purchase thousands of different goods and services and thus have no special interest in legislation affecting any particular product. Most consumers adopt a posture of rational ignorance, because the expected costs of keeping up with special-interest issues usually outweigh the expected benefits.

4. The intense interest that producer groups express in relevant legislation, coupled with the rational ignorance of voters on most issues, leaves government vulnerable to rent seeking by special interests. Elected officials trying to maximize their political support may serve special interests at the expense of the public interest.

5. Bureaus differ from firms in the amount of consumer feedback they receive, in their incentives to minimize costs, and in the transferability of their ownership. Because of these differences, bureaus may not be as efficient or as sensitive to consumer preferences as for-profit firms are.

QUESTIONS FOR REVIEW

1. *(Private and Public Goods)* Distinguish among private goods, quasi-public goods, open-access goods, and public goods. Provide examples of each.

2. *(Free Rider)* Does the free-rider problem arise from the characteristics of consumption rivalry, excludability, or both?

3. *(Median Voter Model)* In a single-issue majority vote, such as the TV example in this chapter, will the median voter always get his or her most preferred outcome?

4. *(Representative Democracy)* Major political parties typically offer "middle of the road" platforms rather than take extreme positions. Is this consistent with the concepts of the median voter and rational ignorance discussed in this chapter?

5. *(Distribution of Costs and Benefits)* Why are consumer interest groups usually less effective than producer lobbies in influencing legislation?

6. *(Distribution of Costs and Benefits)* Which groups typically bear the costs and which groups enjoy the benefits of (a) traditional public goods, (b) special-interest legislation, and (c) competing-interest legislation?

7. *(C a s e **S t u d y** : Farm Subsidies)* "Subsidizing the price of milk or other agricultural products is not very expensive considering how many consumers there are in the United States. Therefore, there is little harmful effect from such subsidies." Evaluate this statement.

8. *(C a s e **S t u d y** : Farm Subsidies)* Subsidy programs are likely to have a number of secondary effects in addition to the direct effect on dairy prices. What impact do you suppose farm subsidies are likely to have on the following?

   a. Housing prices
   b. Technological change in the dairy industry
   c. The price of dairy product substitutes

9. *(Rent Seeking)* Explain how rent seeking can lead to a drop in production of goods and services. What role might the underground economy play in lessening the drop in productive activities?

10. *(The Underground Economy)* What is the underground economy? What is the impact on the underground economy of instituting a tax on a certain productive activity?

11. *(Bureaucracy and Representative Democracy)* How do the incentives and feedback for government bureaus differ from those for profit-making firms?

12. *(Bureaucracy and Representative Democracy)* A firm is described as combining managerial coordination with market exchange in order to produce its good or service. Does similar behavior occur in government bureaus? Explain.

13. *(Optimal Provision of Public Goods)* Using at least two individual consumers, show how the market demand curve is derived from individual demand curves (a) for a private good and (b) for a public good. Once you have derived the market demand curve in each case, introduce a market supply curve and then show the optimal level of production.

14. *(Distribution of Costs and Benefits)* Suppose that the government decides to guarantee an above-market price for a good by buying up any surplus at that above-market price.

Using a conventional supply-demand diagram, illustrate the following gains and losses from such a price support:

a. The loss of consumer surplus
b. The gain of producer surplus in the short run
c. The cost of running the government program (assuming no storage costs)
d. What is the total cost of the program to consumers?
e. Are the costs and benefits of the support program widespread or concentrated?

15. *(Rational Ignorance)* Loren Lomasky, in "The Booth and Consequences" at http://www.magnolia.net/~leonf/sd/tbac.html wrestles with the question of why people bother to vote. Read the article and decide for yourself: Is voting rational?

16. *(Wall Street Journal)* "The Politics & Policy" column in the First Section of the *Wall Street Journal* is a good source for articles on politics at every level. Choose one such article and decide which it describes: special-interest or tradi-

tional public-goods legislation. Classify the benefits and the costs as either concentrated or widespread.

17. The federal budget revenues and expenditures are detailed at http://www.whitehouse.gov/omb/budget. Browse the site and locate the section detailing spending. Find several expenditures that you find interesting. Identify the groups bearing the costs and those reaping the benefits of the expenditures.

*These exercises require access to McEachern Homework Xpress! If Homework Xpress! did not come with your book, visit **http://homeworkxpress.swlearning.com** to purchase.*

1. When the Red River floods, the Prescotts—who live on the east side of the river—and the Walkers—who live on the west side of the river—suffer flood damages. A project to deepen the river by dredging would reduce the damages for both families. The deeper the dredging, the less the damages. The marginal benefits to each family are given in the table. Plot each family's demand curve for the project. Calculate and plot the market demand curve for the project.

Depth in feet	Prescotts	Walkers
0	—	—
10	$10	$6
20	8	3
30	6	0
40	4	0
50	2	0

2. Rice farmers find that they face the market conditions illustrated in the table on the next page. Plot the demand

and supply curves given these data. Identify the market equilibrium price and quantity. Rice farmers are well organized, and have promoted rice consumption with their ad campaign "Rice is nice." Despite this effort, they are not satisfied with the market price and they successfully lobby the government for a price support of $0.80 per bushel. Show the quantity that would be supplied and the quantity that would be demanded at this government-mandated price.

Quantity (millions of bushels)	Price per Bushel	Marginal Cost per Bushel
0	—	$0.00
1	$1.00	0.20
2	0.90	0.40
3	0.80	0.60
4	0.70	0.80
5	0.60	1.00
6	0.50	1.20

3. Rice farmers find that for each $.05 increase in the government mandated price, each farmer's revenues increase by $50,000. The lobbying cost per farmer for each $.05 increment in price support is increasing, as illustrated in the table below, because convincing additional politicians with less interest in the rice industry becomes increasingly expensive. Plot the marginal revenue per increase in the subsidy and the marginal cost per farmer in a diagram, and identify the level of subsidy worth lobbying for.

Subsidy per Bushel	Marginal Cost of Lobbying per Farmer
$0.00	$ 0
0.05	5,000
0.10	15,000
0.15	30,000
0.20	50,000
0.25	75,000
0.30	105,000

Externalities and the Environment

© Tim Brown/Index Stock Imagery

The rivers in Jakarta, Indonesia, are dead—killed by acid, alcohol, and oil. Coral

reefs in the South Pacific have been ripped apart by dynamite fishing. The

tropical rainforest is shrinking because of slash-and-burn claims on the land's re-

sources. In Mexico City, some people buy oxygen tanks for home use because the

air is so bad. And some streams in Colorado are still considered toxic from gold min-

ing that ended more than a century ago. What does all this have to do with econom-

ics? These environmental problems are all negative externalities, which result from

the actions of producers or consumers that affect bystanders. Markets can allocate

resources efficiently only as long as property rights are well defined and can be eas-

ily enforced. But property rights to clean water, air, and soil, to fish in the ocean, to

peace and quiet, and to scenic vistas are hard to establish and enforce. This lack of

property rights to some resources results in externalities.

Externalities may be either negative, such as air and water pollution, or positive, such as the general improvement in the civic climate that results from better education. This chapter discusses externalities and explores how well-designed public policies can increase efficiency by reducing negative externalities and increasing positive externalities. Topics discussed include:

- Exhaustible resources
- Renewable resources
- Common-pool problem
- Private property rights
- Optimal pollution

- Marginal social cost
- Marginal social benefit
- Coase theorem
- Markets for pollution rights
- Environmental protection

Externalities and the Common-Pool Problem

Let's begin by distinguishing between exhaustible resources and renewable resources. An **exhaustible resource** such as oil or coal does not renew itself and so is available in a finite amount. Technology may improve the ability to extract these resources from the ground, but each gallon of oil burned is gone forever. Sooner or later, all oil wells will run dry. The world's oil reserves are *exhaustible*.

Renewable Resources

A resource is **renewable** if, when used conservatively, it can be drawn on indefinitely. Thus, timber is a renewable resource if seedlings replace felled trees. The atmosphere and rivers are renewable resources to the extent that they can absorb and neutralize a certain level of pollutants. More generally, biological resources like fish, game, forests, rivers, grasslands, and agricultural soil are renewable if managed appropriately.

Some renewable resources are also open-access goods, an idea introduced in the previous chapter. An open-access resource is rival in consumption, but exclusion is costly. Fish caught in the ocean, for example, are not available for others to catch, so fish are rival in consumption. Yet it would be difficult for a person or a firm to "own" fish still swimming in the ocean and to prevent others from catching them, so ocean fish are nonexclusive. An open-access good is often subject to the **common-pool problem,** which results because people consume such a good until the marginal value of additional use drops to zero. People will fish the ocean until it becomes "fished out." Open-access goods are overfished, overhunted, overused, and overharvested. Because the atmosphere is an open-access resource, the air gets used as a dump for unwanted gases. Air pollution is a negative externality imposed on society by polluters.

In a market system, specific individuals usually own the rights to resources and therefore have a strong interest in using those resources efficiently. *Private property rights*, a term introduced in Chapter 2, allow individuals to use resources or to charge others for their use. Private property rights are defined and enforced by government, by informal social actions, and by ethical norms. But because specifying and enforcing property rights to open-access resources, such as the air, are quite costly or even impossible, these resources usually are not owned as private property.

Pollution and other negative externalities arise because there are no practical, enforceable, private property rights to open-access resources, such as the air. Market prices usually fail to include the costs that negative externalities impose on society. For example, the price you pay for a gal-

EXHAUSTIBLE RESOURCE

A resource in fixed supply, such as crude oil or coal

RENEWABLE RESOURCE

A resource that regenerates itself and so can be used indefinitely if used conservatively, such as a properly managed forest

COMMON-POOL PROBLEM

Unrestricted access to a resource results in overuse until its marginal value drops to zero

lon of gasoline does not reflect the costs imposed by the dirtier air and the greater traffic congestion your driving creates. Electric rates in the Midwest do not reflect the negative externalities, or external costs, that sulfur dioxide emissions impose on people living down-wind from fossil-fueled power plants. Note that externalities are unintended side effects of actions that are themselves useful and purposeful. Electricity producers, for example, did not go into business to pollute.

Resolving the Common-Pool Problem

Users of the atmosphere, waterways, wildlife, or other open-access resources tend to ignore the impact of their use on the resource's renewal ability. As quality and quantity diminish from overuse, the resource grows scarcer and could disappear. For example, Georges Bank, located off the New England coast, long one of the world's most productive fishing grounds, became so depleted by overfishing that by the 1990s the catch was down 85 percent from peak years.[1] The United Nations reports that 11 of the world's 15 primary fishing grounds are seriously depleted.

By imposing restrictions on resource use, government regulations may be able to reduce the common-pool problem. Output restrictions or taxes could force firms to use the re-source at a rate that is socially optimal. For example, in the face of the tendency to overfish and to catch fish before they are sufficiently mature, the U.S. government has imposed a variety of restrictions on the fishing industry. The laws limit the total catch, the size of fish, the length of the fishing season, the equipment used, and other aspects of the business.

More generally, when imposing and enforcing private property rights would be too costly, government regulations may improve allocative efficiency. For example, stop signs and traffic lights allocate the scarce road space at an intersection, minimum size restrictions con-trol lobster fishing, hunting seasons control the stock of game, and official study hours may calm the din in the dormitory.

But not all regulations are equally efficient. For example, fishing authorities sometimes limit the total industry catch and allow all firms to fish until that total is reached. Conse-quently, when the fishing season opens, there is a mad scramble to catch as much as possible before the industry limit is reached. Because time is of the essence, fishing boats make no effort to fish selectively. And the catch reaches processors all at once, creating congestion throughout the supply chain. Also, each firm has an incentive to expand its fishing fleet to catch more in those precious few weeks. Thus, large fleets of technologically efficient fish-ing vessels operate for a few weeks until the limit is reached then sit in port for the rest of the year. Each firm is acting rationally, but the collective effect of the regulation is grossly inefficient in terms of social welfare. Consider the complicated and sometimes confounding fishing regulations in Iceland:

> The Icelandic government realized that it would have to curb the capac-ity of its own fleet. But the fishermen compensated by buying more trawlers. Then the government restricted the size of the fleet and the number of days at sea; the fishermen responded by buying larger, more efficient gear. The cod stocks continued to decline. In 1984, the govern-ment introduced quotas on species per vessel per season. This was a controversial and often wasteful system. A groundfish hauled up from 50 fathoms [300 feet] is killed by the change in pressure. But if it is a cod and the cod quota has been used up, it is thrown overboard. Or if the price of cod is low that week and cod happens to come in the haddock

1. Deborah Cramer, "Troubled Waters," *Atlantic Monthly* (June 1995): 22–26.

*net, the fishermen will throw them overboard because they do not want
to use up their cod quota when they are not getting a good price.*[2]

Ocean fish remain a common-pool resource because firms have not yet been able to establish and enforce rights to particular schools of fish. But advances in technology may some day allow the creation of private property rights to ocean fish, migrating birds, and other open-access resources. Establishing property rights to cattle on the Great Plains once seemed impossible, but the invention of barbed wire allowed ranchers to fence the range. In a sense, barbed wire tamed the Wild West.

Optimal Level of Pollution

Economics
in the Movies

Though the science is far from resolved, research suggests that the sulfur dioxide emitted by coal-fired electricity generators mixes with moisture in the air to form sulfuric acid, which is carried by the prevailing winds and falls as acid rain. Many argue that acid rain has killed lakes and forests and has corroded buildings, bridges, and other structures. Electricity production, therefore, involves the external cost of using the atmosphere as a gas dump. For example, Ohio is the largest U.S. polluter based on coal-fired plants located there.[3] In this section, we analyze this externality problem.

External Costs with Fixed Technology

Suppose *D* in Exhibit 1 depicts the demand for electricity in the Midwest. Recall that a demand curve reflects consumers' marginal benefit of each quantity. The lower horizontal line

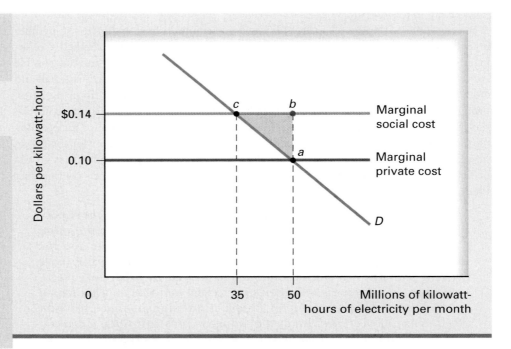

EXHIBIT 1

Negative Externalities: The Market for Electricity in the Midwest

If producers base their output on marginal private cost, 50 million kilowatt-hours of electricity are produced per month. The marginal external cost of electricity reflects the cost of pollution imposed on society. The marginal social cost curve includes both the marginal private cost and the marginal external cost. If producers base their output decisions on marginal social cost, only 35 million kilowatt-hours are produced, which is the optimal output. The total social gain from basing production on marginal social cost is reflected by the blue-shaded triangle.

2. Mark Kurlansky, *Cod: A Biography of the Fish That Changed the World* (New York: Walker & Co., 1997), p. 172.
3. Robert Melnbardis, "Report: Coal, Oil-Fired Power Plants Top Polluters," *Reuters,* 20 July 2001.

reflects the marginal private cost of electricity. If producers base their pricing and output decisions on their private marginal costs, the equilibrium quantity per month is 50 million kilowatt-hours and the equilibrium price is $0.10 per kilowatt-hour. At that price and quantity, the marginal private cost of production just equals the marginal benefit enjoyed by consumers of electricity.

Electricity production involves not only the private cost of the resources employed but also the external cost of using the atmosphere as a gas dump. Suppose that the marginal external cost imposed on the environment by the generation of electricity is $0.04 per kilowatt-hour. When the only way of reducing emissions is by reducing the generation of electricity, then the relationship between the production of electricity and the production of pollution is fixed; the pollution in this case occurs with **fixed-production technology.**

The vertical distance between the marginal private cost curve and the marginal social cost curve in Exhibit 1 shows the marginal external cost of $0.04 per kilowatt-hour. The **marginal social cost** includes both the marginal private cost and the marginal external cost that production imposes on society. Because the marginal external cost is assumed to be a constant $0.04 per kilowatt-hour, the two cost curves are parallel. Notice that at the private-sector equilibrium output level of 50 million kilowatt-hours, the marginal social cost, identified at point *b*, exceeds society's marginal benefit of electricity, identified on the demand curve at point *a*. The 50-millionth kilowatt-hour of electricity costs society $0.14 but yields only $0.10 of marginal benefit. Because the marginal social cost exceeds the marginal benefit, too much electricity is produced.

The efficient quantity of 35 million kilowatt-hours is found where the demand, or marginal benefit, curve intersects the marginal social cost curve. This intersection is identified at point *c*. How could output be restricted to the socially efficient amount? If regulators knew the demand and marginal cost curves, they could simply limit production to 35 million kilowatt-hours, the efficient quantity. Or, on each kilowatt hour, they could impose a tax equal to the marginal external cost of $0.04. Such a pollution tax would lift the marginal private cost curve up to the marginal social cost curve. Thus, the tax would bring private costs in line with social costs.

With a tax of $0.04 per kilowatt-hour, the equilibrium combination of price and output moves from point *a* to point *c*. The price rises from $0.10 to $0.14 per kilowatt-hour, and output falls to 35 million kilowatt-hours. Setting the tax equal to the marginal external cost results in the efficient level of output. At point *c*, the marginal social cost of production equals the marginal benefit. Notice that pollution is not eliminated at point *c*, but the utilities no longer generate electricity for which marginal social cost exceeds marginal benefit. The total social gain from reducing production to the socially optimal level is shown by the blue-shaded triangle in Exhibit 1. This triangle also measures the total social cost of allowing firms to ignore the external cost of pollution. Although Exhibit 1 offers a tidy solution, the external costs of pollution often cannot be easily calculated or taxed. At times, government intervention may result in more or less production than the optimal solution requires.

External Costs with Variable Technology

The previous example assumes that the only way to reduce pollution is to reduce output. But power companies, particularly in the long run, can usually change their resource mix to reduce emissions for any given level of electricity. If pollution can be reduced by altering the production process rather than by simply adjusting the quantity, these externalities are said to be produced under conditions of **variable technology.** With variable technology, the objective is to find the optimal level of pollution for a given quantity of electricity.

FIXED-PRODUCTION TECHNOLOGY

Occurs when the relationship between the output rate and the generation of an externality is fixed; the only way to reduce the externality is to reduce the output

MARGINAL SOCIAL COST

The sum of the marginal private cost and the marginal external cost of production or consumption

VARIABLE TECHNOLOGY

Occurs when the amount of externality generated at a given rate of output can be reduced by altering the production process

Let's look at Exhibit 2. The horizontal axis measures air quality for a given level of electricity. Air quality can be improved by adopting cleaner production technology. For example, coal-burning plants can be fitted with smoke "scrubbers" to reduce toxic emissions. Yet the production of cleaner air, like the production of other goods, is subject to diminishing marginal returns. Cutting emissions of the largest particles may involve simply putting a screen over the smokestack, but eliminating successively finer particles calls for more sophisticated and more expensive processes. Thus, the marginal social cost of cleaning the air increases, as shown by the upward-sloping marginal social cost curve in Exhibit 2.

MARGINAL SOCIAL BENEFIT

The sum of the marginal private benefit and the marginal external benefit of production or consumption

The **marginal social benefit** curve reflects the additional benefit society derives from better air quality. When air quality is poor, an improvement can save lives and thus will be valued by society more than when air quality is already excellent. Cleaner air, like other goods, has a declining marginal benefit to society (though the total benefit still increases). The marginal social benefit curve from cleaner air therefore slopes downward, as shown in Exhibit 2.

The optimal level of air quality for a given quantity of electricity is found at point *a*, where the marginal social benefit of cleaner air equals the marginal social cost. In this example, the optimal level of air quality is *A*. If firms made their production decisions based simply on their private cost—that is, if the cost of pollution is external to the firm—then firms would have no incentive to search for production methods that reduce pollution, so too much pollution would result.

What if the government regulators decree that air quality should exceed *A*? For example, suppose a law sets *A'* as the minimum acceptable level. The marginal social cost, identified as *c*, of achieving that level of air quality exceeds the marginal social benefit, identified

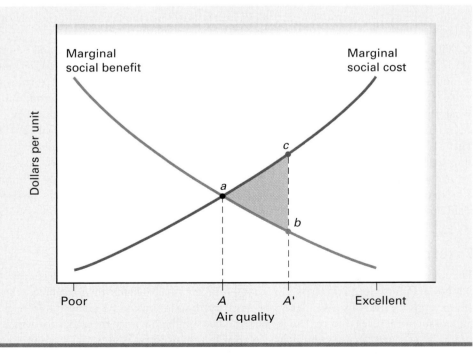

E X H I B I T **2**

The Optimal Level of Air Quality

The optimal level of air quality is found at point *a*, where the marginal social benefit of cleaner air equals its marginal social cost. If some higher level of air quality were dictated by the government, the marginal social cost would exceed the marginal social benefit, and social waste would result. The total social waste resulting from a higher-than-optimal air quality is shown by the pink-shaded triangle.

as *b*. The total social waste associated with imposing a greater-than-optimal level of air quality is shown by the pink-shaded triangle, *abc*. This area is the total amount by which the additional social costs of cleaner air (associated with a move from *A* to *A'*) exceed the additional social benefits. The idea that all pollution should be eliminated is a popular misconception. Improving air quality benefits society only if the marginal benefit of cleaner air exceeds its marginal cost.

What would happen to the optimal level of air quality if either the marginal costs or the marginal benefits of air quality changed? For example, suppose some technological breakthrough reduces the marginal cost of cleaning the air. As shown in panel (a) of Exhibit 3, the marginal social cost curve of air quality would shift downward to *MSC'*, thereby increasing the optimal level of air quality from *A* to *A'*. *The simple logic is that the lower the marginal cost of reducing pollution, other things constant, the greater the optimal level of air quality.*

An increase in the marginal benefit of air quality would have a similar effect. For example, recent research indicates that deaths from heart and lung disease would decrease 0.7 percent in large U.S. cities if suspended particulates decrease by just 1/100,000th of a gram per cubic meter of air.[4] This finding increases the perceived benefits of cleaner air. Thus, the marginal benefit of cleaner air would increase, as reflected in panel (b) of Exhibit 3 by a shift upward of the marginal social benefit curve to *MSB'*. As a result, the optimal level of air quality would increase. *The greater the marginal benefit of cleaner air, other things constant, the greater the optimal level of air quality.*

The atmosphere has the ability to cleanse itself of some emissions, but the destruction of the tropical rainforest has reduced this ability, as discussed in the following case study.

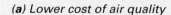

EXHIBIT 3

Effect of Changes in Costs and Benefits on the Optimal Level of Air Quality

Either a reduction in the marginal social cost of cleaner air, as shown in panel (a), or an increase in the marginal social benefit of cleaner air, as shown in panel (b), will increase the optimal level of air quality.

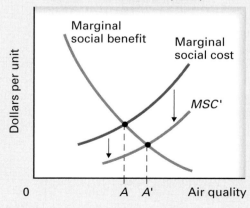

(a) Lower cost of air quality

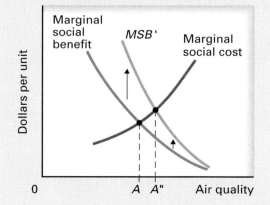

(b) Greater benefit of air quality

4. Jonathan M. Samet et al., "Fine Particulate Air Pollution and Mortality in 20 U.S. Cities, 1987–1994," *New England Journal of Medicine*, 14 December 2000.

Public Policy

Destruction of the Tropical Rainforests

The tropical rainforests have been called the lungs of the world because they naturally recycle carbon dioxide into oxygen and wood, thus eliminating heat-trapping gases and helping to maintain the world's atmospheric balance. These rainforests cover only 6 to 7 percent of the Earth's land surface but contain over half of the world's plant and animal species. The Amazon rainforest, for example, contains the largest collection of plant and animal life on Earth, along with 20 percent of the world's supply of fresh water. Of the tens of millions of species on Earth, scientists have named only about 1.5 million and have studied even fewer in depth.

© Wayne Lawler; Ecoscene/Corbis

The world's rainforests are located in countries that are relatively poor, such as Bolivia, Brazil, Colombia, Indonesia, Sudan, Venezuela, and the Philippines. Landless peasants and settlers burn down these forests to create farmland and pastures. Worse yet, to meet the worldwide demand for timber, loggers strip rainforests. Because the rainforest amounts to an open-access resource where property rights are not easily established, poor settlers and timber companies usually pursue a slash-and-burn approach. The world's tropical forests cover only half the area of 50 years ago, and another 30 million acres are lost each year—an area the size of Pennsylvania.

Burning the world's rainforests spells trouble for the environment. The fires add harmful gases to the atmosphere. The loss of trees reduces the atmosphere's ability to cleanse itself and increases flash flooding and mud slides. Stripped of trees, the land contains huge amounts of carbon subject to oxidization. Soil gets eroded by rains and baked by the sun and runs out of nutrients after just two growing seasons. With nutrients lost, the system is not very resilient—*it takes a century for a clear-cut forest to return to its original state.* The loss of the tropical forests involves other costs. A canopy of trees protects a rich, genetically diverse, ecosystem.

The tropical rainforests, by serving as the lungs of the world, confer benefits around the globe. But these benefits are usually ignored in the decision to clear the land. It's not the greed of peasants and timber companies that leads to inefficient, or wasteful, uses of resources. The problem is that the rainforests and the atmosphere are open-access resources that can be degraded with little immediate personal cost to those who clear the land. The costs of deforestation are imposed on people around the globe.

Poverty in the rainforest countries combined with the lack of legal title to the land encourage people to exploit that timber and soil rather than maximize the long-term value of these resources. For example, a secure property right to the land would reduce the need to clear a lot to claim some value. A farmer with title to the land could even leave a forest bequest to heirs. Research shows that people granted rights to the Amazon rainforest manage their land more conservatively. Property rights promote efficient harvesting of hardwoods and reforestation, allowing the forest to serve as an air filter. For example, the frequency of reforestation among those settlers granted land title was about 15 times greater than among those without title. Without title, the only way to gain some of the land's value is through a slash-and-burn approach. Thus, granting peasants and settlers property rights can help conserve the rainforests.

Other efforts are under way to protect the rainforests. With help from the World Bank and the World Wildlife Fund, Brazil plans to protect an area of rainforest the size of Colorado. And a timber company has given up harvesting rights to what is considered the most pristine rainforest in Africa. The United States now cancels some developing countries' government debts in exchange for their efforts to preserve their rainforests. To help crops that are environmentally friendly, the Rainforest Alliance now certifies farms using such methods. Other ideas are on the drawing board, but a systematic solution is still a long way off.

Sources: R. Godoy, et al., "The Role of Tenure Security and Private Time Preference in Neotropical Deforestation," *Land Economics*, 74 (May 1998): 162–170; Charles Wood and Robert Walker, "Saving the Trees by Helping the Poor," *Resources for the Future* (Summer 1999): 14–17; Jeffrey Ball, "If an Oak Eats CO_2 in a Forest, Who Gets the Emissions Credits?' *Wall Street Journal*, 10 December 2003; Juan Forero, "Seeking Balance: Growth vs. Culture in Amazon," *New York Times*, 10 December 2003; and the Rainforest Alliance at http://www.rainforest-alliance.org/.

The Coase Theorem

The traditional analysis of externalities assumes that market failures arise because people ignore the external effects of their actions. For example, suppose a research laboratory that tests delicate equipment is next door to a manufacturer of heavy machinery. The vibrations caused by the manufacturing process throw off the delicate equipment next door. Professor Ronald Coase, who won the Nobel Prize in 1991, would argue that the negative externality in this case is not necessarily imposed by the heavy machinery—rather, it arises from the incompatible activities of the two firms. The externality is the result of both vibrations created by the factory *and* the location of the testing lab next door. One possible solution might be to modify the machines in the factory; another might be to make the equipment in the testing lab more shock resistant or to move the lab elsewhere.

According to Coase, the efficient solution depends on which party can avoid the externality problem at the lower cost. Suppose it would cost $2 million for the factory to reduce vibrations enough for the lab to function normally. On the other hand, if the factory makes no changes, the lab can't insulate equipment enough to operate accurately, so the lab would have to relocate at a cost of $1 million. Based on this information, the least-cost solution would be for the testing lab to relocate at a cost of $1 million. Coase argues that, as long as transaction costs are low, the parties will reach the efficient solution if one party is assigned the property right. *This efficient solution will be achieved regardless of which party gets the property right.*

Suppose the testing lab is granted the right to operate free of vibrations from next door, so the testing lab can force the factory to reduce its vibration. Rather than cut vibrations at a cost of $2 million, the factory can pay the lab to relocate. Any payment greater than $1 million but less than $2 million will make both sides better off, because the lab would receive more than its moving cost and the factory would pay less than its cost of reducing vibrations. Thus, the lab will move, which is the efficient outcome.

Alternatively, suppose the factory is granted the right to generate vibrations in its production process, regardless of the impact on the testing lab. For the factory, this means business as usual. Because the minimum payment the factory would accept to reduce vibrations is $2 million, the lab would rather relocate at a cost of $1 million. Thus, whether property rights are granted to the lab or to the factory, the lab will move, which is the efficient, or least-cost, solution. The **Coase theorem** says that as long as bargaining costs are small, the assignment of property rights will generate an efficient solution to an externality problem regardless of which party is assigned property rights. A particular assignment of property rights determines only who incurs the externality costs, not the efficient outcome.

Inefficient outcomes do occur, however, when the transaction costs of arriving at a solution are high. For example, an airport located in a populated area would have difficulty negotiating noise levels with all the surrounding residents. Or a power plant emitting sulfur

COASE THEOREM

As long as bargaining costs are low, an efficient solution to the problem of externalities will be achieved by assigning property rights to one party or the other

dioxide would have trouble negotiating with the millions of people scattered across the downwind states. Or peasants contemplating clearing a portion of the tropical rainforest cannot negotiate with the millions, and perhaps, billions, of people ultimately affected by that decision. When the number of parties involved in the transaction is large, Coase's solution of assigning property rights isn't enough.

Markets for Pollution Rights

According to the Coase theorem, the assignment of property rights is often sufficient to re-solve the market failure typically associated with externalities. Additional government inter-vention is not necessary. If pollution can be easily monitored and polluters easily identified, the government may be able to achieve an efficient solution to the problem of pollution simply by assigning the right to pollute. To see how this could work, let's look at an exam-ple. Firms that dump into a river evidently value the ability to discharge waste in this way. For them, the river provides a low-cost outlet for by-products that otherwise would have to be disposed of at greater cost. The river provides a disposal service, and the demand curve for that service slopes downward, just like the demand for other resources.

The demand for the river as a discharge system is presented as *D* in Exhibit 4. The hori-zontal axis measures the tons of discharge dumped into the river per day, and the vertical axis measures firms' marginal benefits of disposing of their waste in this way. The demand curve thus measures the marginal value to firms of using the river as a disposal service. With no restrictions on river pollution—that is, if all firms were free to dump waste into the river—dumping would continue as long as doing so continues to yield some private mar-ginal benefit to producers. This marginal benefit falls to zero in Exhibit 4 when 250 tons per day are discharged.

The river, like the atmosphere and the soil, can absorb and neutralize a certain amount of discharge per day without deteriorating in quality. What if voters make the public choice

EXHIBIT 4

Optimal Allocation of Pollution Rights

Suppose the demand for a river as a discharge service is *D*. In the absence of any environmental controls, polluters would dump 250 tons per day, where the marginal benefit of discharge is zero. If regulatory authorities establish 100 tons as the maximum daily level of discharge and then sell the rights, the market for these pollution rights will clear at $25 per ton. If the demand for pollution rights increases to *D'*, the market-clearing price of pollution rights will rise to $35 per ton.

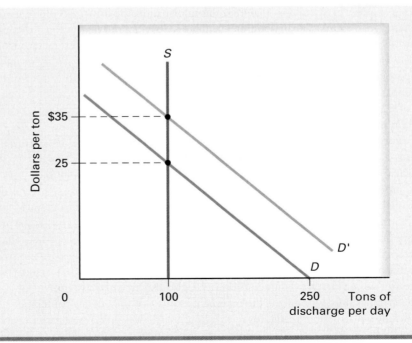

that the river should remain clean enough for swimming and fishing? Suppose engineers determine this level of water quality can be maintained as long as no more than 100 tons are discharged per day. Thus, the "supply" of the discharge service provided by the river is fixed at 100 tons per day, shown by the vertical supply curve, *S*, in Exhibit 4.

If government regulators can easily identify polluters and monitor their behavior, authorities can allocate permits to discharge 100 tons per day. If polluters are simply given these permits (that is, if the price of permits is zero), there will be an excess demand for them, because the quantity supplied is 100 tons but the quantity demanded at a price of zero would be 250 tons. An alternative is to sell permits for 100 tons of pollution at the market-clearing price. The intersection of supply curve *S* and demand curve *D* yields a permit price of $25 per ton, which is the marginal value of discharging the 100th ton into the river each day. To most permit buyers, the marginal value of a permit will exceed $25 per ton.

The beauty of this system is that producers who value the discharge rights the most will ultimately end up with them. Producers who attach a lower marginal value apparently have cheaper ways of resolving their waste problems, including changing production techniques. And if conservation groups, such as the Sierra Club, want a higher river quality than the government's standard, such as water clean enough to drink, they can purchase pollution permits but not exercise them.

What if additional firms spring up along the river and are willing to pay more than $25 per ton for pollution rights? This added demand is reflected in Exhibit 4 by *D'*. This increase of demand would bid up the market price of pollution permits to, say, $35 per ton. Some existing permit holders will sell their rights to those who value them more. Regardless of the comings and goings of would-be polluters, the total quantity of discharge rights is restricted to 100 tons per day, so the river's quality will be maintained. Thus, the value of pollution permits, but not the total amount of pollution, may fluctuate over time.

If the right to pollute could be granted, monitored, and enforced, then what had been a negative externality problem could be solved through market allocation. Historically, the U.S. government had relied on setting discharge standards and fining offenders. But in 1989, a pollution rights market for fluorocarbon emissions was established and was followed in 1990 by a market for sulfur dioxide. During the 1990s, sulfur dioxide emissions in the nation fell by more than half, exceeding the goals of the authorizing legislation. So the market for pollution rights is alive and growing.[5] Even China is now experimenting with this approach.

Pollution Rights and Public Choice

Unfortunately, legislation dealing with pollution is affected by the same problems of representative democracy that trouble other public policy questions. Polluters have a special interest in government proposals relating to pollution, and they fight measures to reduce pollution. But members of the public remain rationally ignorant about pollution legislation. So pollution regulations may be less in accord with the public interest than with the special interests of polluters. This is why a portion of pollution permits are often given to existing firms. For example, under the sulfur dioxide program, the nation's 101 dirtiest power plants receive credits equal to between 30 and 50 percent of the pollution they emitted before the program began. Because they received something of value, polluters were less inclined to oppose the legislation. Once permits were granted, some recipients found it profitable to sell their permits to

---

5. For a discussion of the market for sulfur dioxide emissions, see Paul Joskow, Richard Schmalensee, and Elizabeth Bailey, "The Market for Sulfur-Dioxide Emissions," *American Economic Review* 88 (September 1998): 669–685.

COMMAND-AND-CONTROL ENVIRONMENTAL REGULATIONS

An approach that required polluters to adopt particular technologies to reduce emissions by specific amounts; inflexible regulations based on engineering standards that ignore each firm's unique cost of reducing pollution

ECONOMIC EFFICIENCY APPROACH

An approach that offers each polluter the flexibility to reduce emissions as cost-effectively as possible, given its unique cost conditions; the market for pollution rights is an example

other firms that valued them more. Thus, a market emerged that led to an efficient allocation of pollution permits. According to some analysts, the sulfur dioxide program saves up to $3 billion annually compared with the old system. More generally, a system of marketable pollution rights can reduce the cost of pollution abatement by as much as 75 percent.

Before 1990, **command-and-control environmental regulations** were the norm—an approach that required polluters, such as electric utilities, to introduce particular technologies to reduce emissions by specific amounts. These regulations were based on engineering standards and did not recognize unique circumstances across generating plants, such as plant design, ability to introduce scrubbers, and the ease of switching to low-sulfur fuels. But the market for pollution rights reflects an **economic efficiency approach** that offers each electrical utility the flexibility to reduce emissions in the most cost-effective manner, given its unique operation. Firms with the lowest costs of emission control have an incentive to implement the largest reduction in emissions and then sell unused pollution permits to those with greater control costs.

Now that you know something about the theory of externalities, let's turn to an important application of the theory—environmental protection.

Environmental Protection

Federal efforts to address the common-pool problems of air, water, and soil pollution are coordinated by the Environmental Protection Agency (EPA). Four federal laws and subsequent amendments underpin U.S. efforts to protect the environment: the Clean Air Act of 1970, the Clean Water Act of 1972, the Resource Conservation and Recovery Act of 1976 (which governs solid waste disposal), and the Superfund law of 1980 (legislation focusing on toxic waste dumps). When the EPA was created in 1970, it began with about 4,000 employees and a budget of $1 billion (in 2004 dollars). By 2004, it had about 18,000 employees and a budget exceeding $8 billion.

According to EPA estimates, compliance with pollution-control regulations cost U.S. producers and consumers about $220 billion in 2004, an amount equivalent to 2 percent of gross domestic product, the market value of all final goods and services produced in the economy. We can divide pollution control spending into three categories: spending for air pollution abatement, spending for water pollution abatement, and spending for solid waste disposal. About 40 percent of the pollution control expenditures in the United States goes toward cleaner air, another 40 percent goes toward cleaner water, and 20 percent goes toward disposing of solid waste. In this section, we will consider, in turn, air pollution, water pollution, Superfund activities, and disposing of solid waste.

Air Pollution

In the Clean Air Act of 1970 and in subsequent amendments, Congress set national standards for the amount of pollution that could be emitted into the atmosphere. Congress thereby recognized the atmosphere as an economic resource, which, like other resources, has alternative uses. The air can be used as a source of life-giving oxygen, as a prism for viewing breathtaking vistas, or as a dump for carrying away unwanted soot and gases. The 1970 act gave Americans the right to breathe air of a certain quality and at the same time gave producers the right to emit particular amounts of specified pollutants.

Smog is the most visible form of air pollution. Automobile emissions account for 40 percent of smog. Another 40 percent comes from consumer products, such as paint thinner, fluorocarbon sprays, dry-cleaning solvents, and baker's yeast by-products. Surprisingly, only 15 percent of smog comes from manufacturing. The 1970 Clean Air Act mandated a reduction of 90 percent in auto emissions, leaving it to the auto industry to achieve this target. At the time, automakers said the target was impossible. Between 1970 and 1990, however, average emissions of lead fell 97 percent, carbon monoxide emissions fell 41 percent, and sulfur oxide emissions fell 25 percent. In fact, a recent EPA study concluded that because auto emissions and industrial smoke have been reduced, *air pollution on average is now greater indoors than outdoors*. For example, in the Los Angeles area, a smog alert, meaning the air reached dangerous levels, occurred on a weekly basis during the 1980s, but by 2000 there were no smog alerts. U.S. air quality is now considered good compared to the air quality in much of the world. Only one U.S. city, New York, ranks among the world's 10 worst when it comes to nitrogen oxide, and no U.S. city ranks among the world's 20 worst in sulfur dioxide.

Despite recent improvements in air quality, the United States is still a major source of carbon dioxide emissions. As you can see from Exhibit 5, which shows the world's 20 worst nations in carbon dioxide emissions per capita in 2000, the United States ranks third worst with 5.4 tons per capita. The following case study examines the problem of cleaning up the polluted air in the capital city of one developing country.

City in the Clouds

Mexico City was once known for its spectacular views of snow-capped volcanoes. Now the distant hills seldom appear. The problem? Population surged from 3 million in 1950 to 20 million today. More people mean more industry and more vehicles. Nearly half of Mexico's industrial output is produced in or near Mexico City. Over 3.5 million vehicles (30 percent are more than 20 years old) plus tens of thousands of small, poorly regulated businesses spew a soup of pollution.

The city's geography and altitude compound the pollution problem. Mountains border on three sides, so the wind that blows in from the north (the open side) traps pollution over the city. Worse yet, at 7,400 feet above sea level, the city's altitude reduces the air's oxygen content by about one-quarter. The low oxygen content causes incomplete fuel combustion in engines, and results in yet more pollution. The combination of high pollution, low oxygen, and a tropical sun makes for unhealthy air—which is why some people call the place "Makesicko City."

Traffic is a snarl. The average commuting time is three hours per day, with one-fifth of commuters spending four hours or more. City officials have taken steps to address the common-pool problem, but the task is daunting. Emission limits for new cars were recently imposed but the growing popularity of sports utility vehicles, or SUVs, adds to the problem. They are less fuel efficient, spew more emissions, and take up more space on already crowded roads. In September 2003, some 10 percent of motor vehicles were temporarily ordered off the roads when ozone levels reached 2.5 times acceptable limits.

Part of the problem is that low incomes in Mexico make environmental protection a costly luxury. For example, the minimum wage is the equivalent of about $4 per day. Despite all this, there are some hopeful signs. Catalytic converters, a switch to unleaded fuel, and higher gasoline prices are starting to brighten the picture. The North American Free-Trade Agreement (NAFTA) has encouraged some producers to move closer to the U.S. border. With industry moving out of Mexico City, levels of lead, carbon dioxide, and sulfur dioxide are beginning to show some improvement. Make no mistake, the air in Mexico City

HOMEWORK
Xpress!
econ-apps news

HOMEWORK
Xpress!
Ask the Instructor
Video

Caption (vertical): © Allen Russell/Index Stock Imagry

C a s e **S t u d y**

Public Policy

eActivity
GAIA, a collaborative effort of European research centers and universities, builds multimedia tools for environmental education and management. It presents an interesting case study, "Urban Air Pollution in Mexico City," at http://www.ess.co.at/GAIA/CASES/MEX/index.html. What are the major sources of air pollutants in Mexico City, and what are their primary effects? What plans are there to control emissions? A photographic essay illustrating the problem is archived by the National Geographic Society at http://www.nationalgeographic.com/features/96/mexico/a011.html.

is still bad, but it's better than it was five years ago. For the first time in a long while, a patch of blue sky sometimes shows through.

Sources: Andrew Churg et al., "Chronic Exposure to High Levels of Chronic Air Pollution: A Case Study of Mexico City," *Environmental Health Perspectives*, Vol. 111 (May 2003); Tim Weiner, "Terrific News in Mexico City: Air Is Sometimes Breathable," *New York Times*, 5 January 2001; "Mexico City Declares Air Pollution Emergency, Orders 350,000 Cars Off the Streets," *Associated Press*, 20 September 2002; and Planet Ark at http://www. planetark.org.

EXHIBIT 5   **Fossil-Fuel Carbon Dioxide Emissions per Capita: The 20 Worst Nations**

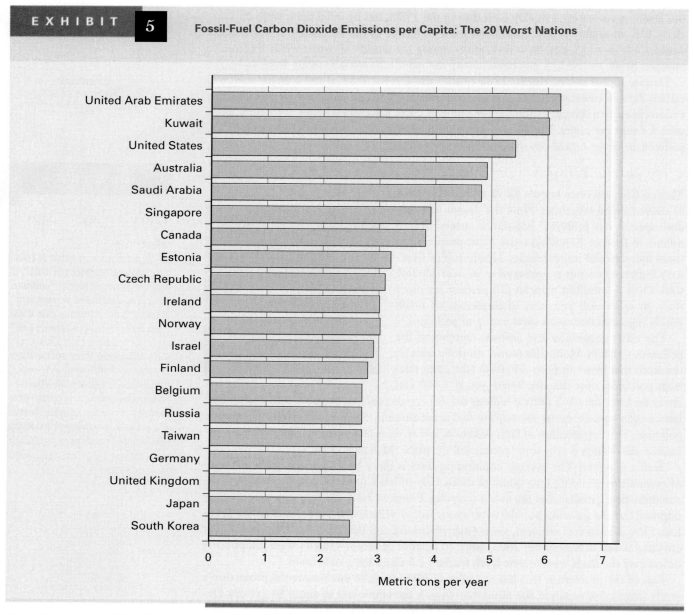

Source: Figures are for 2000 and are from "A Compendium of Data on Global Change" by the Carbon Dioxide Information Analysis Center at http://cdiac. esd.ornl.gov/home.html.

There have been efforts to address air quality on an international scale. A tentative accord reached in Kyoto, Japan, in 1997, would require the 38 industrial countries to reduce emissions of carbon dioxide and other so-called greenhouse gases by one-third over 10 years. The measure would impose a carbon tax on coal, natural gas, and oil. The cost to the U.S. economy could reach $300 billion a year, according to one study. Only industrial countries would be required to reduce emissions; developing countries need not participate. Thus, even if industrial nations met their Kyoto targets, carbon dioxide emissions would continue to rise because most of the projected global increase would come from exempted countries. Critics of the treaty argue that cleaner air should require a greater commitment from the developing world, such as China and India, which are major polluters. Argentina was the first developing nation offering to cut back greenhouse emissions. But the United States and Russia have rejected the treaty, thus dooming it.

Water Pollution

Two major sources of water pollution are sewage and chemicals. For decades, U.S. cities had an economic incentive to dump their sewage directly into waterways rather than clean it up first. The current or tides would carry off the waste to become someone else's problem. Although each community found it rational, based on a narrow view of the situation, to dump into waterways, the combined effect of these individual choices was water pollution, a negative externality imposed by one community on other communities.

Federal money over the years has funded sewage treatment plants, and subsidizing treatment plants has cut water pollution substantially. Hundreds of once-polluted waterways have been cleaned up enough for swimming and fishing. Nearly all U.S. cities now have modern sewage control systems. A notable exception is New York City, which teams up with New Jersey to dump some raw sewage into the Atlantic Ocean, using a discharge point about 100 miles out to sea.

Chemicals are another source of water pollution. Chemical pollution may conjure up an image of a pipe spewing chemicals into a river, but only about 10 percent of chemical pollution in the water comes from point pollution—pollution from factories and other industrial sites. About two-thirds come from nonpoint pollution—mostly runoff from agricultural pesticides and fertilizer. Congress has been reluctant to limit the use of pesticides, although pesticides pollute water and contaminate food. Industrial America seems an easier target than Old MacDonald's farm.

In 1970, Congress shifted control of pesticides from the U.S. Department of Agriculture to the newly created Environmental Protection Agency (EPA). But the EPA already had its hands full administering the Clean Water Act, so it turned pesticide regulation over to the states. Most states gave the job to their departments of agriculture. But these departments usually promote the interests of farmers, not restrict what farmers can do. The EPA now reports that in most states pesticides have fouled some groundwater. The EPA also argues that pesticide residues on food pose more health problems than do toxic waste dumps or even air pollution. The EPA's inspector general said that federal and state officials failed to enforce the nation's clean air and water laws. For example, most streams in Missouri are not clean enough for swimming. So that state failed to achieve the Clean Water Act's central goal.[6]

Hazardous Waste and the Superfund

The U.S. synthetic chemical industry has flourished in the last 50 years, and over 50,000 chemicals are now in common use. Some have harmful effects on humans and other living

6. John Cushman, "E.P.A. and States Found to Be Lax on Pollution Law," *New York Times,* 7 June 1998.

creatures. These chemicals can pose risks at every stage of their production, use, and disposal. New Jersey manufactures more toxic chemicals than any other state and, not surprisingly, has the worst toxic waste burden. Prior to 1980, the disposal of toxic waste created get-rich-quick opportunities for anyone who could rent or buy a few acres of land to open a toxic waste dump. As an extreme example, one site in New Jersey took in 71 million gallons of hazardous chemicals during a three-year period.[7]

Before 1980, once a company paid someone to haul away its hazardous waste, the company was no longer responsible. The Comprehensive Environmental Response, Compensation, and Liability Act of 1980, known more popularly as the Superfund law, now requires any company that generates, stores, or transports hazardous wastes to pay to clean up any wastes that are improperly disposed. A producer or hauler who is the source of even one barrel of pollution dumped at a site can be held liable for cleaning up the entire site.

The Superfund law gives the federal government authority over sites contaminated with toxins. But to get an offending company to comply, the EPA frequently must sue. The process is slow, and nearly half the budget goes to lawyers, consultants, and administrators rather than to site cleanups. The law did not require that benefits exceed costs or even that such comparisons be attempted. Although billions have been spent so far, a recent EPA study concluded that the health hazards of Superfund sites have been vastly exaggerated. Chemicals in the ground often move slowly, sometimes taking years to travel a few feet, so any possible health threat is confined to the site itself. People know when they live near toxic waste sites, and they can exert political pressure to get something done, whereas people exposed to polluted air, water, and pesticide residue may develop health problems but not make the connection to their environment. Thus, people see less reason to press public officials for cleaner air and water. Toxic waste sites, because of their greater political urgency and media appeal, tend to receive more attention than air or water pollution. And with the federal government picking up the tab, localities demand all the cleanup they can get.

Solid Waste: "Paper or Plastic?"

Throughout most of history, households tossed their trash outside as fodder for pigs and goats. New York City, like other cities, had no trash collections, so domestic waste was thrown into the street, where it mixed with mud and manure. Decades of such behavior explains why the oldest Manhattan streets are anywhere from 3 to 15 feet above their original levels. About 200 years ago, people buried their trash near their homes or took it to the town dump. Now U.S. households generate about 4 pounds of garbage per resident per day—more than twice the 1960 level and the most per capita in the world. Much of the solid waste consists of packaging material. The question is, how do we dispose of the more than 200 million tons of household garbage generated in this country each year?

Advanced economies produce and buy more than less developed economies, so there is more to throw away. And because of higher incomes in advanced economies, the opportunity cost of time is higher, so we tend to discard items rather than repair or recycle them. For example, it's cheaper to buy a new toaster for $25 than to pay someone $40 an hour to fix a broken one, assuming you can even find a repair service. (Look up "Appliance Repair, Small" in the *Yellow Pages* of the Internet's Super Pages and see if you can find even one such shop in your area.)

About 70 percent of the nation's garbage is bulldozed and covered with soil in landfills. Although a well-managed landfill poses few environmental concerns, at one time, communities dumped all kinds of toxic materials in them—stuff that could leach into the soil, con-

7. Jason Zweig, "Real-Life Horror Story," *Forbes*, 12 December 1988.

taminating wells and aquifers. So landfills got a bad reputation. The prevailing attitude with landfills is Nimby! (Not in my backyard!). We all want our garbage picked up but nobody wants it put down anywhere nearby.

As the cost of solid waste disposal increases, some state and local governments are economizing, charging households by the pound for trash pickups, and requiring more recycling and returnable bottles. **Recycling** is the process of converting waste products into reusable materials. Nearly half of U.S. households participate in curbside recycling programs. Still, according to the EPA, only about 15 percent of U.S. garbage gets recycled; about 15 percent is incinerated and, as noted already, the remaining 70 percent goes into landfills. Of the recycled material, three-quarters consists of corrugated boxes, newspapers, office paper, newspapers, and other paper products. Some of the paper is shipped to Korea, Taiwan, and China, where it becomes packaging material for U.S. imports such as DVD players and computer components. Exhibit 6 ranks the world's top 20 paper recyclers among advance economies in 2000. Germany heads the list, recycling 70 percent of its paper. The United States ranks 16th, recycling 42 percent, double that of 1985.

Most of the 15 percent of garbage that is incinerated gets burned in trash-to-energy plants, which generate electricity using the heat from incineration. Until recently, such plants looked like the wave of the future, but less favorable tax treatment and environmental concerns over incinerator locations (Nimby strikes again!) have taken the steam out of the trash-to-energy movement.

To repeat, about 70 percent of U.S. garbage goes to landfills, and only 30 percent is incinerated or recycled. In contrast, the Japanese recycle 40 percent of their waste and incinerate 33 percent, leaving only 27 percent to be deposited in landfills. Japanese households sort their trash into as many as 21 categories. Because land is scarcer in Japan—we know this because it costs relatively more—it is not surprising that the Japanese deposit a smaller share of their garbage in landfills.

Some recycling is clearly economical—such as aluminum cans, which are a cheap source of aluminum compared to producing raw aluminum. About two out of three aluminum cans now get recycled, though only 10 states require returnable deposits. The average American uses 12 pounds of aluminum each year in aluminum cans; so about 8 pounds of that is recycled. Recycling paper and cardboard is also economical and occurred long before the environmental movement. Still, such old standbys as paper drives, drop-off bins, and redemption centers still collect more tonnage than curbside programs. Most recycling results from salvaging scrap material from business and industry, a practice that goes back decades.

Governments have tried to stimulate demand for recycled material—for example, by requiring newspapers to use a certain amount of recycled newsprint. Other recycled products are not in such demand. In fact, some recycled products have become worthless and must be hauled to landfills. Recycling imposes its own cost on the environment. Curbside recycling requires fleets of trucks that pollute the air. Newsprint must first be de-inked, creating a sludge that must be disposed. But greater environmental awareness has made consumers more receptive to more efficient packaging material. For example, liquid laundry detergent is now available in a concentrated "ultra" form, which cuts volume in half. And labels for all kinds of products proudly identify the recycled content of the packaging.

Positive Externalities

To this point, we have considered only negative externalities. But externalities are sometimes positive, or beneficial. Positive externalities occur when consumption or production benefits other consumers or other firms. For example, people who get inoculated against a

RECYCLING

The process of converting waste products into reusable material

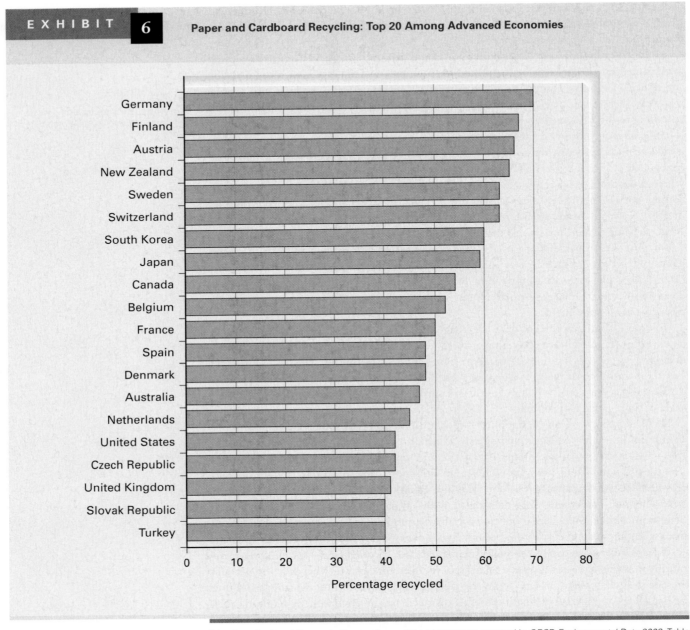

EXHIBIT 6   **Paper and Cardboard Recycling: Top 20 Among Advanced Economies**

Percentage recycled

Source: Figures are rankings among members of the Organization of Economic Cooperation and Development as reported in *OECD Environmental Data 2002*, Table 5.4A, p. 21. This can be found at http://www.oecd.org/document/21/0,2340,en_2825_495628_2516565_1_1_1_1,00.html. Figures are for 2000, except for Canada, which is for 1996, and the United States, which is for 1999.

disease reduce their own likelihood of contracting the disease, but in the process they also reduce the risk of transmitting the disease to others. Inoculations thus provide external benefits to others. Society as a whole receives external benefits from education because those who acquire more education become better citizens, can read road signs, are better able to support themselves and their families, and are less likely to require public assistance or to re-

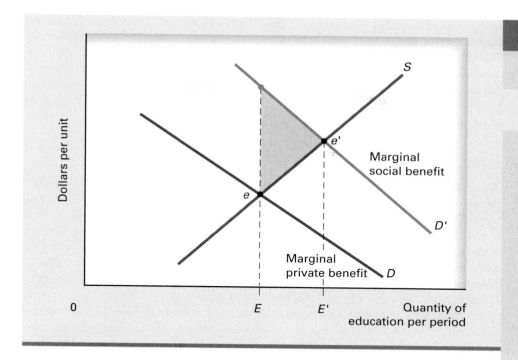

EXHIBIT 7

Education and Positive Externalities

In the absence of government intervention, the equilibrium quantity of education is *E*, at which the marginal private benefit of education equals the marginal cost. Education also confers a positive externality on the rest of society, so the marginal social benefit exceeds the private benefit. At quantity *E*, the marginal social benefit exceeds the marginal cost, so more education increases social welfare. In this situation, government will try to encourage an increase in the equilibrium quantity of education to *E'*, where the marginal social benefit equals the marginal cost.

sort to crime for income. Thus, education provides private benefits but it also confers additional social benefits on others.

The effect of external benefits on the optimal level of consumption is illustrated in Exhibit 7, which presents the demand and supply of education. The demand curve, *D*, represents the private demand for education, which reflects the marginal private benefit for those who acquire the education. More education is demanded at a lower price than at a higher price.

The benefit of education, however, spills over to others in society. If we add this positive externality, or marginal external benefit, to the marginal private benefit of education, we get the marginal social benefit of education. The marginal social benefit includes all the benefit society derives from education, both private and external. The marginal social benefit curve is above the private demand curve in Exhibit 7. At each level of education, the marginal social benefit exceeds the marginal private benefit by the amount of marginal external benefit generated by that particular level of education.

If education were a strictly private decision, the amount purchased would be determined by the intersection of the private demand curve *D* with supply curve *S*. The supply curve reflects the marginal cost of producing each unit of the good. This intersection at point *e* yields education level *E*, where the marginal private benefit of education equals its marginal cost. But at level *E*, the marginal social benefit of education exceeds its marginal cost. Social welfare will increase if education expands beyond *E*. As long as the marginal social benefit of education exceeds its marginal cost, social welfare increases if education expands. Social welfare is maximized at point *e'* in Exhibit 7, where *E'* units of education are provided— that is, where the marginal social benefit equals the marginal cost, as reflected by the supply curve. The blue-shaded triangle identifies the increase in social welfare that results from increasing education from *E* to *E'*.

Thus, society is better off if the level of education exceeds the private equilibrium. When positive externalities are present, decisions based on private marginal benefits result in less than the socially optimal quantity of the good. Thus, like negative externalities, positive externalities typically point to market failure, which is why government often gets into the act. When there are external benefits, public policy aims to increase the level of output beyond the private optimum. For example, governments try to increase education by providing free primary and secondary education, by requiring students to stay in school until they reach 16 years of age, by subsidizing public higher education, and by offering tax breaks for some education costs.

Conclusion

About 6.5 billion people inhabit the globe, doubling in the last 40 years. Over 72 million people are added each year. World population is projected to reach 9 billion by 2050, with most of this growth occurring in countries where most people barely eke out a living. Population pressure coupled with a lack of incentives to conserve open-access resources results in deforestation, dwindling fish stocks, and polluted air, land, and water. Market prices can direct the allocation of resources only as long as property rights are well defined. Pollution arises not so much from the greed of producers and consumers as from the fact that open-access resources are subject to the common-pool problem.

Ironically, because of tighter pollution controls, industrial countries are less polluted than developing countries, where there is more pollution from what little industry there is. Most developing countries have such profound economic problems that environmental quality is not a high priority. For example, when India's Supreme Court recently tried to close some polluting factories in New Delhi, thousands of workers torched buses, threw stones, and blocked major roads, demanding the factories stay open. Although New Delhi's air is so filthy that it often masks any trace of a blue sky, workers believe their jobs are more important. Here's one account of New Delhi's air quality:

> *In the heat of the afternoons, a yellow-white mixture hung above the city, raining acidic soot into the dust and exhaust fumes. At night the mixture condenses into a dry, choking fog that envelops the headlights of passing cars, and creeps its stink into even the tightest houses. The residents could do little to keep the poison out of their lungs or the lungs of their children, and if they were poor, they could not even try.*[8]

WALL STREET JOURNAL
Reading It **Right**

What's the relevance of the following statement from the Wall Street Journal: *"Only when we are sufficiently rich can we start to think about, worry about and deal with environmental problems."*

SUMMARY

1. An exhaustible resource is available in fixed supply, such as crude oil or coal. A renewable resource regenerates itself and so can be used periodically if used conservatively, such as a properly managed forest. Some resources suffer from a common-pool problem because unrestricted access leads to overuse.

2. Production that generates negative externalities results in too much output. Production that generates positive externalities results in too little output. Public policy should tax or otherwise limit production that generates negative externalities and should subsidize or otherwise promote production that generates positive externalities.

3. The optimal amount of environmental quality occurs where the marginal social benefit of an improvement equals its marginal social cost. An upward shift of the marginal benefit curve of environmental quality or a downward shift of its marginal cost curve will increase the optimal level of environmental quality.

8. William Langewiesche, "The Shipbreakers," *Atlantic Monthly* (August 2000): 42.

4. The world's tropical rainforests recycle noxious gases into oxygen and wood. Because rainforests are open–access resources, settlers and loggers cut them down to make a living. This destruction reduces the environment's ability to cleanse itself.

5. The Coase theorem argues that as long as bargaining costs are low, assigning property rights to one party leads to an efficient solution to an externality problem. The market for pollution permits reflects the Coase theorem in action.

6. The nation's air and waterways are getting cleaner. The air is cleaner because of stricter emissions standards for motor vehicles, and waterways are cleaner because of billions spent on sewage treatment plants. Toxic waste sites do not pose as great a health threat as do other forms of pollution such as smog and pesticide residue, but toxic waste gets the media attention.

QUESTIONS FOR REVIEW

1. (*Externalities*) Complete each of the following sentences:

   a. Resources that are available only in a fixed amount are _____ resources.
   b. The possibility that a nonexcludable resource will be used until the net marginal value of additional use equals zero is known as the _____.
   c. Resources for which periodic use can be continued indefinitely are known as _____ resources.

2. (*Resolving the Common-Pool Problem*) Why have authorities found it so difficult to regulate the fishing catch to allow for a sustainable yield?

3. (*Optimal Level of Pollution*) Explain the difference between fixed-production technology and variable technology. Should the government set a goal of reducing the marginal social cost of pollution to zero in industries with fixed-production technology? Should they do so in industries with variable technology?

4. (*C a s e S t u d y*: Destruction of the Tropical Rainforests) Why does a solution to the overharvesting of

timber in the tropical rainforests require some form of international cooperation? Would this be a sufficient solution to the deforestation problem?

5. (*The Coase Theorem*) Suppose a firm pollutes a stream that has a recreational value only when pollution is below a certain level. If transaction costs are low, why does the assignment of property rights to the stream lead to the same (efficient) level of pollution whether the firm or recreational users own the stream?

6. (*The Coase Theorem*) Ronald Coase points out that a market failure does not arise simply because people ignore the external cost of their actions. What other condition is necessary? What did Coase consider to be an efficient solution to a negative externality?

7. (*Positive Externalities*) The value of a home depends in part on how attractive other homes and yards in the neighborhood are. How do local zoning ordinances try to promote land uses that generate external benefits for neighbors?

PROBLEMS AND EXERCISES

8. (*External Costs with Fixed-Production Technology*) Review the situation illustrated in Exhibit 1 in this chapter. If the government sets the price of electricity at the socially optimal level, why is the net gain equal to triangle *abc*, even though consumers now pay a higher price for electricity?

What would the net gain be if the government set the price above the optimal level?

9. (*Negative Externalities*) Suppose you wish to reduce a negative externality by imposing a tax on the activity

that creates that externality. When the amount of the externality produced per unit of output increases as output increases, the correct tax can be determined by using a demand–supply diagram; show this. Assume that the marginal private cost curve slopes upward.

10. (*External Costs*) Use the data in the table below to answer the following questions.

   a. What is the external cost per unit of production?
   b. What level will be produced if there is no regulation of the externality?
   c. What level should be produced to achieve economic efficiency?
   d. Calculate the dollar value of the net gain to society from correcting the externality.

Quantity	Marginal Private Benefit (demand)	Marginal Private Cost (supply)	Marginal Social Cost
0	—	$ 0	$ 0
1	$10	2	4
2	9	3	5
3	8	4	6
4	7	5	7
5	6	6	8
6	5	7	9
7	4	8	10
8	3	9	11
9	2	10	12
10	1	11	13

11. (*External Costs with Variable Technology*) Think of an industry that pollutes the water and has access to variable technology for reducing that water pollution. Graphically illustrate and explain the impact of each of the following, other things constant, on the optimal level of water quality:

   a. New evidence is discovered of a greater risk of cancer from water pollution.
   b. The cost of pollution control equipment increases.
   c. A technological improvement reduces the cost of pollution control.

12. (*Market for Pollution Rights*) The following graph shows the market for pollution rights.

   a. If there are no restrictions on pollution, what amount will be discharged?
   b. What will be the quantity supplied and the quantity demanded if the government restricts the amount of discharge to Q* but gives the permits away?
   c. Where is market equilibrium if the government sells the permits? Illustrate this on the graph.
   d. What happens to market equilibrium if the government reduces the amount of discharge permitted to Q**? Illustrate this on the graph.

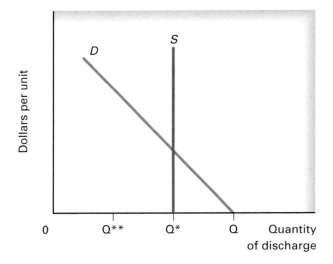

EXPERIENTIAL EXERCISES

13. (*Case Study*: City in the Clouds) Suppose you are the mayor of Mexico City. How can you use some of the techniques outlined in this chapter to control pollution there? (For background information, check http://www.ess.co.at/GAIA/CASES/MEX/index.html.)

14. (*The Common-Pool Problem*) Garrett Hardin's 1968 article, "The Tragedy of the Commons," is available online at http://www.garretthardinsociety.org/articles/art_tragedy_of_the_commons.html. Read this clearly written article, and then describe some examples of the common-pool problem or, as he calls it, the tragedy of the commons.

15. *(External Costs with Fixed Technology)* Read Betty Joyce Nash's "Pollution Allowances Help Clear the Air" at http://www.rich.frb.org/pubs/cross/cross134/2.html. Based on what you've learned in this chapter, evaluate Nash's case for pollution allowances as a way of controlling negative externalities.

16. *(Wall Street Journal)* The Marketplace section of the *Wall Street Journal* is a good place to look for information related to externalities. On a given day, see how many stories you can find that deal with externalities—positive or negative. Are businesses taking steps to "internalize" externalities? What role does technology play in controlling negative externalities?

17. Visit the Environmental Protection Agency's Web site and examine information on general interest programs (at http://www.epa.gov/epahome/general.htm). The EPA has implemented a number of programs aimed at improving air and water quality. Describe one program and the problem it addresses. Graphically illustrate and explain the EPA's approach.

HOMEWORK XPRESS! EXERCISES

These exercises require access to McEachern Homework Xpress! If Homework Xpress! did not come with your book, visit **http://homeworkxpress.swlearning.com** *to purchase.*

1. The production of clean, white paper is really a dirty job. Paper mills generate air and water pollutants. In the diagram, draw a downward sloping demand for paper and a horizontal marginal private cost curve at $20. Identify the private-sector equilibrium level of output of paper. Then add a marginal social cost curve showing that each ton of paper produced generates an additional $2 per ton of external costs. Identify the socially efficient level of output.

2. The runoff of water from streets, lawns, and construction sites is a major source of pollutants for our lakes and streams. Various methods are available for controlling runoff and improving water quality—some cheap, others more costly. In the diagram draw the marginal social cost line that illustrates this. Add a marginal social benefit line that shows how the additional benefits of control decrease. Identify the optimal level of water quality. Suppose the government mandates control efforts that result in a higher level of quality. Illustrate the social waste associated with making the water too clean.

3. Improving the quality of drinking water in developing economies is one of the most beneficial investments that can be made. However, controlling discharges that reduce water quality is costly. Use marginal social cost and marginal social benefits lines to illustrate the optimal level of water quality in any particular area. Then illustrate the effect on the optimal level of water quality of a technological improvement that reduces control costs.

Income Distribution and Poverty

© Amy Sancetta/AP Wide World Photos

Why are some people poor even in the most productive economy on Earth? Who are the poor, how did they get that way, and how long do they remain poor? What's been the trend in poverty over time? How has the changing family structure affected poverty? What public programs aim to reduce poverty, and how well have they worked? Answers to these and related questions are addressed in this chapter, which discusses income distribution and poverty in America.

To establish a reference point, we first examine the distribution of income in the United States, paying special attention to trends in recent decades. We then evaluate the "social safety net"—government programs aimed at helping poor people. We also consider the impact of the changing family structure on poverty, focusing in particular on the increase in households headed by women. We close by examining recent welfare reforms. Topics discussed include:

- Distribution of income
- Official poverty level
- Public policy and poverty

- The feminization of poverty
- Poverty and discrimination
- Welfare reforms

The Distribution of Household Income

In a market economy, income depends primarily on earnings, which depend on the productivity of one's resources. The problem with allocating income according to productivity is that some people have few productive resources to sell. People with mental or physical disabilities and poor education, those facing discrimination, bad luck, or the demands of caring for small children, and the elderly may be less productive or unable to earn a living.

Income Distribution by Quintiles

As a starting point, let's consider the distribution of income in the economy and see how it has changed over time, focusing on the household as the economic unit. After dividing the total number of U.S. households into five groups of equal size, or *quintiles,* ranked according to income, we can examine the percentage of income received by each quintile. Such a division is presented in Exhibit 1 since 1970. Take a moment to look over this exhibit. Notice that households in the lowest, or poorest, fifth of the population received only 4.1 percent of the income in 1970, whereas households in the highest, or richest, fifth received 43.3 percent of the income. The U.S. Census Bureau measures income after cash transfer payments are received but before taxes are paid.

In recent decades, the share of income going to the top fifth has increased, and the share going to the bottom fifth has declined. The richest group's share of income increased from 43.3 percent in 1970 to 49.7 percent in 2002. A primary contributor to the larger share of income going to the highest group has been the growth of two-earner households in that top group. A primary contributor to the smaller share going to the lowest group has been the growth of single-parent households in the bottom group.

Also shown in Exhibit 1 is the share of income going to the top 5 percent of households; that share has grown since 1980, accounting for all the growth of the top 20 percent of households. Because of substantial reductions in the top marginal tax rates in 1981 and 1986, high-income people had less incentive to engage in tax avoidance and tax evasion, so their reported income increased, boosting the share of reported income going to the richest 5 percent of households.

The Lorenz Curve

We have just examined the distribution of income using a bar chart. Another way to picture that distribution is with a Lorenz curve. A **Lorenz curve** shows the percentage of total income received by any given percentage of households when incomes are arrayed from smallest to largest. As shown in Exhibit 2, the cumulative percentage of households is measured along the horizontal axis, and the cumulative percentage of income is measured along the vertical axis. Any given distribution of income can be compared to an equal distribution of income among households. If income were evenly distributed, each 20 percent of households would also receive 20 percent of the total income, and the Lorenz curve would be a straight line with a slope equal to 1.0, as shown in Exhibit 2.

As the distribution becomes more uneven, the Lorenz curve is pulled down to the right, away from the line of equal distribution. The Lorenz curves in Exhibit 2 were calculated for

LORENZ CURVE

A curve showing the percentage of total income received by a given percentage of recipients whose incomes are arrayed from smallest to largest

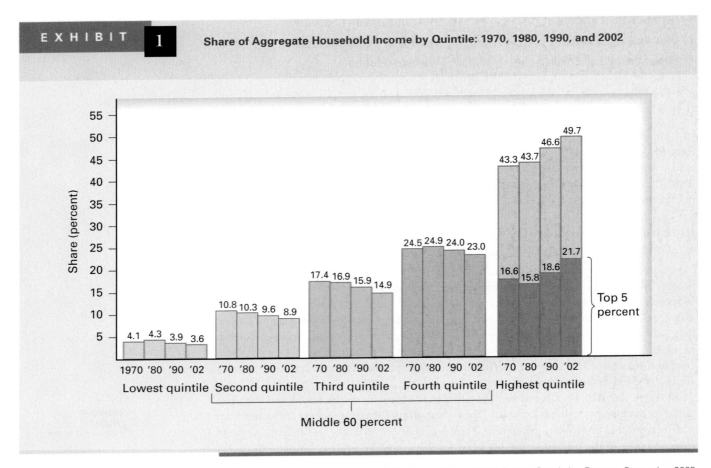

EXHIBIT 1   **Share of Aggregate Household Income by Quintile: 1970, 1980, 1990, and 2002**

Source: U.S. Census Bureau, *Income in the United States: 2002*, Current Population Reports, September 2003, Table A-3, http://www.census.gov/prod/2003pubs/p60-221.pdf.

1970 and 2002 based on the data in Exhibit 1. As a reference, point *a* on the 1970 Lorenz curve indicates that in that year, the bottom 80 percent of families received 56.7 percent of the income, and the top 20 percent received 43.3 percent of the income. The Lorenz curve for 2002 is farther from the line of equal distribution than is the Lorenz curve for 1970, showing that income among households has become more unevenly distributed. Point *b* on the 2002 curve shows that the bottom 80 percent received 50.3 percent of the income and the top 20 percent received 49.7 percent of the income.

A College Education Pays More

Also contributing to the dominance of the top group is a growing premium paid those with college educations. In the last two decades, the median wage (adjusted for inflation) for people with only high school diplomas declined 6 percent, while the median wage for college graduates rose 12 percent. The **median wage** is the middle wage when wages are ranked from lowest to highest. Why have more-educated workers done better? First, trends such as industry deregulation, declining unionization, and freer international trade have reduced the demand for workers with less education. Labor unions, for example, raised the wages of many workers who would have otherwise ended up in the bottom half of the income dis-

MEDIAN WAGE

The middle wage when wages of all workers are ranked from lowest to highest

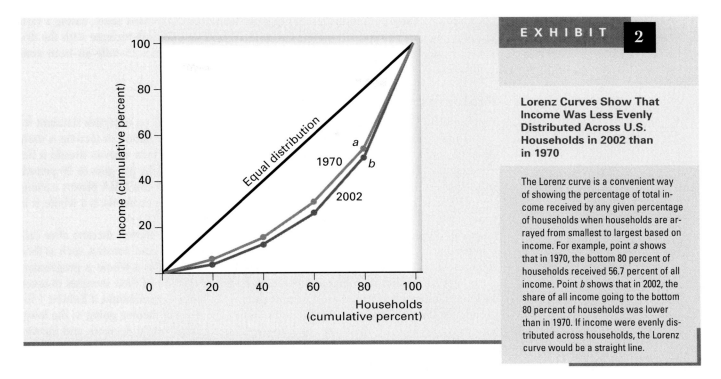

E X H I B I T 2

Lorenz Curves Show That Income Was Less Evenly Distributed Across U.S. Households in 2002 than in 1970

The Lorenz curve is a convenient way of showing the percentage of total income received by any given percentage of households when households are arrayed from smallest to largest based on income. For example, point *a* shows that in 1970, the bottom 80 percent of households received 56.7 percent of all income. Point *b* shows that in 2002, the share of all income going to the bottom 80 percent of households was lower than in 1970. If income were evenly distributed across households, the Lorenz curve would be a straight line.

tribution. But the share of the workforce that is unionized declined from 26 percent in 1973 to only 14 percent in 2002.

Second, new computer-based information technologies have reduced the demand for low-skilled clerical workers, because their jobs became computerized. Computers also offered more timely and accurate information to management, allowing for organizational innovations that made managers and other professionals more productive.[1] So computers reduced the demand for workers with low skills, such as clerical staff and bank tellers, and increased the demand for those who use computers to boost labor productivity, such as managers and accountants.

Third, the supply of less-educated workers increased more than the supply of more-educated workers, thus increasing the rewards of education. For example, compared to average residents, recent U.S. immigrants tend to be less educated, including an estimated 8 million illegal aliens, half of whom are from Mexico. The Hispanic population more than doubled between 1980 and 2000, and the percentage of foreign-born Hispanics increased. Among males age 25 and older, only 57 percent of Hispanics had at least a high school education in 2000, compared with 85 percent of whites and 79 percent of blacks. More generally, the foreign-born share of the U.S. population doubled from 5 percent in 1970 to 11 percent in 2000, the largest share since the 1930s. Thus, immigration has increased the supply of relatively poorly educated workers, which has depressed wages of the less educated generally.

So economic and migration trends in recent years have benefited the better educated, and this helps explain the growing disparity in household income. Income in the United States is less evenly distributed than in other developed countries throughout the world, such as Canada, France, Great Britain, Italy, and Australia, but is more evenly distributed than in most developing countries, such as Brazil, Chile, Mexico, Nigeria, and the Philippines. Some countries also

Net **Bookmark**

Data and analytical reports about income distribution can be found at the U.S. Census Bureau's Web site at http://www.census.gov/hhes/www/income.html. This Income page includes a link to a page devoted to income inequality. There you can find data on the distribution of income by quintile and the report, "The Changing Shape of the Nation's Income Distribution, 1947–98." What is used in this report to measure income distribution? In what year was income least unequal? What is the most recent trend?

1. Timothy Bresnahan, "Computerization and Wage Dispersion: An Analytical Reinterpretation," *Economic Journal* (June 1999).

have far more extensive redistribution programs than does the United States, basing a variety of public policies on income. For example, Finland's traffic fines increase with the driver's income. One young tycoon speeding 43 miles per hour in a 25-mile-an-hour zone paid a $71,400 fine.[2]

Problems with Distribution Benchmarks

One problem with assessing income distributions is that there is no objective standard for evaluating them. The usual assumption is that a more equal distribution of income is more desirable, but is equal distribution most preferred? If not, then how uneven should it be? For example, among major league baseball players, well over half the pay goes to 20 percent of the players. Professional basketball pay skews even more, with top NBA players earning up to 50 times more than the bottom players. Does this mean the economy, as a whole, is in some sense "fairer" than these professional sports?

A second problem is that because Exhibits 1 and 2 measure money income after cash transfers but before taxes they neglect the effects of taxes and in-kind transfers, such as food stamps and free medical care for poor families. The tax system as a whole is progressive, meaning that families with higher incomes pay a larger fraction of their incomes in taxes. In-kind transfers benefit the lowest income groups the most. Consequently, if Exhibit 1 incorporated the effects of taxes and in-kind transfers, the share of income going to the lower groups would increase, the share going to the higher groups would decrease, and income would become more evenly distributed.

Third, focusing on the share of income going to each income quintile overlooks the fact that household size differs across quintiles. Most households in the bottom quintile consist of one person living alone. Only one in 16 households in the top quintile consists of one person living alone. Households in the top quintile average two-thirds larger than those in the bottom quintile, which helps to explain some of the difference in income share going to each quintile.

Fourth, Exhibits 1 and 2 include only *reported* income. If people receive payment "under the table" to evade taxes, or if they earn money through illegal activities, their actual income will exceed their reported income. The omission of unreported income will distort the data if unreported income as a percentage of total family income differs across income levels.

Finally, Exhibits 1 and 2 focus on the distribution of *income*, but a better measure of household welfare would be the distribution of *spending*. Available evidence indicates that *spending by quintiles is much more evenly distributed than income by quintiles.*

Why Incomes Differ

Income differences across households stem in part from differences in the *number* of workers in each household. Thus, *one reason household incomes differ is that the number of household members who are working differs.* For example, among households in the bottom 20 percent based on income, only one in five includes a full-time, year-round worker. Consider the link between median income and the number of workers. The **median income** of all households is the middle income when incomes are ranked from lowest to highest. In any given year, half the households are above the median income and half are below it. The median income for households with two earners is 87 percent higher than for households with only one earner and is about four times higher than for households with no earners.

MEDIAN INCOME

The middle income when all incomes are ranked from smallest to largest

---

2. Seven Stecklow, "Finnish Drivers Don't Mind Sliding Scale, But Instant Calculation Gets Low Marks," *Wall Street Journal,* 2 January 2001.

Incomes also differ for all the reasons labor incomes differ, such as differences in education, ability, job experience, and so on. At every age, people with more education earn more, on average. As noted a few chapters back, those with a professional degree earn about four times more than those with only a high school education. Age itself also has an important effect on income. As workers mature, they acquire valuable job experience, get promoted, and earn more.

Differences in earnings based on age and education reflect a normal *life cycle* pattern of income. In fact, most income differences across households reflect the normal workings of resource markets, whereby workers are rewarded according to their productivity. Because of these lifetime patterns, it is not necessarily the same households that remain rich or poor over time. Indeed, one study of income mobility found that more than three-quarters of people in the bottom 20 percent in 1975 had moved into the top 40 percent for at least one year by 1991.[3] Despite this mobility over time, we can still characterize rich and poor households at a point in time. A high-income household usually consists of a well-educated couple with both spouses employed. A low-income household is usually headed by a single parent who is young, female, poorly educated, and not working. Low incomes are a matter of public concern, especially when children are involved, as we will see in the next section.

Poverty and the Poor

Because poverty is such a relative concept, how do we measure it objectively, and how do we ensure that the measure can be applied with equal relevance over time? The federal government has developed a method for calculating an official poverty level, which serves as a benchmark for poverty analysis in the United States.

Official Poverty Level

To derive the **U.S. official poverty level,** the U.S. Department of Agriculture in 1959 first estimated the cost of a nutritionally adequate diet. Then, based on the assumption that the poor spend about one-third of their income on food, the official poverty level was calculated by multiplying this food cost by three. The U.S. Census Bureau tracks the official poverty level, making adjustments for family size and for inflation. For example, the official poverty level of money income for a family of four was $18,392 in 2002; a family of four at or below that income threshold was regarded as living in poverty. Poverty levels in 2002 ranged from $9,183 for a person living alone to $37,062 for a family of nine. The poverty definition is based on pretax money income, including cash transfers, but it excludes the value of noncash transfers such as food stamps, Medicaid, subsidized housing, or employer-provided health insurance.

Each year since 1959, the Census Bureau has conducted a survey comparing each family's cash income to the annual poverty level applicable to that family. Results of this survey are presented in Exhibit 3, which indicates both the millions of people living below the official poverty level and the percentage of the U.S. population below that level. Periods of U.S. recession are also shown (a recession is defined as two or more successive quarters of declining gross domestic product). Note that poverty increased during recessions.

The biggest decline in poverty occurred before 1970; *the poverty rate dropped from 22.4 percent in 1959 to 12.1 percent in 1969.* During that period, the number of poor people decreased from about 40 million to 24 million. The poverty rate has not shown huge fluctua-

U.S. OFFICIAL POVERTY LEVEL

Benchmark level of income computed by the federal government to track poverty over time; initially based on three times the cost of a nutritionally adequate diet

3. W. Michael Cox and Richard Arm, "By Our Own Bootstraps," *Federal Reserve Bank of Dallas: 1995 Annual Report.*

EXHIBIT 3   **Number and Percentage of U.S. Population in Poverty: 1959–2002**

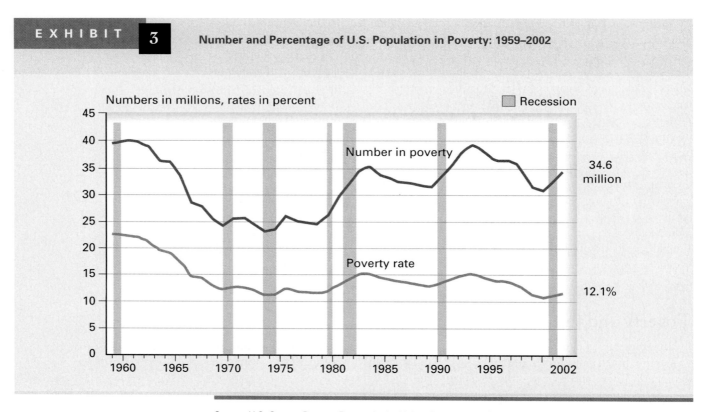

Source: U.S. Census Bureau, *Poverty in the United States: 2002*, Current Population Reports, September 2003, Figure 1, p.3, http://www.census.gov/prod/2003pubs/p60-222.pdf.

tions since that initial drop. After declining from 1994 to 2000, the poverty rate and the number of poor people increased during the next two years because of the national recession in 2001.

Poverty is a relative term. If we examined the distribution of income across countries, we would find huge gaps between rich and poor nations. The U.S. official poverty level of income is many times greater than the average income for three-fourths of the world's population. The U.S. poverty level for a family of four in 2002 works out to be a $12.60 per person per day. Most nations employ a much lower poverty level. For example, the World Bank uses an *international poverty line* of $1 per person per day. Based on that benchmark, about 16 percent of those in China, 35 percent of those in the India, and 47 percent of sub-Saharan Africans lived in poverty.[4]

Programs to Help the Poor

What should society's response to poverty be? The best predictor of family poverty is whether someone in that family has a job. Overall, the poverty rate is about four times greater in families with no workers than in families with at least one worker. One way to reduce poverty, therefore, is to ensure a healthy economy. The stronger the economy, the greater the job opportunities, and the more likely people will find work. Perhaps the best

4. Poverty rates can be found at the World Bank Group's site at http://www.worldbank.org/research/povmonitor/.

indicator of whether or not jobs are readily available is the *unemployment rate*, which shows the percentage or the labor force out of work. The *lower* the unemployment rate, the *higher* the likelihood that someone who wants a job has found one. Thus, the lower the unemployment rate, the lower the poverty rate. Exhibit 4 shows poverty rates and unemployment rates in the United States each year since 1969. As you can see, the poverty rate, shown by the top line, tends to rise when the unemployment rate increases and fall when the unemployment rate declines. For example, between 1979 and 1982 the unemployment rate spiked from 5.8 percent to 9.7 percent. During that period, the nation's poverty rate climbed from 11.7 percent to 15.0 percent. The unemployment rate fell from 7.5 percent in 1992 to 4.0 percent in 2000. During that period, poverty declined from 14.8 percent to 11.3 percent. After 2000, both unemployment and poverty increased with the national recession of 2001.

Thus, the government's first line of defense in fighting poverty is to promote a healthy economy. Yet even when the unemployment rate is low, some people are still poor. Although some antipoverty programs involve direct market intervention, such as minimum-wage laws, the most visible antipoverty programs redistribute income after the market has made an initial distribution. Since the mid-1960s, social welfare expenditures at all levels of government have increased significantly. We can divide these programs into two broad categories: social insurance and income assistance.

Social Insurance

Social insurance programs are designed to help make up for the lost income of people who worked but are now retired, temporarily unemployed, or unable to work because of disability or work-related injury. The major social insurance program is **Social Security,** established during the Great Depression to supplement retirement income of those with a

SOCIAL SECURITY

Supplements retirement income to those with a record of contributing to the program during their working years; by far the largest government redistribution program

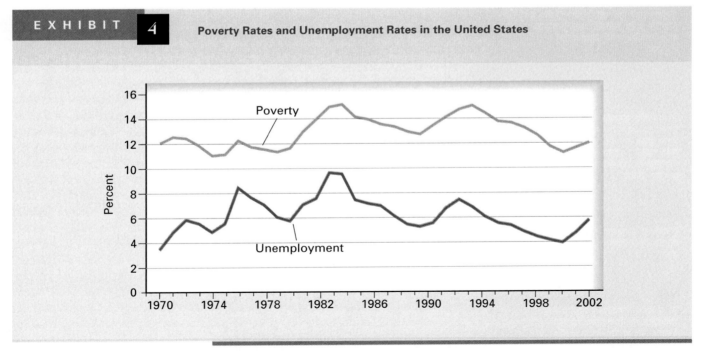

EXHIBIT 4   **Poverty Rates and Unemployment Rates in the United States**

Sources: U.S. Census Bureau and U.S. Bureau of Labor Statistics.

work history and a record of contributing to the program. **Medicare,** another social insurance program, provides health insurance for short-term medical care, mostly to those age 65 and older, regardless of income. There are over 40 million Social Security and Medicare beneficiaries. Other social insurance programs include *unemployment insurance* and *workers' compensation,* which supports workers injured on the job; both programs require that beneficiaries have a prior record of employment.

The social insurance system deducts "insurance premiums" from workers' pay to provide benefits to other retired, disabled, and unemployed individuals. These programs protect some families from poverty, particularly the elderly receiving Social Security, but they are aimed more at those with a work history. Still, the social insurance system tends to redistribute income from rich to poor and from young to old. Most current Social Security beneficiaries receive far more in benefits than they paid into the program, especially those with a brief work history or a record of low wages.

Income Assistance

Income assistance programs—what we usually call welfare programs—provide money and in-kind assistance to the poor. Unlike social insurance programs, income assistance programs do not require recipients to have a history of work or to have contributed to the program. Income assistance programs are means tested. In a **means-tested program,** a household's income and assets must fall below a certain level to qualify for benefits. The federal government funds two-thirds of welfare spending, and state and local governments fund one-third.

The two primary *cash transfer* programs are **Temporary Assistance for Needy Families (TANF),** which provides cash to poor families with dependent children, and **Supplemental Security Income (SSI),** which provides cash to the elderly poor and the disabled. Cash transfers vary inversely with family income from other sources. In 1997, TANF replaced Aid for Families with Dependent Children (AFDC), which began during the Great Depression and originally supported widows with young children. Whereas AFDC was a federal *entitlement* program, meaning that anyone who met the criteria was *entitled* to benefits, TANF is under the control of each state and carries no federal entitlement. The federal government gives each state a fixed grant to help fund TANF programs.

The SSI program provides support for the elderly and disabled poor. It is the fastest-growing cash transfer program, with federal outlays quadrupling from $8 billion in 1980 to nearly $31 billion by 2002, when 6.5 million people averaged $380 per month in federal benefits. SSI coverage has been broadened to include people addicted to drugs and alcohol, children with learning disabilities, and, in some cases, the homeless. The federal portion of this program is uniform across states, but states can supplement federal aid. Benefits in California average twice those in Alabama. Most states also offer modest *General Assistance* aid to those who are poor but do not qualify for TANF or SSI.

The federal government also provides an **earned-income tax credit,** which supplements wages of the working poor. For example, a family with two children and earning $14,500 in 2002 would not only pay no federal income tax but would receive a cash transfer of $4,140. More than 19.2 million recipients received such transfers in 2002, when outlays topped $30 billion, nearly double federal spending on TANF. The earned income tax credit lifts millions of families out of poverty.

In addition to cash transfers, a variety of *in-kind transfer* programs provide health care, food stamps, and housing assistance to the poor. **Medicaid** pays for medical care for those with low incomes who are aged, blind, disabled, or are living in families with dependent children. *Medicaid is by far the largest welfare program, costing nearly twice as much as all cash transfer programs combined.* It has grown more than any other poverty program, quadrupling in the last decade and accounting for nearly a quarter of the typical state's budget (though states receive federal grants covering half or more of their Medicaid budget). The qualifying level of income is set by each state, and some states are strict. Therefore, the proportion of poor covered by Medicaid varies across states. In 2002, about 40 million people received Medicaid benefits at a total cost of over $240 billion; outlays averaged about $6,000 per recipient. For many elderly, Medicaid covers long-term nursing care, which can exceed $100,000 per year. Although half the nation's welfare budget goes for health care, nearly 44 million U.S. residents, or one in seven people, still had no health insurance in 2002.

Food stamps are vouchers that the poor can redeem for food. In 2003, nearly 21.5 million people received food stamps in the average month, down from an all-time high of 27.5 million recipients in 1994. Monthly benefits averaged $82 per person in 2003. Four of 10 people eligible for food stamps do not apply for them.

Housing assistance programs include direct assistance for rental payments and subsidized low-income housing. Spending for housing assistance has more than doubled since 1990. About 10 million people receive some form of housing assistance. Other in-kind transfer programs include the *school lunch program* for poor children; supplemental food vouchers for pregnant women, infants, and children; *energy assistance* to help pay the energy bills of poor families; and *education and training assistance* for poor families, such as Head Start. *In all, there are about 75 means-tested federal welfare programs.*

FOOD STAMPS

An in-kind transfer program that offers low-income households vouchers redeemable for food; benefit levels vary inversely with household income

Who Are the Poor?

Economics
in the Movies

Who are the poor, and how has the composition of this group changed over time? We will slice poverty statistics in several ways to examine the makeup of the group. Keep in mind that we are relying on official poverty estimates, which ignore the value of in-kind transfers, so, to that extent, official estimates overstate poverty.

Poverty and Age

Earlier we looked at poverty among the U.S. population. Here we focus on poverty and age. Exhibit 5 presents the poverty rates for three age groups since 1959: people less than 18 years old, those between 18 and 64, and those 65 and older. As you can see, poverty rates for each group declined between 1959 and 1968. Between the mid-1970s and the early 1980s, the rate among those under 18 trended upward, but then declined from 22.7 percent in 1993 to 16.7 percent in 2002.

In 1959, the elderly were the poorest group, with a poverty rate of 35 percent. Poverty among the elderly has declined to 10.4 percent by 2002, slightly below the rate of 10.6 percent for people 18 to 64 years of age. The decline in poverty among the elderly stems from the tremendous growth in spending for Social Security and Medicare. In real terms—that is, after adjusting for the effects of inflation—those two programs have grown more than twelve-fold since 1959 (Medicare didn't even exist until 1965). *Although not welfare programs in a strict sense, Social Security and Medicare have been hugely successful in reducing poverty among the elderly.*

Poverty and Public Choice

In a democracy, public policies depend very much on the political power of the interest groups involved. In recent years, the elderly have become a powerful political force. The voter participation rate of those 65 and over is higher than that of any other age group. For example, people 65 years of age and older vote at triple the rate of those between 18 and 24

HOMEWORK
Xpress!
econ-apps debate

EXHIBIT 5   **Poverty Rates by Age: 1959–2002**

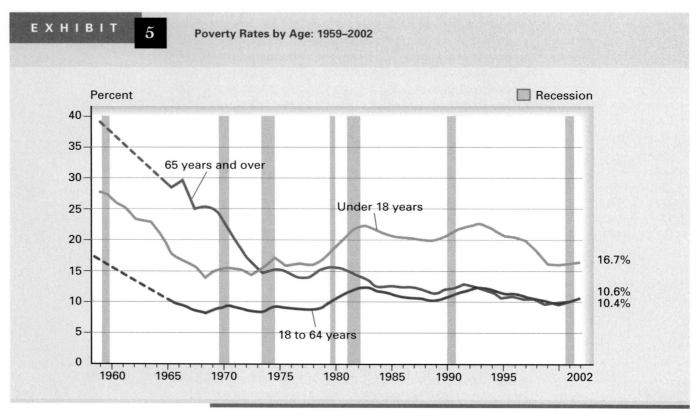

Source: U.S. Census Bureau, *Poverty in the United States: 2002*, Current Population Reports, September 2003, Figure 2, http://www.census.gov/prod/2003pubs/p60-222.pdf.

and four times that of welfare recipients. The political muscle of the elderly has been flexed whenever a question of Social Security benefits are considered.

Unlike most interest groups, the elderly make up a group we all expect to join one day. The elderly are actually represented by five constituencies: (1) the elderly themselves; (2) people under 65 who are concerned about the current benefits to their parents or other elderly relatives; (3) people under 65 who are concerned about their own benefits in the future; (4) people who earn their living by caring for the elderly, such as doctors, nurses, and nursing-home operators; and (5) candidates for office who want to harvest the votes that seniors deliver. So the elderly have a broad constituency, and this pays off in terms of redistribution of wealth to the elderly and in the reduction of poverty among this group.

The Feminization of Poverty

Another way to look at poverty is based on the status of the household head. Exhibit 6 compares poverty rates among families headed by females with no husband present with poverty rates for other families. Two trends are unmistakable. First, poverty rates among families headed by females are much higher than rates among other families—about five times higher on average. Second, poverty rates among female-headed families have declined in the last decade, falling from 39.7 percent in 1991 to 28.8 percent in 2002.

The exhibit compares poverty among female householders to other families. What it doesn't show is the growth in the number of female-headed households. The number of families

Poverty Rates Are Much Higher for Families Headed by Females But Have Declined in the Last Decade

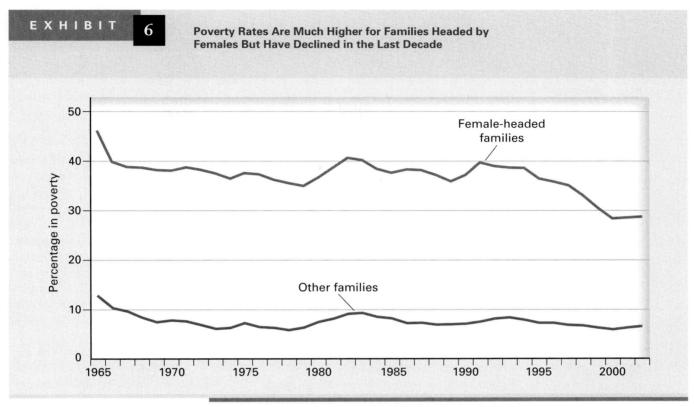

Source: Developed from data in U.S. Census Bureau, *Poverty in the United States: 2002*, Current Population Reports, September 2003, Appendix Table A-1, http://www.census.gov/prod/2003pubs/p60-222.pdf.

headed by women increased 148 percent between 1965 and 2002, while all other families grew just 21 percent. The percentage of births to unmarried mothers is five times greater today than in the 1960s. In 1960, only 1 in 200 children lived with a single parent who had never married. Today, 1 in 10 children lives with a single parent who has never married.

The United States has the highest teenage pregnancy rate in the developed world—twice the rate of Great Britain and 15 times that of Japan. Because the fathers in such cases typically provide little child care or support, children born outside marriage are likely to be poorer than other children. The divorce rate has also increased since 1960. Because of the higher divorce rate, even children born to married couples now face a greater likelihood of living in a one-parent household before they grow up. Divorce usually reduces the resources available to the children.

The growth in the number of poor families since 1965 resulted overwhelmingly from a growth in the number of female householders. The U.S. economy has generated 70 million new jobs in the last four decades. Families with a female householder were in the worst position to take advantage of this job growth. *Children of female householders are five times more likely to live in poverty than are other children. Young, single motherhood is a recipe for poverty.* Often the young mother drops out of school, which reduces her future earning possibilities when and if she seeks work outside the home. Even a strong economy is little aid to households with nobody in the labor force. Worse yet, young, single mothers-to-be are less likely to seek adequate medical care; the result is a higher proportion of premature, underweight babies. This is one reason why the

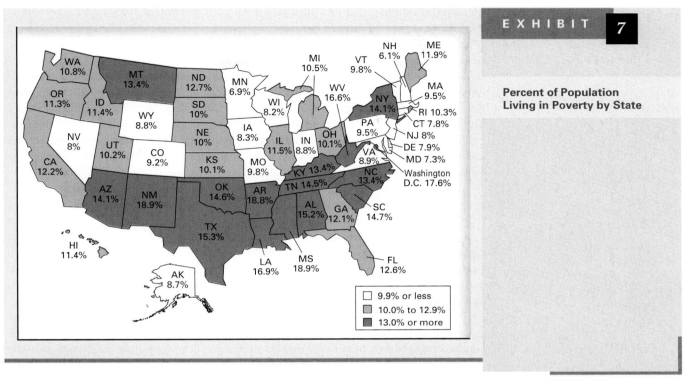

EXHIBIT 7

Percent of Population Living in Poverty by State

Source: *Poverty in the United States: 2002,* U.S. Census Bureau, September 2003, Table 4, http://www.census.gov/prod/2003pubs/p60-222.pdf. Rates are averaged for 2001 and 2002 to provide more reliable figures.

received a lower *quality* of schooling than white workers. For example, black students are less likely to use computers in school. Inner-city schools often have more problems with classroom discipline, which takes time and attention away from instruction. Such quality differences could account for at least a portion of the remaining gap in standardized wages.

Evidence of discrimination comes from studies where otherwise similar white and black candidates are sent to the same source to seek jobs, rent apartments, or apply for mortgage loans. For example, white and black job applicants with similar qualifications and résumés applied for the same job. These studies find that employers are less likely to interview or offer a job to minority applicants. Minority applicants also tend to be treated less favorably by real estate agents and lenders. The President's Council of Economic Advisers concluded that discrimination against members of racial and ethnic minorities, while "far less pervasive and overt" than in the past, still persists.[9]

Affirmative Action

The Equal Employment Opportunity Commission, established by the Civil Rights Act of 1964, monitors cases involving unequal pay for equal work and unequal access to promotion. All companies doing business with the federal government had to set numerical hiring, promotion, and training goals to ensure that these firms did not discriminate in hiring on the basis of race, sex, religion, or national origin. Black employment increased in those firms required to file affirmative action plans.[10] The fraction of the black labor force

9. *Economic Report of the President,* February 1998, 152.
10. James Smith and Finis Welch, "Black Economic Progress After Myrdal," *Journal of Economic Literature* 27 (June 1989): 519–563.

employed in white-collar jobs increased from 16.5 percent in 1960 to 40.5 percent in 1981—an increase that greatly exceeded the growth of white-collar jobs in the labor force as a whole. Research also suggests that civil rights legislation played a role in narrowing the black-white earnings gap between 1960 and the mid-1970s.[11]

Attention focused on hiring practices and equality of opportunity at the state and local levels as well, as governments introduced so-called *set-aside* programs to guarantee minorities a share of contracts. But a 1995 U.S. Supreme Court decision challenged affirmative action programs, ruling that Congress must meet a rigorous legal standard to justify any contracting or hiring practice based on race, especially programs that reserve jobs for minorities and women. Programs must be shown to be in response to injustices created by past discrimination, said the Court.

In summary, evidence suggests that black workers earn less than white workers after adjustment for other factors that could affect wages, such as education and job experience. Part of this wage gap may reflect differences in the quality of education, differences that could themselves be the result of discrimination. Keep in mind that unemployment rates are higher among black people than among white people and are higher still among black teenagers, the group most in need of job skills and job experience. *But we should also note that black families are not a homogeneous group. In fact, the distribution of income is more uneven among black families than it is among the population as a whole.*

On the upside, according to the *Economic Report of the President:* Since 1993, the median income of black families has risen faster than that of white families. The proportion of black families living below the poverty line fell to a record low. And there is a growing middle class among black households. Since 1970, the number of black doctors, nurses, college professors, and newspaper reporters has more than doubled; the number of black engineers, computer programmers, accountants, managers, and administrators has more than tripled; the number of black elected officials has quadrupled; and the number of black lawyers has increased sixfold. Three of the most admired Americans are black—talk show host Oprah Winfrey, basketball legend Michael Jordan, and Secretary of State Colin Powell, who arguably could get elected U.S. president if he chose to run.

Unintended Consequences of Income Assistance

On the plus side, antipoverty programs increase the consumption possibilities of poor families, and this is important, especially because children are the largest poverty group. But programs to assist the poor have secondary effects that limit their ability to reduce poverty. Here we consider some unintended consequences.

Disincentives

Society, through government, tries to provide families with an adequate standard of living, but society also wants to ensure that only those in need receive benefits. As we have seen, income assistance consists of a combination of cash and in-kind transfer programs. Because these programs are designed to help the poor and only the poor, the level of benefits varies inversely with income from other sources. This inverse relationship has resulted in a system where transfers decline sharply as earned income increases, in effect imposing a high marginal tax rate on that earned income. An increase in earnings may reduce benefits from TANF, Medicaid, food stamps, housing assistance, energy assistance, and other programs.

11. David Card and Alan Krueger, "Trends in Relative Black-White Earnings Revisited," *American Economic Review* 83 (May 1993): 85–91.

With a loss in support from each program as earned income increases, working may lead to little or no increase in total income. Over certain income ranges, the welfare recipient may lose more than $1 in welfare benefits for each additional $1 in earnings. Thus, the *marginal tax rate* on earned income could exceed 100 percent.

Holding even a part-time job involves additional expenses—for clothing, transportation, and child care, for instance—not to mention the loss of free time. Such a system of perverse incentives can frustrate people trying to work their way off welfare. *The high marginal tax rate discourages employment and self-sufficiency.* In many cases, the value of welfare benefits exceeds the disposable income resulting from full-time employment.

The longer people are out of the labor force, the more their job skills deteriorate, so when they do look for work, their productivity and their pay are lower than when they were last employed. This lowers their expected wage, making work even less attractive. Some economists argue that in this way, welfare benefits can lead to long-term dependency. While welfare seems to be a rational choice in the short run, it has unfavorable long-term consequences for the family, for society, and for the economy.

Welfare programs can cause other disincentives. For example, children may be eligible for Supplemental Security Income if they have a learning disability. According to one first-hand account, some low-income parents encouraged poor performance in school so their children would qualify for this program.[12]

Does Welfare Cause Dependency?

A relatively brief stay on welfare would be evidence of little dependency. But the same family staying on welfare year after year is a matter of concern. To explore the question of whether welfare causes dependency, a University of Michigan study tracked 5,000 families over a number of years, paying particular attention to economic mobility both from year to year and from one generation to the next.[13] The study first examined poverty from year to year, or dependency within a generation. It found that most received welfare for less than a year, but about 30 percent remained on welfare for at least eight years. Thus, there was a core of long-term recipients.

A serious concern is whether the children on welfare end up on welfare as adults. Is there a cycle of dependency? Why might we expect one? Children in welfare households may learn the ropes about the welfare system and may come to view welfare as a normal way of life rather than as a temporary bridge over a rough patch. Research indicates that daughters from welfare families are more likely than daughters in other families to participate in the welfare system themselves and are more likely to have premarital births.[14] It is difficult to say whether welfare "causes" the link between mother and daughter, because the same factors that contribute to a mother's welfare status can also contribute to her daughter's welfare status. Evidence of a link is weaker when it comes to sons from welfare families.

Welfare Reform

There has been much dissatisfaction with the welfare system, among both those who pay for the programs and direct beneficiaries. Welfare reforms introduced in recent years have been aimed at reducing long-term dependency.

---

12. Jacqueline Goldwyn Kingon, "Education Life: A View from the Trenches," *New York Times,* 8 April 2001.
13. Greg J. Duncan et al., *Years of Poverty, Years of Plenty* (Ann Arbor: University of Michigan Press, 1984).
14. Robert Moffit, "Incentive Effects of the U.S. Welfare System: A Review," *Journal of Economic Literature* 30 (March 1992): 37.

Recent Reforms

Some analysts believe that one way to reduce poverty is to provide welfare recipients with job skills and make them find jobs. Even before the 1996 federal reform of welfare, to be discussed shortly, some sort of "workfare" component for welfare recipients operated in most states. In these states, as a condition of receiving welfare, the head of the household had to participate in education and training programs, search for work, or take some paid or unpaid position. The idea was to expose people on welfare to the job market. Evidence from various states indicates that programs involving mandatory job searches, short-term unpaid work, and training could operate at low cost and could increase employment. The government saved money because those in welfare-to-work programs left welfare rolls sooner.

Reforms at the state level set the stage for federal reforms. By far the biggest reform in the welfare system in the last 70 years came with the 1996 legislation that replaced Aid to Families with Dependent Children (AFDC) with Temporary Assistance for Needy Families (TANF). Whereas the AFDC program set eligibility rules and left federal costs open-ended through matching grants to the states, TANF offers a fixed grant to the states to run their welfare programs. States ended AFDC and began TANF by July 1, 1997. Under the new system, states have much control over their own welfare programs. But concerns about welfare dependency fostered some special provisions. The act imposes a five-year lifetime limit on cash transfers and requires states to move a certain percentage of people from welfare to work.

Aside from the time limits and work participation rates imposed by the federal government, states are free to set benefit levels and experiment however they choose. For example, about half the states impose time limits shorter than five years. Some observers fear that states now have an incentive to keep welfare costs down by cutting benefits. To avoid becoming destinations for poor people—that is, to avoid becoming "welfare magnets"—states may be tempted to offer relatively low benefits. The fear is that states will undercut benefits in what has been called a "race to the bottom."

The following case study surveys some results of welfare reform so far.

HOMEWORK
Xpress!
econ-apps debate

C a s e S t u d y

Public Policy

eActivity

The Urban Institute is a policy research organization working to increase citizens' awareness of important public choices. Go to its Web site at http://www.urban.org and search for its report "Does Work Pay?" See if going to work improves the standard of living for low-income single mothers on welfare who continue to receive assistance from other benefit programs. For more reports about welfare to work, go to Moving Ideas, recommended links on Poverty, Income, and Wealth at http://www.movingideas.org/ideas/subjects/welfare-1.html.

Is Welfare-to-Work Working?

Here are some preliminary conclusions about the course of welfare reform. Work requirements and time limits have resulted in substantial declines in the welfare caseload. The number of welfare recipients peaked in January 1994 at 14.2 million, mostly single women with children. By 2003 the rolls had fallen to 4.9 million—65 percent below the peak. Exhibit 8 shows the percentage of the U.S. population on welfare since 1960. Note the sharp decline in recent years. As a share of the U.S. population, welfare recipients fell from 5.5 percent in 1994 to 1.7 percent in 2003, the lowest rate since 1960. Fortunately, the reforms were introduced during

© Gilles Mingasson/Liaison/Getty Images

an expanding economy, with the unemployment rate the lowest in three decades. But welfare rolls continued to decline, albeit at a slower rate, during the recession year of 2001, and in 2002 and 2003, years when the U.S. economy continued to lose jobs. One study found that those in welfare-to-work programs experienced longer job tenure than other employees.

Because most people on welfare are poorly educated and have few job skills, wages for those who find jobs remain low. Part-time work is common. On the plus side, the earned-income tax credit provides additional income to low-income workers—up to $4,140 in

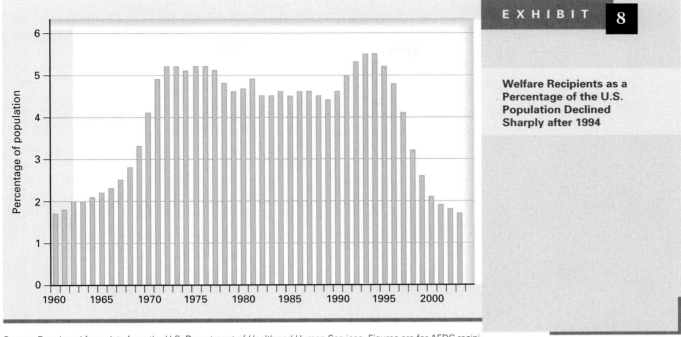

EXHIBIT 8

Welfare Recipients as a Percentage of the U.S. Population Declined Sharply after 1994

Source: Developed from data from the U.S. Department of Health and Human Services. Figures are for AFDC recipients before 1997 and TANF recipients for 1997 and later.

2002. Most of those going to work can continue to receive food stamps, child care, and Medicaid. Because the welfare rolls have declined but federal grants have not, welfare spending per recipient has increased significantly. Most states are combining tough new rules with an expanded menu of welfare services. States have made large investments in work-related services such as job placement, transportation, and especially child care.

Other positive developments include falling rates of crime and drug abuse; the greatest decline in child poverty, especially black child poverty, since the 1960s; and a substantial increase in employment among mothers who head families, especially those who have never married. The proportion of black children living with married parents increased from 35 percent in 1995 to 39 percent in 2000. And a Michigan study found that former welfare mothers with jobs are significantly less likely than mothers still on welfare to report domestic violence or homelessness.

One effect of the work requirements of welfare reform has been to raise the "price" of going on welfare. As one welfare director noted, a lot of people who are leaving welfare are saying, "It's not worth the hassle." We might say that the demand curve for welfare is downward sloping, with "hassle" measuring the price on the vertical axis. The greater the "hassle," the less the amount of welfare demanded. Many on welfare had other ways to support themselves. One expert who counted everything from food stamps to unreported income found cash transfers accounted for only about 34 percent of the average welfare recipient's income. Food stamps provided about 25 percent, and 36 percent came from unreported sources such as secret jobs, boyfriends, relatives, and charities.

Welfare rolls declined more in states where efforts to get people to work are greater. For example, Wisconsin and Minnesota had similar economies, as reflected by identical unemployment rates, but Wisconsin's more aggressive work requirements cut welfare rolls there

WALL STREET JOURNAL

Reading It **Right**

What's the relevance of the following statement from the Wall Street Journal*: "Family households maintained by women without a husband present saw incomes rise 4.0 percent to $28,116 from 1999 to 2000, the Census Department said. Other types of households had no significant change in their median household income."*

three times faster than in Minnesota. Wisconsin's success was no doubt behind President Bush's appointment of that state's governor, Tommy Thompson, to head the Department of Health and Human Services, the agency that runs federal welfare programs. During his 14 years as governor, Thompson reduced welfare payments to parents whose children skipped school and paid teenage parents more if they got married. During his tenure, the number of welfare families in the state dropped from about 100,000 in 1986 to only 16,000 in 2000. Reported cases of domestic violence also declined.

Despite the good news, some poor people are still having a hard time. The demand for emergency shelters increased with the recession of 2001, as did requests for emergency food aid. As mentioned earlier, although Medicaid is by far the most costly welfare program, nearly 44 million Americans still lacked health insurance in 2002. The welfare reform law was set to expire in 2002, but Congress has continued the measure at least through 2004 by a series of extensions.

Sources: Susan Goodin and Margo Bailey, "Welfare and Work: Job-Retention Outcomes of Federal Welfare-to-Work Employees," *Public Administration Review*, January 2001; Tyrone Cheng, "Welfare Recidivism Among Former Welfare Recipients," *Families and Society: The Journal of Contemporary Human Services*; Jan.–Mar., 2003; "HHS Announces Declines in TANF Caseloads," U.S. Department of Health and Human Services, 2 December 2003; and the federal site on welfare reform at http://www.acf.hhs.gov/programs/ofa/welfare/index.htm.

Along with Wisconsin, one of the most successful welfare reforms in the country is in Oregon, as discussed in our final case study.

Oregon's Program of "Tough Love"

Welfare reform in Oregon began in 1994, when the state received a federal waiver to operate under its own rules. The number receiving welfare fell from 116,390 in January 1994 to 42,341 by March 2002, for a drop of 64 percent, also the average U.S. decline. The Oregon decline came not as a result of strict time limits or tougher eligibility standards but by providing strong work incentives and working more closely with welfare beneficiaries. The state combines training and education with help for drug abuse, mental health, domestic violence, and other barriers to employment, even encouraging some people to hold out for better jobs.

© Jim McGuire/Index Stock Imagery.

After leaving TANF for work, people in Oregon continue to qualify for several programs including (1) health benefits for at least a year, (2) child care until income reaches 200 percent of the federal poverty level, (3) food stamps for those who are eligible, and (4) the federal earned-income tax credit, which in effect can raise the wage more than $1 an hour. By working full time at the state's minimum wage of $7 an hour in 2003, a family's living standard would exceed 130 percent of the poverty level. In comparison, the typical family on welfare and food stamps was living at only 75 percent of the poverty level. Thus, work becomes more attractive than welfare. What's more, the average starting wage in the first job after welfare exceeded the minimum wage.

One federal study tracked 5,500 welfare recipients in Oregon over a two-year period, where half the group participated in the welfare-to-work program and half did not. Taking part in the welfare-to-work program increased employment by 18 percent, raised average earnings over the two years by 35 percent, and boosted the proportion of individuals with employer-provided health insurance by 71 percent.

Oregon became the first state to require drug addicts to attend treatment to qualify for welfare. An evaluation of that program found that clients who completed drug treatment earned 65 percent more than similar clients in a comparison group. Those completing treatment for addiction were 45 percent less likely to be arrested and only half as likely to be investigated for child abuse or neglect. The study also found that every dollar Oregon spent on drug treatment saved $5.60 on other social services. The approach in most other states is simply to ban recent drug felons from receiving aid.

The Oregon program offers abundant services, but welfare applicants must first spend a month looking for work before getting help. The federal government requires states to enroll 50 percent of their recipients in job-related activity. Oregon had 89 percent of its recipients in job-related activity. Perhaps the most persuasive evidence that Oregon's approach of tough love is working is that after 18 months, only 8 percent of those who left welfare returned to the rolls. Statewide, the number of child abuse victims fell from 11,241 in 1999 to 8,424 in 2002.

Still, the road to welfare reform has not been smooth, even in Oregon. People coming off welfare often start near the poverty line. A University of Oregon study followed 1,000 Oregon families who left welfare during the first quarter of 1998. After two years, about 70 percent were employed and about 70 percent had health-care coverage, though wages for many still hovered around the federal poverty level.

Sources: Tom Detzel, "Oregon Officials Bracing for Cuts in Welfare Services," *The Oregonian*, 21 September 2003; *National Evaluation of Welfare Strategies*, Manpower Demonstration Research Corporation, June 2000; and Elizabeth Davis and Roberta Walker, "The Dynamics of Child Care Subsidy Use by Rural Families in Oregon," *American Journal of Agricultural Economics*, 15 November 2001. An overview of Oregon's welfare programs is available at http://www.dhs.state.or.us/assistance/. State-by-state caseload information appears at http://www.acf.dhhs.gov/news/tables.htm.

Conclusion

Government redistribution programs have been most successful at reducing poverty among the elderly. But until recently, poverty rates among children increased because of the growth in the number of female householders. We might ask why transfer programs have reduced poverty rates more among the elderly than among female householders. Transfer programs do not encourage people to get old; that process occurs naturally and is independent of the level of transfers. But the level and availability of transfer programs at the margin could influence some young unmarried women as they are deciding whether or not to have a child and may, at the margin, influence a married mother's decision to get divorced.

Most transfers in the economy are not from the government but are in-kind transfers within the family, from parents to children. Thus, any change in a family's capacity to earn income has serious consequences for dependent children. Family structure is a primary determinant of family income. One in six children in the United States lives in poverty. Children are the innocent victims of the changing family structure. Recent welfare reforms are aimed at breaking the cycle of poverty and dependency.

SUMMARY

1. Money income in the United States became less evenly distributed between 1970 and 2002. Since 1959, the poverty rate has dropped most among the elderly, thanks to Social Security and Medicare.

2. Young, single motherhood is a recipe for poverty. Often the young mother drops out of school, which reduces her future earning possibilities when and if she seeks work outside the home. Growth in the number of female

householders in the last three decades increased poverty among children, though that poverty rate has declined since peaking in 1993.

3. The wage gap between black and white workers narrowed between 1940 and 1976, widened until the early 1990s, and has been narrowing again since 1993. Affirmative action programs and gains in education seem to have increased employment opportunities among black workers.

4. Among the undesirable effects of income assistance is a high marginal tax rate on earned income, which discour-

ages employment and encourages welfare dependency. Before recent welfare reforms, about 30 percent of families on welfare remained there for eight years or more.

5. Welfare reforms introduced by the states set the stage for federal welfare reforms aimed at promoting the transition from welfare to work. The states began experimenting with different systems to encourage greater personal responsibility. As a result of state reforms, federal welfare reform, and a strengthening economy, welfare rolls dropped by about 65 percent between 1994 and 2003.

QUESTIONS FOR REVIEW

1. *(Distribution of Household Income)* Look back at Exhibit 1 in this chapter. How would you explain the shift of the U.S. income distribution in the last two decades?

2. *(Lorenz Curve)* What is a Lorenz curve? What does the Lorenz curve in Exhibit 2 illustrate?

3. *(Official Poverty Level)* Although the poverty rate among single mothers has decreased since 1960, the number of poor children from such families has more than doubled. Explain.

4. *(Income Differences)* List some reasons why household incomes differ. Which factors are the most important?

5. *(Official Poverty Level)* How does the U.S. Department of Agriculture calculate the official poverty level? What government assistance programs does the Census Bureau consider when calculating household income? What programs are ignored?

6. *(Programs to Help the Poor)* Distinguish between social insurance programs and income assistance programs. Identify key examples of each.

7. *(Poverty and Age)* Poverty among the elderly fell dramatically between 1959 and 1974 and has continued to decline. However, poverty among that portion of the U.S.

population that is less than 18 years old is no lower today than in the 1970s. Why have the experiences of these two age groups differed?

8. *(Poverty and Public Choice)* Why is it difficult to pass legislation to reduce Social Security or Medicare benefits?

9. *(Poverty and Discrimination)* Which types of discrimination may cause an earnings gap between white and black workers? Consider discrimination in schooling, for example. How would researchers detect such discrimination?

10. *(Disincentives)* How does the implicit tax on earned income (in the form of lost benefits from government assistance programs as earned income increases) affect work incentives? How do some people avoid the implicit tax?

11. *(Welfare Reform)* What has happened to the welfare caseload in recent years? Discuss some differences in results across states.

12. (*C a s e* **S t u d y :** Is Welfare-to-Work Working?) Discuss the key features of welfare reforms introduced by the federal government in 1996. Why were policy makers worried that turning welfare over to the states would result in a "race to the bottom"?

EXPERIENTIAL EXERCISES

13. *(Poverty and the Poor)* Visit the Census Bureau's page on poverty statistics at http://www.census.gov/hhes/www/poverty.html. Look at the Small Area Income and Poverty Estimates, and find the latest poverty estimate for your county. How does the poverty rate there compare with the overall rate in your state and in the United States as a whole?

14. *(Wall Street Journal)* The front page of the Marketplace section of the *Wall Street Journal* often carries articles on income distribution and the personal impact of poverty. Pay particular attention to the "Work & Family" and "Business and Race" columns in the Wednesday paper. How are the actions of U.S. businesses affecting income distribution and poverty?

HOMEWORKXPRESS! EXERCISES

These exercises require access to McEachern Homework Xpress! If Homework Xpress! did not come with your book, visit **http://homeworkxpress.swlearning.com** *to purchase.*

The distribution of income among quintiles can be illustrated using a Lorenz curve.

1. In the diagram draw a line representing an equal distribution of income. Then add Lorenz curves for 1980 and 2005 based on the hypothetical data in the table.

Households (cumulative percent)	Income (cumulative percent) 1980	Income (cumulative percent) 2005
0	0	0
20	10	5
40	20	15
60	35	30
80	60	50
100	100	100

2. In the diagram for this exercise is a line representing an equal distribution of income. Sketch a Lorenz curve representing a typical distribution of income in the United States. Brazil is noted for having one of the most unequal distributions of income among major economies. Add a Lorenz curve for Brazil illustrating how the distribution there is significantly more unequal than in the United States.

International Trade

© Gary Conner/Index Stock Imagery

This morning you pulled on your Levi's jeans from Mexico, pulled over your Benetton sweater from Italy, and laced up your Timberland boots from Thailand. After a breakfast that included bananas from Honduras and coffee from Brazil, you climbed into your Volvo from Sweden fueled by Venezuelan oil and headed for a lecture by a visiting professor from Hungary. If the United States is such a rich and productive country, why do we import so many goods and services? Why don't we produce everything ourselves? And why do some groups try to restrict foreign trade? Answers to these and other questions are addressed in this chapter.

The world is a giant shopping mall, and Americans are big spenders. Americans buy Japanese cars, French wine, Chinese kitchen gadgets, European vacations, and thousands of other goods and services from around the globe. But foreigners buy American products too—grain, personal computers, aircraft, movies, trips to New

York City, and thousands of other goods and services. In this chapter, we examine the gains from international trade and the effects of trade restrictions on the allocation of resources. The analysis is based on the familiar tools of demand and supply. Topics discussed include:

- Gains from trade
- Absolute and comparative advantage revisited
- Tariffs
- Import quotas
- Welfare loss from trade restrictions
- Arguments for trade restrictions

The Gains from Trade

A family from Virginia that sits down for a meal of Kansas prime rib, Idaho potatoes, and California string beans, with Georgia peach cobbler for dessert, is benefiting from interstate trade. You already understand why the residents of one state trade with those of another. Back in Chapter 2, you learned about the gains arising from specialization and exchange. You may recall how you and your roommate could maximize output when you each specialized. The law of comparative advantage says that the individual with the lowest opportunity cost of producing a particular good should specialize in producing that good. Just as individuals benefit from specialization and exchange, so do states and, indeed, nations. To reap the gains that arise from specialization, countries engage in international trade. *With trade, each country specializes in the goods that it produces at the lowest opportunity cost.*

A Profile of Exports and Imports

Just as some states are more involved in interstate trade than others, some nations are more involved in international trade than others. For example, exports account for about one-quarter of the gross domestic product (GDP) in Canada and the United Kingdom; about one-third of GDP in Germany, Sweden, and Switzerland; and about half of GDP in the Netherlands. Despite the perception that Japan has a huge export sector, exports make up only about one-seventh of its GDP.

U.S. Exports

In the United States, exports of goods and services amounted to about 10 percent of GDP in 2003. Although small relative to GDP, exports play a growing role in the U.S. economy. The left panel of Exhibit 1 shows the composition of U.S. merchandise exports by major category. Capital goods account for 41 percent of all exports. Capital goods include high-tech products, such as computers and jet aircraft. Next most important are industrial supplies and materials, at 24 percent of the total. Together, capital goods and industrial supplies and materials make up 65 percent, or nearly two-thirds, of U.S. exports. Thus, most U.S. exports help foreign manufacturers make stuff. Consumer goods (except food, which is included in another category) account for only 13 percent of exports. This category includes entertainment products, such as movies and recorded music.

U.S. Imports

U.S. imports of goods and services were 14 percent relative to GDP in 2003. The right panel of Exhibit 1 shows the composition of U.S. merchandise imports. Whereas consumer goods accounted for only 13 percent of U.S. exports, they are the largest category of imports at 27 percent of the total. Imported consumer goods include electronics from Taiwan, shoes from Brazil, and kitchen gadgets from China. The next most important category of imports, at

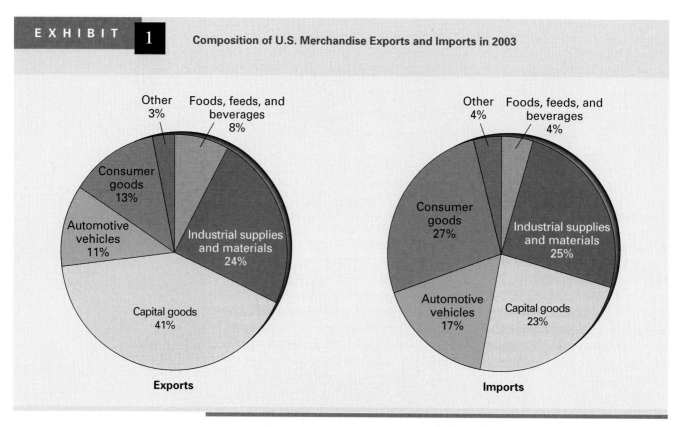

Source: Based on government figures reported by Christopher Bach, "U.S. International Transactions, 2003," *Survey of Current Business* (April 2004), Table D, p. 63.

25 percent, is industrial supplies and materials, such as crude oil from Venezuela and the Middle East and raw metals, including lead, zinc, and copper, from around the world. Ranked third is capital goods, at 23 percent, such as printing presses from Germany. Note that automotive vehicles are only 11 percent of exports but 17 percent of imports.

Raw Materials

Let's focus just on raw materials. Exhibit 2 shows, for 12 key commodities, U.S. production as a percentage of U.S. consumption. If production falls short of consumption, the United States imports the difference. For example, because America grows coffee only in Hawaii, U.S. production is only 1 percent of U.S. consumption, so nearly all coffee is imported. The exhibit also shows that U.S. production falls short of consumption for oil and metals such as lead, zinc, copper, and aluminum. If production exceeds consumption, the United States exports the difference. For example, U.S.-grown wheat amounts to 184 percent of U.S. wheat consumption, so nearly half of U.S.-grown wheat is exported. U.S. production also exceeds consumption for other crops, including cotton, oil seeds (soybeans, sunflower seeds, canola), and coarse grains (corn, barley, oats). In short, when it comes to basic commodities, the United States is a net importer of oil and metals and a net exporter of crops.

Trading Partners

To give you some feel for America's trading partners in 2003, here are the top 10 destinations for U.S. goods in order of importance: Canada, Mexico, Japan, Great Britain, Germany,

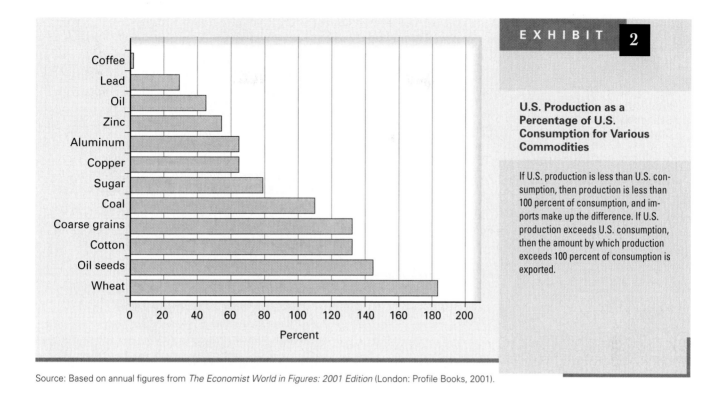

Source: Based on annual figures from *The Economist World in Figures: 2001 Edition* (London: Profile Books, 2001).

EXHIBIT 2

U.S. Production as a Percentage of U.S. Consumption for Various Commodities

If U.S. production is less than U.S. consumption, then production is less than 100 percent of consumption, and imports make up the difference. If U.S. production exceeds U.S. consumption, then the amount by which production exceeds 100 percent of consumption is exported.

China, South Korea, France, the Netherlands, and Taiwan. The top 10 sources of U.S. imports consist of Canada, China, Mexico, Japan, Germany, Great Britain, South Korea, Taiwan, France, and Italy. China makes the biggest jump in the ranks, going from sixth as a destination for U.S. exports to second as a source of U.S. imports.

Production Possibilities Without Trade

The rationale behind most international trade is obvious. The United States grows little coffee because our climate is not suited to coffee. More revealing, however, are the gains from trade where the comparative advantage is not so obvious. Suppose that just two goods—food and clothing—are produced and consumed and that there are only two countries in the world—the United States, with a labor force of 100 million workers, and the mythical country of Izodia, with 200 million workers. The conclusions derived from this simple model have general relevance for international trade.

Exhibit 3 presents production possibilities tables for each country, based on the size of the labor force and the productivity of workers in each country. The exhibit assumes that each country has a given technology and labor is fully and efficiently employed. If no trade occurs between countries, Exhibit 3 presents each country's *consumption possibilities* table as well. The production numbers imply that each worker in the United States can produce either 6 units of food or 3 units of clothing per day. If all 100 million U.S. workers are in the food industry, they produce 600 million units per day, as shown in column U_1 in panel (a). If all U.S. workers make clothing, they turn out 300 million units per day, as shown in column U_6. The columns in between show some workers making food and some making clothing. Because a U.S. worker can produce either 6 units of food or 3 units of clothing, *the opportunity cost of 1 more unit of food is ½ unit of clothing.*

| EXHIBIT | 3 |

Production Possibilities Schedules for the United States and Izodia

(a) United States

	Production Possibilities with 100 Million Workers (millions of units per day)					
	U_1	U_2	U_3	U_4	U_5	U_6
Food	600	480	360	240	120	0
Clothing	0	60	120	180	240	300

(b) Izodia

	Production Possibilities with 200 Million Workers (millions of units per day)					
	I_1	I_2	I_3	I_4	I_5	I_6
Food	200	160	120	80	40	0
Clothing	0	80	160	240	320	400

Suppose Izodian workers are less educated, work with less capital, and farm less-fertile soil than U.S. workers (think of China), so each can produce only 1 unit of food or 2 units of clothing per day. If all 200 million Izodian workers specialize in food, they can produce 200 million units of food per day, as shown in column I_1 in panel (b) of Exhibit 3. If they all make clothing, total output is 400 million units of clothing per day, as shown in column I_6. Some intermediate production possibilities are also listed in the exhibit. Because an Izodian worker can produce either 1 unit of food or 2 units of clothing, *the opportunity cost of 1 more unit of food is 2 units of clothing*.

We can convert the data in Exhibit 3 to a production possibilities frontier for each country, as shown in Exhibit 4. In each diagram, the amount of food produced is measured on the vertical axis and the amount of clothing on the horizontal axis. U.S. combinations are shown in the left panel by U_1, U_2, and so on; Izodian combinations are shown in the right panel by I_1, I_2, and so on. Because we assume that resources are perfectly adaptable to the production of each commodity, each production possibilities curve is a straight line reflecting a constant opportunity cost.

Exhibit 4 illustrates the possible combinations of food and clothing that residents of each country can produce and consume if all resources are fully and efficiently employed and there is no trade between the two countries. **Autarky** is the situation of national self-sufficiency, in which there is no economic interaction with foreign producers or consumers. Suppose that U.S. producers maximize profit and U.S. consumers maximize utility with the combination of 240 million units of food and 180 million units of clothing—combination U_4. This will be called the *autarky equilibrium*. Suppose also that Izodians are in autarky equilibrium, identified as combination I_3, of 120 million units of food and 160 million units of clothing.

AUTARKY

A situation of national self-sufficiency; there is no economic interaction with foreigners

Consumption Possibilities Based on Comparative Advantage

Economics in the Movies

In our example, each U.S. worker can produce more clothing and more food per day than can each Izodian worker, so Americans have an *absolute advantage* in the production of both goods. Recall from Chapter 2 that having an absolute advantage means being able to produce something using fewer re-

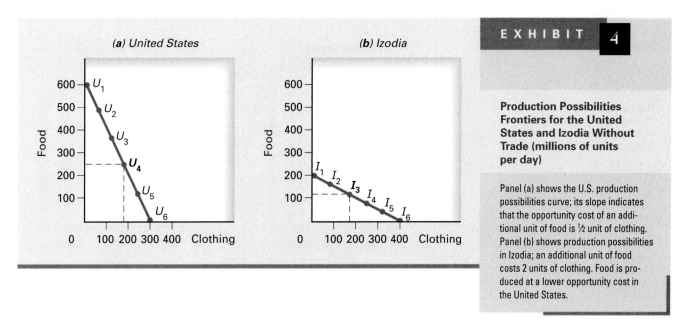

EXHIBIT 4

Production Possibilities Frontiers for the United States and Izodia Without Trade (millions of units per day)

Panel (a) shows the U.S. production possibilities curve; its slope indicates that the opportunity cost of an additional unit of food is ½ unit of clothing. Panel (b) shows production possibilities in Izodia; an additional unit of food costs 2 units of clothing. Food is produced at a lower opportunity cost in the United States.

sources than other producers require. Should the U.S. economy remain in autarky—that is, self-sufficient in both food and clothing productions—or could there be gains from trade?

As long as the opportunity cost of production differs between the two countries, there are gains from specialization and trade. The opportunity cost of producing 1 more unit of food is ½ unit of clothing in the United States compared with 2 units of clothing in Izodia. *According to the law of comparative advantage, each country should specialize in producing the good with the lower opportunity cost.* Because the opportunity cost of producing food is lower in the United States than in Izodia, both countries will gain if the United States specializes in food and exports some to Izodia, and Izodia specializes in clothing and exports some to the United States.

Before countries can trade, they must somehow agree on how much of one good exchanges for another—that is, they must establish the **terms of trade.** As long as Americans can get more than ½ unit of clothing for each unit of food, and as long as Izodians can get more than ½ unit of food for each unit of clothing, both countries will be better off by specialization and exchange rather than autarky. Suppose that market forces shape the terms of trade so that 1 unit of clothing exchanges for 1 unit of food. Americans thus trade 1 unit of food to Izodians for 1 unit of clothing. To produce 1 unit of clothing themselves, Americans would have to sacrifice 2 units of food. Likewise, Izodians trade 1 unit of clothing to Americans for 1 unit of food, which is only half what Izodians would sacrifice to produce 1 unit of food themselves.

Exhibit 5 shows that with 1 unit of food trading for 1 unit of clothing, Americans and Izodians can consume anywhere along their blue consumption possibilities frontiers. *The consumption possibilities frontier* shows a nation's possible combinations of goods available as a result of production and foreign trade. (Note that the U.S. consumption possibilities curve does not extend to the right of 400 million units of clothing, because that's the most Izodians can produce.) The amount each country actually consumes will depend on the relative preferences for food and clothing. Suppose Americans select combination *U* in panel (a) and Izodians select point *I* in panel (b).

Without trade, the United States produces and consumes 240 million units of food and 180 million units of clothing. With trade, the United States specializes in food by producing

TERMS OF TRADE

How much of one good exchanges for a unit of another good

Production (and Consumption) Possibility Frontiers with Trade (millions of units per day)

If Izodia and the United States can trade at the rate of 1 unit of clothing for 1 unit of food, both can benefit. Consumption possibilities at these terms of trade are shown by the blue lines. The United States was previously producing and consuming U_4. By trading with Izodia, it can produce only food and still consume combination U, which has more food and more clothing than U_4. Likewise, Izodia can attain preferred combination I by trading its clothing for U.S. food. Both countries are better off as a result of international trade.

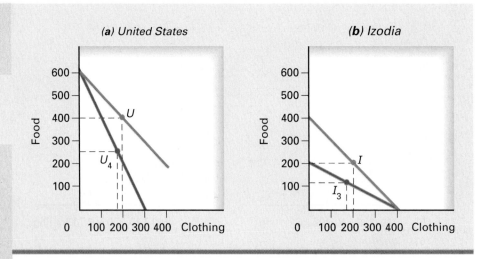

600 million units; Americans eat 400 million units and exchange the rest for 200 million units of Izodian clothing. This consumption combination is reflected by point U. Through exchange, Americans increase their consumption of both food and clothing.

Without trade, Izodians produce and consume 120 million units of food and 160 million units of clothing. With trade, Izodians specialize to produce 400 million units of clothing; they wear 200 million units and exchange the rest for 200 million units of U.S. food. This consumption combination is shown by point I. Through trade, Izodians, like Americans, are able to increase their consumption of both goods. How is this possible?

Because Americans are more efficient in the production of food and Izodians more efficient in the production of clothing, total output increases when each specializes. Without specialization, total world production was 360 million units of food and 340 million units of clothing. With specialization, food increases to 600 million units and clothing to 400 million units. Thus, both countries increase consumption with trade. *Although the United States has an absolute advantage in both goods, differences in the opportunity cost of production between the two nations ensure that specialization and exchange result in mutual gains.* Remember that comparative advantage, not absolute advantage, creates gains from specialization and trade. The only constraint on trade is that, for each good, *total world production must equal total world consumption.*

We simplified trade relations in our example to highlight the gains from specialization and exchange. We assumed that each country would completely specialize in producing a particular good, that resources were equally adaptable to the production of either good, that the costs of transporting goods from one country to another were inconsequential, and that there were no problems in arriving at the terms of trade. The world is not that simple. For example, we don't expect a country to produce just one good. Regardless, the law of comparative advantage still leads to gains from trade.

Reasons for International Specialization

Countries trade with one another—or, more precisely, people and firms in one country trade with those in another—because each side expects to gain from exchange. How do we know what each country should produce and what each should trade?

Differences in Resource Endowments

Trade is often prompted by differences in resource endowment that results in differences in the opportunity cost of production across countries. Some countries are blessed with an abundance of fertile land and favorable growing seasons. The United States, for example, has been called the "breadbasket of the world" because of its rich farmland ideal for growing corn. Coffee grows best in the climate and elevation of Colombia, Brazil, and Jamaica. Honduras has the ideal climate for growing bananas. Thus, the United States exports corn and imports coffee and bananas. Differences in the seasons across countries also serve as a basis for trade. For example, during the winter, Americans import fruit from Chile, and Canadians travel to Florida for sun and fun. During the summer, Americans export fruit to Chile, and Americans travel to Canada for camping and hiking.

Mineral resources are often concentrated in particular countries: oil in Saudi Arabia, bauxite in Jamaica, diamonds in South Africa. The United States has abundant coal supplies, but not enough oil to satisfy domestic demand. Thus, the United States exports coal and imports oil. More generally, *countries export products they can produce more cheaply in return for those that are unavailable domestically or are more costly to produce than to buy from other countries.* Remember, trade is based on comparative advantage, which is the ability to produce something at a lower opportunity cost than other producers face.

Economies of Scale

If production is subject to *economies of scale*—that is, if long-run average cost falls as a firm expands its scale of operation—countries can gain from trade if each nation specializes. Such specialization allows firms in each nation to produce more, which reduces average costs. The primary reason for establishing the single integrated market of the European Union was to offer producers there a large, open market of over 450 million consumers so that producers could achieve economies of scale, and thereby produce at a lower opportunity cost than faced by foreign producers. Firms and countries producing at the lowest opportunity costs are most competitive in international markets.

Differences in Tastes

Even if all countries had identical resource endowments and combined those resources with equal efficiency, each country would still gain from trade as long as tastes differed among countries. Consumption patterns differ across countries and some of this likely results from differences in tastes. For example, the Czechs and Irish drink three times as much beer per capita as do the Swiss and Swedes. The French drink three times as much wine as do Australians. The Danes eat twice as much pork as do Americans. Americans eat twice as much chicken as do Hungarians. Soft drinks are four times more popular in the United States than in Europe. The English like tea; Americans, coffee. Algeria has an ideal climate for growing grapes, but its large Muslim population abstains from alcohol; thus, Algeria exports wine.

Trade Restrictions and Welfare Loss

Despite the benefits of international trade, nearly all countries at one time or another erect trade barriers. Trade restrictions usually benefit some domestic producers but harm some other domestic producers and all domestic consumers. In this section, we will consider the effects of restrictions and the reasons they are imposed.

Tariffs

A *tariff,* a term first introduced in Chapter 3, is a tax on imports. (Tariffs can apply to exports, too, but we will focus on import tariffs.) A tariff can be either *specific,* such as a tariff of $5 per barrel of oil, or *ad valorem,* such as 10 percent on the import price of jeans. Consider the effects of a specific tariff on a particular good. In Exhibit 6, *D* is the U.S. demand for sugar and *S* is the supply of sugar from U.S. growers (there were about 10,000 U.S. sugarcane growers in 2004). Suppose that the world price of sugar is $0.10 per pound, as it was recently. The **world price** is determined by the world supply and demand for a product. It is the price at which any supplier can sell output on the world market and at which any demander can purchase output on the world market.

With free trade, U.S. consumers can buy any amount desired at the world price of $0.10 per pound, so the quantity demanded is 70 million pounds per month, of which U.S. producers supply 20 million pounds and 50 million pounds are imported. Because U.S. buyers can purchase sugar at the world price, U.S. producers can't charge more than that. Now

WORLD PRICE

The price at which a good is traded on the world market; determined by the world supply and world demand for the good

---

EXHIBIT   **6**

HOMEWORK **Xpress!** *Graphing*

Effect of a Tariff

At a world price of $0.10 per pound, U.S. consumers demand 70 million pounds of sugar per month, and U.S. producers supply 20 million pounds per month; the difference is imported. After the imposition of a $0.05 per pound tariff, the U.S. price rises to $0.15 per pound. U.S. producers increase production to 30 million pounds, and U.S. consumers cut back to 60 million pounds. Imports fall to 30 million pounds. At the higher U.S. price, consumers are worse off; their loss of consumer surplus is the sum of areas *a*, *b*, *c*, and *d*. Area *a* represents an increase in producer surplus; this area is transferred from consumers to producers. Area *b* reflects the higher marginal cost of domestically producing sugar that could have been produced more cheaply abroad; thus *b* is a net U.S. welfare loss. Area *c* shows government revenue from the tariff. Area *d* reflects the loss of consumer surplus resulting from the drop in consumption. The net welfare loss to the U.S. economy consists of areas *b* and *d*.

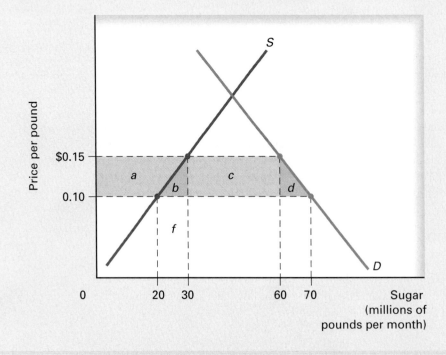

suppose that a specific tariff of $0.05 is imposed on each pound of imported sugar, raising its price from $0.10 to $0.15 per pound. U.S. producers can therefore raise their own price to $0.15 per pound as well without losing customers to imports. At the higher price, the quantity supplied by U.S. producers increases to 30 million pounds, but the quantity demanded by U.S. consumers declines to 60 million pounds. Because quantity demanded has declined and quantity supplied by U.S. producers has increased, U.S. imports fall from 50 million to 30 million pounds.

Because the price is higher after the tariff, consumers are worse off. Their loss in consumer surplus is identified in Exhibit 6 by the combination of the blue- and pink-shaded areas. Because both the U.S. price and the quantity supplied by U.S. producers have increased, U.S. producers' total revenue increases by the areas *a* plus *b* plus *f*. But only area *a* represents an increase in producer surplus. The increased revenue represented by the areas *f* plus *b* merely offsets the higher marginal cost of expanding U.S. sugar production from 20 million to 30 million pounds per month. Area *b* represents part of the net welfare loss to the domestic economy because those 10 million pounds could have been imported for $0.10 per pound rather than produced domestically at a higher marginal cost.

Government revenue from the tariff is identified by area *c,* which equals the tariff of $0.05 per pound multiplied by the 30 million pounds that are imported, or $1.5 million per month. Tariff revenue represents a loss to consumers, but because the tariff goes to the government, it can be used to lower taxes or to increase public services, so it's not a loss to society. Area *d* shows a loss in consumer surplus because less sugar is consumed at the higher price. This loss is not redistributed to anyone else, so area *d* reflects part of the net welfare loss of the tariff. Therefore, areas *b* and *d* show the domestic economy's net welfare loss of the tariff; *the two triangles measure a loss in consumer surplus that is not offset by a gain to anyone in the domestic economy.*

In summary: Of the total loss in U.S. consumer surplus (areas *a, b, c,* and *d*) resulting from the tariff, area *a* is redistributed to U.S producers, area *c* becomes government revenue, and areas *b* and *d* are net losses in domestic social welfare because of the tariff.

Import Quotas

An *import quota* is a legal limit on the amount of a particular commodity that can be imported. Quotas usually target imports from certain countries. For example, a quota may limit automobiles from Japan or shoes from Brazil. To have an impact on the domestic market*,* a quota must be less than would be imported under free trade. Consider a quota on the U.S. market for sugar. In panel (a) of Exhibit 7, *D* is the U.S. demand curve and *S* is the supply curve of U.S. sugar producers. Suppose again that the world price of sugar is $0.10 per pound. With free trade, that price would prevail in the U.S. market as well, and a total of 70 million pounds would be demanded. U.S. producers would supply 20 million pounds and importers, 50 million pounds. With a quota of 50 million pounds or more per month, the U.S. price would remain the same as the world price of $0.10 per pound, and quantity would be 70 million pounds per month. In short, a quota of at least 50 million pounds would not raise the U.S. price above the world price. A more stringent quota, however, would reduce imports, which, as we'll see, would raise the U.S. price.

Suppose U.S. trade officials impose an import quota of 30 million pounds per month. As long as the U.S. price is at or above the world price of $0.10 per pound, foreign producers supply 30 million pounds. So at prices at or above $0.10 per pound, the total supply of sugar to the U.S. market is found by adding 30 million pounds of imported sugar to the amount supplied by U.S. producers. U.S. and foreign producers would never sell for less than $0.10 per

E X H I B I T   7

Effect of a Quota

In panel (a), *D* is the U.S. demand curve and *S* is the supply curve of U.S. producers. When the government establishes a sugar quota of 30 million pounds per year, the supply curve from both U.S. production and imports becomes horizontal at the world price of $0.10 per pound and remains horizontal until the quantity supplied reaches
50 million pounds. For higher prices, the supply curve equals the horizontal sum of the U.S. supply curve, *S*, and the
quota. The new U.S. price, $0.15 per pound, is determined by the intersection of the new supply curve, *S'*, with the
U.S. demand curve, *D*. Panel (b) shows the welfare effect of the quota. As a result of the higher U.S. price, consumer surplus is cut by the shaded area. Area *a* represents a transfer from U.S. consumers to U.S. producers.
Triangular area *b* reflects a net loss; it represents the amount by which the cost of producing an extra 10 million
pounds of sugar in the United States exceeds the cost of buying it from abroad. Rectangular area *c* shows the gain
to those who can sell foreign-grown sugar at the higher U.S. price instead of the world price. Area *d* also reflects
a net loss—a reduction in consumer surplus as consumption falls because of the price increase. Thus, the blue-
shaded areas illustrate the loss in consumer surplus that is captured by domestic producers and those who are
permitted to fulfill the quota, and the pink-shaded triangles illustrate the net welfare cost of the quota on the
U.S. economy.

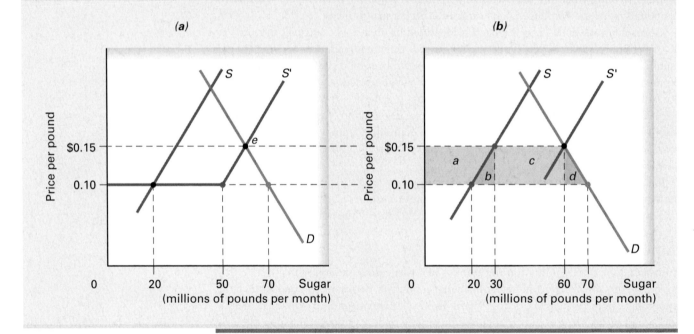

pound in the U.S. market because they can always get that price on the world market. Thus,
the supply curve that sums domestic production and imports is horizontal at the world price
of $0.10 per pound and remains so until the quantity supplied reaches 50 million pounds.

Again, for prices above $0.10 per pound, the new supply curve, *S'*, adds horizontally the
30-million-pound quota to *S*, the supply curve of U.S. producers. The U.S. price is found
where this new supply curve, *S'*, intersects the domestic demand curve, which in the left
panel of Exhibit 7 occurs at point *e*. *By limiting imports, the quota raises the domestic price of sugar
above the world price and reduces quantity below the free-trade level.* (Note that to compare more
easily the effects of tariffs and quotas, this quota is designed to yield the same equilibrium
price and quantity as the tariff examined earlier.)

Panel (b) of Exhibit 7 shows the distribution and efficiency effects of the quota. As a result of the quota, U.S. consumer surplus declines by the combined blue and pink areas. Area

a becomes producer surplus and thus involves no loss of U.S. welfare. Area *c* shows the increased economic profit to those permitted by the quota to sell Americans 30 million pounds at $0.15 per pound, or $0.05 above the world price. If foreign exporters rather than U.S. importers reap this profit, area *c* reflects a net loss in U.S. welfare.

Area *b* shows a welfare loss to the U.S. economy, because sugar could have been purchased abroad for $0.10 per pound, and the U.S. resources employed to increase sugar production could have been used more efficiently producing other goods. Area *d* is also a welfare loss because it reflects a reduction in consumer surplus with no offsetting gain to anyone. Thus, areas *b* and *d* in panel (b) of Exhibit 7 measure the minimum U.S. welfare loss from the quota. If the profit from quota rights (area *c*) accrues to foreign producers, this increases the U.S. welfare loss.

Quotas in Practice

The United States has granted quotas to specific countries. These countries, in turn, distribute these quota rights to their exporters through a variety of means. *By rewarding domestic and foreign producers with higher prices, the quota system creates two groups intent on securing and perpetuating these quotas.* Lobbyists for foreign producers work the halls of Congress, seeking the right to export to the United States. This strong support from producers, coupled with a lack of opposition from consumers (who remain rationally ignorant for the most part), has resulted in quotas that have lasted for decades. For example, sugar quotas have been around more than 50 years. In 2003 the world price of sugar averaged about $0.07 a pound, but U.S. businesses that need sugar to make products, such as candy, paid about $0.21 a pound, costing consumers an extra $2 billion a year.[1]

Some economists have argued that if quotas are to be used, the United States should auction them off to foreign producers, thereby capturing the difference between the world price and the U.S. price. Auctioning off quotas would not only increase federal revenue but would reduce the profitability of quotas, which would reduce pressure on Washington to perpetuate quotas.

Tariffs and Quotas Compared

Consider the similarities and differences between a tariff and a quota. Because both have identical effects on the price in our example, they both lead to the same change in quantity demanded. In both cases, U.S. consumers suffer the same loss of consumer surplus, and U.S. producers reap the same gain of producer surplus. The primary difference is that the revenue from the tariff goes to the government, whereas the revenue from the quota goes to whoever secures the right to sell foreign goods in the U.S. market. *If quota rights accrue to foreigners, then the domestic economy is worse off with a quota than with a tariff.* But even if quota rights go to domestic importers, quotas, like tariffs, still increase the domestic price, restrict quantity, and thereby reduce consumer surplus. Quotas and tariffs can also raise production costs. For example, U.S. candy manufacturers face higher production costs because of sugar quotas, as do U.S. automakers because of steel quotas. Finally, and most importantly, quotas and tariffs encourage foreign governments to retaliate with quotas and tariffs of their own, thus shrinking U.S. export markets, so the loss in welfare is greater than shown in Exhibits 6 and 7.

Other Trade Restrictions

Besides tariffs and quotas, a variety of other measures limit free trade. A country may provide *export subsidies* to encourage exports and *low-interest loans* to foreign buyers to promote

1. "America's Sugar Daddies," *New York Times*, 29 November 2003.

exports of large capital goods. Some countries impose *domestic content requirements* specifying that a certain portion of a final good must be produced domestically. Other requirements concerning health, safety, or technical standards often discriminate against foreign goods. For example, European countries prohibit beef from hormone-fed cattle, a measure aimed at U.S. beef. Purity laws in Germany bar many non-German beers. The European Union bans Brazil nuts, claiming the shells contain a cancer causing agent. Until the European Community adopted uniform standards, differing technical requirements forced manufacturers to offer as many as seven different versions of the same TV for that market. Sometimes exporters will voluntarily limit exports, as when Japanese automakers agreed to cut exports to the United States. The point is that *tariffs and quotas are only two of many devices that restrict foreign trade.*

Recent research on the cost of protectionism indicates that international trade barriers slow the introduction of new goods and improved technologies. So, rather than simply raising domestic prices, trade restrictions slow economic progress.

Freer Trade by Multilateral Agreement

Mindful of how high tariffs cut world trade during the Great Depression, the United States, after World War II, invited its trading partners to negotiate lower tariffs and other trade barriers. The result was the **General Agreement on Tariffs and Trade (GATT),** an international trade treaty adopted in 1947 by 23 countries, including the United States. Each GATT member agreed to (1) reduce tariffs through multinational negotiations, (2) reduce import quotas, and (3) treat all members equally with respect to trade.

Trade barriers have been reduced through trade negotiations among many countries, or "trade rounds," under the auspices of GATT. Trade rounds offer a package approach rather than an issue-by-issue approach to trade negotiations. Concessions that are necessary but otherwise difficult to defend in domestic political terms can be made more acceptable in the context of a package that also contains politically and economically attractive benefits. Most early GATT trade rounds were aimed at reducing tariffs. The Kennedy Round in the mid-1960s included new provisions against **dumping,** which is selling a commodity abroad for less than is charged in the home market. The Tokyo Round of the 1970s was a more sweeping attempt to extend and improve the system.

The most recently completed round was launched in Uruguay in September 1986 and ratified by 123 participating countries in 1994. The number of signing countries grew to 142 more recently. This so-called **Uruguay Round,** the most comprehensive of the eight postwar multilateral trade negotiations, included 550 pages of tariff reductions on 85 percent of world trade. The Uruguay Round also created the World Trade Organization (WTO) to succeed GATT.

The World Trade Organization

The **World Trade Organization (WTO)** now provides the legal and institutional foundation for world trade. Whereas GATT was a multilateral agreement with no institutional foundation, the WTO is a permanent institution in Geneva, Switzerland. A staff of about 500 economists and lawyers helps shape policy and resolves trade disputes between member countries. Whereas GATT involved only merchandise trade, the WTO also covers services and trade-related aspects of intellectual property, such as books, movies, and computer programs. Quotas will eventually be phased out by the WTO, but tariffs will remain legal. Average tariffs will fall from 6 percent to 4 percent of the value of imports (when GATT began in 1947, tariffs averaged 40 percent).

GENERAL AGREEMENT ON TARIFFS AND TRADE (GATT)

An international tariff-reduction treaty adopted in 1947 that resulted in a series of negotiated "rounds" aimed at freer trade; the Uruguay Round created GATT's successor, the World Trade Organization (WTO)

HOMEWORK Xpress!
Ask the Instructor Video

DUMPING

Selling a product abroad for less than charged in the home market

URUGUAY ROUND

The most recently concluded multilateral trade negotiation under GATT; this 1994 agreement cut tariffs, formed the World Trade Organization (WTO), and will eventually eliminate quotas

WORLD TRADE ORGANIZATION (WTO)

The legal and institutional foundation of the multilateral trading system that succeeded GATT in 1995

Whereas GATT relied on voluntary cooperation, the WTO settles disputes in a way that is faster, more automatic, and less susceptible to blockage than the GATT system was. The WTO resolved more trade disputes in its first decade than GATT did in nearly 50 years. Since 2000, developing countries have filed 60 percent of the disputes. But the WTO has also become a lightning rod for globalization issues, as discussed in the following case study.

The WTO and the "Battle in Seattle"

When WTO members met in Seattle in November 1999 to set an agenda and timetable for the next round of trade talks, all hell broke loose, as 50,000 protesters disrupted the city. Most were peaceful, but police made more than 500 arrests over three days, and property damage reached $3 million. T-shirts sold the week before the meeting dubbed the event the "Battle in Seattle," and so it was. The less-peaceful protestors targeted multinational companies, smashing windows at Starbucks, McDonald's, Nike Town, and Old Navy, and burning khakis in front of the Gap. Across the Atlantic, about 2,000 protested in London, where 40 were arrested for overturning vehicles and starting fires.

© Todd Bigelow/Aurora Photos

The "Battle in Seattle" was by far the largest demonstration against free trade in the United States. Organizers used free trade as a recruiting and fund-raising focus for a variety of groups, including labor unions and environmental groups. Protestors could pick their favorite cause—union members' fear of losing jobs overseas, environmentalists' fear that producers would seek out countries with lax regulations, and other groups' fear of developments such as hormone-fed beef and genetically modified food. (If you want to sample their concerns, plug "stop the WTO" into any Internet search engine.)

Protestors would probably have been surprised to learn that WTO members are not of one mind about trade issues. For example, the United States and Europe usually push to protect worker rights around the world, but developing countries, including Mexico, Egypt, India, and Pakistan, object strenuously to discussing worker rights. These poorer nations are concerned that the clothing, shoes, and textiles they make have not gained access to rich nations quickly enough. Many developing countries view attempts to impose labor and environmental standards as just the latest effort to keep poor countries poor.

Without international groups such as the WTO to provide a forum for discussing labor and environmental issues around the world, conditions in poor countries would probably be worse. Working conditions, especially in poor countries, have been slowly improving, thanks in part to trade opportunities along with pressure for labor rights from WTO and other international groups. For example, Cambodia is one of the poorest countries in the world, but the highest wages in the country are earned by the 1 percent of the population working in the export sector. For example, Deth worked in the June Textile factory in Cambodia sewing T-shirts and shorts, mostly for Nike and the Gap. She worked from 6:15 A.M. to 2:15 P.M. with a half hour for lunch, extra pay for overtime, and double pay for working holidays. Though her pay was low by U.S. standards, it supported her family and was more than twice what judges and doctors averaged in Cambodia. Her pay and working conditions were also far more attractive than in her previous line of work—prostitution. Factories tend to hire young women, a group that otherwise has few job opportunities. Factory jobs have provided this group with status and social equality they never had.

Child labor still occurs in poor countries, but it's more likely to be on the family farm than in a factory. One in six 10- to 14-year-olds in Cambodia works, the highest rate in Southeast Asia. But the manufacturing and trade sectors account for only about 10 percent of Cambodia's estimated 600,000 child workers, according to the United Nations Development Program. The rest work on family farms or fisheries, with some hired out to neighboring families for work. Some children try to use fake IDs to get hired in factories, where the minimum age is 15. The trade-barrier reductions from the Uruguay Round are projected to boost world income by $510 billion in 2005 (the target date for full implementation), or about $100 per person on Earth. In Cambodia and in other poor countries around the world this extra income could be a lifesaver.

The Seattle WTO meeting adjourned without a date or an agenda for the next round of trade talks, so demonstrators succeeded in disrupting deliberations. In part because of media pressure, Nike ended its contract with the June Textile factory in Cambodia. Deth was worried. "I don't know what the fate of my children will be if I lose my job," she told *Asiaweek*.

After failing to get off the ground in Seattle, the current round of WTO talks was finally launched two years later in Doha, Qatar. In setting the groundwork for the **Doha Round,** members agreed to improve market access around the world, phase out export subsidies, and substantially reduce distorting government subsidies in agriculture. But that round has not gone smoothly so far. Talks in Cancun ended bitterly in September 2003. Headed by Brazil, a group of developing countries demanded stronger commitments from the richer countries to curb agricultural subsidies in the United States, Europe, and Japan. These subsidies harm farmers in poor countries.

Sources: Brian Lindsey, "The Miami Fizzle—What Else But Cancun Redux," *Wall Street Journal*, 28 November 2003; Gina Chon, "Dropped Stitches," *Asiaweek*, 22 December 2000; Nicholas Kristoff, "Inviting All Democrats," 14 January 2004; David Postman and Linda Mapes, "Why WTO Unified So Many Foes," *Seattle Times*, 6 December 1999; and the Web site for the World Trade Organization at http://www.wto.org.

DOHA ROUND

The current multilateral trade negotiations, which aims at lowering tariffs on a wide range of industrial and agricultural products; the first trade round under WTO

Common Markets

Some countries have looked to the success of the U.S. economy, which is essentially a free trade zone across 50 states, and have tried to develop free trade zones of their own. The largest and best known is the European Union, which began in 1958 with a half dozen countries and has expanded to 25. The idea was to create a barrier-free European market like the United States in which goods, services, people, and capital are free to flow to their highest-valued use. Twelve members of the European Union have adopted a common currency, the *euro,* which replaced national currencies in 2002.

The United States, Canada, and Mexico have developed a free trade pact called the North American Free Trade Agreement (NAFTA). Through NAFTA, Mexico hopes to attract more U.S. investment by guaranteeing companies that locate there duty-free access to U.S. markets, which is where over two-thirds of Mexico's exports go. Mexico's 110 million people represent an attractive export market for U.S. producers, and Mexico's oil reserves could ease U.S. energy problems. The United States would also like to support Mexico's efforts to become more market oriented, as is reflected, for example, by Mexico's privatization of its phone system and banks. After a decade of NAFTA, agricultural exports to Mexico doubled, as did overall trade among the three nations, but Americans bought much more from Mexicans and Canadians than the other way around.

Free trade areas are proliferating. The United States and other countries are negotiating the Central American Free Trade Agreement, or CAFTA. A half dozen Latin American countries form Mercosur, the association of Southeast Asian nations make up ASEAN, and South Africa and its four neighboring countries make up the Southern African Customs

Union. Regional trade agreements require an exception to WTO rules because bloc members can make special deals among themselves and thus discriminate against outsiders. Under WTO's requirements, any trade concession granted one country must usually be granted to *all other* WTO members.

Arguments for Trade Restrictions

Trade restrictions often appear to be little more than handouts for the domestic industries they protect. Given the loss in social welfare that results from these restrictions, it would be more efficient simply to transfer money from domestic consumers to domestic producers. But such a bald transfer would be politically unpopular. Arguments for trade restrictions avoid mention of transfers to domestic producers and instead cite loftier goals. As we shall now see, some of these arguments are more valid than others.

National Defense Argument

Some industries claim they need protection from import competition because their output is vital for national defense. Products such as strategic metals and military hardware are often insulated from foreign competition by trade restrictions. Thus, national defense considerations outweigh concerns about efficiency and equity. How valid is this argument? Trade restrictions may shelter the defense industry, but other means, such as government subsidies, might be more efficient. Or the government could stockpile basic military hardware so that maintaining an ongoing productive capacity would become less essential, though technological change soon makes certain weapons obsolete. Because most industries can play some role in national defense, instituting trade restrictions on this basis can get out of hand. For example, U.S. wool producers gained protection at a time when some military uniforms were made of wool.

Infant Industry Argument

The infant industry argument was formulated as a rationale for protecting emerging domestic industries from foreign competition. In industries where a firm's average cost of production falls as output expands, new firms may need protection from imports until these firms grow big enough to be competitive. Trade restrictions let new firms achieve the economies of scale needed to compete with mature foreign producers.

But how do we identify industries that merit protection, and when do they become old enough to look after themselves? Protection often fosters inefficiencies. The immediate cost of such restrictions is the net welfare loss from higher domestic prices. These costs may become permanent if the industry never realizes the expected economies of scale and thus never becomes competitive. As with the national defense argument, policy makers should be careful in adopting trade restrictions based on the infant industry argument. Here again, temporary production subsidies may be more efficient than import restrictions.

Antidumping Argument

As we have noted already, *dumping* is selling a product abroad for less than in the home market. Exporters may be able to sell the good for less overseas because of export subsidies, or firms may simply find it profitable to sell for less in foreign markets where demand is more price elastic—that is, firms price discriminate. Critics of dumping call for a tariff to raise the price of dumped goods. But why shouldn't U.S. consumers pay as little as possible, even if these low prices result from a foreign subsidy or price discrimination? If dumping is *persistent,* the increase in consumer surplus would more than offset losses to domestic producers. *There is no good reason why consumers should not be allowed to buy imports for a persistently lower price.*

An alternative form of dumping, termed *predatory dumping,* is the *temporary* sale abroad at prices below the home market or even below cost to eliminate competitors in that foreign market. Once the competition is gone, so the story goes, the exporting firm can raise the price in the foreign market. The trouble with this argument is that if dumpers try to take advantage of their monopoly position by sharply increasing the price, then other firms, either domestic or foreign, could enter the market and sell for less. There are few documented cases of predatory dumping.

Sometimes dumping may be *sporadic,* as firms occasionally try to unload excess inventories. Retailers hold periodic "sales" for the same reason. Sporadic dumping can be unsettling for domestic producers, but the economic impact is not a matter of great public concern. Regardless, all dumping is prohibited in the United States by the Trade Agreements Act of 1979, which calls for the imposition of tariffs when a good is sold for less in the United States than in its home market. In addition, WTO rules allow for offsetting tariffs when products are sold for "less than fair value" and when there is "material injury" to domestic producers. For example, U.S. producers of lumber and beer have accused their Canadian counterparts of dumping.

Jobs and Income Argument

One rationale for trade restrictions that is commonly heard in the United States, and was voiced by WTO protestors, is that they protect U.S. jobs and wage levels. Using trade restrictions to protect domestic jobs is a strategy that dates back centuries. One problem with such a policy is that other countries will likely retaliate by restricting *their* imports to save *their* jobs, so international trade is reduced, jobs are lost in export industries, and potential gains from trade fail to materialize. That happened during the Great Depression.

Wages in other countries, especially developing countries, are often a small fraction of wages in the United States. Looking simply at differences in wages, however, narrows the focus too much. Wages represent just one component of the total production cost and may not necessarily be the most important. Employers are interested in the labor cost per unit of output, which depends on both the wage and labor productivity. Wages are high in the United States partly because U.S. labor productivity remains the highest in the world. High productivity can be traced to education and training and to the abundant computers, machines, and other physical capital that make workers more productive. U.S. workers also benefit from a stable business climate.

But what about the lower wages in many developing countries? These low wages are often linked to workers' lack of education and training, to the meager physical capital available to each worker, and to a business climate that is less stable and less attractive for producers. But once multinational firms build plants and provide technological know-how in developing countries, U.S. workers lose some of their competitive edge, and their relatively high wages could price some U.S. products out of the world market. This has already happened in the stereo and consumer electronics industries. China now makes 80 percent of the toys sold in the United States. Some U.S. toy sellers, such as the makers of Etch A Sketch, would no longer survive if they had not outsourced manufacturing to China.

Domestic producers do not like to compete with foreign producers whose costs are lower, so they often push for trade restrictions. But if restrictions negate any cost advantage a foreign producer might have, the law of comparative advantage becomes inoperative and domestic consumers are denied access to the lower-priced goods.

Over time, as labor productivity in developing countries increases, wage differentials among countries will narrow, much as wage differentials narrowed between northern and southern U.S. states. As technology and capital spread, U.S. workers, particularly unskilled workers, cannot expect to maintain wage levels that are far above those in other countries. So far, research and development has kept U.S. producers on the cutting edge of technological developments, but staying ahead in the technological race is a constant battle.

Declining Industries Argument

Where an established domestic industry is in jeopardy of closing because of lower-priced imports, could there be a rationale for *temporary* import restrictions? After all, domestic producers employ many industry-specific resources—both specialized machines and specialized labor. This physical and human capital is worth less in its best alternative use. If the extinction of the domestic industry is forestalled through trade restrictions, specialized machines can be allowed to wear out naturally, and specialized workers can retire voluntarily or can gradually pursue more promising careers.

Thus, in the case of declining domestic industries, trade protection can help lessen shocks to the economy and can allow for an orderly transition to a new industrial mix. But the protection offered should not be so generous as to encourage continued investment in the industry. Protection should be of specific duration and should be phased out over that period.

The clothing industry is an example of a declining U.S. industry. The 22,000 U.S. jobs saved as a result of one recent trade restriction paid an average of about $23,000 per year. But a Congressional Budget Office study estimated that, because of higher domestic clothing prices, U.S. consumers paid between $39,000 and $74,000 per year for each textile and apparel job saved. Trade restrictions in the U.S. clothing and textile industry are being phased out beginning in 2005 under the Uruguay Round of trade agreements.

Free trade may displace some U.S. jobs through imports, but it also creates U.S. jobs through exports. When people celebrate a ribbon-cutting ceremony for a new software company, nobody credits free trade for those jobs, but when a steel plant closes, everyone talks about how those jobs went overseas. What's more, many foreign companies have built plants in the United States and employ U.S. workers. For example, a dozen foreign television manufacturers and all major Japanese automobile manufacturers now have U.S. plants.

The number of jobs in the United States has more than doubled since 1960. To recognize this job growth is not to deny the problems facing workers who are displaced by imports. Some displaced workers, particularly those in blue-collar jobs in steel and other unionized industries, are not likely to find jobs that will pay as well as the ones they lost. As with infant industries, however, the problems posed by declining industries need not require trade restrictions. To support the affected industry, the government could offer wage subsidies or special tax breaks that decline over time. The government has also funded programs to retrain affected workers for jobs that are in greater demand.

Problems with Protection

Trade restrictions raise a number of problems in addition to those already mentioned. First, protecting one stage of production usually requires protecting downstream stages of production. Protecting the U.S. textile industry from foreign competition, for example, raises the cost of cloth to U.S. apparel manufacturers, reducing their competitiveness. Thus, if the government protects domestic textile manufacturers, the domestic garment industry also needs protection. Second, the cost of protection includes not only the welfare loss arising from the higher domestic price but also the cost of the resources used by domestic producers and groups to secure the favored protection. The cost of *rent seeking*—lobbying fees, propaganda, and legal actions—can equal or exceed the direct welfare loss from restrictions. A third problem with trade restrictions is the transaction costs of enforcing the myriad quotas, tariffs, and other trade restrictions. A fourth problem is that economies insulated from foreign competition become less innovative and less efficient. And a final problem with imposing trade restrictions is that other countries usually retaliate, thus shrinking the gains from trade. Retaliation can set off still greater trade restrictions, leading to an outright trade war. Consider the recent steel tariffs discussed in the following case study.

Bush's Steel Tariffs

The U.S. steel industry has been suffering a long, painful decline for decades—a death from a thousand cuts. From 1997 to 2001, about 30 percent of U.S. steel producers filed for bankruptcy, including Bethlehem Steel and National Steel. During that same stretch, 45,000 steel jobs disappeared, leaving about 180,000 jobs remaining. Imports accounted for 30 percent of the U.S. market, with most of that steel coming from Europe.

Industry leaders turned to the White House for help. Many of the jobs lost were in "rust-belt" states, such as Ohio, West Virginia, and Pennsylvania, states that President George W. Bush hoped to win in his 2004 reelection bid. We can only speculate what role politics played in the decision, but in March 2002, the Bush administration imposed tariffs on imported steel, claiming imports caused "material injury" to the U.S. steel industry. The tariffs, which ranged from 8 to 30 percent on 10 steel categories, were scheduled to last three years.

As expected, the tariffs cut imports and boosted the domestic price of steel. By 2003, steel imports reached their lowest level in a decade. The higher price of steel helped U.S. steel makers but made steel-using industries less competitive on world markets. For example, the tariffs added about $300 to the average cost of a U.S. automobile. According to one conservative estimate, the tariffs lost 15,000 to 20,000 jobs in the steel user industries.

The European Union and other affected nations complained to the WTO. In November 2003, the WTO ruled that the tariffs violated trade agreements. The European Union, with about 300,000 steel jobs at stake, announced that if the tariffs were not lifted by mid-December 2003, EU countries would retaliate with tariffs on U.S. exports. Japan and South Korea also threatened retaliatory tariffs.

In early December 2003, the Bush administration repealed the tariffs, arguing that they had served their purpose. Approximately $650 million in higher tariffs had been collected during the 20 months they were imposed. The steelworkers union called the repeal "an affront to all workers." But union members should not have been surprised in light of the WTO ruling, the threatened retaliation from abroad, and the fact that several months earlier, the steelworkers union endorsed a Democrat for president.

Sources: Neil King et al., "U.S. Steel Tariffs Ruled Illegal, Sparking Potential Trade War," *Wall Street Journal*, 11 November 2003; Carlos Tejeda, "After Removal of Steel Tariffs, Many Are Without Scrap Heap," *Wall Street Journal*, 15 December 2003; Carlos Tejeda, "Tariffs Retreat May Affect Talks," *Wall Street Journal*, 8 December 2003; and "Rolled Over," *Economist*, 6 December 2003.

Case Study

Public Policy

*e*Activity

For more on the union perspective about the repeal of the steel tariffs visit the AFL-CIO's Web page on the issue at http://www.aflcio.org/issuespolitics/manufacturing/ns12042003.cfm, which includes links to additional union statements. For the European view visit the BBC World News to read about the proposed retaliatory tariffs at http://news.bbc.co.uk/1/hi/business/3243423.stm and look at a Q&A about the trade dispute at http://news.bbc.co.uk/1/hi/business/3291675.stm. On what basis did the Europeans select the goods on which to impose the countervailing duties? Why do you think President Bush changed his mind about the tariffs?

© Photodisc/Getty Images

Import Substitution Versus Export Promotion

An economy's progress usually involves moving from agriculture and raw material to manufacturing then to services. If a country is fortunate, this transformation occurs gradually through natural market forces. Sometimes governments push along the evolution. Many developing countries, including Argentina and India, pursued a strategy called **import substitution,** whereby the country manufactured products that until then had been imported. To insulate domestic producers from foreign competition, the government imposed tariffs and quotas. This development strategy became popular for several reasons. First, demand already existed for these products, so the "what to produce" question was easily answered. Second, import substitution provided infant industries a protected market. Finally, import substitution was popular with those who supplied capital, labor, and other resources to the favored domestic industries.

Like all protection measures, however, import substitution erased the gains from specialization and comparative advantage among countries. Often the developing country replaced low-cost foreign goods with high-cost domestic goods. And domestic producers, shielded from foreign competition, usually failed to become efficient. Worse still, other countries often retaliated with their own trade restrictions.

Critics of import substitution claim that export promotion is a surer path to economic development. **Export promotion** concentrates on producing for the export market. This development strategy begins with relatively simple products, such as textiles. As a developing country builds its technological and educational base—that is, as the developing economy learns by doing—producers can then export more complex products. Economists favor export promotion over import substitution because the emphasis is on comparative advantage and trade expansion rather than on trade restriction. Export promotion also forces producers to grow more efficient in order to compete on world markets. Research shows that global competition boosts domestic efficiency.[2] What's more, export promotion requires less government intervention in the market than does import substitution.

Of the two approaches, export promotion has been more successful around the world. For example, the newly industrialized countries of East Asia (Taiwan, South Korea, Hong Kong, and Singapore) have successfully pursued export promotion, while Argentina, India, and Peru have failed with their import-substitution approach. Since 1965, the four newly industrialized economies of East Asia raised their average real incomes from only 20 percent of industrial economies to over 70 percent. Most Latin American nations, which for decades had favored import substitution, are now pursuing free trade agreements with the United States. Even India is dismantling its trade barriers.

IMPORT SUBSTITUTION

A development strategy that emphasizes domestic manufacturing of products that were imported

EXPORT PROMOTION

A development strategy that concentrates on producing for the export market

Conclusion

International trade arises from voluntary exchange among buyers and sellers pursuing their self-interest. Since 1950 world output has risen sevenfold, while world trade has increased seventeenfold. World trade offers many advantages to the trading countries: access to markets around the world, lower costs through economies of scale, the opportunity to utilize abundant resources, better access to information about markets and technology, improved quality honed by competitive pressure, and lower prices for consumers. Comparative advantage, specialization, and trade allow people to use their scarce resources most efficiently to satisfy their unlimited wants.

2. See Martin Baily and Hans Gersbach, "Efficiency in Manufacturing and the Need for Global Competition," in *Brookings Papers on Economic Activity: Microeconomics,* M. Baily, P. Reiss, and C. Winston, eds. (Washington, D.C.: Brookings Institution, 1995), 307–347.

Despite the clear gains from free trade, restrictions on international trade date back centuries, and pressure to impose trade restrictions continues today. Domestic producers (and their resource suppliers) benefit from trade restrictions because they can sell their products for more. Protection insulates domestic producers from the rigors of global competition, in the process stifling innovation and leaving the industry vulnerable to technological change elsewhere. Under a system of quotas, the winners also include those who have secured the right to import goods at the world prices and sell them at the domestic prices. Consumers, who must pay higher prices for protected goods, suffer from trade restrictions, as do the domestic producers who use imported resources. Other losers are U.S. exporters, who face higher trade barriers as foreigners retaliate with their own trade restrictions.

Producer groups have a laser-like focus on trade legislation, but consumers remain largely oblivious. Consumers purchase thousands of different goods and thus have no special interest in the effects of trade policy on any particular good. Congress tends to support the group that makes the most noise, so trade restrictions often persist, despite the widespread gains from free trade.

SUMMARY

1. Even if a country has an absolute advantage in all goods, that country should specialize in producing the goods in which it has a comparative advantage. If each country specializes and trades according to the law of comparative advantage, all countries will have greater consumption possibilities.

2. Tariff revenues could be used to lower taxes or fund government programs. Quotas benefit those with the right to buy goods at the world price and sell them at the higher domestic price. Both tariffs and quotas harm domestic consumers more than they help domestic producers, although tariffs at least yield government revenue, which can be used to fund valued public programs or to cut taxes.

3. Despite the gains from free trade, trade restrictions have been imposed for centuries. The General Agreement on Tariffs and Trade (GATT) was an international treaty ratified in 1947 to reduce trade barriers. Subsequent negotia-

tions lowered tariffs and reduced trade restrictions. The Uruguay Round, ratified in 1994, lowered tariffs, phased out quotas, and created the World Trade Organization (WTO) as the successor to GATT.

4. Arguments used by producer groups to support trade restrictions include promoting national defense, nurturing infant industries, preventing foreign producers from dumping goods in domestic markets, protecting domestic jobs, and allowing declining industries time to wind down.

5. Import substitution is a development strategy that emphasizes domestic production of goods that are currently imported. Export promotion concentrates on producing for the export market. Over the years, export promotion has been more successful than import substitution because it relies on specialization and comparative advantage.

QUESTIONS FOR REVIEW

1. *(Profile of Imports and Exports)* What are the major U.S. exports and imports? How does international trade affect consumption possibilities?

2. *(Reasons for Trade)* What are the primary reasons for international trade?

3. *(Gains from Trade)* Complete each of the following sentences:

   a. When a nation has no economic interaction with foreigners and produces everything it consumes, the nation is in a state of _____.

   b. According to the law of comparative advantage, each nation should specialize in producing the goods in which it has the lowest _____.

   c. The amount of one good that a nation can exchange for one unit of another good is known as the _____.

   d. Specializing according to comparative advantage and trading with other nations results in _____.

4. *(Reasons for International Specialization)* What determines which goods a country should produce and export?

5. *(Tariffs)* High tariffs usually lead to black markets and smuggling. How is government revenue reduced by such activity? Relate your answer to the graph in Exhibit 5 in this chapter. Does smuggling have any social benefits?

6. *(Trade Restrictions)* Exhibits 6 and 7 show net losses to the economy of a country that imposes tariffs or quotas on imported sugar. What kinds of gains and losses would occur in the economies of countries that export sugar?

7. *(The World Trade Organization)* What is the World Trade Organization (WTO) and how does it help foster multilateral trade? (Check the WTO Web site at http://www.wto.org/.)

8. *(Case Study: The WTO and the "Battle in Seattle")* Why did protesters demonstrate during the WTO meetings in Seattle in November 1999?

9. *(Arguments for Trade Restrictions)* Explain the national defense, declining industries, and infant industry arguments for protecting a domestic industry from international competition.

10. *(Arguments for Trade Restrictions)* Firms hurt by cheap imports typically argue that restricting trade will save U.S. jobs. What's wrong with this argument? Are there ever any reasons to support such trade restrictions?

11. *(Case Study: Bush's Steel Tariffs)* How did Bush's steel tariff affect the domestic steel industry, the workers in the steel industry, and consumers?

PROBLEMS AND EXERCISES

12. *(Comparative Advantage)* Suppose that each U.S. worker can produce 8 units of food or 2 units of clothing daily. In Fredonia, which has the same number of workers, each worker can produce 7 units of food or 1 unit of clothing daily. Why does the United States have an absolute advantage in both goods? Which country enjoys a comparative advantage in food? Why?

13. *(Comparative Advantage)* The consumption possibilities frontiers shown in Exhibit 4 assume terms of trade of 1 unit of clothing for 1 unit of food. What would the consumption possibilities frontiers look like if the terms of trade were 1 unit of clothing for 2 units of food?

14. *(Import Quotas)* How low must a quota be to have an impact? Using a demand-and-supply diagram, illustrate and explain the net welfare loss from imposing such a quota. Under what circumstances would the net welfare loss from an import quota exceed the net welfare loss from an equivalent tariff (one that results in the same price and import level as the quota)?

15. *(Trade Restrictions)* Suppose that the world price for steel is below the U.S. domestic price, but the government requires that all steel used in the United States be domestically produced.

    a. Use a diagram like the one in Exhibit 5 to show the gains and loses from such a policy.

    b. How could you estimate the net welfare loss (deadweight loss) from such a diagram?

    c. What response to such a policy would you expect from industries (like automobile producers) that use U.S. steel?

    d. What government revenues are generated by this policy?

16. *(Import Substitution Versus Export Promotion)* Two strategies frequently used to stimulate economic development are export promotion and import substitution. Describe the advantages and disadvantages of each strategy.

EXPERIENTIAL EXERCISES

17. *(Arguments for Trade Restrictions)* Visit the Office of the U.S. Trade Representative at http://www.ustr.gov/. The U.S. Trade Representative is a cabinet member who acts as the principal trade advisor, negotiator, and spokesperson for the president on trade and related investment matters. Look at some of the most recent press releases. What are some of the trade-related issues the United States is currently facing?

18. *(Wall Street Journal)* The *Wall Street Journal* is one of the world's best sources of information regarding international trade. A good place to look is the International page inside the First Section of each day's edition. Look at today's issue and find an article dealing with trade barriers—tariffs, quotas, and so on. Model the trade barrier using a graph, and try to determine who benefits and who bears the costs. If you are lucky, the article will provide sufficient information to allow you to actually estimate costs and benefits in dollar terms. If you can't find a relevant article in today's paper, go to previous issues until you come up with one.

HOMEWORK XPRESS! EXERCISES

These exercises require access to McEachern Homework Xpress! If Homework Xpress! did not come with your book, visit **http://homeworkxpress.swlearning.com** *to purchase.*

1. Canada and Bolivia both can produce two goods—chairs and sweaters. The production possibilities for each are shown in the diagram. Identify how many sweaters Canada can produce if it produces 30 chairs. Add a consumption possibilities curve if each country specializes and trades 1 chair for 10 sweaters. Identify how many sweaters Canadians can have if they keep 30 chairs and trade the rest for sweaters.

2. Demand and domestic supply curves for crude oil in the nation of Yacimiento are shown in the diagram. The world price for crude oil is $20 per barrel. Identify the quantity demanded and domestic quantity supplied at this price. The government decides to lessen dependence on imported oil by imposing a $10 per barrel tariff on imported crude. Identify the quantity demanded and domestic quantity supplied with the tariff. Shade the area representing government revenue generated by the tariff.

3. Demand and domestic supply curves for crude oil in the nation of Yacimiento are shown in the diagram. The world price for crude oil is $20 per barrel. Identify the quantity demanded at the world price. The government decides to lessen dependence on imported oil by imposing a quota on imports of .25 billion barrels. Draw the part of the new supply curve that will intersect the demand curve. Identify the new price of oil in Yacimiento and the quantity demanded at this price.

Glossary

A

ability-to-pay tax principle Those with a greater ability to pay, such as those with a higher income or those who own more property, should pay more taxes

absolute advantage The ability to produce something using fewer resources than other producers use

accounting profit A firm's total revenue minus its explicit costs

adverse selection Those on the informed side of the market self-select in a way that harms those on the uninformed side of the market

agent A person or firm who is supposed to act on behalf of the principal

allocative efficiency The condition that exists when firms produce the output most preferred by consumers; marginal benefit equals marginal cost

alternative goods Other goods that use some or all of the same resources as the good in question

annuity A given sum of money received each year for a specified number of years

antitrust policy Government regulation aimed at preventing monopoly and fostering competition in markets where competition is desirable

association-is-causation fallacy The incorrect idea that if two variables are associated in time, one must necessarily cause the other

asymmetric information One side of the market has more reliable information about the product than does the other side

autarky A situation of national self-sufficiency; there is no economic interaction with foreigners

average revenue Total revenue divided by output, or $AR = TR/q$; in all market structures, average revenue equals the market price

average total cost Total cost divided by output, or $ATC = TC/q$; the sum of average fixed cost and average variable cost, or $ATC = AFC + AVC$

average variable cost Variable cost divided by output, or $AVC = VC/q$

B

backward-bending supply curve of labor As the wage rises, the quantity of labor supplied may eventually decline; the income effect of a higher wage increases the demand for leisure, which reduces the quantity of labor supplied enough to more than offset the substitution effect of a higher wage

balance of payments A record of all economic transactions between residents of one country and residents of the rest of the world during a given period

barrier to entry Any impediment that prevents new firms from entering an industry and competing on an equal basis with existing firms

barter The direct exchange of one good for another without using money

behavioral assumption An assumption that describes the expected behavior of economic decision makers, what motivates them

benefits-received tax principle Those who receive more benefits from the government program funded by a tax should pay more taxes

binding arbitration Negotiation in which union and management must accept an impartial observer's resolution of a dispute

bond Certificate reflecting a firm's promise to pay the lender periodic interest and to pay a fixed sum of money on the designated maturity date

bounded rationality The notion that there is a limit to the information that a firm's manager can comprehend and act on

budget line A line showing all combinations of two goods that can be purchased at given prices with a given amount of income

bureaus Government agencies charged with implementing legislation and financed by appropriations from legislative bodies

C

capital The buildings, equipment, and human skill used to produce goods and services

capture theory of regulation Producers' political power and strong stake in the regulatory outcome lead them, in effect, to "capture" the regulating agency and prevail on it to serve producer interests

cartel A group of firms that agree to coordinate their production and pricing decisions to act like a monopolist

circular-flow model A diagram that outlines the flow of resources, products, income, and revenue among economic decision makers

Clayton Act of 1914 Beefed up the Sherman Act; outlawed certain anti-competitive practices not prohibited by the Sherman Act, including price discrimination, tying contracts, exclusive dealing, interlocking directorates, and buying the corporate stock of a competitor

Coase theorem As long as bargaining costs are low, an efficient solution to the problem of externalities will be achieved by assigning property rights to one party or the other

collateral An asset pledged by the borrower that can be sold to pay off the loan in the event the loan is not repaid

collective bargaining The process by which union and management negotiate a labor agreement

collusion An agreement among firms to increase economic profit by dividing the market or fixing the price

command-and-control environmental regulations An approach that required polluters to adopt particular technologies to reduce emissions by specific amounts; inflexible regulations based on engineering standards that ignore each firm's unique cost of reducing pollution

commodity A standardized product, a product that does not differ across producers, such as bushels of wheat or an ounce of gold

common-pool problem Unrestricted access to a resource results in overuse until its marginal value drops to zero

comparative advantage The ability to produce something at a lower opportunity cost than other producers face

competing-interest legislation Legislation that confers concentrated benefits on one group by imposing concentrated costs on another group

complements Goods, such as milk and cookies, that are related in such a way that an increase in the price of one shifts the demand for the other leftward

conglomerate merger A merger of firms in different industries

consent decree The accused party, without admitting guilt, agrees to stop the alleged activity if the government drops the charges

constant long-run average cost A cost that occurs when, over some range of output, long-run average cost neither increases nor decreases with changes in firm size

constant-cost industry An industry that can expand or contract without affecting the long-run per-unit cost of production; the long-run industry supply curve is horizontal

constant-elasticity demand curve The type of demand that exists when price elasticity is the same everywhere along the curve; the elasticity value is constant

consumer equilibrium The condition in which an individual consumer's budget is spent and the last dollar spent on each good yields the same marginal utility; therefore, utility is maximized

consumer surplus The difference between the maximum amount that a consumer is willing to pay for a given quantity of a good and what the consumer actually pays

core competency Area of specialty; the product or phase of production a firm supplies with greatest efficiency

corporate stock Certificate reflecting part ownership of a corporation

corporation A legal entity owned by stockholders whose liability is limited to the value of their stock

craft union A union whose members have a particular skill or work at a particular craft, such as plumbers or carpenters

cross-price elasticity of demand The percentage change in the demand of one good divided by the percentage change in the price of another good

D

deadweight loss of monopoly Net loss to society when a firm uses its market power to restrict output and increase price

demand A relation between the price of a good and the quantity that consumers are willing and able to buy during a given period, other things constant

demand curve A curve showing the relation between the price of a good and the quantity demanded during a given period, other things constant

demand for loanable funds The relationship between the market interest rate and the quantity of loanable funds demanded, other things constant

dependent variable A variable whose value depends on that of the independent variable

derived demand Demand that arises from the demand for the product the resource produces

differentiated oligopoly An oligopoly that sells products that differ across suppliers, such as automobiles or breakfast cereal

discounting Converting future dollar amounts into present value

diseconomies of scale Forces that may eventually increase a firm's average cost as the scale of operation increases in the long run

disequilibrium The condition that exists in a market when the plans of buyers do not match those of sellers; a temporary mismatch between quantity supplied and quantity demanded as the market seeks equilibrium

dividends After-tax corporate profit paid to stockholders rather than retained by the firm and reinvested

division of labor Organizing production of a good into its separate tasks

Doha Round The current multilateral trade negotiations, which aims at lowering tariffs on a wide range of industrial and agricultural products; the first trade round under WTO

dominant-strategy equilibrium In game theory, the outcome achieved when each player's choice does not depend on what the other player does

dumping Selling a product abroad for less than charged in the home market

duopoly A market with only two producers; a type of oligopoly market structure

E

earned-income tax credit A federal program that supplements the wages of the working poor

economic efficiency approach An approach that offers each polluter the flexibility to reduce emissions as cost-effectively as possible, given its unique cost conditions; the market for pollution rights is an example

economic growth An increase in the economy's ability to produce goods and services; an outward shift of the production possibilities frontier

economic profit A firm's total revenue minus its explicit and implicit costs

economic regulation Government regulation of natural monopoly, where, because of economies of scale, average production cost is lowest when a single firm supplies the market

economic rent Portion of a resource's total earnings that exceeds its opportunity cost; earnings greater than the amount required to keep the resource in its present use

economic system The set of mechanisms and institutions that resolve the what, how, and for whom questions

economic theory, or economic model A simplification of reality used to make predictions about cause and effect in the real world

economics The study of how people use their scarce resources to satisfy their unlimited wants

economies of scale Forces that reduce a firm's average cost as the scale of operation increases in the long run

economies of scope Average costs decline as a firm makes different products rather than just one

efficiency The condition that exists when there is no way resources can be reallocated to increase the production of one good without decreasing the production of another

efficiency wage theory The idea that offering high wages attracts a more talented labor pool, making it easier for firms to hire and retain more-productive workers

elastic demand A change in price has a relatively large effect on quantity demanded; the percentage change in quantity demanded exceeds the percentage change in price; the resulting price elasticity has an absolute value exceeding 1.0

elastic supply A change in price has a relatively large effect on quantity supplied; the percentage change in quantity supplied exceeds the percentage change in price; the resulting price elasticity of supply exceeds 1.0

entrepreneur A profit-seeking decision maker who organizes an enterprise and assumes the risk of its operation

entrepreneurial ability Managerial and organizational skills needed to start a firm, combined with the willingness to take risks

equilibrium The condition that exists in a market when the plans of buyers match those of sellers, so quantity demanded equals quantity supplied and the market clears

excess capacity The difference between a firm's profit-maximizing quantity and the quantity that minimizes average cost

exclusive dealing A supplier prohibits customers from buying from other suppliers of the product

exhaustible resource A resource in fixed supply, such as crude oil or coal

expansion path A line connecting points of tangency that identify the least-cost input combinations for producing alternative output rates; the expansion path need not be a straight line, though it generally slopes upward

explicit cost Opportunity cost of resources employed by a firm that takes the form of cash payments

export promotion A development strategy that concentrates on producing for the export market

externality A cost or a benefit that falls on a third party and is therefore ignored by the two parties to the market transaction

F

fallacy of composition The incorrect belief that what is true for the individual, or part, must necessarily be true for the group, or whole

featherbedding Union efforts to force employers to hire more workers than wanted or needed

Federal Trade Commission (FTC) Act of 1914 Established a federal body to help enforce antitrust laws; run by commissioners assisted by economists and lawyers

firms Economic units formed by profit-seeking entrepreneurs who use resources to produce goods and services for sale

fiscal policy The use of government purchases, transfer payments, taxes, and borrowing to influence economy-wide activity such as inflation, employment, and economic growth

fixed cost Any production cost that is independent of the firm's rate of output

fixed resource Any resource that cannot be varied in the short run

fixed-production technology Occurs when the relationship between the output rate and the generation of an externality is fixed; the only way to reduce the externality is to reduce the output

food stamps An in-kind transfer program that offers low-income households vouchers redeemable for food; benefit levels vary inversely with household income

foreign exchange Foreign money needed to carry out international transactions

free-rider problem Because a public good is nonexclusive, people may try to reap the benefits of the good without paying for it

G

game theory An approach that analyzes oligopolistic behavior as a series of strategic moves and countermoves by rival firms

General Agreement on Tariffs and Trade (GATT) An international tariff-reduction treaty adopted in 1947 that resulted in a series of negotiated "rounds" aimed at freer trade; the Uruguay Round created GATT's successor, the World Trade Organization (WTO)

golden rule of profit maximization To maximize profit or minimize loss, a firm should produce the quantity at which marginal revenue equals marginal cost; this rule holds for all market structures

good A tangible item used to satisfy human wants

graph A picture showing how variables relate in two-dimensional space; one variable is measured along the horizontal axis and the other along the vertical axis

H

Herfindahl-Hirschman Index, or HHI A measure of market concentration that squares each firm's percentage share of the market then sums these squares

hidden actions One side of an economic relationship can do something that the other side cannot observe

hidden characteristics One side of the market knows more than the other side about product characteristics that are important to the other side

horizontal axis Line on a graph that begins at the origin and goes to the right and left; sometimes called the x axis

horizontal merger A merger in which one firm combines with another that produces the same product

hypothesis A theory about relationships among key variables

I

implicit cost A firm's opportunity cost of using its own resources or those provided by its owners without a corresponding cash payment

import substitution A development strategy that emphasizes domestic manufacturing of products that were imported

income assistance programs Welfare programs that provide money and in-kind assistance to the poor; benefits do not depend on prior contributions

income effect of a price change A fall in the price of a good increases consumers' real income, making consumers more able to purchase goods; for a normal good, the quantity demanded increases

income effect of a wage increase A higher wage increases a worker's income, increasing the demand for all normal goods, including leisure, so the quantity of labor supplied to market work decreases

income elasticity of demand The percentage change in demand divided by the percentage change in consumer income; the value is positive for normal goods and negative for inferior goods

increasing-cost industry An industry that faces higher per-unit production costs as industry output expands in the long run; the long-run industry supply curve slopes upward

increasing marginal returns The marginal product of a variable resource increases as each additional unit of that resource is employed

independent variable A variable whose value determines that of the dependent variable

indifference curve A curve showing all combinations of goods that provide the consumer with the same satisfaction, or the same utility

indifference map A set of indifference curves representing each possible level of total utility that can be derived by a particular consumer from consumption of two goods; a map of the consumer's tastes for the two goods

individual demand The demand of an individual consumer

individual supply The supply of an individual producer

Industrial Revolution Development of large-scale factory production that began in Great Britain around 1750 and spread to the rest of Europe, North America, and Australia

industrial union A union of both skilled and unskilled workers from a particular industry, such as autoworkers or steelworkers

inelastic demand A change in price has relatively little effect on quantity demanded; the percentage change in quantity demanded is less than the percentage change in price; the resulting price elasticity has an absolute value less than 1.0

inelastic supply A change in price has relatively little effect on quantity supplied; the percentage change in quantity supplied is less than the percentage change in price; the price elasticity of supply has a value less than 1.0

inferior good A good, such as used clothes, for which demand decreases, or shifts leftward, as consumer incomes rise

Information Revolution Technological change spawned by the invention of the microchip and the Internet that enhanced the acquisition, analysis, and transmission of information

initial public offering (IPO) The initial sale of corporate stock to the public

innovation The process of turning an invention into a marketable product

interest Payment to resource owners for the use of their capital

interest rate Interest per year as a percentage of the amount saved or borrowed

interlocking directorate A person serves on the boards of directors of two or more competing firms

isocost line Line identifying all combinations of capital and labor the firm can hire for a given total cost

isoquant A curve that shows all the technologically efficient combinations of two resources, such as labor and capital, that produce a certain amount of output

L

labor The physical and mental effort used to produce goods and services

labor union A group of workers who organize to improve their terms of employment

law of comparative advantage The individual, firm, region, or country with the lowest opportunity cost of producing a particular good should specialize in that good

law of demand The quantity of a good demanded during a given period relates inversely to its price, other things constant

law of diminishing marginal rate of substitution The amount of good A a consumer is willing to give up to get one more unit of good B declines as the consumption of B increases

law of diminishing marginal utility The more of a good a person consumes per period, the smaller the increase in total utility from consuming one more unit, other things constant

law of increasing opportunity cost To produce each additional increment of a good, a successively larger increment of an alternative good must be sacrificed if the economy's resources are already being used efficiently

law of supply The quantity of a good supplied during a given period is usually directly related to its price, other things constant

leisure Time spent on nonwork activities

linear demand curve A straight-line demand curve; such a demand curve has a constant slope but usually has a varying price elasticity

loanable funds market The market in which savers (suppliers of loanable funds) and borrowers (demanders of loanable funds) come together to determine the market interest rate and the quantity of loanable funds exchanged

long run A period during which all resources under the firm's control are variable

long-run average cost curve A curve that indicates the lowest average cost of production at each rate of output when the size, or scale, of the firm varies; also called the planning curve

long-run industry supply curve A curve that shows the relationship between price and quantity supplied by the industry once firms adjust fully to any change in market demand

Lorenz curve A curve showing the percentage of total income received by a given percentage of recipients whose incomes are arrayed from smallest to largest

M

macroeconomics The study of the economic behavior of entire economies

marginal cost The change in total cost resulting from a one-unit change in output; the change in total cost divided by the change in output, or $MC = \Delta TC / \Delta q$

marginal Incremental, additional, or extra; used to describe a change in an economic variable

marginal product The change in total product that occurs when the use of a particular resource increases by one unit, all other resources constant

marginal rate of return on investment The marginal revenue product of capital expressed as a percentage of its marginal cost

marginal rate of substitution (MRS) A measure of how much of one good a consumer would give up to get one more unit of another good, while remaining equally satisfied

marginal rate of technical substitution (MRTS) The rate at which one resource, such as labor, can substitute for another, such as capital, without affecting total output

marginal resource cost The change in total cost when an additional unit of a resource is hired, other things constant

marginal revenue The change in total revenue from selling an additional unit; in perfect competition, marginal revenue is also the market price

marginal revenue product The change in total revenue when an additional unit of a resource is hired, other things constant

marginal social benefit The sum of the marginal private benefit and the marginal external benefit of production or consumption

marginal social cost The sum of the marginal private cost and the marginal external cost of production or consumption

marginal tax rate The percentage of each additional dollar of income that goes to the tax

marginal utility The change in total utility derived from a one-unit change in consumption of a good

marginal valuation The dollar value of the marginal utility derived from consuming each additional unit of a good

market A set of arrangements through which buyers and sellers carry out exchange at mutually agreeable terms

market demand Sum of the individual demands of all consumers in the market

market failure A condition that arises when the unregulated operation of markets yields socially undesirable results

market power The ability of a firm to raise its price without losing all its customers to rival firms

market structure Important features of a market, such as the number of firms, product uniformity across firms, firms' ease of entry and exit, and forms of competition

market supply The sum of individual supplies of all producers in the market

market work Time sold as labor

means-tested program A program in which, to be eligible, an individual's income and assets must not exceed specified levels

median income The middle income when all incomes are ranked from smallest to largest

median voter model Under certain conditions, the preferences of the median, or middle, voter will dominate other preferences

median wage The middle wage when wages of all workers are ranked from lowest to highest

mediator An impartial observer who helps resolve differences between union and management

Medicaid An in-kind transfer program that provides medical care for poor people; by far the most costly welfare program

Medicare Social insurance program providing health insurance for short-term medical care to older Americans, regardless of income

merchandise trade balance The value of a country's exported goods minus the value of its imported goods during a given period

microeconomics The study of the economic behavior in particular markets, such as that for computers or unskilled labor

minimum efficient scale The lowest rate of output at which a firm takes full advantage of economies of scale

mixed system An economic system characterized by the private ownership of some resources and the public ownership of other resources; some markets are unregulated and others are regulated

monetary policy Regulation of the money supply to influence economy-wide activity such as inflation, employment, and economic growth

money income The number of dollars a person receives per period, such as $400 per week

monopolistic competition A market structure with many firms selling products that are substitutes but different enough that each firm's demand curve slopes downward; firm entry is relatively easy

monopoly A sole producer of a product for which there are no close substitutes

moral hazard A situation in which one party, as a result of a contract, has an incentive to alter their behavior in a way that harms the other party to the contract

movement along a demand curve Change in quantity demanded resulting from a change in the price of the good, other things constant

movement along a supply curve Change in quantity supplied resulting from a change in the price of the good, other things constant

N

natural monopoly One firm that can serve the entire market at a lower per-unit cost than can two or more firms

natural resources So-called gifts of nature used to produce goods and services; includes renewable and exhaustible resources

negative, or inverse, relation Occurs when two variables move in opposite directions; when one increases, the other decreases

nonmarket work Time spent getting an education or producing goods and services for personal consumption

normal good A good, such as new clothes, for which demand increases, or shifts rightward, as consumer incomes rise

normal profit The accounting profit earned when all resources earn their opportunity cost

normative economic statement A statement that represents an opinion, which cannot be proved or disproved

O

oligopoly A market structure characterized by a few firms whose behavior is interdependent

open-access good A good that is rival in consumption but nonexclusive, such as ocean fish

opportunity cost The value of the best alternative forgone when an item or activity is chosen

origin On a graph depicting two-dimensional space, the zero point; the point of departure

other-things-constant assumption The assumption, when focusing on the relation among key economic variables, that other variables remain unchanged

outsourcing A firm buys inputs from outside suppliers

P

partnership A firm with multiple owners who share the firm's profits and bear unlimited liability for the firm's debts

patent A legal barrier to entry that grants its holder the exclusive right to sell a product for 20 years from the date the patent application is filed

payoff matrix In game theory, a table listing the payoffs that each player can expect based on the actions of the other player

per se illegal In antitrust law, business practices that are deemed illegal regardless of their economic rationale or their consequences

perfect competition A market structure with many fully informed buyers and sellers of a standardized product and no obstacles to entry or exit of firms in the long run

perfectly discriminating monopolist A monopolist who charges a different price for each unit sold; also called the monopolist's dream

perfectly elastic demand curve A horizontal line reflecting a situation in which any price increase reduces quantity demanded to zero; the elasticity has an absolute value of infinity

perfectly elastic supply curve A horizontal line reflecting a situation in which any price decrease drops the quantity supplied to zero; the elasticity value is infinity

perfectly inelastic demand curve A vertical line reflecting a situation in which any price change has no effect on the quantity demanded; the elasticity value equals zero

perfectly inelastic supply curve A vertical line reflecting a situation in which a price change has no effect on the quantity supplied; the elasticity value is zero

populist legislation Legislation with widespread benefits but concentrated costs

pork-barrel spending Special-interest legislation with narrow geographical benefits but funded by all taxpayers

positive economic statement A statement that can be proved or disproved by reference to facts

positive rate of time preference Consumers value present consumption more than future consumption

positive, or direct, relation Occurs when two variables increase or decrease together; the two variables move in the same direction

predatory pricing Pricing tactics employed by a dominant firm to drive competitors out of business, such as temporarily selling below marginal cost or dropping the price only in certain markets

present value The value today of income to be received in the future

price ceiling A maximum legal price above which a good or service cannot be sold; to have an impact, a price ceiling must be set below the equilibrium price

price discrimination Increasing profit by charging different groups of consumers different prices when the price differences are not justified by differences in production costs

price elasticity formula Percentage change in quantity demanded divided by the percentage change in price; the average quantity and the average price are used as bases for computing percentage changes in quantity and in price

price elasticity of demand Measures how responsive quantity demanded is to a price change; the percentage change in quantity demanded divided by the percentage change in price

price elasticity of supply A measure of the responsiveness of quantity supplied to a price change; the percentage change in quantity supplied divided by the percentage change in price

price floor A minimum legal price below which a good or service cannot be sold; to have an impact, a price floor must be set above the equilibrium price

price leader A firm whose price is adopted by other firms in the industry

price maker A firm that must find the profit-maximizing price when the demand curve for its output slopes downward

price taker A firm that faces a given market price and whose quantity supplied has no effect on that price; a perfectly competitive firm

prime rate The interest rate lenders charge their most trustworthy business borrowers

principal A person or firm who hires an agent to act on behalf of that person or firm

principal-agent problem The agent's objectives differ from those of the principal's, and one side can pursue hidden actions

prisoner's dilemma A game that shows why players have difficulty cooperating even though they would benefit from cooperation

private good A good that is both rival in consumption and exclusive, such as pizza

private property rights An owner's right to use, rent, or sell resources or property

producer surplus A bonus for producers in the short run; the amount by which total revenue from production exceeds variable cost

product market A market in which a good or service is bought and sold

production function The relationship between the amount of resources employed and a firm's total product

production possibilities frontier (PPF) A curve showing alternative combinations of goods that can be produced when available resources are used fully and efficiently; a boundary between inefficient and unattainable combinations

productive efficiency The condition that exists when market output is produced using the least-cost combination of inputs; minimum average cost in the long run

profit The reward for entrepreneurial ability; the revenue from sales minus the cost of resources used by the entrepreneur

progressive taxation The tax as a percentage of income increases as income increases

proportional taxation The tax as a percentage of income remains constant as income increases; also called a flat tax

public good A good that, once produced, is available for all to consume, regardless of who pays and who doesn't; such a good is nonrival and nonexclusive, such as national defense

public utilities Government-owned or government-regulated monopolies

pure capitalism An economic system characterized by the private ownership of resources and the use of prices to coordinate economic activity in unregulated markets

pure command system An economic system characterized by the public ownership of resources and centralized planning

Q

quantity demanded The amount demanded at a particular price, as reflected by a point on a given demand curve

quantity supplied The amount offered for sale at a particular price, as reflected by a point on a given supply curve

quasi-public good A good that is nonrival in consumption but exclusive, such as cable TV

quota A legal limit on the quantity of a particular product that can be imported or exported

R

rational ignorance A stance adopted by voters when they find that the cost of understanding and voting on a particular issue exceeds the benefit expected from doing so

real income Income measured in terms of the goods and services it can buy

recycling The process of converting waste products into reusable material

regressive taxation The tax as a percentage of income decreases as income increases

relevant resources Resources used to produce the good in question

renewable resource A resource that regenerates itself and so can be used indefinitely if used conservatively, such as a properly managed forest

rent Payment to resource owners for the use of their natural resources

rent seeking Activities undertaken by individuals or firms to influence public policy in a way that will increase their incomes

resource complements Resources that enhance one another's productivity; an increase in the price of one resource decreases the demand for the other

resource market A market in which a resource is bought and sold

resource substitutes Resources that substitute in production; an increase in the price of one resource increases the demand for the other

resources The inputs, or factors of production, used to produce the goods and services that people want; resources consist of labor, capital, natural resources, and entrepreneurial ability

retained earnings After-tax corporate profit reinvested in the firm rather than paid to stockholders as dividends

right-to-work states States where workers in unionized companies do not have to join the union or pay union dues

rule of reason Before ruling on the legality of certain business practices, a court examines why they were undertaken and what effect they have on market competition

S

scarcity Occurs when the amount people desire exceeds the amount available at a zero price

screening The process used by employers to select the most qualified workers based on readily observable characteristics, such as a job applicant's level of education and course grades

secondary effects Unintended consequences of economic actions that may develop slowly over time as people react to events

service An activity used to satisfy human wants

Sherman Antitrust Act of 1890 First national legislation in the world against monopoly; prohibited trusts, restraint of trade, and monopolization, but the law was vague and, by itself, ineffective

shift of a demand curve Movement of a demand curve right or left resulting from a change in one of the determinants of demand other than the price of the good

shift of a supply curve Movement of a supply curve left or right resulting from a change in one of the determinants of supply other than the price of the good

short run A period during which at least one of a firm's resources is fixed

shortage At a given price, the amount by which quantity demanded exceeds quantity supplied; a shortage usually forces the price up

short-run firm supply curve A curve that shows the quantity a firm supplies at each price in the short run; in perfect competition, that portion of a firm's marginal cost curve that intersects and rises above the low point on its average variable cost curve

short-run industry supply curve A curve that indicates the quantity supplied by the industry at each price in the short run; in perfect competition, the horizontal sum of each firm's short-run supply curve

signaling Using a proxy measure to communicate information about unobservable characteristics; the signal is more effective if more-productive workers find it easier to send than do less-productive workers

slope of a line A measure of how much the vertical variable changes for a given increase in the horizontal variable; the vertical change between two points divided by the horizontal increase

social insurance Government programs designed to help make up for lost income of people who worked but are now retired, unemployed, or unable to work because of disability or work-related injury

social regulation Government regulations aimed at improving health and safety

Social Security Supplements retirement income to those with a record of contributing to the program during their working years; by far the largest government redistribution program

social welfare The overall well-being of people in the economy; maximized when the marginal cost of production equals the marginal benefit to consumers

sole proprietorship A firm with a single owner who has the right to all profits and who bears unlimited liability for the firm's debts

special-interest legislation Legislation with concentrated benefits but widespread costs

specialization of labor Focusing work effort on a particular product or a single task

strategy In game theory, the operational plan pursued by a player

strike A union's attempt to withhold labor from a firm to stop production

substitutes Goods, such as Coke and Pepsi, that are related in such a way that an increase in the price of one shifts the demand for the other rightward

substitution effect of a price change When the price of a good falls, consumers substitute that good for other goods, which become relatively more expensive

substitution effect of a wage increase A higher wage encourages more work because other activities now have a higher opportunity cost

sunk cost A cost that has already been incurred in the past, cannot be recovered, and thus is irrelevant for present and future economic decisions

Supplemental Security Income (SSI) An income assistance program that provides cash transfers to the elderly poor and the disabled; a uniform federal payment is supplemented by transfers that vary across states

supply A relation between the price of a good and the quantity that producers are willing and able to sell during a given period, other things constant

supply curve A curve showing the relation between price of a good and the quantity supplied during a given period, other things constant

supply of loanable funds The relationship between the market interest rate and the quantity of loanable funds supplied, other things constant

surplus At a given price, the amount by which quantity supplied exceeds quantity demanded; a surplus usually forces the price down

T

tangent A straight line that touches a curve at a point but does not cut or cross the curve; used to measure the slope of a curve at a point

tariff A tax on imports

tastes Consumer preferences; likes and dislikes in consumption; assumed to be constant along a given demand curve

tax incidence The distribution of tax burden among taxpayers; who ultimately pays the tax

technologically efficient Produces the maximum possible output given the combination of resources employed; that same output could not be produced with fewer resources

Temporary Assistance for Needy Families (TANF) An income assistance program funded largely by the federal government but run by the states to provide cash transfer payments to poor families with dependent children

term structure of interest rates The relationship between the duration of a loan and the interest rate charged; typically interest rates increase with the duration of the loan

terms of trade How much of one good exchanges for a unit of another good

tit-for-tat In game theory, a strategy in repeated games when a player in one round of the game mimics the other player's behavior in the previous round; an optimal strategy for encouraging the other player to cooperate

total cost The sum of fixed cost and variable cost, or $TC = FC + VC$

total product The total output produced by a firm

total revenue Price multiplied by the quantity demanded at that price

total utility The total satisfaction a consumer derives from consumption; it could refer to either the total utility of consuming a particular good or the total utility from all consumption

traditional public-goods legislation Legislation that involves widespread costs and widespread benefits—nearly everyone pays and nearly everyone benefits

transaction costs The costs of time and information required to carry out market exchange

transfer payments Cash or in-kind benefits given to individuals as outright grants from the government

trust Any firm or group of firms that tries to monopolize a market

tying contract A seller of one good requires a buyer to purchase other goods as part of the deal

U

U.S. official poverty level Benchmark level of income computed by the federal government to track poverty over time; initially based on three times the cost of a nutritionally adequate diet

underground economy An expression used to describe market activity that goes unreported either because it is illegal or because those involved want to evade taxes

undifferentiated oligopoly An oligopoly that sells a commodity, or a product that does not differ across suppliers, such as an ingot of steel or a barrel of oil

unit-elastic demand The percentage change in quantity demanded equals the percentage change in price; the resulting price elasticity has an absolute value of 1.0

unit-elastic demand curve Everywhere along the demand curve, the percentage change in price causes an equal but offsetting percentage change in quantity demanded, so total revenue remains the same; the elasticity has an absolute value of 1.0

unit-elastic supply The percentage change in quantity supplied equals the percentage change in price; the resulting price elasticity of supply equals 1.0

unit-elastic supply curve A percentage change in price causes an identical percentage change in quantity supplied; depicted by a supply curve that is a straight line from the origin; the elasticity value equals 1.0

Uruguay Round The most recently concluded multilateral trade negotiation under GATT; this 1994 agreement cut tariffs, formed the World Trade Organization (WTO), and will eventually eliminate quotas

utility The satisfaction or sense of well-being received from consumption

V

variable A measure, such as price or quantity, that can take on different values

variable resource Any resource that can be varied in the short run to increase or decrease production

variable technology Occurs when the amount of externality generated at a given rate of output can be reduced by altering the production process

vertical axis Line on a graph that begins at the origin and goes up and down; sometimes called the y axis

vertical integration The expansion of a firm into stages of production earlier or later than those in which it specializes, such as a steel maker that also mines iron ore

vertical merger A merger in which one firm combines with another from which it had purchased inputs or to which it had sold output

W

wages Payment to resource owners for their labor

winner's curse The plight of the winning bidder who overestimates an asset's true value

winner-take-all labor markets Markets in which a few key employees critical to the overall success of an enterprise are richly rewarded

world price The price at which a good is traded on the world market; determined by the world supply and world demand for the good

World Trade Organization (WTO) The legal and institutional foundation of the multilateral trading system that succeeded GATT in 1995